# Standard History Of Memphis, Tennessee: From A Study Of The Original Sources

A. R. James

**Nabu Public Domain Reprints:**

You are holding a reproduction of an original work published before 1923 that is in the public domain in the United States of America, and possibly other countries. You may freely copy and distribute this work as no entity (individual or corporate) has a copyright on the body of the work. This book may contain prior copyright references, and library stamps (as most of these works were scanned from library copies). These have been scanned and retained as part of the historical artifact.

This book may have occasional imperfections such as missing or blurred pages, poor pictures, errant marks, etc. that were either part of the original artifact, or were introduced by the scanning process. We believe this work is culturally important, and despite the imperfections, have elected to bring it back into print as part of our continuing commitment to the preservation of printed works worldwide. We appreciate your understanding of the imperfections in the preservation process, and hope you enjoy this valuable book.

# Standard History

*of*

# Memphis, Tennessee

From a Study of the Original Sources

Edited by
JUDGE J. P. YOUNG

Knoxville, Tennessee
Published by H. W. Crew & Co.
1912

Copyrighted 1912
by
H. W. CREW & CO.

Knoxville Printing & Box Co.
Printers and Binders
Knoxville, Tenn.

# INTRODUCTION

Patriotism or devotion to one's country is a sentiment. It is not due to self interest nor other sordid motive, but is born of the story of her origin and of the achievements of the brave and enterprising ancestral stock, which, out of small beginnings, established and organized and wrought a nation. Every great city is in semblance a small nation, both in government and the loyal co-operation of its people for the common good. And the same patriotic devotion, born of the same sentiment does, or should prevail in every city as in every nation.

As our civilization grows older our larger cities are taking more interest in the story of their own origin and development, and concerning some of them many historical volumes have been written, dealing with almost every incident of fact and legend that could be traced. And in many notable instances of cities the greater the knowledge of her history, the greater the pride and love and devotion of her people.

Our own City of Memphis, though rated young among her Eastern sisters in America, is yet one of the most ancient, considering the discovery of her site, and the building of the first habitations of the white man here, on the whole American continent. When it is recalled that the adventurous Hernando De Soto built a cantonment for his troops here and established a little ship-yard, in which he constructed four piragues or barges, large enough to transport across the Mississippi River in time of high water, five hundred Spanish soldiers, as many more Indian vassels and one hundred and fifty horses, with baggage and other military equipment, in a few hours, and that all this occurred seventy-nine years before the landing of the Mayflower at Plymouth Rock and twenty-four years before the building of the first hut and stockade at St. Augustine, Fla., it will be realized that our story dates far back in ancient American history.

Following up this fact much space has been given to the wonderful march of De Soto from Tampa Bay, Fla., to the Chickasaw Bluffs, literally hewing his way as he came with sword and halberd through swarming nations of brave Indians; and to showing that he marched directly from the Chickasaw towns in northeast Mississippi to the Chickasaw Bluffs; and to presenting in fullest detail from the Spanish Chroniclers what De Soto and his people did while on the Bluffs where Memphis now stands. And it was deemed proper also to tell with equal detail of the voyages of Marquette and Joliet and La Salle, past the lonely Chickasaw Bluffs, and of the coming of Le Moyne Bienville with a large army and the construction of a great fortress here, heavily mounted with artillery, in the endeavor to overcome the heroic Chickasaws who resented the French invasions in the effort to conquer their country and to found a great French Empire in Western America. And the story also is told of the effort of Governor Don Manuel Gayoso to establish in like manner a Spanish Empire west of the Mississippi River before the Americans could take hold.

Indeed few American cities possess so romantic a story and the archives, not only of the United States, but of France and Spain also are yet rich in historical material awaiting the historian with time and opportunity for investigation.

When the American pioneer came to the Chickasaw Bluffs and began to plan a city and then to cut away the forests and build, the narrative became more complex. The records at a frontier post, where the printing press had not yet appeared, were few and tradition is unreliable. To weigh and compare the fantastic legends and stories from memory that have come down to us, with the official records and authentic documents that survive, required patient care and discrimination and much that has been heretofore published as history has been rejected when found to be doubtful at least, or actually untrue.

With the founding of newspapers the story became more lucid. But to collect and edit the great mass of undigested material and weave it into a connected story, has been a herculean task that should not have been crowded into a year of time. There are necessarily imperfections and omissions in such a work which a generous public, we trust, will overlook. It has been the purpose of the editor to collect, in condensed form, as much of all this story as could be compressed into one volume, leaving to the future historian the enlargement of the concise outline into the several volumes that would be necessary to convey the narrative in fullest detail. Our present beautiful city, with its wonderful river and parks and driveways and libraries and public buildings is worthy of far greater efforts than we have been able to bestow upon it in the work.

If the people of Memphis shall be inspired by any part of the story, written in this book, to greater and more patriotic endeavors, not only to enlarge and adorn their already beautiful city, but to elevate her whole population to the highest plane of intellectual and moral progress and civic righteouness, the editor will feel richly paid for his humble but laborious work.

The editor desires to express the obligation he is under for the cheerfully rendered assistance of all the citizens of Memphis, and the city authorities to whom he applied, for use of documents and records. And especially does he desire to express his obligation to Miss A. R. James, Assistant Writer and Compiler, to whose intelligence, aptitude and energy the public is indebted for much of the story of municipal progress since the founding of the city, as well as of the sanitary and educational development of Memphis and the growth of classical, musical and histrionic art among her people.

J. P. YOUNG.

Memphis, Tenn., August 29, 1912.

# DEDICATION

To the pioneers who founded and the brave sons who builded and loyally stood by Memphis in her hours of adversity and pestilence as in her days of victory and triumph, this volume of her history is affectionately dedicated.

# CONTENTS

## CHAPTER I

The Chickasaw Bluffs and the Aborigines. The Great, Silent Continent. Habits and Customs of the Indians. Choctaw Legend of the Bluffs. The Story of DeSoto. With Pizarro in Peru. He Plans the Conquest of Florida. DeSoto's Dream of Gold. His Army and Knightly Commanders. The March Through Florida. Cruelties of the Spaniards. Toils and Sufferings of the Troops. On the Savannah River. DeSoto Turns Westward. The Battle of Mauvila. DeSoto Enters Mississippi. He Winters at Chicaça. Terrible Battle with the Chickasaw Indians. Sad Plight of the Spaniards. The Battle of Alibamo. The March to the Chickasaw Bluffs. DeSoto Discovers the Mississippi River. Chisca's Fortress on Jackson Mound. Story of the Discovery by the Spanish Chroniclers. DeSoto's Sojourn Here. He Builds Huts and Then Boats. He crosses the River and Disappears in the West .................... 9

## CHAPTER II

The Chickasaw Bluffs Under Spain. The Coming of the Frenchmen. Voyage of Marquette and Joliet. The Journey of LaSalle. The Site of Fort Prudhomme. The Town of Mitchigamea. The Mouth of the Mississippi River. The Country Claimed for France. Bienville at the Bluffs. The Voyage up the River. The Building of Fort Assumption. War with the Chickasaws. Failure of Bienville. Diary of his Sojourn on the Chickasaw Bluffs. Terrible Indian Customs. Again Under the Dominion of Spain. Cession of the Country to Great Britain. The Province of Carolina. Grant of Charles II to the Lords Proprietors. Once More Under the Dominion of Spain. Don Manuel Gayoso De Lemos. Fort San Fernando de Barancas. Trouble with the Spaniards. Arrival of Captain Isaac Guion. The Americans Take Possession. The Chickasaw Bluffs Become Part of Tennessee. Our Chickasaw Allies. American Forts Here. ................. 31

## CHAPTER III

Land Grants by the State of Tennessee. John Rice and John Ramsey Grants. Purchase of West Tennessee from the Chickasaws. Judge John Overton Purchases Rice Grant. Takes in with him Andrew Jackson. Sketch of John Rice. The Birth of Memphis. Map of New Town. Appearance of the Surroundings. Narrative of Colonel James Brown. The Name of Memphis. Establishment of Shelby County. The First Court of Laws. The First County Tax Levy. The First Marriage. ...............................52

---

## CHAPTER IV

Incorporation of Memphis. Resentment of the Inhabitants. Sketch of First Charter. First Board of Mayor and Aldermen. Limits of the Corporation Fixed. Outline of First Tax-Levy. Second Board of Aldermen. Memphis Made a City. Isaac Rawlings Mayor. City Divided into Wards. Fire Department Established. Citizens Oust the Gamblers. Young Memphis a Free Soil Town. Removal of the Indians to the West. Rivalry Between Memphis and Randolph. Mississippi Claims Site of Memphis. Tax Assessment of 1840. War With the Flatboatmen. Memphis Gets the Great Navy Yard. The City Limits Extended. "South Memphis" and "Pinch." Incorporation of South Memphis. The First Telegraph Line. Troubles Over Slavery. The Wolf River Canal Project. The First Bond Issue. The Charters of 1848 and 1849. .....................70

---

## CHAPTER V

The Census of 1850. The Building of Plank Roads. Rapid Growth of the City. Extension of the Telegraph System. The First Railroad to the Atlantic. Great Railroad Jubilee in Memphis. The Financial Panic of 1857. Crime in Memphis. Uprising of the People and Mob Violence. Rescue of Able by N. B. Forrest. The Problem of Street Paving. The Bust of Andrew Jackson. More Troubles Over Slavery. The John Brown Raid and Its Consequences. The First Paid Fire Department. ..........92

## CHAPTER VI

Mutterings of the Coming Civil War. Secession Activities in Memphis. Great Torch Light Processions of the Unionists and Secessionists. Secession Defeated at the Polls. Resolutions of the Secessionists. The Leaders of the Disunion Party. The Call of Mr. Lincoln for Troops. Secession of Memphis from State. Tennessee Finally Secedes. The Vote in Memphis. Preparations for War. The Southern Mothers. ......................................111

---o---

## CHAPTER VII

Memphis Captured by the Federal Fleet. Exciting Scenes in the City. Memphis Under Military Law. Sherman in Command. His Cruelty and Tyranny. Seizure of the Municipal Government by Military Commander. Close of the Civil War. Reconstruction Measures. Trouble with the Negroes. Great Riot in the City. The Freedman's Bureau. Brownlow's Militia Police. The Ku Klux Klan. Peace at Last. The City Begins to Grow Again. Trouble About Finances. Small Pox, Cholera and Yellow Fever Appear. ......126

---o---

## CHAPTER VIII

John Loague, Mayor. Financial Difficulties. Census of 1875. New Charter. The Flippin Administration. Schemes to Retire City Debt. Sale of Navy Yard. Surrender of Charter Considered. Great Epidemic of Yellow Fever Begins. Panic and Stampede of Citizens. Terrible Scenes of Suffering and Death. Howard Association and Relief Committees. Heroism of the Workers. The Tragedy of Death and Burial. The Daily Press Faithful. Generosity of Non-Residents. Loyal Negro Militia. Death Roll of the Howards. End of the Epidemic. Thanksgiving for Relief. ..............................................161

## CHAPTER IX

Debt and Disaster Follow the Fever. Surrender of the City Charter. The Taxing District Act. Struggle with Creditors. How Memphis had been Robbed. The Taxing District Officials. How Memphis was Redeemed. Another Epidemic Breaks Out. Efficient Sanitary Measures Discussed. The Meeting of Refugees in St. Louis. Colonel Waring Plans Sewer System. Work on the Sewers Begun. Character of the System. The People Take Heart. Progress of Reconstructing the City Government. D. P. Hadden, President. The Old Debt Refunded. New Water System Established. Artesian Wells Sunk. .......... 185

## CHAPTER X

Memphis Rising From Her Ashes. Census of 1880. Details of the Sewer System. The Bethell Administration. Increase of Property Values. The Cotton Trade. Big Fires in Memphis. The Mississippi River Bridge. Ceremonies of the Opening. Electric Car Service Inaugurated. Protest Against Taxing District Form of Government. Taxing District Proves a Success. Form of Taxation Unjust to Memphis. Gamblers Again. Law and Order League. Sam Jones in Memphis. Other Lecturers and Moral Workers. The Legislature Restores Titles of City, Mayor and Vice-Mayor. Clapp Elected Mayor. Artesian Water Company, Telephones and Electric Lighting. Back Tax Collector Appointed. Memphis to Levy Her Own Taxes. New City Hospital. Interstate Drill and Encampment. Flood of Mississippi River. Yellow Fever Scare. Bank Clearings. ................................... 212

## CHAPTER XI

J. J. Williams Elected Mayor. Death of Senator Harris. T. B. Turley Appointed Senator. Gambling Houses Closed. Further Extension of the City Limits. Collection of Taxes Authorized. Sewer Extension. Visit of President McKinley. Great Confederate Reunion. Williams is Reelected Mayor. Municipal Ownership of Water Works. Purchase of the Old Plant. Attempt to Amend Charter. Memphis Streets Renamed. Quarantine. ................... 247

## CHAPTER XII

**J. H. Malone Elected Mayor. Attack Upon Charter. Commission Government Established and Declared Unconstitutional. Reduction of Tax Rate. Flippin Compromise Bonds Refunded. Police Department Work. Improvement of Water System. The City's Real Estate. Front Foot Assessment Law. Pensioning Policemen. City Limits Again Extended. Greater Memphis. Resume of Progress, 1909.** ............................................. 263

## CHAPTER XIII

Commission Form of Government Established. Provisions of the Act. Election of E. H. Crump, as Mayor. Williams Vigorously Contests the Election of Crump. Contest Withdrawn. Reduction of Tax Rate. Extension of Sewer System to Annexed Territory. Mounted Police Station. Vast Construction of New Streets. The City Greatly Beautified. Prohibition in Memphis. Curious Result of the Law. Juvenile Court Established. Splendid Work Among Children. Mounted Police Force. Modern Fire Equipment. Stupendous Municipal Improvements. Increase of Bond Issues. Purchase of Tri-State Fair Grounds. Crump Reelected. Tremendous Flood of Mississippi River. Part of City Overflowed. Water System Contaminated ..................................... 277

## CHAPTER XIV

Architecture and Public Buildings ................... 307

## CHAPTER XV

Parks and Promenades .............................. 323

## CHAPTER XVI

Military History ................................... 336

## CHAPTER XVII

Transportation .................................... 374

## CHAPTER XVIII

Education ........................................ 397

## CHAPTER XIX

The Press ........................................ 444

## CHAPTER XX

Literature ....................................... 462

## CHAPTER XXI

Art, Music and Drama ............................. 469

## CHAPTER XXII

Churches of Memphis .............................. 499

## CHAPTER XXIII

The Bench and Bar ................................ 520

## CHAPTER XXIV

Medical History .................................. 539

## CHAPTER XXV

Societies and Clubs .................................. 553

## CHAPTER XXVI

Banks and Insurance ................................ 579

## CHAPTER XXVII

Commerce and Manufactures ......................... 586

# ILLUSTRATIONS

Young, J. P., portrait.........................Frontispiece

|  | Facing Page |
|---|---|
| Map of the City............................... | 60 |
| Buckingham, M. S., portrait.................... | 584 |
| DeSoto, Ferdinand, portrait.................... | 13 |
| Fisher, F. N., portrait......................... | 392 |
| Forrest, N. B., portrait........................ | 355 |
| Galloway, R., portrait......................... | 334 |
| Garnsey, Cyrus, Jr., portrait................... | 576 |
| Hanson, C. C., portrait........................ | 439 |
| Harrison, Walter H., portrait................... | 443 |
| Henning, B. G., portrait....................... | 549 |
| Jackson, Andrew, portrait...................... | 58 |
| Keating, J. M., portrait........................ | 177 |
| LeMaster, E. B., portrait....................... | 258 |
| Love, Geo. C., portrait......................... | 305 |
| Malone, Jas. H., portrait....................... | 263 |
| Maury, R. B., portrait.......................... | 574 |
| Meriweather, N., portrait....................... | 197 |
| McFarland, L. B., portrait...................... | 328 |
| Omberg, J. A., portrait......................... | 579 |
| Overton, John, portrait......................... | 69 |
| Pickett, A. B., portrait......................... | 491 |
| Randolph, Wm. M., portrait..................... | 162 |
| Speed, R. A., portrait........................... | 396 |
| Taylor, A. R., portrait.......................... | 371 |
| Toof, S. C., portrait............................ | 449 |
| Tutwiler, T. H., portrait........................ | 395 |
| Winchester, James, portrait..................... | 63 |
| Wright, E. E., portrait.......................... | 538 |
| Wright, Luke E., portrait....................... | 183 |

# CHAPTER I

The Chickasaw Bluffs and the Aborigines. The Great, Silent Continent. Habits and Customs of the Indians. Choctaw Legend of the Bluffs. The Story of DeSoto. With Pizarro in Peru. He Plans the Conquest of Florida. DeSoto's Dream of Gold. His Army and Knightly Commanders. The March Through Florida. Cruelties of the Spaniards. Toils and Sufferings of the Troops. On the Savannah River. DeSoto Turns Westward. The Battle of Mauvila. DeSoto Enters Mississippi. He Winters at Chicaça. Terrible Battle with the Chickasaw Indians. Sad Plight of the Spaniards. The Battle of Alibamo. The March to the Chickasaw Bluffs. DeSoto Discovers the Mississippi River. Chisca's Fortress on Jackson Mound. Story of the Discovery by the Spanish Chroniclers. DeSoto's Sojourn Here. He Builds Huts and Then Boats. He crosses the River and Disappears in the West.

WHEN the light of history first began to illumine the story and traditions of the lower Chickasaw Bluff on the Mississippi River on the day that DeSoto arrived, May 8, 1541, the civilization of western Europe was yet young. Henry the Eighth was king of England and Queen Elizabeth still a young child. Shakespeare was yet to be born twenty-three years later, Galileo and Kepler, the fathers of modern astronomy, twenty-three and thirty years later respectively, Cromwell after fifty-eight years, Milton after sixty-seven years and Sir Francis Bacon, the proposer of inductive reasoning, the basis of all modern science, was not to open his eyes upon the world for yet twenty years to come.

For centuries America had slept, a great, silent continent, undisturbed by the boom of guns or the crash of arms. There was no traffic along highways and rivers and her stillness was unbroken by any sound louder than the yell of the savage or the bark of the wolf. Her inhabitants were red nomads, of savage habits, but great mentality, and popularly known as Indians, as they were supposed at first to be connected in some way on the west with the East Indies. These were thinly scattered throughout the territory now occupied by the United States, living for protection mostly in groups of villages, constructed of upright logs or poles, the huts being covered with sections of bark taken from certain trees and sometimes defended by stockades of logs laboriously chopped down with the stone hatchets of the Indians and buried deeply at one end in the ground. These Indians possessed no iron out of which to forge tools or weapons, the tips to the latter, usually arrows only, being wrought as in the stone age, of flint and their hatchets in many instances being made of green porphyry brought from great distances, but more often of flint ground or rubbed smooth.

Their villages were commonly imbedded at some central point in the country occupied by the tribe and between the borders of their territory and that of the next tribe was usually a neutral strip of considerable and sometimes vast extent, claimed by one or both contiguous tribes as a hunting ground, but never permanently occupied. About their villages were extensive cleared fields in which they raised crops of maize, called by the Indians mahiz, which means Indian corn as now known. They likewise grew large quantities of beans, pumpkins and squash, which, together with nuts and dried meats prepared from the wild game of the forest, afforded them subsistence. The southeastern Indian tribes, and probably others also, prepared oils from the nuts of the woods, such as walnuts, pecans and hickory nuts, which were pronounced by the early Spaniards to be a very fine relish, and they made large quantities of oil from the fat of bears, which they used as lard. The family ties were very strong with most tribes of Indians and their tenderness and affection for their children was a striking trait of these people.

Confining our inquiry to those tribes which had relations with the Chickasaw bluffs, that part of the United States between the Savannah River and the Mississippi and south of the Tennessee River was, in 1541, covered by a distinctive racial population known as Appalachees. Between the Tennessee and Cumberland Rivers, and southeastward into North Alabama and Georgia and in East Tennessee the Cherokees were then located. The Appalachees were divided into a number of tribes which were bound by no political ties and were very exclusive. Among these were the Seminoles of Florida, the Uchees in Northern Georgia, the Mauvila or Mobilians in Southern Alabama, the Chickasaws in North Mississippi and West Tennessee, the Creeks or Muscogees in Georgia and Southeastern Alabama, the Choctaws in Central Mississippi and Alabama, and the Natchez in Southern Mississippi and Louisiana. The Akansas and Quapaws, of Siouan stock and of the same blood as the Omahas, occupied the west bank of the Mississippi opposite Memphis and at the date of DeSoto's arrival the large tribe occupying, with its chief town and fortress known as Chisca, the site of modern Memphis, seemed to be subject to the tribes across the river under a great chief known as the lord or chief of Pacaha or, by other chroniclers called Capaha, probably the Spanish for Quapa, which was likewise the name of a town. This tribe at the lower Chickasaw bluffs was not related to the Chickasaws and was probably a colony of the trans-Mississippi settlers. The brave Chickasaws whose northern resident limit was in part the Tallahatchie River were then, as always afterwards, though few in numbers, the dominant race of Indians south and west of the Tennessee River and indeed, of the present Eastern Gulf States, though West Tennessee was in the time of DeSoto, as in the days of LaSalle and Bienville claimed, but used only as a hunting ground by them.

All these tribes kept up a pretty constant communication with each other, their embassies or delegations of chief men, passing over vast distances, undisturbed by the tribes through whose territory they traveled, always on foot, as they possessed neither horses nor cattle. But they would frequently, through some real or fancied slight or injury, go to war with each other and they always guarded their well-known boundaries, as well as their more vaguely defined hunting grounds, with jealous care and determination.

Choctaw legend gives to the site of Memphis a fantastic interest in its narrative of mythical events of great antiquity. The legend relates that many centuries ago the Choctaws and Chickasaws, led by two brothers, Chacta and Chicsa, came from the far west. On crossing the Mississippi River they found the country occupied by the Nahonla, giants who were very fair and had come from the East. There was also a race of giants here who were cannibals and who kept the mammoths, animals whose great bones are found everywhere in the clay and gravel deposits of the lower Mississippi Valley, herded, and used them to break down the forests, thus causing the prairies. At last all the cannibals and their gigantic mammoths, except one of the latter, which lived near the Tombigbee River, became extinct. The Great Spirit attempted to destroy him with lightning, but he foiled the bolts by receiving them on his head. Finally being hard pressed by the Great Spirit, he fled to the Socta-Thoufah, "steep bluffs," (now Memphis), cleared the river at a bound and hied him away to the Rocky Mountains.*

It was through tribes like these above described that DeSoto hewed his bloody way from Tampa Bay, Florida, to the Mississippi River, lured by that "auri sacra fames," the accursed thirst for gold, undergoing the most dreadful toil and suffering, but never finding the gold, El Dorado the Golden, or the riches embodied in the wild dream of Cabeza de Vaca. He was moreover unconscious of the fact as he journeyed and toiled that the soil of the lands beneath his feet has proven one of the world's greatest sources of wealth, and that a single cotton crop raised on these same lands now produces more gold than existed in all Europe during his era.

As the lower Chickasaw bluffs first came into prominence in the world's history on the arrival of DeSoto, a brief abstract of his journey and exploits will be here given, derived from

*One may readily discover the origin of this legend in the coming of DeSoto with his horses and guns across the Tombigbee and his crossing the river at Memphis.

FERDINAND DE SOTO.

the original narrative of "The Portuguese Gentleman," Ranjeld, DeSoto's private secretary, Biedma and Garcilaso de la Vega all, except the last named, companions of his march, and whose writings have come down to us and now exist in several splendid translations.* But this will be preceded by a short sketch of his life.†

Hernando DeSoto, frequently written Ferdinand DeSoto, was, according to the narrative of the Portuguese Gentleman, or the Gentleman of Elvas, the anonymous knight who was a companion on his great march through Florida, born at Xeres de Badajos in Spain, but the date of his birth is not by him given. Garcilaso de la Vega, commonly known as the Inca, gives his birthplace at Villa nueva de Barcarota, and Herrara assigns the same town as the birthplace and the date is fixed at about 1501. Buckingham Smith asserts that he was born at Xeres in the province of Estremadura, and the Encyclopedia Brittanica names Xeres de Caballeros in Estremadura as the place where he first saw the light and the year 1496 as the date. He was said to have been of gentle birth on both his father's and mother's side, but was without means, his whole possessions, according to the Knight of Elvas, being his sword and buckler. DeSoto was indebted to his patron Pedro Arias de Avila, generally written Pedrarias Davila, whose attention he had attracted, for the means of acquiring his education. With Davila he went when a mere youth, to the "Indies of the Ocean,"‡ or the West Indies, of which his patron had been appointed governor and was by the governor appointed to the command, as captain, of a company of cavalry. Soon after, by order of Davila, he took part with Pizarro in the Conquest of Peru. Here he greatly distinguished himself and attracted

---

*The editor gratefully acknowledges his indebtedness, in obtaining correct data, to the splendid translations of the narratives of the Knight of Elvas, Biedma and Ranjel, collected in the Narratives of the Career of DeSoto by Edward Gaylord Bourne and published in the Trailmakers series in two volumes, A. S. Barnes & Co., New York, 1904, and to the earlier works of Theodore Irving.

†The editor does not apologise for this sketch of DeSoto and his long march from Tampa Bay, Florida, to the Chickasaw Bluff. It is logically the initial story in the History of Memphis.

‡Portuguese Narrative, page 7.

the attention of that shrewd but accomplished cut-throat who "soon singled him out from the hardy spirits around him and appointed him his lieutenant. Was there a service of special danger to be performed, DeSoto had it in charge; was there an enterprise requiring sound judgment and careless daring, DeSoto was sure to be called upon."*

DeSoto, narrates Garcilaso de la Vega, commanded one of the troops of horse which captured the Inca, Atahualpa and put to rout his army. He finally shared in the spoil wrung from this unfortunate prince and in the looting of Cuzco. He is alleged in the Spanish chronicles to have been the officer who indicated on the wall of the great room in the Inca's palace, by the reach of his arm and sword, the line to which the room was required to be filled with gold for his ransom, by the unfortunate monarch. He later returned to Spain laden with wealth, his share amounting to 180,000 cruzados or crowns of gold.† Here he lived at the court of the emperor in almost imperial style and loaned of his money to the shrewd Charles V. Soon after he was married to Dona Ysabel, daughter of his former patron Davila and was appointed by the emperor, Charles V, Governor and Captain General of Cuba and Florida with the more exalted civic title of Adelantado or President of Florida.

DeSoto, after some delay, determined to attempt the conquest of Florida, chiefly by reason of the reports brought from there by Cabeza de Vaca, one of the four survivors of the ill-fated Narvaez expedition, which led him to believe that the land contained rich treasures of gold.‡ DeSoto for this purpose organized at his own expense an expedition composed of six hundred hardy adventurers,§ including many knights and soldiers of distinction and a brilliant escort of Portuguese hidaljos or gentlemen under Andre de Vasconcelo, and with these he sailed in seven ships April 6, 1538, from San Lucar de Borrameda for Santiago de Cuba and after nearly a year's sojourn in that island sailed May 8, 1539, for Florida and landed May 25, at Tampa Bay.

*Irving's Conquest of Florida, page 36.
†Portuguese Narrative, page 8.
‡Portuguese Narrative, page 8.
§Garcilaso says this force was 950 strong. Irving, page 41.

DeSoto had, besides his foot soldiers, 224 horses, having lost 19 at sea. He also drove with his command a herd of hogs, partly for the support of his army, if meat should not be found, and partly with which to stock a colony if he should deem it expedient to found one. His march is one of the most remarkable for its toils and hardships and barrenness of results in all history, and strongly emphasized the imperious will as well as the greed of the adventurer. By some historians it is called DeSoto's crazy march, but if he did not discover "El Dorado, the Golden," which he is believed to have sought, he unquestionably found what is to us vastly more important, the site of our splendid city. He also gave accurate information to all Europe of the nature of the interior of the country now constituting the East Gulf States of the American Union, with its rich plains and forests and mighty water courses, as well as of its brave aboriginal inhabitants, for the mastery of which Spain, France and England struggled for more than two centuries, when it was finally wrested from all of them by the young American Republic.

DeSoto lost no time in getting off on his long march from the landing place at Tampa. The landing was made May 30, 1539 at a village called Ocita and the march was begun June 1. The Spaniards on June 4, recaptured a Spanish captive named Juan Ortiz, who became their guide and interpreter. The Indians were brave and resentful and attacked the detachments of Spanish soldiers wherever found and this in turn moved the Spanish soldiers to reprisals and they inflicted the greatest cruelty on the brave Indians. The Spaniards killed many wantonly, running them down with their horses and spearing them when overtaken and also chased them with their Irish greyhounds, a species of large fierce dog, and caused the dogs to tear numbers of them in pieces. The line of march was through a rough, swampy country and the midsummer sun was hot, causing great suffering to the troops. The route from Tampa was in a long sweeping curve to the eastward and northward through many Indian villages, among others

Mocoço. Urri-Barra-Caxi* and Ocali to Vitachuco, where the Spaniards had a fierce battle. Here DeSoto turned northwestwardly and probably crossing the Suwanee River above the old town of that name, reached, after a long march and many vicissitudes, the site of the modern city of Tallahassee. This was called Anhayca by the Gentleman of Elvas and Iviahica by Ranjel. Here DeSoto wintered in the Province of Apalachee.

The journey was resumed March 3, 1540,† in a northeastwardly direction, the line of march taking them almost in a straight line from Tallahassee, Florida, to the Savannah River some miles below Augusta, Georgia, crossing in their route the Ocmulgee and the Oconee, probably not far above the junction of these rivers, and the Ogeechee. The march was attended with much toil and sometimes almost with starvation. The principal Indian towns passed were Achise, Cofaqui and Cofachiqui, the latter thought to be about twenty-five miles below Augusta on the east side of the Savannah River.

On May 13, 1540, DeSoto left Cofachiqui and marching northwest he crossed the country of Achelaque or Cherokee, a very poor and unproductive district, and reached the province of Xualla or Choualla, skirting the Savannah River and its northern tributaries, and rested May 21, in a town of the same name, probably in the vicinity of Clarksville, Georgia. Thence turning westward they marched through a rich province and across a chain of low, uninhabited mountains. They now passed through Conasaqua to Chiaha where, June 5, 1540, they again rested. Leaving Chiaha June 28, they followed the course of the Coosa River southwestward through the village of Acoste July 2, and the present city of Rome in the extensive and fertile province of Cosa, or Coça, according to Ranjel, and reached Ulibahali September 2, 1540, and thence moved forward to Talisé, reaching there September 18.

DeSoto's march was now continually down the Coosa River and he finally reached the fortified town of Tuscaloosa

*Ranjel calls this place Orra-Porra-Cogi, and the Portuguese Gentleman, Paracaxi.
†Ranjel.

or "Black Warrior," which Ranjel calls Athahachi, October 10, and still proceeding he arrived at the great Indian fortress of Mauvila, about twenty-five miles above the junction of the Alabama and Tombigbee Rivers. The Spaniards since leaving Cofachiqui on the Savannah River had been received in a friendly spirit by the Indians and had had little fighting. But under the inspiration of the great Indian Chief, Tuscaluza, the storm broke at Mauvila, into which town some of the Spaniards, including DeSoto, had been cunningly decoyed by Tuscaluza under pretense of showing them greater hospitality, and a terrible battle followed. This short sketch will not permit the details of this great conflict. After nine hours fighting DeSoto succeeded in burning the town, with its lightly built straw-thatched houses, and slew 2,500 or 3,000 of Tuscaluza's warriors. DeSoto lost only twenty-two of his own protected and mail-clad knights and cross-bowmen, killed, but one hundred forty-eight others received six hundred eighty-eight arrow wounds, while seven horses were killed and twenty-nine others wounded. The Spaniards also lost all their baggage which they had carelessly carried into the town and deposited in a building.

Resting here a month to recuperate DeSota left Mauvila, determined in a dare-devil spirit to spy out the whole land and marching northwestward and conforming to the course of the Tombigbee River he again encountered the Indians, this time probably Choctaws, at the Black Warrior River a short distance above its mouth. He was delayed several days to build two rafts or piraguas, with which to cross. Finally effecting a crossing here December 9, he moved forward and entered the state of Mississippi a short distance east of the present city of Columbus. He reached the Tombigbee, called by the Spaniards the River of the Chicaças, probably between the present town of Waverly and the mouth of Tibbee Creek, a short distance above Columbus. The Indians here, still of the Choctaw tribe, again opposed the crossing and DeSoto was delayed until he could build another raft or flat with which he ferried his men over the wide, deep stream. Baltasar de Gallegos was sent with thirty horsemen up the stream to find a ford and turn the Indian position, which he did, but not before DeSoto had forced a passage with his footmen. Gallegos crossed almost certainly at the old Choctaw crossing or ford at or near Lincacums shoals. Claiborne says, "DeSoto probably entered the present state of Mississippi at Columbus, and followed an Indian trail or buffalo path some five miles up to Lincacums shoals, just about the mouth of the Tibbee and a little below the present town of Waverly. The Tombigbee here is bifurcated by an island, the first obstruction below Buttahatchie. The gravel discharged from this stream lodged against the island and rendered both channels fordable a great part of the year, and this is the only point where the Spaniards could have forded in December. It was the crossing used by the Choctaws when going to the villages and hunting grounds east of the Tombigbee. The trail struck here a stretch of prairie, between Tibbee and Hanging Kettle creeks, and crossed the present Mobile and Ohio Railroad at Lookhattan, thence a little west of the railroad by Mulden, Prairie Station and Egypt.

"The early settlers of this portion of Mississippi remember the well-worn, beaten trail, long disused but distinctly defined, and can to this day trace it from plantation to plantation.

"On leaving Egypt the trail tended northwest up the ridge known as Featherstone's ridge, through a series of glades three or four miles west of Okolona, and up the second bottom on the east side of Sookatonchee Creek. There it struck Pontotoc ridge four miles east of the ancient Chicasa council house. Near this point stood the first Chicasa town, and in this vicinity the Spaniards went into winter quarters.

"At that period a portion of the Chickasaws still resided in the mountain region of East Tennessee, but a large body of them had taken possession of a territory where DeSoto found them, and their principal settlement or town, or series of villages, was on the ridge from the ancient council house (near Redland) north fifteen miles (near Pontotoc) and northwest on the 'mean prairie' eight or ten miles, within a few miles of Tallahatchie River. On the southern bluff was the Alabama fort or town, the stronghold of the tribe of that name, in alliance with the Chickasaws.

"Four miles east of the ancient council house on the Pontotoc ridge, near the source of Sookatonchee Creek are the vestiges of a fortified camp, evidently once strongly entrenched, after the European style of that day, with bastions and towers. Leaden balls and fragments of metal have been often found in these ruins. The inclosure was square and the whole area, as evidenced by the remains, would have afforded shelter to the Spaniards and their live stock.

"The ancient chronicles described the Chicasa town near which DeSoto halted, as containing two hundred houses, shaded by oak and walnut trees and with rivulets on each side. These requisitions are filled in the locality referred to. Beautiful groves of oak and hickory (which the Spaniards called walnut) abound, and living streams running west to the Yazoo and east to the Tombigbee."*

Professor Theodore Hayes Lewis, in his article on the route of DeSoto, in Volume 6, Publications of the Mississippi Historical Society, furnishes this data: "Chicaca was a town of two hundred fires and was situated on a hill extending north and south, which was watered by many little brooks. It was located about one mile northwest of Redland on the S.½ of the S.W.¼ of Section 21, and the N.½ of the N.W.¼ of Section 28, town. 11, range 3, E., in Pontotoc County."

The crossing was effected by DeSoto December 16, 1540 (Ranjel), in all likelihood at or in the immediate vicinity of Columbus. He immediately rode forward to find a suitable town for winter quarters, as the weather was becoming cold, and late at night entered a small, deserted village of twenty houses (Ranjel), where Baltasar De Gallegos joined him the next day. This was not the capital of Chicasa as some assume from the somewhat confused accounts of the narrators. Garcelaço says, (Richelet's translation, tome 2, p. 352) that after he crossed the river they marched four days and reached the capital of the Chicaças, a town of two hundred fires, and

*Claiborne's Mississippi as a Province, Territory and State, page five.

important respects from the version of Theodore Irving, 1851. Richelet says:

"I return to where I was in my history. The Spaniards in leaving Alibamo, marched across a waste country bearing always towards the north in order to get further and further away from the sea, and at the end of three days they came in view of the capital of Chisca, which bears the name of its province and of its ruler. This town is situated near a river which the Indians called Chucagua, the largest of all those encountered by our people in Florida. The inhabitants of Chisca, unaware of the coming of the troops, by reason of the war which they were waging with their neighbors, were taken by surprise. The Spaniards plundered them and took several of them prisoners. The rest of them fled, some into a forest between the village and the river, and others to the house of the Cacique, which stood upon a high mound commanding a view of the whole place. The Cacique was old, and then sick upon his bed, in a condition of great weakness. He was of such small stature and of such meagre visage that in that country the like had never been seen. Nevertheless at the sound of the alarm and being surprised that his subjects were being plundered and being taken prisoners, he arose, walked out of his chamber with a battle axe in his hand and made the threat that he would slay all who might enter his lands without his leave. But as he was about to go forth from his house to confront the Spaniards, the women of his household, aided by some of his subjects who had made their escape from the Spaniards, restrained him. With tears in their eyes they reminded him of the fact that he was feeble, without men at arms, his vassals in disorder, and not in condition for fighting and that those with whom he had to do were vigorous, well disciplined, great in number and, for the most part, mounted upon beasts of such speed that none could ever escape them. That it was necessary, then, to await a favorable occasion for their revenge and to deceive their enemies in the meantime by fair appearances of friendship, thus preventing the destruction of himself and his subjects.

"These considerations caused Chisca to pause, but he was so chagrined by the injury which the Spaniards had done him, that instead of being willing to listen to the envoys of the general in their demands for peace, he declared war upon them, adding that he hoped within a short while to cut the throat of their captain and all those with him.

"DeSoto, however, was not astonished at this, but sent others and they made excuses for the disorder created upon their arrival, and repeated the demand for peace.

"For it was clear to DeSoto that his men were discouraged on account of the constant skirmishing, and were encumbered with sick men and sick horses; that in less than six hours there had come to the side of the Cacique not less than four thousand men, quite well equipped; that in all probability he would get together a very much larger number; besides, that the lay of the land was very favorable to the Indians, and very unfavorable to the Spaniards, on account of the thicket surrounding the town, which would make it impossible to use his cavalry; that finally, instead of making progress by fighting, the Spaniards were working their own destruction from day to day. These were the considerations which induced the general to offer peace.

"But the larger part of the Indians who were assembled to deliberate upon the subject had quite contrary views. Some were for war, believing that to be the only means of recovering their goods and delivering their companions from the power of the Spaniards. They declared that there need be no fear of such people; that such earnest demands for peace as the Spaniards made afforded certain proof of their cowardice; finally, that it was fitting to apprise them of the courage of those whom they had just attacked by giving battle in turn, to the end that no stranger in future would have the temerity to enter their domain. But the other side contended that peace was their only means of getting back their property and their imprisoned countrymen; that if there should be a battle their misery would only be increased by reason of fire and the loss of their crops, (which were still unharvested), resulting in ruin to the entire province and the death of many of their people.

"For they said inasmuch as their enemies had come as far

as their country, through so many trials and perils and through so many fierce tribes, their courage could not be fairly doubted. Thus they said that without any other proofs, peace ought to be made, and that if they were afterwards dissatisfied they could break the truce to a much better advantage than they could on that day make war. This opinion prevailed and the Cacique, dissembling his resentment, asked the envoys what they thought to gain by this peace, which they seemed to desire so much. They answered, their lodging in the town, together with supplies for passing on. Chisca agreed to all on condition that they should set at liberty those of his subjects whom the Spaniards held prisoners, return all the goods that they had seized, and not enter into his house; and he warned them that the only alternative would be war of extermination. The Spaniards accepted peace on these conditions and released the subjects of Chisca, for they had no lack of Indian servants, and returned all the booty—consisting only of some sorry deerskins and clothing of small value. Thereupon the inhabitants abandoned the town with the supplies which they had and the Spaniards remained six days, treating their sick. On the last day DeSoto got leave from Chisca to visit him in his house, and after he had thanked him for the favor done his troops he withdrew, proceeding the next day upon his journey of discovery."

Besides Garcilaso, whose narrative has just been given, three companions of DeSoto also told the story of the approach to and occupation of the town of Chisca on the lower Chickasaw Bluff, now the site of Memphis. Inasmuch as some writers have endeavored to show from these narratives that DeSoto probably reached the Mississippi River at or about the thirty-fourth parallel of latitude and not at Memphis, the narratives will be given here in full[*] in order that the reader may judge for himself of the correctness of the conclusion drawn by the editor in common with Ramsey and Claiborne, that the lower Chicasaw Bluff, with its big mound, was the place where DeSoto first saw the great inland river.

The first of these narratives to be quoted is that of the

*By permission of the publishers, A. S. Barnes & Co., N. Y.

Gentleman of Elvas, usually referred to as the Portuguese Gentleman. This narrative is as follows:

"He accordingly set out for Quizquiz and marched seven days through a wilderness having many pondy places, with thick forests, all fordable however on horseback except some basins or lakes that were swum. He arrived at a town of Quizquiz without being descried and seized all the people before they could come out of their houses. Among them was the mother of the Cacique; and the Governor sent word to him by one of the captives to come and receive her with the rest he had taken. The answer he returned was that if his lordship would order them to be loosed and sent, he would come to visit and do him service.

"The Governor, since his men arrived weary and likewise weak for want of maize and his horses were also lean, determined to yield to the requirement and try to have peace; so the mother and the rest were ordered to be set free and with words of kindness were dismissed. The next day, while he was hoping to see the chief, many Indians came with bows and arrows to set upon the Christians, when he commanded that all the armed horsemen should be mounted and in readiness. Finding them prepared, the Indians stopped at the distance of a cross-bow shot from where the Governor was, near a river-bank, where, after remaining quietly half an hour, six chiefs arrived at the camp, stating that they had come to find out what people it might be; for they had knowledge from their ancestors that they were to be subdued by a white race; they consequently desired to return to the Cacique to tell him that he should come presently to obey and serve the Governor. After presenting six or seven skins and shawls brought with them they took their leave and returned with the others who were waiting for them by the shore. The Cacique came not, nor sent another message.

"There was little maize in the place and the Governor moved to another town, half a league from the great river, where it was found in sufficiency. He went to look at the river and saw that near it there was much timber of which piraguas might be made, and a good situation in which the camp might be placed. He directly moved, built houses, and settled on a plain a cross-bow shot from the water, bringing together all the maize of the towns behind, that at once they might go to work and cut down the trees for sawing out planks to build barges. The Indians soon came from up the stream, jumped on the shore and told the Governor that they were vassals of a great lord named Aquixo, who was the suzerain of many towns and people on the other shore; and they made known from him that he would come the day after, with all his people to hear what his lordship would command him.

"The next day the Cacique arrived with two hundred canoes filled with men having weapons. They were painted with ochre, wearing great bunches of white and other plumes of many colors, having feathered shields in their hands, with which they sheltered the oarsmen on either side, the warriors standing erect from bow to stern, holding bows and arrows. The barge in which the Cacique came had an awning at the poop in which he sat; and the like had the barges of the other chiefs; and there from under the canopy where the chief man was the course was directed and orders issued to the rest. All came down together and arrived within a stone's cast of the ravine, whence the Cacique said to the Governor, who was walking along the river bank with others who bore him company, that he had come to visit, serve and obey him; for he had heard that he was the greatest of lords, the most powerful of all the earth and that he must see what he would have him do. The Governor expressed his pleasure and besought him to land that they might the better confer; but the chief gave no reply, ordering three barges to draw near wherein was a great quantity of fish and loaves like bricks, made of the pulp of ameixas (persimmons), which, DeSoto receiving, gave him thanks and again entreated him to land.

"Making the gift had been a pretext to discover if any harm might be done; but finding the Governor and his people on their guard the Cacique began to draw off from the shore, when the crossbowmen, who were in readiness, with loud cries shot at the Indians and struck down five or six of them. They retired with great order, not one leaving the oar, even though the next one to him might have fallen and covering themselves they withdrew. Afterwards they came many times and landed; when approached they would go back to their barges. These were fine looking men, very large and well formed; and what with the awnings, the plumes and the shields, the pennons and the number of people in the fleet, it appeared like a famous armada of galleys.

"During the thirty days that were passed here four piraguas were built, into three of which one morning three hours before daybreak, the Governor ordered twelve cavalry to enter, four in each, men in whom he had confidence, that they would gain the land, notwithstanding the Indians, and secure the passage or die. He also sent some crossbowmen on foot with them, and in the other piragua oresmen to take them to the opposite shore. He ordered Juan de Guzman to cross with the infantry, of which he had remained captain in the place of Francisco Maldonado; and because the current was stiff they went up along the side of the river a quarter of a league and in passing over they were carried down so as to land opposite the camp; but before arriving there at twice the distance of a stone's cast, the horsemen rode out from the piraguas to an open area of hard and even ground, which they all reached without accident.

"So soon as they had come to the shore the piraguas returned, and when the sun was up two hours high the people had all got over. The distance was near half a league; a man standing on the shore could not be told whether he was a man or something else from the other side. The stream was swift and very deep; the water always flowing turbidly brought along from above many trees and much timber, driven onward by its force."

The narrative of Biedma is much briefer than the other two and is thus given:

"We traveled eight days with great care in tenderness of the wounded and sick we carried. One midday we came upon a town called Quizquiz and so suddenly to the inhabitants that they were without any notice of us, the men being away at work in the maize fields. We took more than three hundred women and a few skins and shawls they had in their houses.

There we first found a little walnut of the country (pecans), which is much better than that here in Spain. The town was near the banks of the river Espiritu Santo (The River of the Holy Spirit.) They told us that it was, with many towns about there, tributary to the lord of Pacaha, famed throughout all the land. When the men heard that we had taken their women they came to us peacefully, requesting the Governor to restore them. He did so and asked them for canoes in which to pass that great river. These they promised, but never gave; on the contrary they collected to give us battle, coming in sight of the town where we were; but in the end, not venturing to make an attack, they turned and retired.

"We left that place and went to encamp by the riverside to put ourselves in order for crossing. On the other shore we saw a number of people collected to oppose our landing, who had many canoes. We set about building four large piraguas, each capable of taking sixty or seventy men and five or six horses. We were engaged in the work twenty-seven or twenty-eight days. During this time the Indians every day at three o'clock in the afternoon would get into two hundred and fifty very large canoes they had, well shielded, and come near the shore on which we were; with loud cries they would exhaust their arrows upon us and then return to the other bank. After they saw that our boats were at the point of readiness for crossing they all went off leaving the passage free. We crossed the river in concert, it being nearly a league in width and nineteen or twenty fathoms deep."

The last of these narratives is by Ranjel, the secretary of DeSoto, who thus narrates the occurrences at the Chickasaw bluffs:

"Saturday, the last of April, the army set out from the place of the barricade and marched nine days through a deserted country and by a rough way, mountainous and swampy, until May 8, when they came to the first village of Quizqui, which they took by assault and captured much people and clothes; but the Governor promptly restored them to liberty and had everything restored to them for fear of war, although that was not enough to make friends of these Indians. A league beyond this village they came to another with abundance of corn and soon again after another league upon another likewise amply provisioned. There they saw the great river. Saturday, May 21, the force went along to a plain between the river and a small village and set up quarters and began to build four barges to cross over to the other side. Many of these conquerers said that this river was larger than the Danube.

"On the other side of the river about seven thousand Indians had got together with about two hundred canoes to defend the passage. All of them had shields made of cane joined so strong and so closely interwoven with such thread that a cross-bow could hardly pierce them. The arrows came raining down so that the air was full of them and their yells were something fearful. But when they saw that the work on the barges did not relax on their account, they said that Pacaha, whose men they were, ordered them to withdraw and so they left the passage free. And on Saturday, June 8, (June 18), the whole force crossed this great river in the four barges and gave thanks to God because in His good pleasure nothing more difficult could confront them. Soon, on Sunday, they came to a village of Aquixo. Tuesday, June 21, they went from there and passed by the settlement of Aquixo, which is very beautiful and beautifully situated."

Comparing these four narratives, which are in peculiar agreement with each other, except the last, it can readily be seen that Ranjel, in speaking of the villages a league apart to which the Spaniards moved in turn for the purpose of obtaining provisions, was merely describing the usual group of villages which went to make up a settlement among these Indians such as the Spaniards found at the Chickasa towns in Pontotoc County, Mississippi, and in no way contradicts the other narratives. The fact seems to be that DeSoto came upon the town of Chisca where the great mound was and still remains, which was near the wide river with a forest between and then, without reaching the river, he moved from village to village on the bluff for more convenient access to corn or maize, by which his army was supported, and finally pitched his camp under the bluff at the foot of a ravine probably near the mouth of Wolf River and within cross-bow shot of the water, where he constructed and launched his boats. Again the Gentleman of Elvas narrates that: "The Rio Grande being crossed, the Governor marched a league and a half to a large town of Aquixo, which was abandoned before his arrival."

And this statement again tends to locate the crossing at Memphis, as, from the opposite bank, it is four and a half miles or a league and a half to the high point at Mound City, Arkansas, where a great mound still stands and which was the site of another Indian village in ancient times. And from Mound City westward in a winding course a ridge extends which affords probably the only dry crossing through the swamps from the river west to the highlands, during high waters which usually prevail at that season of the year, between Cairo, Illinois and Helena, Arkansas.

# CHAPTER II

The Chickasaw Bluffs Under Spain. The Coming of the Frenchmen. Voyage of Marquette and Joliet. The Journey of LaSalle. The Site of Fort Prudhomme. The Town of Mitchigamea. The Mouth of the Mississippi River. The Country Claimed for France. Bienville at the Bluffs. The Voyage up the River. The Building of Fort Assumption. War with the Chickasaws. Failure of Bienville. Diary of his Sojourn on the Chickasaw Bluffs. Terrible Indian Customs. Again Under the Dominion of Spain. Cession of the Country to Great Britain. The Province of Carolina. Grant of Charles II to the Lords Proprietors. Once More Under the Dominion of Spain. Don Manuel Gayoso De Lemos. Fort San Fernando de Barancas. Trouble with the Spaniards. Arrival of Captain Isaac Guion. The Americans Take Possession. The Chickasaw Bluffs Become Part of Tennessee. Our Chickasaw Allies. American Forts Here.

DE SOTO was Adelantado of Florida and all interior America was Florida to him, so that he left no record of having claimed by virtue of discovery for his sovereign the vast wilderness which he traversed on his way from Tampa Bay to the Mississippi River. But by international right Spain was the owner and her king the sovereign of these great solitudes until dispossessed by later adventurers of other nations.

After the departure of DeSoto the Indians lived undisturbed on the lower Chickasaw Bluff and roamed the surrounding solitudes in quest of game or in warfare with their neighbors for one hundred thirty-two years. In the meantime the Atlantic coast line had been settled and the French were extending their dominions beyond the Great Lakes in the northwest, but no white man since DeSoto's time had ventured down the great inland river. In May, 1673 Father Marquette, a noted Jesuit priest and missionary of restless energy and wandering proclivities, with a Quebec trader named Louis Joliet and five other Frenchmen began ascending the Fox River from Lake Michigan in two canoes and about the tenth of June made a portage to the Wisconsin River and, descending that stream, on June 17, 1673, entered the Mississippi. Rowing slowly down the stream past the mouth of the Pekitanoui or Missouri, and the Ouabouskigou, or the Ohio, which they noted, the voyagers passed the lower Chickasaw Bluff early in July, 1673, but made no stop. Soon after they passed the village of Mitchigameas, now Helena, Arkansas, below the mouth of the St. Francis River, and finally stopped about the site of the last of the villages of the Akansea below the mouth of the river of that name and about latitude 33° 40', but Father Marquette's map shows this village to be on the east side of the Mississippi River.* Remaining here until July 17, the missionary and his party began their journey northward again and once more passed the lower Chickasaw Bluff but no record is made of a stop here. His map, however, contains certain symbols indicating high lands on the east bank about this latitude.

Nine years later a more important personage, Sieur Robert Cavelier de la Salle, also attempted the exploration of the Mississippi River and carried out his enterprise with perfect success. He had with him twenty-three Frenchmen, including Sieur Henri de Tonti, and Father Piere Zenobé Membré, a recollet missionary, eighteen Indians, ten Indian women and three children, in all fifty-four persons. Reaching the Mississippi River by way of the Seignelay or Illinois River, on February 6, 1682, he left there in canoes on February 13, and rode slowly down to the mouth of the Ohio, stopping at intervals to hunt. Father Membré, in his narrative of the voyage, says: "From the mouth of this river you must advance forty-two leagues without stopping because the banks are low and marshy and full of thick foam, rushes and walnut trees."

*John Gilmary Shea's translation and authentic map of Father Marquette voyage, 1852. The original map was preserved at St. Mary's College, Montreal.

Forty-two French land leagues is equal to one hundred five miles, the exact distance from Cairo to the first Chickasaw Bluff, ten miles above Randolph, Tennessee, which stands on the second Chickasaw Bluff, and forty-two miles above Memphis by land courses.

Here LaSalle stopped to hunt on the first high ground below the Ohio River, and one of his men, Piere Prudhomme, got lost in the woods on February 24, according to Father Membré.

Finding some Chickasaw Indians in the vicinity LaSalle became alarmed and thinking they had captured his hunter and that they might attack his little escort he threw up a "fort and intrenchments," probably a stockade with a low parapet around it, and set out with a party to hunt for Prudhomme. Having at length found the lost hunter and some of the Indians, from whom he learned that their villages were four and a half days' journey of twenty-five or thirty miles each to the southeast, he finally left Fort Prudhomme about March 3, and proceeded on his journey down the river.* Proceeding forty French land leagues or one hundred miles further after leaving Fort Prudhomme, but making no stop at Memphis, or the lower Chickasaw Bluff, LaSalle reached the village of the Mitchigameas, now Helena, Arkansas, about March 12, and remaining there two days took possession of the country on the west bank of the Mississippi River in the name of his sovereign,

*Narrative of Father Membre, by John Gilmary Shea, 1852. The distance from the mouth of the Ohio River, forty-two leagues or 105 miles, and the fact of its being the first highland after leaving the Ohio, shows that the site of Fort Prudhomme was at the first Chickasaw Bluff and not at the fourth or lower bluff, as some writers allege. This fort was indeed a landmark for many years at the first Chickasaw Bluff, where the Confederates during the Civil War built Fort Wright, ten miles above Randolph and not far above Fort Pillow. A map in Abbe Prevost's History General of Voyages and Discoveries, 1749, shows the fort at the first Chickasaw Bluff; and the diary of a French officer who was with Bienville at the lower bluff in 1739, reprinted in Claiborne's History of Mississippi, refers to Prudhomme Heights several times as being on the river above Fort Assumption on the lower Chickasaw Bluff, where Memphis now stands. The statement that LaSalle established a trading post at Fort Prudhomme is a pure fiction. When returning up the river in June, 1682, he was taken ill at or about the site of Fort Prudhomme 100 leagues below the mouth of the Illinois River, (land courses), and remained there forty days.

After thus solemnly declaring the rights of his sovereign Louis XIV, of France, to the whole of the Mississippi Valley lying between the Alleghanies and the Rocky Mountains, LaSalle returned to Canada, passing up the Mississippi River to the Illinois and thence to Lake Michigan, not stopping at the lower Chickasaw Bluff but at the first Chickasaw Bluff or Fort Prudhomme, where he was seriously ill for more than a month.

Other Frenchmen, after LaSalle's return, made voyages down the Mississippi, notably De Tonti, who passed down in 1686 and again in 1700, in an endeavor to find his friend LaSalle, who had sailed from France with ships and a colony to enter the mouth of the Mississippi, but failed to find it and landed further west.

The next white man who is certainly known to have visited and taken possession of the lower Chickasaw Bluff after DeSoto left here was Jean Baptiste Le Moyne de Bienville, a distinguished French colonial governor and soldier, who arrived here in 1739. Bienville, then Governor of Louisiana, became involved in a war with the unconquerable Chickasaw Indians, whose group of villages were still where DeSoto found them, scattered in a long line from Redland near Pontotoc, Mississippi, to a point about three miles northwest of Tupelo in Lee County, Mississippi. Moving with an army up the Tombigbee River from Mobile, Bienville had ordered D'Artaguette to support him with a force from the post at the Illinois fort to be landed at Fort Prudhomme on the first Chickasaw Bluff and to march thence and form a junction with him in the vicinity of the Chickasaw villages. Bienville was delayed and D'Artaguette arriving at Fort Prudhomme May 10, and at the objective point six days before Bienville reached there, attacked the Chickasaws May 20, 1736 and was terribly defeated, being himself wounded and captured and with thirteen companions, burned at the stake. Bienville arriving on May 26, and unaware of the defeat of his lieutenant, attacked the Chickasaw towns and was himself disastrously defeated and compelled to retreat to Mobile. But Bienville possessed the nature of a bulldog and burning with shame and thirsting for vengeance, he induced the French court to send him fresh troops. With these, Bienville, in July, 1739, proceeded up the Mississippi River in a fleet of pirogues, with a large force of troops and auxiliaries, including a contingent of about sixteen hundred Indian allies. Another force from the Illinois and Canada, under De la Buissonniére and three hundred northern Indians under Sieur de Longueuil had arrived first by his order and a fort was built on the face of the bluff in the middle of August, called Fort Assumption. Bienville is estimated to have brought here twelve hundred white men and twenty-four hundred Indians, though from the details given by subordinate officers of the decimation of his army by malarial fevers, and the desertion of considerable bodies of Indians, it is not probable that he had here at any one time more than two thousand men. Bienville himself was delayed in collecting other Indian allies among the Akanseas and arrived here on November 14, 1739.

In a journal kept by a young French officer under De Noailles d'Aime, Bienville's chief commander, and reprinted in Claiborne's History of Mississippi, from a translation of the original French manuscript, many interesting and curious details are given of the sojourn of Bienville's forces on the site of the City of Memphis. Before quoting from his journal it may be stated that Bienville's intention was to collect an overwhelming force here and marching overland to the Chickasaw villages, the scene of his first defeat, to avenge himself for his overthrow and that of his lieutenant, D'Artaguette, in May, 1736. He had been misled by his engineer, Deverge, who induced him to believe by his rudely constructed map that the Chickasaw towns were only about half the distance that they really were from Fort Assumption. Bienville spent the fall and winter here in laborious but futile endeavors to discover or cut out a practicable highway to the Chickasaw towns, the main group of which were, as above stated, about ninety-seven miles from the Chickasaw Bluff in an airline, but one at least of which must have been, from the descriptions of the French and Indian scouts, on the south side of the Tallahatchie River near the site of the Indian fort called Alibamo, or

Alimamu, attacked by DeSoto on his approach to the bluff, as above described. There was a trail, in fact, from the first Chickasaw Bluff to the Chickasaw towns which was used by D'Artaguette even for his baggage wagons. This passed some distance east of Memphis and was the trail sought but never discovered by Bienville. It probably crossed the Tallahatchie River at New Albany, Mississippi.

The young French officer, whose name has not been preserved, among other things in his diary, describes Fort Assumption as constructed on our bluff. He says:

"This fort has been constructed at the foot of the steeps of Margot River (Wolf River), three-fourths of a league to the right and in the middle days of August, which latter circumstance has been the origin of its name Assumption. It is constructed of piles, three bastions bearing on the plain and two half bastions on the river, which is reached by seven different and wide slopes of one hundred and forty feet each. In the center of these slopes have been constructed bakeries and ovens scooped out of the walls of earth. The right was occupied by the battalion of regulars, and the left by various stores and the Colonial and Swiss troops. The remainder of the forces were encamped on the exterior, including the Canadians and savages, who encircled the whole of our left to the river."

This description does not leave us in any doubt as to the location of this fort. It was described as being three quarters of a league to the right, that is from the head of the bluffs or steeps, which was in the vicinity of the south bank of Bayou Gayoso, near its mouth and just beyond our county jail. Three-fourths of a French land league at that date was about one and eighty-seven hundredths of an English mile, and this would put the site of Fort Assumption on the edge of the bluff and somewhere between Georgia Street and Jackson Mound, which point is also just west of the site of the Indian village of Chisca, first captured by DeSoto on his arrival.

The diary further along proceeds as follows:

"On the 27th there was found at a distance of one-fourth of a league from our camp a reed, through which had been passed a piece of English cloth in the shape of a pouch and filled with tobacco. At the top was an ear of corn, and beneath a bear skin, the whole encircled by a ring of some kind. Five Chic. savages had recently brought these enigmatical emblems which signified peace, both, according to the interpretation of our savages and the people of the colony. By the ear of corn they mean that they desire to eat of the same bread; by the tobacco, smoke together; and by the bearskin within the circle, sleep under the same roof. This is a sufficient indication that they are much impressed with their own weakness, although we must give them credit for much hardihood and intrepidity, for not fearing to approach a spot about which five hundred savages are continually roaming."

Other paragraphs describe the darker side of the savage nature. The narrator says:

"On the 24th of November, we dispatched a party of fifty men upon the tracks of the 'Chicachat.' On the same day, at seven in the evening, we received a courier from a body of our Indians, who had fallen upon the 'Chics' and captured one man and two women (one of the latter being quite young), and killed another man whose scalp, ears, tongue and a portion of the heart they had sent us, the courier in the meantime having eaten a small portion of the heart whilst announcing the arrival of his comrades in the course of the next morning. * * * * * As they had decided firstly to put the man to death, they placed him opposite their cabin upon a couple of deer-skins, and between three fires to shield him from the coldness of the night, during which they sang and danced around him, occasionally throwing themselves upon him like rabid dogs and biting him in the thighs to keep him awake, assuring him in the meanwhile that as soon as the sun appeared he would be tied to the stake. Notwithstanding the awful treatment he neither complained nor spoke one word. * * * * * On the 26th, at nine in the morning, he was tied to a stake, which consists of two poles or trees four feet apart, to each of which was fastened one arm and a cross piece below on which rest the feet. They then applied bars of red hot iron upon all the most sensitive parts of his body. He was exposed to these atrocities for three hours, at the end of which he expired."

The greater part of the succeeding narrative is taken up with the various endeavors to find a feasible way to the Chickasaw towns which would admit of the usual army transport and with the description of the incidents connected with the life of the army here with their brutal Indian allies. On the 24th of December a French engineer, Saucier, endeavored to find the road made by D'Artaguette on his march from the first Chickasaw Bluff to the Chickasaw towns, but without avail. On the 14th of January, a scouting party reported having discovered "a body of one hundred men to the north of our fort in the direction of the Prudhomme Heights," and another scout reported having found a Chickasaw canoe on the bank of the river in the direction of Prudhomme Heights, which is convincing proof that Fort Prudhomme was not at the lower Chickasaw Bluffs.

And so the winter wore away without action, which greatly disgusted the Indian allies who were becoming very restless at the delay. On the 6th of February Bienville finally dispatched Mons. de Celeron with two hundred Frenchmen and three hundred Indians to attack the Chickasaw towns, but in fact that commander had secret instructions to make peace with the Chickasaws. Bienville was reluctantly forced to admit to himself that by reason of the disintegration of his forces from sickness and desertion he could not hope to successfully overcome the determined Chickasaws, and when on the 20th of March, Celeron returned with his whole force, after having treated with the Chickasaws for peace, bringing with him three of their chiefs as envoys, and three Englishmen, who came to claim damages for horses which had been killed by the savages, Bienville eagerly summoned a council to make peace with the Chickasaw commissioners. This was done, the Indians agreeing to surrender five Natches refugees whose domicile with the Chickasaws was the real beginning of the first war, and being the only remnants of that tribe still with them, and the French agreeing on their part to appease and withdraw their ferocious Indian allies, whose swarming scouting parties had kept the Chickasaw towns in a state of siege for many months and prevented their hunting for game, which had caused great distress among them. By the 31st of March all of Bienville's troops had departed from the bluff, spitefully carrying the three English traders with them as prisoners of war, and on April 9, Bienville reached New Orleans with his whole force, the sole trophies of his great movement to overwhelm the Chickasaws being the five Natchez prisoners and the three English captives. The aged Bienville never recovered from the last crushing failure, and returning to France, was coldly received by the French court and spent his remaining days in quiet retirement after forty-four years of laborious work for his colony and king. He finally died in Paris in 1768.

After this second failure of Bienville to conquer the Chickasaws, that virile tribe was left to its freedom again, which they employed for the next fourteen years in committing depredations along the shores of their great river on the boats of traders and other French voyagers from the chain of forts on the upper river and its tributaries to the French forts in the Natchez district and below.

The new French governor of Louisiana, Marquis de Vaudreuil, made a final effort to destroy them by an expedition on the line of Bienville's old route, the Tombigbee River, in 1754, but signally failed as his predecessors had done and the Chickasaws were thenceforward left undisturbed by the French. This noted tribe of warlike people had broken lances with and foiled DeSoto, fought desperate battles with the Cherokees, Creeks, and Choctaws and several French armies and defeated all of them. But with the English and after them the Americans, they had always been friendly and because of this fact the final settlement of West Tennessee and North Mississippi by the Anglo Saxon race was accomplished without a recorded massacre or racial tragedy between the settlers and the savage but proud tribe.

On November 3, 1762, eight years after De Vaudreuil's unsuccessful venture the French king, wearied with the costly struggle to maintain colonies in America, by a secret treaty ceded without consideration all his colonial possessions on this continent to Spain, which act of cession made the locality of Memphis again a part of a Spanish province. But on February 16, 1763, a general treaty of peace was made in Paris between Great Britain, France and Spain, by which France, joined by Spain, ceded to Great Britain all her enormous possessions on the east side of the Mississippi River, including both Canada and Louisiana, except the small district known as the Island of New Orleans, which went to Spain. Besides this, Spain obtained all the vast domain west of the Mississippi River except the "Oregon country."

Thus our district first came under the actual dominion of the English crown. Great Britain had indeed claimed this territory long before La Salle seized it in behalf of his sovereign, Louis XIV, in 1682. Queen Elizabeth had granted it to Sir Walter Raleigh in 1584 and Charles I, had granted it to Sir Robert Heath. On March 24, 1663, Charles II constituted the whole territory from the Atlantic seaboard to the "South Seas," and from the 31° to the 36° of north latitude as a province, called Carolina in honor of himself, and granted it to Lord Clarendon and others, designated as the "Lords Proprietors." By a subsequent grant dated June 30, 1665, which refers to the letters patent of March 24, 1663, Charles enlarged the grant so as to embrace all the territory "within the dominion of America," etc., from north latitude 29° to north latitude 36° 30'. This remarkable grant embodied an imperial domain, including North and South Carolina, Georgia, Tennessee, Alabama, Mississippi, Louisiana and Arkansas and parts of Florida, Missouri and California.*

However, North Carolina, later the northern division of the province of Carolina, never claimed under this grant any further west than the Mississippi River. But the French got possession of the west end of the province and held it until the treaties of 1762 and 1763 above mentioned. By the treaty of 1763 the crown of Great Britain came into its own again and the title of the province of North Carolina to its western lands beyond the Alleghenies, accrued to it in full under its

---

*Goodspeed, History of Tennessee, 1887, p. 166.

old grants of 1663 and 1665. By the treaty of 1783 at the close of the Revolutionary War, Great Britain ceded this western appendage of North Carolina to the United States and subsequently the state of North Carolina, by virtue of an act of cession passed by the Legislature, December, 1789,† made a formal deed of conveyance through its national senators, Samuel Johnson and Benjamin Hawkins, of this western extension of its public lands from its present western boundary to the Mississippi River, to the United States. And on April 2, 1790 Congress accepted the deed and constituted, May 26, 1790, of the imperial domain thus acquired, the "Territory South of the Ohio River." This territory was finally admitted into the Union as the sixteenth State on June 1, 1796.

But though taken into the bounds of the State of Tennessee, constituted in June, 1796, the site of Memphis on the lower Chickasaw Bluff was yet to undergo some vicissitudes before it came absolutely under the control of the United States.

Florida had been taken from Great Britain by the Spanish admiral, Galvez in 1781, during the Revolutionary War. By the treaty of peace between Great Britain, the United States and Spain in 1783, the former had recognized the conquest of Florida by Spain and ceded the territory which it had laid off as Florida and West Florida to that country. The cession of West Florida by Great Britain was made with an indeterminate northern boundary and Spain consequently claimed the land far to the north of the 31° of north latitude, Great Britain's original boundary of West Florida. Spain also endeavored to control the navigation of the Mississippi River. This incensed the western American settlements. Spain endeavored to pacify them by advantageous commercial privileges on the Mississippi River and sought by intrigue to acquire the western portion of the United States as it existed at that date and to separate it from the Atlantic States. To this end Baron Carondelet, the new Spanish governor of Louisiana, 1792, bent his endeavors. But the French, now at

†The first Act of Cession was passed by North Carolina at Hillsborough, in April, 1784 and repealed October 22, 1784.

war with Spain, also endeavored to incite an invasion of Louisiana and Florida, by the western frontiersmen and to, if possible, separate the western states from the Union and form with them an alliance with Louisiana under the protectorate of France. This French movement, engineered by the French minister at Washington, Genet, alarmed Spain and she began to strengthen her forts on the west side of the Mississippi River as high up as New Madrid, Missouri. She also entered into a treaty with the Chickasaw Indians and obtained permission to establish a fort on the east side of the river at the lower Chickasaw Bluff near the mouth of Wolf River and the bluff was ceded to Spain by the Chickasaws for that purpose, the alleged purpose being to protect Louisiana from invasion by the United States. This fort was erected in 1795 by the then Spanish Governor of Louisiana, Don Manuel Gayoso de Lemos, Ramsey says, "Upon the peninsula formed by the junction of the Margot (Wolf) River and the Mississippi" and was called Fort San Fernando de Barancos. Is it now definitely known that this redoubt, as well as Fort Adams built two years later by Captain Isaac Guion, the first American commander here, occupied the present site of the Shelby County jail, below the mouth of Wolf River.

This bold act of aggression by Gayoso constituted an invasion of the territory of the United States and was not to be endured. The American government claimed the whole territory on the east side of the Mississippi River down to the 31° of north latitude and being also inspired by the urgent appeals of the western frontiersmen, at once took steps to secure it.

General Wilkinson, who had succeeded General Anthony Wayne in command of the United States army, wrote this letter to Captain Isaac Guion conveying instructions to that accomplished officer as to securing the territory of the United States bordering on the Mississippi River below the mouth of the Ohio. The letter is furnished by Claiborne in his History of Mississippi as a Province, Territory and State, page 178, as follows:

"Fort Washington, May 20, 1797.
"It being deemed essential that the troops of the United

States should take possession of the certain military posts on the Mississippi, within our territorial limits, heretofore held by the Spanish garrison, I have thought proper to appoint you to this very honorable and important service, relying, with entire confidence on your intrepidity, talents, zeal, patriotism and discretion.

"You are to embark for this place on the 26th instant, with such party as may be assigned to you, in charge of your ordinance, stores and implements of every kind, and to proceed, without halt, to Fort Massac. Arrived there you will report to the commanding officer (Captain Z. M. Pike), and deliver the orders for him which accompany these instructions. These orders are to be promptly executed, and so soon as the detachment provided for can be organized and mustered and the additional ordinance and stores, to be taken from Massac, can be put on board, you will proceed on your voyage.

"You are to sail under the flag of the United States, displayed conspicuously on your barge, and on approaching any Spanish post, on the side of Louisiana, you are to give seasonable information by a subaltern, of the object of your movement and announce your disposition to offer a salute provided you are assured it will be returned gun for gun. No objection to your further progress can justify you in halting, unless it amounts to an official prohibition in writing, covering a menace of opposition by force of arms or a shot fired into your flotilla or across your bows.

\* \* \* \* \* \* \* \* \*

"It may, however, be presumed that no impediment will be thrown in your way, and that you will proceed without interruption to Wolf River, at the head of the lower Chickasaw Bluff, where you are to halt and distribute the goods intended for the Chickasaws. This being done you are to proceed to the Spanish post at the Walnut Hills and if it shall have been evacuated you will take possession. Should it be found in the occupation of the Spaniards you will demand possession in the name of the United States, in conformity with the treaty."

The letter then proceeds with explicit instructions to Captain Guion as to the necessity of the utmost vigilance and circumspection in his intercourse with and treatment of the Spanish military forces and the inhabitants of the country in the Natchez district. A few days later Baron Carondelet wrote to General Wilkinson in relation to these ominous movements, which had been ordered and rumors of which had reached him, urging the general to suspend the advance of his troops, "whose presence might possibly disturb the tranquility of the province and the good understanding that now prevails." But the movement of the troops was not withheld.

Reverting to the occupation of the lower Chicasaw Bluff by Governor Gayoso in 1795, Claiborne, the Mississippi historian, quotes a letter written by Governor Gayoso to his wife, from Fort Ferdinand at the mouth of Wolf River May 31, 1795, as follows:

"Yesterday I passed from my post of Esperanza over to the Chicacha Bluffs, where I now write. I hoisted the King's flag and saluted it in the most brilliant manner from the flotilla and the battery. It being St. Ferdinand's day (the name of my Prince), I gave the post that name. It was a pleasant day, and withal my birthday, and nothing was wanting to complete my happiness but your presence. The chiefs are to visit me tomorrow, and then I shall count the days, the hours and moments until I can be with you."

Thus affairs stood at the Chickasaw Bluff, the fort being under command of Captain Bellechasse, a Spanish officer, when Captain Guion received his instructions to go there and take possession of it. Captain Guion proceeded promptly from Fort Washington, now Cincinnati, and stopped at Fort Massac to take aboard his artillery. When he reached New Madrid he was halted by the Spanish commandant, who objected to the further progress of his expedition but who finally consented to his going as far as Fort Ferdinand at the lower Chickasaw Bluff, on Captain Guion's agreement to proceed no further until the matter should be referred to the Spanish officials. Captain Guion, having been instructed to be very discreet in dealing with the Spaniards on the west bank of the river or, as derisively put by the frontiersmen, "do nothing to offend the dons," made the best he could of this permission, gave his pledge and proceeded down the river. He reached the lower Chickasaw Bluff on July 20, 1797. He there found that Captain Bellechasse, the Spanish commandant, had dismantled the Spanish fort, Ferdinando de Barancos, and taken position at Hopefield, then called Esperanza, on the west bank of the river and just above Memphis. It may be further noted here that the Spanish troops left Esperanza and floated down the river on September 1st following, thus abandoning both their eastern and western fortified posts at the Chickasaw Bluffs, though they continued to own the territory west of the river.

Captain Guion found great unrest prevailing among the Chickasaw Indians in their territory to the southeast of Memphis. As part of this early history of Memphis under American rule this letter of Captain Guion to General Wilkinson, dated August 14, 1797, is quoted from Claiborne's History of Mississippi:

"Owing to apprehensions of an attack by the Creeks on their town, the Chickasaws did not appear here until the tenth instant. Yesterday Piamingo, the mountain leader, arrived in bad health. The Wolf's Friend preceded him two days and is here with all his people and a very disorderly, turbulent and troublesome clan they are. Great discord prevails in this nation, owing probably to the intrigues of the Spaniards, and the want of information and energy somewhere else. General Colbert, who was here a few days since, with about one hundred of his people, manifested a very friendly disposition, and gave me permission to remove my troops and stores from this bank to the bluff where the Spanish fort recently stood and to erect there such works as I thought fit, observing that it would be extraordinary to deny to us, who were born on the same side of the water, a privilege that had been granted to those born on the other side of it. I immediately set a party to get pickets for a temporary cover for our stores and camp, a very heavy job, for they had to be got a mile up the River Margot (Wolf), rafted down and drawn up the bluff by hand. I have, however, inclosed a sexangular stockade, of which the plan is transmitted.

"The Wolf's Friend, who has great influence is by no

means inclined to the United States. There is an evident coolness between him and the mountain leader. I do not know how it will end. I shall use every exertion to reconcile these discords. I despair however of effecting anything with the former without using a more potent argument than words. A few hundred dollars is the best 'talk' for him.

"On the twelfth Colonel Howard, with five galleys and about one hundred Spanish infantry, arrived from above at the post of Hopefield on the opposite bank of the Mississippi. They have been very civil and a salute has been received and returned. Our troops are daily falling down with intermittents, the prevailing malady of this country."

Another letter quoted by Claiborne and further illustrating the early relations between the American troops and the Chickasaw Indians at the bluffs, is as follows:

"Fort Adams, Chickasaw Bluffs, Oct. 22, 1797.

"Contrary to my expectation the Mountain Leader, (Piamingo), the King, and the Wolf's Friend, with their followers, did not present themselves here to receive their goods, until the twelfth instant. Piamingo apprehended an incursion by the Creeks and had remained at home to repel it. Wolf's Friend, who is a warm partisan of the Spaniards, and a cunning, mischievous fellow, regulated his movements by their advices and arranged to come in about the time the Spanish galleys and troops from St. Louis were to arrive at the post of Esperanza, opposite this. A supply of goods from New Orleans for the Chickasaws, had for some time been stored at Esperanza, but they had delayed the distribution, believing that our lot was very inferior to theirs, and that the contrast would make its impression, which would be supported by the new arrival of soldiers. The Wolf's Friend had assured the commandant at Esperanza that we should not be permitted to remain. August 12th, Colonel Charles Howard, with one hundred men and five galleys, arrived at Esperanza from St. Louis. Wolf's Friend immediately crossed over. On his return he said he wished to make a talk, and desired that his friend Colonel Howard should be present. I appointed the 16th to give time to have William Colbert and Piamingo present. Colonel Howard with two of his officers came over in the morning. He apologised for his visit and said it was only to gratify Wolf's Friend, who had insisted upon it, and he hoped that when he distributed the presents at Esperanza, I would be his guest. This I promptly declined but observed that I had no objection to his presence, as I had no secret intrigues or policy to carry out with the Indians and should merely recommend them to observe order among themselves and peaceful relations with both Spaniards and Americans. William Colbert, anticipating Wolf's Friend's design, opened the conference with a bold and animated talk. Addressing himself to that chief he said, 'I know your object is to expel the Americans and bring back your friends the Spaniards. But this shall not be while I live. The works now being built here were begun with my consent. I and my people gave our consent and our promise and I would like to see the man or the chief who can make that promise void. The Americans may go away if they choose to go. I hear you talk of force. You will do well to count the warriors of this nation. Before you can drive the Americans you must first kill me and my warriors and bury us here.'

"This was followed by a brief but pointed talk from Piamingo to the same purpose. Wolf's Friend remained moody and silent and his Spanish friends, who had come to hear a very different story, were greatly disconcerted. Next day our goods were distributed and as they were more liberal in quantity and more substantial and valuable than the Spanish distribution, the effect was fine.

"I find at this place four white families who came here two and three years ago. The man of most consequence is Kenneth Ferguson, a Scotchman and agent of Panton, Leslie & Company, of Pensacola—very active in the Spanish interest. He is extensively engaged in the Indian trade and sells at most exorbitant rates. Another of these people is William Mizell, a native of North Carolina, who was at Pensacola, under British protection, when it surrendered to the Spaniards. He is no friend to them, and I find him very useful as an interpreter, as he has resided fifteen years among the Chickasaws and speaks their language well."

When Captain Isaac Guion set out from Fort Adams at the Chickasaw Bluff in November, 1797, to go down the river and take possession of the Natchez district, he left a detachment of artillery under Lieutenant Campbell in charge of the fort. The fort was in 1801, removed from its site at the present jail to the bluff near Jackson Mound, by order of General Wilkinson on account of the excessive malarial sickness prevailing among the garrison at the mouth of Wolf River and a new fort was erected between Jackson Mound and the present big Mississippi River bridge, which was called Fort Pickering in honor of Honorable Timothy Pickering, President Washington's secretary of state. Additional troops were sent there, namely, one company of artillery, commanded by Captain Pierce and also one company of infantry, commanded by Captain Meriwether Lewis, the lieutenants being Steele and Fero. Before this, however, Captain Zebulun M. Pike was in command here and about 1800 a fort had been erected near the old site of Fort Adams called, in his honor, Fort Pike. Captain Sparks of the Third United States regiment, was in command at Fort Pickering on November 23, 1801, when that post was visited by Governor W. C. C. Claiborne of the Mississippi Territory at that date, as reported by him to President Madison and in the same letter Governor Claiborne recommended the expediency of more military posts on the Mississippi River, saying that boats were often stranded or sunk or disabled by the illness of their crews and, except at Fort Pickering, there were no stations where relief could be obtained. The Governor added, "A few posts to render aid in such cases, with hospital stores for the sick, would greatly promote the commerce and the peopling of this remote territory. The humanizing effect on the Indians of such stations would soon be felt." He also reported in that letter that opposite the lower Chickasaw Bluff there was a small blockhouse garrisoned by a sergeant and twelve men, meaning the Spanish post of Esperanza.

These excerpts from Claiborne's History of Mississippi

illustrate the character of the military post and its appointments, maintained at the Chickasaw Bluffs on the Mississippi River from their occupation by Captain Guion in 1797, until the purchase of West Tennessee from the Chickasaw Indians by Governor Isaac Shelby of Kentucky and General Andrew Jackson, commissioners on behalf of the United States, on October 17, 1818, at which time West Tennessee and the lower Chickasaw Bluff were first formally and officially opened to settlement by the American pioneer. The brave Chickasaws, who were always friendly to the Americans, had seen to it that no part of their ancient territory should be appropriated by the white man until their own title had been legally extinguished by a purchase negotiated with them by the United States.

In the Navigator, a little book published first in Pittsburg in eleven editions from 1801 to 1811, a map of the river at the lower Chickasaw Bluff is given and among other things these notes:

"Fort Pike formerly stood just below Wolf River; but a better situation was pitched upon and a fort built two miles lower down the bluff, called Fork Pickering. It occupies the commanding ground of the fourth Chickasaw Bluff on the left bank of the Mississippi. The United States have a military factor here, with a few soldiers. The settlement is thin and composed of what is called the half breed; that is, a mixture of the whites and Indians, a race of men too indolent to do any permanent good, either for themselves or society. A landing may be had a little above Fort Pickering but it is not a very good one."

# CHAPTER III

Land Grants by the State of Tennessee. John Rice and John Ramsey Grants. Purchase of West Tennessee from the Chickasaws. Judge John Overton Purchases Rice Grant. Takes in with him Andrew Jackson. Sketch of John Rice. The Birth of Memphis. Map of New Town. Appearance of the Surroundings. Narrative of Colonel James Brown. The Name of Memphis. Establishment of Shelby County. The First Court of Laws. The First County Tax Levy. The First Marriage.

---

LONG preceding these events the State of North Carolina, as we have before seen, claimed this western territory north of the thirty-fifth parallel and embracing the present district of West Tennessee, by virtue of its grant from the Crown of England, as far as the eastern shore of the Mississippi River, and before its cession to the United States of its western territory in December, 1789, it had made to various people sundry grants in this territory of lands, regardless of the unquestionable title of the Chickasaw Indians, who were the actual owners of the ground and had never parted with their rights.

So we find that on the 23rd of October, 1783, a tract of five thousand acres of land abutting on the Mississippi River and embracing the landing at the mouth of Wolf River at the lower Chickasaw Bluff was entered by John Rice, a citizen of North Carolina, in the land office in Hillsboro, North Carolina. We further find that this land was surveyed by Isaac Roberts, deputy surveyor for the Western District, State of North Carolina, on December 1, 1786, by virtue of a land warrant from the state entry taker, Number 382, dated the 24th day of June, 1784. Upon this entry and survey a grant was made by the State of North Carolina, Number 283, on the 25th of April, 1789, evidenced by a formal written document signed by Sam Johnson, Governor, Captain General and Commander-in-Chief, and attested by J. Glasgow, Secretary, which document is the celebrated John Rice grant, the land granted embracing a large portion of the site of the present city of Memphis.

On the same day a land warrant, Number 383, was issued to John Ramsey, by John Armstrong, entry officer of claims for the North Carolina western lands, for five thousand acres, entered on the 25th of October, 1783, said five thousand acres adjoining on the south for part of its depth the John Rice grant, above referred to, but a grant in pursuance of this entry was not issued until the 30th of April, 1823.

As these several grants of lands, made in violation of the ownership and title of the Chickasaw Indians who were then in possession of the same, constitute the original title or titles of the people of the present city of Memphis to all of their lands and holdings within such limits, and as there were no conflicting Spanish or French grants of the same lands, it is deemed proper to here give them in full as a part of the history of the city.

The Rice grant is as follows:

"State of North Carolina, No. 283.
"To all to whom these presents shall come, Greeting:
"Know ye, that we, for and in consideration of the sum of ten pounds for every hundred acres hereby granted, paid into our Treasury by John Rice, have given and granted, and by these presents do give and grant unto the said John Rice, a tract of land containing five thousand acres, lying and being in the Western District, lying on the Chickasaw Bluff. Beginning about one mile below the mouth of Wolf River, at a white oak tree, marked J. R., running north twenty degrees east two hundred and twenty-six poles; thence due north one hundred and thirty-three poles; thence north twenty-seven degrees west three hundred and ten poles to a cottonwood tree; thence due east one thousand and three hundred and seventy-seven

and nine-tenths poles to a mulberry tree; thence south six hundred and twenty-five poles to a stake; thence west one thousand three hundred and four and nine-tenths poles to the beginning, as by the plat herewith annexed doth appear, together with all woods, waters, mines, minerals, hereditaments and appurtenances to the said land belonging or appertaining; To hold to the said John Rice, his heirs and assigns forever—yielding and paying to us such sums of money yearly, or otherwise as our General Assembly from time to time shall cause. This grant to be registered in the Register's office of our said Western District within twelve months from the date hereof; otherwise the same shall be void and of no effect.

"In testimony whereof we have caused these our letters to be made patent and our Great Seal to be hereunto affixed. Witness Samuel Johnson, Esquire, our Governor, Captain General and Commander-in-Chief, at Halifax, the twenty-fifth day of April, in the XIII year of our Independence, and of Our Lord, one thousand seven hundred and eighty-nine.

By his Excellency's command,
J. Glascow, Secretary.                    Sam Johnson."

This grant was based upon an entry and survey made in 1786, as follows:

"State of North Carolina,
Western District.

"By virtue of a warrant from the State Entry Taker, Number 382, dated the twenty-fourth day of June, one thousand seven hundred and eighty four, I have surveyed for John Rice five thousand acres of land, lying on the Chickasaw Bluff; beginning about one mile below the mouth of Wolf River, at a white oak tree, marked J. R., running north twenty degrees east, two hundred and twenty-six poles; thence due north one hundred and thirty-three poles; thence north twenty-seven degrees west, three hundred and ten poles to a cottonwood tree; thence due east one thousand three hundred and seventy-seven and nine-tenths poles to a mulberry tree; thence south six hundred and twenty-five poles to a stake; thence west one thousand three hundred and four and nine-tenths poles to the beginning.

"Surveyed December 1st, 1786.
                    Isaac Roberts, D. S.
John Scott,         }
Thomas Jamison,     }  S. C. C."

"Orange County, Register's Office,
                    August 14th, 1789.
"The within grant is registered in Book M, Folio 117.
                    By John Allison, P. R.
"State of Tennessee, Shelby County,
                    Register's Office, 14th May, 1820.
"The foregoing grant is duly registered in my office this 5th May, 1820.                    Thos. Taylor, R. S. C."

The John Ramsey grant, Number 19,060, for that part of the city lying south and adjoining the Rice grant for part of its length is as follows:

"The State of Tennessee:

"To all to whom these presents shall come, Greeting:

"Know ye, that in consideration of Warrant No. 383, dated the 24th day of June, 1784, issued by John Armstrong, Entry Officer of Claims for the North Carolina Western lands, to John Ramsey, for five thousand acres, and entered on the 25th day of October, 1783, by Number 383, there is granted by the said State of Tennessee, unto the said John Ramsey and John Overton, assignee, etc., a certain tract or parcel of land, containing five thousand acres by survey, bearing date the first day of March, 1822, lying in Shelby County, eleventh district, ranges eight and nine, sections one and two, on the Mississippi River, of which to said Ramsey four thousand two hundred and eighty-five and five-seventh acres, and to said Overton seven hundred and fourteen and two-sevenths acres, and bounded as follows, to-wit: Beginning at a stake on the bank of said river—the southwest corner of John Rice's five thousand acre grant, as processioned by William Lawrence in the year 1820 —running thence south eighty-five degrees east, with said Rice's south boundary line, as processioned aforesaid, one hundred and seventy-five chains to a poplar marked R; thence south two hundred chains to an elm marked F. R.; thence west, at sixty-two chains, crossing a branch bearing south, at seventy chains crossing a branch bearing southeast, at one hundred and nineteen chains, crossing a branch bearing south, and at one hundred and sixty chains a branch bearing south—in all two hundred and seventy-three chains to a cottonwood marked F. R. on the banks of the Mississippi River; thence up the margin of said river, with its meanders, north seven degrees east eleven chains, etc., etc. (Here follows the magnetic bearings of the east bank of the Mississippi River), to the beginning; with the hereditaments and appurtenances appertaining.

"To have and to hold the said tract or parcel of land, with its appurtenances, to the said John Ramsey and John Overton and their heirs forever.

"In witness whereof, William Carroll, Governor of the State of Tennessee, has hereunto set his hand and caused the great seal of the State to be affixed, at Murfreesboro, on the 30th day of April, in the year of Our Lord, 1823, and of the Independence of the United States the forty-seventh. By the Governor.                                    William Carroll.

Daniel Graham, Secretary.

"I, Alexander Kocsis, Register of the land office, for the District of Middle Tennessee, do hereby certify that the foregoing is a true copy of Grant No. 19,060, of the State of Tennessee, to John Ramsey and John Overton, as the same stands recorded in my office, in Book V, page 415. Given under my hand, at office, this 15th day of June, 1867. Alexander Kocsis, By A. Gattinger, Deputy.              Register Land Office."

State of Tennessee, Shelby County."

"The foregoing instrument, with Clerk's certificate, was filed in my office for registration on the 6th day of March, 1872, at 10:40 o'clock a. m., and noted in Note Book No. 7, page 120, and was recorded on the 7th day of March, 1872.

John Brown, Register.
By J. C. Buster, Deputy Register."

The area covered by the territory south of the Rice grant and lying between Bellevue Boulevard, the east line of the Ramsey grant, Trezevant Avenue on the east and the present city limits on the south, was made up of several small grants to the following people, to-wit: Anderson B. Carr, Thomas Hickman and Nicholas Long.

It will be observed that both the Rice and Ramsey grants were conveyances by the State of North Carolina of all the rights which it claimed or possessed under the old grant from the Crown of England, in 1762, of all territory west of its then western limits to the "South Seas," which were supposed to lie far to the west of the Mississippi River. But these lands, insofar as West Tennessee is concerned, were at that time the private property of an unconquered and unconquerable Indian race, the Chickasaws, which were then friendly towards the United States, and North Carolina had no legal right to grant away their territory, either to John Rice, John Ramsey or the United States of America, which she had actually done as we have before seen at about the same period of time. The United States, however recognized this valid title of her Indian friends, the Chickasaws, and appointed a commission to negotiate with the Indians for the sale of all their lands lying between the Tennessee, Mississippi and Ohio Rivers and north of the thirty-fifth parallel of latitude, which commission negotiated with the Chickasaw Indians at their treaty grounds two or three miles west of Tupelo, Mississippi, October 19, 1818, a sale and cession of all these lands to the United States for a consideration of $300,000, to be paid in fifteen annual installments of $20,000 each. Besides this gross sum the Indians, with cunning craft, insisted on and secured from the commissioners certain additional sums which, under their untutored process of reasoning, were due them, growing out of the following train of incidents, viz: Debt of Chief (General) William Colbert to Captain John Gordon, $1,115; debt due Captain David Smith for supplies furnished to himself and soldiers who had helped the Chickasaws in a war with the Creeks; due Oppassantubbee for a tract of land reserved for him under the treaty of 1816, $500; due Captain John Lewis for saddle lost in the service, $25; due Chief John Colbert for sum stolen from him in theatre in Baltimore, $1,089. There were also certain reservations to various members of the tribes and annuities to the chiefs. They also overreached the commissions in trading about the last or 15th annuity of $20,000. Colbert begged for another "cent" when the fourteenth annuity had been agreed upon which Jackson, much puzzled, granted. The Indians then claimed that that agreement meant another $20,000 annuity. Governor Shelby became angry and refused and the treaty came near failing. But Jackson, by giving his personal bond for the $20,000, if Congress failed to provide for it, appeased the angry governor and the treaty was signed.

The commissioners on the part of the United States were General Andrew Jackson, later one of the proprietors and founders of Memphis, and later still President of the United States, and Governor Isaac Shelby, of Kentucky, one of the heroes of the decisive Battle of King's Mountain, North Carolina, the turning point in the American Revolution. Having previously, in 1796, admitted the State of Tennessee to the American Union and designated its western boundary as the Mississippi River, and its limits as embodying all the lands thus purchased from the Chickasaws, the United States made no claim of proprietorship in these lands except in a national sense, and left Tennessee to deal with the question of original title as between itself and the early settlers. Tennessee never questioned the grants of North Carolina to Rice, Ramsey, Hickman, Carr, Long and numerous others in the ceded territory made before the Indian titles were extinguished and the land ceded to the United States by the Chickasaws and those five first named grants to John Rice, John Ramsey, Thomas Hickman, A. B. Carr and N. Long, are today and have always been recognized as the original and legal muniments of title to all lands on which Memphis is now situated, the title of the Chickasaws merging in the title derived from the State of North Carolina.*

John Rice, the grantee of the first grant above named, never lived to realize the value of the splendid domain which

---

*The State of North Carolina, however, in her deed of cession of the territory now covered by the State of Tennessee, to the United States, reserved to her grantees the title to all lands theretofore granted by her to sundry individuals in the ceded territory. This deed of cession was made in December, 1789.

*Andrew Jackson*

## History of Memphis, Tennessee.

They also overreached the commissions in trading ... last or 15th annuity of $20,000. Colbert begged ... "cent" when the fourteenth annuity had been ... which Jackson, much puzzled, granted. The ... claimed that that agreement meant another ... Governor Shelby became angry and refused ... treaty came near failing. But Jackson, by giving his ... bond for the $20,000, if Congress failed to provide for ... the angry governor and the treaty was signed.

The commissioners on the part of the United States were General Andrew Jackson, later one of the proprietors and ... of Memphis, and later still President of the United States, and Governor Isaac Shelby, of Kentucky, one of the heroes of the decisive Battle of King's Mountain, North Carolina, the turning point in the American Revolution. Having previously ... 1796, admitted the State of Tennessee to the ... and designated its western boundary as the ... and its limits as embodying all the lands thus ... the Chickasaws, the United States made no ... prietorship in these lands except in a national ... ft Tennessee to deal with the question of original ... ween itself and the early settlers. Tennessee never ... ed the grants of North Carolina to Rice, Ramsey, Hickman, Carr, Long and numerous others in the ceded territory ... before the Indian titles were extinguished and the land ... ed to the United States by the Chickasaws and those five ... st named grants to John Rice, John Ramsey, Thomas Hickman, A. B. Carr and N. Long, are today and have always been recognized as the original and legal muniments of title to all lands on which Memphis is now situated, the title of the ... ging in the title derived from the State of North ...

... the grantee of the first grant above named, ... realize the value of the splendid domain which

... State of North Carolina, however, in her deed of cession of ... covered by the State of Tennessee, to the United ... to her grantees the title to all lands theretofore ... sundry individuals in the ceded territory. This ... was made in December, 1789.

*Andrew Jackson*

he had obtained from the State of North Carolina. He migrated from North Carolina to Nashville soon after obtaining his grant of this and other large bodies of land in Middle and West Tennessee and later engaged in large commercial enterprises, according to the standards of that day, and was killed by the Indians in 1791 while transporting his goods up the Cumberland River, at a point about where the city of Clarksville now stands. He had left a will devising to his brother, Elisha Rice, his grant of five thousand acres on the Chickasaw Bluff, and this grant was in 1794 conveyed by Elisha Rice to Judge Overton for a consideration of $500.00, though his brother John had originally paid to the State of North Carolina ten pounds for every one hundred acres of the grant, a sum amounting in all to five hundred pounds sterling or about twenty-five hundred dollars. Judge Overton made certain his title by also obtaining conveyances from the other three surviving brothers of John Rice, who were the remaining heirs of his estate. The day following the purchase of this land Judge Overton conveyed an undivided one-half interest in the Rice grant to his warm friend and almost lifelong companion, General Andrew Jackson.

John Rice with great sagacity had located his grant so as to embrace the mouth of Wolf River and the then only available landing on the Mississippi River, although the lands were rough and broken to a considerable extent at and near the Mississippi River front on that part of the lower Chickasaw Bluffs, although he might, if he had chosen, have entered the lands embraced in the Ramsey grant next adjoining him a little lower down and obtained much smoother and more elevated property. But as he foresaw the development at that early period must begin where the landing facilities were greatest and this actually followed, as every student of the history of Memphis now knows.

Immediately upon the extinguishment of the Chickasaw title to West Tennessee lands in 1818, immigration began to flow towards the Mississippi River, the hardy pioneers by hundreds seeking homes in that nature favored territory. Among the first to come was Judge John Overton and soon after,

General Jackson. The latter had disposed of portions of his half interest, William Winchester obtaining one-fourth and General James Winchester one-half, a half of which he held in trust for the heirs of a deceased brother, and General Jackson retained one-fourth. Judge Overton and his colleagues, General Winchester and General Jackson, immediately became very active and proceeded to lay off a town on the river front section of the Rice grant as soon as the correct lines of the grant could be ascertained. There was some difficulty in determining the actual bounds of this land which was described as beginning "about one mile below the mouth of Wolf River at a white oak tree marked J. R.," but after numerous measurements and surveys, by reason of the fact that the mouth of Wolf River was a shifting point from time to time, owing to the alternate encroachments and recession of the low water line of the Mississippi River in the alluvial lands under the upper end of the Chickasaw Bluffs, it was finally determined about May, 1819, to locate the town first from Auction Street on the north to the present north line of Union Avenue on the south and from Front Street on the west to the alley east of Second Street on the east. This plan of the new town was wrought into shape by William Lawrence, the surveyor, and a map prepared of the town, subsequently to the first draft of which an extension was made of the territory from Auction Street northward to Bayou Gayoso, which new territory was likewise divided into lots and streets. A copy of this map is here published, showing the exact location and plan of the town of Memphis and its extension, and showing its streets, alleys, squares and blocks, its splendid system of parks or public squares and grand promenade on the river front and the then relative positions of the mouth of Wolf River, the course and curves of Bayou Gayoso near its mouth, and the outline of the bluff, which then overhung the water-line of the river from a point near the foot of Jackson Street southward.

The partition of the lands which the proprietors of Memphis then held as tenants in common, which took place in 1829, and the ratification of the dedication to public use forever of

# PLAN of MEMPHIS

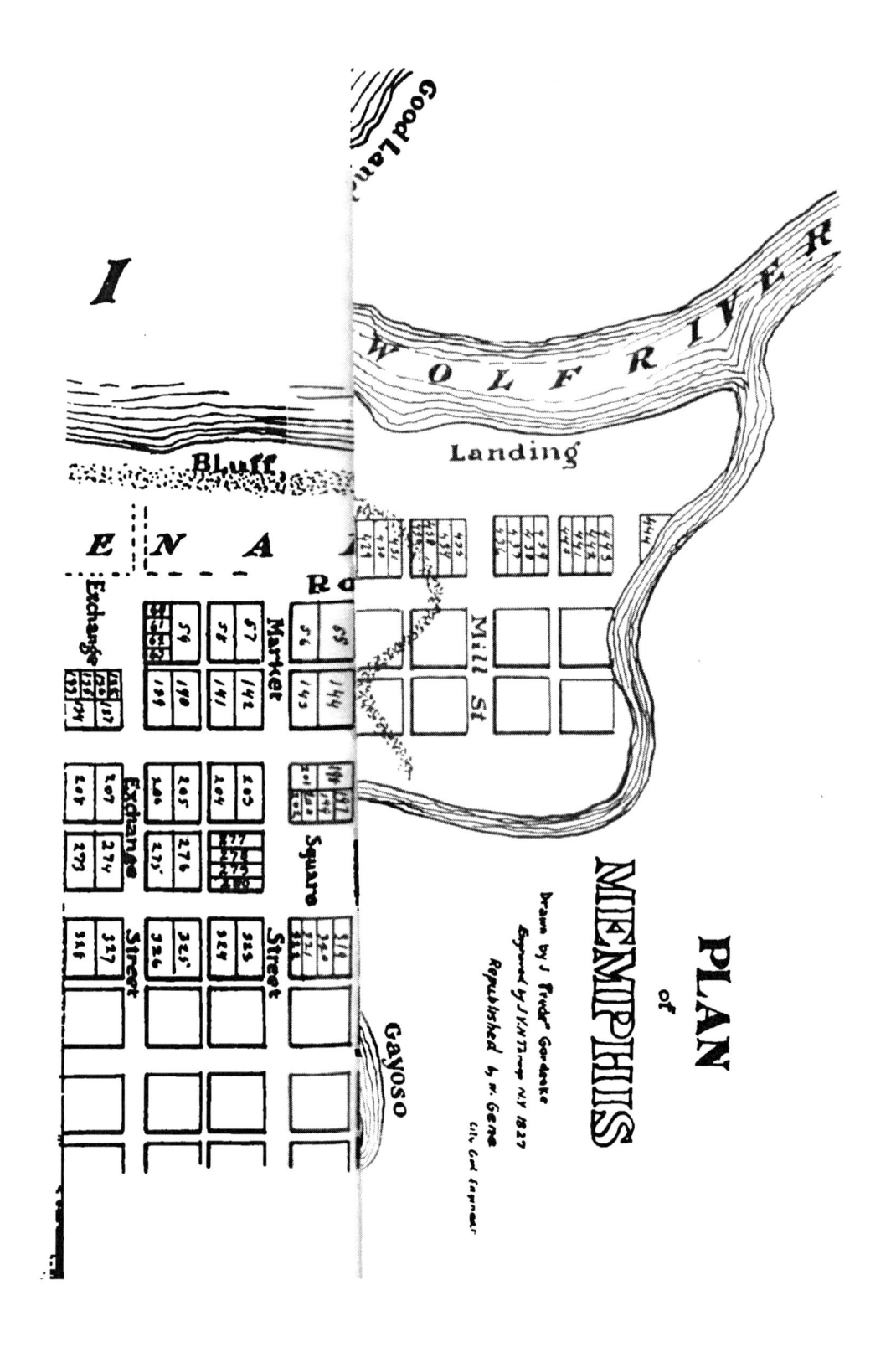

the squares and promenade will be treated further along in this narrative.

Colonel James Brown, an early locater and surveyor of lands in the western district of Tennessee, thus tells of some of the important events which immediately followed the laying out of the town of Memphis in the early part of the year 1819. He says:

"Judge John Overton, of Nashville, Tennessee, one of the proprietors of the new town of Memphis, was here with his plan of the upper part of Memphis, (now Pinch), and on several days had offered some of his lots for sale; very few were sold and they for small prices, I rather think from thirty and forty dollars to one hundred dollars would cover the range of prices. I was well acquainted with the Judge (grandfather to our present State Senator), and well recollect his estimate of the ultimate value of the location as a town, saying that it would some day be the greatest city in the United States, and rival the ancient city of Memphis on the River Nile, for which it was named.

"Judge Overton did not seem to be discouraged at the low prices and short sales, and only offered the lots for sale to afford all who might be disposed to invest, an opportunity to do so. He said that he knew it took many people to make a large town and the country contiguous must be settled before it could grow much.

"He was quite liberal in donating lots to nearly all of the old settlers. To T. D. Carr he gave two lots whereon to build a tavern for the accommodation of the persons attending the land office. It consisted of six or eight one-story round-pole cabins, very low, and floored with old boat plank, the cracks daubed with clay, after the manner of Indian huts. To A. B. Carr he gave one lot for the location of a horse-mill and one lot out on Bayou Gayoso for a tan-yard site."

To this excerpt taken from the June number, 1875, of The Old Folks Record, a historical mazagine then published in Memphis, will be added other quotations from the same narrative and reminiscences of Memphis and West Tennessee, by Colonel James Brown, the pioneer surveyor of this locality, which describes with extreme vividness the condition of affairs existing at the lower Chickasaw Bluffs during the year 1819, in May of which year the original town of Memphis was first laid off, as before stated.

Colonel Brown says, in his extremely interesting narrative:

"On the 19th of October, 1818, Isaac Shelby and Andrew Jackson, as commissioners on the part of the United States, made a treaty with the Chickasaw Indians for all that part of their territory north of the southern line of the State of Tennessee, beginning on the 35th parallel of north latitude, where the same crosses the Tennessee River; thence west with said line to where the same strikes the Mississippi River at or near the Chickasaw Bluffs; thence up the Mississippi River to the mouth of the Ohio; thence up the Ohio to the mouth of the Tennessee River; thence up the Tennessee to the beginning. This treaty was forwarded to Washington City for the consideration of the Executive of the United States, and was approved by the President, James Monroe, and proclaimed as such on the 7th of January, 1819. At this time I was associated with my uncle, Joseph B. Porter, and his son, J. T. Porter, for the purpose of locating land warrants and establishing North Carolina grants surveyed some thirty years previous. As soon as the news reached us, (then residing in Maury County, Tennessee), we set out for the newly acquired territory.

"The southern boundary of Tennessee not having been as yet extended any further west than the Tennessee River, we began at that point, it being the northwest corner of the State of Alabama previously established and the lands in Alabama had been in market. Here we ascertained the variation of the dividing line between Tennessee and Alabama, as accurately as we could, and extended the same westwardly to the Mississippi River, striking nearly opposite the lower end of President's Island, about four miles south of old Fort Pickering, arriving there, part of us on the sixth and part on the seventh of March, 1819. This line was run for our own information and not as an established line, but some time in the summer following the official line was run by General James

ASTOR, LENOX
TILDEN FOUNDATION

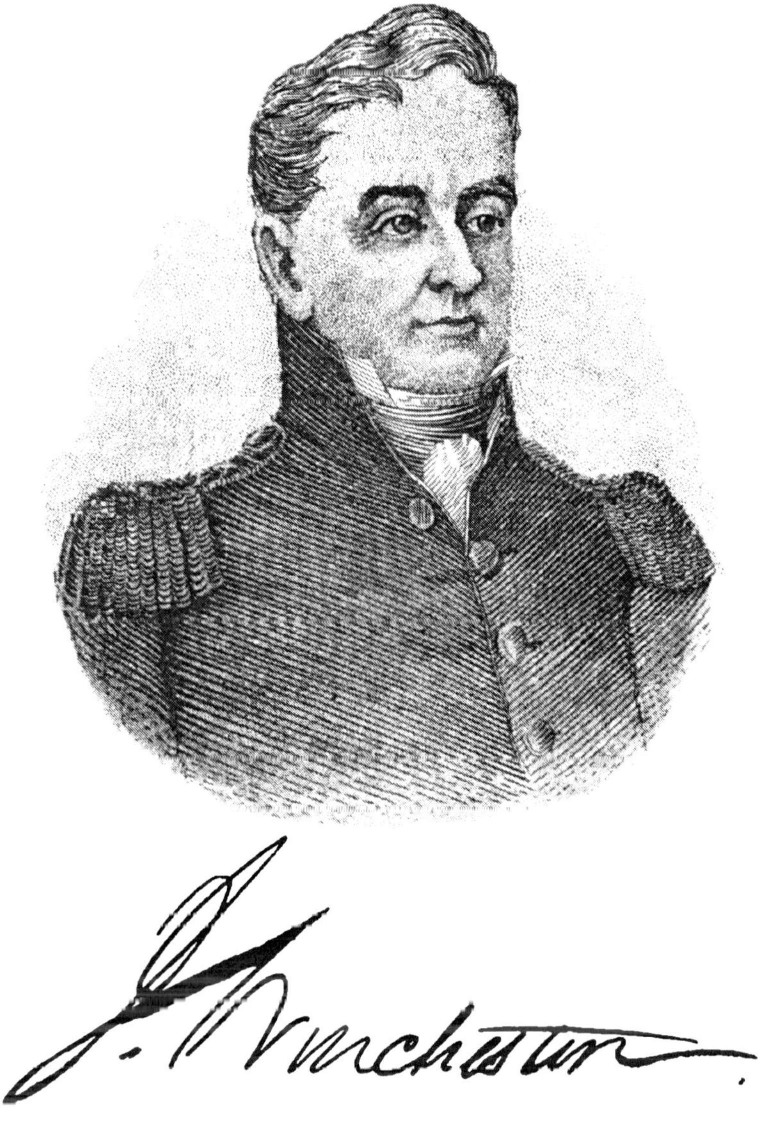

Winchester as commissioner of the United States, with whom James Blakemore, I believe, was the surveyor.

"At this time there were but three white men residing in this part of the purchase, Thomas D. Carr, A. B. Carr and a hired man named Overton, excepting those who were connected with the Indians, Tom Fletcher (who was raised in the Nation), Pat Meagher and his family, Joab Bean, a blacksmith and resident gunsmith, to repair the guns for the Indian hunters. No roads led to or from the Chickasaw Bluffs, as it was then called; only an Indian path or trail, called the Cherokee trace, leading from Tuscumbia, over which the Cherokees emigrated west of the Mississippi River a few years previous by the use of pack-horses entirely; also an Indian trail leading out southeastwardly to the Indian towns on what is now called the Pontotoc Ridge and formerly the Chickasaw agency.

"This entire country and part of North Mississippi was never occupied by the Indians as residents, but only as hunting grounds. The town of Memphis was laid out about the month of May, 1819.

"In Book A, of the Records of Shelby County, page 133, Andrew Jackson, John Overton and James Winchester conveyed to trustees the five thousand acre tract originally entered in the name of John Rice, including the mouth of Wolf River, on a part of which they designed to lay off a town, south of Wolf River and within one mile of the Mississippi River. In the same book, page 201, is recorded a deed from Memphis proprietors to B. Fooy for Lot Number 53, in accordance with title bond dated the 22nd of May, 1819, for lot Number 53, in the town called Memphis.

"From the records referred to, it is evident that the town of Memphis was established, surveyed and named about May, 1819, and as shown in the last number of your record, the county was organized first of May, 1820; at which time I doubt whether there was twenty actual settlers in the county, or within any other settlement within seventy-five miles. I did not know of any nearer than the middle fork of the Forked Deer River, some ten miles northeast of where Jackson is now, there was one or two settlers that raised corn during that year, 1819. The Messrs. Carrs had arrived at this place but two or three weeks previous to our arrival. They were traveling in a small boat from Virginia to Louisiana and on the way heard that the Chickasaws were negotiating for the sale of their country. They stopped here to settle, if it was true, and our arrival gave them the first reliable intelligence of that fact, which was soon affirmed by the arrival of other parties on the same business that we were. Among them that I now recollect was Gideon Pillow, (father of our General G. J. Pillow), William Bradshaw, J. C. McLemore, James Vaulx, R. Hightower and sons.

"At this time, March, 1819, the Mississippi River current set very strong into the then mouth of Wolf, which was some one hundred yards north and about the same distance west from the northern termination of the high ground, with a narrow bench of low bottom extending down the river some 150 to 200 yards to where the current struck the bluff. The bank all along there was giving way rapidly and soon all disappeared to the bluff but in a short period the current slackened about the mouth of Wolf and struck the bluff lower down and a sandbar formed along the upper part of the bluff and mouth of Wolf, and in the course of fifteen to twenty years formed the bar now called the Batture and Navy Yard, and thereby throwing the mouth of Wolf over a quarter of a mile into what fifty years ago was the main channel of the Mississippi River. The landing at the mouth of Wolf was very difficult for flatboats, owing to the strong current but the landing at, or a little above Fort Pickering was very good, having a gentle, smooth current passing along the bank without caving.

"The descent from the top of the bluff was down a gentle sloping hollow. The old fort, or rather blockhouse, was still standing. The road from Fort Pickering to the mouth of Wolf was a narrow path along the top of the bluff, through a dense forest of timber and cane, some places very thick and others thin cane; in one place, perhaps half way between the points, there had been a recent slide or caving in of the bluff, taking off the road for some hundred yards or more, and perhaps two or three acres of land."

And thus it was that twenty-nine years after North Carolina ceded her claim to the United States and Tennessee was made a territory, and twenty-three years after she was admitted to the Union as the State of Tennessee, Memphis was laid out.

Several names had been suggested for the new town: "Jackson," for General Andrew Jackson, one of her founders; "Chickasaw," which was thought by some to be the most appropriate name for this site and "Memphis," on account of her situation on the river being so similar to that of old Memphis in Egypt, on the Nile. The last was chosen by "Old Hickory" himself, it is said, who claimed for the new town such future greatness as the past greatness of the other Memphis. This controversy over names took place in 1819, when the city was laid out, but Memphis was not finally decided upon until May, 1819, the meaning of the name pleasing the founders and really gaining the choice more than the signification of her situation. This meaning, variously interpreted, is "The Good Place," "Good Abode," or "The Abode of the Good One."

It seems that the first joint conception of a town on the lower Chickasaw bluffs took place in January of the year 1819 and was embodied in the instrument referred to by Colonel James Brown, in the excerpt quoted above, as recorded in Book A, page 133 of our Shelby County records. The clause in question is as follows: "Andrew Jackson, John Overton and James Winchester agreed on the sixth of January, 1819, the same being filed for record on January 1, 1823, probate being in person by Jackson in open circuit court, Davidson County, Tennessee and by Overton and Winchester in open circuit court Williamson County, Tennessee, relative to laying out a town on that part of premises described in Number 1 herein, lying south of Wolf River and within one mile of the Mississippi River, provided, that in case of the death of one or two of the parties hereto, the survivors shall have full power to lay off and dispose of lots in said town, and that no future transfer of interest in said plan shall affect the terms in this agreement which is to remain in force for ten years."

Just at the time that the town of Memphis was laid off and received its name, ignoring the wretched group of aboriginal huts and Indian traders who swapped blankets, beads and tobacco and whiskey for pelts with the Chickasaw Indian hunters at the old landing by the mouth of Wolf River, the Legislature thought it wise and progressive to establish a county extending eastward from the Chickasaw Bluff so that the state would not be hampered in its administration of the new and promising territory. It is not so historically stated but there is little question that the far-seeing mind of Judge John Overton of Nashville, suggested this legislation. On November 24, 1819, the General Assembly of Tennessee passed an act establishing a new county on the Mississippi River, to be called Shelby County in honor of the great Kentucky governor and Revolutionary soldier, Isaac Shelby who, together with General Andrew Jackson, and on the 19th of October of the preceding year negotiated with the Indians the purchase by the United States of what is now West Tennessee and Western Kentucky.

And so, just one year after the plans of the future city were drawn and the lots staked off on the bluff, Honorable Jacob Tipton, as commissioner of the State of Tennessee, appeared May 1, 1820 at the site of the new town, produced his commission and caused proclamation to be made for the organization of a court of pleas and quarter sessions for the County of Shelby and then proceeded to the qualification of Anderson B. Carr, Marcus B. Winchester, William Irvine, Thomas D. Carter and Benjamin Willis as justices of the peace, administered the oath of office to them as such justices, and then made proclamation of the opening of the court. The above named gentlemen, together with Jacob Tipton, ex-officio member, at once elected William Irvine as chairman, John Read, clerk *pro tem* and Major Thomas Taylor, sheriff.

These gentlemen having qualified and entered upon their duties on the same day, the County of Shelby was born. The court at once proceded to business, the first item being to authenticate a deed of conveyance from William Thompson to

Anderson B. Carr. The next day the court proceeded to the appointment of permanent officers for the county and qualified William Lawrence as clerk; Samuel R. Brown, sheriff; Thomas Taylor, register; Alex. Ferguson, ranger; William A. Davis, trustee; Gideon Carr, coroner; William Bettis and William Dean, constables; and John P. Perkins, solicitor.

A few other items of their legislative work will be referred to. On the 3rd of May, John Montgomery and John P. Perkins were admitted to practice in the court, and were thus the first recognized lawyers in West Tennessee. Joseph James was the first man licensed to keep an ordinary or house of entertainment in the country and William Irvine was authorized to keep a public ferry at the river landing, known as Irvine's, being forced to give bonds for keeping the river banks in proper order and providing suitable boats, and thus Mr. Irvine was likewise the first wharf-master. The rates of board and lodging at the public houses for man and beast was fixed by law, by the order of the court, and the tax-levy for the year 1820 was laid as follows:

On each 100 acres of land ........................... $ .18¾
On each town lot ................................. .37½
On each white poll ............................... .12½
On each black poll ............................... .25
On each wholesale and retail store, peddler and hawker 5.00

This levy was made August 3, 1820 and on the same day the court tried its first prisoner under indictment, Patrick Meagher, for retailing spirits, who pleaded guilty and was fined one dollar and costs.

The court then turned its attention to the question of a courthouse for holding its august sessions and ordered that T. D. Carr, Esquire, be authorized and empowered to contract with some workman "to build and erect a temporary log courthouse, jury-room and jail on Market Square in the town of Memphis, and hereby appropriate one hundred and seventy-five dollars for erecting and building the same."

As compared with our modern million and a half dollar courthouse, this structure was indeed primitive, but the laws seem to have been enforced inside those log walls with a vigor and determination that forms a model for all time to come.

Mr. James D. Davis, in his Old Times Sketches, says that the first court was held at a log house on the north side of Winchester Street in the rear of the brick building which now stands at the northeast corner of Main and Winchester Streets, but it being questioned as to whether a court should be held elsewhere than in Court Square, the $175.00 building was built in that square, where it remained for many years and was used for a long time as a school-house. But the records of the court show that on February 5, 1821, the court met at the house of William Lawrence and that on May 7, 1821, the court met in the courthouse in the town of Memphis; also that on May 9, the order for building the courthouse, jury-room and jail was rescinded and $125.00 was appropriated for building a jail. Where the courthouse was first actually erected, the record does not show, but the court did provide on November 7, 1821, the prison bounds as "beginning and running so as to include the public square on which the courthouse now stands."

On May 1, 1820, the first authorized marriage in Memphis was celebrated, the contracting parties Overton W. Carr and Mary Hill, the marriage rites being performed by Jacob Tipton, Justice of the Peace.

The Chickasaw Bluffs were now occupied by a town in name at least, which was also the county seat of the County of Shelby, and all they seemed to lack was a sufficient population to make good their claims. In 1825 the town of Memphis is alleged to have shown a census return of 308, but this included of course, both the Indian and Negro population, the former being more or less transient and occupying the bluffs from time to time on trading expeditions, in which they camped in the usual style in the vicinity of the landing near the mouth of Wolf River. There were some Indian residents and some of these had sold their huts or shacks to enterprising immigrants, who did not otherwise possess the means of building themselves homes. This species of squatter sovereignty, though the titles of the purchases were undoubtedly legal, caused some trouble between the proprietors of Memphis and

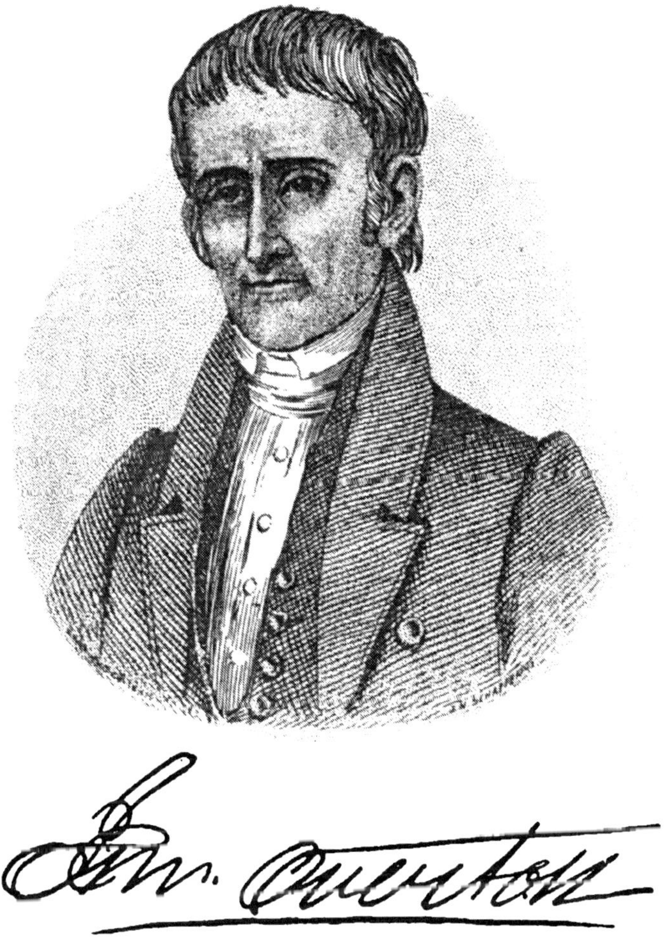

the holders of these lots or patches of ground, as they occupied in many instances more or less of the city lots, as designated on the new map of Memphis.

It will be remembered that John Rice received his grant and sold his tract to Judge John Overton while the lands on the Chickasaw Bluffs were still held by the aboriginal inhabitants who had up to that time never parted with their titles and when, in 1818, these Indians ceded their territory in West Tennessee to the United States Government the grantee of course obtained the only actual and legal title to the land. The United States made no grants or conveyances of these lands and the Indian residents, who had not abandoned their lands under this cession to the United States, but retained and occupied their tenures, beyond question had a better title to the ground than did John Rice, whose grant was from the State of North Carolina, before the Indians had parted with their titles, not to North Carolina, but to the United States, and neither John Rice nor his grantees had ever got possession of the ground so occupied by the Indians. But the matter was ultimately settled by the conveyance of certain of the town lots by the proprietors to the claimants.

# CHAPTER IV

Incorporation of Memphis. Resentment of the Inhabitants. Sketch of First Charter. First Board of Mayor and Aldermen. Limits of the Corporation Fixed. Outline of First Tax-Levy. Second Board of Aldermen. Memphis Made a City. Isaac Rawlings Mayor. City Divided into Wards. Fire Department Established. Citizens Oust the Gamblers. Young Memphis a Free Soil Town. Removal of the Indians to the West. Rivalry Between Memphis and Randolph. Mississippi Claims Site of Memphis. Tax Assessment of 1840. War With the Flatboatmen. Memphis Gets the Great Navy Yard. The City Limits Extended. "South Memphis" and "Pinch." Incorporation of South Memphis. The First Telegraph Line. Troubles Over Slavery. The Wolf River Canal Project. The First Bond Issue. The Charters of 1848 and 1849.

---

THE Legislature of Tennessee passed an Act December 9, 1826, incorporating the town of Memphis. As only a few of the inhabitants,—chiefly the younger and more progressive men,—had been consulted with regard to this incorporation as a town, the new charter came as a surprise to most of the people. In consequence it met with considerable resentment from some of the unconsulted and offended members of the small community. Among these indignant men was Isaac Rawlings, one of the most influential men of the locality, but one of the old-time sort, ever suspicious of innovations of any kind that might disturb the ease of people prone to remain in a rut. But often excellent people remain in narrow pathways because there is no incentive to turn them aside, but when persuaded to leave the old trail, they find new and better ways and learn that they can add to their own comfort and profit by branching out, as well as to their usefulness to others. So it later proved with this worthy old pioneer, Mr. Isaac Rawlings.

A public meeting was called and speeches were made for and against the new corporation. Isaac Rawlings was made chairman of this meeting and he made a speech against the new act, denouncing it as "a trick of the proprietors." He held that the small community could not support a city government; that it must grow in population and wealth before such an act should be considered. He said that it would be an advantage only to the proprietors and well-to-do class, while the poor on the outskirts of the proposed town would suffer hardships thereby. Speakers on the other side put forward the advantages of a corporation and offered to leave out the poor "on the outskirts" to satisfy Mr. Rawlings and his partisans.

One of the strongest supporters of the new charter was Marcus B. Winchester, a young man of education, refinement and progressive spirit. His energetic methods of doing business and pushing affairs had disturbed Rawlings and his followers from the advent of that young gentleman to the "Bluff," but as time progressed and the city enlarged, becoming more and more important and flourishing under the new charter, Mr. Rawlings saw the benefits and was big enough to acknowledge it, though he harbored a feeling of resentment and jealousy toward Marcus Winchester for a long time.

O. F. Vedder gives the substance of the first charter of Memphis, as follows:

Section 1, incorporated the town and conferred upon it its name, but fixed no boundaries. Section 2, gave the town authorities power to pass all kinds of needful legislation for the government of and preservation of the health of the town. Section 3, required the sheriff of the county to hold an election on the first Saturday of March, 1827, and on the same day in every subsequent year, for members of the board of aldermen, at which election any person holding a freehold in the town, who was entitled to vote for members of the general assembly should be qualified to vote for mayor and aldermen. Section 4, read: "That the seven persons having the highest number of votes at any election shall be taken to be elected, and the sheriff of said county shall within two days thereafter, and a majority being present, proceed to elect a mayor from their own body for said corporation for the time the aldermen were elected.''

On account of the delay of the charter the election of 1827 did not take place until April 26, instead of the first of March as specified in the charter. This election was held at the old courthouse and the first board of aldermen elected for the city of Memphis were: M. B. Winchester, Joseph L. Davis, John Hooke, N. B. Atwood, George F. Graham, John R. Dougherty and William D. Neely. This board held its first meeting May 9, 1827 and they elected for the first mayor of the infant city, Marcus B. Winchester, who had been so largely instrumental in having it made a town. His administration confirmed all that his former conduct toward the little town had bespoke, that he was one of her best friends and most earnest workers.

At this first meeting of the board the certificate of election was presented, signed by Nathan Anderson, Isaac Rawlings, A. Rapel and S. F. Brown, sheriff.

The first resolution passed was to the effect that it was important to the interest of Memphis that ordinances be adopted for the government of the town. An election was announced for May 12, when the treasurer, recorder and town constable should be elected. At the appointed time the election took place, when Isaac Rawlings was elected treasurer, Jacob L. Davis, recorder, and John J. Balch, constable.

Another meeting of the board was held May 30, at which time the question came up of the legality of their organization. The charter had set the first Saturday in March for the election and it had not taken place until April the 26th. The matter was exhaustively discussed and finally dismissed, with these reasons or pleas: "That the charter did not reach Memphis until after the first Saturday of March; that it was evidently the intention of the Legislature that the corporation should be organized during the current year; that the judges held the election legal, and the sheriff had so certified; hence, it was declared proper on the part of the board that they consider themselves a legal body, and proceed to pass the ordinances needed by the new town."*

There is no record nor tradition that this action of the board was ever disputed.

The first ordinance passed was for the classification of property into taxable and non-taxable possessions. Those liable to taxation were classed thus: "All town lots; all free males between the ages of twenty-one and fifty; all slaves between the ages of twelve and fifty, wholesale and retail stores, including medicine stores, peddlers and hawkers; members of the learned professions, who practice the same for profit; tavern keepers; retailers of spirits; stud horses and jacks. Taxes were levied in the following proportions: Improved lots with buildings, ten cents on the one hundred dollars; unimproved lots ten cents; each free male inhabitant, twenty-five cents; each slave twenty-five cents; each wholesale and retail store, eight dollars; each trading boat, peddler or hawker, ten dollars; each lawyer or doctor practicing for profit, two dollars; each tavern keeper, three dollars; each retailer of spirits, without tavern license, ten dollars."†

An ordinance fixed the corporation limits as follows:

"Beginning at the intersection of Wolf River with the Mississippi River; thence with Wolf River to the mouth of Bayou Gayoso; thence with said bayou to the county bridge; thence with the line of the second alley east of and parallel with Second Street to Union Street; thence, at right angle to Second Street, to the western boundary of the tract of land granted to John Rice by the grant number 283, dated April 25, 1789; thence with the said western boundary up the Mississippi River to the Wolf River."‡

At this meeting of the board a public printer was chosen and bonds were required of the recorder to the amount of $500, and the treasurer was to give bond for double the sum likely to come into his hands during the current year. All ordinances passed at this meeting were signed by all the members of the board, including the mayor.

*Vedder. †Vedder. ‡Vedder.

The two first years of her existence Memphis had a population of 53, which increased rapidly until, by 1827, the year she received her first charter, there were estimated to be more than 500 inhabitants.

The first board of mayor and aldermen of this little western town started to work under difficulties, with little money and many needs, as Memphis, like other infants, needed much expenditure to bring her to useful maturity. As the town grew the authorities appropriated what they could for public benefits and at a meeting held in October they gave eighty dollars for improving Chickasaw Street and one hundred and twenty dollars for building a wharf at the lowest steamboat landing.

When the second election was held in the city the aldermen elected were M. B. Winchester, Samuel Douglass, William A. Hardy, John D. Graham, Augustus L. Humphrey, Joseph L. Davis and Robert Fearn. They again chose Marcus B. Winchester for mayor. During this year the office of town surveyor was created and provision made for a superintendent of graveyards.

When Memphis had enjoyed two years of corporate government it was conceded to be successful and improvements were manifest. In the second corporate year the charter was amended, giving Memphis all the powers of the older city, Nashville, thus constituting it a city. The charter of this year also provided that the mayor should not hold office under the United States Government, and on March 4, 1829, when another municipal election took place, Winchester could not be elected mayor, as he was postmaster. The mayor elected for this year was Isaac Rawlings, he by this time being one of the staunchest supporters of the corporation that he had so vehemently fought two years before. His service was so satisfactory that in 1830, he was again elected by his fellow aldermen as mayor. During this administration a town hall was erected on the southeast corner of Market Square and was a great pride to the little city on the Mississippi.

In August of this year Memphis was divided into three wards: "Ward No. 1 comprising all that part of Memphis northeast of a direct line from the Mississippi River to Overton Street; thence with said street to the Bayou Gayoso. Ward No. 2, all that part of the aforementioned line to Overton Street, to Bayou Gayoso and northeast of a direct line from the Mississippi to Winchester Street, and thence with Winchester Street to the eastern boundary of the town. Ward No. 3, all that part of Memphis south of the last mentioned line.''

The next year Seth Wheatley was elected mayor and the year following, 1832, Robert Lawrence. The succeeding election brought Isaac Rawlings back to the head of the aldermen's table as mayor, which seat of honor he held for three consecutive terms.

Improvement of streets, paying bills and assessing taxes chiefly occupied the august city board during this administration, but one other important accomplishment was the organization and equipment of the city's first fire-engine company, a vital addition to the town's safety but, as was common with fire companies in those days, this organization became a political power, largely influencing the control of municipal elections.

Early court proceedings and justice in the young city were often crude, as the citizens and people to handle affairs were themselves often so. For instance, once in the early twenties a jury was trying a man for his life. Six were for acquittal and six for conviction. Finding that they could not come to an agreement it was proposed that a game of "seven-up" decide the question. The game proved a close and exciting one and ended for acquittal. Such was justice with men accustomed to gambling. As men's lives trend, so their viewpoints are formed.

Gambling was prevalent all along the Mississippi River in those days and continued to be so for a number of years. The gamblers multiplied and became such a power for evil that towns began driving them out forcibly unless they would agree to leave peaceably. In 1835 many of them had gathered in Vicksburg, Mississippi, where they became such a menace that they were ordered by the town authorities to leave, and those who refused to do so were hung. That drove the survivors from the Mississippi town and they were also ordered to leave other places, after which Memphis became overrun with them. Human birds of prey are as great a menace to a community as are eagles and hawks to unoffending domestic fowls, and the respectable citizens of Memphis felt outraged that this class of society should prey upon the decency and good government of the city. Efforts were made to oust them to no avail until there was finally a public meeting of reputable men, after which the gamblers were ordered to leave or expect the treatment received by some of their fellows in Vicksburg. That threat, which bade fair to be carried into effect, had the desired result and for a while Memphis was freed from that element.

In 1834 candidates for the state constitutional convention in Memphis were all abolitionists and the man elected, Adam Alexander, was strong in announcing his views against slavery, but he was opposed to emancipation until a scheme of practical colonization had been determined upon. The fact that he was elected proves that his was the sentiment most prevalent in the community at that time. Another proof of the feeling in favor of emancipation in that period is that "many petitions were sent to the convention from a number of counties, praying that some system of gradual emancipation be agreed upon."

But acts of extremists did much to reverse the prevalent feeling and to embitter the white people in the South. One of these was the uprising of Nat Turner in 1831 in Virginia, and was really the beginning of intensified feelings of hatred between the two races and between the North and South. The slavery code became more rigidly enforced in Southern States, as a means of protection to the whites, although many influential Southern people continued to plead for emancipation, declaring slavery to be a drawback to any country, harmful both to whites and blacks. Most people favored Jefferson's plan of gradual emancipation in order that the negro should thereby be fitted for life in a civilized country, where customs were so different from those of the savagery they had left in the jungles of Africa.

One resolution adopted in a Southern meeting for emancipation, read:

"Resolved, *That slavery is morally, politically and economically wrong,* and that its abolition by the approaching convention will be proper, expedient and practical." But this sentiment for justice gave way to feelings of resentment and revenge as fanatics in the North and South tried to stir up negro insurrections, and it became common for such agitators to be whipped and driven from the South. But not in the South alone did this treatment endure. It is well known how Garrison, for his extreme abolitionism and scathing sentences, was dragged through the streets of Boston and all but killed. For like offences MacIntosh was burned to death in St. Louis and Lovejoy murdered by a mob in Illinois. In Connecticut, Prudence Crandall was imprisoned for teaching colored children to read, while at that time Frances Wright had the permission of Shelby County and the help of Memphis people to do the same thing as extensively as she chose, in her colony at Germantown, Tennessee. Miss Crandall was afterwards mobbed and ordered to leave the State of Connecticut and was in danger of her life.

It was an outcome of this bitterness of feeling being brought to bear that caused Tennessee about this time to take away from free negroes the privilege of the ballot, in opposition to Section 8, of the Bill of Rights, "that no free man shall be disseized of his freehold, liberties or privileges, or outlawed or exiled, or in any manner destroyed or deprived of his life, liberty or property, but by the judgment of his peers or the law of the land."

The question of race supremacy seems to have been a strong one in United States History, and many dissensions arose in those days of the first half of the Nineteenth Century concerning dealings between the whites and negroes and between the whites and Indians. The Indians were driven back, back, as white men advanced and became numerous and in 1835 the Chickasaws, who had held the bluffs on the Mississippi River many generations before white men knew these heights at all, were removed from their Mississippi reservation farther west, to what was called the Indian Territory. This action of the Government was strongly opposed by many white people and stands "as one instance of the white man's perfidy and oppression."*

The population of Memphis by this time had increased to 1,239.

In the early thirties a strong rivalry sprang up between Memphis and Randolph, a town forty-two miles northeast of Memphis, situated much like the latter on a high bluff on the Mississippi River. This was the second formidable rival of Memphis, the first being Raleigh Springs in the same county and eleven miles northeast of the Bluff City.

In 1827 the county-seat had been changed from Memphis to Raleigh, which had made the latter a rival to be feared. Many people moved from Memphis to the new county seat, but its situation for business was not so good as that of Memphis, and this in time told in favor of Memphis, as she grew again while Raleigh dwindled, business being a greater force in the building of a city than capitalship.

But Randolph, equal in situation—and some said better— became formidable indeed, and for years Memphis suffered greatly from the preference of traders for Randolph, many ignoring her entirely for the landing higher up the river. Randolph continued to grow and flourish until the great financial calamity of 1837. That crash, brought about by "wild-cat" banking, carried disaster all over the country. That year's sufferings, brought on by speculators trying to carry on banking without convertible security, is a matter of history and many business houses and individuals were financially ruined.

At the time of this disaster, Randolph was a rapidly growing little city, having twenty-two business houses, all of which were doing well, the town being at that time the real business center of this section of the country. But this crash so affected her business interests that a decline commenced from which she never recovered. By degrees her trade came to Memphis

*Keating.

and her misfortune became the latter's good fortune. This disaster, carrying failure and ruin in all directions, really started the flow of business to Memphis. From that time the substantial commerce of our city really began and she made such rapid strides that soon Randolph ceased to be a competitor at all.

Young Memphis also had three rivals on the Arkansas side of the river—Mound City, which flourished for a while; Hopefield, really giving for a time the hope that its name implied but ending in hope; and Pedraza, formerly Foy's Point, which had in still earlier days been an important landing and trading center. Still another rival had birth in Mississippi, founded by Mississippi planters, who objected to paying fifty cents a bale for storing, handling and insuring cotton in Memphis, but "Commerce," as the Mississippi town was named, was not a success and Memphis continued to handle, store and insure Mississippi cotton.

Sectional jealousies did much to retard progress in the early history of Memphis. Jealousy was displayed between some of the leading citizens; it was much in evidence between sections of the city; rival towns sprang up and even the State was charged with slighting the western city. In January, 1830, $150,000 of unappropriated funds from the sale of Hiawassee lands was placed at the disposal of the state. Of this amount $60,000 was appropriated to Middle Tennessee, the same to East Tennessee and for West Tennessee only $30,000.

West Tennessee chafed at such slights and while Seth Wheatley was mayor of Memphis—1831-1832—the city expressed much dissatisfaction at her standing in the state. The discontent took on such proportions that discussions of the advantage of forming a new state arose. This new state was to include West Tennessee, all of Kentucky that was bounded by the Ohio, Tennessee and Mississippi Rivers, and that part of Mississippi known as The Indian Reserve. The names suggested for this new state were the same as had been discussed for naming the infant Memphis in 1819—Jackson, Chickasaw and Memphis—the last leading in popularity.

General Andrew Jackson favored the idea of this new state, but the discussion was dropped and no action ever taken.

During this same administration Tennessee, Mississippi and the Chickasaw Indians had a wrangle about the ownership of Memphis. Tennessee claimed that the town was within her territory, Mississippi that it was within hers and the Indians that it was on part of their reservation. A new survey was made which left the city four and a half miles further north of the boundary line between Tennessee and Mississippi. This put the city wholly in Tennessee and entirely out of the Indian Reserve.

Although many rough characters came to Memphis in her youth, as is usual with new settlements, she was fortunate in having some most excellent leaders. Among these was a quartette of men, entirely different as individuals and sometimes antagonistic, but always one on the subject of Memphis and her advancement, namely, Andrew Jackson, the rugged hero of that time, nicknamed "Old Hickory;" Isaac Rawlings, sometimes narrow but ever stanch and honest; Marcus B. Winchester, an unselfish citizen and a finished gentleman; and Judge John Overton, the scholarly lawyer and shrewd man of business. These were four friends of which any town might boast, and much of the city's importance was built upon the foundation laid by these men. Judge Overton was a close friend of Jackson's and often helped the less learned old hero with papers and other things that required the scholar more than the soldier and pioneer. And as the Judge was a close and unselfish friend to the other man, so was he as unselfish and true to the young city whose fortunes he had undertaken to share and to uplift.

Up to 1840 the growth of Memphis was very slow but the decade beginning with that year was a healthful one for the struggling city. Property had increased a great deal in value and the mayor, Thomas Dixon, and aldermen had more money at their disposal for civic improvements. The census showed a population of 1,799.

O. F. Vedder gives the tax list of 1840, as follows: "Four hundred and ninety-nine town lots, value $552,425, taxes

$4,143.18; two hundred twenty-one slaves, value $107,500, taxes $268.75; three hundred twenty-four white polls, $324.00; six carriages, $24.00."

By 1841 the duties of the mayor had so increased with the growth of the city that the sentiment of the people was taken in regard to making the office one with monetary reward, the mayor previous to that time having given his services to the city. The vote was in favor of paying the chief officer for his services and in November of that year it was decided to allow $500.00 per year for this purpose.

William Spickernagle was the first to occupy this salaried position and he entered upon his duties with a determination to straighten out a number of city affairs. One of these was a difficulty with flatboatmen heretofore unmastered. In the early days of Memphis most of her traffic was carried on by flatboats, consequently much of the city revenue should have been from this source. The flatboatmen were usually a lawless set who objected to the small wharfage exacted and refused to recognize any authority of the wharf-master to collect it from them, banding together to resist him, even using violence when necessary to gain their end. Mayor Spickernagle realized how much was lost to the city treasury by this species of lawlessness from men who enjoyed city privileges as much as any other class of people here and made their own living from Memphis trade, and took the matter in hand.

A dauntless wharf-master, Colonel G. B. Locke, was appointed, to be paid twenty-five per cent of all his collections. These collections were to be made by force, if necessary, and two volunteer military companies offered their services. The boatmen, seeing that a wharf-master noted for fearlessness, a city government and the military were organized against them, succumbed and paid the trifling tax required, but a few desperadoes continued to resist and openly defied the wharf-master. The military was called out. Citizens also came to his aid and, although outnumbered by the boatmen, after a severe encounter in which the leader of the beligerants was killed, order was restored and Memphis thereafter profited from her flatboat revenue. It is told that the wounded leader before dying said that he wished he had paid the tax, as he would not have missed the money and most of his profits were gained from Memphis, but that he did not want to "give in."

It was in this year that Congress appointed commissioners to locate a navy yard somewhere in the Mississippi Valley. Public-spirited citizens of Memphis became alert and advocated their city as a suitable site for this navy yard, which bespoke progress and success for the place where it should be located.

On September 23, 1841, a meeting was held by the board of mayor and aldermen to take action on the navy yard, and the following preamble and resolutions were adopted:

"*Whereas*, the government of the United States has passed an act promising the establishment of an armory on the western waters, and believing the local situation of Memphis is advantageously situated for such an establishment, therefore

"*Resolved*, That the mayor be authorized to appoint a committee of five citizens, to draw up a memorial to the President of the United States, setting forth the claims of Memphis and the advantages she possesses for such an establishment."

The commissioners, after examining the Mississippi River from the mouth of the Ohio down, reported the best location to be at the mouth of Wolf River at Memphis, Tennessee. Memphis considered this a great honor and advantage and was glad to convey to the United States, for $25,000, the tract of ground surveyed by the committee appointed by Congress for a navy yard and depot, provided the same should be required within three years for the establishment of such navy yard and depot. In December, 1844, the transfer was made and the Government took possession of the property. A rope walk and the neccessary buildings were constructed, all being completed in 1846. This addition promised to be a vast benefit to Memphis, and the navy yard became a busy place. A great iron steamship, the "Alleghany," was built and equipped here, except her hull. She cost the Government $500,000 but did not prove satisfactory. Some other work was carried on but the navy yard was never a success.

By that time feelings of enmity between the South and the North had begun to be strong and this Southern navy yard was neglected by the government to such an extent that it never repaid the outlay in fitting it up. The appropriations made for its support were so small that they barely paid the officers' salaries, and later the government refused to keep it in operation. In 1853 Congress passed a resolution "to donate the entire navy yard property at Memphis to the city authorities," a gift Memphis did not want, although it had cost the United States $1,500,000. It was impossible for the little city to keep a navy yard operative, so the property was used for shops, storing cotton, and a few other purposes, by rapid degrees going to decay.

But Memphis had not depended upon this navy yard for her progress. She had plodded on, ever adding to her business and civic improvements. In 1842 her charter was amended, by which act the city was divided into five wards, each ward entitled to elect two aldermen. This act also changed the city's boundaries and gave to the people the power of electing the mayor. The boundaries were given as follows: "North by Bayou Gayoso, east by Bayou Gayoso, south by Union Street, west by the main channel of the Mississippi and Wolf River to the mouth of the Bayou Gayoso."

Memphis had wretched streets and the city authorities seemed never able to spend enough to improve them much, but in 1845, when J. J. Finley was mayor, action was taken for their improvement and considerable work on them was accomplished, as well as provision made for an annual appropriation for the same purpose.

During this part of the century citizens all over the country were imbued with the spirit of improvement and in November, 1845, the great International Improvement Convention met in Memphis, presided over by the Honorable John C. Calhoun, the noted South Carolina statesman. This important meeting gave Memphis more eclat than she had before enjoyed and among her guests were some of the most prominent men in the

United States. One of the improvements discussed at this meeting was making a deep waterway from the Great Lakes to the Gulf of Mexico. This meeting benefitted Memphis and brought many of her citizens to realize the advantages that might be gained by a united and harmonious city.

It has been told that from her earliest days rivalry between the sections of Memphis existed, and this state of affairs did not improve as the years continued to pass. Some bitterness was first brought about by the proprietors, or early owners of Memphis property, each of whom wanted the city planted on the spot most advantageous to himself, and the people of each section would wrangle for roads and other improvements to be brought to their parts of the town. Bitterness grew until rivalry became a retarding influence in the city's growth. North and South Memphis people became so rancorous that in either section it was considered degrading to live in the other. South Memphis people dubbed North Memphis "Pinch," derived from what some South Memphians termed the "pinched" condition of some of the poor families living on Wolf River; the name was afterwards applied to all Wolf River inhabitants and then to all of North Memphis. In retaliation the Pinchites called South Memphis "Sodom," because of the alleged wickedness of the place.

Memphis first had her greatest strength in the northern part of the city, but by 1835 quite a community occupied the section south of Union Street and antagonism there grew severe against North Memphis or "Pinch." The growth of each section, as well as the growth of the enmity between them, was at white heat for about a decade from this year when a crisis came and it was thought necessary to form two cities. So in 1846 the Legislature passed an Act incorporating South Memphis, with a mayor and eight aldermen, the city to be divided into four wards, laid off into blocks, 1 to 67, all south of Union Street and east of Bayou Gayoso. This charter was afterwards amended and included Fort Pickering as far as Jackson Street and eastward to LaRose Street. January seventeenth of this year an election for the new town officers was held, when Sylvester Bailey was elected mayor and A. B.

Shaw, H. H. Means, George W. Davis, Wardlaw Howard, J. E. Merriman, John Brown, J. P. Keiser and James Kennedy, aldermen.

In September of this year Joseph Wright took a census which showed the population of Memphis to be, including South Memphis, Chelsea in North Memphis and all divisions of the city, 7,782.

National as well as municipal dissensions arose when, in 1842, trouble with Mexico came. People became much excited. Memphis raised a company of soldiers to go to Texas and these, together with a company from Randolph, left on the steamer "Star of the West," amid shoutings, farewells and Godspeeds of the people.

South Memphis grew and property increased much in value in that section of the city. The Gayoso House, destined to be one of the greatest hotels in the South, was begun in 1842. This hotel was beautifully situated, being built in a stately grove, overlooking the Mississippi River. Churches and other buildings were going up rapidly and the board of mayor and aldermen made appropriations for street improvements, which were much needed. A steamboat wharf had been graded and the Market Street wharf was completed.

The first telegraph line to New Orleans was completed in 1843, which made the people of the two Mississippi River cities feel much closer drawn together. This telegraph was erected and owned by a Memphis company, Thomas H. Allen, a substantial citizen of Memphis, being president.

Strangers with money having heard of the possibilities of Memphis, came to "look around" and some of them being favorably impressed, stayed to invest their money and make their homes in Memphis.

The following year saw the Gayoso House completed and opened to the public and it was during this same year that the United States made the big appropriation for a navy yard that promised so much and fulfilled so little.

During this same year, 1844, James Knox Polk, a Tennesseean, was elected President of the United States by the Democratic party, his defeated opponent being Henry Clay, the great Whig leader. Polk was known to favor the annexation of Texas.

This campaign brought out more sentiment in regard to slavery than had yet been done and abolitionism grew in the North and declined in the South. The annexation of Texas became a tremendous question. The slave states wanted the additional power that the big new territory would give them and the abolition states did not want the annexation for the same reason. Slavery became the greatest bone of contention in the country, becoming an important question in politics, churches and the social world and remained so for many years to follow.

The idea had been conceived that a canal from Wolf River above Stanley's Ford, about eleven miles east of Memphis, dug westward to the Mississippi River or to the mouth of Wolf River, would be a great advantage to Memphis in that it would furnish water for the city and power for manufacturing and other purposes. This canal was hotly discussed by the papers and people and on November 4, 1842, the *Appeal* published a map showing the proposed route and the specifications of Colonel Morrison, who had made a survey. Colonel Morrison asserted that a canal eleven miles long, forty feet wide at the top and twenty-six feet wide at the bottom and four feet deep, could be dug for $50,000. It was to have a permanent dam at Wolf River and a fall of forty-two and seventy-two one-hundredth feet, equal to four hundred horse-power. This, he said, would furnish power to the then proposed armory and navy yard and would run eight pairs of six feet millstones, five hundred thousand spindles for spinning cotton and one hundred power looms. Mayor Hickman and the aldermen advocated this project and many of the people became enthusiastic over it, though others opposed it. The Legislature took it up and in 1843 passed an act empowering the corporation of Memphis to build the canal and the mayor and aldermen were authorized to levy and collect a tax for the purpose of putting it through. It really seemed that the contemplated improvement would become a reality but the scheme lagged along until 1845, when it was again revived and Mayor J. J. Finley advertised in the *Appeal* "for bids for the construction of a canal from Wolf River to the city of Memphis; sealed proposals to be received up to the twentieth of July; the work to be paid for in the bonds of the corporation, having twenty years to run, the interest to be paid at Philadelphia semi-annually." Another survey was made and enthusiasm again aroused but that was as far as the matter went, though interest continued to be manifested at intervals.

Mayor Finley announced to the public that the city was out of debt and that its revenue had increased forty per cent per annum for the past four years, amounting to $25,000. The population by this time had increased to 3,500.

When General Andrew Jackson passed from this life on June 8, 1845, the whole nation mourned his loss, none more than little Memphis, whose beginning was largely due to his efforts, though later, when his private affairs became so strictly national, he had ceased to have connection with the town of his early interest and love.

Texas was admitted to the Union in 1845 and April 24, 1846, when war was declared by Mexico with the United States, Memphis became the center of much martial excitement. Almost nothing but war was discussed and Colonel Keating says that an earthquake on May 7, received only two lines mention in the paper. Military companies were formed both by native and foreign citizens and troops of soldiers left here for the scene of action, effusively patriotic and showered all along their route by attention from patriotic ladies and other citizens.*

As the war progressed most of the battles proved victorious for the United States, each of these successes receiving Memphis enthusiasm. In February, 1847, the battle of Buena Vista was won by General Taylor, after which that leader became a popular hero. Following this victory came Cerro Gordo, April 18, 1847, and in August of this same year Contreras and Churubusco were taken. August also gave the United States Santa Fé and New Mexico. September 14, the City of

---

*See chapter on the Military History of Memphis for the deeds of these volunteers.

Mexico was captured, all these making the year 1847 rich in victories for the United States. The following year a treaty of peace was obtained between our country and Mexico, President Polk proclaiming peace between the two countries July 4th. This war had cost the United States one hundred million dollars and the lives of thirteen thousand soldiers,[†] but it gave her a great increase in territory. Besides Texas and that which came from the victories of war, this country paid three million dollars at the close of the war and pledged herself for twelve million dollars in three annual installments and assumed three million, five hundred thousand dollars of debts due from Mexico to American citizens.

The new accessions gave to us Texas, Arizona, New Mexico, Nevada, Utah, Colorado, Wyoming, Kansas and California.

Despite the excitement and interference of business caused by this war, in Memphis, the city continued to grow and her people to agitate business and general improvements, some of which were carried out and some others of which are still agitated, more than half a century later.

As already stated, the great Commercial Convention of 1845 held in Memphis, had given to the city a dignity not before felt and told the country at large of her advantageous situation for a city of importance, while it awoke the residents to the futility and even absurdity of the sections pulling apart, and so did much toward bringing about a feeling of municipal harmony.

John Timothy Trezevant, who was elected mayor of South Memphis in 1847, was an unselfish, public-spirited man and while in office used his influence and arguments to bring about an amicable feeling between Memphis and South Memphis. He urged that their interests were the same and that unity would be more advantageous to both. The new town of South Memphis had not been a success, standing alone as most of the merchants still preferred "Pinch," so that mutual interests ought to bring the sections together. His

[†] Hart's Essentials in American History.

efforts and those of other broad-minded citizens bore fruit which ripened rather slowly but did finally come to full maturity.

Memphis kept getting deeper into debt and by September, 1847, her indebtedness amounted to $80,000, which caused considerable discontent. This delinquency and the fear of more debt caused the Wolf River canal project not only to be deferred but almost abandoned, although at a meeting of the board of mayor and aldermen January 26, 1847, it was learned that they had received five bids for contracts for building the canal, the lowest being $104,000, to be paid in bonds. Of course none of these was accepted. But, despite debt, civic improvements went forward. Bonds were issued this year by Mayor Banks to the amount of $92,000 for various improvements. There was some irregularity about the issuance of these bonds, they having been irregularly numbered on the Register's books. They were issued for grading Center landing; for a medical college; for grading and graveling streets; for plank roads leading in different directions from the city and for the Exchange Building. The bonds for this building were issued to W. A. Bickford who, with this assistance from the council, erected a block of buildings on Exchange Square, from Poplar to Exchange Streets. In this important addition to Memphis, accommodations were provided for a city hall and court rooms, a council chamber and mayor's office, besides a hall for the medical college and other accommodations. In consideration of these municipal betterments Mr. Bickford was given a lease on the ground, part of Exchange Square, for ninety-nine years.

A telegraph was completed between Memphis and Nashville, bringing these two cities closer together and making their interests more at one. About this same time papers all over the country were getting the New York dispatches to Cincinnati concerning foreign affairs, and in this way they got foreign news in about twenty-two days. This was important to Memphis as it increased the prominence of her market and cotton dealers were especially benefitted.

Again the charter of Memphis underwent a change, the

Legislature, January 21, 1848, passing an act that reduced all previous charters of Memphis into one. This new Act defined the city limits as "Beginning at a point in the middle of the Mississippi River, opposite to the center of Union Street; thence eastwardly with a line passing through the center of Union Street to the western bank of Bayou Gayoso; thence down said bayou with the western bank of the same to the point of its intersection with Wolf River; thence down Wolf River with its northwesterly bank to its intersection with the Mississippi River; thence down the Mississippi River to a point opposite the north side of Market Street; thence to a point in the main channel of the Mississippi River opposite to the said north side of Market Street; and thence down the said main channel of the said river to the place of beginning."

The charter of this date also limited the tax-levy to "three fourths of one cent upon all property taxable for State purposes and the city council was given authority to borrow money to the amount of the annual revenue of the city, and no more in any one year, to establish hospitals." It also authorized the establishment of a system of free schools, the first free schools of the city. Ward boundaries were also changed in this year in order to more equally distribute city representation in the board of aldermen.

A year later this charter was thrust aside for an entirely new Act of the Legislature, incorporating both Memphis and South Memphis into one city, under the name of the city of Memphis, as by 1849 the desire for unity of all the sections had grown strong. A few were not pleased with this union and even fought it, but in all communities may be found stubborn and near-sighted natures that will not give up a first opinion even when shown by actual failure that their methods are retarding the public good. But a year later, when a vote was taken for the consolidation of the city it was almost unanimous in favor of union.

Sectional strifes continued even after the union was made but perfect harmony could scarcely be expected to follow immediately on the trail of recent bitter dissensions. The board of mayor and aldermen sometimes had difficulty in appeasing the different sections and sometimes in agreeing among themselves.

The first city council included all the former aldermen of the two cities, making twenty-four in all, and this same number was continued in the election of the following year, 1850, when Edwin Hickman was elected mayor.

The boundaries of the newly united city were given as follows: "Beginning in the middle of the Mississippi River, opposite the mouth of the Bayou Gayoso; thence due east to and with Bayou Gayoso to Auction Street; out Auction and Raleigh Road to Avenue east (Dunlap), of town reserve (Manassas); thence south with said avenue to the South Memphis tract; thence with its east line to its southeast corner; thence west with the south line to the east line of Butler tract, thence to its southeast corner; thence with its south line to center of the Mississippi River; thence with the river to the place of beginning, excluding the navy yard."

## CHAPTER V

The Census of 1850. The Building of Plank Roads. Rapid Growth of the City. Extension of the Telegraph System. The First Railroad to the Atlantic. Great Railroad Jubilee in Memphis. The Financial Panic of 1857. Crime in Memphis. Uprising of the People and Mob Violence. Rescue of Able by N. B. Forrest. The Problem of Street Paving. The Bust of Andrew Jackson. More Troubles Over Slavery. The John Brown Raid and Its Consequences. The First Paid Fire Department.

THE new decade and half century seemed auspicious for the united city. She had then a population of 8,841, of these 6,355 being white. The board of mayor and aldermen seemed wide-awake and they issued bonds in 1850 to the amount of $119,000 for civic improvements. Plank roads were constructed or extended to the most important points in Tennessee and Mississippi and the river trade was, one writer says, "doubling upon itself every year."*

Memphis people realize more and more the benefits derived from the union of the two small towns and the Bluff City was beginning to really be a power. The states around her were settling rapidly. Tennessee, Mississippi and Arkansas had become important cotton states and Memphis was their central market. The city showed progress and improvement in all directions and Colonel Keating says of her growth in the early fifties, "Business grew in volume and value to an extent not then surpassed by Cincinnati, St. Louis or even New Orleans herself."

*These plank roads, or more properly, planked roads, the roadway being laid with heavy planks, were constructed to Big Creek and Raleigh in Shelby County, LaGrange in Fayette County, Tennessee, and to Holly Springs and Hernando, Mississippi.

Memphis had been fortunate in her leading men and at this period she had some of the best. People who had her interest at heart had always been very much in earnest, sparing neither themselves nor their money in her behalf. These friends had realized the possibilities of a great city, despite the drawbacks that came up so frequently and worked to overcome the latter and make the possibilities grow into realities. This was recognized beyond the city too, and papers of other cities frequently had favorable paragraphs about Memphis or her citizens. The Nashville *Banner,* in 1850, had these words for a Memphis man of business: "Memphis can boast of a single citizen who in the past eighteen months has aided public enterprise more liberally in proportion to his wealth than perhaps any individual in the South," meaning R. C. Brinkley. A few others were quite as liberal as Mr. Brinkley and Memphis seemed on the upward bound.

But Memphis and the country had a curse—slavery! Slavery had been introduced into the land as a convenient and profitable form of labor. The negro had been enslaved from time immemorial, both by more enlightened races and by victorious tribes of his own race, so when he was introduced into the United States as a slave it was in accordance with a custom then pervading the world. Slavery had been a matter-of-fact institution when the human race had been chiefly physical and physical might was power, but as spiritual life grew and broadened human minds began to look up and beyond self and selfish comfort to a respect of the rights of others. People were learning the Golden Rule and slavery could not endure with this advancement. But though the world as a whole had made great moral strides and freedom for all men was asserting its right and being advocated in all civilized regions, people were very human still, and by degrees the cause of slavery in the New World grew to be more a theme of antagonism and enmity than the freeing of a race.

Abolitionists had formerly been as common in the South as in the North, but as murder and other evils grew out of abolition fanaticism in slave states, Southerners lost sight of the original cause of abolitionism to free the slaves, in the feeling of defense for state rights and home. So, while the abolitionist was elected to office in Memphis in 1834 and chiefly on account of his avowed tenets, such an election in the fifties would have been impossible. This bitterness between the sections increased until such hatred existed that in the South to be called a Northerner was an opprobrium of the direst sort and vice versa. Politics of the two sections became rapidly antagonistic and speakers on both sides used strong denunciatory language. The territory gained from Mexico had become the source of fiery controversy as to whether it should be entered slave or free.

But the time for final outburst had not yet come and above the surging undercurrent of prognostication and unrest Memphis continued to grow and prosper and her people to think of strictly home subjects. Nor was charity for the poor forgotten and in 1850 Memphis women gave a "Fair" in Odd Fellows Hall, from which they netted two thousand dollars for the unfortunates. Other enterprises, charitable and civic, went forward with the decade.

Mayor A. B. Taylor, in his first message, in 1852, stated the annual expenses of the city to be $75,000.

In 1853 the judiciary bill was amended so as to provide "that the qualified voters of Shelby County shall elect a judge of the Common Law and Chancery Court of the City of Memphis." Also, that "the qualified voters of the counties of Shelby, Fayette, Tipton and Henderson, shall elect a judge for the eleventh Judicial Circuit, composed of said counties," and "the qualified voters of the fifth, thirteenth and fourteenth Civil Districts in Shelby County, in which Memphis and Fort Pickering are situated, shall elect a judge of the Criminal Court of Memphis and also an attorney-general for said Criminal Court."

Another new city charter came to Memphis in 1854, the Legislature of that year having passed an Act for such a measure, including the navy yard in the corporation. And with increased territory came increased population; the inhabitants numbered this year 12,687.

As this decade advanced Memphis made tremendous strides

in business and the city fathers made big plans for improvements, some of which were accomplished. Whole blocks of business buildings were erected and so great was the demand for the houses under construction that much of the labor on them was done by gaslight. The first five-story building in the state was erected in Memphis in 1856.

New residences sprang up all over the city too to supply the many new residents who came to make Memphis their abode. Telegraph lines continued to draw Memphis into closer touch with other cities; in 1857 Henry A. Montgomery, an enterprising citizen, completed a telegraph line between Memphis and Tuscumbia, Alabama, and the year following he completed another line to Little Rock, with a branch line at Helena, Arkansas. The railroads were causing much of the rapid advancement going on. These brought towns into closer communication and made traffic easy on the land, while steamboats in increasing numbers continued to ply the river north and south, conveying passengers and traffic.

In 1857 the Memphis and Charleston Railroad was completed and its completion brought great rejoicing in Memphis, in Charleston and in towns all along the road. In May a big celebration in recognition of this feat was held in the Bluff City when prominent men from both the ocean and river cities took part and hundreds of visitors came to witness the ceremonies. Senator James C. Jones, who had driven the first spike in the first rail of the road, was also honored by being allowed to drive the last, and this completing spike was driven amid very enthusiastic demonstrations. Senator Jones addressed the crowd, presaging a great future for Memphis, now joined to the Atlantic Ocean. The *Appeal* stated that over twenty-five thousand people participated in the celebration. Many speeches were made in Court Square, all full of enthusiasm over connecting the Mississippi River with the ocean and of bringing "the ancient and chivalrous city of Charleston on the sounding shores of the Atlantic," to Memphis, the vigorous and growing younger city on the Great River. The *Appeal* said, "We rejoice at the annihilation of distance and the approximation of neighboring districts which hitherto, mountain, river and slow locomotion have kept apart and sundered." The paramount ceremony of this day's exercises was the pouring into Mississippi waters of two hogsheads of ocean water brought from Charleston for the purpose. This was managed by the fire companies, firemen of the Phoenix Company using their engine, gorgeously decorated for the occasion. Visiting firemen were tendered the honor of using the hose and throwing the salty water into the river. As the stream shot through the air and then mingled with the waters of the river, a great shout went up from the throats of thousands of people witnessing the scene from wharf, bluff, boat, Front Row windows or other places within sight, where human beings could find accommodation. Later in the month Mayor William Porcher Miles of Charleston invited the Memphis mayor and all who would go, to Charleston to another celebration in honor of the completion of the road where, when the demonstration took place, enthusiasm proved quite as rousing as it had at Memphis.

The Memphis and Charleston Railroad had been the cause of agitation for twenty-five or more years, or ever since the first railroad—the Memphis Railroad Company—had been chartered by the State in 1831, changed in 1833 to the Atlantic and Mississippi Railroad Company, so the final completion of the line was of course a cause of much satisfaction to the projectors, the owners and the people who were to be benefitted. The president of this road was Mr. Samuel Tate.

Crops of the South were abundant, each successful year adding to Memphis growth and prosperity and continuously adding to her importance as a market. In 1857 this rapid growth had a check, brought about by bank failures throughout the country. There was a great decline in railroad stocks and State stocks in the eastern cities fluctuated eight per cent in a single week. All securities except those of the Federal Government, felt the tremendous force of depression and the business outlook of our little city on the Mississippi took a tumble with its real estate, which had been booming and now went down with a crash. But the government called in its securities for payment, hoping thus to relieve the stringency of the market by throwing upon it $20,000,000 in gold, and when this call came from the Secretary of the Treasury, there was rejoicing by the Democrats, who contrasted the condition with that of 1837, when the Government money was locked up in suspended banks in every part of the country.

But this money depression, while it necessarily affected business, did not stop civic improvements in Memphis, though they continued more slowly for a time.

Several murders and other crimes brought about by drinking and gambling, aroused the people to a determination to put such outrages down, so an organization was formed, as had been done in an earlier period of Memphis history, to drive the gamblers from town. Gamblers and debauchees, like other evils, are not easily eradicated when once they seem to get a grasp, but they can be defeated by determined citizens, if the paid officers fail in their duty, and this organization of respectability annoyed the gamblers of Memphis to such an extent that many of them left town and those remaining were not so sure of the firm footing they had before enjoyed—at least for a time.

Some murders had been committed in the vicinity and gone unpunished so, during this time, when people were incensed over the manner in which crimes were being perpetrated, John Able shot and killed one Everson, the community was in no mood to let it pass lightly. Able's father had killed a man in a saloon not long previous to this killing of Everson and both the senior and junior Able were gamblers and considered undesirable characters. Young Able was arrested and taken to jail but a large crowd had gathered round the Worsham House on the corner of Main and Adams Streets, where the killing had occurred. As the men increased in numbers their dispositions increased in resentment which grew into revenge and then to fury. Cries arose of "Mob him!" "Kill him!" "He'll be turned loose!" "Take the law in our own hands and get rid of murderers and gamblers!" These men, seeking justice and desirous of ridding their town of crime grew as murderous as the object of their revenge and were willing to hang him without a trial, in the name of justice! Oh, Justice, how many evils have been done in thy name! Such inconsistencies occur along the pathway of civilization with a people seeking but not yet grown to a full knowledge of what real civilization is.

Just when the men had allowed their anger and excitement to reach white heat and were ready to rush to the jail for their unlawful purpose, a large, handsome, commanding figure appeared on the balcony of the hotel and raised his hand for silence. This man was not accustomed to making speeches but he comprehended the necessity of quick action here and his appearance and commanding attitude silenced that mass so completely that every high-pitched word he uttered could be distinctly heard. In a few terse sentences he pointed out the unlawfulness of the act contemplated and emphasized that it would make matters much worse to mob the criminal than to allow him to have a fair trial. Objections were given utterance that there was no justice to be had in the courts but the man in the balcony said, "There is to be a mass meeting at the Exchange Building tomorrow evening for the purpose of reasonably discussing a plan for enforcing the laws and putting down crime. Wait until then and do not increase the city's burden by restoring to mob law, that is no law at all!"

Strange to say, that furious mass dispersed almost immediately and awaited the meeting of the following night.

When the evening for the mass meeting of citizens came the hall of the Exchange Building was filled and overflowing before the time appointed. When the proceedings commenced the crowd had grown restless and the mob spirit of the previous day was again manifesting itself. Mayor Baugh stated the object of the gathering to be that of providing means for enforcing laws and preserving peace and order in the city. He made a few remarks but could feel the undercurrent of impatience through the crowd and before the meeting had made much headway cries burst from the audience for revenge and taking the law into the hands of the people. A man from Mississippi arose and offered to lead any hundred men to the jail to get Able and hang him. Before officers could arrest this disturber of the peace, one after another offered to join him until the whole throng in and out of doors caught the spirit of disorder and got beyond control. The mayor and other men on the rostrum tried in vain to restore order and reason. They found themselves helpless as well as the policemen who put forth their puny efforts to quell the mob. The men rushed forth and straight toward the jail. Alderman Hughes and Colonel Saffrans tried desperately to quiet the crowd but their words were wasted or not heard.

"They must be stopped, but how can it be done?" exclaimed the helpless mayor. A vice-president of the meeting —the same man who had quelled the crowd before the Worsham House twenty-four hours before—asked the mayor why he did not stop the crowd at the jail. The officials looked at this questioner as though they thought he might be insane and one asked why he did not do it himself, as he was a citizen. Turning quickly to the mayor this big man asked, "Does being a citizen give me authority to rescue Able?" The chief officer told him that it did, but that one man or even their whole body would be helpless before that furious mob. "All right," responded the man with set jaw, flaming eyes and face red with determination. "I'll try," and he rushed from the building.

When he reached the jail the jailer had been forced to give up his keys, Able's cell had been opened and the culprit rushed in his night clothes to the navy yard, where the rope had already been placed around his neck. Able's mother and sister were frantically pleading with the mobbers to spare the young man and he was trying in a feeble way to plead his cause and to soothe these relatives. He was allowed five minutes to speak and he used the time trying to point out the justice of a trial, but his words were drowned to all except the few nearest him and they were not to be moved from their purpose. The rope was thrown over a beam and men were pulling it to draw up the unfortunate man when the tall, brawny citizen rushed through the crowd straight to the victim, the flash of a keen knife-blade was seen and it severed the rope. After this bold act the citizen grasped the criminal by his arm and facing the astonished crowd exclaimed, "I am going to take this boy back to jail and keep him there until he has a trial!" The very daring of the act kept the crowd back for several seconds but as soon as a realization of the situation came to them there were cries of revenge and urgings to kill both the victim and his rescuer. "Give us the murderer!" yelled several, "we'll get him anyhow!" "If you do," defiantly answered the recapturer, "it will be over my dead body!" and the man stood like a bulwark between Able and that raging crowd. "I came to turn him over to the proper authorities," he continued after other requests and threats, "and I'm going to do it or die in the attempt!"

The intrepidity of this one daring soul actually awed some of the mobbers and they moved away but others rushed at him and only by quick thrusts and dodges did he escape being severely wounded or killed. He saw between himself and the jail an impassable jam of people determined on keeping him away. Glancing around his quick mind conceived the idea of eluding the crowd in the dim light and almost as quick as his thought followed the act of rushing suddenly forward and taking shelter between two piles of lumber. There he thrust Able behind him and with his powerful left arm and hand parried the blows of his pursuers. His scheme succeeded; those nearest him, that saw his act and knew the place of shelter were swept forward by the rushing crowd behind, who did not know what had become of Able and his rescuer, but supposed they were in close pursuit of the lost object of revenge, and actually rushed madly over or around the men they meant to catch.

When the press had left him free to move the man hurried to the jail where he succeeded in getting the prisoner locked safely in his cell. But the mob was not long learning the truth and then their rush was for the jail. The jailer and other inmates were terrified at the ominous sounds without, but if the rescuer felt terror he did not show it. Ascertaining that his pistol was in proper order he stepped out onto the jail steps and facing that seething mob of three thousand human beings, threatened to shoot the first man who approached. Almost unreasonable as it may seem, that one man could stand against three thousand furious rioters, this hatless, disheveled, torn, cut, determined man did that very thing. Some stones were thrown and a shot fired toward the man on the steps, but the determination for right and justice won and by degrees the whole three thousand dispersed and the man on the steps stood alone, the murderer behind him safe in his cell and the mob retreating before him. That man was Nathan Bedford Forrest, who, at a then not far-distant year was to be selected a leader and general in defense of his state and country and to be followed into battle by many men of that very mob.

The Adams Express Company opened offices in Memphis in 1858, and established agencies in all the surrounding towns that could be reached by river or railroad. So now, with railroads, steamboats, telegraph and express privileges, the town had become a city, destined to be the greatest, said the people and papers, on the "artery" of the country, the Mississippi River.

During the legislative session of 1857 and 1858 two more wards were created in Memphis, making eight in all.

Memphis had an enormous problem,—her streets. Much money had been spent by the city for graveling, but the clay was so deep and soft that a foot of gravel would sink in a few years. In 1858 the graveling was covered by two feet of mud on Main Street and in some places had gone to a depth unknown, leaving mud-holes great enough to swallow a team. It was a common occurrence during wet weather for men, boys and slaves to lend helping hands and shoulders to unfortunate animals and vehicles that had become stalled on business and residence streets and it is recorded that a mule was drowned in a mudhole at the corner of Main and Monroe. There are also stories told by reliable citizens of oxen, mules and horses being prized out of mud on Main Street near Madison, and of a white boy being barely saved by a negro. That is a queer picture for us to contemplate today as we see electric-cars, carriages, and automobiles traveling easily and safely along that busy part of the city on asphalt streets. We who enjoy the easy travel of solid streets and roads today have small conception of the trials of our forefathers battling with the mud that swamped Memphis in those early days, and later.

But we owe the comfort of eventual good thoroughfares to their continual paving, mending, filling, experimenting.

We are wont in this life to go easily along, enjoying the comforts built for us by our predecessors, rarely thanking them; usually, if thinking of their efforts at all, smiling at their crude improvements, boasting, in our supercilious way, of our superiority over all that has gone before. We forget, or perhaps some of us have never been thoughtful enough to know that without the hard work, the discoveries, the blunders, the successes of our forefathers, our present advantages and luxuries would have been impossible.

The heavy traffic of Memphis made it necessary for something substantial and lasting to be done with the streets so the city fathers of 1858 consulted engineers and other authorities of different parts of the country. After much discussion of granite cobble-stones, cedar blocks and other materials, gravel was again decided upon, though there was protest against it, and uptown Memphis was newly graveled to be in a short time again covered by mud and slush. Two years after this $500,000 was appropriated for the streets and wharves, this time up-town paving to be of cobble-stones.

So Memphis struggled and progressed, as circumstances allowed, her people fighting their mud and other inconveniences, ever striving to bring the town to the dignity of cityhood.

Politics kept pace with business, Whigs and Democrats strenuously advocating their different views, but on the birthday of Henry Clay, who had so lately been an idol of the country, both these parties met in amicable hospitality at the Commercial Hotel to commemorate the day and do honor to the orator and statesman who they alike admired, though all there had not agreed with his politics.

In August of 1858 the yellow fever became so serious in New Orleans that many Memphis citizens felt the necessity of quarantine and agitated taking measures to that effect. The question was brought up before the board of mayor and aldermen and a resolution to lease ground on President's Island for quarantine buildings was discussed, but some of the members opposed it. One of them said, "I never knew any good to come from quarantine. If Providence intended the fever to come here, it would come in spite of all we could do."

But the awful yellow plague continued to spread and, despite the opposing aldermen, the mayor was authorized to lease property on Bray's Island at $600 per annum for quarantine purposes, but the ground was never used. Alas, Memphis! If your people could have foreseen the future with its terrible yellow-fever days, would they have been so indifferent, and would they have thought that a kind Providence does not bring disease and suffering, but allows neglect and carelessness to be punished by plagues and other *effects?* The disease that year became rampant and spread to Natchez, Vicksburg and other towns above New Orleans, defying all treatment, and as there were many refugees in Memphis, the outlook for the city was alarming. But she escaped that year.

The same August in which so many victims succumbed to the yellow demon brought world-wide rejoicing over the success of the Atlantic cable. The man who brought this great invention to a successful issue, Cyrus W. Field, had toiled long and thanklessly, having met with two failures that had caused the world to lose faith in him, but the world is usually a disheartening step-mother, not sympathetic enough to encourage unless she sees that success is inevitable. But success came to Field in 1858 and Memphis was not behindhand in honoring the patient and triumphant inventor, who had been born in the year of her own birth. Mayor Baugh of the little city on the Mississippi, directed by the board of aldermen, sent this message to the mayor of Manchester, England: "The city of Memphis on the shore of the Mississippi, the largest interior depot of cotton in America, sends her greetings to the city of Manchester, the largest manufacturing city of that staple in Great Britain, and desires to mingle her congratulations with those of her trans-Atlantic sister upon the successful establishment of the ocean telegraph."

By 1859 the country was in a state of sectional upheaval, but in January of that year many patriotic citizens and guests were brought together in Court Square in Memphis to witness the unveiling of the marble bust by Frazee of Andrew Jackson,—"Old Hickory,"—whom Memphians loved for the services he had rendered to their city in her infancy; whom Tennesseeans loved for his devotion to the State; and whom Americans loved for his untiring allegiance to his country. His country had meant more to him than life. For her he had suffered the horrors of war, having with him, to share those trials, many of Tennessee's brave sons with equally brave sons from other states of his beloved motherland. Those true men suffered, as is the soldier's fate, but they won for the country they defended more security and a stronger union. The result of the Battle of New Orleans, January 8, 1815, where six thousand soldiers under Jackson against twelve thousand under Pakenham, secured that important stronghold to our Country and made lasting our possession of the great Father of Waters. So this marble bust, unveiled in Memphis fourteen years after the hero's death, was turned with its face to the river which he loved, defended and secured.

Several times during Jackson's career secessions had been threatened for various causes by different states, and that hardy American had abhorred such a possibility. "Our Federal Union, it must and shall be preserved," were his well-known words and, in 1859, when feeling had grown bitter between the sister states, these words were placed below the bust of this great Southerner.*

Strange inconsistencies occur along the generations, and this inscription, chosen for that monument at that time, was strange. Not that all the witnesses of that day's ceremonies approved of secession, for indeed, the majority of them did not and approved with all their hearts the inscription, "The Federal Union, it must be preserved," but turbulence was fast gathering and in a little over two years from that time the general Southern feeling had changed and war was in the land.

*The words on the pedestal of the Frazee bust "The Federal Union, it must be preserved," were a careless misquotation. See History of Andrew Jackson by A. C. Buell, (Charles Scribner's Sons, New York, 1904) Vol. II, page 241, where will be found the full story of the Jefferson banquet and the language used.

Had Jackson lived a score of years longer, would his sentiment have changed too? That of course cannot be known; he loved his country and he loved his native and adopted Southern States. Thousands who served bravely and honorably in the war between the states had, during Jackson's lifetime and later, said that the Union must be preserved, and then fought to sever it. During the four years that brothers waged that fearful war, and hatred and vengeance routed love and peace, the solemn bust of "Old Hickory" stood in Court Square in Memphis, calmly facing the West, as though he would say that there lay much of the future greatness of his country when the bitter family quarrel should be over, but he looked out over the words: "The Federal Union, it must be preserved." It was preserved, but, oh! the cost!

Municipal prosperity and interest gradually lessened and gave way under the terrible pressure of national turbulence. Worse and worse became the hatred between the North and the South, more and more did Northern abolitionists rant against slavery and denounce Southerners as tyrants, barbarians, etc., and more and more did Southern "fire-eaters" shout against intrusion and oppression and for secession and independence.

Many Southern people, before antagonism between the sections became so rank, had advocated, planned, and some had worked to bring about a gradual emancipation whereby the slaves would be freed as they had been in other states and countries, and yet their owners not be left impoverished. The slave's condition compared more than favorably with that of other laborers of the world's various systems, and so the accusation of universal cruelty practiced in the South was not calmly received. Slavery had been introduced into the United States by a former generation and had *grown* to be part of the condition of Southern living, and, as a tumor, or other abhorrent excrescence that has been accumulating for years is not dissipated at once, so many thinkers North and South, notably Abraham Lincoln, advocated gradual emancipation.

Memphis, in the heart of the cotton-belt, contained naturally all "Southern institutions, and no other Southern city was in more danger from the unsettled state of affairs than she.

Here came also abolition agitators and occasionally Memphis sent some such offender from her precincts with instructions not to return on penalty of harsher treatment for a second offense. It was common at that time for fanatical members of the abolition brotherhood to insinuate themselves into Southern homes and then at any opportunity presented,—usually at night after the family slept,—try to incite the negroes to uprisings against their owners, or persuade them to run away.

In October of 1859 all former deeds of abolitionists were cast into shadow by the bold daring of one in Virginia, John Brown. This fanatical old man made a raid on Harper's Ferry and his boldness, though failing in its aim, shook the whole country, intensifying bitterness and making the Mason and Dixon line one of live electric wires.

This impracticable old man, after committing and suffering from much bloodshed in Kansas, where he had obtained the sobriquet of "Ossawottamie Brown," from his deeds committed at the place of that name, moved to Harper's Ferry, Virginia. He laid a deep plot to incite the negroes to insurrection, and had sent to him there at intervals boxes of pikes made expressly for arming the slaves. He also had boxes of guns, ammunition, blankets and other army equipment sent to Harper's Ferry, ostensibly as household goods. He posed as a farmer wishing to locate, and as a geologist interested in the minerals of that locality. He carried out this deception by often wandering about the mountains with hammer and chisel. He lived in that way some time, receiving support from abolition friends in New England and elsewhere, and had some confederates with him, men who had been making a business of mingling with the people and learning the neighborhood. Brown thought that if the negroes were once aroused and armed they would make war on their owners, subdue the whites and so be free. After freeing the slaves in this state he hoped to push his warfare on and on, gathering recruits as he went, until the slaves should all be freed. By the 16th of October he must have felt sure of his readiness for the remarkable mode of warfare contemplated, for on the morning of that day, before dawn, he seized the United States arsenal with part of his force of twenty-two men, having sent some of them to different parts of the neighborhood to get slaves and take some influential white men prisoners, that he might use them as hostages. Several men were killed by the insurgents near the arsenal, one of them a free negro. When daylight came and an understanding of his actions dawned on the people, militia was called out and the whole surrounding country was aroused. Brown kept his captives imprisoned and armed the negroes with pikes with instructions to use the same for their defense, but the slaves for whose benefit all these plans had been laid, were not in the least enthusiastic, most of them refusing to do any fighting or even arm themselves. It was afterward noted that not a single slave rallied to the old man's cause and the chief object of those he had brought to the arsenal seemed to be to get back to their homes, some of them even running away for that purpose.

The engine house was used as a prison for the captives and for a fort, which Brown refused to surrender when ordered to do so, barricading the doors and shooting into the troops surrounding the arsenal at intervals during the day. Colonel Robert E. Lee was sent from Washington with a batallion, but he did not reach Harper's Ferry until evening. Nothing was accomplished that night and the people in the engine house spent a very uncomfortable time, but at daylight of the next day Colonel Lee demanded the surrender of the insurgents. Brown refused and the marines selected by Colonel Lee, under their commander, Lieutenant S. G. Green, stormed the engine-house and after several lives had been lost, among them Brown's son, and the old man himself badly wounded, the insurgents were captured. They were first turned over to the authorities at Washington to be tried for seizing a Federal arsenal and resisting Federal troops, but Virginia demanded the disturbers as her prisoners for killing some of her citizens and trying to incite insurrection among the slaves, and they were surrendered to her.

John Brown's raid was a failure that ended in the hanging of the leader and several of his confederates at Charleston,

Virginia, after a trial in which they were defended by Northern attorneys.

Brown's wife was allowed to visit him in Charleston where she was courteously received and treated during her stay. She was with her husband before his death and, accompanied by some abolition friends who had gone with her to Virginia, took the body to North Elba, New York, the trip, after crossing the Mason and Dixon line being one of ovation all the way.

The feeling engendered by Brown's bold attempt did not die with him on the scaffold. Enmity that had existed between the North and South before was after this occurrence intensified to an alarming degree. The North in general looked upon Brown as a martyr and some enthusiasts placed his scaffold by the cross of Christ in importance, while at the South and in Memphis he was considered an incendiary of the most vicious sort and was as much abhorred as he was adored in the North. All Northern strangers were looked upon with suspicion and the South was never sure of her safety from invasion while abolitionists in the North increased and continued to incite the people with assertions of the barbarisms of the South.

The decade of the sixties brought very different results from anything of which the builders of the fifties had dreamed. Municipal affairs had been poorly managed in Memphis and people were dissatisfied and becoming indignant. In 1860 the taxable wealth of Memphis had increased to $21,500,000, having been only $4,600,000 ten years previous, and yet citizens contended that it was impossible to see where the city was being benefitted. The men in office were accused of bungling in every way, especially in not using the city's money to the best advantage. These men, said to be good managers in their own affairs, seemed incapable of managing the affairs of the city and were getting her deeper into debt all the time. The population of this year, as shown by the United States census, had increased to 22,643, more than double the census of 1850.

Streets were in bad condition, street lights unsatisfactory and the fire department was so poorly managed that much property was thought to be unnecessarily burned. In a single fire $100,000 worth of property had been destroyed, the fire service not having been adequate.

The first fire brigade of Memphis had been composed of volunteer citizens with pails of water. As Memphis grew this primitive mode of putting out fires was insufficient, but the town was small and money not plentiful enough to buy a fire-engine. But the subject was frequently discussed; some of the citizens wanted a tax for the purpose of having a fire department, and others said the proprietors ought to furnish it. The discussions and occasional losses by fire continued until 1830, when a second-hand engine was purchased in Cincinnati by George Aldred, at the time acting as an alderman of Memphis. The bringing of this small instrument to Memphis was quite an event, though some pranks were played by making it "squirt" muddy water on people and in buildings, which actions did not add to the respectability of the men who took it from the river up the bluffs. On all public occasions there are some people who will carry their enthusiasm to the point of license.

James D. Davis says that the "Little Vigor," as the new engine was named, was not "over three feet high, worked by two long cranks extending from her sides and capable of furnishing room for eight men, by which power she could throw water over the tallest house on the bluff, and although somewhat defaced, seemed very substantial, and made quite a handsome appearance, while the general opinion seemed to be that she was just the thing we needed."

Firemen continued to be volunteers but they had a better method for extinguishing the flames. This was the only safeguard from fires until 1838, when the "Deluge," a larger and better engine was bought by the city authorities, and the still volunteer servers of the public hurried from their business or beds at sound of the fire alarm, to the engine-house, where they as quickly as possible got the engine and apparatus, rushed to the scene of conflagration, themselves hauling the engine, and proceeded to throw the stream of water upon the flames.

As Memphis grew there were of course more and larger

buildings, closer together, and this fire service became as inefficient as the old bucket brigade had been in earlier years. Occasional destructive fires caused the people to cry for an up-to-date fire department and by the latter part of the fifties this cry was loud, especially after the $100,000 loss above mentioned. So in January of 1860 the board of mayor and aldermen organized a paid fire department and ordered steam fire-engines, despite the fact that the city was deeply in debt.

By November of this year the city's debts amounted to $596,742, besides railroad stock subscriptions for which she was responsible. A comptroller had been considered for some time so in November of 1860 one was appointed and he, the last of the year, began to investigate financial affairs.

# CHAPTER VI

Mutterings of the Coming Civil War. Secession Activities in Memphis. Great Torch Light Processions of the Unionists and Secessionists. Secession Defeated at the Polls. Resolutions of the Secessionists. The Leaders of the Disunion Party. The Call of Mr. Lincoln for Troops. Secession of Memphis from State. Tennessee Finally Secedes. The Vote in Memphis. Preparations for War. The Southern Mothers.

AS MONTHS advanced bitterness between the North and South increased to such an extent that interest in private and municipal affairs was almost entirely supplanted by the absorbing questions of Union and Secession, the organizing of military companies, etc. The Union spirit which had been so strong a few years before in Memphis was giving place to the spirit of Southern independence and men who had formerly been strong for Union were making speeches for Secession.

Secessionists and Unionists vied in speeches and other demonstrations and on many nights both forces held forth in different parts of the city. Business came almost to a standstill and the absorbing theme of everybody's thoughts was "Secession" or "Union." Influential men on both sides were invited to address the masses and many able speeches were made.

At a secession meeting held in January, 1861, the following resolutions were drawn up by the committee appointed for the purpose:

"*Whereas*, all attempts to settle the question of slavery have been rejected by the Black Republicans during the present session of Congress, and, whereas, we despair of obtaining our rights in the Union, therefore be it

"*Resolved,* That the convention of the people of Tennessee, to assemble on the 25th of February, should, immediately after its organization, prepare to pass an ordinance declaring the State of Tennessee no longer a part of the United States of America, and thereafter take immediate action for the formation of a confederacy with our Southern sisters.

"*Resolved,* That ours is a government deriving its just powers from the consent of the people governed and it was never contemplated that its laws should be enforced or its institutions maintained by standing armies; and the doctrine of coercion, by which a seceding state, if conquered, would become a subjugated province, is wholly repugnant to the spirit of the Federal compact, and meets our unqualified disapprobation.

"*Resolved,* That we most heartily and earnestly deprecate any plan which looks to a union of the border slave and non-slaveholding states for the formation of a central confederacy, and that we regard the only true position for Tennessee to occupy is in a Southern confederacy, which shall have for its bond of union the present federal compact."[*]

When the committee that formed these resolutions returned to the crowded hall the resolutions were read and adopted unanimously, a circumstance that would have been improbable a month earlier and impossible six months before. This committee comprised M. C. Galloway, Andrew Taylor, N. B. Forrest and John W. Somerville, at least two of these men having been formerly in favor of adhering to the Union.

Lincoln's election was a terrible shock to the South, as he was head of the Republican party and that party had been formed for the purpose of opposing the South and her institutions.

During the campaign of 1860, the Republican party, which had been considered insignificant in the beginning, had made rapid strides and ended by electing its first president. This was taken by the South as a challenge and she accepted it.

Southern States began to secede in February of 1861, and delegates from the seceded States met at Montgomery,

[*]Memphis *Appeal* of Sunday, January 27, 1861.

Alabama, to organize a provincial government. Before the Republican President was inaugurated Jefferson Davis had been elected by the Southern Convention and installed into office as President of the new Confederate States of America. This installation took place on the 18th of February. Alexander H. Stephens was elected Vice-President and Mr. Davis selected his cabinet. A constitution was modeled on that of the United States, a few changes being made to suit the conditions of the new Confederacy.

Of course all this made the South and especially Memphis, a troubled hive and people were in a frenzy of excitement, enthusiasm and expectation.

The city was much interested in the daily proceedings of the new Government at Montgomery and many Memphis men and women went to attend the inauguration of Jefferson Davis and Alexander H. Stephens. Both these men had been strong advocates for the preservation of the Union but upon the secession of their respective states they had cast their lots with their homes. When the secession of Mississippi was pending, Jefferson Davis had plead before the United States Senate for a compromise to arrest the proceedings, had acknowledged himself ready to vote for the Crittenden Resolution and to stand by the Union; but when all hope for a compromise was over and Mississippi joined the Confederacy he withdrew from the United States Senate, making upon that occasion a calm and logical speech justifying his action.

February 6, 1861, the Unionists of Memphis had a big street demonstration, to witness which thousands of Memphis people gathered. Many stores and residences were brilliantly lighted and large and small United States flags floated all along the line of the torch-light procession. This procession was led by a double file of torch-bearers and following them was a band playing "My Country 'Tis of Thee." Then came transparancies with mottoes for the Union and another band played "Star Spangled Banner." More transparancies followed and torch-bearers came, bearing flags as well as torches. One flag was so large that it took several bearers to keep it upright.

Some of the mottoes to be seen were: "Union is good for the Constitution." "Our Rights in the Union." "Tennessee's Strength is in Union." "Secession is Treason." "Don't Run Away from your Independence." "Reason and Compromise." "United We Stand, Divided We Fall." There were many others, as well as cartoons bearing on subjects of the time.

One feature of this procession was a large skiff fitted up as a brig and profusely decorated with flags and lights. Carriages held business and professional men who bowed and waved their loyalty as they rode along.

Two nights after this manifestation the Secessionists had a parade and demonstration even greater than that of the Unionists had been. Their participators were, said the *Appeal*, "from the laborer and mechanic to the merchant and capitalist." The illuminations of this night were elaborate, gas-jets in many places formed into beautiful designs, torches flaring, spitting and spilling in all directions, candles doing their modest part behind window-panes and huge bonfies roaring at street-crossings.

This night's parade was headed by six decorated marshals on spirited horses. Following them were many torch-bearers; big transparencies with secession mottoes; an immense decorated skiff; color draped omnibuses filled with people, one of these containing seven young girls dressed to represent the seceded States; a train of carriages bearing ladies with flags and behind them was a long line of horsemen riding in column of twos. A band played "Dixie," an air then becoming popular, and was wildly greeted. The Star of the West was represented; "Bleeding Kansas" was pictured and South Carolina was represented by a palmetto flag and the words: "Southern Independence;" and there were many devices on wheels to attract the throng gathered along the streets.

A few of the mottoes used in this procession and on the store-fronts, were: "We have exhausted argument, we now stand by our arms." "A United South will Prevent Civil War." "Secession our Only Remedy." "Anti-Coercion." "Southern Rights and Southern Honor before Union." "Appeal, Avalanche and Enquirer all go for Secession." "People's Candidates for the Convention: Marcus J. Wright, Humphery R. Bate, Solon Borland and D. M. Currin." "Vote Tomorrow for White Man's Rights."

But though Tennessee was much divided in her sentiment she was only slowly growing in the spirit of secession. At the election in this state, held February 9, 1861, to pass upon the question of secession and to determine the question of "Convention" or "No Convention" for that purpose, the convention was defeated by a vote of 91,803 to 24,749, and in Memphis, where secession had seemed assured, a Union candidate for the State Convention was elected by a majority of 722 votes. The Unionists voted down the convention while electing delegates to represent them in such convention.

This defeat was a sore surprise and disappointment to the Secessionists but failure in this instance did not dampen their ardor. Meetings and speakings continued and Memphis papers had such daily announcements as "Secession Meeting of Merchants and Business Men." "Mechanics and Workingmen's Southern Rights Association." "The Irish Against Coercion." "Mass Meeting of German Adopted Citizens." "French Citizens Meet to Down Foreign Dominion in their Adopted Country."

Many citizens wanted Memphis to have an independent ballot for secession and then, if the vote was in favor of secession, have the city made part of Mississippi, that she might belong to the Confederacy, whatever the state did. Trade had given place to the excitement of the time. Local affairs held little interest for the people, even so important an affair as the opening of the Mobile and Ohio Railroad, which made an important connecting line, claiming only a lukewarm interest, says Colonel Keating, from people who had been all but wild over such improvements before.

The Secessionists held a great mass meeting February 13, 1861, when the following resolutions were passed and signed. As this was the leadership of the revolutionary party in Memphis which ultimately brought about secession in Tennessee and embraces many prominent names of that and a later day, the resolutions and some of the names are here given:

"MEMPHIS SECESSION DIRECTORY.
For 1861.

"The following was copied from the Memphis Weekly *Avalanche*, of February 26, 1861.

"The following is a complete copy of the names signed to to accompanying resolutions which were adopted at a meeting held at Odd Fellow's Hall, on the 13th day of February, 1861:

"*Resolved,* That those who, on the 9th of this month, cast their votes in favor of the Secession ticket in the State of Tennessee, hereby ratify and confirm, in their full length and breadth, the principles and opinions to which the Secession party stood pledged in the late canvass.

"*Resolved,* That having perfect confidence in the judgment and patriotism of the citizens of Tennessee, and believing that a vast majority thereof are unalterably opposed to a submission to, and union with, an incoming administration, elected by a sectional majority, whose success was based upon a platform denying the slave states an equal right and just protection to property guaranteed by our Constitution; and that the honor and interest, and safety of Tennessee, demand that she should not separate from her sister slave-holding States, we do hereby pledge ourselves to the citizens of Tennessee and to the whole South, that we will not submit to any other than the rights demanded by the seceding states.

*Resolved,* That deploring the result of the recent election in this state, and believing that very many of our citizens who, by their vote, contributed to that result, are as fully imbued with patriotic pride and devotion to the rights of the South, as those who differed with them as to the best mode of vindicating the same, we cordially request all such and particularly all those whose votes on the 9th instant pledged them to sustain the Secession party to enroll their names on the tables of the secretaries of this meeting, to the end that no encouragement to Northern aggression, and no concession of Southern rights can be inferred from the result of the recent canvass.

"*Resolved,* That we believe that when our Union friends of Tennessee, whose tardy action we regret, shall be convinced that their rights and the sacredness of slavery, will not be recognized by the non-slaveholding States, or the policy of the next administration, we trust that they will make good their pledges and unite with us in a cordial effort to place Tennessee in a proper situation in a Southern Confederacy.

"*Resolved*, That all opinions in favor of any coercion to be used against any portion of the South, whether the same come from Abe Lincoln, his Black Republican cohorts, or elsewhere, receive our unmitigated contempt and the defiance of every true Southron.

"We, the undersigned citizens of Memphis, most heartily endorse the resolutions above:

| | | |
|---|---|---|
| J. W. Armstrong, | F. M. Anderson, | T. J. Allen, |
| R. B. Brow, | J. W. S. Browne, | R. D. Baugh, |
| J. H. Botto, | W. F. Boyle, | W. C. Bryan, |
| W. S. Brooks, | G. R. Bridges, | F. G. Capers, |
| D. Caldwell, | J. W. Frazer, | M. A. Freeman, |
| H. Ferguson, | T. R. Farnsworth, | T. A. Fisher, |
| T. J. Finnie, | R. M. Flournoy, | F. M. Gailor, |
| D. F. Goodyear, | J. H. Goodbar, | B. Graham, |
| T. H. Logwood, | F. M. Leath, | A. H. Lake, |
| H. C. Lewis, | B. M. Massey, | A. D. Morrison, |
| W. H. Malone, | M. Magevny, | W. W. McLemore, |
| G. McFarland, | C. A. Newton, | J. H. Oliver, |
| B. J. Olmsted, | John G. Pittman, | B. K. Pullen, |
| W. G. Richardson, | George R. Redford, | Thos. Randolph, |
| W. Speckernagle, | J. Speckernagle, | S. C. Snyder, |
| R. H. Taylor, | A. Julius Taylor, | Jas. T. Titus, |
| F. Titus, | S. C. Toof, | A. C. Treadwell, |
| Hugh Tate, | J. J. Williams, | J. D. Williams, |
| W. S. Williams, | C. L. Williamson, | S. A. Wills, |
| M. J. Wright, | Robt. Wormly, | H. C. Young, |
| Jas. Young, | Chas. W. Quinn, | S. S. Clark, |

and about eight hundred other Memphis names, all of which can be seen on the original paper, published in 1861.

Such was the state of feeling in Memphis—one of unrest, uncertainty and almost revolution. Military companies were organizing, as war seemed inevitable, especially after Fort Sumter was taken at Charleston, which event threw people all over the South and North into a fever of disquiet and expectation.

Ammunition, fire-arms and other army equipments were being collected in the Bluff City and by April 28, 1861, Mr. W. G. Ford secured from Louisiana a battery of thirty-two pound guns, three thousand Mississippi rifles and five hundred thousand cartridges.

On April 10, 1861, the steamer H. R. W. Hill arrived at Memphis and her captain, who had hoisted a Confederate flag on his yawl while in St. Louis and had been rudely handled for his daring, was received by a throng of people at the Memphis bluff. He was saluted by many rounds of cannon and presented with a handsome Confederate flag.

On April 15th President Lincoln had called upon the states for 75,000 volunteers for three months' service, demanding that each state furnish its quota. Tennessee, not having seceded, was required to furnish 2,000 of these soldiers, but the spirit of Tennessee had undergone such severe tests during the past few weeks that the majority of her inhabitants felt indignant at being demanded to help coerce the South, even though the state was still in the Union. Governor Harris sent answer to Washington, "Tennessee will not furnish a single man for coercion, but 50,000, if necessary, for the defense of our rights and those of our Southern brethren."

This response accorded with the general sentiment of the people and was received with wild enthusiasm in Memphis. The citizens had a mass meeting in the Exchange Building to settle the question of secession, where it was unanimously resolved that if Tennessee should remain in the Union Memphis would secede from the state and give herself to Mississippi. Speeches were plentiful and fiery at this meeting, in which many men declared themselves turned from Unionists to Secessionists. The sentiment of these was expressed by Mr. J. G. Holland when he said, "I was a Union man up to two and a half o'clock p. m. today—an ardent and zealous one,—but now I will raise my voice for the Union of the *South*."

Col. R. F. Looney, a former Union man, responded to a

call for a speech in which he said, "I am forced now, as a true Southern man, to repudiate all allegiance to the Lincoln government and henceforth raise my cry for resistance against despotism or coercion for the Southern Confederacy."

Major Bartlett advocated establishing a battery on the bluff for the city's defense, which proposition was met with enthusiasm. One speaker referred to Jefferson Davis as "the chivalric leader of the Southern forces," and the walls shook from thunders of applause.

Mr. Hill of Illinois said, "I pledge the people of Southern Illinois to oppose the war scheme of the abolition despot and assist in driving back his minions from the crusade of Southern subjugation," and he expressed the feeling of many Northerners living in the South at that time.

A committee was appointed at this meeting to inform President Davis "That the city of Memphis has seceded from the late United States forever—and that she places herself under the government of the Confederate States and will respond to any call for aid from him." There was great enthusiasm on the reading of this resolution, three thousand men making a roar that sent its thunder far and lasted many minutes.

The call of the Northern President for 75,000 soldiers caused the Southern President to give a counter call for 35,000 volunteers, and the response to this later call was quite as tempestuous as that at Washington, and Montgomery became another seething camp of soldiers, many more than the required 35,000 pouring in from all the Southern States.

President Lincoln's demand for troops was followed a few days later by a proclamation which ordered the blockade of Southern ports and suspended the writ of *habeas corpus,* This added gunpowder to the flames and caused many more Unionists to turn to the Southern cause. Numbers of soldiers and officers left the United States army and one day twenty men left the ranks at Washington to go to Montgomery and enlist there. A recorder said that this score made an aggregate of two hundred and eighty army recruits for the Southern government from the Federal capital up to that date. Many people throughout the Northern States held to state rights and there were public speeches and Northern editorials denouncing the President's action as tyrannical and beyond the power of that officer. Some preachers in Northern pulpits omitted their usual prayer for the President of the United States, which caused a sensation among church-goers that ended in divisions of the different orthodox churches.

Of course all this stir made it necessary for the slave states to decide whether or not they should remain in the Union and within the next two months several states withdrew from the United States and joined the Southern Confederacy. Virginia seceded April seventeenth and on the twenty-third Robert E. Lee, who had refused the tender of Commander-in-Chief of the Federal forces, and entered the cause of his birth-land, was assigned to the command of the Virginia troops. Arkansas withdrew May 6, and North Carolina May 20.

On June 8, Tennessee cast her last vote on secession and this time the opinions of her voters had undergone serious change since the time of her previous vote. Then, the majority had been in favor of remaining in the Union and now the vote of the people stood 108,418 for separation and 53,336 against.* In Memphis only five votes were cast against secesssion. As the figures for the State vote show, there still remained many Unionists in the state, and perhaps it will not be amiss to precede events by stating that 37,000 of Tennessee's sons joined the Union army, most of these being from East Tennessee, and 100,000 the Confederate Army, many of these also from the eastern part of the state.

Memphis, recognized as a strong strategic point, by June had become a military center and the headquarters of Major-General Pillow, commander of the Army of Tennessee. By Kentucky remaining neutral it was evident that this state would be one of the fields of action and that it was necessary to prepare for defense. Tennessee was poorly equipped for war but her people set to work to do what they could. Bureaus of military supplies were established and armories were created. As many of the skilled mechanics had fled

*Number afterward declared by the Secretary of State.

north at war's certain approach, Southern men and women took up their work and soon doctors, lawyers, mechanics, planters, merchants and women of many classes of society were trained in the gun-making craft, casting cannon and manufacturing percussion caps, powder and balls. Colonel Keating says: "Merchants, planters, doctors and lawyers found themselves possessed of forces hitherto latent, which were speedily turned to account, and the result was not only the formation of depots of supply, but the partial equipment of the hurriedly improvised army which a suddenly precipitated revolution had called forth."

In August the Confederate Congress ordered two gunboats built for the defense of Memphis, appropriating $125,000 for the purpose.

Memphis received news of the Battle of Manassas July 21, the day of the battle, and for several days particulars continued to come in. The victory caused great rejoicing in the city and many Memphians said, "I told you the North could not fight and that we would soon make them run." A street in Memphis was named Manassas, as a memorial of that victory, and the people were still enthusiastic over the conquest, when news came of another victory at Belmont. More demonstrations and rejoicings were indulged in and Southern people were now convinced that the "Yankees can never whip." They read the papers eagerly to learn how their soldiers under Generals Cheatham, Polk and Pillow drove Grant's men to their boats in the greatest confusion, and how the Federals hastily retreated to Cairo, Illinois, but these rejoicings were greatly reduced by the sad letters which followed, telling of the dead and wounded. Boats were sent up from Memphis and returned loaded with wounded men who were immediately taken to the hospital of the "Southern Mothers" in the Irving Block, to a Catholic hospital conducted by the Sisters of St. Agnes Academy and to many homes. Actual contact with the suffering, dying and dead took away much of war's glory for our women who attended the unfortunate soldiers day and night.

Thankful for the victories that the South had won and

realizing that more carnage was to come, President Davis proclaimed November 15th a day of humiliation, prayer and fasting, and services were held in churches in Memphis and throughout the Southland.

More calls were made by the Confederate States for volunteers and each state's call received ready response, but by the close of 1861 those in authority realized that their reserve supply of men had grown small and one-third of those enlisted were unarmed, while the North had tens of thousands in reserve and almost the world to call upon, besides a powerful navy and unlimited supplies of war equipment. Thus, even so early in the war the South stood frightfully exposed and almost tottering, but she did not know it.

The new Confederate States of America, with eleven states and a population of 9,000,000, was opposed by twenty-three states with a population of 22,000,000. But the precipitation had come and the South thought herself strong enough to resist any power.

Memphis, on account of her situation, became a dependence of the Southern and a desire of the Northern country. She was a military center and furnished many soldiers and supplies to the cause her state had espoused. Her officials, ministers, and citizens in general became almost entirely absorbed in the country's trouble at the expense of private and civic affairs. Many of the churches took up subscriptions for the Confederate Treasury and this letter to one of the said churches shows the gratitude felt at these efforts:

"Treasury Department, C. S. A.,

Richmond, June 19, 1861.

"I. B. Kirkland, Esq., Memphis, Tenn.

"Sir:—This Department acknowledges with pleasure the receipt of your letter of the 15th inst., inclosing $250, and more to follow, a portion of the amount subscribed to the Treasury of the Confederate States by the congregation of the Second Presbyterian Church of Memphis.

"The sympathy of the Christian denominations of our country is highly appreciated by the Government which acknowledges its dependence for success upon the 'ruler of nations.'

Very respectfully, your obedient servant,
C. G. MEMMINGER,
Secretary of the Treasury.''

As men neglected business, so women forgot home duties in their work for the army and wounded. At a meeting of the Southern Mothers Association June 24, 1861, some of their work was reported in the minutes of the previous week, as follows:

"On Monday afternoon the called meeting of the secretary assembled, about twenty being present. Mrs. S. C. Law, president, took the chair, and the secretary, who had been absent for several meetings on account of family affliction, resumed her duties. The meeting being called to order, the secretary read the minutes of the previous two meetings. The secretary stated that Thos. Gallagher, of the Crockett Rangers now in camp at Randolph, had died at the house of one of the members, J. N. Patrick. He accidentally received a wound in camp and was taken by a comrade to the house of Mrs. Magevney, on Union Street. Moved by his captain to the house of his mother, where he died. He was buried in Elmwood Cemetery, Mr. Flaherty furnishing, without charge, coffin and hearse, and the 'Mothers' who had nursed him attended to the grave.

"The President reported that a telegram had been received by surgeon general of Tennessee that an Arkansas regiment, Colonel Hindman, would return from Virginia with thirty sick. The surgeon requested the society to receive them. Hurried preparations were made about ten o'clock at night and the meeting informed that the men were then at the rooms, receiving every care from visiting and standing committees and our noble and most indefatigable surgeon Dr. G. W. Curry, to whom the ladies are under many obligations for disinterested and efficient service and excellent advice. The standing committee consisted of Mrs. Law, Mrs. Shanks, Mrs. Greenlaw and Mrs. Vernon and was reinforced by a visiting committee for the week consisting of Mrs. Doyle, Mrs. Kirk and Mrs. Gondar. A committee of two ladies for each day was appointed to send food prepared to the rooms.

"A call was made through the papers for increased contributions, which was promptly responded to by donations of money, furniture, food and other necessaries. The meeting adjourned to meet every week during the summer, at the residence of the secretary."

The following report was read:

"Since fitting up rooms seventy-two soldiers have been received into them, receiving the best medical attention and kindest and most efficient nursing. Seventeen have been discharged, one died and buried by the Mothers. Eighteen removed from rooms to private homes* * * Conduct of men has been, without exception, manifestation of gratitude for services and high appreciation of motives of those engaged in the work. A large number of ladies relieve each other day by day in nursing and arrangements are rapidly approaching the perfection of system to which their officers hope to attain. Ladies in the country can aid by sending chickens, fresh meat, fruit, milk and butter to the rooms. Dr. Erskine has given efficient attention to the sick in the house of the secretary. Drs. Hopson and Shanks have also offered to attend the sick at the houses of some of their patrons. The military board have given medicine. Both ice companies large quantities of ice. The gas company is giving gas and putting up fixtures. Many merchants have contributed money and goods. Mr. W. G. Proudfit authorized the President to draw upon him to any amount, and the use of rooms is the donation of Messrs. Greenlaw. All these things show that the great heart of Memphis is in the work, and soldiers brought here may rely on the Mothers for attention."

This report partly shows where the "great heart of Memphis" was throbbing, so is it any wonder that municipal affairs were cast into the background and that such matters became more and more tangled?

The board of mayor and aldermen continued to have meetings but did little work and were still under opprobrium for poorly managed city affairs. It is recorded that at a meeting of the board June 6, 1861, one of the aldermen objected to charges to the city of whips, gold pens, silver pencil-cases and pocket-knives, and at this same meeting it was shown that the chain-gang cost Memphis more than it was worth to city work. On the 13th of this month the board could not meet the first draft of $1,000, of the $75,000 that had been voted for the city's defenses, but by the 19th they paid this first draft, which was needed to meet the expenses of the miners and sappers who had been employed on the fortifications. At this same time they refused to pay $262.00 for sixty-four tent-spikes which had been made by order of the mayor at the request of the military board.

On July 3 of this year John Park was sworn in as mayor and three days later the city council reduced school expenses $12,000, the school tax having been struck from the levy.

In August Comptroller Lofland, who had been appointed the previous year to straighten out Memphis finances, gave his report, showing an excess of receipts over appropriations, which was said to be the first time in such a report in the history of Memphis, but two months later he reported an outstanding indebtedness of $307,000, for which no provision had been made. This year the board of mayor and aldermen reduced city property assessments fifteen per centum.

Even this early in the war many people had become inpoverished, so the mayor was authorized to distribute fifty dollars a week among the poor. In addition to this help different organizations of the city gave concerts and other entertainments for the benefit of widows and orphans of soldiers.

Nearly all the voting population was in the army, so when, this summer, Isham G. Harris was elected Governor of Tennessee, Memphis had only 731 votes for him, that being nearly the full extent of the vote cast.

# CHAPTER VII

Memphis Captured by the Federal Fleet. Exciting Scenes in the City. Memphis Under Military Law. Sherman in Command. His Cruelty and Tyranny. Seizure of the Municipal Government by Military Commander. Close of the Civil War. Reconstruction Measures. Trouble with the Negroes. Great Riot in the City. The Freedman's Bureau. Brownlow's Militia Police. The Ku Klux Klan. Peace at Last. The City Begins to Grow Again. Trouble About Finances. Small Pox, Cholera and Yellow Fever Appear.

---

BY 1862 the South realized that the war was a much more serious matter than she had dreamed. When, in the beginning, she asserted that the North would not fight and the first victories seemed to confirm the assertion, she did not remember that her enemies were largely of the same Revolutionary stock as her own people and that failure to them only meant more determination to win. The Northern President called for more troops for three years' service and they came.

The great plan was to reach the heart of the Confederate States and, as the closing in upon them went gradually on, Memphis saw her precarious position, especially after New Orleans was taken and the upper river defences fell. On came the Federal fleet down the river, few men and boats to impede its progress, until June 6, Memphis was reached. The battle of that day and the taking of Memphis by the Federals is told in another part of this work.

After the new order of Affairs the Memphis board of mayor and aldermen found little work to do and soon none at all. Military rule became the government of the city and Federal soldiers, well dressed and well provided for, reminding Memphis people of her own scantily supplied soldiers, were to be seen on all sides.

The little city that had so lately been aiding the Confederate cause in every way she could, was now subjected to severe punishments for all such aid detected. But her spirit remained the same and the Federals, who had been told they would receive a warm welcome from the "many subdued Unionists" in the Bluff City, found only "a dead city and a stiff-necked people," as one of them expressed it.

After the river battle before Memphis and the victors had taken possession of the town, business houses were closed and the people kept aloof from the enemy. When a squad was sent to remove the Confederate flag from the mast on Front Row, the crowd refused to let it be done until two companies of marines were marched from one of the transports to the spot. Then, after a hot dispute of several minutes which threatened to be a riot, it was cut down amid hisses and execrations of the crowd and huzzahs for Jeff. Davis and the Confederacy.*

A correspondent of the Cairo *Gazette* who came to Memphis to note the state of affairs, wrote: "There has not been the slightest manifestation of Union feeling. The stores are all closed * * * * As yet the extraordinary Union welcome we were to receive has not been accorded." And later this same correspondent wrote: "In all Memphis there is only one flag to be seen, and that is the Union flag in front of a saloon." Later a Union flag was hoisted over the Union and Planters Bank. A telegram sent North June 11, had these words: "The *Argus* is still quite outspoken in its secession sympathy. The *Avalanche* is more guarded." The *Appeal* had moved to Grenada on the approach of the Federals, as told in another chapter.

Soon, however, merchants from the North came and with them came provisions such as Southern people had not seen for many days. June 16, the postoffice, which had been closed, was reopened, but was very quiet at first. Later one hundred and thirty lock-boxes were engaged and one report gave 1,200 letters as the number mailed.

*Memphis *Appeal*.

On the twenty-sixth of June Colonel Slack, who had been placed in charge of Memphis by the Federal Government, gave his permission for an election to be held in Memphis for electing municipal officers. The voters in this election were required to take the oath of allegiance to the United States. There were about seven hundred votes cast and John Park was reelected mayor.

In July General Grant took command. He issued an order that expelled from the city all persons in any way connected with the Confederate civil or military government. He also expelled from office "all persons holding state, county or civic offices who claim allegiance to the said so-called Confederate Government, and who have abandoned their families and gone South."

Grant was succeeded by General Alvin P. Hovey and he added to Grant's order the requirement that "every man between the ages of eighteen and forty-five take the oath of allegiance, or leave the city."

These measures forced many into the Confederate Army and created feelings of hatred toward the new Union rule.

The Irving Block, which had been used as a Confederate hospital, was now converted into a prison, where Confederate soldiers or other persons caught aiding the Confederate Army were confined.

When General Sherman came to control the city July 21, he was so unreasonably displeased because Southerners did not take the Federal soldiers to their hearts and homes that he made harsh and strict laws, adhering to them even when it took cruelty to do so. The history of this officer's mode of warfare shows that he never stopped at cruelty. Writing of the feeling of the people here at that time he said: "It is idle to talk about Union men here: many want peace and fear war and its results; but all prefer a Southern, independent government, and are fighting or working for it."

With all the patriotism he felt for his own cause he seemed utterly uncomprehensive of this feeling of Southerners, and resented it most vindictively. Again he wrote, after his arrival in Memphis: "When we first entered Memphis, July

21, 1862, I found the place dead; no business doing, the stores closed, churches, schools and everything shut up. * * I caused all the stores to be opened, churches, schools, theatres and places of amusement, to be reestablished. * * * * I also restored the mayor (whose name was Parks) and the city government to the performance of their public functions and required them to maintain a good civic police."

But General Sherman, and not the mayor, governed the city. On August 11, he wrote: "There is not a garrison in Tennessee where a man can go beyond the sight of a flagstaff without being shot or captured."

Upon receiving numerous complaints from citizens and farmers of useless destruction of their property by his soldiers he replied in the *Bulletin*, September 21: "All officers and soldiers are to behave themselves orderly in quarters and on the march; and whoever shall commit any waste of spoil, either in walks of trees, parks, warrens, fish-ponds, houses and gardens, cornfields, inclosures or meadows, or shall maliciously destroy any property whatever belonging to the inhabitants of the United States unless by order of the commander-in-chief of the armies of said United States, shall (besides such penalties as they are liable to by law) be punished according to the nature and degree of the offense, by the judgment of a general or regimental court-martial. * * * * When people forget their obligations to a government that made them respected among the nations of the earth and speak contemptuously of the flag which is the silent emblem of that country, I will not go out of my way to protect them or their property. I will punish the soldiers for trespass or waste, if adjudged by a court-martial, because they disobey orders; but soldiers are men and citizens as well as soldiers, and should promptly resent any insult to their country, come from what quarter it may. * * * * Insult to a soldier does not justify pillage, but it takes from the officer the disposition he would otherwise feel to follow up the inquiry and punish the wrong-doers.

"Again, armies in motion or stationary must commit some waste. Flankers must let down fences and cross fields; and when an attack is contemplated or apprehended, a command will naturally clear the ground of houses, fences and trees. This is waste, but it is the natural consequence of war, chargeable to those who caused the war. So in fortifying a place, dwelling houses must be taken, materials used, even wasted, and great damage done, which in the end may prove useless. This, too, is an expense not chargeable to us, but to those who made the war; and generally war is destruction and nothing else."

While in Memphis General Sherman was vigilant in keeping supplies of all kinds from passing out of the city to supply the Confederates, but sometimes the guard was eluded and articles necessary for the comfort of Confederate soldiers were taken through the lines. When these performances were detected the offenders were severely punished or, if the offender could not be found, military laws were made more rigid and often innocent people made to suffer. At one time Sherman ordered forty persons to leave Memphis because they had husbands or sons in the Confederate Army, or because they were "Rebel" sympathizers. Citizens who would not take the oath of allegiance to the United States were forced to pay rent for their own dwellings and stores. He also issued an order to the effect that heads of families nearest whose residences the dead body of a Federal soldier or a Unionist might be found, were to be held responsible and punished accordingly.

When the relish of war had penetrated this stern soldier's nature it glutted him and he knew no quarter, no mercy, no pity for one in distress, if that one, man, woman or child, was an enemy. Such was the spirit of warfare with Indian and other savage natures long ago. One writer said of Sherman:[*] "I challenge the world to produce a person who will say that Sherman was ever touched by the pleadings of any woman, even though she asked for what belonged to her. Like the cobra, he plunged his deadly fangs into everything that moved within his reach." He expressed his own insatiableness in a letter to Brigadier-General J. A. Rawlings:[†] "I know that

[*]Captain James Dinkins.     [†]September 17, 1863.

at Washington I am incomprehensible, because at the outset of the war I would not go it blind and rush headlong into a war unprepared and with an utter ignorance of its extent and purpose. I was then considered *unsound;* and now that I insist on war pure and simple with no admixture of civil compromise, I am supposed vindictive. You remember that Polonius said to his son Laertes: 'Beware of entrance to a quarrel; but, being in, bear it that the opposed may beware of thee.' What is true of a single man is equally true of a nation. * * * * I would make this war as severe as possible, and show no symptoms of tiring till the South begs for mercy."

General Sherman used the slaves during his rule in Memphis for public work. He ordered that "all negroes who apply for work shall be employed as laborers on the fortifications, and draw rations, clothing, and one pound of tobacco per month, but no wages will be allowed until the courts determine whether the negro is slave or free. Officers are forbidden to employ them as servants. The negroes employed as laborers will be allowed to return to their masters at the close of any week, but owners are not allowed to enter the lines in search of slaves. The post quartermaster is also authorized to employ negroes on the same conditions and, when necessary, to take them by force. Division quartermasters may employ negroes to drive teams and attend horses. Commanders of regiments may cause negroes to be employed as cooks and teamsters, not exceeding sixty-five for each regiment. In no case will any negro employed under the above conditions be permitted to wear arms or wear uniforms."

The mud in Memphis at this period was terrible, the streets being almost impassable. An English press correspondent named William H. Russell, then touring the South, wrote of our unattractive city:

"I wonder why they gave it such a name of old renown,
This dreary, dismal, muddy, melancholy town?"

A letter from a woman in January, 1863, written to a friend away from Memphis, describes the city as desolate in appearance and in reality. She wrote: "All residences between Tennessee and Shelby Streets from Vance out toward

Fort Pickering, have been destroyed, and their former site is now filled with fortifications and tents of the enemy." The trees and shrubbery were also destroyed in this district.

The illness and fatality of Federal soldiers in Memphis was great in 1863 in the hospitals, 112 deaths being reported for the week ending March 14th. Many residences were demanded for hospitals and other uses of the soldiers, and the above mentioned lady writing to a friend, describes the situation thus:*

"An officer walks in and says: 'Your house is wanted for General ———'s headquarters. He gives you three days to move out and orders that no provisions or stores, or furniture be moved.' All slaves, carriages and horses are taken possession of, and sentinels placed round the house to enforce obedience to orders. When the premises are no longer needed, the silver plate, queensware and best articles of furniture are packed up to grace the mansions of the plunderers in the North. In this way many have been stripped of everything. * * * * Books, pianos, music and many other things which these generals and colonels have no use for, are destroyed. Books are used for waste paper and pianos are beaten to pieces with axes. * * * * Negro men are taken to work on fortifications and their families are crowded into uncomfortable and unwholsome quarters to suffer and die of neglect and despondency. * * * * Few people have the possession and use of their own property. Nearly all the stores and warehouses are either used or rented by the Federal government, which makes no repairs and pays no taxes. * * * * Union meetings are frequently held, and sometimes processions, but nearly everybody engaged in them are newcomers and strangers."

As 1863 advanced, Memphis was filled with Northern men and women and all of her conditions were so changed that she had little resemblance to the city of two years previous. The newcomers received little social recognition from the native residents and some of them resented it, giving expression to their resentment in revengeful acts and words.

*Appeal, March 26, 1863, published at Grenada.

Others, of course, of higher caliber, understood and even sympathized with the invaded, proud and impoverished Southerners.

Some of these new residents petted negroes to such an extent that both the black and white Southerners would get disgusted. One negro woman said to her mistress, "Dose Yankees overdoes!"* It was common for a Federal soldier to step aside to give passage to a negro woman and then crowd by a white woman, even pushing her aside. It was also common for school girls and others to be forced to step into the mud to allow soldiers, afoot and on horses, to pass on the sidewalks, despite an order against riding on side-walks. But some of the newcomers were as extreme in their hatred of the negroes as was the other class in their sentimental love. Southerners were often engaged in taking up for their servants and defending them against this unreasonable loathing. A Federal beat a negro man unmercifully and vowed he would give every other negro who crossed his path the same kind of treatment. After this quarrel a Memphian told the negro he had not been well treated by his Yankee friend. The negro replied, "Oh, Massa, de Yankee's is jes' mad caze dey cain't take Vicksburg."†

In this same year a lady went to one of the fortifications to ask for her servants. The provost-martial did not see her but a subordinate told her that she might get them if they would go with her. She went to the slaves and told them that she needed their help and wanted them to go home but they refused. She urged them further but made no threats, all the communication being before the guard sent with her. They refused again so she went away with the guard who had conducted her there. After she was gone one of the negroes said braggingly, "She couldn't make me go!" A guard hearing what the man said reported it immediately and an officer was sent to arrest the woman. She was put under arrest before reaching home and told that she was to be taken to the Irving

*Told by a lady who lived here at the time.
†*Appeal*, April 17, 1863.

Block. She asked to be allowed to first get her baby but was refused.*

Sherman's reign did not last always and when Major-General Hurlbut was sent to relieve him in December, 1862, Memphis people felt thankful. This change of officers did not mean that harsh rule was at an end but conditions were somewhat relieved and, as Colonel Keating says, "the people breathed more freely."

Hurlbut was replaced by General C. C. Washburne. Both of these officers adhered to the military laws that had been laid down for the government of the city.

People came continually from the North and the Southerners were subjected to continual oppression. Colonel Keating says of this period: "The experiences of Memphis during the Federal occupation were bitter beyond belief, and the humiliations put upon her citizens were some of them as brutal as they were careless and wanton. She was a conquered city, and her citizens, such of them as remained, were in their own homes by permission, seemingly in the Federal view as suspects; but this did not justify the extremities of petty and exasperating annoyances, the denial of any rights whatever but that of merely living, a compulsory restraint being put upon every man and woman who desired to earn a living, and pursue any avocation for profit or for gain."

After Andrew Johnson was made military governor of the State, laws against disunionists became iron-clad. An oath to support the Union was necessary before a man could be an officer in the State, or vote. The numerous Union men who had come to Memphis and were living here agreed with these measures, but it must have been difficult to put the native residents entirely under subjection for July 2, 1864, after more than two years of military discipline and limited municipal government, Major-General Washburn set aside the civil government and its newly elected officers and issued this "Special Order:"

*Appeal, January 26, 1863.

"HEADQUARTERS DISTRICT OF WEST TENNESSEE,
(Special Order No. 70.)   Memphis, Tenn., July 2, 1864.

"1. The utter failure of the municipal government of Memphis for the past two years to discharge its proper functions, the disloyal character of that government, its want of sympathy for the government of the United States, and its indisposition to coöperate with the military authorities, have long been felt as evils which the public welfare required to be abated. They have grown from bad to worse until a further toleration of them will not comport with the sense of duty of the commanding general. The city of Memphis is under martial law, and municipal government, existing since the armed traitors were driven from the city, has been only by sufferance of the military authorities of the United States. Therefore, under the authority of general orders No. 100, dated War Department, Adjutant General's office, April 24, 1863:

"It is ordered that the functions of the Municipal government of Memphis be, and they are hereby suspended until further orders.

"The present incumbents are forbidden to perform any official acts or exercise any authority whatever; and persons supposed to be elected officers of the city at an election held on June 30, 1864, will not qualify. That the interests and business of the city may not be interrupted, the following appointment of officers is made:

"Acting mayor, Lieutenant-Colonel Thomas H. Harris, assistant adjutant general United States volunteers; recorder, F. W. Buttinghaus; treasurer, James D. Davis; comptroller, W. O. Lofland; tax collector, F. L. Warner; tax collector on privileges, John Loague; chief of police, P. M. Winters; wharfmaster, J. J. Butler, who will be fully respected in the exercise of the duties assigned them; and all records, papers, moneys and property in any manner pertaining to the offices, governments and interests of the city of Memphis, will be immediately turned over by the present holders thereof to the officers above appointed to succeed them. Said officers will be duly sworn in the faithful discharge of their duties and will be required to give bonds to the United States in the sums at present prescribed by law and the city ordinances for such officers respectively.

"The officers herein named and appointed will constitute a board which shall discharge the duties heretofore devolving upon the board of aldermen, and the acting mayor shall be chairman thereof; and their acts, resolutions and ordinances shall be valid and of full force and effect until revoked by the commanding general of the district of West Tennessee, or superior military authority.

"By order of Major-General C. C. Washburne.

W. H. Morgan, Maj. and Asst. Adj't-Gen'l.
Official: W. H. Morgan, Asst. Adj't-Gen'l."

July 16, "Special order No. 83," modified Order No. 70, by providing for a provisional board of mayor and aldermen, thus:

"I. Paragraph I of special orders No. 70, from these headquarters, dated July 2, 1864, is hereby so modified as to constitute the persons hereinafter named, a council to discharge the duties heretofore devolving upon the board of mayor and aldermen of the city of Memphis, and they, with the acting mayor, are hereby invested with all the powers heretofore exercised by the said board of mayor and aldermen, and shall receive the usual compensation, and be known as the provisional mayor and council of the city of Memphis"

Then followed a list of all the officers appointed.

This patched-up sort of government was not beneficial to the city and Memphis degenerated, lack of improvements and general neglect naturally leading to decay and a dreadful condition of streets and property. Taxes were only partially collected and those collected were not judiciously spent.

In January, 1865, at the Union convention held in Nashville, among other disabilities imposed upon Southerners, voting was restricted to

"(1) Unconditional Union men; (2) to those who since the war had come of age; (3) to persons of proved loyalty from other states; (4) to Federal soldiers; (5) to loyal men who had been forced into the Confederate Army; (6) to persons known to the election judges to have been true friends of the

United States; (7) it disfranchised ex-Confederates of high rank for fifteen years and others for five; and (8) it imposed the test oath on all voters. A bill was also passed declaring that negroes had a right to vote under the Constitution, which was the same as that of 1796, under which free negroes had voted."*

In April of this year the war ended. That should have been the beginning of better times for the South as well as for the North, but alas! Many politicians who had not served their country in the war were eager to pack their carpet-bags and hie to the devastated country where most of the best people were disfranchised and the childish negro men had been lifted to the pinnacle of voting, a height they little comprehended, and which their new masters—in reality, though not in name— the "carpet-baggers," took advantage of to the end of serving their own purposes.

April 14, Abraham Lincoln was killed. That tragedy and the death of one who had so faithfully studied the problem of the readjustment of the States, proved a greater loss to the South than to the North. History tells us how vengeance was visited upon the already stricken country and how innocent persons were put to death, martyred and otherwise punished for that terrible killing and the whole Southern country made to suffer hardships even as great as those of the war.

On July 3, 1865, military rule in Memphis ended, Major-General John E. Smith, who then commanded the troops stationed here, revoking special orders 70 and 83, and turning over all books, papers and authority to the new city officers. These recently-elected officers were John Park, mayor; John Creighton, recorder; B. G. Garrett, chief of police.

Memphis started under this new government with conditions so changed that it was difficult for the officers to know how to conduct affairs. Labor was different, citizenship was different and business seemed to be unbalanced.

Business was chiefly carried on with Northern capital as Southerners had become impoverished, especially all those who had taken part in the Confederate Army or had in any

*Keating.

way aided that cause. Property of all such actors or sympathizers was consumed by the direct war-taxes that had been levied by the Federal government. The owners could not pay these taxes and the property was sold at public auction. Many of the carpet-baggers of that time, as well as respectable Northern people became rich from the misfortunes of Memphians who were unable to retain their property and powerless to prevent the sales.

Lawyers who had been Confederate soldiers could not practice in the courts and most of the respectable element of the town was disfranchised. Negroes had been given the franchise and other men who enjoyed this privilege were largely of a low element who had come into Memphis. Many of these came in from the river and afterwards proved to be very undesirable citizens.

James F. Rhodes speaks of the legislation in the South of that time as "enfranchising ignorance and disfranchising intelligence," and he continues, "It provided that the most degraded negro could vote while Robert E. Lee, Wade Hampton, Alexander H. Stephens and Governor Joseph E. Brown could not. * * * * It followed that the ignorant Congo Negro was a better citizen for the upbuilding of the new State than a man of the highest intelligence and largest political experience, who had sided with the Confederacy. Obviously this view was more partisan than patriotic."

There were many foreign laborers in Memphis at this time, these being chiefly of the fixed foreign type. The Irish laborer had an unreasonable hatred for the negro and rivalry between them became so great as to be another problem in the city's welfare.

Though Memphis was said to have returned to civil government, Major-General Stoneman was stationed here with white and negro troops and the latter proved a source of much annoyance to Memphis people.

Policemen had been largely appointed from the Irish voters and they and the negro soldiers became avowed enemies.

Some of the white Northerners who had come to Memphis to teach or preach to the colored people, with no knowledge of the negro character, still in a childish stage of development, were continually firing their students with the idea that they were better than their former owners and that they must assert their rights and their superiority on all possible occasions. Many of the Northern whites were above this, of course, and many of the negroes could not be induced to injure or even speak against their "white folks," but the lawless part of the community grew in strength until life for respectable people, white and black, became a problem difficult to be solved.

Many of the rabble part of discharged soldiers from the Union army had gathered in Memphis and some of the negroes, intoxicated with their new freedom, and intoxicated with liquor much of the time, did not make a desirable element in a community and their lawlessness found many vents. Living in the country or even suburbs was really dangerous at that time. Numbers of homes of ex-Confederates were burned for no cause except the spite of the incendiary, and on several occasions white people were shot down by drunken and sober negro soldiers. Many families were compelled to abandon their country homes and move into town for safety.

The Freedman's Bureau, originated for a worthy purpose, and at first conducted in a manner beneficial to blacks and whites, became a machine of much corruption. Mr. G. S. Shanklin, writes of the Freedman's Bureau as "the manufacturer of paupers and vagabonds, the fruitful source of strife, vice and crime," and Colonel Keating states: "It assumed to regulate labor, substituting for the free will of the late slave the one-man direction of officials who cloaked their rapacity and money-greed behind a zeal sustained by sectional hate, and the hot fanaticism of the abolition furies whose passions were not satisfied with the manumission of the negro, and could only be so by the degradation of the whites. Many of the agents of this Bureau made a fence of the Redeemer's name, behind which to caricature his compassion and humanity, and enact, surrounded by all conceivable devices, sham sympathy, which for a time only concealed their villanies long enough, however, to enable them to maintain their ill-gotten and ill-managed political power, and by it rob the victims of their pseudo-philanthropy."

President Johnson, through whose agency so many "reconstruction" hardships had come upon the Southland, with his talent for changing views, again became the South's friend and then used his power to raise it from misfortune. He said now that he wished the South to "be remitted to its former status in the Union, with all its manhood."

The year after the war Memphis was truly an afflicted city. In the throes of carpet-bag misrule, the best of her population unable to take any part in public affairs, officers and voters mostly made up of comparative strangers and riffraff, and all city matters in chaos,—it was depressing to think of the outcome. A bomb goes its distance and then bursts. So it was with the Memphis political and social bomb at that period. It was speeding its way from the mortar of confusion, and in May, 1866, exploded its destructive casing and shrapnel, scattering death among innocent and guilty alike.

In Fort Pickering there were 4,000 negro soldiers, pervaded with an exaggerated idea of their own importance, who were continually insulting white women as well as white men, and the fact that they were being encouraged by white people, aroused the indignation of respectable white Southerners toward them and the hatred of ignorant classes of white people toward all negroes. Thoughtful people of Southern and Northern birth tried to prevent outrages arising from the fast-crystalizing hatred, by petitioning the President of the United States for their removal. President Johnson referred this petition to the secretary of war and he to General Thomas, who declined to grant it. When this fact became known it only increased the insolence of the black troops. General Stoneman was in charge of the department of Tennessee, with his headquarters at Memphis. He tried to enforce discipline and did to a degree, but his own attitude toward Southerners was not especially friendly.

In April of that unfortunate year the four negro regiments causing most of the disturbance were mustered out of service, but after their discharge they continued to lounge around the fort, awaiting their pay, and wandering through the city, more dangerous under the loose discipline they now enjoyed than before. They frequented low houses, drank a great deal and so annoyed the poorer class of white people that some of them resented it to the point of chastising several of the obstreperous blacks. This aroused the negroes to fierce wrath and they swore vengeance.

On the afternoon of May 1, 1866, one hundred or more of these soldiers were "on a spree" and making great disturbance in South Memphis, not far from the fort. About three o'clock a policeman arrested one of the negroes who had been very unruly and the soldiers rescued him, for which they cheered loudly and made great threats about what they meant to do to white people and to the policemen especially. An hour later six policemen went to the neighborhood and two of them arrested two particularly boisterous soldiers. This caused the others to crowd about with yells of "Stone 'em!" "Shoot 'em!" "Club 'em!"

As these officers went along the four who had dropped behind joined them and the six kept the crowd off, but soon about forty of the soldiers began to fire their revolvers, while others threw rocks or missles or brandished sticks. The officers then turned and fired into the crowd. One of the policemen was shot and soon after one of the soldiers, which caused them to make a rush down Causey Street for the police. Many shots were fired on both sides. After dark the negro soldiers went into the fort and were not out again that night, but the police and white people of the class that make up a mob, gathered in numbers and fury. About ten o'clock they returned to the scene of the former trouble but found no negroes abroad with hostile intent. Then they broke up into squads and some of these passion-aroused creatures wreaked their vengeance on innocent negroes, burning their homes, robbing and killing many of the inmates.

The next morning, Wednesday, May 2, the mob broke loose again and committed deeds as disgraceful as those of the night before. Sheriff Winters had got together a posse, after having failed to get military assistance from Major-General Stoneman, and tried, with the police, to put down the riot. However, a large number of them joined the mob, flagrantly deserting the cause for which they had been called out. These deserters, made up largely of foreigners, now had an opportunity to vent their spite on the negroes and did it, without regard to the innocence or guilt, sex or age of their victims, the only offense needful being a dark skin. The sheriff rescued one colored man from four men and tried to quell the general disorder, but was powerless with his handful of men.

Wednesday night the mob was out again. Seeing Mr. M. C. Gallaway, editor of the *Avalanche*, a paper Southern in its sympathies, some of the men tried to lift him to their shoulders and persuade him to lead the mob to the office of the *Post*, a republican paper, and demolish that office. He refused and appealed to the men not to attempt such a thing, trying to make them comprehend how harmful such a proceeding would be. Mr. Gallaway afterward testified that he did not know a man in the mob. After the crowd left him they shot at two negroes. The colored population was very scarce that night, the mass of them being secreted by white people in their homes. A striking fact connected with this riot was that of the two thousand or more ex-Confederate veterans resident in the city, not one raised his hand against the negroes but, in hundreds of instances, sheltered them in their homes.

By Thursday the mob was under control, though there were a few spurts of feeling on that day.[*]

This riot, like other occurrences in Southern cities during that strained period of "reconstruction" was the outcome of extreme prejudice on both sides. It was disgraceful in itself, as all passionate revolutions are, but did not brand all Memphis people, as was claimed by some papers and political parties. At the time of its outbreak there was extreme antagonism between the negroes and a large element of white people, especially the Irish laboring class, who have never been known

---

[*]This description is taken from the testimony of Major D. Upman, a United States officer and strong Union man; Dr. S. J. Quimby, a five months' resident of Memphis, from Center Harbor, Mich., who served in the Union army from 1862 to the close, part of the time commanding colored troops; and others.

to affiliate with people of an inferior race. From one-half to two-thirds† of the better class of white men were disfranchised, so that the men in political power were largely from the inferior class of society, such officers frequently being unequal to their duties and not men who would have been selected by the two thousand or more disfranchised Confederate officers and soldiers living in Memphis at the time.

The Memphis police force in 1866 comprised 180 men, of these 167 being Irish, 8 American and 5 of unknown nationality. The firemen in April and May, 1866, numbered 46, of whom 42 were foreign born, 3 Americans and one unknown. As this was the official material the sheriff and mayor had for their posses, the futility of their efforts can be understood. It was much like taking a troop of lions to guard a herd of unruly cattle.

Mr. G. S. Shanklin, member of the Select Committee, afterward selected by Congress to investigate the Memphis riots, said: "It is most conclusively shown by all the testimony in this investigation that this mob was exclusively composed of the police, firemen, rowdy and rabble population of the city of Memphis, the greater part of whom are voters in the city of Memphis, under the franchise law of the State of Tennessee, enacted by what is known and called the 'radical Brownlow party,' and intended to disfranchise all persons in that State, who had in any manner aided, encouraged or abetted the late rebellion, and thereby place the political and civil power of the State in the hands of and under the control of those they call true loyal men."

The mayor and sheriff have been harshly criticised for not quelling the riots, and even accused of abetting it, but both these officers tried to get the coöperation of the military in restoring order on the first day. At the breaking out of the riots Tuesday afternoon, May 1, Sheriff Winters appealed to Major-General Stoneman for troops but that officer refused aid, saying that he wished to see if the city could govern herself and stop disturbances, as Southern people had boasted she could, if the United States troops were removed. The

†Shanklin.

same afternoon, shortly after the sheriff's call, Mayor Park sent this communication to Major-General Stoneman:

"Mayor's Office, City of Memphis, May 1, 1866.

"General: There is an uneasiness in the public mind, growing out of the occurrences of today, which would be materially calmed if there was an assurance of military coöperation with the civil police in suppressing all disturbances of the public peace. I should be happy to have it in my power to give this assurance at once. It would intimidate the lawless, and serve to allay the apprehensions of the orderly. I therefore request that you will order a force of, say, two hundred men, commanded by discreet officers, to be held ready to coöperate with the constabulary force of the city in case of any further continued lawlessness.

"I am, general, very respectfully, your obedient servant,

John Park, Mayor."

General Stoneman responded, as follows:

"Headquarters Department of Tennessee,

Memphis, Tennessee, May 1, 1866.

"Dear Sir:—I am in receipt of yours of this instant. In reply I have the honor to inform you that the small force of regular infantry stationed at this post, in all not more than one hundred and fifty strong, will be directed to hold itself in readiness to coöperate with the civil authorities of Memphis in 'case of further continued lawlessness.' This force is in camp at the fort, where you can communicate with the commanding officer in case you shall find that you need his assistance and support. I should prefer that the troops be called upon only in case of an extreme necessity, of which you must be the judge.

"I am very respectfully, your obedient servant,

Geo. Stoneman, Major-General Commanding."

Two days later, May 3, some Memphis citizens had a meeting at the courthouse, after which this letter and resolutions were sent to Major-General Stoneman:

"Memphis, Tennessee, May 3, 1866.

"Sir:—I am requested by the citizens composing a meeting held this morning at the courthouse to lay before you the following resolutions which passed unanimously, and to request from you your coöperation in any measures that may be taken in pursuance thereof,

Respectfully yours,

R. C. Brinkley."

"*Resolutions.*

"Resolved, That the mayor of the city and the sheriff of the county together with the chairman of this meeting, (W. B. Greenlaw,) be authorized to summon a force of citizens of sufficient number to act in connection with the military, which shall constitute a patrol for the protection of the city, to serve such time as the mayor, sheriff, and chairman of the meeting shall direct.

"Resolved, That the chairman, (W. B. Greenlaw,) J. H. McMahan, S. P. Walker and R. C. Brinkley, be requested to wait upon General Stoneman and inform him of the proceedings of this meeting.

W. B. Greenlaw, Chairman.

R. C. Brinkley, Secretary."

Major General Stoneman, U. S. A.

Commanding Department of Tennessee."

In his testimony afterward taken by the Select Committee, appointed by Congress to investigate the riots, General Stoneman said, "When this resolution was transmitted to me, I told them I had determined to take the thing into my own hands, and that I should have to set all civil government aside."

His written response to the above communication, was:

"Headquarters Department of Tennessee.

Memphis, Tennessee, May 3, 1866.

"To the Mayor, City Council and all civil authorities of the County of Shelby, and City of Memphis:

"Gentlemen: Circumstances compel the undersigned to interfere with civil affairs in the city of Memphis. It is forbidden for any person, without the authority from these headquarters, to assemble together any posse, armed or unarmed, white or colored. This does not include the police force of the city, and will not so long as they can be relied upon as preservers of the peace.

"I am, gentlemen, very respectfully,

Your obedient servant,

Geo. Stoneman, Major-Gen'l Commanding."

General Stoneman seemed to be somewhat vindictive in his conduct. In his testimony he said that Union officers were not welcome in Memphis society and that Southern people were less loyal than they had been six months previous to that time. He also complained that they were ever ready to cheer "Dixie" and to hiss "Yankee Doodle," and that the only flags to be seen in the city were the one at his headquarters, one at the Freedmen's Bureau and one in front of the Republican paper, the Post. He sent word to the manager of the theatre that he would interfere if national airs were again hissed. He showed little understanding of human nature in condemning a feeling that had been part of the nature of Southern people for over four years and he seemed not to comprehend that it had taken just such treatment to make Southern people "less loyal than they had been six months before."

Mr. Shanklin wrote:

"No city in the Mississippi Valley can claim a more intelligent cultivated and refined society, or more active and efficient business men can be found, than in the city of Memphis. The growth of the city is rapid, the masses of the population are industrious, orderly and moral, and with these classes the sentiment of condemnation of the riot is universal; then why should they suffer reproach or condemnation? They were deprived by the law, in the enactment of which most of them had no voice, civil or legal power; they had but recently emerged from military control and government. The military was then present for the purpose of aiding in the enforcement of the law and preventing disorder; and whilst they in a large body offered their services to General Stoneman, and to be under his control, and such officers as he might appoint over them, to aid in suppressing the mob, these proffered services having been declined by General Stoneman, it is fair to presume that they came to the conclusion that it would have been improper for them to interfere in the matter."

The outlook for Memphis was not promising. Leaders of the government misunderstood conditions in the South, were unable to grasp them or felt only rancor toward ex-Confederates. The best material of Southern citizenship,—the men who were capable of the best feeling, best reasoning and judgment, and who, since they knew the cause they had fought and suffered for to be lost, were the sort to look the inevitable in the face and go to work on new lines to readjust affairs to suit the changed conditions, were, according to the law, placed lower than the ignorant, the childish and rabble material of the community. James Ford Rhodes, writing of this period, says: "It may be affirmed with confidence that there was nothing in the condition of the South which required the stringent military rule provided for in the Reconstruction acts."

All Northern men were not in sympathy with these "stringent" measures, and Mr. Rhodes quotes Governor Andrews of Massachusetts as saying: "The true question is now, not of past disloyalty, but of present loyal purpose," to which he himself adds: "On the practical question of loyalty the Southern men were sound."

Abraham Lincoln must have realized the state of disruption that would be brought about by the mismanagement of reconstruction when he said in his last public speech, April 1, 1865, "We shall sooner have the fowl by hatching the egg than by smashing it." This just man also said: "We can't undertake state governments in all these Southern states. Their people must do that, though I reckon that at first they may do it badly."

Insults to Confederate soldiers continued at intervals but, as inharmony is not the true and God-given state of man, it cannot always last, and adjustment was slowly asserting itself. In June of this chaotic year of the riots and other race and political disturbances, it was decided that all criminal cases in which negroes were parties were to be turned over to the civil authorities of Memphis, and these officers were also authorized to take charge of the medical and other hospital stores which had been under the charge of the Freedmen's Bureau.

But the Bureau was only dying, not dead. On the thirteenth of this month Brigadier-General Runkle, who was in charge of Bureau affairs at Memphis, issued an order that "all contracts with negroes must be registered and approved by the Freedmen's Bureau, otherwise they would have no binding force."*

This order retarded adjustment between the races and was the indirect cause of more bad feeling. The police of the city were organized into a force that amounted to militia and they and the citizens became very antagonistic. Later, officers and police became implicated in crimes that brought them into even more disrepute. The unscrupulous among these men used, so far as possible, the power given them by the "Brownlow radical administration." The commissioner† was charged with "forgery, bribery and robbery, and with two of his detectives,‡ was placed under bonds, and the grand jury found two bills against them,"§ but this case, with others against the "radicals" could not be sustained, especially after November, when the Legislature passed an act "disqualifying and prohibiting all Confederate soldiers and sympathizers serving as jurors."‖

The "radicals," "carpet-baggers," or "scalawags," as they were variously called, usually narrow and fanatical, could not grasp the true status, and so Southern respectability was forced into the background while those in charge officially had full sway. They succeeded in getting the entire country into a muddle, deeper into debt and filling their own pockets. Again quoting Mr. Rhodes: "Military government at the South may be described as possessing all powers and no responsibilities."

John Park was continuously elected mayor of Memphis until after the war and when the conflict came to an end he remained in office a year longer than his expired term, owing

---

*Keating.    †Beaumont.    ‡Pratt and Norton.    §Keating
‖Old Folks Record.

to the fact that no election was held that year. On October 15, 1866, W. O. Lofland was elected to the office for two years, that time being determined the following year, 1867, by the Legislature for the term of mayor's office.

This same Legislature enlarged the boundaries of Memphis as follows:

"From mouth of Wolf River to Brinkley Street, thence east to Mosely Avenue, thence south to old Raleigh road, thence east to Brinkley Avenue, thence south to its termination, thence to Dunlap Street, thence to west boundary of Elmwood Cemetery, thence to Walker Avenue, thence west to Bayou Gayoso, thence to Gaines Street, thence by this street to Mississippi River, thence by the river to the beginning. The added territory to compose the Ninth and Tenth wards, Madison Street dividing them."*

The county seat was also moved from Raleigh this year back to Memphis.

The city debt was all this while increasing enormously. The papers tried to make the people realize the seriousness and detriment to the city of this debt, but affairs were in too much turmoil generally and too much distrust was abroad for matters to be set straight or even attempted by the people then. However, this very state of affairs was waking citizens to more determination to get the city government into their own hands, and some of the state senators and representatives were beginning to work to the end of placing the people in power over the State.

President Johnson, with all of his erratic behavior and unpopularity was at this time doing what he could to lift the white man's burden in the South. In Memphis he became as popular as he had been unpopular, and a mass meeting was held in Court Square, where his new policy of restoration was publicly sanctioned and delegates elected to a convention that was to be held in Philadelphia for the purpose of uniting in a "National Union Party," all in favor of the President's policy. Forty-one Democratic members of Congress signed

*Old Folks Record.

an address to the people of the United States, approving the call of this convention, the aim of which was to bring harmony to the distracted country. These signers endorsed all of its principles, Southerners accepting much that was distasteful and even humiliating, for the sake of bringing about a more livable condition of government in their land.

This National convention, held in June, helped to break down the barrier between the sections and gave a blow to the rabid radicalism which was threatening even the Constitution.

Soon after this Memphis gave her first public greeting to a Union soldier,—General Frank P. Blair. He was cordially received by the mayor and aldermen and was warmly greeted as he arose to address the people.

Confederate soldiers, who had so long remained silent, began to show interest in affairs and when General Blair again visited the city they gave him a hearty welcome and General Forrest this time introduced him to an audience.

Colonel Keating says of these pacifying events, "The ice was at last broken. Brownlow and his Legislature were no longer to have things their own way."

But this change for the better was only beginning. Continued night stealing, burning and other depredations by negroes was rarely punished, which gave them more and more a sense of license and insolence, and had become such a nuisance and even terror that strategy was resorted to by men who understood their superstitious natures. A secret order for frightening them into their homes at night was formed and became known as the Ku Klux Klan.

The object of the organizers of this order was to bring tranquility and safety to the community, nor was their method new, though their particular klan was. Numerous such orders have come down to us through history, notably the Nihilists of Russia, Alumbrados of Spain and other orders organized for religious freedom.

The Ku Klux Klan was secretly and mysteriously conducted and its members could not be caught. These men would ride about the country at night in fantastic garb, pretending to be the spirits of departed Confederate soldiers, come back to avenge outrages on their people. Some of them had a method of seeming to elongate themselves and others had concealed bags into which they would empty one or more buckets of water, seeming to the astonished onlookers to be drinking it. Soon the colored population could not be induced to leave their houses at night and some white people were quite as much afraid.

L. C. Lester and D. L. Wilson give this explanation of the object and results of this peculiar order:

"Whatever may be the judgment of history, those who know the facts will ever remain firm in the conviction that the Ku Klux Klan was of immense service at this period of Southern history. Without it, in many sections of the South, life to decent people would not have been tolerable. It served a good purpose. Wherever the Ku Klux appeared the effect was salutary. For a while the robberies ceased. The lawless class assumed the habits of good behavior."

After the Klan has achieved its purpose it went out of existence in 1869, and its members ceased their self-imposed discipline. The Ku Klux Klan has often been maligned and men were arrested, after the order had disbanded, for misconduct done under the guise of the former Klan. Lester and Wilson say of this: "No single instance occurred of the arrest of a masked man who proved to be—when stripped of his disguises—a Ku Klux."

At a Ku Klux convention held in Nashville in 1867, where numerous and prominent Memphis men were in attendance, their principles were thus stated:

(1) To protect the weak, the innocent and the defenseless, from the indignities, wrongs and outrages of the lawless, the violent and the brutal; to relieve the injured and the oppressed; to succor the suffering, and especially the widows and orphans of Confederate soldiers.

(2) To protect and defend the Constitution of the United States, and all laws passed in conformity thereto, and to protect the States and people thereof from all invasion from any source whatever.

(3) To aid and assist in the execution of all constitutional laws, and to protect the people from unlawful seizure, and from trial except by their peers in conformity to the laws of the land.

Instead of having treasonable designs, as had been preferred against them, their creed is additional proof of fidelity to the United States.

*Creed.*

We, the order of the \* \* \* , reverentially acknowledge the majesty and supremacy of the Divine Being, and recognize the goodness and providence of the same. And we recognize our relation to the United States Government, the supremacy of the Constitution, the Constitutional laws thereof, and the Union of States thereunder.

But behind it all was a determined purpose to rid the "reconstructed" Southern States of carpet-bag government and misrule, and this was ultimately accomplished.

The last of this decade of the sixties, with its war effects, was as disastrous for Memphis as the war itself. Municipal and financial affairs were in deplorable condition, an epidemic of yellow fever in 1867 claimed 550 victims and several big fires added to the stress of losses already experienced.

The people were discouraged, but were sustained by the greatest gift to human beings,—Hope!

Each year seemed to strengthen affairs a little and better feeling between Northerners and Southerners was making its way. Carpet-bag rule was weakened and the South was beginning to stand up again. By 1870 all her states had been readmitted to the Union and she was avowedly and really ready to take her part in the welfare of the common country.

The year 1870 started with John W. Leftwich as mayor, he having succeeded W. O. Lofland. In that year the Memphis board of rulers was changed from that of "Mayor and Aldermen" to "Mayor, Board of Aldermen and Board of Common Councilmen," all these together denominated the General Council. Each ward was entitled to one alderman, elected for two years, and two councilmen, elected for one year. The city boundaries were also reduced at this time thus:

## History of Memphis, Tennessee.

Beginning at a point on the west line of the State of Tennessee, where the center of Kerr Street, produced, would strike the Mississippi River; thence eastward on a line with the center of Kerr Street, if extended, would strike the town reserve; thence southward, along the said east line of the town reserve, to the middle of the old Raleigh road, or Johnson's Avenue; thence eastward along the middle of the old Raleigh road to a point where the center line of Dunlap Street, produced, northward, would intersect the same; thence southward along the said produced line, and the middle line of Dunlap Street to the middle of Union Avenue; thence westward along the middle of Union Avenue to the middle of Walnut Street; thence southward along the middle of Walnut Street to the middle of the old Fort Pickering Railroad; thence westward along the middle of the old Fort Pickering Railroad, or Broadway, to the middle of Bayou Gayoso; thence southward, up said bayou, and along the middle of the same, to Jackson Street; thence along the middle of Jackson Street and the prolongation of said street, to the west line of the State of Tennessee; thence northward with the west line of the State of Tennessee to the beginning.

The valuation of real and personal property in Memphis for this same year, was:

"fixed at $24,783,190, upon which was levied a tax of $486,881, divided as follows: For schools, $74,359; interest tax, $239,049; city tax, $173,482. The value of real and personal property in the city of Memphis as returned by the assessor from and inclusive of 1860 and 1870, was as follows: 1860, $16,897,000; 1861, $21,153,000; 1862; $18,297,000; 1863, $16,693,000; 1864, $15,026,000; 1865, $15,574,000; 1866, $17,823,000; 1867, $30,819,900; 1868, $28,564,000; 1869, $28,528,000; 1870, $24,783,000."*

In January of 1870 John Johnson was elected mayor of the city and served two terms, or four years. The Federal census of this year gave Memphis a population of 40,226. Of this number 24,755 were white; 15,471, colored; 6,780, foreign; 3,371, Irish; 2,144, German.†

*Vedder. †Keating.

This showed an increase of nearly 18,000, although the Ninth and Tenth wards had been taken from the corporation. This official census encouraged the people as it proved that the town was at least active and they trusted to its becoming sane and harmonious soon.

"Reconstruction," so called, was ended in Tennessee and although carpet-bag rule had depleted Memphis, the people felt relieved, took heart and hoped to do their little part in the working out of the Nation's welfare.

The Charter Amendment provided that day and night police, exclusive of the chief, should consist of one policeman to every 1,000 inhabitants under the Federal census. The Board of Commissioners were to elect the chief of the Fire Department, and to adopt rules of discipline, which they required the chief to enforce. There were to be enough firemen to manage all the equipment and to extinguish fires, but no more, and they were also to be employed by the Commissioners.

One of the first duties imposed on the General Council was to establish work-houses and houses of correction.

Municipal enterprise was going forward. Work was being done on the streets and the Popular Street turnpike was nearing completion. Two railroads that had been discussed and agitated in former years were begun,—one to Selma, Alabama, and the other to Paducah, Kentucky.

The new mayor was much handicapped by the condition in which he found affairs. In his first report he stated that the city was "without a dollar of cash in her treasury and her credit so impaired that she was really paying at least two prices for all services rendered, or supplies purchased; her bonds, authorized to be issued to fund due outstanding indebtedness, having been and being disposed of by her own officers at less than fifty cents on the dollar to pay current expenses; and though ostensibly the pay of the city employees and supplies obtained were at cash rates, yet, by allowances thereon in various ways, and for heavy interest on loans, and fabulous discount on bonds sold, the cost to the city was eventually more than double the amount nominally paid. Her floating debt, then over $600,000 in excess of all assets applicable for its liquidation, was being increased in the ratio of 100 to 65, by being exchanged for her own six per cent bonds, so that, in taking up $65 of debt in one shape, she issued to the fortunate holders thereof, $100 in a much better form. The floating debt at that date being, in round numbers about $1,200,000, with assets applicable to its reduction to only half that amount, and that inequality between debt and means continuously and rapidly increasing, it must be obvious to any one who will impartially examine this matter, that this pretense of merely taking up floating indebtedness by issuance of six per cent bonds when in the exchange there was really so great an increase, would, by a continuance of the system (the city's credit rapidly depreciating as her necessities increased) soon have led to financial ruin and actual bankruptcy."

The city's total debt July 1, 1870, amounted to $4,785,000, her assets, all told, to $882,488.*

Mr. Johnson considered this state of affairs appalling, as well he might, and proposed that the city be run on a cash basis until finances were in better condition, but the people did not join with him and he was "hampered and hindered by ward politicians."†

$500,000 more of bonds were issued for funding purposes. Taxes were high but debt increased and poor management was fast hurrying Memphis to bankruptcy and humiliation. Distrust was felt on all sides and the mayor himself was charged with fraud in regard to "the payment of some Memphis coupons in the hands of the state,"‡ but he was exonerated by Mr. William M. Farrington, president of the Union & Planters Bank, in a manner so satisfactory to the public that he was reelected mayor at the next municipal election.

Crimes were so numerous during this time that many arrests were made and it became necessary to hold so many criminals that in August of 1871 Judge Flippin lectured on the state of affairs and warned those in charge of the jail to be vigorous "in preventing criminals from escaping and mur-

*Keating.  †Ibid.  ‡Keating.

derers too much freedom in the jail and from preventing women from having free access to them."

The levy of taxes became so heavy that citizens protested strongly, even appealed to the Supreme Court and Legislature for redress, but the Supreme Court sustained the city government and declared their legislation constitutional. But even the excessive taxes could not meet expenses and suits were brought against the city for debts. One contractor brought suit for $448,000, for Nicholson pavement, and obtained judgment.*

In the midst of her own troubles news came to Memphis of the terrible Chicago fire and she raised over $50,000 for the benefit of the thousands made homeless by that catastrophe. Little did she think then that the sufferers from that great conflagration would, in a few years, be called upon to help her own stricken people.

While this burden of excessive taxes was being borne by the people, who were striving to build up their unfortunate city, the fact was published by the grand jury that the County Court had not been spending as much for public improvements as the city and county had been charged for. The tax-collector was declared to be a defaulter to the amount of $100,000 and the amount was afterwards found to be three times that sum.

When their officials could not be trusted the people knew their troubles were not decreasing. While they were taxed beyond the rates of larger cities, still municipal affairs were woefully neglected. The streets were in poor condition, filth was allowed to accumulate in yards, alleys and even streets, and sewerage was scarcely regarded at all. As effect is sure to follow cause, Memphis paid the penalty for this neglect.

The beginning of 1873 seemed to point to an unraveling of municipal tangles and to city prosperity, but plans of men are as naught when Nature punishes. It is then that we realize that merely human existence is very uncertain, and that to be well in this span of life we must regard the laws of decency and right as pointed out to us by Mother Nature herself. The unsanitary conditions of Memphis, the foul air that had been

*Ibid.

allowed to hover over her homes and streets,—all the general neglect, brought their lesson to Memphis.

As the last decade had been one of war and poorly managed reconstruction, this one seemed to be destined for one of pestilence. Before the winter of early 1873 was over small-pox laid seize to the city; in June and July it was followed by a "malignant type of Asiatic cholera,"* and in August came yellow fever.

When yellow fever was pronounced epidemic, September 14,† the people were terror-stricken and in a very short while the population was reduced to 25,000, and many of these left later. Business of course was almost entirely suspended, the law of self-preservation usurping all other interests. Of those left 4,204 were stricken with the disease, of which number 1,244 died.‡

Memphis was in poor condition to care for an epidemic, but a Citizens' Executive Committee was organized and they set valiantly to work to care for the stricken, soliciting aid from abroad. All the states responded to this call and several European countries sent large subscriptions. The Howard Association, which had been formed for the especial purpose of aiding yellow fever epidemics, called its forces together the day after the announcement of the epidemic. Only eight of its original members responded to the roll-call, but more joined the association and they were soon engaged in their noble work. The eight members on hand when the meeting was called were: J. G. Lonsdale, Sr., Dr. P. P. Frame, A. D. Langstaff, W. J. B. Lonsdale, J. P. Robertson, E. J. Mansford, A. G. Raymond and Fred Gutherz. The new members were: W. J. Smith, J. J. Murphy, B. P. Anderson, J. G. Simpson, W. P. Wilson, G. W. Gordon, J. H. Smith, E. B. Foster, A. E. Frankland, W. S. Rogers, W. A. Holt, F. F. Bowen, J. F. Porter, R. T. Halstead, T. R. Waring, S. W. Rhode, W. J. Lemon, W. G. Barth, L.

*Father D. A. Quinn.
†According to Dowell. He also says that the first case appeared August 1, and the last November 9.
‡Dowell gives these figures as the nearest estimate, not including those that died before September 14, and after November 9, although there were deaths both before and after those dates, but no official record was kept of them.

Seibeck, J. E. Lanphier, J. H. Edmondson, John Johnston (attorney), J. W. Cooper, F. A. Tyler, Jr., C. A. Laffingwell, H. D. Connell, P. W. Semmes, D. E. Brettenum and D. B. Graham.* They only had $130 in the treasury but their call for aid was quickly responded to by contributions of money, clothing and provisions of all sorts from all over the country.

Several physicians who had had experience with the disease came to the city and many other helpers came at the call of distress. Besides the workers of the Howard Association and the Citizens' Committee, the Odd Fellows, Masons, priests and sisters of the Catholic church, and others volunteered service, and contributions from Protestant, Catholic and Jewish churches, from the secret organizations, trade organizations, police, firemen, city, county, State and all states, came pouring in. Ministers of all denominations could be seen among the patients, some having come from afar to take part in allaying the suffering. All feelings between the North and the South were forgotten and "carpet-baggers," "scalawags," foreigners, —all classes and nationalities thought only of the suffering and became brothers.

Women of station in society joined in the work and often beside them and the religious workers, would toil a former "outcast," tending the needs of patients, closing the eyes that were blind to earthly scenes, or otherwise assisting in their self-sacrificing and volunteer work for others. Many of these unselfish ones laid their lives on the altar of sacrifice, perhaps after bringing to convalescence many others.

When, in November, the epidemic was declared to be a horror of the past, the General Council passed resolutions of thanks to all the states and countries that had sent succor during the disheartening seige.

People came back much depressed, but Colonel Keating tells us that the merchants were only inconvenienced and almost uninjured.

When the year ended confidence had been regained and 1874 showed noteworthy increase in business improvements, but the city government was still a cause of complaint. A

*Keating.

writer in "Old Folks Record" in 1874, said: "We need legislative reform. Our city government should be simplified. As it is, too many members of our city legislature have axes to grind, and they are ground at the expense of their fellow citizens." This writer advocated one tax-collector instead of four or five, and continued: "We could dispense with some of our courts and incidental expenses. We could reform our jury system, and in this particular save thousands of dollars.

"Let our city and county be managed as a frugal farmer manages his farm, and there will be no drawback in their progress.

"Let our people be persuaded that our offices and courts and government are for them, and not for the officers."

The city's monthly outlay at that time was said to exceed $35,000, much more than the depleted and debt-encumbered corporation could afford. Taxes continued to be a great burden and for 1873 amounted to $4.00 on the $100, on a tax valuation of $28,217,000, and in addition to this extortionate levy, the mayor was demanding the collection of $977,000 of back taxes. For this purpose the General Council issued distress warrants, after the United States court had issued a writ of mandamus against the city for $514,900, for the Nicholson pavement contractor before mentioned.

Crime still stalked through the town, but the officers had grown very determined and were doing what they could to lessen its evils by enforcing strict laws against carrying concealed weapons and bringing all criminals to justice. Judge Flippin again lectured to the city and appealed to the sense of civic pride and right in the citizens to do all in their power to eradicate crime and build up poor Memphis, who had had many terrible experiences to hold her back on the road to progress.

Confidence between the white people and negroes was gaining ground and the latter had learned to a great extent that their former owners were not enemies, though many of them had never thought so. Occasional riots were threatened and a serious one in 1874 occurred in Gibson County in which several negroes were killed.

Memphis people held a mass meeting to denounce this affair and try to establish harmony, especially now that the state had returned to Democratic government and conditions generally had improved or, at least were improving, in the South. At this meeting were many former Confederate soldiers and some of the speakers were ex-President Jefferson Davis, Isham G. Harris and General Forrest.

Finances did not improve and the city debt loomed, a bigger obligation than Memphis could pay, and it was growing greater all the time.

# CHAPTER VIII

John Loague, Mayor. Financial Difficulties. Census of 1875. New Charter. The Flippin Administration. Schemes to Retire City Debt. Sale of Navy Yard. Surrender of Charter Considered. Great Epidemic of Yellow Fever Begins. Panic and Stampede of Citizens. Terrible Scenes of Suffering and Death. Howard Association and Relief Committees. Heroism of the Workers. The Tragedy of Death and Burial. The Daily Press Faithful. Generosity of Non-Residents. Loyal Negro Militia. Death Roll of the Howards. End of the Epidemic. Thanksgiving for Relief.

---

JOHN LOAGUE, who had succeeded John Johnson as mayor, was a good financier and his most earnest work in his new office was to reduce Memphis' debt and the overwhelming burden of her taxes. In his first message to the General Council he set forth in plain figures the enormity of the debt which was crushing the town. In a second message he questioned the legality of some of the bonds and thought the courts could not force Memphis to pay more than she had received from them, which would be about forty-two per cent. A few months later this determined mayor issued another message in which he "urged the appointment of a commission of eminent citizens to unite with the creditors of the city in a convention to consider the debt and agree and determine upon a plan by which it might be refunded at a rate, below its face value, that would bring it within the reach of the city to pay."*

This plan was agreed upon and Mayor Loague recommended G. A. Hanson, I. M. Hill, E. M. Apperson, P. C. Bethel, J. M. Keating and A. J. Keller for such commissioners. They were appointed by the General Council and given power to act.

*Keating.

The total debt of the city amounted to $5,651,165.* These commissioners went to New York to consult some of the creditors, but failed to get them to agree to anything less than the face value of the bonds. This failure was discouraging but the mayor set to work to use strenuous means to lessen the city's burdens. After much controversy by and between the General Council, even sometimes almost to the point of combat, it is recorded, Mr. Loague was authorized "to issue scrip for the certificates held by the tax-payers who had paid the Nicholson pavement tax."†

There were suits then pending in the United States court against the city and William M. Randolph was employed to defend Memphis.

Financial difficulties of the Nation coming on at this time, the Memphis officials found their task of straightening out home affairs all the more perplexing. Of the Country's trials during this decade James Ford Rhodes says: "These five years [1873-1878] are a long dismal tale of declining markets, exhaustion of capital, a lowering in value of all kinds of property, including real estate, constant bankruptcies, close economy in business and grinding frugality in living, idle mills, furnaces and factories, former profit-earning iron mills reduced to the value of a scrap-heap, laborers out of employment, reductions of wages, strikes and lockouts, the great railroad riots of 1877, suffering of the unemployed, depression and despair."‡

Financial complications occupied the General Council at the expense of other city needs, but some attention was paid to sanitation. The neighborhood where yellow fever had started in 1873 was cleaned up and the Board of Health exerted itself in various directions.

The County Court, despite the County's financial misfortunes, purchased the old Overton Hotel for a courthouse and voted $20,000 for the building of a new insane asylum, to be conducted upon more thoughtful and humane methods than formerly.

A census was taken in 1875 and gave 40,230, an increase

*Ibid. †Ibid.
‡Rhodes' History of the United States—Volume VII.

Wm. M. Randolph

of only four in five years, the smallest gain Memphis had ever made in any other five or even one year since her beginning. Had it not been for the disastrous epidemic of 1873 the city would no doubt have grown as she had heretofore, and as her physical situation indicated that she should. But sickness, war, misgovernment, abnormal taxes, debt, had discouraged the people and they were not as alert and energetic as they should have been. After the experience of 1873 the place should have been put in thorough sanitary condition, but as one summer passed after another and the fever did not return, premises, alleys, vacant lots and other localities became unclean and general neglect grew from bad to worse with only an occasional spurt of activity on the part of the Board of Health.

Memphis seemed to be rushing pell-mell into ruin from many causes. Property-holders were growing or had grown indignant at the looseness of municipal management and were beginning to assert themselves through the public press and otherwise. Most of the office-holders were not tax-payers and the majority of the voters owned no property. These, it was claimed, thought more of personal gain than of the city's good. The rent derived from property in many cases did not pay taxes, repairs and insurance. In consequence, persons not already property-holders, preferred renting to investing their money in Memphis real-estate. Manufacturers were driven away and no inducements were held out to others to come. Few buildings were erected and mechanics were idle or left the city. Capital and labor both suffered as one necessarily affects the other.

Citizens came to the conclusion that if the city was in such a deplorable condition under existing circumstances, surely a change was needed. A people's Protective Union was formed, and the members recommended reforms for the city government, affecting such items as taxes and their collection, salaries and fees of city officials, juries and jury-service, vagrancy, the establishment of a reformatory prison and other needs.

The new charter contained some reforms. For instance, a Board of Fire and Police Commissioners were to govern and control the police and fire departments and the members were prevented from taking any part, as formerly, in politics, more than casting votes at elections. It limited the city tax to $1.60 and prevented city officials from having any interest in city bonds.

This revised charter was approved by Mayor Loague but opposed by the Council, and brought up lively controversies. City Attorney G. A. Hanson and Comptroller Newsom did not agree in their figures as to the city's indebtedness. Hanson reported the debt to be $6,500,000 in round numbers, with an interest of $390,000, while Newsom reported it to be $5,522,362.22, against which he said were assets amounting to $1,675,208.39. The Council was opposed to Attorney Hanson and a committee, appointed by it, endorsed Newsom's statement and disputed Hanson's, whereupon the latter resigned.

The People's Protective Union sent a request, through a committee, to the Council to employ a city attorney of high grade to handle efficiently the suits and mandamus proceedings that hovered as dark shadows over the city. Besides this request for the appointment of an able lawyer, the committee set forth the grievances of the people thus:

"The financial condition of the city of Memphis has reached a crisis, threatening wholesale confiscation, and the expulsion of the people from their homes, alarming to every citizen having the interest of the city at heart. The remorseless Shylocks who speculate in city bonds at twenty-one cents demand their payment dollar for dollar and expect by the writ of mandamus to override the law limiting the rate of taxation and compel the collection of a tax sufficient for its immediate payment. If this is the law, and it is to be enforced, it amounts to virtual confiscation, and the people, especially the poor, will be turned into the streets, and their humble homes, the fruit of years of hard toil and frugality, will pass for a mere song into the hands of greedy speculators in city bonds. It is well known that a large amount of the debt of the city is illegal, and was imposed upon a people having no voice in its creation through military rule and through the instrumentality of elections held in violation of law, and conducted in fraud and violence, while a large majority of tax-payers were disfranchised and denied the right of voting upon the very proposition to issue the bonds. In the election for the million dollar issue in 1868, some man who paid thousands of dollars of taxes annually, was driven from the polls with insult when he offered to vote against the issue of bonds. A large amount of the debt of the city has been created not only without authority, but in positive violation of law. Every dollar of the scrip issued by the military government, and subsequently funded, is illegal. * * * * Those who speculate in the life-blood of the city, and some who esteemed it no dishonor to neglect the payment of their private debts, prate about the honor and credit of the city, and insist upon the 'pound of flesh,' though the operation reduced the people to penury and serfdom to the bondholder. Such people talk of the innocent holder, as if none but bondholders were innocent, and the people a set of knaves, seeking to evade the payment of just debts. We proclaim and insist that the victimized and plundered people are the innocent parties, and the bondholders were bound to know of the fraud and outrage perpetrated upon a helpless people.''

Mayor Loague appointed Judge Sam P. Walker to the position of city attorney, that able lawyer resigning the chancellorship to accept it. He took matters seriously in hand and won several suits that saved the city thousands of dollars.

Mayor Loague, in his last report tendered to the city, showed how the expense of city government had lessened, and the mayor succeeding him, Judge John R. Flippin, and his new council, started in with determination for even stricter economy and reforms for bringing the city out of her difficulties. These new officials found affairs worse than Comptroller Newsom's report had led them to believe, and nearer the condition that ex-City Attorney Hanson had declared. Mayor Flippin in his first report gave the city a debt at $5,600,000, of which $600,000 was matured coupons bearing interest at the rate of seven per cent. The annual interest of the city amounted to $350,000, while annual expenses were $300,000. In order to meet all the indebtedness for the year and pay expenses it would require $1,400,000, and the city was not equal to it.*

*Figures quoted in Keathing's History of Memphis.

Mayor Flippin proposed "to retire all the debt over $5,000,000 by delinquent taxes; then from the gross sum deduct one third, leaving $3,333,333, fund this in $100 bonds due in 30 years, interest on them payable when drawn, as per schedule given. From these draw annually paying four per cent on numbers drawn, using not less than $140,000 for the last ten years."*

The mayor's plan was much discussed but was thought not feasible and was not adopted. Judge Flippin then went to New York for the purpose of making a settlement with the bond-holders. They agreed to scale at sixty cents on the dollar.

After this compromise the General Council authorized the mayor to prepare a bill for the next Legislature for the purpose of carrying it out.

The Navy Yard was sold during this administration, in 1876, to Amos Woodruff and J. J. McCombs for $117,000, they being allowed to give notes from date of purchase, bearing six per cent interest. This sale terminated long discussions and litigation which had cost Memphis $540,000.†

The Board, though running on economical lines, allowed a few civic improvements. The levee was repaired and added to, Main and Madison Streets were partly paved and numerous bridges were built throughout the city. But the population did not increase, those remaining grew poorer, taxes were extortionate without much to show for expenditures, property continually decreased in value, the funding of the big debt was discouragingly slow, the United States court mandamus writs had become urgent and city conditions were as bad as could be.

Mayor Flippin worked zealously trying to get rid of the city debt and carried on much correspondence with the bond-holders and talked to them personally when possible, making trips to Charleston, Baltimore and New York for that purpose. By the close of 1877 he had succeeded in funding more than

*Keating.
†Keating.

$1,000,000 of the obligations, but even this great accomplishment was small when compared with all that was to be done.

Several meetings were held by the Chamber of Commerce and the Cotton Exchange to weigh affairs and try to bring about a solution and remedy. These meetings brought forth suggestions of dissolving the corporation of Memphis, and by consulting with able attorneys, Judges J. W. Clapp and H. T. Ellett, it was learned that "Public corporations are but part of the machinery employed by the sovereign power of the State for the purposes of government, and as they are created and exist only by law, they may be changed and destroyed by law." Also, "The city of Memphis, then, is but the creature of the Legislature, and though our State Constitution is peculiar in its provisions as to the creation and destruction of corporations, which may or may not include public corporations, yet its corporate franchises may, by proper legislation, be suspended or taken away; its corporate limits extended or curtailed; its name changed, and its legal existence annihilated at the pleasure of the Legislature, and with or without the consent of its inhabitants."

To the questions of citizens as to the consequences ensuing from such dissolution, the attorneys responded that the city's "personal estate vests in this country in the people, and in England in the crown, and the debts due to and from the corporation are totally extinguished."

In such case franchises, they said, are taken from the corporation dissolved, still, "This rule has been repudiated as to private corporations in this state, and almost universally, and whilst the franchises of a corporation that has forfeited its charter are taken away, the existence of the corporation is prolonged by the statute until its debts are paid or its effects disposed of for the benefit of its creditors."

These lawyers gave much study to the questions in controversy and handed in quite an elaborate document, over their signatures, of the digested law, In continuation of the matter already quoted, they replied in part:

"Whilst the Legislature may accept the surrender of its charter by a municipal corporation and terminate its legal existence, it can enact no law that impairs the obligation of any contract which the municipality has, by authority of law, entered into. * * * * Whilst the Legislature may abolish the charter of the city of Memphis, it cannot disannul its contracts, nor cancel its debts, nor can it deprive its creditors of the remedies to which they are entitled under their contracts. It may change the form of the remedy, and may, perhaps, substitute one less stringent and efficient, but unless a substantial remedy be left, it is apprehended the act would be held void by the courts. * * * * When a creditor deals with a municipal corporation, he knows that it is the creature of the legislative will and may therefore be presumed to take the risk of the repeal of the charter and the loss of his remedy as a part of the law of his contract. * * * * The municipal officers, who were such at the time of the passage of the act annulling the charter, might be judicially determined to be still in office and subject to the mandates of the courts as to the levy and collection of taxes for the purpose of paying the debts of the city. * * * * Were the city charter abolished, the Legislature, in the exercise of its unrestrained power of taxation, except as limited by the State Constitution, could, we presume, by special legislation for the territory now within the city limits adopt a plan of local taxation sufficient to meet the expenses incident to such public regulations as might be necessary for the protection of the persons and property of the inhabitants, and might, perhaps, if it chose to do so, levy a special tax upon such inhabitants, or upon their property and pursuits, for the purpose of providing a fund to pay off the indebtedness of the city at the time of the repeal of its charter."

After this answer was received and considered a committee consisting of W. P. Proudfit, F. S. Davis, J. W. Clapp, II. T. Ellett, B. Bayliss and D. P. Hadden, was appointed to formulate a plan of action in conformity therewith. The city attorney, S. P. Walker, was requested to draft a bill, which he did and presented at a meeting of the Chamber of Commerce, Cotton Exchange, citizens and officials. The caption of this bill gives its purport and is as follows:

"AN ACT to repeal the charter of certain municipal corporations, to remand the territory embraced within the corporate limits of such municipalities to the government of the county courts, to enlarge the powers of such county courts and to levy and dispose of special local taxes upon the persons and property located within the territorial limits of such municipalities."

This bill was approved by three of the committee and many others, but the mayor and many with him, repudiated such a step on the part of the city. Men spoke for and against such action and on a vote being taken the bill was defeated by nearly two to one. This vote was reconsidered, however, and the committee instructed to have five hundred copies, together with the legal opinion of Judges Clapp and Ellett, printed and sent to the senators and representatives for their consideration. The bill was opposed in the Legislature and those members attempted to pass another bill appointing a receiver for Mempihs, but this failed, as the Governor did not sign it.

The General Council, most of whom were against dissolving the city government, passed resolutions opposing the bill. They were of the opinion that Mayor Flippin was handling the enormous debt problem efficiently and that with time, judicious perseverance would lift the incubus from Memphis.*

This by no means ended considerations of dissolving the charter and the subject continued to be agitated, especially after the United States court issued a peremptory order for the Nicholson pavement debt of $200,000 to be paid immediately, the money to be obtained by levying a special tax. This order aroused the people to frenzy. Indignation meetings were held and Major Minor Meriwether, representing the People's Protective Association, addressed the General Council, explaining how impossible it was for the people to meet this and other enormous demands. He urged a repeal of the charter as a necessity for getting city affairs settled and perhaps keeping the people from rebellion.

Following this were weeks of altercation and reasoning,

*The description of these proceedings was obtained chiefly from Colonel Keating's History of Memphis.

during which time it was decided to cut down the salaries of city employes from ten to twenty per cent, reduce salaries of school-teachers and take salaries entirely away from the Sinking Fund Commissioners.

Collection of back taxes was again agitated and the people wrangled and planned and blundered until the stealthy yellow enemy that had remained away five years, giving the city time to rid herself of dirt, came back in the midst of the financial confusion, political wrangles, dirty streets, filthy alleys, open vaults of putrefaction, stench, and said, "Stop your human chatter! After your sinful neclect of God's first law and a city's highest need, order and cleanliness, I claim this town as mine!"

Dr. R. W. Mitchell, president of the Board of Health, who had been urging and pleading for quarantine and appropriations for sanitary precautions, discouraged by failure to obtain any assistance from the General Council, resigned his position. When the first suspicious case of fever appeared in the city, the officials became alarmed, refused the resignation of Dr. Mitchell and agreed to meet his demands. The whole city went to work with feverish energy to clean up. Politics, debt, disagreements, amusements, business,—everything else gave way before fear and efforts to prevent an epidemic. It was too late!

Reports came daily from New Orleans and other places, showing a constant increase in the spread of the disease and mortality. Memphis people became excited. Quarantine restrictions were enforced and the Board of Health, that had so lately begged in vain for assistance and coöperation, now had their hands upheld by the General Council and the citizens. Merchants, who a short while before, had thought they could spare no money for anything, subscribed liberally to supply the means that the city lacked.

A steamboatman at the city hospital had a suspicious case of illness and on August 2, it was pronounced yellow fever. Other cases occurred but were kept suppressed until August 14, when an Italian snack-house keeper, Mrs. Bionda, was reported as having a well-defined case of the dread disease.

This caused general alarm and many sought safety in flight.

The day after Mrs. Bionda's case twenty-two others were announced and panic ensued. On the following day, the sixteenth, thirty-three new cases were reported, and the people rushed from the city like mad. Fear, more contagious than the disease, possessed men and women, and the predominant impulse was to flee. Houses were not only left in haste, but many of them were left open, with silver-plate in dining-rooms, elegant rugs, curtains, pictures and other valuable furnishings forgotten and barely enough clothing taken to supply immediate needs, while the owners rushed for trains that could not supply all the demands. Seats, aisles, platforms and roofs of all cars were crowded and men who could not obtain entrance by doors climbed through car-windows, despite all protests from people in the packed seats. Courtesy was forgotten and often, even the common feelings of humanity. Self preservation reigned as law.

Policemen were stationed at trains to enforce order, but when men found their entrance to cars interfered with they cared not for law and order; they considered that life hung in the balance, and many obtained admittance for themselves and families by the use of fire-arms. The officers saw the futility of trying to keep people back and they, themselves in sympathy with the crowd, simply tried to keep order until the trains would push out. And push out they did, more packed than they had ever been before, as fast as managers could get them ready, though all too inadequate was the service.

Those who could not get away on trains left in carriages, buggies, wagons, vans,—even drays were pressed into passenger service, while others walked, not even knowing where they were going, their only object being to get away from the pestilence. Many who would have gone could not because themselves or families were overtaken by the now striding plague. Some, however, were not even held by family ties and one of the saddest pictures of the whole horrible time that we contemplate at this distant day is that of persons leaving relatives and friends to suffer and die unattended save by the noble strangers who stayed or came to help while others fled. It is recorded that even men left their wives and fathers their families and a few, away at the time of the stampede refused to come to afflicted wife or children or both. It is pitiful when narrow human nature supplants the nobler nature of man made in God's image, but when we do behold that Image, the contemplation exalts even human nature in our minds. Though there were a few deserters, we are told that no wife deserted her husband and, at a later time Governor Marks, in his address made at the laying of the corner-stone of the Memphis Custom House, said: "In the history of the pestilence I read that parents deserted their children, children their parents, husbands wives, but that no wife deserted her husband. * * * * When you erect your monument to commenorate the heroes of the pestilence of 1878, in justice to the noble women of Memphis, let it be written upon that monument that 'Thermopylae had her deserter, but the wives of Memphis had none.'"

As the disease spread here other towns and cities became alarmed for their own safety and quarantine laws caused many Memphis refugees to be turned away, in some places even shot-guns being used to show the determination of the inhabitants. Many of these rejected and helpless safety-seekers camped in the woods, without necessary equipment for the crudest comforts, or later joined one of the camps provided for refugees.

By August 26, the rush from the city was over, though some still sought safety in unquarantined places. The panic being over, those left settled down to the inevitable. Business and traffic of course, were paralyzed, streets deserted, houses desolate, many standing open and none properly protected against dust or thieves. Politics, the $5,000,000 debt, inadequate or extortionate taxes, cries of people for improvements or justice,—these and all other things were forgotten, and only the alleviation of human suffering or the saving of human life was considered.

In one week the population had been reduced to 19,600, 14,000 of these being negroes. Of the less than 6,000 white people 4,204 died, and of the negroes 946 died. Up to the epidemic of this year colored people had been thought to be immune, and even then the purely African type usually escaped and when they had it the disease did not prove fatal. The hybrid part of the population was not so fortunate and many of them succumbed. About two hundred and fifty white people escaped the disease, most of these having had it in previous epidemics.

On the 17th of August the Citizens Relief Committee organized and its members were soon doing what they could to relieve the stricken, keep order and take systematic charge of all money and provisions sent to them. The Howard Association was called together and these good men were soon hand in hand with the Relief Committee in their brave work.

Many people of this generation do not even know what the Howard Association was and it is but fair to devote a little space to them in passing. This organization originated in New Orleans in 1853, among the clerks of N. B. Kneass. The mother of two of these young men had been a resident of San Domingo where yellow fever was a common malady and she had learned to treat it successfully. When the epidemic afflicted New Orleans in 1853, these young men went about distributing the medicines prepared by this good woman, giving much relief, though that year claimed 7,970 victims in the Crescent City. Other young men joined these, some from wealthy families, and they organized under the name of the Howard Association, choosing the name of the greatest philanthropist, John Howard. As the Association grew, physicians, nurses and medicine were furnished by it and agencies were formed in all towns where there with liklihood of the yellow pest. The sole purpose of the association was to aid in this one disease and whenever it made its appearance Howard members assembled for work. In 1867 a call was made in Memphis for this association and members met to form a working order in the Bluff City. These first Memphis members were: R. W. Ainslie, William Everett, H. Lonergan, John Heart, C. T. Geoghegan, J. K. Pritchard, A. D. Langstaff, J. B. Wasson, J. P. Gallagher, Jack Horne, E. J. Mansford, John Park, Rev. R. A. Simpson, Dr. P. P. Fraime, J. P. Robertson, T. C.

McDonald, J. T. Collins, E. M. Levy, W. A. Strozzi, E. J. Corson, Dr. A. Sterling, A. A. Hyde, G. C. Wersch, W. S. Hamilton, A. H. Gresham, Fred Gutherz, W. J. B. Lonsdale and J. G. Lonsdale, Sr.

As soon as these men were organized they notified the public that they were ready to furnish necessities, which they did as long as the fever lasted. When that year's pestilance was over the members adjourned, subject to call whenever yellow fever sufferers claimed their services again. A charter was not granted to the Memphis association until 1869.

As has been related, these self-sacrificing men were next called together for work in 1873, when the few members remaining responded, new members joined and they went to work.

The next call came in 1878, when, on the fourteenth day of August, the members again answered roll-call, added new names to the roll and, under the first vice-president, A. D. Langstaff, launched upon their duties, to face the worst epidemic the heroic men of any of the Howard associations had yet encountered. According to the Howard custom, the city was divided into districts and members assigned to each. Cases from each district were reported at headquarters, each investigated at once and the necessary supplies were furnished.

The first week after the fever started in Memphis in 1878, 1,500 were reported sick, ten dying every day. The second week registered 3,000 cases, with fifty deaths a day. The following week showed a still greater mortality, which continued to increase until the middle of September, when the average deaths per day were two hundred, with between 8,000 and 10,000 sick. September fourteenth was the day of greatest mortality, when considerable over two hundred deaths were reported.

The plague had a fearful hold and threatened to depopulate the town. As such stupendous increase came fear seized physicians and nurses, which caused them to succumb more easily to the disease than at first, and so their ranks were rapidly thinned. There were much uncertainty about methods. Some patients died under treatment that seemed to cure others. Doctors consulted, but there were many disagreements and much of the treatment was guess work or experiment, but they worked conscientiously and did the best they could.

Dr. Robert W. Mitchell, an experienced and scientific physician, had a corps of efficient workers under him and they had great success in treating the disease. Dr. G. B. Thornton, in charge of the City Hospital, was much overworked, as well as those who aided him. How those faithful hospital doctors and nurses did work, stopping only when the disease they were fighting claimed them for its own. Doctors, nurses, the organization workers, ministers, priests, church sisters and other volunteers worked, forgetting exhaustion and their own needs in trying to make up for the inadequacy of their forces.

By the last of August the workers were falling rapidly, some of them going until they fell prostrate. By the middle of September nineteen Howards were dead or sick. The noble President of the Association, Butler P. Anderson, who had gone to Grenada to help the sufferers there, had returned to Memphis, taken the fever and died. Mr. Langstaff was stricken and his place was filled by ex-Mayor John Johnson. Early in October only three officers of the Howard Association were on duty and many members of the other working orders were down or gone to rest after giving their lives for others.

The Citizens Relief Committee was conspicuous for its broadcast work, as were the Masons, Odd Fellows, Knights of Pythias, Knights of Honor, the Father Matthew Society, the Hebrew Hospital Association, the Typographical Union, Telegraphers, Southern Express Company, the railroad companies and many private volunteer workers,—physicians, nurses and ministers of all denominations.*

Poor and rich alike accepted the services of these laborers and indeed were at their mercy. The patients were no longer patrons, they were all the children of the relief societies and these organizations were supplied by the world.

*Out of ten members of the Odd Fellows Relief Committee by the sixth week of the epidemic only one was left, John A. Linkhauer, and he carried on the relief work alone.

Memphis seemed a doomed city. Her streets were deserted except for the nurses, doctors and occasional other pedestrians, and it has been said that even dogs, cats, rats and other animals became so oppressed by the general gloom that they left by hundreds. Many of course starved, as the few people left were so intent in their ministrations to human charges that they usually forgot the animals.

At midday the streets showed life when negroes and some white people went to the relief headquarters for daily rations. When they were gone the death-like silence fell again and one man said his own footsteps on the pavement would sometimes startle him.

Doctors met at night for consultation and this put a bit of social refreshment into their overworked lives. Their days were ghastly enough with the moaning, dying and dead on every hand, the deserted, hot, dusty streets, the oppressive atmosphere, even worse than that of a battle-field after the battle, the sorrowful, hopeless faces of convalescents, bereft of whole families, perhaps, little children left orphans and penniless, who so lately had been blest with homes, with all that that word implies,—gloom, devastation, pall,—it was more terrible than any of the other discouraging experiences these heroic men and women had been through during the past two decades. Human life seemed so pitiful, so useless at times, and yet they worked, these men and women, hoping for the end and for brighter days after all the horrible gloom. Can Memphis ever be grateful enough to those devoted souls who dropped at their posts, succumbed or rose from their beds, still weak from the ravages of the pest, and went to work again. Occasionally they met in the silent streets, spoke, shook hands, compared notes, laughed, maybe shed tears, saw the wagon-loads of piled-up coffins go by to await their turns at the cemeteries for interment, paid little heed to the irreverence with which these were treated, passed on and worked!

Sometimes it was many hours before bodies could be buried, owing to the difficulty of getting men to dig the graves. These grave-diggers were a courageous few and their work during the dark days of 1878 deserves to be remembered by

J. M. Keating,

Memphis people. All day bodies were deposited in the graveyards, sometimes buried with funeral rites and sometimes without. Catholic priests were vigilant in this respect and many bodies Catholic and Protestant, received a last religious service from watchful priests, that would otherwise have gone into their last earthly beds unattended.

Colonel Keating says that the Elmwood Cemetery bell "was for a long time tolled by a lovely girl, who for weeks was her father's only help. She kept the registry of the dead, and knew what the havoc of the fever was; yet she remained at her self-selected post, her father's courageous clerk, until the fell disease overcame her physical energies. But she recovered, and after a few days resumed her place, keeping tally of the dead until the plague itself was numbered with the things that were. No bell save that of death was tolled. The churches were closed."

While these awful tales told of the past harrow us to a degree, there was a time when they were in the present,—now! and the now of a horrible time is much more terrible than future generations, told of the happenings, can realize.

Many other places were visited by the plague that same year, notably New Orleans and Grenada, Mississippi, but Memphis paid the greatest penalty of all. Colonel Keating calls this 1878 epidemic "the horror of the century, the most soul-harrowing episode in the history of the English-speaking people in America," and he had reason to know of it as he stayed through the whole terrible siege, being one of the few who escaped having the disease.

This splendid man, who has preserved a history of the plague for future generations, is one of the heroes of Memphis. If he had done nothing else for this city than what he did during the epidemics she has endured, he would deserve a monument.

In this particular year, as the populace fled for safety and the disease progressed, Colonel Keating felt that it was essential to keep the world informed of each day's occurrences, so he kept his paper alive in addition to his offices as member of the Citizens Relief Committee. Men stayed with him on

*J. M. Keating,*

Memphis people. All day bodies were deposited in the graveyards, sometimes buried with funeral rites and sometimes without. Catholic priests were vigilant in this respect and many bodies Catholic and Protestant, received a last religious service from watchful priests, that would otherwise have gone into their last earthly beds unattended.

Colonel Keating says that the Elmwood Cemetery bell "was for a long time tolled by a lovely girl, who for weeks was her father's only help. She kept the registry of the dead, and knew what the havoc of the fever was; yet she remained at her self-selected post, her father's courageous clerk, until the fell disease overcame her physical energies. But she recovered, and after a few days resumed her place, keeping tally of the dead until the plague itself was numbered with the things that were. No bell save that of death was tolled. The churches were closed."

While these awful tales told of the past harrow us to a degree, there was a time when they were in the present,—now! and the now of a horrible time is much more terrible than future generations, told of the happenings, can realize.

Many other places were visited by the plague that same year, notably New Orleans and Grenada, Mississippi, but Memphis paid the greatest penalty of all. Colonel Keating calls this 1878 epidemic "the horror of the century, the most soul-harrowing episode in the history of the English-speaking people in America," and he had reason to know of it as he stayed through the whole terrible siege, being one of the few who escaped having the disease.

This splendid man, who has preserved a history of the plague for future generations, is one of the heroes of Memphis. If he had done nothing else for this city than what he did during the epidemics she has endured, he would deserve a monument.

In this particular year, as the populace fled for safety and the disease progressed, Colonel Keating felt that it was essential to keep the world informed of each day's occurrences, so he kept his paper alive in addition to his offices as member of the Citizens Relief Committee. Men stayed with him on the press work, brave men, deliberately facing danger that the outside world might be served. Colonel Keating says of this class of workers: "The printers and telegraphers suffered more than any other classes. * * * * The nature of their employment exposed them more than any other classes, save the doctors and nurses, to the fever poison. They fell very fast. Only one of all those employed by the telegraph company escaped, and of the editors, compositors and pressmen of the daily press, only one escaped of the *Ledger,* four of the *Avalanche* and two of the *Appeal.* Their numbers thus so rapidly decreased, these heroic men continued not only to fulfil the duties expected of them by a public, impatient for every fact and incident of the epidemic, but nursed their sick and buried their dead. Though often wearied to exhaustion, ready to fall for want of strength, they continued to send messages, and print papers and to succor those who had claims upon them."

This is a tribute to his co-workers, truly earned, but he fails to tell of his individual work. He also was often "wearied to exhaustion," but he did not falter. His history does not record the day that he went to the *Appeal* office and found that of the force he was the only one left. Other duties as well as press work were demanding him but he said, "The paper must be printed, and I am the only one who can do it." His message was one that the world was expecting and he felt the urgency of giving it. Memphis refugees looked for it as they did for nothing else. Each day the readers learned what was being done in the unfortunate city and the lists of dead and convalescent were eagerly scanned in Canada and all the states. People wept or rejoiced as they read names of relatives or friends in one list or the other and waited impatiently for the next day's intelligence. Colonel Keating did not allow them to be disappointed. He wrote his editorial, the reports and all matter needed, set the type, worked the press, printed the sheets, folded them and gave his small but valuable sheet to the waiting world that day and other days.

"Worse indeed," says James Ford Rhodes, "than the desolation of the war was that of the Negro-carpet-bag rule from 1868 to 1874," and poor Memphis, who had suffered them all, in 1878 could say, "and even worse than carpet-bag rule is this awful pestilence!"

But the heavier the gloom the more beautiful are the rays of good that filter through its depressing weight. The rays in those dark days that made themselves manifest were unselfishness and brotherly sympathy. Selfish humanity goes on in its daily business, considering only its own welfare, but when a great human crisis comes the merely human, selfish nature is replaced by the god-nature that asserts itself. At such times people become brothers in the true sense.

In 1878, when our country and the world learned of the terrible strait Memphis and the South was in, all animosity, all sectional feeling and every other sentiment save that of sympathy, were forgotten and help such as the outside world could give, poured in to strengthen the efforts of those brave souls who had sacrificed themselves to the cause of suffering humanity. Money was sent from near and far. The Howard Association alone used $500,000 during that one epidemic. They employed 2,900 nurses and furnished doctors, nurses and supplies to 15,000 people. The Citizens Relief Committee spent $93,914.11 and issued 745,735 rations. Altogether during that siege Memphis received nearly a million dollars in money, clothing Medicine and other supplies. The world contributed to the entire South that year $4,548,700, for the relief of yellow-fever patients.

One train came to Memphis loaded almost entirely with coffins, a grewsome but very acceptable gift at that time. All sorts of people and all sorts of institutions were interested in the various contributions. Many were collections of mayors of cities and towns, others of churches of all denominations, of secret societies, men's and women's clubs and church societies. Lecturers gave lectures and artists gave concerts or other entertainments for the sufferers. Contributions came accompanied by letters from "young ladies;" "young men," "the children;" "little girls;" "colored contributions;" "employees;" "ministers;" "soldiers;" "Jews;" "Quakers;"

and some of the contributions were the proceeds of special sales for the purpose.

Nashville came to the aid of the children who had been orphaned and these little ones were put into her asylums or into private homes, where some have grown up as the adopted and loved children of the people who took them.

Some misguided human beings commit depredations even in the midst of distress, but fortunately these are a minority. Some of these weeds of humanity appeared in Memphis during those direful days, and planned for much mischief to gain their selfish ends. The negroes, the ignorant mass of whom had been given such false ideas of their importance, were now instigated by a few white men to take possession of the commissary department and to overpower the white people. They were told and made to believe that the fact of their not having the fever as white people did, proved that God meant for them to have the land and that they could take it now that the white people were so weakened and helpless. It is easy to imagine the added horrors if these fiends and foragers could have got the upper hand. But they reckoned more foolishly than they knew and were defeated by the vigilance of the Citizens Relief Committee and the Howard Association, both of which organizations were most looked to for succor and protection.

The police and fire forces were so reduced that the associations had to provide for guarding the city. Some thieves stole Howard nurse badges and so were enabled to enter homes and looted them, but steps were quickly taken by the Relief Committee to drive them from town. The police were instructed to arrest all persons on the streets after nine o'clock at night, unless the pedestrians could give satisfactory reasons for being abroad. At Court Square were stationed two negro military companies composed of trustworthy members of the race. At Camp Joe Williams the Bluff City Grays were placed with instructions to be ready to take the train kept for them immediately, if they were needed. The highly trained Chickasaw guards were ordered to Grand Junction, where they were to be in readiness if called. A Raleigh company of over a hundred volunteered their services when needed, and another company south of Memphis volunteered and kept in readiness for the call. In the city were not more than one hundred white men that could have been mustered but they were to be relied upon. If the necessity arose for their services the signal was to be three taps of the fire-bell, when they were to hasten to the express office on North Court Street.

One day, when men and women were lined up for their daily apportionment, a bullying black, instigated by a white ruffian, and several of his own color near, attacked the colored sentry at the commissary entrance. It was probably the beginning of a general rush to overpower the small force at headquarters, but the sentry was not to be intimidated, and immediately shot his assailant. Then arose a wail of women and howl of men that portended trouble, but the negro soldiers rushed to the scene. The mob soon comprehended that these soldiers were for order, and in nowise inclined to join in any irregularity, so they were checked in the very beginning of their uprising. The disturbance brought out the members of the Relief Committee who were in the building, and General Luke E. Wright, one of the most earnest of the self-sacrificing band of workers, raising his voice above the Bedlam of tongues, thanked the sentry for his prompt action and then, turning to the soldiers, commended them for their soldierly behavior. He then told the crowd that any depredations from thieves or any other attempted mob violence would be met as summarily as in this case, and that in a very short while military enough could be called to destroy their whole force. It is recorded that the white man who urged the negro to make his attack, disappeared, and was never heard from again.

This occurrence, with the assurance that court, or no court, lawlessness was not to be tolerated, brought about a beneficent result and the would-be looters knew that although the respectable element was small they were determined and able to defend themselves.

It was unfortunate that those who were working so unselfishly to save their fellows and the life of the city, and who were so sorely needed for their daily tedious rounds, should have the additional responsibility of keeping order. One can not but wonder that at such a time there could be human beings so low as to add crime to universal sorrow and helplessness, but weeds flourish in all sorts of soil. There seems to be no doubt that if it had not been for the vigilance of the Relief Committee a riot would have added to the horrors of the city, perhaps ending in its total destruction, for when useless, non-producing ignorance gets the upper hand, temporary liberty is only license and during the period of such license it knows no cessation nor feeling of compassion or order.

Memphis can scarcely realize the debt of gratitude she owes to such men as General Wright, Colonel Keating, Mr. Langstaff, Dr. Mitchell, Dr. Thornton, and the scores of noble souls who stayed and actually saved the city for future usefulness. Fortunately Colonel Keating has preserved for us the names of the men and women who worked and died and worked and lived for Memphis in those strange dark days.

The commissary department was so well managed and the outside world so generous that all the patients and others in the city were supplied with necessities and even luxuries such as ice, fruit, wine and other sick-room supplies were not wanting. The efficient men who had distribution in charge so directed that, as Colonel Keating says, "every pound and ounce of food or bushel or cord of fuel or suit or part of a suit of clothes was accounted for." By this system the bounty of the states and Europe was not wasted and nourishment and supplies went where it was intended that they should. The commissary clerks died rapidly but, as in the ranks of battle, their places would be filled, though the recruits would often have to serve day and night to supply the demands. The men who gave their time and sometimes their lives to this work had no recompense save that of the consciousness of doing what they could to help others.

By October 7, new cases of the fever had fallen to fifty-seven and deaths on that day to twenty-four, so the Howards having, what with other organizations, more supplies than were needed for the Memphis demands, President Langstaff organized relief trains to be run on the Memphis & Charleston,

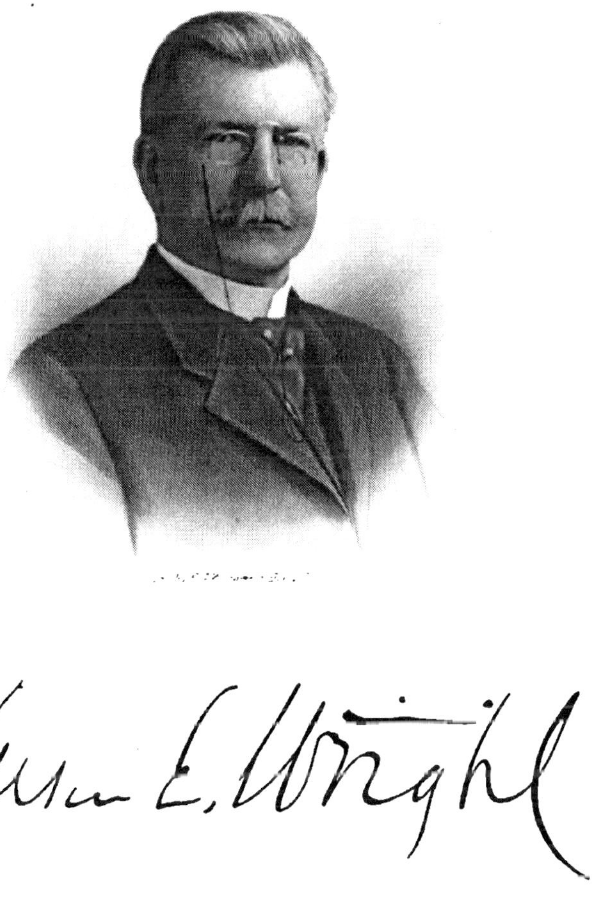

Mississippi & Tennessee, and Louisville, Nashville & Great Southern, to supply calls from surrounding towns. These trains carried physicians, nurses, medical supplies and provisions. The Association had done some work for outsiders before, but not until the plague had abated in the larger city had they been able to take many supplies for other places.

As October advanced the fearful heat abated, cases continued to diminish and the faithful few who had been keeping the world informed were able to say that the siege was almost over. On the twenty-ninth of this month the Board of Health declared the epidemic at an end. The nurses were paid and discharged; the physicians also dismissed; the medical department and its agencies closed. Some cases occurred later but they were scattered,—just remnants of the awful visitation. However, so long as there was a need for help it was supplied, although organized work of the associations was closed.

The Howards who reported for duty and then faithfully fulfilled that duty were, as given by Colonel Keating: A. D. Langstaff, W. J. Smith, J. H. Edmundson, J. H. Smith, John Johnson, A. M. Stoddard, J. W. Cooper, B. P. Anderson,* W. D. McCallum,* Louis Frierson, D. G. Reahardt, W. S. Rogers, F. F. Bowen, J. G. Lonsdale,* E. B. Mansford,* N. D. Menkin,* J. T. Moss, S. M. Jobe,* R. P. Waring, J. Kohlberg, Charles Howard, J. W. Page, T. R. Waring, P. W. Semmes, W. A. Holt, E. B. Foster,* J. W. Heath,* Fred Cole,* A. F. C. Cook,* W. S. Anderson, C. L. Staffer, W. Finnie. The honorary members who reported for duty were: Dr. Luke P. Blackburn of Kentucky, Major W. T. Walthall, Captain P. R. Athy, and the Reverends W. E. Boggs, S. Landrum* and E. C. Slater.*

The surviving members of the Relief Committee were: Luke E. Wright, D. T. Porter, J. M. Keating, James S. Prestidge, Ed. Whitmore, W. W. Thatcher, Casey Young, C. F. Conn, D. F. Goodyear and Captain J. C. Maccabe. The members of this committee who gave their lives were: Charles G.

*Died from the fever.

Fisher, J. G. Lonsdale, Jr., William Willis, S. M. Jobe and the Reverend Doctor Slater.*

The ordeal was over but there was another ordeal to come! People began coming home. Nearly all of them wore black and the crowded cars were as sombre in appearance as in feeling. The city was more desolate than ever before and the inhabitants hardly knew how to take up the threads of life again. So many homes were wrecked, all had borne losses. Thanks to the vigilance of the good people who had stayed, few houses had been molested and many that had been left open had been found closed and so saved from thieves, dust and weather.

The order of the time was sadness, but human nature is plastic and easily shapes itself to circumstances. Interests came back, threads that had been entirely lost were taken up again and Memphis became an active community once more, though much reduced in the number of her inhabitants. Once more the business wheels began to revolve and city officials turned from the work of getting their homes started again to municipal affairs. If these had been staggering before they seemed dead now.

On Thanksgiving Day, November 28, a mass-meeting was held, when public acknowledgment was made and thanks tendered to the world for the help so lately extended to stricken Memphis, and especially to those noble men and women who had given their lives and labors.

*The account of this epidemic is gathered chiefly from Colonel Keating's history of that year's dreadful experience, a remarkable record valuable to Memphis for all time, and from conversations with people who remained here during the siege or were among the refugees. It would take a volume like Colonel Keating's own to do justice to the terrible catastrophe.

# CHAPTER IX

Debt and Disaster Follow the Fever. Surrender of the City Charter. The Taxing District Act. Struggle with Creditors. How Memphis had been Robbed. The Taxing District Officials. How Memphis was Redeemed. Another Epidemic Breaks Out. Efficient Sanitary Measures Discussed. The Meeting of Refugees in St. Louis. Colonel Waring Plans Sewer System. Work on the Sewers Begun. Character of the System. The People Take Heart. Progress of Reconstructing the City Government. D. P. Hadden, President. The Old Debt Refunded. New Water System Established. Artesian Wells Sunk.

AFTER domestic and business affairs were again fairly launched, more attention was paid to sanitation than had been before, and there was certainly much to be done in this line. The city had little money to use, as her repeated calamities had left her bankrupt and, under the burden of an enormous debt,—the only thing that had not decreased during the plague,—that hung over her like a great pall.

It was evident that under the then existing government there was no way of escaping the Tennessee and United States writs of mandamus, which were demanding all the taxes collected and would leave nothing for carrying on the city, nor allow her anything with which to take precautions against future scourges of disease. Creditors became clamorous for their money, despite the general mourning and financial embarrassment of the people, and men saw that nothing short of complete change in government would or could work out a solution and get the disabled town in condition to escape annihilation.

The ablest men in the city discussed the matter and a

meeting was called when people listened to a bill that had been prepared by Colonel George Gantt, and a discussion in which the true state of affairs was set forth and a dissolution of the charter earnestly recommended.

The bill drafted before the epidemic by S. P. Walker was reexamined and revised by able legal men, prominently among them Judge C. W. Heiskell and Colonel Gantt. The new bill as revised, was adopted and ordered presented to the members-elect of the Legislature, for their consideration. These members had been elected with a view to their approval of the bill and now they were urged to push it through immediately.

On January 29, 1879, the bill was passed, but not approved by Governor Marks until January 31. During this delay of two days Memphis officials resigned and the city government became thoroughly disorganized.

Humiliations seemed to pile up for poor Memphis. Now she was not even a city,—had been reduced to a Taxing District. Her charter of incorporation passed in 1826, and approved and extended at later intervals, had been dissolved. her population "resolved back into the body of the state," her offices all abolished and her municipal affairs were to be managed b ythe state. But it has been shown how unsettled conditions during and after the war, fraud, misgovernment and pestilence had made such ravages on the town that she had been left stranded and the Taxing District Act* seemed the only lever to assist in setting her again afloat.

This new bill provided that taxes for the support of the government of the Taxing District "shall be imposed directly by the General Assembly of the State of Tennessee and not otherwise." But an amendment of this Act† gave the Taxing District more power to handle her own affairs.

Instead of a Board of Mayor and Aldermen or the General Council, as heretofore, the Taxing District was to be regulated and administered by the "Legislative Council of the Taxing District," to consist of "the commissioners of the fire and

*Capter XI of the Acts of the Legislature of 1879, p. 15.
†Chap. LXXXIV, of the Acts of the Legislature of 1879, p. 98.

police board and the supervisors of the board of public works."

Provision was made for "A board of health, to consist of the chief of police, a health officer and one physician, * * * * who shall be ex officio president of the board."

A board of public works, consisting of five supervisors, was also provided for.

Section 3, of this bill defined the powers of the government of the Taxing District, which were much the same as those of the former city, giving "power over all affairs in the taxing district in which the peace, safety and general welfare of the inhabitants is interested."

The President of the Board of Fire and Police Commissioners was also judge of the police court and tried all offences against the District ordinances. He was also a justice of the peace, having criminal jurisdiction within the limits of the District. When the same act was an offense against the State and District, he had the right to try both offenses; when against the state only he could fine, if the party submitted, otherwise the accused was held to the criminal court.

Section 4, defined the powers and restrictions of the Legislative Council, this being "restricted to the business alone of making ordinances or local laws for the Taxing District, except as hereinafter provided."

Section 5, fixed the salary of the president at $2,000 per annum, demanding that he "shall devote his entire time and attention to the duties of his office." This $2,000 was to be his only compensation, any fees that he might make as justice of the peace, to be credited on his salary "and if such fees amount to $2,000 or more per annum, he shall receive no other compensation."* The salaries of the commissioners are also provided for and fixed at $500 per annum.

Section 5, also provided the number of fire and police commissioners, their ages, duties and mode of appointment. They were authorized to elect a president from their number after each biennial election, such president to be the executive officer of the Taxing District. The said commissioners were also

*The first part of this paragraph is taken from the original Act, and the latter part from the Amendatory Act.

authorized to appoint a secretary at a yearly salary of $1,800, and they were given "power to appoint all officers and subordinates in the police and fire service, including the Chief of Police, and to suspend and discharge the same at will." Also to make rules for the discipline of policemen and firemen.

In Section 6, the Commissioners are given supervision over streets, drains, sewers and all sanitary measures, lighting, bridges, wharves, etc., and are authorized to "employ a competent civil engineer at a salary not exceeding $2,000 per annum.

The remaining sections, with the amendments, elaborate on the duties of the Commissioners and all officials, their oaths, elections, levy of taxes for streets, hospital purposes, wharfage, contracts and other Taxing District necessities.

Judge C. W. Heiskell gives a comprehensive statement of the Taxing District and its government in a few words, as follows:

This government is simply an agent of the state government, without the power of credit or taxation, and the evils consequent thereto. It owns no property, except for governmental purposes alone. It can issue no bonds and has no power to pay them if they are issued. It contracts no debt, except as against particular taxes levied by the state itself, to pay them year by year. It therefore pays as it goes—the only true policy for individuals and states. What improvements it makes it pays for, and if it has no money to pay, it waits till it has. Launched under such auspices, it is hoped that it will prove a lasting blessing, and that economy, honesty and enterprise, cleanliness and sanitation, good streets, and an efficient fire and police protection, will close its gates on the pestilence forever, and open wide the doors of health and lasting prosperity.

Creditors were not pleased at this new state of Memphis affairs and attempted to test this new law creating taxing districts in every court until the Supreme Court of the United States declared it entirely constitutional. Colonel Gantt worked hard to gain this opinion and many declared that his argument before the United States Supreme Court on the constitutionality of the law establishing taxing districts, turned the scales that logically compelled the Judicial finding.

This new settlement brought great relief to Memphis people and assured them of more time and money for civic improvements and defense against future attacks of pestilence.

Doctor Porter said of the new form of government: "The object in creating the Taxing District was not to repudiate the debt of the old city of Memphis, but to have a cheap and efficient system of government, so as to put the municipality in a good sanitary condition, pave the streets, and enable us to pay that debt upon terms that may be agreed on by the commissioners that may be appointed, and the creditors."

When the bondholders could no longer mandamus the citizens of Memphis to provide for their improvident debts, they petitioned the General Assembly of the state to give them power to collect their money, in which petition they stated that their debts were lawfully created and that "there is no substantial ground on which it can be claimed that such debts, or any part or portion of any of them are not justly owing."

In the cross-petition of the citizens to that of the bondholders, and in response to the above charge, they answered: "There is much of the debt that is not *justly* owing, but very largely fraudulent. As a sample, we submit the following statements:

"*First Statement*—On the 10th of June, 1868, Joseph A. Mabry, holding $275,000 of city script, and others holding large amounts, submitted a written proposition to the acting mayor to accept city bonds for their debts, giving $65 of script for each $100 of bonds, a loss to the city of 35 cents on the dollar, when the amount paid for the indebtedness was not exceeding 30 cents for a dollar, thus making a $1000 bond cost $216. This proposition was accepted, and it is stated that the arrangement was consummated, without any authority from the Board of Mayor and Aldermen. This fact appears from the report of a committee raised by the Board of Mayor and Aldermen in 1872, four years after the transaction. That report is in these words:

" 'Your committee are unable to find on the records of the city any resolution authorizing such contract, nor does it appear from the records that any meeting from the Board of Aldermen was held on the 10th day of June, 1868, as stated in the indorsement,' (the Mayor's endorsement accepting the proposition.)

"By this arrangement, $568,000 six per cent bonds were issued to take up $369,000 of open accounts. In other words to settle $369,000 of debt, the bonds and interest would cost us $1,590,400.

"*Second Statement*—In June, 1867, $897,000 of paving bonds were authorized to be issued. Under this authority sixty-two bonds, ($62,000) were actually sold at the following prices:

| "Bonds | Proceeds | Proceeds on the Dol. | Loss on Dol. |
|---|---|---|---|
| $ 4,000 | $ 643.34 | 16 cents | 84 cents |
| 3,000 | 670.00 | 22 " | 78 " |
| 5,000 | 941.67 | 19 " | 81 " |
| 5,000 | 753.57 | 15 " | 85 " |
| 7,000 | 1,682.10 | 24 " | 76 " |
| 8,000 | 1,746.95 | 22 " | 78 " |
| 1,000 | 450.00 | 45 " | 55 " |
| 8,000 | 2,710.00 | 34 " | 66 " |
| 3,000 | 900.00 | 30 " | 70 " |
| 8,000 | 1,432.75 | 18 " | 82 " |
| 4,000 | 812.67 | 20 " | 80 " |
| 2,000 | 64.12 | 3 1-5c | 96 4-5c |
| 4,000 | | | 100 " |
| $62,000 | $12,807.17 | Av. 20 3-5 cents | 79 2-5c |

After setting forth these statements and other conditions, the petitioners continued:

"And so, petitioners, through your honorable body and the highest judicature of the country, having obtained some surcease from their intolerable burdens, hope your honorable body will not again enslave them, but allow them to maintain their vantage ground, and make such a settlement of the debts of the dead city of Memphis as will be just and fair to the creditor, and not compel petitioners to desert their homes, or give them over to the merciless exaction of those who in time past have shown no mercy."

The peitioners showed the former excessive expenses of the old city government and the much reduced amounts for carrying on the same functions under the Taxing District. After stating the greedy demands of the bondholders to levy taxes, they stated:

"It can easily be demonstrated that a tax sufficient to meet the demands of bondholders, together with the state and county taxes, would amount to confiscation—speedy and irretrievable. * * * And in after years—well it is unnecessary to calculate them, for the first year would finish us."

Setting forth the city's wrongs and hardships, they contined:

"Had it not been for the charity of our fellow citizens throughout the whole country [during the epidemics] we would not have been able to bury our dead—and in the midst of it all the insatiate clamor of creditors, not for justice, not for compromise, not for a fair compensation, but for the pound of flesh which they have from the beginning claimed, was it not time for us to ask your honorable body, the State Legislature, to take back our franchises, and give us another and different municipal instrumentality by which we could preserve ourselves from absolute destruction?"

Again:

"It should not be forgotten that the policy pursued by these creditors, in connection with the great plagues that from time to time have afflicted this community, has reduced the population from fifty thousand to a little more than thirty thousand inhabitants, and its taxable values from $30,000,000 to the nominal amount of $13,900,000, but to the actual amount of only about *eleven millions* that can be relied on to produce revenue; and that the relief extended to these creditors should be made with reference to this diminished capacity to bear burdens, it being a state of things which they aided largely, by the course they pursued, in bringing about."

This petition, which was quite lengthy, was signed by twenty-five citizens of the Taxing District.

The Taxing District officers of 1880 were:

*Board of Fire and Police Commissioners*—D. T. Porter,

president, salary $2,000; John Overton, Jr., salary $500; M. Burke, salary $500; C. L. Pullen, secretary, salary $800.

*Board of Public Works*—C. M. Goyer, chairman; R. Galloway, W. N. Brown, John Gunn, J. M. Goodbar. These members received no salary.

The Legislative Council was composed of the two boards in joint session, Hon. D. T. Porter, Chairman.

Dr. D. T. Porter was elected first President of the Board of Police and Fire Commissioners, and we learn from his report, tendered to the Governor of Tennessee, as required by Section 13 of the Act creating the Taxing District of Shelby County, Tennessee, Dec. 1, 1880, something of the work following the organization of the Taxing District. He says in part:

"While a rate of taxation was fixed, the assessment of property and merchants' capital was not provided for, which necessitated an amendment, which was passed March 13th. Very soon thereafter the validity of the Charter or Act creating the Taxing District was contested, which stopped the payment of taxes. The Supreme Court decided in our favor on the fourth day of June, 1879, during which time a very small amount of revenue was received, and, in order to run the government, Hon. John Overton, Jr., and myself borrowed about $7,900. After that time taxes were being promptly paid until the 10th of July, 1879, when the yellow fever made its appearance, which prevailed until about the 1st of November. During that time the payment of taxes ceased again, and business of every kind was almost entirely suspended."

In April of 1879 there was a meeting of Taxing District citizens in the Greenlaw Opera House, called for the purpose of coöperation in providing ways and means for preventing yellow fever. Colonel Keating delivered an address on the benefits of sanitary work to prevent the introduction and spread of diseases, which created enthusiasm among his audience and brought immediate subscriptions of several thousand dollars for a fund for the purpose. The Auxiliary Sanitary Association was organized and officers elected, James S. Prestidge, president, and the association declared itself ready to work with the city to make Memphis a clean and non-epidemic city. The members of this new organization were: James S. Prestidge, president; Colton Greene, J. W. Dillard, N. Fontaine and H. Furstenheim, vice-presidents; W. W. Thatcher, treasurer; A. D. Langstaff, secretary; John T. Willins, assistant secretary; Elias Lowenstein, Dave Eisman, J. S. Watkins, Sr., Luke E. Wright and J. M. Keating, executive committee; D. P. Hadden, L. Hanauer, H. M. Neely, J. Fowlkes and J. E. Beasley, finance committee; Dr. R. W. Mitchell, Dr. Overall and Dr. W. B. Winn, committee on sanitation.

A valuable auxiliary these self-sacrificing and worthy citizens made, but summer was too near for their work, which had been begun at once, to advance far that year. Their industrious emptying of cesspools and general cleaning up was stopped, as Doctor Porter said tax-collecting was, by the reappearance of yellow-fever. In April the woman who had charge of the Linden Street school had a case of suspicious fever and she was reported to Doctor Thornton, of the Board of Health. She died and, to allay excitement, it was given out that her case was malarial fever.

The weather was getting warm, so emptying of vaults and otherwise stirring up filth was postponed for cooler days. The spring of that year was unusually warm and in May, another case of suspicious fever was reported in South Memphis. On the 26th this man died, having black vomit, and a few days after his decease another case of the disease occurred. In June several cases were diagnosed and in July the disease broke out in different parts of the town. The doctors no longer denied the nature of these maladies but instead, advised and urged depopulation of the city. By August there were only 16,000 people left out of 40,000, the estimate of the previous June. Nearly 16,000 of the refugees took advantage of the camps around the city and so avoided the isolated suffering and neglect of the year before. The State Board of Health passed strict quarantine laws which were rigidly enforced, to prevent the spread of the disease to neighboring towns.

The epidemic this year lasted from its early start until November 10, but was of a much milder form than it had been in 1873 and 1878. There were 2,010 cases of the disease, 587 of which were fatal. The per centum of white people attacked was 30¼, and of colored, 6½. The percentage of deaths among the whites was 36.21 and of black 16.04. *

The Howards and other organizations were again at the post of duty and self-sacrifice, and Doctor Thornton was as untiring in his labors as he had been the year before. Under his direction the Taxing District Board of Health, together with the State and National Boards of Health, made great strides in sanitary work, the beginning of a system that was to rid the city of the plague and enable her to recuperate and take her place as the important city she was entitled to be.

Memphis seemed a ruined city, one with a stigma that would make her the shunned of all home-seekers, but her problem was only a repetition of the experiences of cities before, some of them important centers of America. London and Paris had their plagues in former times, after which strenuous measures were taken to clean the cities, and other European and Asiatic municipalities had been called to account in the same way. The important city of Philadelphia once had her time of reckoning, when it was not known whether or not she would survive. In the last part of the Eighteenth Century, after this city had been ravaged by *yellow fever,* her citizens rallied their forces and her valuable son, Benjamin Franklin, urged cleanliness and a supply of pure water to be brought to the city in pipes, as the wells then in use he thought partook of the filth that soaked into the ground. He also advocated that the streets be paved and city ground be made as solid as possible in order to carry off rain and snow to prevent their soaking into the earth and carrying with them impurities to the wells. In 1789 he wrote: "I recommend that at the end of the first hundred years, if not done before, the corporation of the city employ a part of the hundred thousand pounds in bringing by pipes the water of Wissahickon Creek into the town, so as to supply the inhabitants." In 1798, Doctor Brown of New York, said that he considered much of the sickness of that city, especially "the yellow fever which had recently made great

*From the table of the State Board of Health, taken by Mr. John Johnson.

ravages there," to be caused from the use of impure water, caused by the sinking of filth into the soil.*

So Memphis, younger than these cities, had learned her lesson at great cost, as they had done, and now was her time to act and to rectify former carelessness.

Refugees who were in St. Louis in 1879, had meetings to discuss the future of Memphis and decided that complete sanitation and pure water were the only solutions of the problem.† They determined to spare no expense within reason for an efficient sewer system and to petition the Legislature to aid in carrying out the work. Memphis must be saved soon or entirely lost. As she stood now, strangers would not go to her and present inhabitants were leaving by hundreds to seek more healthful homes. Business people and property-holders were desperate, hence the call of these meetings in another city before the return of the people to their homes. Memphis citizens in St. Louis formed committees to start to work immediately upon returning to the desolated Taxing District, or just as soon as cool weather would permit general renovation. These committees were the Executive Committee, the members of which were W. H. Proudfit, Ben Eiseman, I. N. Snowden, Dr. D. T. Porter, M. Gavin, H. Furstenheim, John Overton, Elias Lowenstein, W. N. Brown, W. W. Thatcher, John W. Cochrane and John K. Speed; the Committee on Calling an Extra Session of the Legislature, composed of George Gantt, Jerome Hill, Julius A. Taylor, J. M. Keating, A. J. Kellar, J. Harvey Mathes, J. S. Brigham, George R. Phelan and George B. Peters; Committee on Loans and Finance—Napoleon Hill, Amos Woodruff, W. M. Farrington and Hugh L. Brinkley; Committee on Engineering and Surveying—Colton Green, M. Burke, O. H. P.

*Charles Hermany's Water Report to the Water Works & Sewerage Commissioners of Memphis.—1868.

†Nothing was known at that time of the mosquito as the mischievous factor in the dissemination of yellow fever. But the proposed remedy of "complete sanitation and pure water" nevertheless proved the most important boon to Memphis, as regarded its healthfulness, that had ever been proposed and carried into effect. Aside from yellow fever, these indispensable requisities of comfortable living and good health have reduced the death rate from general causes more than one-half and made of a plague spot one of the most healthful cities in North America.

Piper; Committee on Legislation and Laws—Luke E. Wright, Judge John M. Lea, Thomas B. Turley, John T. Fargason and John Johnson.

While these men were making home plans the National Board of Health had a meeting in Washington,—October 13,—to discuss Memphis, and a committee was appointed to make a sanitary survey of the Taxing District. This committee comprised Dr. J. S. Billings of the United States Army, Dr. R. W. Mitchell, of Memphis, and Dr. H. A. Johnson, of Chicago.[*]

The State Board joined these national and city workers and they investigated a thorough sewer plan and a house to house inspection, to be rigidly enforced, the Taxing District president and other officers joining heartily in the too-long-delayed campaign.

Memphis inhabitants had not all returned to their homes when the house-to-house inspection began, under the personal direction of Doctor Mitchell.

On November 22, the American Public Health Association met in Nashville. Col. George E. Waring, Jr., an experienced civil engineer of Newport, R. I., had been invited by Doctor Cabell, president of the association, to offer a plan of sewerage to be considered and discussed. His paper was listened to with interest and his plan not discussed, but adopted by the commissioners from Memphis. These men invited Colonel Waring to make a special plan for sewering Memphis with the new, small-pipe, separate system he proposed. Later, the committee of the National Board of Health that visited Memphis engaged him as consulting engineer. Numerous meetings were held in Memphis, when all sorts of sewer systems were discussed. These discussions terminated with a general agreement to adopt the Waring system of sewers, and the inventor was employed to put in this system.[†]

The National Board, impressed by the necessity of prompt

[*] Colonel George E. Waring said that "it was out of this epidemic 1878 that the National Board of Health grew."

[†] Colonel Waring was well known in Memphis. He had commanded a brigade of Federal cavalry operating about Memphis. He was often engaged in fierce combats with General Forrest and, though generally worsted, was a brave and chivalrous soldier.

Niles Meriwether

action, made its examinations at once and prepared their report, a copy of which was furnished Governor Marks. They recommended the ventilation of all houses, disinfection of houses throughout, tearing down many unsanitary buildings, cleaning wells and cisterns, cleaning out and filling with fresh earth all excrement vaults and the introduction of Colonel Waring's sewer system.

The work on the sewers was begun January 21, 1880, and went on fairly well, though much interferred with by the incessant rains of the early spring of that year. But "within four months after breaking ground," wrote Colonel Waring, "we had laid the whole of the west main, the submain east of the bayou, and all of the laterals shown on the map of 1880, making a total length of over 18 miles with 152 flush-tanks and with four-inch house-connecting drains extending from the sewer to the sidewalk, or in alleys to the line of each private property."

Colonel Waring remained in Memphis during the first part of the work on the sewers, but the efficiency of the city engineer, Mr. Niles Meriwether, and his better knowledge of handling some of the inexperienced assistants and laborers necessarily employed, obviated all necessity for the superintendence of the inventor and the greater part of the responsibility of the work devolved upon Mr. Meriwether and his assistants, though Major Humphreys was "engineer in charge" until 1883, when the entire responsibility devolved upon Mr. Meriwether. Mr. A. J. Murray was assistant engineer.

This system of sewerage, known as the Waring System, was one not heretofore used to any extent, and hence uncertain, but it seemed reasonable and the fact that it was cheaper than the big-pipe sewerage recommended it to a city impoverished as Memphis had been. But, aside from economy, arguments in favor of the new system won the ears of the committee and the public, who, as before stated, acted upon the plan immediately. Colonel Waring at a later date wrote of the prompt action of Memphis at that time: "That such a town, impoverished by a dishonest government, disheartened by the most serious epidemic extending over two years, and without financial credit, should have done so promptly and so thoroughly the work that it did do must ever redound to the great credit of its people and of its rulers."

Waring's plan provided for six-inch vitrified pipes, which discharged into pipes of eight inches diameter, these sub-mains increasing to ten and twelve inch pipes where the flow was greater. The mains were from twelve to fifteen inches and when the mouth was neared the increase grew to twenty inches of brick inclosure. The small pipes were easily ventilated and their glazed smoothness allowed sewerage to pass through easily. The workmen were instructed not to allow the slightest roughness in joining the pipes, as even a small defect of this sort would gather and hold silt and rubbish.

These pipes were for sewerage only, excluding surface and underground drainage, but they were regulated and cleansed from flush-tanks and ventilators, so they could be kept constantly cleaned and half full of water. The pipes or drains for disposing of storm-water was an independent system, and discharged into the bayou. It was argued that the storm water should be used as flush for the sewers, but experienced engineers said that plan had never worked well as such supply of water was not constant; that the sudden rush smeared the pipe and as it receded left the smeared matter to ferment or make a slime that became offensively odorous and escaped through the ventilators as misnamed "sewer-gas," while systematic flushing from tanks provided for the purpose, kept the pipes well washed and then half or nearly half full of water, that a constant flow might be had. Ventilation was obtained through the numerous house drains.

Mr. F. S. Odell, who was one of the able assistants on the Memphis work, said that "the advantage of this system over the ordinary system of large sewers is two-fold. It is cleaner and cheaper—cleaner because the pipes are kept constantly flushed and thoroughly ventilated; cheaper because there is a vast difference between the cost of a large brick sewer, with its man-holes and receiving basins, and a small pipe-sewer, with its simple fresh-air inlets. The difference is very apparent when it is considered that the total cost of twenty miles of sewers in Memphis, for labor, materials, engineering, superintending and incidentals, including the two main sewers, was about $137,000."

Charles Hermany, in his report to the Memphis Water Works and Sewerage Commissioners, had this to say: "As sanitary measures, large sewers are very objectionable, for the reason that the ordinary flow of sewerage spreading over the inverts of large sewers has not sufficient volume and scouring efficacy to remove promptly the heavier particles of undecomposed animal and vegetable matter constantly finding their way into them. The constant accumulation of such matter during the dry season of each year, when the flow of sewage does not keep the main sewers clean, would convert them, as it were, into 'elongated' cess-pools, and thus originate or aid in prolonging epidemics to a fearful extent. To keep sewers of this magnitude clean by flushing them with water from the public water supply, would involve an expense for elevating water for this purpose alone."

This small-pipe system brought another good than that for which the engineers were working. In the big sewers it is necessary that men go into them often, and by manual labor rid them of their filth. This is exceedingly unpleasant, unwholesome and dangerous work, and an abolishment of such labor is a benefit to humanity.

Charles H. Latrobe, C. E., of Baltimore, Md., who, after the Memphis sewers had been working successfully, came to examine them, said: "I examined the action of the flush-tanks, which I found discharged with the most perfect regularity, being under complete control as to the amount of water used. I also examined personally into the condition of the main and outlet sewers, both of the fifteen-inch pipe and the twenty-inch brick sewer. The sewers were running at the time of my inspection three fourths full with a swift current. Nothing solid could be detected, not even paper, in the flow. Nor was it in the least offensive. This condition existed, I was told, as a rule in all parts of the system. I also measured the flow, and was astonished at its regularity. My conclusions were that the Memphis system answered fully the purpose for which it was intended, and which is primarily the object of all sewerage systems, but which seemed to me to be attained more perfectly in this case than in any other I had ever known of—viz: to carry off domestic and industrial wastes with rapidity and without offense to their destination. So regular and rapid was the flow through the pipes of the Memphis system that no time was given for putrefaction to take place between the time at which the waste products entered the system and were delivered into Wolf River."

This innovation in sewerage was watched with interest by engineers all over the civilized world, especially in England, where a separate system had never been used and where the engineers had grave doubts of its working efficacy. In France the new system was looked upon favorably and Mr. E. Lavoinne, chief engineer of the department of Rouen, said "that the sewerage of the city of Memphis had solved the sewerage problem for Paris."*

Doctor Porter, in the Taxing District report of December 1, 1880, already referred to, had this to say of the streets and sewers: "Very little paving or other work was done until January, 1880; since which time over five miles of stone pavement have been completed, and twenty-four miles of sewers, and about the same number of miles of sub-soil drains have been completed, the sewers to convey sewage into the river, and the subsoil drains to drain and purify the soil. Both are acting splendidly. Our thanks are due Col. George E. Waring, Jr., of Newport, R. I., for this admirable system of sewerage and subsoil drains. I think other cities would do well to investigate before adopting any other system."

Other cities did adopt the system and eight years after the adoption by Memphis, the inventor wrote: "The sewers of Memphis have now been in operation for eight years. Their original extent has been more than doubled. That they have been successful is shown not only by their increased use there, but by the quite remarkable extension of the use of the system throughout the country." During that time the Waring system had been put into thirty-seven other towns, these scattered

*Waring, in "Sewerage and Land-Draining."

all over the United States, and plans had been made for eighteen other places.

Colonel Waring concludes his extensive book of 1889 on "Sewerage and Land Drainage," thus: "The city [Memphis] would not have adopted this plan but for its sore need and its great poverty. Work of the same sort had never been done before anywhere in the world. Other engineers predicted the failure of the system. Notwithstanding their predictions, it succeeded, and those who once opposed it have since adopted it. Memphis itself, now rich and prosperous, still adheres to the plan, and has more than doubled the length of pipe laid in 1880* * * * the total length of sewers of this system now in completely successful operation in the United States is between 250 and 300 miles. * * * * No engineer who has had experience with its working would think of giving it up."

Mr. Niles Meriwether, who superintended the work of laying the sewers from the beginning, found it necessary from time to time, as the work progressed and grew in magnitude, to enlarge the supply pipes. Of the system he entirely approved and of it said, six years after its introduction: "Thus far no fault can be found with the manner in which this system has worked. The excessive quantity of mud in the water is our chief cause of trouble, the small, three-quarter inch supply pipes of the flush-tanks being clogged with mud, making it necessary to replace these in high places with large pipes. With clear-settled or filtered water all this trouble will cease and the whole system will work to a charm."

So the manifold misfortunes and poverty of Memphis caused her to be the starting place of a system of cleanliness that was to become widespread and benefit much of the civilized world. All animal excrement and other waste matter not carried through the sewers was to be carted away and the condition of premises was to be rigidly inspected by the Board of Health. The inspectors appointed for this work were Doctors G. D. Bradford, S. H. Collins, H. Ess, G. W. Overall and W. B. Winn, of Memphis, and Drs. P. B. McCutchen and F. W. Parham, of New Orleans, who were assisted by a corps of twenty-six able helpers.

These inspectors found some deplorable conditions in cellars and yards. Among these finds were 1,184 public nuisances; 124 stagnant pools, 369 cisterns and wells within ten feet of vaults, 3,039 within from ten feet to fifty feet from them, and many of these vaults were under houses and in cellars, some holding collections of filth of many years accumulation.

The Taxing District officers tried to use her money to advantage. Improvements in all the municipal branches went forward and residents were requested and required to put private property in sanitary condition. The report of the city engineer, Mr. Meriwether, to the President of the Taxing District, Dec. 1, 1880, tells of some of the important work done and money expended from Feb. 1, 1879 to Dec. 1, 1880. To quote from that report: "The total expenditures have been $199,533.35 * * * * * $160,296.02 have been expended in the purchase of materials (stone, gravel, etc.), and the paving of streets—a total of 5 28-100 miles having been paved, equal to 99,903 square yards. Of this amount about 38,000 square yards, or about 1 7-10 miles were block stone, and the remainder Telford and Macadam form. The statement also shows that 4 23-100 miles of Nicholson pavement have been taken up, the greater part of which has been replaced with stone pavements. Much of this work was done under great disadvantages of bad weather, and the trials and troubles occasioned by the fever of 1879.

"Considering all the difficulties encountered, a great deal has been accomplished, and the citizens of the District have reason to be proud of the work of the past twenty-two months."

This report also showed that twenty bridges and culverts had been built and repaired in the twenty-two months; that 2,800 cubic yards of rip rap stone had been used and 15,800 square yards of the wharf had been paved, thirty anchor-rings placed, a large amount of piping for cleaning and fire purposes, besides much repairing,—this outside of the sewering.

Major Humphreys reported up to July 1, 1881, the putting in of 3,579 water-closets, 2,408 sinks, 133 urinals, 267 bath tubs, 200 wash-basins, 17 privy-sinks and 14 cellar-drains, and he added the words: "The system of sewers appears to give entire satisfaction both to the city government and citizens generally."

All branches of civic improvements were receiving their due attention during this time of agitating and putting in sewers, and a few excerpts from Doctor Porter's report to Governor Marks will suffice to show how the Taxing District officials and others were performing their several duties. He says, in praise of his helpers:

"The police department, under P. R. Athy, as chief until August 1st, when he was elected sheriff, and since that time under W. C. Davis, as chief, has been admirably managed, and the officers and men have performed their duties well and faithfully. * * * * The fire department, under M. McFadden, as chief, has been very efficient, and officers and men have done their duty nobly and efficiently. * * * * To these departments our people owe a debt of gratitude for their vigilance and promptness in protecting life and property, especially during the epidemic.

"C. L. Pullem, secretary, has rendered me invaluable aid. * * * * * *

"Judge C. W. Heiskell, district attorney, has done his whole duty, promptly and efficiently.

"Major N. Meriwether, district engineer, has performed the arduous duties of his office satisfactorily and well.

"Dr. G. B. Thornton, President of the Board of Health, has been active and vigilant in performing his duties, and has had an immense amount of work done. Capt. D. F. Jackson, health officer, has rendered him valuable assistance."

After commending other individuals and organizations, he continues: "The people have been the great friend of the government, not only obeying the laws, but by paying their taxes promptly and making liberal subscriptions for paving and sanitary work. Besides paying their taxes they have expended from $150,000 to $200,000 in cleaning out, disinfecting and filling up privy vaults, making connections with the sewers, and other valuable sanitary work during this year—this, too, after two successive epidemics of yellow fever, which prostrated business and reduced values of property, etc., very largely."

Of the financial condition of the new government he said:

"All employees of the government have been promptly paid, and the Taxing District can pay all its liabilities on demand, except what it owes to Overton, Burke and Porter, about $40,000, temporarily loaned to finish paving and continue the sewer work while the weather was suitable, which will be paid in a few weeks.

"All contracts are made on a cash basis."

Doctor Porter thanked the Governor for his interest in Memphis, thus:

"Our people owe your Excellency a debt of gratitude that cannot be expressed by words only, for assistance you rendered at the breaking out of the yellow fever in 1879, which enabled me to protect life and property; for the powerful appeal made to the people of Tennessee for money and supplies to aid in feeding and caring for our people in camps; for your very generous offer to aid me in taking care of the same without limit as to the amount, if reasonable, for calling the Legislature together in extra session to pass our sewer bill; and for many other acts of kindness."

Doctor Porter's work had been through a trying period and he had never held public office before, but by giving all of his time to the problem he was helping to solve, he started the new government on the road to success.

Doctor Porter was succeeded in 1882 by Hon. D. P. Hadden. The officers and members of the Legislative Council for the Taxing District this year were elected by popular vote, as had been provided in the Taxing District Act. D. P. Hadden, R. C. Graves and M. Burke were elected the Board of Fire and Police Commissioners and James Lee, Jr., Lymus Wallace, Charles Kney, Henry James and M. Gavin, the Board of Public Works.

At the first meeting held by the Police and Fire Commissioners, D. P. Hadden was elected President. Mr. Hadden was a unique character but a strong man and well fitted to take up the arduous work of the Taxing District.

The great problem was still the Memphis debt, which had not yet been satisfactorily arranged. In 1882 the Legislature empowered a liquidating board to settle the liabilities at 33 1-3 cents on the dollar. The board comprised J. R. Godwin, J. J. Duffy and H. F. Dix. This act was generally so unsatisfactory to the creditors that only a small part of the debt was thus funded. The following year another act was passed whereby a new liquidating board was authorized to compromise the debt at 50 cents on the dollar. The members appointed on this board were D. P. Hadden, S. P. Walker and C. W. Heiskell. By December, 1884, $4,589,881.38 of the old debt was refunded and a debt of $2,396,299.67 was created against the Taxing District.

Some of the creditors were still stubborn and refused the fifty per cent compromise, so in 1885 another board was allowed by the Legislature to still further negotiate for final settlement. This board was made up of Napoleon Hill, I. N. Snowden, Thomas B. Turley, J. R. Godwin and the three police and fire commissioners, who were James Lee, Jr., H. A. Montgomery and D. P. Hadden. These men were to compromise on the best terms they could, and after much controversy and arguments of length they settled the remaining debt of $1,049,940.80 by the issuance of $773,830 in bonds against the Taxing District. The bonds of the three refunding boards made $3,102,930.14, the whole debt of the Taxing District.*

By November, 1886, there was only $150,000 of the old city debt left, most of that in bonds not then due.† By 1888 there was outstanding $3,241,710.85 of new bonds to mature in 1907, 1913 and 1915, the annual interest on the amount being $148,648, which, Colonel Keating said in 1888, was "met promptly every six months at maturity."

Mr. Hadden's first report, to Governor Alvin Hawkins, successor to Governor Marks, who had been such a friend to Memphis, showed the Taxing District to be succeeding as a government. The president said, "The present form of government becomes more and more satisfactory with each day of its existence. It is less cumbrous, and so far superior to

*Gathered from Vedder and Taxing District Reports.
†Vedder.

the old municipal form of government that I will venture to say no thinking citizen desires its dissolution. The old system was complicated, and made necessary the establishment of many offices which are not now required. * * * * Again it has been sufficiently proven that the present method of electing officers by the voice of the whole people is far preferable to the the old system of election by wards." Of the Board of Health he said: "The Board of Health, composed of Dr. G. B. Thornton, president; Dr. J. H. Purnell, secretary; D. F. Jackson, health officer, and W. C. Davis, chief of police, is active, vigilant and effective in all things pertaining to local sanitation. * * * * Its efficacy in the past two years in all respects has been thoroughly tested as a public health organization, and it has given entire satisfaction to the government and our citizens generally."

He commended other public workers and said of the District Attorney, "Judge C. W. Heiskell, Taxing District Attorney, has fulfilled the duties of his office in a highly satisfactory manner to the government and its citizens. In all matters affecting the Taxing District government, from its incipiency to the present hour, he has been its warm friend, defender and legal adviser and he is more familiar with all the legal points affecting its interests than any member of the government."

In his report of 1884 President Hadden complained of the poor method of collecting taxes, by which delinquency became so enormous. He stated that in the then six years of the existence of the Taxing District there was a "delinquent tax list of $134,526.08 for general purposes and $28,602.32 for the purpose of paying interest on the compromise debt of the Taxing District." Two years later he showed the accumulated delinquency to be $125,288.32, and to these figures he added the words: "Experience teaches us that under the present laws and present mode of collecting taxes our city government will always have to carry about $150,000 of delinquent back taxes. About as much as is collected from the preceding years will offset the delinquency for the current years."

Further on in this 1886 report he cautioned: "We would

not overlook the fact that being a prosperous and rapidly growing city we have much to do to meet the demands of this growth and prosperity. Our greatest need at present is good, pure, wholesome water."

But although there were still glaring needs, the growth of the city was an assured fact and the president said, in recognition of this: "The past two years have been the most prosperous and most important in the history of Memphis. This seems to have been brought about by the general outside feeling that Memphis possesses the location of a great railroad center. Congress recognizing this fact, has recently passed a bill providing for the construction of a railroad bridge over the Mississippi River at this point. This bridge will be completed within the next three years, or sooner, if possible, as the demands of trade are now requiring it, and the various railroad interests both east and west of the Mississippi will be focalized at Memphis, thereby forever fixing her commercial supremacy in the great Mississippi Valley."

Obtaining pure water was quite as potent a municipal necessity as disposing of the dirt, so this subject went hand in hand with the sewers.

In 1868 Mr. Charles Hermany, then civil engineer of Memphis, after investigating the supply and quality of water to be obtained for the city, recommended that Wolf River water be used. A water company was formed and in 1870 they obtained a charter from the Legislature, under the name of the Memphis Water Company. A pumping station was erected on the south bank of Wolf River and the company laid seventeen miles of pipe to supply the city with river water.* Previous to this time only cisterns and wells had supplied the inhabitants with water and some of these were far from sanitary.

This company did not succeed financially and their plant was sold in 1879 to a newly organized company for $200,000. This new organization was also named The Memphis Water Company.

March 6, 1880, the water works were again sold, this time for only $155,000. Of this new company, which was composed

*Lundee's Report on the Water Works System of Memphis.

of business men, Judge T. J. Latham was elected president.*

After the epidemics had brought forth the sewer system more water was needed for the flush-tanks, house-flushes and other domestic purposes, so the Memphis Water Company extended its pipes and started negotiations with the Taxing District for the public supply of water. This contract was not completed until May, 1882. After this water-piping increased rapidly, but the water was sometimes so muddy as to be very unsatisfactory. Three years after the consummation of this contract, which was to remain in force for twenty years, there were citizens' meetings for the purpose of providing ways and means of getting better water. The Legislative Council of the Taxing District appointed a committee of ten to investigate water supplies in the vicinity. General Colton Greene was engaged to report to this committee, which he did in February, 1886. After hearing from General Greene the committee pursued its further investigation and reported in December of the same year to the Legislative Council. Three sources of water supply were considered, namely, that of the Mississippi River, of Horn Lake and of Wolf River, higher up stream than where the supply was then obtained. In any case it would be necessary to provide for filtration.

Wells had been suggested to the committee, but wells at that time were not thought feasible, especially as The Memphis Water Company had experimented with wells and reported them failures. They rejected driven wells as "impracticable for local reasons," and artesian wells because of their "uncertainty and unreliability."

After much discussion of all the systems presented, this committee recommended "Wolf River, at a point above and near to the L. & N. R. R. crossing, as the proper source of supply," and they advised the adoption of the plan of the water works described by Gen. Colton Greene.

While this committee was busy with its discussions and recommendations against the wells, Mr. R. C. Graves, superintendent of the Bohlen Huse Ice Company, had a well sunk

*Keating.

on Court Street for "obtaining water for condensing purposes, to a depth of 354 feet."*

This well proved a success and came to be much discussed, casting other recommended systems for the city supply of water into shadow. A company was organized to supply the Taxing District from wells, and upon successful experiments they were able to contract with the authorities in July, 1887. This new company took the name of "The Artesian Water Company," and agreed to supply water to the city and to individuals. This interferred with the Wolf River Company, so they too sank wells. Consolidation of interests was considered, but that plan was not fully agreed upon until 1889. In April of that year the two companies combined and soon after this consolidation the Wolf River plant became a thing of the past.

In 1890 a first-class pumping station was started, and the Memphis water supply became one of the best supplies in the world. Mr. Lundee gives this description of how the wells give forth their supply:

"To the bottom of each well tube, in the case of the water works wells, is attached a strainer, consisting of a long section of brass tubing having fine slots cut in it, which permit the water to pass but hold back the sand. These slots are liable to become filled up, especially if the well should be in proximity to a clay pocket in the sand. When this occurs the water is held back and consequently the yield of the well is diminished. Various methods are adopted for cleaning the strainers. * * * * The water is pumped directly into the distributing mains. * * * * The major quantity leaving the pumping station is primarily taken by a 36-inch pipe which runs west along Auction Street and south along Front and Shelby Streets, connecting with a standpipe about two miles distant from the station, situated on a lot at Tennessee and Talbot Streets. * * * * From this pipe subdistribution is made. The standpipe is of steel construction, twenty feet in diameter and 160 feet high. The function of the standpipe is simply that of a pressure regulator and in a limited degree acts as a reservoir."

Experts from different sections examined the Memphis

*Lundee's Report.

artesian water and all pronounced it excellent, some the best city supply in the world. Of the yield, Mr. Lundee says: "The supply is inexhaustible and it is limited only as the supply from any spring or river has its natural limitations by the rate at which it is called on to yield water. Thus the water, while there is no reason for not using it liberally, ought not to be unnecessarily wasted."

In the contract between the Taxing District and the Artesian Water Company, the latter contracted to furnish, twelve months from the time of the contract, "good, clear, pure and wholesome water of the character examined and approved" by the board of inspectors in a previous report, from "deep wells of the depth of about 400 feet below the level of Court Square in said Taxing District or deeper, if necessary." Besides private supply they contracted to furnish water for fire-hydrants, flush-tanks, to be flushed once or twice every twenty-four hours, dumping stations, public municipal offices, police stations, municipal hospitals, engine-houses, public fountains—not over two,—sanitary stables, levee washing, flushing gutters, public drinking-fountains—not over twelve, etc.

So the eighties seemed to be untangling all the knotty problems of the two previous decades that had hampered Memphis and made her very existence doubtful.

The Board of Health reports from year to year show improved conditions and much work along sanitary lines. In 1885 Dr. Thornton said in his annual report: "The year was an exceptionally healthy one. * * * * The total freedom from epidemic disease, with a lower death rate calculated upon the same estimated population, must be due, in a large measure, to the improved sanitary condition of the city, the enforcement of the health ordinances and operations of the health department.

"With a steadily increasing population, which is apparent and conceded, and which is attested by improvements in every part of the city, the number of deaths for the year is 193 less than for 1884, and only 81 in excess of 1883. This, I think, demonstrates very clearly an improved condition of the public health of the city."

In each year's report Doctor Thornton compliments sanitary and sewerage work in the Taxing District but deplores always the unsanitary condition of Bayou Gayoso and the dilapidated and unsanitary condition of the City Hospital.

In 1888 yellow fever was reported in Jacksonville, Fla., Decatur, Ala., Jackson, Miss., and other Southern points, so quarantine became strict in Memphis and a refuge hospital, to be placed in a safe locality, was advocated. Mr. Niles Meriwether had a plan for such a hospital "of eight rooms, with halls, verandas, etc., * * * * estimated to cost $3,000." There were a few suspicious cases of fever in Memphis that season, but the decade ended free from pestilence with a small death rate and the Bluff City had come in a few years time to be pronounced one of the most healthful cities in the country, instead of one of danger.

In his fourth biennial report, Jan. 1, 1889, President Hadden gave the happy statement: "It is gratifying to report that the debt of the old city of Memphis is practically settled—probably ten thousand dollars yet outstanding. The compromise bonds are above par."

He said he "would also state that during the last two years a new gas company has been introduced into our city, and also a new water company, and our citizens are to be congratulated upon having at present an abundant supply of pure artesian water, overflowing from thirty-two wells. This is the greatest boon our city has ever possessed. * * * * We are also to be congratulated that work has been commenced upon a railroad traffic bridge across the Mississippi at this point, which will add greatly to our material prosperity. Our city has enjoyed perfect health during the past two years, and we know of no city that has such a bright future and possesses so many elements of prosperity and future greatness."

# CHAPTER X

Memphis Rising From Her Ashes. Census of 1890. Details of the Sewer System. The Bethell Administration. Increase of Property Values. The Cotton Trade. Big Fires in Memphis. The Mississippi River Bridge. Ceremonies of the Opening. Electric Car Service Inaugurated. Protest Against Taxing District Form of Government. Taxing District Proves a Success. Form of Taxation Unjust to Memphis. Gamblers Again. Law and Order League. Sam Jones in Memphis. Other Lecturers and Moral Workers. The Legislature Restores Titles of City, Mayor and Vice-Mayor. Clapp Elected Mayor. Artesian Water Company, Telephones and Electric Lighting. Back Tax Collector Appointed. Memphis to Levy Her Own Taxes. New City Hospital. Interstate Drill and Encampment. Flood of Mississippi River. Yellow Fever Scare. Bank Clearings.

---

AS MEMPHIS had from her beginning, after every backset, taken new life so, even after she had seemed to be left in ashes she revived, and out of the ruins rose, like the ever mythical-truthful phoenix. Hope, her shining though sometimes cloud-hidden star, rose higher and clearer in the sky as the eighties progressed, and Memphis again asserted herself.

This city was a need of the country and it was inevitable that she should take her place in the work of the Nation. There was no other important city within two hundred or more miles of her bluffs. Her situation made her the entrepot of several states and western produce could come most conveniently to this market. She was a valuable point between St. Louis and New Orleans and by right, if freed from misfortunes that had held her back, should become as great and important as either of these cities.

Mississippi, with its wealth of cotton, lay just south of

her borders, her own great state, that was yearly developing in untold riches, lay north and east, while Arkansas, a state beginning to be recognized as one of the richest of the country, was to be joined to the Bluff City by a great steel bridge. These advantages could not but receive recognition from the business world and, as assurance spread that pestilence and unreasonable debt were no longer hindrances to her citizens, her residents were encouraged and new people began to come.

In 1880 the population had been reduced from 40,226 in 1870, and 40,230 in 1875,* to 33,592. By 1885, the estimated population was 60,000, and each year of confidence added to the number until by 1890 there were 64,495. In 1880 Memphis had been practically a city in the mud, but the efficient work year by year of the city engineer and his assistants had brought many good streets, bridges, culverts, miles of sewers, drains and other conveniences, as shown in the lucid annual reports of Mr. Meriwether.

President Hadden, in his report of December 1, 1884, to Governor Bate, said of Mr. Meriwether's work: "I am satisfied that no city ever received more or better work for the same amount of money than has been accomplished by this able engineer. He in connection with Mr. Anthony Ross, his assistant, have vastly extended and improved our sewer system, which has done so much to improve the health of our city since its introduction four years ago."

In this same report Mr. Hadden praised the Board of Health work and said: "The garbage system of this city we think excels in efficiency any city that we know of, and our own people as well as those who visit us, express the belief that we are the cleanest city in the country. This entire department receives the personal attention of that able sanitarian Dr. G. B. Thornton, who is the president of our local Board of Health, which is composed of Dr. G. B. Thornton, Dr. George S. Graves, secretary, D. F. Jackson, Health Officer, and W. C. Davis, Chief of Police."

As Memphis grew and the sewer-pipes became vehicles of

*This standstill of population from 1870 to 1875 was due to the yellow fever epidemic of 1873.

more and more sewage the six-inch pipes were found to be inadequate. Obstructions sometimes occurred of sticks, bones and other objects getting caught cross-wise in the small pipes. It was necessary to locate and remove all these, which added considerably to the cost of the maintenance, the cost of these removals averaging $13.50 each.

In a report "compiled and prepared under the supervision of Niles Meriwether," by his assistant, James H. Elliott, in 1891, it was set forward that "the unit or six-inch pipe is too small, as nearly all of the stoppages occur in them; very few in large pipes where properly laid. * * * * As early as 1882 the main sewers were at times taxed to their full capacity. In 1885-86 the main sewers had become so overcharged as to make it necessary to tap them at several points north of Monroe Street."

Manholes, which had been left out when the Waring system was laid, because of the saving of expense, were now necessary and many were put in along the old line of work and in the new. These soon proved their efficacy by reducing the cost of removals of stoppages, as well as enabling better observation of the pipes and so fewer obstructions had to be dealt with.

Mr. Elliott had to say of the plumbing of that period: "Attention is called to the great improvement in our plumbing work. To the untiring energy of the inspector, Mr. William Lunn, and his hearty interest in his work is this great improvement greatly due; and it may also be added that we have in this work, as a rule, the hearty coöperation of the plumbers, who have come to realize that they have, if possible, as much or more interest in first-class plumbing and good sanitary work."

The cost of the sewering during that decade amounted to $399,314.18, an average per mile of about $8,100.

Mr. Meriwether said: "It would seem that we have now reached a period in the growth of the city when it has become necessary to build in the near future one or two large intercepting sewers, discharging by independent outlets directly into the river, for which surveys and plans should be made as soon as the time and means will permit. * * * * These sewers should be made sufficiently large to accommodate territory beyond our present limits that may be brought in within a few years."

When the Waring system of pipes was put in only the southern part of the city profited from the work. The northern part, known as Chelsea, remained unsewered, except for private pipes, so Mr. Meriwether now advocated sewering that portion of the city with the Waring system, but with the mistakes of the first work rectified. These mistakes had not been many and the system had worked admirably on the whole. Colonel Waring himself, who came to Memphis in the early nineties to examine the system after thirteen years' trial, said:

"If time has shown that something less than absolute perfection was secured, here and there, I think it may still be said, that considering all the circumstances, we did reasonably well. The work then done had its desired effect of aiding to improve the sanitary condition of Memphis, and of showing to the world, that this condemned city had taken on a new life, that it was earnest in its determination to overcome the disastrous effects of its epidemics, and that it offered a hopeful field for enterprise. During the thirteen years that have since passed, it has maintained its promise, and from that moment of its regeneration, it has gone bravely on and has, by its prosperity, astonished the world, which in 1879, would have been glad to see it swept off the face of the earth, as a dangerous public nuisance."

In 1888 the Council ordered a survey of a system of sewerage in Chelsea, which was made and a plan submitted by Mr. R. F. Hartford of Chattanooga, Tennessee. Mr. Hartford consulted Mr. Meriwether and, considering the defects of the old system, they worked out an improved plan.

The Chelsea work was begun but progressed slowly the first year, retardation being enforced by the delay in getting pipe. Over 3,000 feet of pipe were laid in 1889 and a year later Mr. Meriwether said, "For the coming year, 1891, we start out with a well-organized force at work on the Chelsea system. The work should be pushed to completion the coming year, if possible."

The Chelsea work and that all over the city went rapidly

forward, each portion of the city suggesting by its position or peculiarities its special needs.

In 1890 Dr. J. E. Black was president of the Board of Health, and he continued the work begun by Doctor Thornton as well as he could with the small force allowed for his work. The house-to-house inspection was persevered in, much to the discomfort of careless house-keepers and other thoughtless persons.

The population had more than doubled in ten years and larger forces became urgent in all the city departments.

The chief officers of the Taxing District at that time, January, 1890, were: Fire and Police Commissioners,—W. D. Bethel, president; J. T. Pettit, vice-president; Martin Kelly. Supervisors of Public Works,—T. J. Graham, Samuel Hirsch, E. J. Carrington, George Haszinger, George E. Herbers.

These two boards composed the Legislative Council, with Honorable W. D. Bethell, president.

Other city officers were,—Henry J. Lynn, secretary; William M. Sneed, attorney; Niles Meriwether, chief engineer; A. T. Bell, assistant engineer; W. C. Davis, chief of police; James Burke, chief of fire department; W. B. Rogers, president of the board of health; William Krauss, secretary of board of health; Dr. J. E. Black, surgeon in charge of the City Hospital.

Doctor Rogers' first report shows work done in many branches, especially praising the inspection work of Mr. William Lunn, inspector of plumbing. Doctor Rogers, as Doctor Thornton had been doing for several years, condemned in earnest language the city hospital, recommending that it be burnt to the ground and a new and modern one erected.

Doctor Rogers' sanitary work extended itself to the humane effort of lifting poverty above some existing horrible conditions to cleaner habitations that would improve the inmates morally by making them more thoughtful of their surroundings and more active in keeping themselves decent. All work done for the betterment of humanity in one direction bears fruit in other directions as well.

One of the first things this officer did was to ascertain how far the ordinance allowed the Health Board to go and then, using his authority to the fullest extent, he worked faithfully for bettering conditions wherever he could. Among other renovations he condemned "numerous decaying rookeries in which were cuddled hundreds of human beings; reveling in filth and breathing most unhealthful atmospheres."

Doctor Krauss examined the water from cisterns and wells, many being condemned and ordered filled with fresh earth in consequence of these examinations. He recommended the artesian water in use as "absolutely pure."

Dr. W. B. Rogers was followed in office by Dr. Shep. A. Rogers, who continued the city health work faithfully. One of this president's most earnest appeals was for a milk-inspector properly equipped with Babcock apparatus, and that his duties be not only to inspect the milk, but to visit and inspect the dairies. He also asked that abattoirs be established at some point along the river below the city, and that the unsanitary slaughter houses then existing be abandoned.

In 1893 Doctor Thornton again took charge of the Health Department, under better auspices than formerly. This year the sanitary force was strengthened, consisting of G. B. Thornton, M. D., president; J. J. McGowan, M. D., secretary; D. F. Jackson, health officer; W. C. Davis, chief of police; W. L. Clapp, mayor, ex-officio member; Miss Verner Jones, clerk. The sanitary police officers were O. B. Farris, John McPartland, W. A. Casey, Thomas McCormick and E. F. Cunny.

The total number of deaths reported for the year 1893 was 1,235—the smallest number reported since 1882, when the population was very much smaller.

Dr. Thornton resumed his condemnation of the condition of many parts of Bayou Gayoso and of the wretched old city hospital building.

The decade just closed, that had made such strides in business and better conditions generally, and brought Memphis to the favorable recognition of the world once more, still had its official trials, as what city has not? One of these at that time was serious shortage in the Taxing District finances. The grand jury appointed for investigating this affair found a deficit of $10,377.80 in the station house fund between 1886 and 1889. After this unfortunate discovery the jury was instructed to investigate further back and found that dishonesty or carelessness had robbed the city of considerable of her revenue.

On January 9, 1890, Honorable W. D. Bethell had been elected to succeed President Hadden, and on the 15th of the same month was inducted into office.

Of President Hadden's retirement the Appeal had this to say:

"After 8 years of service the Hon. D. P. Hadden retires from the presidency of the Taxing District. During this period he has shown himself a tireless officer. His individuality is of so pronounced a type that he has made himself famous. The Administration of the city government for the last eight years, has been distinctly his administration. His will has controlled the council. * * * * He has enjoyed demonstrations of the popular regard such as has rarely been experienced by public officials. He can point with satisfaction to many good results of his administration."

In his parting speech, the last time he officiated as Police Judge, Mr. Hadden said:

"I feel sad at leaving two such departments, but the will of the people seems to be that I should do so; and I certainly resign the position which I hold with much more pleasure than I experienced when I took it up. * * * * I go forth without any ill feeling towards any one. * * * * I well know how tempestuous is the sea of politics, and how many have been wrecked thereon, but I claim that I was not sailing the bark of government upon this sea, and have ever looked upon it as a purely business government."

Several northern and other papers writing of Memphis at this period likened her to great cities of the country and spoke of her as a "future Chicago of the southwest," the "future metropolis of the Mississippi Valley," a "great city of the future," and one author and poet* called her "The Collossus of the Valley."

President Bethell, in his first report to Governor Buchan-

*James R. Randall.

an, called attention to the growth of Memphis and the growing needs as a consequence, thus:

"The reports of these two years are very suggestive, and in a growing city, full of enterprising and public-spirited people, will doubtless show the necessity for increased provision for enlarged public works during the incoming two years, and I trust it will please your Excellency to invite the attention of the Legislature of the State to these growing demands upon our city's public service, and allowing for its rapid growth, year by year, to make provision accordingly, by wise and liberal legislation."

The total outstanding bonded indebtedness in 1890 was $3,248,977.11. By 1891 several thousand of these outstanding bonds had been called, leaving the amount outstanding, $3,230,042.93.

Much of the street work done in the city was performed by the criminals or chain-gang, and this supplied the double service of keeping these unfortunates busy and forcing them to serve the city to which they were an expense. Of these workmen, Mr. Meriwether said in his report of January 1, 1891:

"In working the chain-gang every effort has been made to obtain the greatest amount of service, and in such directions as would do the most good; and a great deal has been accomplished with that force during the year. The carpenter and bridge and street forces have done a large and unusual amount of work. There is no ward in the city in which more or less work has not been done by all of the above forces: grading and cleaning streets and alleys and repairing same, building bridges, culverts and drains, putting down crossings, setting curbing and other miscellaneous work. We have endeavored to do the greatest amount of work with these forces, and as impartially as possible."

He also wrote, realizing the rapid growth of the city and consequently the need of increase in materials and working forces:

"The question as to the best plan of grading and paving all the streets and alleys of the city in the shortest possible time, is now one of absorbing interest. The steady growth of the city and the great volume of business that has followed in the past two or three years, would seem to demand a change in our methods in this respect. There is no question that we need more paved streets and a better class of work, at least upon all of the central traffic streets of the city. The subject is one requiring the greatest care and deliberation. * * * * Our progress made in the past ten years has been commendable, but something more is now required and the question is, upon what plan is it best to proceed?"

He commends the work of his assistants, thanks them and concludes the report with a summary of the work done by his different departments from February, 1879 to December 31, 1890, the total of all these amounting to $399,314.18.

Chief of Police Davis in his report to President Bethell also urged increase of facilities to accord with the city's rapid growth. He said:

"I urgently call your attention to the necessity of furnishing the department with more men, as you see from the roster we have only thirty-eight patrolmen, nineteen on each relief. We need at least twenty more men, which would be twenty-nine for each relief, which is less than three men to each ward. This is quite few enough, considering the extent of territory to patrol and the time taken up attending to the wants of the public at the depots of the ten railroads coming into our city, where some forty passenger trains arrive and depart daily. If the enactment giving us additional territory shall become a law, we shall need at least twelve mounted policemen—six on each relief—to patrol the new district. * * * * The patrol wagon so long needed and furnished the department a few months ago is a great benefit, bringing the prisoner quickly to the Station House, leaving the officer on his beat, and sparing him many hard struggles in bringing drunk and disorderly persons to the Station House; but the full benefit of the wagon cannot be realized until we have established a police signal system. At present the police have to depend on private telephones to call for the wagon, and when the call is most urgent the officer may have to await the convenience of others before he can be accommodated."

Chief Davis, often heartsick at the downfall of youth in the city, urged upon the Council the necessity of a reformatory for boys. To quote from this plea:

"In years past I have urged the establishment of a house of correction for boys; the necessity still becomes greater for such an institution. The Mission Home and House of the Good Shepherd take care of many of the wayward girls we have to look after, but the viciously inclined boy roams about the streets, plunging into every kind of vice. For him we have no place except the rock-pile, where he is associated with still more hardened criminals than himself; where instead of being reformed, is prepared as he grows older to take position among the mature criminals in the penitentiary. Something should be done for the restoration and protection of these poor boys."

One arrest recorded about this period was of a negro boy six years of age who had battered a somewhat larger boy's face with a brick. The little fellow was fined ten dollars. He had no father and his mother was a poor charwoman, so he had to work out his fine on the rock-pile, with older criminals who, amused at his infancy, enjoyed joking with and about him, not at all to his benefit. A judge who would thrust into such company a baby, that would in all probability grow to maturity, perhaps a menace to the city that had allowed him to develop in crime, was not appreciative of his power for good or evil. Chief Davis could see the hurtful consequences of such procedures and petitioned that they might be averted.

For the year 1890 the Chief said that on the whole "we had had but little serious crime during the year."

In his report for the following two years we find him still pleading for more modern and efficient appliances and methods, according with the growth of the city, which he said already compared favorably with larger cities. In this report he thanked the Council for what they had allowed for the furtherance of improvement.

We have seen how, many years ago, the Memphis wharf-master had numerous trials in collecting the required fees from flatboat-men for the city, and how he finally come out victorious. All the years since then wharfage had continued to be an item in Memphis revenue, and at the close of 1890 Wharfmaster Simon W. Green showed his collections during the year to have been $10,141.95.

Memphis real estate had increased very much during the years from her awakening in 1880 to the nineties. Real estate transfers showed that during the years 1890 and 1891 the property changing hands in Memphis aggregated $5,183,830.

A few items of interest recorded in 1892 by business men, help to show the growth of the Taxing District. The enhancement of real estate values from 1882 to 1892 had been 500 per cent, and much property was paying from 25 to 30 per cent on prices paid for it in the early eighties. The Peabody Hotel, which at one time had brought little to its owners was reputed in 1892 to be returning a rental of $50,000 a year.

People in general had lost all fear of Memphis as an abiding place, as was proved by the numbers that came for the purpose of settling and stayed.

Business in all branches was not only hopeful but continually increasing. Building was progressing more than ever before and on greater scales. Workmen were in such constant demand that in 1890 Memphis had two labor agencies, which could scarcely supply the demand for labor.

To get an idea of the increase in business we can consult a few figures gathered by business men in 1892: In 1880 the cotton trade, which comprised nearly all the business of Memphis at that date, aggregated for the season 470,000 bales, valued at $23,000,000, while for the season of 1891-92, the aggregate was 770,000 bales, valued at over $30,000,000.

The banking capital was estimated in 1880 to be about $1,500,000, and in 1892 it had increased to $7,200,000.

Besides these improvements the lumber trade had grown to be so important as to make Memphis one of the lumber centers of the world, and the grocery business, both wholesale and retail, had grown enormously.

Another indication of the city's growth from the time of her calamities to the early nineties was the increase in the postal business, the figures in 1890 and 1891 showing an aggregate that equaled those of the city's most flourishing banks.

The United States census for 1890 gave a population of 64,589 and in 1892 the population was estimated from the city directory to be 85,000.

The nineties showed Memphis to have many new industries and these were constantly increasing. Her municipal advantages were among the first of the country. Taxes had been reduced from $2.35 to $1.80, which encouraged home-seekers and people wishing to invest money.

The fire department continued to grow in efficiency and although some destructive fires occurred they were better handled than formerly. In April, 1891, Hill, Fontaine & Company's cotton-shed, situated in the old navy yard, was struck by lightning, which started a conflagration. This occurred about eleven o'clock at night and the shed was filled with cotton, so the flames spread rapidly, but the firemen succeeded in confining the damage to the shed. This fire caused the greatest loss of that year.

On the night of February 8, 1892, a fire swept the block bounded by Main, Monroe, Second and Union Streets. This fire started in the auction rooms of Rosin & Hurst, and created a loss of a million dollars. Among the buildings destroyed were Luehrman's Hotel, Lemon & Gale's wholesale drygoods house, Langstaff Hardware Company, Wetter & Company, Beine-Bruce Hat Company, Jack & Company, Wilkerson & Company, Levy Trunk Factory and several smaller firms. This destructive conflagration was supposed to have been started by an electric wire.

The following year this same re-built block was much damaged by another destructive fire, the Wetter block being again demolished, other serious losers by these flames being the Y. M. C. A. and the Pythian Journal. Several persons being entrapped by this fire and consequently injured by jumping to safety, much blame was attributed to the neglect of fire-escapes and criminal negligence was charged. This unhappy experience started strict enforcement of the laws regarding fire-escapes.

In April, 1892, flames were discovered by the night-watchman, at 2:30 a. m., in an unfinished seven-story building on

Adams Street, and before the firemen could reach it much damage had been done. Chief Burke said of this fire, in his report to the Legislative Council:

"This building formed a veritable flue, no doors or windows in, and the flooring, which was only partially laid, covered with highly inflammable material, pine-shavings, etc. This fire was discovered in its incipiency by the watchman at the Adams Street engine-house, the alarm promptly given and responded to, but owing to the condition of the building, within ten seconds from the time the fire was discovered, the flames had reached the roof and communicated to the adjoining buildings. It required almost superhuman efforts on the part of every member of the department to extinguish this fire. We had no ladders at that time sufficiently long to enable the men to reach an advantageous position, a fact detrimental to the interests of the city, which has since been remedied, thanks to your honorable body in purchasing an aerial truck."

In November of this same year the Chief said of the new equipment:

"We had an opportunity to test the new aerial truck on the night of November 2, at a stubborn fire which originated on the third floor of the building occupied by Fly, Hobson & Company. By means of the aerial used as a water-tower, we were enabled to extinguish, with a comparatively trifling loss, what at one time looked as if it would prove to be a disastrous conflagration."

In consequence of these and other serious losses, Chief Burke said in his report:

"I feel it my duty to reiterate the recommendations made in my last report, viz., that at least two more engine companies and one chemical company be placed in the suburban districts, as with the limited number of men and pieces of apparatus now constituting the fire department, it is a matter of impossibility or rather poor judgment, to reserve any in case of an alarm being sounded from the business portion of the city. * * * * A valuable adjunct to every well-equipped fire department is the latest improved 'water-tower.' In other cities the efficacy of these machines has been proved on numerous occasions. This city has suffered losses in the past which could have been saved if one of these 'towers' had been in service."

He explained how a building could be flooded with one of these towers and so save the spread of disaster, and recommended "the purchase of one of these 'towers' as soon as possible."

In January of 1893 there was another big and destructive fire in which several prominent business houses and some smaller ones were demolished or severely damaged. The firemen worked desperately and bravely this night, saving much property and perhaps nearly the whole business section of the city. When the flames reached Dean & Carroll's paint store most of the attention was centered on that place and the efforts of the hard-worked men really succeeded in quenching the flames before they reached the cellar in which was stored thousands of pounds of the combustibles and explosives kept in paint stock. The firemen were much exhausted by that night's labor and Chief Burke was injured by a falling brick.

1892 brought forth the consummation of the great achievement long contemplated and anticipated by hundreds of people, —that of joining Tennessee and Arkansas together. In May, 1892, the great cantilever bridge that accomplished this feat was finished and on the 12th of that same month the bridge was formally opened. The *Commercial* called this structure a "notable triumph of engineering and mechanical skill."

It had taken three and a half years to construct this steel connection, the work having been carried on from both ends simultaneously, until the middle span met. Its finished length from end to end, was 15,635 feet, or nearly three miles, and it contained 7,000 tons of steel, while in its construction had been used 2,000,000 feet of lumber.

Building a bridge across the Mississippi at Memphis had first been agitated in 1856, but some engineers at that time thought the expense of such a structure would not pay for itself, while still others thought the scheme wholly unfeasible. But the subject was not dropped and continued to be brought forward at intervals until 1885, when an act was passed and approved by Congress, authorizing the construction of a bridge at this point. Following this act William G. Ford, Reese B. Edmondson and others obtained a charter in Tennessee and Arkansas, but lack of funds caused the matter to stand still until three years later, when James Phelan introduced a bill in the Congress, authorizing the construction of a bridge across the Mississippi River at Memphis, by the Kansas City and Memphis Railway and Bridge Company. This act, which came to be known as the "Phelan Bill," passed and was approved April 24, 1888.

The act required that the bridge be seventy-five feet above high water mark, across the entire bed of the river, which provision, later carried out, caused it to extend a long way high over the Arkansas swamps. Many engineers were consulted and finally the plans of Morrison and Nettleton were accepted, the contractors to be two brothers, Andrew and William Baird.

When this long-wished-for convenience was completed, naturally the people desired a celebration and they had a pretentious one. Numerous eminent people were invited for the opening and thousands of other visitors came.

On the morning of May 12, 1892, a parade two miles in length passed through the streets of Memphis, headed by twenty-four policemen, mounted four abreast, the leading four being Chief Davis, Captain O'Haver, Captain Hacket and Sergeant Horan. Following them was the Grand Marshal, Colonel Hugh Pettit, and his assistant marshals, General G. W. Gordon, Captain W. W. Carnes, John M. Tuther, E. A. Keeling and Honorable Zachary Taylor. Then followed the National Guards of Tennessee, commanded by Colonel Arthur Taylor. Arnold's band filled the air with music and after them came more military, some of these being visitors to the city. The civic societies were imposing in their regalias and they were followed by the fire department with their burnished engines and other equipment, headed by Chief Burke. The Colored Chickasaw Band made their instruments do justice to the occasion and following them distinguished guests rode in carriages, other carriages conveying city officials, committees, citizens, etc. After this long line of carriages came the artistic floats on which were represented the industries of Memphis. These were interesting as well as beautiful, and were enthusiastically received by the spectators.

At and near the bridge gathered great crowds to witness, or to try to witness the ceremonies of opening the bridge for traffic. The papers estimated this crowd to number 25,000 people.

Soon after ten o'clock eighteen locomotives slowly entered the bridge and steamed back and forth, snorting and causing many of the onlookers to wonder what they were about. What they really were doing was testing the strength of the structure that had been built for their accommodation. Each span was tested and proved satisfactory. The total weight of these iron horses was 3,000,000 pounds.

After this test was over a decorated car, the "Tennessee train," on which the Tennessee Governor, Adjutant General Norman, Inspector-General Weakly, Quartermaster Frank and many other distinguished guests and Memphis people, went to the middle of the bridge. There this car was met by the "Arkansas train," on which were the Arkansas Governor and his party. When these cars met Governor Buchanan rose and said, "Governor Eagle, in the name of the State of Tennessee, I bring you greeting." Governor Eagle responded: "In the name of Arkansas I accept it. I trust that the two great states may ever be upon the same sisterly terms, their relations ever becoming closer."

After these greetings there was a cheer and both cars returned to Memphis, where a platform of people awaited them. Colonel J. R. Godwin was chairman of the committee on this platform, and with him sat prominent guests from many states.

After the Arkansas and Tennessee governors and their parties were greeted, speeches were made. Governor Buchanan set forth the advantages to come from the new bridge, and his speech was followed by one from Governor Eagle, quite as patriotic and enthusiastically received. Other orations followed, in which were given much of the history of early days in the Bluff City, of navigation, development of the South and National progress in general, while much hope was expressed for the future.

Chief Engineer Morrison and General Nettleton received much praise for their success in carrying the work of the bridge to completion and both of these modest workers displayed embarrassment in responding. One of them said that his business was not speech-making and hence his embarrassment.

The night pageant was an impressive one. This procession was led by city officials and contained artistic floats and inspiring music. The first float represented "Aurora" and following the Queen of Early Day were floats containing allegorical displays, giving the history of Memphis from aboriginal days.

It was recorded that out of all the throng in Memphis on Bridge Opening Day there was not a drunken disturbance.

The then new electric car service proved itself very efficient and these cars were to many of the visitors even more interesting than the big bridge, as they had never before seen horseless or muleless street conveyances. There were a few amusing incidents of people who walked long distances rather than trust themselves on these cars and some visitors left satisfied to only look at these new rapid carriers of street passengers. Stories were circulated of watches being stopped, eyesight ruined, people terribly shocked and even killed by the electric currents that *passed through these cars*. But despite the timid ones the cars were said to have carried on that date 126,000 passengers.

The gunboat "Concord" came to Memphis in honor of the celebration and was the first sea-going vessel many of the people had ever seen. It was much visited and its officers and crew received considerable attention.

A round of festivities was given to visitors and many of the strangers expressed admiration for Memphis and for Memphis people.

During the time committee meetings were held for various purposes, among these being one for discussing the possibility and practicability of a deep-water way through the Mississippi River.

The Bridge celebration attracted much attention to the

Bluff City and the business exchanges received numerous letters from people impressed by the growing importance of the place and wishing to invest capital.

Memphis had grown and was continuing to grow so rapidly and her place in the world seemed now so sure that her officials and citizens were advocating a change from the taxing district government, as the time for its expediency was thought to have passed. There was much discussion over the subject, the consensus of opinion seeming to be that Memphis should have her identity restored. It was argued that the object for which the taxing district government had been formed was accomplished and that to longer remain under such jurisdiction was subservient and reflected upon Memphis abroad. The Commercial said it was time for Memphis to be divorced from the County and that she should fix her own tax-rate, collect her own taxes and spend them for her own improvements. This paper called for the opinions of citizens and many were given, mostly in favor of abandoning the taxing district form.

General Peters said that St. Louis and Louisville had had similar experiences and that those now flourishing cities dated their prosperity from the time that each became separated from the county.

Mr. J. S. Menken said that the taxing district government "accomplished much good, but it has fulfilled its mission, and is now unequal to our requirements." He advocated "home rule." Of taxing Mr. Menken said, "Such bungling and ignorance as are exemplified in some of our revenue laws are difficult to parallel in the statute books of the country. It appears as if the makers of those laws had resolved to kill all enterprise, to ignore justice, and place a fine on honesty."

Mr. Robert Galloway said, "I see no reason for our going to Nashville every two years to have our 'country cousins' from all parts of the State, many of whom know absolutely nothing about city government, fix our rate of taxation." He also advocated a change in the taxing system, saying, "No matter what change we make, we can't be worsted."

Chairman Harrell, of the County Court, only objected to the taxing power. He said: "It places us in an embarrassing attitude abroad to have the budget of the city's expenses audited and passed upon by the State Legislature. If it would be possible to maintain the present form of government with the power to levy taxes delegated to the local authorities, I would be heartily in favor of it. It is the cheapest government on earth, and is less liable to fraud and corruption."

County Clerk T. B. Crenshaw declared the taxing district form of government "undemocratic."

Other officials and business men gave opinions, and while a few desired the taxing district form of government, all wanted a change in the taxing system.

Mr. Clapp, making a speech in contemplation of running again for the presidency, said of the taxing district government, "This may have been suitable enough, and satisfactory in results, when the cities of the State were little more than villages; but when a city comes to be a metropolis, embracing population, wealth and taxable property greater in number and value than many of the counties combined, and with widely diverging interests and requirements, the absurdity of the system is manifest. * * * * It is not easy to conceive of anything more illogical and oppressive than the situation of your city dangling on the apron strings of her Nashville nurses. The subserviency of the city to the county may be more tolerable than to the State, because the benefits are more frequent and of direct application, but the relationship is hardly less oppressive."

Mr. Clapp gave as illustration some of the business pursuits of Memphis, and showed the amount of revenue of each to the state, county and city, half of which are here given:

|  | State Rate | Co. Rate | City Rate |
|---|---|---|---|
| Breweries | $ 200 | $ 200 | $ 100 |
| Cold Storage Company | 1,000 | 1,000 | 50 |
| Construction Company | 100 | 100 | None |
| Gas Company | 700 | 300 | 25 |
| Liquor, Wholesale | 300 | 150 | 10 |
| Lightning Rod Agents | 150 | 50 | 15 |
| Land Stock Company | 75 | 75 | None |
| Telephone Co. (1500 in use) | 750 | 750 | 250 |

| | | | |
|---|---|---|---|
| Water Company | 800 | 800 | 200 |
| Grand Opera House Theatre.. | 200 | 200 | 75 |
| | $4,275 | $3,625 | $ 725 |

In view of these figures one does not wonder at the general desire of citizens for a change in the tax-rate.

Mr. Clapp set forth other inequalities and oppressions. In the course of his speech he said: "The city provides good streets, over which the business may be economically done, and has them cleaned and lighted; gives fire and police protection; supplies the population for trade and consumption and can with some conscience exact a privilege, but pray what help or assistance is given by the other governments to the dealer?"

At this time Memphis had her moral troubles as well as political, as had so often happened before in her history. Gambling and other immoral practices had become so open-faced and prevalent as to cause law-abiding citizens to become alarmed for the youth of the city and to take measures for improving conditions. Some blamed the city administration, saying that the officials cared more for retaining a "fat office" than for enforcing the laws.

In January, 1893, at a meeting of the Council, the questions of gambling and other evils were brought before the members, and President Clapp made a lengthy speech on the subject. He said:

"* * * No city has ever authoritatively claimed to have suppressed these evils, nor will this be entirely or partially accomplished to the full satisfaction of every class in the community, until poor human nature undergoes a transformation. Your present fire and police commissioners, whose duty it is, through the constituted departments to look after these social evils are but men, no better nor worse than sagacious officials, charged with similar duties in other cities. * * * Such authority and information as the board could command led to the conclusion that in every city of respectable size, in all the states and nations, these 'social evils' were regulated and controlled, but not suppressed."

Mr. Clapp said that the evil of gambling had perplexed Memphis as far back as the oldest living citizen and officer could remember and that it had been impossible to put it down, though the city had regulated, fined, etc. He said that in previous years, when gambling houses had been closed and gamblers ordered to leave town, "where there was formerly one gambling house there were then five or more gambling rooms." As a preventive of this evil he said that "the commissioners agreed that the chief of police might permit the most reliable and trustworthy of the gaming men, who lived in Memphis, to open their houses and play four games, which, in the opinion of the police, offered the least opportunity for fraud or cheating."

After more arguments in favor of "suppression," he concluded with:

"I therefore submit the question to the council, with this suggestion: Should you be of the opinion that it is best for the city and her people, then request the Legislature now in session to repeal so much of the city's charter as gives the fire and police commissioners any power to regulate or control, and leave the charter to provide, as does the law of the state, for suppression only."

This opinion of the Taxing District president was hailed with delight by the gamblers and other moral law breakers, and variously received by citizens. Members present at this meeting discussed the subject and the president's opinion. Mr. Haszinger asked, "Do you think gambling can be suppressed?" and upon the president saying that he thought it possible, Mr. Haszinger replied, "Well, I don't!"

Others agreed with the president and others did not and arguments were vehement for a while.

The message stirred up the citizens at large, as it had the Council, and upon request, men wrote their views to the papers. One of these, Mr. R. G. Craig, wrote: "If every voter who has an interest in the lawful pursuits of our city and county would take care to exercise his right and privileges, I feel sure men would be elected who would enforce proper measures for the proper government of our city and suppress criminal development."

W. H. Leath, said: "I am opposed to gambling in all its forms, but I have no suggestion to make to President Clapp. I think he is opposed to gambling himself, but the question is how to handle the matter. There are many complications arising that are hard to deal with."

S. H. Dunscomb, said: "I don't approve the action of the Council on gambling. I think where there are laws they should be enforced."

Joseph Reynolds: "I am opposed to gambling in all its forms, or anything that looks like it. It is all nonsense that it can't be stopped. I know it can, for I have seen towns where it was not allowed, and they were as large and as lively as Memphis. It simply means the law enforced to the very letter."

Judge C. W. Heiskell responded: "I see Mr. Clapp fortifies himself behind a long established custom, which I think would be more honored in the breach than in the observance. * * * * I would like to ask the gentlemen of the council if they would invite Christian people to Memphis when they establish it as their policy that gamblers are to be given a *quasi* legal status in the city? Do they not think that it would invite Christian citizenship if they would, as they have the power to do, suppress gambling as the charter authorizes? Do they not think further that not only Christian people but all other people would have more respect for law and the constituted authorities if those authorities would execute the law against law-breaking?"

J. P. Young replied: "Mr. Clapp is mistaken in his premises. Open gambling houses can be suppressed. A notice to the chief of police from the proper authorities would enable him to close up every house in Memphis within twenty-four hours. * * * * As long as the felony statute stands it is as much a crime to gamble in Memphis as in any other town in Tennessee."

M. B. Trezevant said: "I don't see how gambling can

be justified in any way. * * * * Gambling is by no means a necessary evil."

D. M. Scales: "I am unable to see how a municipal corporation can license a crime forbidden by the laws of the State."

On January 31, a "Law and Order League" was organized over Joseph Specht's on Madison Street. Judge Heiskell was elected president, Col. John W. Dillard, vice-president and G. T. Fitzhugh, secretary.

Much enthusiasm was expressed by the members of this organization, and committees were formed as follows:

*Executive*: Napoleon Hill, chairman; G. W. McCrea, J. M. Greer, J. M. Steen, L. Lehman, T. C. Hindman, W. B. Glisson.

*Financial*: W. F. Taylor, chairman; J. M. Goodbar, J. C. Norfleet, Tom Gale, J. P. Edmondson.

*Constitution and By-Laws*: E. W. Carmack, chairman; J. H. Watson, John Johnson.

Secretary Fitzhugh submitted seventy-five names of men wishing to become members of the league, and he was instructed to enroll them.

The *Scimitar* advocated the Law and Order League and denounced the gamblers, as did their contemporary, the *Commercial*. Mr. A. B. Pickett, of the *Scimitar*, had this to say of existing evils:

"We have tried to make it very clear, since we began on the gambling question, how corrupt is the city. People ought to know about the evil that they may correct it. * * * * The extravagant burdens of taxation, the corner groceries and the power of political rings growing out of that thing have polluted the city, county and state. * * * * We have no personal malice in doing what we think right as a public journal. * * * * We are banking on the *Commercial* to stand by us in this work."

On the evening of February 21, 1893, there was a rousing meeting of the Law and Order League in Jefferson Club Hall, which was packed to overflowing. Many votes for the betterment of conditions were taken that night and it is recorded that every ballot was unanimous.

It would be fortunate if a community in choosing its leaders could always get those who would hold the good of their charges above selfish ends, and would respect the law they are expected to uphold and fairly administer. The reverse of this is sometimes true and Memphis has had numerous misfortunes of this sort. During this part of her history, when so many good men were trying to make the city a clean one morally, some considered only selfish or even dishonest gains and smiled at the efforts for moral uplift. A prominent lawyer of that period was disbarred because of dishonest and unprofessional conduct, while a judge of the criminal bench so perverted his power in a tyrannical and despicable manner that it finally became its own foil and caused him to be tried by an indignant people, the result being impeachment and expulsion from office.

Such misguided characters often mar the progress of cities, but they cannot continue their work indefinitely as right will find them out. In history it would be pleasing to record only the good, especially as it is the strong, but history tell of the things that are or have been, even though the telling is sometimes unfortunate or unpleasant.

While Memphis was thus trying to rid herself of evil influence the evangelist, Sam Jones, came within her bounds and in his unique and strictly "Sam Jones way" did his part to make people "quit their meanness." He preached daily and nightly to packed houses and in his unvarnished, straightforward manner held hundreds of people spellbound. On the first of these visits he was tendered the largest church, the First Methodist, but when the new Auditorium on the corner of Main and Linden Streets was completed he was invited to open it and even in that commodius structure it was found almost as difficult to seat the thousands as the church had found in seating its hundreds. Men and women of all grades and professions attended these meetings and the coldest and rainiest days and nights found full attendance. The success of this man was remarkable.

He scored Memphis officials and berated the saloons and gamblers, sometimes using expressions in doing so that few would have dared use in the pulpit. One of his pointed thrusts was: "You are afraid of hurting your business and making enemies, you are afraid of losing votes if you stand up for the right."

Again: "You will never drive gambling out of the town until the members of the church quit gambling for cut-glass vases. You will never drive the saloon out as long as the deacon keeps a demijohn in the closet." "If whiskey ran ankle deep in Memphis, and each front door had a dipper tied to it, you could not get drunk quicker than you can in Memphis now."

He advocated that all the ministers become members of the Law and Order League, and that all respectable men in Memphis belong to it, and not be afraid. "An honest man," he said, "is willing to know what and where he is." He said that many of the people sang "Hold the Fort,—for I am going the other way."

He thought that the real starting-point of morality and decency was in the home and said, "God help you parents to see that it is right in the homes, and that when the homes are right, everything will be right."

In these attempts at moral cleaning up women were not idle. They urged their husbands, fathers, brothers, sons and friends on in the work and they themselves came forward in a public way more than ever before in Memphis history. In 1892 the Association for the Advancement of Women met here, when many distinguished women from all over the world were Memphis guests. Most of these women had been earnest workers in the cause of allowing suffrage to women as one means of purifying social conditions, and there were, during their stay here, more well-received speeches on this and other moral subjects than ever before in the Bluff City. The daily papers, all at that time more or less opposed to woman suffrage, praised these intellectual women and gave much space to their lectures, their work, ability and themselves as individuals.

A few seasons later Miss Susan B. Anthony and Mrs. Carrie Chapman-Catt were guests in Memphis again, when they had not only good audience but enthusiastic gatherings. Mrs. Lide Meriwether introduced both of these speakers and one of the dailies in mentioning this Memphis woman who had done so much for the cause of Temperance and justice for women, called her "deservedly popular" and praised her achievements.

Mrs. Meriwether did much, and some have said more than any other woman in the state to get the law known as the "age of consent law" raised from infancy,—ten years,—to an age when girls would at least be beyond the baby, doll-playing age. This age was first raised through the efforts of the untiring workers of that time to sixteen years and a few years later to eighteen years.

Governor McMillan, under whose administration this last was accomplished, argued that he thought a wrong whereby a young person's whole future life was marred should be of as much importance in the laws of the land as those of larceny, vagrancy and other petty crimes. He said that if a boy twenty years and eleven months old made a business transaction on credit, neither he nor his parents could be held responsible for the obligation, but that if his much younger sister had her life wrecked by some man old enough to be her father, neither she nor her parents had any redress whatever. He thought this unjust, as did many other good men and they, being larger and more progressive than the then-existing law, listened to parents and other moral reformers and had the age when an inexperienced girl could be said by law to consent to her degradation, raised to eighteen years, an age when she could at least comprehend that there were human beings immoral enough to prey on inexperience. Another Memphis "Mother in Israel" who worked hard for the moral uplift of both sexes was Mrs. Elizabeth Lyle Saxon.

Women usually work hardest for moral reforms and charity, and they take advantage of opportunities offered them for this work. In 1895 the Commercial offered to give women the Valentine edition of their paper, to be conducted by women throughout. This offer was gladly accepted and on February 14, after much labor, a mammoth paper was produced, containing original articles, sketches, drawings, stories, poems and many pages of advertisements. One department was devoted to men and many literary and other men contributed meritorious articles. Arts and industries had departments, all of which were well conducted. The space allotted to the War Between the States and other memorials was conducted by Mrs. Luke E. Wright, Mrs. Kellar Anderson, Mrs. J. H. Humphries and Mrs. M. L. Beecher. This department was deservedly popular, and these ladies, having experienced the war's disadvantages, knew how to conduct the work.

The Board of Managers of this paper comprised: Mesdames C. N. Grosvenor, W. M. Farrabee, J. M. Judah, Cooper Nelson, J. W. Allison and James M. Greer. The business managers were Mesdames C. B. Galloway and M. M. Betts and the treasurer, Mrs. C. F. M. Niles.

The women were grateful for the liberal patronage this paper received and all of the proceeds of the big volume-paper went to the United Charities.

The city was not cleared of evil influences and undesirable characters, but the work of good citizenship had its weight and many conditions were bettered. She was partially restored to cityhood and again held her place as a civic, independent center.

In 1893 the Legislature passed an act declaring that "the president and vice-president of the board of fire and police commissioners of the city of Memphis shall be hereafter designated respectively mayor and vice-mayor of the city of Memphis." And,—"That at the expiration of the respective terms of office of the president and vice-president of the board of fire and police commissioners of the city of Memphis, their successors respectively, shall be elected by popular vote, in the manner provided in said acts. The mayor of said city to be voted for and elected in and by that name at the expiration of the term of the now president of said board, and the vice-mayor to be elected in and by that name at the expiration of the term of the now vice-president of said board. The said board shall remain constituted as heretofore, of three fire and police commissioners, the said mayor and vice-mayor to remain and be, as heretofore, commissioners and members of said board."

In the race for the next election of city officers in 1893, three men were candidates for the mayoralty, namely, W. L.

Clapp, J. J. Williams and D. P. Hadden. The faction headed by each of these men held enthusiastic meetings and it was a spirited race. Many of the Law and Order League members worked for Mr. Hadden, as they said he was a positive character, not afraid to act, and would enforce law and collect the taxes.

Mr. Clapp was elected and with him Mr. Jeptha Fowlkes, vice-mayor.

City improvements went on as steadily as means would allow and Memphis was becoming more and more habitable. The city engineer reported that in 1892 $116,473.37 had been spent on pavements, while that year's work on sewers had made the complete length of the city's system 54.6 miles.

The Artesian Water Company, with Judge T. J. Latham as president, and Mr. R. C. Graves, vice-president, continued to grow and by 1892 there were 41 artesian wells, ranging from 350 to 500 feet in depth and covering an area of about 23 acres.

Telephones increased rapidly in use and from luxuries had become necessities to business houses and many homes.

Electric lights continued to improve and became popular as illuminating power for residences, stores and streets.

Electric lights were first introduced into Memphis in 1882 by the Brush Electric Light and Power Company. Three years later a competitor in this business came,—the Thompson-Houston Electric Company. Later the Brush Company bought the stock of the Thompson-Houston Company and the two companies became incorporated as the Memphis Light and Power Co. The officers of this company in 1891 were S. T. Carnes, president and general manager, S. H. Brooks, vice-president, W. W. Carnes, secretary and D. T. Porter, treasurer.

The electric car service also continued to improve, as shown in the chapter on transportation.

January 3, 1895, Mayor Clapp said there was not a cent of floating debt against the city, as Memphis had paid for all material supplied during 1894, despite the fact that receipts had been limited.

Still, Memphis had causes for complaint. In this same

month of January the Mayor and Mr. Hu Brinkley presented several Memphis bills to the Legislature at Nashville, the most important being that "To amend the general assessment law of 1889; also to amend the Taxing District Act so as to enable the legislative council of Memphis to fix the tax levy instead of the assembly."

The "debt" and taxing system continued to keep Memphis hampered and her officials and citizens in a wrangle that seemed destined never to have an end.

In 1895 the Legislature appointed a back-tax collector for Memphis and the city council opposed it and appointed a collector of their own. Mr. Clapp complained that collection of taxes by the state was tyranny and that "the city of Memphis, in common with the other cities of the state, has power through its own selected agency and employes to collect its delinquent taxes." He complained that no matter how much Memphis needed these taxes, she must wait and let her expenses, incurred for officers, teachers, etc., etc., remain unpaid until the state turned over the money; that during the period of four years proposed for the term of the tax collector of the state, "there will come into his hands on the basis of the average delinquencies for the past three years $450,000; and it is believed to be impossible to suggest a plausible, much less a valid or logical, reason why the power to collect this amount of taxes should be taken out of the hands of the chosen representatives of the city and lodged in the hands of a state officer, a resident of Nashville, and wholly foreign to every interest of the city except such as might be assumed to exist in any non-resident of the city clothed with so vast a power over the city's interests."

In May of this year the legislature amended the act denying Memphis the power of levying her own taxes and conferred upon her taxing power "to be free from restrictions and limits imposed" before that time.

The reader has perhaps noted how Dr. G. B. Thornton, year after year, decried the old City Hospital, setting forth its wretched condition, and petitioned for a new building, and how his successors in office reiterated his statements. It was a trying time for those earnest workers who felt the necessity of surrounding the sick with sanitary and pleasant conditions, but they were finally rewarded. The Legislature of 1895 passed an act authorizing Memphis to levy an ad valorem tax of nine cents for the years of 1895, 1896 and 1897 for a new hospital, "the proceeds thereof to be appropriated and devoted exclusively to the building and equipping of a new hospital, and to the purchasing of a new hospital site, if, in the judgment of the Legislative Council, a new site should be deemed more desirable than the present one."

The old hospital was torn away, a new site purchased and a splendid new building, the plan of which was selected from a number of excellent plans submitted, was erected. After completion this hospital became one of the most important adjuncts of the city, and is one of the best arranged and equipped buildings for its purpose in the country, where hundreds of people have since received attention and comforts that have brought them back to useful life or made their last earthly days more pleasant than they would otherwise have been.

This hospital has pay and free service, the latter receiving no less careful attention than that for which patients are fortunate enough to pay. Two long wings extend from the central building, on either side, facsimiles of each other, one for white and the other for colored patients. The building is so arranged that other wings can be added from the central structure, as increased patronage or demands might require. Every room in the building has outside ventilation and sunshine some part of the day.

When the edifice was near completion, Mrs. W. L. Surprise was appointed by the fire and police commissioners to the position of matron of the institution. Her first duty was to purchase all the bedding and hospital linen, the purchase and care of which was a greater responsibility than one without experience of such domestic duty can easily realize.

In January, 1899, an ordinance was passed to establish a medical staff to take charge of the City Hospital, and these physicians assumed their duties March 1, following.

W. C. Davis was appointed superintendent and his report, tendered to the mayor and councilmen, showed the first year's work to be productive of much good. Of the medical staff he said, "It affords me much pleasure to say that the staff have performed their duties well and without compensation."

In connection with the Hospital a Training School for Nurses was established, the nurses to serve, under professional direction, in the institution while receiving their training.

The report of Superintendent Davis for 1899 showed the number of patients received during the entire year to have been 2,452, all of whom had recovered except 242. Of these, 385 were from Mississippi, 275 from Arkansas and 738 from other states besides Tennessee. Memphis had furnished only 403 of these patients. The cash taken in from pay patients during that year was only $3,009.93.

May 10, 1895, the Interstate Drill and Encampment opened at Montgomery Park, and was the occasion of much interest and enjoyment to Memphis people and visitors. Among the military companies was the famous Veteran Chickasaw Guards, whose achievements in former days had won them much recognition.

Miss Helen Gould, one of the numerous distinguished guests expected, could not attend the encampment, but she sent a solid silver urn, skillfully chased and gold-lined, with these lines engraved upon it:

"Presented to the Veteran Chickasaw Guards by Miss Helen M. Gould on the occasion of the Interstate Drill and Encampment, held at Memphis, Tenn., May 10th to 21st, 1895."

There were daily drills at the park and several brilliant parades of visiting and home troops through the streets.

On Confederate Day, May 18, the business houses closed and a general holiday was enjoyed in honor of the Southern soldiers.

May 20, there was a Grand Review of all the troops, the soldiers making a splendid spectacle in full dress.

During these patriotic May days the Chickasaw Guards were enthusiastically received wherever they appeared, but for one time they did not carry off first honors, which was a disappointment to Memphis people. They were in Class A, but did not head the list.

On the last day there was a great sham battle and award of prizes. The Thurston Rifles of Omaha carried off first honors and the best-drilled individual soldier was Private H. K. Williams of this well-drilled company.

The Memphis Neely Zouaves led in the Zouave class, and Company A of the Memphis Confederate Veterans led in the Hardee tactics class.

Going back to municipal affairs, we find that in June of 1895, there were complaints because no work had been done on the streets, sewers, bridges and other civic necessities during the year, and a long list of petitions for improvements was presented to the city council by tax-payers who suffered inconvenience from this sort of neglect. Some of the petitions received attention, while others continued causes of complaint.

Despite all drawbacks, however, the council declared that Memphis had made unusual progress in the past sixteen years and by the close of 1895 she was able to refund $1,300,000 of her bonds, thus saving $30,000 of annual interest.

In the spring of 1896 there was an unnusually high flood that left much devastation and suffering in its wake. The breaking of several levees caused great destruction of property. Many animals were drowned and some people lost their lives in the flood torrents, but most of the people were saved. Memphis cared for over 6,000 of the refugees that year whose homes and other earthly possessions had been swept away.

After this affairs went along with comparative smoothness until the fall of 1897, when a yellow fever scare retarded business somewhat.

In September of that year a number of cases of this dread disease were reported in New Orleans, Mobile and other Southern cities, especially along the Gulf coast. There were some deaths and in October the disease spread considerably. Quarantine was very strict in Memphis but the yellow pest crept in. The fact was kept out of the papers for a while and the yellow fever deaths were reported as malarial fever, but the Board of Health demanded that it be made known.

Such knowledge frightened many people and there was an exodus of thousands, but most of the populace acted on the advice of the Board of Health, stayed at home and attended strictly to sanitation and cleanliness, as this was urged by the health officers to be the best quarantine, although the other sort was strictly enforced.

Some papers declared quarantine unnecessary and very disastrous to business, but it lasted all through October and was not lifted until November 5th.

The tension through October was great but an epidemic was averted although Memphis had so many more people than she had during her former disastrous experiences from this plague. Some physicians said such a catastrophe was averted because of the cleaner condition of the city, while others declared that the cool-headedness of the people who remained in the city helped more than anything else. "Fear," said one, "is a greater devastator than disease itself," and fear was not allowed to enter to the extent of getting the upper hand that year.

Three new cases were reported the day before the quarantine was lifted and there were a few scattered cases after, but danger was declared past and people came flocking home.

After this unsettling experience was over business was resumed with renewed vigor and the people advocated adding many of the suburbs to the corporation of the city, as the greater number of inhabitants lived beyond the city limits. This was necessary, many of the citizens claimed, that more of the inhabited territory might have civic improvements and enforced sanitation.

There were croakers who declared that the following year would produce an epidemic worse than any ever known before because there were so many more people but the majority were optimistic and they were correct for the year following was free from fever, as have been the fifteen years ensuing. An occasional quarantine has been enforced because yellow fever has made a feeble appearance further south, but just as this plague grew to be a thing of the past in New York, Philadelphia and other Northern cities, so it has become a pest and dread of the past to Memphis. It is claimed that the discovery of the yellow fever mosquito will put an end to the plague in future.

On November 18, 1897, there was a conference in the city hall between the city council and two committees of suburban residents, presided over by Mayor Clapp, for the purpose of discussing the annexation of more territory to the city of Memphis. This was an enthusiastic meeting, with many speeches, suggestions, objections, etc. Some advocated that the limits be extended only a short distance while others objected that this would be no advantage, as many people would then build just outside the limits to avoid city taxes and that in a few years conditions from lack of sanitation would be the same as those then in the outskirts of town.

Large extensions would of course necessitate extending sewers and water-pipes at great expense and there were arguments for and against the advisability of this action.

Those in favor of extending the lines won in the arguments for in February, 1898 the Legislature passed an act extending the limits of Memphis, thus:

Beginning at a point on the east bank of Wolf River, at the west end of the south line of Maple Street if extended west to Wolf River, running thence eastward with the south line of Maple Street if extended to the west line of Breedlove Avenue; thence south with the west line of Breedlove Avenue to the south line of Vollentine Avenue; thence east with the south line of Vollentine Avenue to the west line of Watkins Avenue; thence south along the west line of Watkins Avenue to the north line of the right of way of the Raleigh Springs electric line; thence east with the north line of said right of way to the west line of Cooper Avenue; thence south with the west line of Cooper Avenue to the north line of Central Avenue; thence west with the north line of the Central Avenue, to a point north of the west line of Brown Avenue; thence south with the west line of Brown Avenue to the south line of the right of way of the Nashville, Chattanooga & St. Louis Railroad Company; thence west with the south line of said right of way to a point opposite the west line of Rayner Avenue;

thence south with the west line of Rayner Avenue to the north line of the right of way of the Memphis & Charleston Railroad Company; thence east along the north line of said right of way to a point opposite the west line of Ragan Avenue; thence south along the west line of Ragan Avenue to the north line of Austin Avenue; thence west along the north line of Austin Avenue to the west line of Raleigh Avenue; thence south along the west line of Raleigh Avenue if extended to the northeast corner of Calvary Cemetery; thence westward along the north line of said cemetery to its northwest corner; thence south along the west line of said cemetery one thousand feet to the center of Kerr tract; thence west with the center line of Kerr tract to the east bank of the Mississippi River; thence northward with the meanderings of the east bank of the Mississippi River to the south line of Wolf River where it empties into the Mississippi River; thence northeast up the meanderings of said bank of Wolf River to the point of beginning.

The Act authorizing these boundaries also authorized the city of Memphis to divide her territory "into such wards as may be necessary or may attach parts of the same to the wards now in existence."

The annexed territory was to be exempt from paying former debts of the city and from taxation for police, fire and light departments for ten years.

Despite the fever scare, the clearings of Memphis for November, 1897 exceeded those of November, 1896, $1,856,240.60, those for 1896 showing $10,635,361.04. And the bank clearings for the week ending December 11, 1897, were $3,386,523.77, while the same week the previous year showed $2,930,454.64 and the same week in 1895 showed $2,624,143.45.

# CHAPTER XI

J. J. Williams Elected Mayor. Death of Senator Harris. T. B. Turley Appointed Senator. Gambling Houses Closed. Further Extension of the City Limits. Collection of Taxes Authorized. Sewer Extension. Visit of President McKinley. Great Confederate Reunion. Williams is Reelected Mayor. Municipal Ownership of Water works. Purchase of the Old Plant. Attempt to Amend Charter. Memphis Streets Renamed. Quarantine.

ON JANUARY 6, 1898, J. J. Williams was elected mayor of Memphis, D. P. Hadden, vice-mayor and W. B. Armour, secretary. The board of fire and police commissioners of this administration comprised the three just named and Hu L. Brinkley. The supervisors of Public Works were E. C. Green, B. R. Henderson, G. D. Raine, William LaCroix, H. H. Litty, P. J. Moran, Thomas Clark, E. J. Carrington and W. B. Armour, clerk.

Dr. Heber Jones was president of the Board of Health and Dr. Marcus Haase, secretary.

Jerome E. Richards was Chief of Police. Wm. F. Carroll, Chief of the Fire Department.

John H. Watkins, City Attorney, A. T. Bell, City Engineer. W. C. Davis, Superintendent of the City Hospital.

These and all other city officials went into office January 17, 1898.

On the night of February 3, Memphis did honor at the Auditorium to one of her sons, Thomas B. Turley, who had been appointed by Governor Robert L. Taylor to succeed the late, lamented Senator Isham G. Harris. Mayor Williams introduced Judge Greer as chairman of the meeting, and Judge Greer, in his own inimitable manner introduced the guest of honor, Senator Turley.

When the new senator stepped before the audience applause and cheering made it impossible for him to be heard for some time, but finally the audience subsided and Mr. Turley thanked the people for this reception and for all they had done for him.

After Memphis boundaries had been extended the city went to work to improve Greater Memphis. The increased property value amounted to $8,000,000. Memphis was now the largest city in the state and had much to do to get all within her boundaries in running order.

One of the first benefits to suburbanites who had come into the corporation was diminishing their car-fares by getting transfers to the different lines of the city. They also profited from the extension of streets, sewers, lights and educational facilities.

Early in February all the gambling houses were closed and their proprietors thrown out of business, if preying on the possessions of others can be called a business. This promptitude of the new city administration surprised the gamblers, but many of them said it was only a temporary suspension and waited around to see whether they would be allowed to resume or if, as the *Commercial* expressed it, they would have to "seek pastures new."

February 15, the Battleship Maine was blown up in Havana harbor, and Memphis, with all the Country, became very patriotic and little was discussed beside this catastrophe. The accident theory was at first accepted but the people soon grew to believe that treachery lay at the bottom, especially when Spain commenced to send war boats and torpedoes to Havana. Investigation proceedings were instituted and the spirit of war and revenge became rampant until war was finally declared.

For months papers teemed with war news almost to the exclusion of other events. War was east of us in Cuba and west in the Philippines, and many of our young men were called both ways. West Tennessee militia companies centered in Memphis and for a while the Bluff City seemed to have revived the days of the sixties except that this time her boys all wore the blue.

But the fields of action were distant and Memphis, with her additional territory, had much home work to do. In 1898 her limits had been extended, as we have seen, and the city officials had put in many improvements, besides keeping up those of the old part of the city. In January, 1899 the Legislature passed another bill extending the limits still further, thus:

"Commencing where the north line of Trigg Avenue touches the Mississippi River at low water mark; thence east with the north line of Trigg Avenue to Raleigh Avenue; thence east with the north line of Trigg Avenue if extended to the intersection of the Pidgeon Roost road and Cooper Avenue; thence north with the west line of Cooper Avenue to the intersection of Old Raleigh road; thence north to a point where Vollentine Avenue, if extended east, would intersect the west line of Cooper Avenue as produced; thence west along said south line of Vollentine Avenue as produced east, to Marley Avenue; thence west on the south line of Vollentine Avenue produced west, to the south line of Brinkley Street; thence west along the south line of Brinkley Street as now opened and as produced west, to the east bank of Wolf River at low water mark; thence in a southerly direction along the east bank of Wolf River to the Mississippi River; thence along the east line of Mississippi River at low water mark to the point of beginning."

Another act passed at the same session enabled the city to levy her own taxes for her own purposes, and in April of the same year the Legislature authorized "That all commissions, which have been paid or turned over to the County of Shelby, for the collection of the taxes of the city of Memphis, since January 1, 1899, shall be refunded by the county to the city of Memphis, and hereafter no commissions for the collection of the taxes of the city of Memphis shall be paid to the County of Shelby, or collected out of its current taxes or by the county trustee."

Memphis was also empowered by Act of this same Legislature, to provide for the collection of her current and delinquent taxes and was "vested with the power to establish the office of tax receiver," and to elect or employ said tax collector by her legislative council.

She was vested with full city powers as to appointing the time and place for collecting taxes, to fix delinquencies, penalties, costs, advertisements, etc. She was "vested with full and complete power to establish, by ordinance, and to enforce in any manner advisable any and all measures necessary or expedient for the collection of the current and delinquent taxes of such city, and all such measures and acts of all officers and persons acting thereunder shall be as valid and binding as if such measures were enacted by the Legislature."

Although still under the weight of the debt begun in her helpless days, Memphis was practically restored to the full privileges of cityhood, and was no longer dubbed merely a taxing district, though in fact it continued to be one in modified form.

The "Williams administration" started in to do conscientious work and much was accomplished under the difficulties prevailing.

Mr. Williams, in his report for 1899, said:

"By the addition of twelve square miles of territory, part of which was thickly settled, having many miles of unpaved streets totally lacking in sewers or any other means of sanitation, wholly without provision for lights, fire or police protection, and having a very limited mileage of water or gas pipes, there was thrust upon our shoulders a very mountain of responsibility and difficulty, the magnitude of which few of our people are conscious of. * * * * If we had all the money wanted the needed improvements could be rapidly accomplished; but, our tax rate, while lower than in former years, is as high as our people are willing to bear. I therefore recommend that the rate of taxation for general purposes remain the same as it was last year, and that by a judicious appointment of the budget and an economical administration of affairs, the improvements demanded by our people be pushed to the utmost limits of our resources."

During this year thirty-six miles of sewers were laid, costing $141,930.99, as against twenty miles for the previous year, costing $166,955.49.*

The Board of Health had a good report for the work of the year 1899, both in the old and annexed territory. Among other improvements for the latter, two crematories had been built, as cremating garbage had now become a prevalent system in Memphis.

The sanitary inspector of the health department, Dr. J. L. Andrews, expressed gratification for the fact that citizens and property owners had generally been prompt in making sewer connections and in complying with other demands. These owners had been rewarded by having their property increased in value from ten to twenty-five per cent.

The *Sanitarian*, a periodical of New York, had to say of the condition of Memphis at that time: "The health of Memphis is of abiding interest as an object lesson for sanitarians, and it is gratifying to observe that her health authorities are constantly alive to the importance of cleanly local conditions."

The Artesian Water Company reported 125,835 feet or 25 miles of water-pipes laid in 1899.

The street commissioner, Mr. George Haszinger, reported that there had been grading, rounding up of dirt streets, cleaning gutters, filling sewer ditches and approaches to new bridges mainly in the annexed territory, but sufficient money had not been allowed to insure half the work needed, some of the streets in the annexed portions of the city being in very bad condition. Mr. Haszinger recommended a new sweeping machine, new carts for hauling sweepings and a stable owned by the city for housing city street cleaning property.

The police and fire departments made good showings for the closing of the century, according to their facilities, but both these departments felt the need of additions to their forces, the added miles of city territory requiring it. Chief Richards said of this:

"The area of territory to be patrolled and protected was increased from four miles (the area of the old city limits) to

*Engineer's Report.

sixteen miles, which additional territory was annexed by an act of the Legislature, and embraced all the thickly settled suburbs to the north, east and south of the old city limits. This annexation made the increase of the force imperative, and one sergeant and eighteen men were added to the regular patrol force, which, up to March 1, 1899, was limited to forty-five men."

The entire number of patrolmen of that time was only sixty-three for both reliefs which, Mayor Williams said was "wholly inadequate to properly guard the territory of sixteen square miles."

Chief Richards suggested that in order to get conscientious work from policemen they should be paid sufficient to enable them to support families and, when too old to work, should be pensioned on half pay, when the better part of their lives had been spent in the service.

He praised the detective force, through whose agency he reported $15,656.85 worth of property to have been restored to the owners.

Of the police matron the chief said: "I cannot speak in too high terms of praise of the work performed by Miss M. E. Roark, the police matron. Her position is a most trying one, and is not confined alone to the searching of females who have been arrested. Abandoned infants, homeless girls, poverty-stricken families, and all the misery that follows broken homes, deserted wives and helpless children, it has been her task to succor and relieve."

A report of her work showed 140 white and 360 colored female prisoners searched.

| | |
|---|---|
| Strangers cared for in Matron's Apartment | 504 |
| Girls placed in Reformatories | 18 |
| Employment secured for Girls and Women | 74 |
| Children cared for | 50 |
| Children placed in Orphan Asylums | 14 |
| Infants given to families for adoption | 24 |
| Homes found for children between the ages of four and 14 | 10 |
| Infants that died while in her charge | 2 |

This did not include medicine and clothing distributed among the poor whom she visited.

Chief Carroll of the Fire Department, reported sixty-five as his total force, including himself. Much of the vigilance of this department has been spent in discovering and removing or remedying defects and dangerous conditions of property. There were 442 of these reported and the chief said, "An ounce of prevention is worth a ton of cure."

Six hundred and six plugs and hydrants were at the service of the Fire Department at that time, and their property at the close of the century was valued at $191,300.00.

Mayor Williams said: "The rapid growth of the old city, as well as the addition of the annexed territory, demand a greater number of fire-engines and the maintenance of the facilities of this department at the highest standard."

Several large fires and many small blazes, some of which would have resulted direfully but for the quick work of the firemen, were reported for 1899, the total fire loss for that year showing $906,452.14, as against insurance for $1,500,891.73.

The City Secretary, W. B. Armour, showed that on January 1, 1900, there was $11,140.23 on hand, after the expenses of the city had been paid, besides $58,000 of annexed territory taxes that had been repaid, according to an act of 1899,[*] making that requirement.

The total receipts shown for this year were $925,936.40 and the disbursements $873,658.64.

Mayor Williams, in concluding his report for the year ending December 31, 1899, said to the councilmen:

"In conclusion, allow me to remind you that we have in our hands the welfare of a great and prospering city. The responsibility upon us is great. Numerous questions of the very highest importance demand our earnest and immediate action. The people have recently expressed their confidence in us. Let us handle these questions in a way which will demonstrate that we deserve their confidences. Each of us is entitled to a full expression of his views, but due considera-

[*]House Bill 124, Acts of 1899, approved Jan. 25th.

tion for each other and the harmonious action of the Council as a whole is necessary to the public weal."

With the opening of the new century the one-time unfortunate Memphis had left fears behind and seemed to be steadily climbing the road to prosperity. The eyes of the world seemed to be turned upon her and many newspapers commented on her achievements and future. The census of 1900 gave the city a population of 102,320, which caused great rejoicing, but in fact the city census had been fraudulently "padded" about 20,000 names, as the people of the city only found out a decade later.

Her growth during the past decade showed an increase on the face of the figures of fifty-nine per cent while in truth it was only twenty-nine. However, eleven steam-railways steamed in and out her confines and the river facilities were excellent.

The Nineteenth Century had been a wonderful span of time for humanity, having brought more advancement than any other in the world's history. All sciences had made great strides; many helpful discoveries had lightened many forms of labor and brought luxuries before undreamed of; art had both made much advancement and resuscitated bygone skill; universal peace had grown in favor and the brotherhood of man had gained a firm foundation.

In April of 1901 President McKinley, his wife and their party visited Memphis and were cordially received. From the station they were escorted by Company A, Confederate Veterans, who formed a guard around the President's carriage, all the way to Court Square.

In Court Square a stand had been erected for the speaking, where Mayor Williams presented the President to the great throng gathered to see and hear him. The mayor gave a graceful introduction, to which the President responded quite as gracefully. He paid high tribute to Tennessee and to Tennessee soldiers, then showed he knew something of Memphis history by mentioning her bitter trials of past years. He praised her for overcoming difficulties as she had, predicting for the Bluff City a great future. He called Memphis the leading commercial city of the Middle South, and in paying tribute to her bravery and energy, said: "No other city in your country has suffered more than Memphis and no other city has overcome so completely adversity as Memphis." He expressed high regard for General Luke E. Wright who, he said, was doing his duty in the Philippines, just as he had done it in Memphis.

The President and his wife received many honors while here, for which they expressed appreciation, and no celebrated visitors ever left kindlier feelings in the hearts of their hosts than these two and their distinguished party. So it was with doubly deep sorrow that Memphians heard a month later of the serious illness of Mrs. McKinley, and later in the year of the terrible assassination of Mr. McKinley, one of the noblest souls that had ever held high office.

On the day of his funeral, September 19th, Memphis respected his memory by closing her business houses in the afternoon and draping them in mourning. The churches also had services on that day and church and fire bells tolled during the time of the funeral procession. At a mass meeting held for the purpose, resolutions of sorrow on the death of the President were drawn up and passed.

In May, 1901, the Confederate Reunion was held here, and Memphis had been preparing for the reception and entertainment of the soldiers for months. Eighty thousand dollars had been contributed for the purpose and conspicuous in the contributions was a check for $1,000 from Robert Church, an ex-slave who, by his industry, had made for himself a fortune in Memphis. His contribution was accompanied by a letter, showing high merit and refined feeling.

All the railroads reduced rates for the Reunion and these trains, with extra cars and schedules, came to the city with load after load of visitors, the number during the Reunion being 125,580,[*] more guests than she had inhabitants. This included eighteen thousand veterans.

The city was beautifully decorated in honor of the soldiers, some of the arches being feats of artistic skill, while bunting

[*] "Commercial Appeal."

and flags,—Confederate and Union,—waved in all directions.

General John B. Gordon of Georgia, was at that time Commander-in-Chief of the Confederate Veterans and he received much attention and many honors. The papers were filled with Reunion affairs, war reminiscences and pages and pages of pictures of soldiers, officers, sponsers, etc.

In the address of welcome to the Veterans, Mayor Williams said many loving things, expressing the general feeling of the people,—which was one of reverence and tenderness for the men who had lost a cause and then suffered untold humiliations heaped upon them by the worst element of their enemies.

But these men have again reached a state of citizenship as high as they and their fathers had enjoyed before the war. Sons and daughters of these heroes, born Americans and loyal to their birth, yet revere and honor their fathers who fought for a cause they believed to be just, and are keeping green the memory that would otherwise die before many more years.

Bishop Gailor addressed the Sons of Veterans in an eloquent speech, as he can so well do, especially when talking to young men. At the conclusion of this address he said: "There is no virtue more manly or more precious than filial reverence for the traditions of one's own people, and there is no patriotism so enduring and so reliable as that which begins with and proceeds from the honest, the firm, the unswerving affection for one's own section and one's native land."

On May 30, there was a mammoth parade, greeted and cheered by thousands, especially that part of the procession made up of the soldiers. Cheers, tears, yells, waving and all possible demonstrations greeted them.

Many tributes were paid during the Reunion to the South's leaders and the Confederate Veterans were never and will never be more honored than they were in May, 1901, in Memphis, by the thousands who revered and loved them so.

Great efforts were made in 1901 to lesson evils and promote all kinds of municipal benefits. An act was passed this year enabling Memphis to levy an ad valorem tax of $1.00 on the $100.00 of all taxable property within the city limits, to improve streets, highways and bridges and to complete the sewer system.

During this same year the city won a suit requiring real estate agents and others to consider city health, comfort and convenience in laying off subdivisions, and all other precautions possible were taken to keep up the standard of city health and to increase it.

Growth was shown by the constant increase of population, which had passed the 100,000 point, by the phenomenal building permits, growth of manufactures and by the increase in Bank and Clearing House receipts. During the last five years of the Nineteenth Century bank clearings had increased nearly sixty per cent, and the Clearing House showed in May, 1901, $12,157,500.58, as against $9,949,648.76 for May, 1900, and this, after caring for over 100,000 visitors at the Reunion.

At this time Memphis was the leading manufacturing city in the state and she owned much of her precedence in this and other advancement to the Industrial League.

In January, 1902, an election was held for Mayor, when Mr. Williams was reelected with the entire Democratic ticket, having had little opposition, for a term of four years. It was said that the four years of the Williams administration ending with December, 1901, were among the most prosperous in the history of Memphis.

Sanitation in Memphis at this time was said to be a "model for the world."

The people complained of high taxes and the high price of water and lights, and the municipal ownership of these conveniences grew in favor. In 1898 the Legislature had passed a bill authorizing the city of Memphis to control her own water works, and under a contract between the water works and Memphis the city was given the right to buy the existing plant. Judge Latham said that meters would obviate all trouble and he urged their use. He said that under the then existing system there was so much waste of water that the company could not afford to cut the rates as the city demanded without bankrupting the water company, but that meters would reduce individual consumption and so the general expense.

Meters were put in where people wanted them but their use was discouraged. Dr. Jones, President of the Board of Health, said that the meters would bring about more evils than cures and the plan became so unpopular that Judge Latham refused any further controversy on the subject. A committee was appointed in February, 1902, composed of E. B. LeMaster, chairman, B. R. Henderson and Ed. F. Grace, to investigate the situation. They made a report the following May, and after setting forth the conditions of the contract between the city and the Water Company, existing conditions of the meters, flat rates, water quality, etc., they recommended that the city either buy the water plant then in existence or construct one of their own.

The mayor was opposed to municipal ownership and most of the councilmen agreed with him, but some argued that it was the only wise solution of the problem and citizens generally favored it, so it was the plan finally agreed upon. The committee was authorized to negotiate with the Water Company and in December, 1902, Mr. Armour, the City Secretary received a communication from the Water Company accepting the proposition of the city to buy the plant and to "pay off in cash the floating indebtedness of the company."

On January 27, 1903, the committee, of which Mr. LeMaster was chairman, held a meeting to receive bids for $1,250,000 water bonds. Three bids were made but rejected, and the committee was authorized to sell the "$1,250,000 of 4 per cent 30-year water bonds at the best price obtainable, but at a price not less than par."

After much controversy and many business transactions, matters were finally settled and the city possessed the water plant with all its properties, since which time water has been furnished at as low rate as possible to good business judgment, and wrangling in that branch of municipal affairs has ceased.

In 1902 the Water Company had sunk six new wells and in 1905 eight more were sunk, as the former wells were inadequate to supply the greatly increased demand for water.

In April, 1902, all the gambling houses were closed and, as of old, the gamblers waited around for the time to come

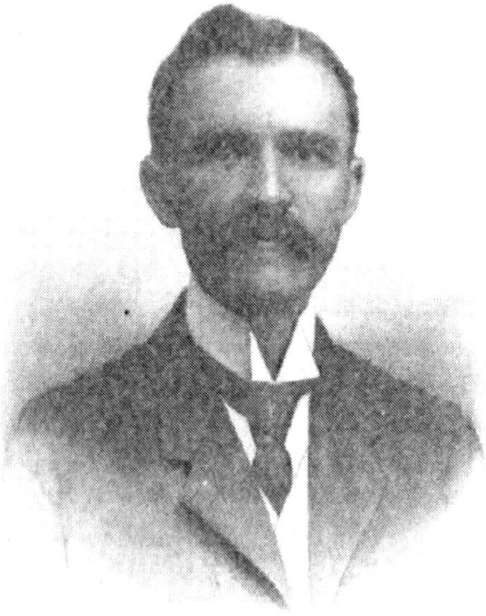

E. B. Le Master

when they could open their houses or rooms again. This time, however, they stayed closed so much longer than on former occasions that in February, 1903, the gamblers appealed to the city council, promising to keep orderly houses, refuse to allow intoxicated persons into their places or youths under twenty-one, and to close at the hour of night required. These men argued that closing their houses had injured the city in many ways and had caused suffering to the families of the gamblers. One wonders that men having such a fluctuating existence should not change their employment. Each year added to the uncertainty of their positions and laws were gradually closing round them.

In 1905, when some of them had grown to believe that they again had a foothold in Memphis, the Legislature passed an act authorizing taxing districts to suppress gaming houses and punish gaming by fine and imprisonment, this act taking from taxing districts the "power to control and regulate" and to make it their duty to suppress gaming houses.*

The trusts, so steadily gaining power all over the country, affected Memphis as well as other places and the increase in cost of living was very noticeable.

The year 1903 found the street-car service very insufficient for city needs. In September of that year the company added thirty new cars and it was required under the franchise of the company that they do $100,000 worth of street paving. In December this company was given a fifty-year franchise. In 1905 it changed hands after which further improvements were made.

A bill was framed for the Legislature of 1903, amending the Memphis charter, but many people objected to its provisions and at the same time it went to the Capitol, a petition went, signed by 13,000 Memphis citizens, to defeat the same. One of the objectionable provisions was the creation of the office of tax-assessor; that officer to be elected by the council. Many citizens said that this and other objects of the bill would bring back some of the old conditions before 1879. After much fighting for and against, the bill was passed with a proviso

---
*Acts of 1905.

that it should be submitted to Memphis people for approval or rejection at an election to be held in July. At this time the tax-assessor was to be elected by the people, but in the meantime one was to be employed by the city government of their own choosing.

Scarcity of money was very apparent in 1903 and the mayor felt the necessity of curtailing asphalt and other city work, but there was a great demand for building and the general growth of the city was steady. The amusements were all well patronized, the streets were crowded and old residents saw many more new than familiar faces on the streets. The postal increase was large, bank clearings excellent and the public school system had grown to be more extensive than that of any other city in the state.

The Commercial Appeal said at this time: "You can hear the town growing early in the morning before the street-cars are running."

Mayor Williams entered upon his second term without opposition, but politics later caused dissensions, as is so often the case where there are many men of many minds. These dissensions continued and increased as the years went on.

The News made war on the Williams administration, accusing it of profligate expenditure of the city's money, etc., while others complained because the mayor tried to reduce expenses. He said there should be no extensive civic improvements while the city funds were so low. The added territory gave more responsibility, more work to be done and more people to be satisfied or dissatisfied.

The bank clearings of 1904 exceeded those of 1903 twenty-two per cent, and the increase for ten years previous was 171 per cent, while the Clearing House showed an increase of $48,000,000 over 1903. Building permits for this same year showed $3,274,398.35 and the volume of trade, $436,000,000.

In 1905 Memphis streets were renamed and the names placed on corners. Those running north and south were called streets and those running east and west, avenues. Many old land-marks like DeSoto, Hernando, and others originally named for early settlers and builders of Memphis had their names changed, which change was not to the liking of many old residents.

In the summer of 1905 yellow fever made its appearance in New Orleans and other Southern points, but the *Commercial Appeal* said "Memphis is serene."

The mosquito theory was prevalent by that time and the health officers in their house to house inspection saw that no water was allowed to stand in pools, barrels, or otherwise. Cisterns were condemned as mosquito breeders and people forced to use city water. Dr. Albright, president of the State Board of Health at that time, declared Memphis to be "a health resort," so favorable were her health reports.

Many business people were opposed to quarantine, but after a mass meeting held to discuss the subject, the matter was left in the hands of Mayor Williams and Dr. Jones, President of the Board of Health. They decided quarantine to be safe and that too much was at stake to act recklessly.

Meetings were held by business exchanges, city officials and others, all coming to the final agreement that while quarantine would inconvenience business and travelers, it and cleanliness were the safest methods. Quarantine went into effect July 29, and after being enforced became very strict. It was not lifted until October. Rumors got abroad occasionally that someone had the disease in Memphis but these were wholly false and the fever did not get into the city at all.

On November 23, following the excellent management of the "fever scare," there was a meeting held in the Cotton Exchange Building, where Dr. Heber Jones was presented with a check of $10,000, a gift from Memphis citizens, in appreciation of his splendid services to the city. Doctor Jones had given up a very large and lucrative practice to become President of the Board of Health, that he might serve the city, and had been unsparing of himself in pursuing the duties he had taken upon himself, and the fact of the yellow fever being kept entirely from our borders and so preventing untold calamity to the city, was most largely due to his vigilance.

In presenting him with the check Mr. Caldwell made the presentation speech and gave the doctor a book containing the names of several hundred subscribers to the gift. After Doctor Jones responded, expressing deep feeling for Memphis people and their appreciation of his services, he was tendered an ovation.

In 1905 the Circuit Court work had become so heavy that three new divisions were added, Judge Walter Malone being appointed to the second division, Judge A. B. Pittman to the third and Judge H. W. Laughlin to the fourth. The judge of the fourth division was given jurisdiction of divorce proceedings before that time vested in the second circuit court, which was abolished.

*James H. Malone*

# CHAPTER XII

J. H. Malone Elected Mayor. Attack Upon Charter. Commission Government Established and Declared Unconstitutional. Reduction of Tax Rate. Flippin Compromise Bonds Refunded. Police Department Work. Improvement of Water System. The City's Real Estate. Front Foot Assessment Law. Pensioning Policemen. City Limits Again Extended. Greater Memphis. Resume of Progress, 1909.

IN THE fall of 1905, Messrs. J. J. Williams and James H. Malone had an animated race for the mayoralty. There were rousing mass-meetings for nights before the election and each candidate set forth in his platform unfailing attention to streets and other civic improvements, schools, taxes, etc. The election was held November 9, and Mr. Malone was elected. The opposing faction claimed that his election was fraudulent and tried to keep the new mayor from going into office, but he entered upon his turbulent duties in January, 1906. Much work was accomplished during that year, despite the depleted treasury and political upheaval, and Mr. Malone carried on with zest improvements begun by Mr. Williams, besides instituting many new ones.

Enemies of his administration did not cease to contend that the election had been fraudulent, and they elected to the Legislature of 1907 members who promised to have the city charter annulled, that the mayor and other officials might be removed from office and others put in their places. They succeeded temporarily in their plan, passed the commission bill and Mayor Malone was ejected from office. The case was appealed to the Supreme Court and there it was decided that the newly made commission form of government was unconstitutional, so two months after the Malone officials had been put out of office they returned to take up the broken threads of their work. This disorganization of government had not been beneficial to the city and hampered the administration, but by degrees matters became adjusted and the administration continued its work.

There were disheartening conditions in some respects. City debts amounted to $200,000, some of these being of several year's standing. In order to do the essential work on streets, bridges, sewers, etc., it was necessary to make an overdraft of $87,950.18, while the fire, police and health departments were each forced to make overdrafts to meet their expenses.

Mayor Malone believed in the granolith sidewalks, that his predecessor had introduced and he had many miles of board, cinder and old brick sidewalks replaced with the smooth, satisfactory walks of granolith. He also had old wooden bridges removed and concrete put in their places and muddy streets, walks and roads lessened appreciably as this administration progressed in its work.

In the beginning of his term Mr. Malone could see no way to reduce taxes and carry on city expenses, but as good management lessened these and adjustments in general grew, the taxes were lowered in 1907 to $1.97, and a year later to $1.91, the lowest taxes Memphis had had for thirteen years. The mayor complained that the railroads, street railways, light, telegraph and telephone companies did not pay their share of city taxes, and at the beginning of 1908, the assessments of these different companies was increased nearly $2,000,000. Mayor Malone's report showed that "The city derived from these public utility corporations in 1907 in ad valorem taxes $96,722.04, which includes the North Memphis levee, park and Cossitt Library special taxes."

In 1905 the Legislature had repealed the variable ward tax-rates of the city and provided that all wards of the city should be uniformly taxed. This in turn was repealed in 1907, but it was not enacted that the former three rates should be revived and they were not. Later the bill was passed for a commission form of government, which also sanctioned uniform taxation throughout the city and this has since been the rule.

The Mayor's report showed that during 1906-7, $196,000 of the "Flippin Compromise Bonds" had been cancelled and retired, leaving still outstanding $551,000, all bearing six per cent interest. Later, "the refunding bonds to redeem the Flippin Compromise Bonds were sold for $1,025.70 each, so that applying the premium received on the bonds it only became necessary to issue $537,000 of these bonds, this reducing the principal of the indebtedness $14,000. These new bonds mature in 1939 and bear only 4½ per cent interest, whereas the Flippin bonds bore six per cent."

It was shown that the indebtedness of the city was then one-thirteenth of the taxable values, while in 1879 it had been one-third.

The Police Department had in 1908 a force of 146, with George T. O'Haver, chief. Chief O'Haver gave an excellent report of the work done in his department during 1907, showing that the department had gradually been increased, but he complained that the force was still far from being numerically sufficient. He stated that Memphis, on account of her geographical position, is a difficult city to patrol and protect, as criminals and fugitives from Tennessee, Arkansas, Mississippi and Alabama come here or often get into mischief here while enroute to other cities. To quote from Chief O'Haver: "Memphis is along the great highway of travel between the North and South, also the East and West, and with its eleven railroads and water transportation, navigable all the year, it presents an attraction to thieves to commit depredations not possessed by any other city, and the means for criminals to escape on account of its proximity to other states are unsurpassed."

The amount of stolen property recovered that year by the fourteen detectives was $22,705.60 and these "plain clothes men" captured many noted criminals in Memphis. One of the duties of the detectives is to protect the traveling public at railroad stations day and night. The chief praised Miss Mary E. Roark's work and said: "She has ever proved equal to the exigencies of the occasion, no matter if the distressed was a reputable woman or one of the unfortunates of the world."

The department at that time had forty police signal boxes,

which had proved all that had been argued for them when the council had been importuned to get them. The Gamewell system had been adopted by Memphis, built at a cost of $10,000, and the forty boxes in operation enabled policemen in all twenty-two wards of the city to keep in touch with one another.

Of the police station building, Chief O'Haver said: "Central Station still remains the nightmare of the department. Its dangerous condition, together with its lack of facility to properly shelter officers and men, and also those arrested, continues to deserve the severe criticisms that grand juries for teh past ten years have never failed to call public attention to, both to its insanitary surroundings and insecurity."

Owing to the crowded condition of the uptown district, the properly policing that portion of the city, as well as policing parks and other places of amusement, caused parts of the city to be neglected, and the Chief said that some people, ever ready to criticise the police service, do not take into consideration, or perhaps do not know, how difficult it is to give proper police protection to a large city, with all of its various demands, without sufficient men to do the work.

Chief O'Haver also thought that everything should be done to raise the standard of the policemen themselves, such as paying them good salaries and enabling them to look forward, after years of faithful service, to pensions for their old age or disability.

The Board of Health used quite an overdraft on their funds during the year 1908, but they did much toward cleaning up the city and worked hand in hand with the Council in getting the city as a whole in good condition. Doctor Raymond was president of the board at that time, and he was an earnest worker.

Among improvements that he and his assistants accomplished was the removal of garbage boxes from streets and putting them in alleys and back-yards, and having the wooden ones, as they wore out, substituted by galvanized iron cans. The removal of these boxes took from the streets many unsightly nuisances. Alleys received careful inspection and those up town, especially, were thoroughly cleaned and ordered kept so. Some of the street workmen were appointed to this special work and were called the "alley gang." This gang removed during 1907 25,000 cartloads of dirt of various sorts.

Food inspection had become strict and the city attorney, Mr. Thos. H. Jackson, said that enforcing the laws in regard to milk and other pure food restrictions took much of the time of himself and his assistants.

In 1906 the city authorities decided that the "tunnel" system of obtaining water for the city supply was not the best method. It was impossible to abandon the system, as the city plant, with its tunnels and lifts was too extensive for this, but all new works were to be put in according to more advanced methods. In 1906 three air-compressors and pumps were put in in New South Memphis, and in January, 1907, a new "air-lift" plant was erected at the corner of Central and Tanglewood Avenues. It consisted "of five 150-horsepower boilers, five air compressors with a capacity of 500 cubic feet free air per minute each and five 1,000,000-gallon pumps. The maximum capacity of this plant is about 7,500,000 gallons daily, with a normal capacity of 5,000,000 gallons." Six wells were connected with this plant and all were pronounced good.

The water commissioners, comprising Messrs. Wirt J. Wills, James S. Davant and Robert E. Lee, were of opinion that this new water system solved the water problem for Memphis.

Besides this new work, improvements had been made in other ways, all the property of the Department kept in thorough repair, and the water pumped was increased 1,000,000 gallons per day, making the daily pumpage 14,000,000, all of which the commission claimed made "1907 the banner year for the Department."

The reduction in rates since the city bought the water plant had been 34 per cent and yet, by 1907 the commissioners declared that the revenue of the Department had increased until it was equal to what it had been under private ownership. The supply continued in its purity and chemists of America and Germany pronounced it the best public water in the United States. The commissioners gave the value of the water plant to be $6,000,000.

Much work had been accomplished on streets and bridges and sewers had been greatly extended. City Engineer J. H. Weatherford complained that the supervision of the city government over new subdivisions had not been enforced as to width and location of streets. In closing his report he advised: "As it is probable that the city limits will be again extended in the near future I would respectfully recommend that some legislation be secured to the end that the city may have some positive control of the location and width of streets opened for public use."

The City Hospital had an excellent report for the year 1907 and although still not self-sustaining, was steadily climbing to that point. The amount received for pay-patients during the year was $56,512.50, and the year's expenses had amounted to $81,417.42. Doctors and nurses had been added to the service of the hospital, and of these the superintendent, Mr. John H. Kibler, said: "I have nothing but praise for the staff-physicians, interns and co-laborers in the care of the sick and injured."

The number of patients received during the year were 2,874 and those treated numbered 3,918. Of this number 3,624 were cured. The greatest number of patients had been, contrary to former reports, from Memphis, these numbering 2,009, the remaining 864 being from Tennessee, Mississippi, Arkansas and other states.

Miss Nell A. Peeler, superintendent of nurses, reported good work from the graduate and pupil nurses, ending: "I desire to speak in the highest praise of our Training School Faculty and the entire staff, for their painstaking and untiring instructions, both at the bedside and in the class room. This enables us to be successful in giving to the public nurses who are competent and thorough."

The real estate and buildings owned by the city of Memphis in 1907, amounted to $5,733,800.00.

Despite any and all drawbacks, Mr. Malone said: "We have every reason to be encouraged for the future and should enter upon the duties of the current year [1908] with renewed energy and hope," and in his next report he declared: "The year 1908 opened under auspicious circumstances."

During 1908 the Mayor proposed that the city limits be extended, both to raise the census of 1910 and from a sanitary and police standpoint, as the immediate suburbs had become very thickly settled, all these inhabitants being strictly Memphis people, making their living in the city, having fire protection without paying city taxes, and enjoying other advantages the city gives.

The front-foot assessment law was enforced in Memphis this year and brought about much complaint, as any new form of taxation always arouses a people, no matter how much good the tax might do the city. This law provided that abutting owners of property should pay two-thirds of the expense of street improvement work done in front of their property, and sixty per cent of the owners on any street could petition for the improvement of their street. In this last case the mayor thought the city should be given the initiative of judging which streets needed attention first. The city, in addition to its one-third of the entire expense of work under this law was "liable for certificates of indebtedness used to cover the cost of the other two-thirds falling on the property holder. In addition to this it is ruled by our legal department that in case it becomes necessary to relay water-pipes or to lay down sewers in advance of a permanent improvement on the street, that the city must pay the entire cost thereof, and no part thereof is chargeable to the property owner. It will thus be seen that as compared with other cities an undue portion of the cost of improvements must fall on the city."

So long as the Flippin Bonds were current, Memphis could not issue any liability bonds, but these being refunded in 1908, the city had the power to issue general liability bonds, the first time she had enjoyed that privilege for forty years. During this period of two score years all improvements had been made by direct taxation. "In the meantime the city was allowed in all these years to collect in addition privilege taxes, and the

Legislature likewise levied special taxes, such as for Parks, Cossitt Library, North Memphis Levee, etc."*

Mr. Malone urged the issuance of bonds for city improvements and said in defense of the act:

"We have gone through war, pestilence and financial panic; in short, we have borne the heat and burden of the day, and have now in the rough a city of the most flattering possibilities of any in this broad land, and why should we not make it a finished city?

"We certainly will hand it over to the generation that succeeds us as a valuable asset, and surely our successors can care for the small liability with such a splendid inheritance.

"There will be opposition to the issue of any bonds. We have the pessimist and doubter always with us. There are men still living who violently opposed sewering the city, although it was the only redemption of the city from pestilence. Likewise the purchase of our present water system, so superbly successful and an absolute necessity for our health, was vigorously opposed, and the same pessimists held up their hands in horror when it was proposed to purchase our magnificent large parks, which have been so well brought into public use as to meet universal approval."

Granolith sidewalks grew in favor and they, with all the other civic improvements going forward certainly benefitted Memphis so materially that one of the inhabitants of early days coming back to visit her many mudless streets and sidewalks would have marveled indeed, and might have thought that an earthquake had occurred and left the city a rocky foundation instead of the bottomless clay and mud of his own time.

In 1908 Chief O'Haver was succeeded in office by that faithful servant who had served Memphis so long as an officer of the peace, Chief W. C. Davis. In a report given in June, 1909, this ever just man said:

"In presenting the statistical figures, I wish to give credit to ex-Chief of Police, George T. O'Haver, who as head of the department all during the year 1908, is entitled to all praise for

*From speech of Mayor Malone, given to Business Men's Club in November, 1908.

the efficiency shown and for the discipline of the department during the year past. He resigned last February, after an honorable career as a police officer of the city extending over a period of thirty-two years."

By this time Memphis contained twenty-two square miles and had become a very difficult and expensive problem for her city fathers to manage. Her size and importance entitled her to first-class advantages of all kinds and her people wanted her to have them. Chief Davis said:

"Citizens generally are fast realizing that municipalities are costly luxuries, when being conducted on lines of latest improved methods in all branches of government, and there is no reason why Memphis should not compare favorably with other metropolitan cities, both as to the strength of its police force and its most modern equipments."

The pension so long asked for policemen and firemen was given in 1909 by an act of the Legislature in which:

"The city of Memphis is hereby empowered to create a fund for the purpose of pensioning members of the police and fire departments of the city, and to compensate members of said departments or their families in case they are killed or injured in the discharge of their duties as members of the said department."

Section 3, of this Act provided "That the city shall have power in cases where any member of said departments shall have been injured, in the discharge of his duty, to make provision for his compensation."

Section 4, "That the city have power in cases where any member of said departments shall have been killed, in the discharge of his duty, to make provision for the compensation of his family."

Section 6, "That the city shall levy a special tax of not more than one cent on the $100 of taxable property for the purpose of creating a fund with which to meet the expenses and carry out the purposes of this Act."

Mr. Jackson, the City Attorney, had much work during 1908 and 1909 straightening city law affairs and trying to keep them straight. There were many law-suits to handle and of his assistants in the work he said, in his report to the Mayor and Council:

"In speaking of these matters I desire to call the attention of your honorable body to the fact that Mr. Marion G. Evans and Mr. James L. McRee, my assistants, have done more than their share of the work and labor in the trial and disposition of the matters set forth in this report. The industry and ability of these two gentlemen has made it possible for this department to handle the immense amount of work entailed upon it."

Mr. Jackson gives some idea of his work in the closing paragraph of his report, as follows:

"I have been constantly called upon for advice and services by the various departments of the city government. Among the more important of these matters have been the preparation of the Union Depot ordinance, which required the greatest care and very laborious work. I have also been called upon to look into the extents and limits of the Southern Railway's right of way through the City of Memphis, and the right which that railroad had to extend the limits of its right of way. I have also been called upon to examine the authorities and advise the city with reference to its right to require the railroad companies to rebuild the Madison Street bridge. I have been called on to draw contracts and ordinances at various times. The Engineering Department, the City Judge, the License Inspector, the Building Inspector and the City Register have called upon us for opinions and advice at various times."

Reverting to the water department, its largest well was dug in 1908, on Central Avenue. The pipe leading to this new water supply measured thirteen inches, inside diameter, and the yield from the well was 2,500,000 gallons per day. There were also laid during this year twelve miles of mains, giving 191 miles in the entire water system.

The growth of this department under municipal ownership and management continued favorable and never ceased to be a satisfactory arrangement. The secretary of the water department, Mr. Sanford Morison, said that "Notwithstanding the various reductions in rates, gross earnings for 1904 were

$378,340.04. For the year 1908 the gross earnings were $383,881.40."

Mr. Morison's general balance sheet showed the property in 1908 to be worth $3,080,446.87.

During the term of the Legislature of 1909 numerous bills concerning Memphis were passed, some of these being of vital importance to the city. One of these, passed February 27, and approved March 6, changed the limits of the city, as follows:

"Beginning on the line of midstream of the Mississippi River at a point where the south line of the Speedway is laid off immediately east of Moore Avenue if extended west would intersect said midstream line, and running thence east with the south line of the said Speedway (said Speedway being known here as 'Kerr Avenue') to the southeast corner of said Speedway and Victor Avenue; thence east with the south line of said Speedway to a point where it turns north; thence north to the southeast intersection of said Speedway and Kerr Avenue; thence east with the south line of Kerr Avenue to the northeast corner of Cavalry Cemetery; thence north to the south line of the Speedway (known here as 'Austin Avenue') thence east with the south line of the Speedway to the southeast corner of said Speedway and Locke Avenue; thence due east to the east line of Trezevant Avenue; thence north to the east line of Trezevant Avenue to the south line of the Speedway; thence east with the south line of the Speedway to the east line of the Speedway; thence north following the east line of the said Speedway (said Speedway being known as 'Trezevant Avenue'), to the northeast corner of Trezevant and Summer Avenue; thence north with the east line of Trezevant Avenue to the old Raleigh Road (also known as 'Jackson Avenue'); thence west with the north line of the old Raleigh Road or Jackson Avenue to a point where it intersects the west line of Springdale Avenue; thence north with the west line of Springdale Avenue to the northwest intersection of the said Springdale Avenue and the right of way of the Louisville and Nashville Railroad; thence west to the northeast corner of the present city limits; thence westwardly on the north line of the present city limits (being the south line of Volentine Avenue) to a point where the west line of Jones Avenue if projected south would intersect said north line of present city limits; thence north to the northwest intersection of Jones Avenue and the New Raleigh Road; thence west on a direct line to the southwest corner of Maple and Chestnut Streets; thence west with the south line of Maple Street to the southeast corner of Maple Street and Thomas Street; thence west on a direct line to midstream of Wolf River; thence southwardly with the meanderings of the midstream line of Wolf River and Manigault Canal to the line of midstream of the Mississippi River; thence southwardly with the meanderings of the midstream line of the Mississippi River to the point of beginning."

The last year of the Malone administration saw quite as much accomplished as the previous year and some of the work progressed faster than formerly. The government was conducted on a cash basis which, Mr. Malone said, was "the only true policy." Still, overdrafts were drawn and owed in the different departments, the Engineering Department alone, owing, by 1909, an overcheck of nearly $500,000.

Among other improvements for streets attention was turned to getting rid of dust. Sprinkling obviated much of this evil but on warm days the water soon soaked into the streets or evaporated and on driveways much traveled, dust could not be kept down long even by heavy sprinkling. Crude oils had been tried to some extent by a hand system and had been partly successful, but raw oils and tar were found to be hurtful to the streets. A distilled tar, made from bituminous coal, had proved so satisfactory in other places that Memphis decided to use it and an automatic tar-spraying machine was purchased by the city, on Mr. Malone's recommendation and proved successful and economical when it arrived in 1910.

The rate of taxes was fixed for 1909 at $1.76. The taxable property in Memphis at that time was valued at $84,058,431.46, an increase of $43,740,221.46 since 1900.*

The debts of the city at this time, not backed by property subject to sale, amounted to $3,195,000.

In 1908 a woman sanitary inspector had been appointed by

*Mr. Malone's Message.

the Fire and Police Commissioners and by the end of 1909 her report showed that she had filled a real need. Among other accomplishments this active woman investigated the condition of factories and stores where women were employed and remedied many evils found thereby, some of these conditions having been almost unbelievable. Many Memphis employers, like those of other parts of the world, grow in prosperity without considering the comfort or convenience of those who are assisting in their business growth, unless forced to do so. Mayors and other city officials have it in their power to remedy many of these evils and Memphis employees as well as the public at large have much cause for gratitude, in this respect, to the late mayors and commissioners of the city.

This inspector also discovered numerous unsanitary kitchens and other places not so apt to be discovered by men, which were ordered cleaned and kept so. She also aided much in keeping the pure food laws enforced.

The chief sanitary inspector was changed from a physician who, on account of his practice, could give only limited time to city duties, to a layman who could give all of his time to the work and supervision of the work of those under him.

For many years subways for street-cars and other vehicles of travel had been advocated, as accidents often occurred where these crossed railroad tracks. Two unsuccessful ordinances had been passed for constructing subways, but on December 24, 1909, an ordinance was passed which provided for the building of eleven subways in Memphis, the bulk of the cost to be borne by the railroads, including incidental damages. As the cost of these constructions amounts to millions of dollars, the advantages to Memphis from a financial point of view, in addition to lessening danger to an untellable degree, is very great.

These new subways were to be a continuation of a system already begun, two having been built and others ordered.

It was a boast of the Malone administration that they left $240,000 in bank for their successors and that during the period of their supervision there had been no misappropriations; also that the city books had at all times been open to inspection.

One achievement of Mr. Malone's which was not required by his official duties, but that took much time and trouble, was the beginning of a collection of portraits of the mayors of Memphis.

After much inquiry, request, correspondence, etc., fourteen portraits were secured, painted and placed in the city hall in the courthouse. On December 12, 1909, there was an article in the *Commercial Appeal,* giving cuts of these portraits and a short sketch of each mayor represented. On December 28 of that year, Senator Turley presented the portraits to the city in a most excellent address.

These portraits include: Marcus B. Winchester, Edwin Hickman, Addison H. Douglass, John Johnson, John R. Flippin, John Overton, W. D. Bethel, Isaac Rawlings, Gardner B. Locke, John Park, John Loague, D. T. Porter, David P. Hadden, W. L. Clapp.

Another portrait has since been added, that of Seth Wheatley, and one of Mr. Malone has been painted but not yet presented to the city.

It is well for the city to revere those who have helped in her building and as mayors have much to do with this development, it seems a justifiable tribute to have them so honored. Would that we might have all our benefactors, men and women, kept before succeeding generations.

# CHAPTER XIII

Commission Form of Government Established. Provisions of the Act. Election of E. H. Crump, as Mayor. Williams Vigorously Contests the Election of Crump. Contest Withdrawn. Reduction of Tax Rate. Extension of Sewer System to Annexed Territory. Mounted Police Station. Vast Construction of New Streets. The City Greatly Beautified. Prohibition in Memphis. Curious Result of the Law. Juvenile Court Established. Splendid Work Among Children. Mounted Police Force. Modern Fire Equipment. Stupendous Municipal Improvements. Increase of Bond Issues. Purchase of Tri-State Fair Grounds. Crump Reelected. Tremendous Flood of Mississippi River. Part of City Overflowed. Water System Contaminated.

---

AN ACT of fifty-three sections, passed April 24, and approved April 27, amended the charter so as to make several changes in the city government. In Section 2, of this Act the name of the "Board of Fire and Police Commissioners" was changed to the "Board of Commissioners of the City of Memphis." This new board of Commissioners was to consist of five members, one of these the Mayor.

To quote from Section 1 of this Act:

"The first Board hereunder shall consist of the four members of the present Legislative Council of the City of Memphis, whose terms expire in November, 1911, and of a Mayor, who shall be elected by the people of the city of Memphis on the first Thursday after the first Monday in November, 1909. The qualifications of said Mayor and of the members of said Board of Commissioners shall be those now required by law for the members of the present Legislative Council, and the Mayor shall have the additional qualifications now provided by law for said office; *provided, however,* that no person shall be ineligible to said office because of having heretofore held said office."

Section 3 provided, "That the said Board of Commissioners shall have and exercise all the powers and discharge all the duties now vested in and imposed upon the present Board of Fire and Police Commissioners, the present Board of Public Works, and the Present Legislative Council, together with such other powers and duties as are hereinafter prescribed."

Section 4: "The Board of Public Works is hereby abolished, and the powers and duties now vested in and imposed upon said Board and the several members thereof by law are hereby vested in and imposed upon the said Board of Commissioners and the several members thereof."

The Board of Health management was thus changed in Section 5: "The Board of Health as at present constituted is hereby abolished, and in lieu thereof is established a subordinate department to be known as the 'Health Department,' to be under the supervision and control of the Department of Public Affairs which said department shall perform the duties and functions heretofore performed by the Board of Health."

Section 7, fixed the salary of the Mayor at $6,000 per annum and that of the other members of the Board at $3,000 and further provided that "No member of said Board of Commissioners shall, directly or indirectly, receive any other or greater compensation than that just provided."

Section 9 provided "That at the first meeting of the said Board of Commissioners or at some meeting within thirty days thereafter there shall be elected by said Board the following officers, whose terms of office and whose annual compensation shall be as herein indicated, as follows:

"City Attorney, two years, $3,600; City Judge, two years, $2,500; City Engineer, two years, $3,000; City Clerk, two years, $3,000; Chief of Police, one year, $2,700; Chief of Fire Department, one year, $2,700; City Paymaster, two years, $2,000; City Chemist, one year, $2,400; Superintendent of Health Department, two years, $3,000; Clerk of City Court, one year, $1,800; City Plumbing Inspector, one year, $1,500; City Meat Inspector, one year, $1,500; City Boiler Inspector, one year, $1,680; Collector of License and Privilege Taxes, one year, $1,500; Wharfmaster, one year, $1,500; Marketmaster, one year, $1,200; City Veterinary Surgeon, one year, $1,200; Gas and Electric Light Inspector, one year, $1,500; City Harnessmaker, one year, $1,200; Inspector of Weights and Measures, one year, $1,800; Superintendent of City Hospital, one year, $1,500; Electric Inspector, one year, $2,000; Building Inspector, one year, $2,500.''

In case of varied opinions as to departmental duties, Section 16 of this Act provided ''That whenever a difference of opinion shall arise as to what department embraces a particular work or matter, either because the same is not herein specially provided for or because of the difference of opinion as to the proper construction of the foregoing sections, the question shall be determined by the Board of Commissioners in regular session, and their conclusion shall be final and binding.''

Memphis was authorized by this Legislature of 1909 to issue bonds for a police station and engine house and a ''Police Station Building Commission,'' was also appointed, consisting of Messrs. Dwight M. Armstrong, Henry E. Craft and Dave Halle, to serve ''until the police station building * * * * shall have been completed and turned over to the city of Memphis.'' This also included the Engine House.

Mr. Malone was succeeded in office January 1, 1910, by E. H. Crump, who was elected under the Commission form of Government, making him mayor and commissioner of Public Affairs and Health. Mayor Crump defeated J. J. Williams.

The old controversy as to the validity of this form of government arose and kept the new administration much vexed but the new commissioners started into their work vigorously, notwithstanding, and continued to accomplish city improvements begun in the last administration and to introduce new ones. Their right to transact business was denied by their opponents and everything that depended upon the legality of the charter was attacked until late in June, when the Supreme Court sustained the charter and decided other cases in favor of the Commission form of Government.

It was charged that the election itself had been fraudulent, which accusation brewed and simmered until October, 1910, when the long complicated case of Crump vs. Williams was brought in Judge J. P. Young's First Division of the Circuit Court. Technicalities became so involved that the attorneys had much ado to untangle the web and to present the case in proper form before the court.

In order to settle the question of the votes beyond a doubt, Judge Young ordered a recount of all the ballots and an investigation of the names of the voters in all the questioned wards, a tedious operation that was much complained of but which settled the controversy, bringing the wrangling to an undisputed end. The recount showed that Mr. Crump was elected mayor by an increased majority. Mr. Williams gracefully withdrew his contest.

After this legal controversy was over the new administration began work vehemently on municipal affairs and the improvement of the city sprang forward with a bound.

Some of the things accomplished in the years 1910 and 1911, were: collection in the fee-earning departments of more money than had been previously collected; reduction of taxes to $1.59; collection of the full amount of turnpike dues from the County Court, amounting to $22,500; the removal of many unsightly shacks, which were replaced by more modern and sanitary buildings; extension of the sewer system to the territory annexed in 1909; creation of the office of purchasing agent for the city, whose duty it is to buy all city necessities after bids have been taken, thus saving money for the city; erecting a mounted police station on Barksdale Avenue; remodeling the old section of the City Hospital and building another wing; constructing 30.6 miles of streets and paving 9.60 miles under the front-foot assessment plan; and succeeding in securing from banks 3½ per cent interest on city money, on deposit.[*]

Municipal ownership of the Light plant has been agitated and continues to be discussed as a great benefit to the city, the success of water ownership being held up as an example. Much

[*] From statements in a booklet entitled "One Year Eight Months under Commission Form of Government."

has also been said about reducing telephone rates so that all citizens may have them and all patrons enjoy better service.

The present administration believe they have solved the intricate city-bookkeeping problem, and the mayor says that "under Ennis Douglass, city clerk, and Albert D. Perkins, bookkeeper," the system "will compare favorably with that used in any big wholesale house in the country."

Mayor Crump, in proof of the fact that he thinks first of the city's good in what he does, states that he has not ridden on a railroad pass during his connection with the city government, nor accepted free favors from any corporation, man or set of men; that he has refrained from associating himself with any concern that might have business dealings with the city, and that, despite false charges, neither he nor any member of the administration has been guilty of any sort of graft.

During this administration much work has been done on the subways and great is the benefit accrued and yet to be realized from them.

The conduit system of wires has also been extended and by degrees unsightly poles and criss-cross wires are being lost from view. The poles that must remain are painted and made as pleasing to the eye as possible. Many ugly light-posts have been removed and symmetrical, pleasing ones put in their places. Everything that adds to the beauty of the city is educational to its people and, with improving aesthetic taste, comes a refining of the whole public nature. Through physical beauty our people may come to a moral beauty worthy of a municipality striving to climb the hill of progress. The mayor, city commissioners and public-minded citizens of Memphis have spent thought, time and money in trying to beautify her precincts and the beneficiaries feel grateful as they drive or walk through the beautiful streets on clean, smooth roadways or grass-bordered walks; stroll or rest in the splendid parks or study nature in the wild places of some of them; enjoy the luxury of city benefits, given in artistic form, and behold buildings and sculpture worthy a larger and older city than ours.

Inasmuch as lawlessness and trouble with saloons and

gamblers have been chronicled at intervals through this history, it is but fair to mention the present condition of affairs, as it presents a curious phase of the latest attempt at statewide prohibition. When the prohibition law went into effect in Tennessee in 1911, Memphis saloon-keepers, supposing that the law passed by the Legislature of the State must be a final dictum, at least until some legislative act of the future should repeal it, were ready to leave the city. Many had already left and some of these men had put their capital into other kinds of business. For a time it looked as if saloons and gambling were to be evils of the past in Memphis and it was rare that a drunken man was to be seen. Even some people who did not approve of the principle of prohibition declared it good to see the places closed where youth was so often tempted. But it was whispered, then spoken aloud, that this law was not a popular law and that therefore the saloon-keepers should not be forced to obey it. Many business men openly asserted these views and the press took up the cry. Saloons were reopened surreptitiously at first, but seeing that no attempt was made to close them their proprietors became bolder and by degrees opened wide the doors that the law said must be closed. Others followed the example of the leaders and soon the city was as "wide open" as to saloons, as it had ever been. Whichever theory is correct as to the merits of the prohibition law, open defiance of law, in whatever way that defiance may be practiced, is most prejudicial to a city and gives her citizens a growing contempt for law in general.

Memphis has now been nearly a century fighting for and against the moral part of her development and one can but wonder at the final outcome.

One institution has come into being under Mr. Crump's administration that is calculated to perform a work of untold good and to counteract many evil influences that surround young boys and girls in unfortunate environments, and that is the Juvenile Court.

Much is already known of the workings of the Juvenile Court from Judge Lindsey and other great souls who have wrought so much benefit to humanity by its force and it is good for Memphians to know that we have here more than a nucleus of a most excellently conducted court for the young. The need of such a safe-guard has been felt in Memphis for a great many years and in 1905 the first enactment was passed by the state providing for it. The good of that proceeding, however, stopped with the enactment itself, as no advantage was taken of its privilege to establish such a court.

In 1907 this Act was amended so that only counties containing 100,000 or more inhabitants could establish such courts, jurisdiction being conferred upon all city courts of such counties. Still no juvenile court became part of the Memphis city government and child "criminals" were tried in police courts or committed by judges to an Industrial school or other place of confinement. In 1909 the law was again amended, giving juvenile courts to counties of 150,000 or more inhabitants, and this amended act made it compulsory that all children under sixteen years of age be tried for misconduct only by an officer given the authority of a juvenile judge.

Memphis still hesitated and did not put into form a court for the betterment of her children, but interest had been aroused in the subject and it had obtained numerous friends.

Ten days after Mr. Crump entered upon his duties as mayor, the Juvenile Court of Memphis was established under his authority, with Judge Kelly on the bench. Judge Kelly was interested in his young charges from the beginning and the court was soon accomplishing much good.

The first Advisory Board consisted of Mrs. T. H. Scruggs, chairman, Mrs. Benjamin West, secretary, and Mr. George W. Pease. These members held office for one year and helped many boys and girls during their term of service.

The first probation officers were Messrs. William Eifler, H. H. Chamberlain and R. L. Christy. These officers were detailed from the police department and all proved excellent factors in the new work, contrary to the prediction of some who said that men from the police force could never serve efficiently in juvenile court work.

In 1911 the Juvenile Court Act was again amended and

this time was quite fully treated, having become an important part of the law's business.

All delinquent and dependent children up to the age of sixteen years are taken in charge by this court. A delinquent child is one "who violates any law of the state or any city or town ordinance, or who is incorrigible, or is a persistent truant from school, or who associates with criminals or reputed criminals or vicious or immoral person, or who is growing up in idleness or crime, or who frequents, visits or is found in any disorderly house, bawdy house or house of ill fame * * * * or in any saloon, barroom or drinking shop or place. * * * * or who patronizes, frequents, visits or is found in any gaming house * * * * or who wanders about the streets in the night time without being on any lawful business or occupation, or who habitually wanders about any railroad yards or tracks or climbs on moving trains * * * * or who habitually uses, vile, obscene, vulgar, profane or indecent language,"* etc.

A dependent child is "any child who, for any reason, is destitute or homeless or abandoned or dependent upon the public for support, or has not proper parental care or guardianship or who is found begging or receiving or gathering alms * * * * or who is found living in any saloon, disorderly house * * * * or with any vicious or disreputable person, or whose home, by reason of neglect, cruelty, drunkenness, or depravity on the part of its parents, guardian or other person in whose care it may be, is an unfit place for such a child, and any child under the age of fourteen (14) years who is found begging, peddling or selling any article or singing or playing any musical instrument upon the streets * * * * or who is used in aid of any person so doing."*

Any reputable resident in the city or county, having knowledge of a delinquent or dependent child, may notify the Clerk of the Juvenile Court, filing with him a petition setting forth the facts of the case.

It is the duty of the clerk, when any child is to be brought before the court, to notify a probation officer, whose duty it then becomes to investigate the case, and "to be present in

*Public Acts of 1911.

court to represent the interest of the child when the case is heard, to furnish such information and assistance as the court may require, and to take charge of any child before or after the trial, as may be directed by the court."

When a child is found by this court to be either delinquent or dependent, "the court may make an order committing the child to the care of some suitable state institution or to the care of some reputable citizen of good moral character, or to the care of some institution provided by law, or to the care of some suitable association willing to receive it, embracing in its objects the purposes of caring for or of obtaining homes for dependent or delinquent children." The city judge is required to "hold his court for the trial of juvenile offenders in a separate place and at a separate time from the courts for the trial of other offenders."

There are many other details to this Act but these quoted give a general idea of the scope of the work of the Juvenile Court.

In 1911 this court was reorganized in Memphis and after the reorganization Mayor Crump appointed Mr. Thomas B. King, chairman, Mrs. Benjamin West, secretary and Mr. G. W. Pease, the other member of the Board. In August of 1911 Judge Kelly was succeeded on the bench by Judge William J. Bacon.

The work went bravely on, Judge Bacon giving much time and thought to judging the young people who came under his direction here, and gaining many confidences from the unmatured young beings who only needed stimulant of the right sort and encouragement to start them on the road to useful man or womanhood.

In the fall of 1910, a colored department of the Juvenile Court was started and the detention home taken in charge by Julia Hooks, a woman who has been working for the betterment of her race for over forty years. Her husband, Charlie Hooks, was made probation officer.

During 1911 Charlie and Julia Hooks had in their charge 288 colored children, all detained from two to ten days. These children had been dependents, or guilty of offenses from petty larceny to murder. Twenty-nine of them were babies and homes were found for all the twenty-nine. Julia said that colored people love children and it is never difficult to find homes for the foundlings. One six-year old had been rescued from an uncle who used the boy to climb into windows and steal goods, many of which were taken in the day time and concealed in a false bottom to the wagon in which the uncle hauled wood.

So far in this year over 180 colored children have been cared for in this department of the Juvenile Court.

Surely no work of any Memphis administration has been of so great importance as this of rescuing the children. If more money were spent on child-work now, less would be spent on prisons and criminal proceedings in the future. We build many improvements for future generations to enjoy and think little of the generations themselves. The greatest human work is building human character and strengthening the moral fiber of the race.

Returning to older municipal affairs, Memphis now has a most excellent police force, numbering 200 patrolmen, mounted police and detectives, with the chief and other officers. The Memphis force makes a splendid appearance when in drill and Major Kit Deffry is employed to drill the men according to military tactics.

The mounted force also receive careful drilling and these men themselves are selected for their good forms, intelligence and good character. They do credit to their drill-master, their city and their calling. These officers of the peace have regular cavalry drilling from Sergeant W. Lee, a United States cavalry man, and in case of riots or other uprisings they and the patrolmen could act as a unit of soldiers.

The fire department is also "up-to-date" and that means much in our age of invention and convenience. The horses of this department are magnificent specimens but they are greatly reduced in numbers by the use of motor power. The engines are works of skill, beauty and strength, as is all the other apparatus, and the engine-houses do credit to their builders. The latest of these is a beautiful white marble-front building next to the elegant new police-station already referred to.

The aerial ladders and other modern equipments would be a marvel to the aldermen of by-gone years who worked so hard to get the "Little Vigor" in order to help Memphis people save their property.

This department is equipped with the Gamewell system of fire alarms and is of course in touch with all the private telephones in the city. It also has access to 225 miles of water mains, with nearly 1,500 hydrants and fifty storage cisterns, ranging from 17,500 to 70,000 gallons.

Engineering work of the past two years has been vast. Since the introduction of tar macadam for streets in 1910, it has proved successful and so has been used a great deal; also creosoted wooden blocks which are placed over a concrete foundation, have proved satisfactory street material. Many of the new neighborhoods taken into the corporation in 1909 have been sewered, and a large sewer-main has been run up Nonconnah Creek, that that remote part of the city may be connected with the city sewerage. This pipe enables the city to dispense with the pumping-station on Wilson Avenue, the one at Kyle Street and the Southern Railway.

During the twenty months for which Mr. Crump reported, one hundred and five streets were paved under the front-foot assessment plan; thirty-four streets and alleys were graded, paved, curbed and guttered; 37.29 mile of sewers laid; 11.7 streets resurfaced; 85 streets and alleys spread with gravel; 14.4 miles of dirt streets rounded up; 30.6 total mileage of completed street pavements laid. Work in all these departments is being assiduously continued, and 1912 has seen much addition to the above.

The city's legal business has so increased that a second assistant attorney has been added to the force of which Charles M. Bryan is city attorney, Leo Goodman, assistant and William M. Stanton, second assistant. It is the duty of the second assistant to look after unpaid taxes, and his first year of work showed an increased collection that proved his need.

In the Health Department, of which Dr. M. Goltman is superintendent, John C. Bell, secretary, Dr. Cummings Harris, health officer, Miss Teresa Manley, bookkeeper, and Mr. June

Sneed, chief sanitary officer, improvements are being made in many directions. The garbage system is being improved and contains about 85 routes, north and south. It is the rule of this department that every portion of the city be visited every day, but the force is not large enough to enable this to be done.

Milk and other pure food laws are strictly enforced and results are beneficial to the city thereby.

A number of bonds have been issued during this administration which, some complain, raises the city debt to appalling figures, but each bond was issued for a specific benefit and, as Mr. Malone expressed it during his administration, with the indebtedness is left an inheritance of great value in the work done.

A street, alley, highway and subway bond of $750,000 has been issued to carry on street improvements and to pay the city's share of the subway expense. This bond was recommended by a citizen's committee of tax payers and was passed by the Legislature of February, 1911.

Another bond, issued by request of the Water Commission, and recommended by a citizens' committee "to extend mains into territory where sewers had been laid, and where the health department was demanding water in the interests of sanitation," was passed last year by the Legislature. This bond is to the amount of $250,000 of negotiable coupon bonds of $1,000 each, to bear interest of not more than 4½ per cent.

A school bond issue of "$250,000 gave the means to complete the new high school, erect a grammar school and make repairs on numerous other buildings."

The Tri-State Fair bond was recommended by the city commissioners and decided on after a meeting of citizens, who indorsed the issuance of such bonds. The Tri-State Fair, given annually in Memphis, has proved to be a successful enterprise and one calculated to bring much future good not only to Memphis, but to all three of the States represented in the enterprise.

$275,000 of negotiable coupon bonds have been issued "for the purpose of acquiring property to be used as public recreation parks and playgrounds, and for the maintenance and equipment of same.''

The City Treasurer has been made the ''tax collector and disburser of the municipal taxes of the city of Memphis including all funds derived from assessments for street improvements and proceeds of all bond sales. He shall have and possess all the powers and be subject to all the duties and obligations now vested in or imposed upon the Treasurer or tax receiver of said city, and his compensation for such service is fixed at three thousand dollars ($3,000) per annum.'' The said City Treasurer and tax collector is nominated by the Commissioner of Accounts, Finances and Revenues, and elected by the Board of Commissioners of the city of Memphis.

Mayor Crump succeeded himself in office in 1912, with Mr. R. A. Utley as vice-mayor.

Chief Davis was succeeded by W. J. Hayes, as Chief of Police, Chief Davis to go to the sub-station. Chief Davis has served Memphis on the police force for forty-two years, entering upon his duties in January, 1870. In 1880 he was appointed chief, and again, after having served as Wharfmaster, Hospital Superintendent and Court Square Guard, in 1908. His service as chief alone has covered eighteen years, and he has witnessed and helped in the development of his department of municipal discipline in Memphis.

The new chief has served a number of years on the force and comes to his new office from that of Inspector of Police. His has also been an up and down experience on the force.

The winter of 1911-12 was an unusually severe one all over the country and the upper Mississippi River was filled was ice, as were its upper tributaries. Ice and snow accumulated for months and in the spring heavy rains fell. The result was a tremendous flood which grew into proportions never before known in the history of the Mississippi Valley. Those of 1858 and 1882 gave forth as great an onrush of waters, but in some respects this flood of 1912 surpassed both of those record breakers.

Levees that had been thought impregnable broke as the waters surged southward and pressed with a terrific force against these safeguards, and each break carried tremendous destruction in its wake, making hundreds of people homeless.

These homeless ones had to be cared for, and as their distresses became known and surmised, Memphis saw the necessity for quick action, in order to save human beings and their stock. By April the situation had grown alarming and a mass meeting was held in Memphis for the purpose of providing ways to help the sufferers. A committee was appointed to solicit funds and provide for their use. This committee consisted of Mr. James F. Hunter, Chairman, and Messrs. W. R. Barksdale, C. O. Scholder, F. G. Barton, Fred B. Jones, T. R. Boyle and R. G. Brown. This committee met April 8, organized and began active duty at once. The first work they did was to have skiffs made and to press other boats into immediate service. With these they rescued people, cattle and other animals in the St. Francis Basin, inundated from the breaking of levees, where loss was very great. People were rescued from tops of houses, trees and floating debris, some of these unfortunates being in half-starved and nearly frozen condition.

The rescue work was pushed speedily and the next task was to provide a place for the shelter of all who were taken up or who were known to be homeless. Clothing and food had also to be provided, most of the rescued having nothing but the bedraggled clothing on their bodies.

Mayor Crump and Vice-mayor Utley coöperated with the committee and they, together with Messrs. J. A. Riechman and Frank Omberg, established a Refugees' Camp at Montgomery Park, and gave it their strict personal attention. In that inclosure over 1,700 people were housed, clothed and fed for six weeks, besides a large number of cattle and stock sheltered and fed for that time.

Realizing the stupendous task of caring for all these beings, military discipline was established and an excellent sanitary system was instituted, in consequence of which the camp was managed throughout with order and satisfaction and won the compliment of being the best managed camp of all that were organized in the valley.

In answer to the call for funds, food and clothing, Memphis and other places responded liberally, and abundance came flowing in without the necessity of any personal solicitations. These contributions were handled by the Committee and the Associated Charities, which organization worked with the city through the whole undertaking.

Some food was sent by individuals and business firms, all of which was gratefully received, but the daily rations were furnished by the government. These consisted of substantial and pure food, served in two plentiful meals a day, and pint bottles of certified milk were furnished for all the babies. Each mother of a babe left the mess-hall after the four o'clock meal, with a pint bottle of this pure rich milk for night use for her little one.

The Government sent aid so promptly that the people felt very grateful, and the work between the Government employes and the committee here was so harmonious that Memphis felt a great bond had been established with the National as well as between the state and municipal government.

Major J. E. Normoyle of the Government Commissary department had his headquarters in Memphis and much credit is due him for the able manner in which he organized the working forces and for the well-managed distribution of supplies. The Memphis Committee were in personal touch with Major Normoyle while he was in Memphis, and in daily communication with him when he went South, in obedience to a call for help in alleviating suffering there, which had become appalling. When this excellent manager left Capt. S. McP. Rutherford took charge of the Memphis district and all went well under his good management. He was ably assisted by Capt. J. A. Logan, Mr. Cooke, Sergeant Edward McCormack and Corporal Henry Brouch.

The territory looked after by Memphis workers was divided into three sections. That section of the river from the city to seventy-five miles north was taken in charge by Messrs. D. H. White and C. O. Scholder; that portion south to Bledsoe's Landing, Arkansas, was under the supervision of Messrs. W. R. Barksdale and Doc Hottum, and the interior country in

East Arkansas, west of Memphis, was in charge of Mr. F. G. Barton.

Major C. D. Smith is due much credit for the valuable aid he rendered in caring for the destitute, as well as those efficient workers, Messrs. James Barton, George W. Blackwell, George T. Webb, Miss Helen Forsdick and others that gave untiring assistance to the cause.

After the waters subsided and the refugees were sent back to their homes, many individual cases of those who had been made destitute by the flood, continued to be cared for, this attention being chiefly turned over to the Associated Charities of Memphis whose employes, headed by Mr. Kranz, served untiringly through the whole period, and they cared for the destitute from many sections.

The flood brought more problems to Memphis than that of caring for the refugees. This visitation of the waters lasted through a long and trying period. The flood stage was passed at this point March 22, after which date the water rose steadily until far into April, before it began to go down again. So much work and expense had been spent on the levees that it was thought they would withhold any flood that might come, but such an unusual catastrophe as the flood of this year was not contemplated. Forty two feet is the mark considered dangerous at Memphis, and when that was reached, the rise continued daily until April 6, when the gauge was 45.3. This was a stage three feet feet higher than the levees had been built to hold. On this date a levee gave way nine miles north of Memphis and another broke about that distance south. These breaks lowered the river but caused the most disastrous damage ever known in the unfortunate districts back of the crevasses, the water rushing in with a fury that carried destruction to everything before it. The United States local forecaster, Mr. S. C. Emory, said that had the levees not broken, the water would have reached a stage of 48 feet.

The fall was slow even after the breaks, and not until May 22, did the water lower to 33 feet, having been above the danger level for sixty-one days. The flood of 1882 was above flood-stage four days longer. The flood of that year, those of

1844 and 1858 and the one of this year are the greatest deluges of the Mississippi River on record.

Most of Memphis is too high to be reached by flood-waters, but a section of less than forty acres in North Memphis and a few other outlying places are low and they were inundated. North Memphis was more overflowed this year than ever before. About twenty-five blocks suffered from this damage, many residences and business buildings being submerged and some mills stopped. Injury to the Gas Works caused the city to be shut off from that supply for many days, a great inconvenience to people dependent on gas for cooking, heating and lighting purposes. Fortunately the electric lights were serviceable through the whole time.

The worst effect to Memphis was contamination of her water supply. Some of the artesian wells supplying the city were in the overflowed district of North Memphis. As the river rose the sewage-pumping station was put out of service and much of the sewage of the city was discharged into the flood waters. When this fact became known it was not thought that any of the wells could be contaminated, but the unusual appearance of the water coming from the Auction Street pumping station about the first of April caused questions to arise, and as this appearance continued and increased, investigation was made. Examination of the water on April 3, showed it to be polluted and later analyses showed the same condition. Soon after this discovery much intestinal trouble became prevalent, followed by an epidemic of typhoid fever, and people in the down-town district were cautioned not to use the water or to boil it before doing so.

By reducing the pressure of the Auction Avenue station and raising it at all other stations, all the impure water was driven into the business section, for use in case of fires and other emergencies not personal. In the residence districts water-pipes were gated off tightly from the pipes connecting with the North Memphis supply and the street-sprinkling department carried pure water for drinking and cooking purposes, to people living in the business district or bordering it.

It was impossible to find the cause of the contamination

while the flood lasted, and all that could be done was to ascertain by constant analyses which water was polluted and which pure. As soon as the flood receded the Water and Health departments began investigations of all the wells and other openings of the artesian supply in North Memphis, and the Health Department took measures to clean and disinfect all streets and residences that had been lately inundated.

Mr. George W. Fuller, consulting engineer of New York City, was asked by the Water Department to come to Memphis the latter part of April for investigation and to make a report on the conditions he found. He arrived April 27th, and with the coöperation of the Health Department, spent three days making a thorough examination, giving his report to the public, May 1st.

He congratulated the work of investigation already made, and said that the City Board of Health had practically completed all of the inspections when he arrived. This inspection had led to the discovery of an opening in Shaft Number 13 on Third Street, thirteen inches long and from four to eight inches in width, through which polluted water had reached the Auction Avenue pumping station.

This break is supposed to have been made three years ago presumably by a steam roller, when the street level was raised above the shaft to make it part of the bayou levee. This long hidden defect in a shaft of such importance to the city water supply certainly represents great negligence on the part of some one, charged with the vital duty of inspection.

Besides this opening it was found that water entered the tunnel below the cover of the same shaft. Mr. Fuller estimated the total opening to be more than eighty square inches in area. He was assured that this opening was the cause of the direful effects of the pollution that caused so much trouble. This defect is at an elevation 40.5 on the river guage.

Mr. Fuller said that "in all probability water did not immediately enter this opening when the river reached this stage, as it was necessary first for the water to wash a pathway from the gutter to the opening on the opposite side of the shaft."

After finding entrance the contaminated water continued to pour into the well until the flood dropped below that guage, which covered a period of nearly three weeks.

Close investigations disclosed no other defective shafts, but the Auction Avenue pumping station itself showed that seepage had entered the dry well in which the pumps are located. It is thought that some of this seepage reached suction wells and added to the contamination.

Mr. Fuller recommended that strict precautions be taken with North Memphis water until the Health Department was thoroughly satisfied with all analyses. He said: "I see no signs of the water and health department officials being derelict in handling the situation, although it is plain that added precautions must be taken to guard against a similar misfortune in the future."

He also recommended that sewers be carefully inspected and kept in thorough condition, and that there be no more use of vaults and surface wells, so that "there will be absolutely no chance whatever for surface pollution to reach the North Memphis water supply."

Mr. Fuller continued: "Employes should be cautioned to take every step possible to avoid polluting wells, shafts, drifts or tunnels when they are working around and in them."

Of our other wells he said: "There is no evidence whatever to indicate that there has been any contamination whatever of the water from the segregated wells of those at East Memphis or South Memphis. They are located well above the flooded area and every analysis that has been made has shown a pure water which may be used with entire confidence."

On the question of abandoning the North Memphis well this engineer said: "It has been very fortunate for your city that you have had other sources of supply than that at North Memphis, and if you can give ordinary water service from sources other than North Memphis at reasonable cost it would be wise to do so. * * * *

"On the other hand, I am clearly of the opinion that it is not necessary or advisable to abandon the North Memphis supply. It is highly urgent to watch it with great care, but even if it is necessary to sterilize the water regularly from that source, as is done in scores of places elsewhere, it is a valuable piece of property which I would not think for a moment of abandoning."

He recommended flushing all pipes, saying: "I consider it highly important to begin at once to flush thoroughly all the water-pipes into which water has been delivered during the past few weeks from the Auction Avenue pumping station. This had best be done by delivering sterilized water from the pumps at their full capacity and opening fire hydrants and plumbing fixtures in different districts, so as to remove all iron deposits and pollution from the bayou water that may have become lodged on the interior surfaces, not only of the street mains, but also the service pipes of the consumers. * * * * When this district is thoroughly flushed another district adjoining it should be similarly treated and so on until all pipes have been thoroughly flushed to points most remote from the pumping station."

Dissatisfaction has been expressed by some of the citizens, that the city should have been subjected to such an experience as the neglected shaft caused which, for a while looked very serious indeed, when so much of the tax-payers' money goes for salaries of inspectors of various sorts, but after the defective shaft was discovered, work went vigorously forward to rectify all errors and this accident will probably insure all the more caution and thorough inspection in all branches of city work in the future.

The city continues to expand. Our own dailies show general growth and papers of other localities compliment the Bluff City.

Following is a list of the mayors, aldermen, councilmen and commissioners of the City of Memphis from 1827:

March, 1827, to March, 1828:—Mayor, M. B. Winchester. Aldermen, Joseph L. Davis, John Hook, N. B. Atwood, Geo. F. Graham, John R. Dougherty, Wm. A. Hardy, Nathaniel Anderson and Littleton Henderson.

March, 1828 to March, 1829:—Mayor, M. B. Winchester. Aldermen, Samuel Douglass, Wm. A. Hardy, John D. Graham,

Augustus L. Humphrey, Joseph L. Davis and Robert Fearn.

March 1829 to March, 1830:—Mayor, Isaac Rawlings. Aldermen, M. B. Winchester, A. L. Humphrey, J. L. Davis, J. F. Schabell, James L. Vaughn, J. D. Graham and Wyatt Christian.

March, 1830 to March, 1831:—Mayor, Isaac Rawlings. Aldermen, John Kitchell, A. L. Humphrey, D. King, E. Young, J. L. Davis, H. W. Mosely, John Coleman, David W. Wood, Geo. Aldred and J. F. Schabell.

March, 1831 to March, 1832:—Mayor, Seth Wheatley. Aldermen. Geo. Aldred, Martin Swope, Ulysses Spaulding, A. L. Humphrey, L. Henderson and Thomas Phoebus.

March, 1832 to March, 1833:—Mayor, Robert Lawrence. Aldermen, John Kitchell, E. Coffee, C. C. Locke, J. C. Walker, L. Henderson and J. A. H. Cleveland.

March, 1833 to March, 1834:—Mayor, Isaac Rawlings. Aldermen, Littleton Henderson, John F. Schabell, Samuel Runkle, Hezekiah Cobb, John W. Fowler, Elijah Coffee and Joseph Cooper.

March, 1834 to March, 1835:—Mayor, Isaac Rawlings. Aldermen, Jedediah Prescott, H. Cobb, M. B. Winchester, John W. Fowler, Littleton Henderson and John F. Schabell.

March, 1835 to March, 1836:—Mayor, Isaac Rawlings. Aldermen, John F. Schabell, James Rose, Joseph Cooper, H. Cobb, Silas T. Toncray, S. M. Nelson and Hugh Wheatley.

March, 1836 to March, 1837:—Mayor, Enoch Banks. Aldermen, Silas T. Toncray, Hannibal Harris, Seth Wheatley, M. B. Winchester, Hugh Wheatley, James Rose, John Hare, S. M. Nelson, R. G. Hart and Joseph Cooper.

March, 1837 to March, 1838:—Mayor, John H. Morgan. Aldermen, Frank McMahan, S. T. Toncray, A. H. Bowman, L. C. Trezevant, Charles Stuart, Zachariah Edmunds, Joseph Cooper, Barnett Graham, H. Cobb and James D. Currin.

March, 1838 to March, 1839:—Mayor, Enoch Banks. Aldermen, Jedediah Prescott, James D. Currin, Lewis C. Trezevant, Lewis Shanks, A. H. Bowman, Edwin Hickman and Gray Skipwith.

March, 1839 to March, 1840:—Mayor, Thomas Dixon.

Aldermen, Jedediah Prescott, Joseph Wright, Samuel Hayter, E. Hickman, C. Stewart, C. B. Murray, William Spickernagle.

March, 1840 to March, 1841:—Mayor, Thomas Dixon. Aldermen, Michael Leonard, Joseph Wright, C. B. Murray, Jacob M. Moon, T. C. McMakin, E. Hickman, L. C. Trezevant, W. B. Garrison.

March, 1841 to March, 1842:—Mayor, William Spickernagle. Aldermen, Joseph Wright, Michael Leonard, L. C. Trezevant, J. N. Moon, Charles Stewart, F. P. Stanton, J. Prescott, H. Cobb, John Trigg.

March, 1842 to March, 1843:—Mayor, Edwin Hickman. Aldermen, C. C. Mahan, V. Ferguson, C. Bias, C. Lofland, E. H. Porter, Wm. Chase, A. Walker, J. C. Davenport, M. Gabbert, W. B. Waldran, H. Cobb, L. Shanks, W. A. Bickford, W. Test, J. Prescott, John Wood, Eugene Magevney.

March, 1843, to March, 1844:—Mayor, Edwin Hickman. Aldermen, J. Prescott, H. Cobb, William Spickernagle, C. Bias, Wm. Chase, E. H. Porter, John Woods, E. Magevney, W. B. Waldran, Calvin Goodman, L. Shanks, Thomas Whitelaw, L. R. Richard.

March, 1844, to March, 1845:—Mayor, Edwin Hickman. Aldermen, Wm. Spickernagle, J. D. Allen, Lewis Shanks, Joseph Wright, Wm. Connell, Charles A. Leath, E. Magevney, J. B. Outlaw, J. T. N. Bridges, M. B. Sappington, Wm. F. Allen, John A. Allen, Calvin Goodman, W. B. Waldran, Dr. Jeptha Fowlkes, John Trigg, David Looney, L. Shanks.

March, 1845 to March, 1846:—Mayor, J. J. Finley. Aldermen, Jos. D. Allen, William Goodman, Jos. Wright, Daniel Hughes, Jeptha Fowlkes, Wm. Chase, David Looney, J. R. Maltbie, E. F. Watkins, Calvin Goodman, Gardner B. Locke, D. S. Greer, E. M. Apperson, Lewis Shanks, Miles Owen, J. Delafield.

March, 1846 to March, 1847:—Mayor Edwin Hickman. Aldermen, Joseph D. Allen, Michael Leonard, Jeptha Fowlkes, Daniel Hughes, D. O. Dooley, E. H. Porter, E. Magevney, Wm. Carter, Wiley B. Miller, Samuel Mosby, E. Banks, A. O. Harris, V. D. Barry.

March, 1847 to March, 1848:—Mayor, Enoch Banks. Aldermen, Joseph D. Allen, J. W. A. Pettit, J. Fowlkes, Daniel Hughes, Wm. Connell, V. D. Barry, S. A. Norton, Joseph I. Andrews, Samuel Mosby, W. B. Miller.

March, 1848 to March, 1849:—Mayor, Gardner B. Locke. Aldermen, Benj. Wright, J. W. A. Pettit, Jeptha Fowlkes, Daniel Hughes, James Wright, V. D. Barry, R. L. Kay, E. Magevney, J. M. Patrick, S. B. Williamson.

March, 1849 to July, 1850:—Mayor, E. Hickman. Aldermen, H. Cobb, T. James, L. Shanks, J. Weller, E. H. Porter, H. B. Joyner, V. Rhodes, E. McDavitt, R. A. Parker, H. G. Smith, D. Looney, A. O. Harris, N. B. Holt, S. W. Jefferson, A. B. Taylor, G. W. Murphy, W. Carr, J. L. Webb, H. L. Guion,

July, 1850 to July, 1851:—Mayor, E. Hickman. Aldermen, Thomas Conway, John Kehoe, E. McDavitt, E. H. Porter, S. W. Jefferson, A. D. Henkle, S. P. Walker, D. Looney, A. B. Shaw, J. Waldran, G. W. Smith, A. B. Taylor.

July, 1851 to July, 1852:—Mayor, E. Hickman. Aldermen, F. Titus, T. Conway, E. H. Porter, E. McDavitt, S. W. Jefferson, A. D. Henkle, David Looney, S. P. Walker, J. M. Patrick, A. B. Shaw, Wm. Ruffin, G. W. Smith, W. S. Cockrell, A. Woodruff, J. D. Danbury.

July, 1852 to July, 1853:—Mayor, A. B. Taylor. Aldermen, J. Kehoe, B. Wright, A. Woodruff, R. W. Thompson, A. D. Henkle, M. Eagan, S. P. Walker, J. D. Danbury, A. B. Shaw, T. W. Hunt, A. N. Edmunds, M. Jones, A. P. Merrill, F. Lane, J. M. Patrick, A. G. Underwood.

July, 1853 to July, 1854:—Mayor, A. B. Taylor. Aldermen, Thos. Conway, Dr. L. Shanks, E. McDavitt, W. M. Maddox, E. Magevney, S. W. Jefferson, S. P. Walker, A. Whipple, T. W. Hunt, J. M. Patrick, Marcus Jones, John Wiley, R. W. Thompson, John Park, Charles Jones.

July, 1854 to July, 1855:—Mayor, A. B. Taylor. Aldermen, John L. Saffarans, Dan'l Hughes, S. B. Curtis, John Neal, A. Street, A. M. Hopkins, A. A. Smithwick, J. L. Morgan, J. M. Patrick, James Jenkins, W. E. Milton, A. H. Douglass, A. Woodruff, W. Houston, J. D. Danbury.

July, 1855 to July, 1856:—Mayor, A. H. Douglass. Aldermen, John L. Saffarans, Dan'l Hughes, S. B. Curtis, John Neal,

A. Woodruff, Jas. Elder, W. R. Chandler, J. D. Danbury, James Jenkins, Jno. L. Morgan, W. E. Milton, F. M. Copeland, A. B. Shaw.

July, 1856 to July, 1857:—Mayor, T. B. Carroll. Aldermen, John L. Saffarans, Daniel Hughes, S. B. Curtis, L. J. Dupre, W. F. Barry, James Elder, C. M. Fackler, T. J. Finnie, Jno. Smoot, A. B. Shaw, D. Bogart, F. M. Copeland, A. H. Douglass, R. Wormeley.

July, 1857 to July, 1858:—Mayor, R. D. Baugh. Aldermen, Dan'l Hughes, J. S. Irwin, A. Street, W. O. Lofland, A. Woodruff, R. S. Jones, Thos. J. Finnie, I. M. Hill, F. M. E. Falkner, T. A. Hamilton, John Martin, F. M. Copeland.

July, 1858 to July, 1859:—Mayor, R. D. Baugh. Aldermen, J. O. Drew, Daniel Hughes, A. Street, R. H. Norris, Chas. Kortrecht, N. B. Forrest, James Elder, T. J. Finnie, T. A. Hamilton, A. H. Douglass, G. P. Foute, D. H. Townsend, John B. Robinson, F. M. Copeland, Jno. Neal, S. W. Jefferson, S. T. Morgan.

July, 1859 to July, 1860:—Mayor, R. D. Baugh. Aldermen, Jno. O. Drew, Samuel Tighe, A. Street, N. B. Forrest, James Elder, C. Potter, T. A. Hamilton, A. H. Douglass, W. E. Milton, Marcus Jones, I. N. Barnett, Wm. Farris, J. C. Griffing, W. M. Perkins, D. H. Townsend, S. T. Morgan, W. O. Lofland, C. Kortrecht.

July, 1860 to July, 1861:—Mayor, R. D. Baugh. Aldermen, Daniel Hughes, P. T. O'Mahoney, S. T. Morgan, R. S. Joyner, J. J. Worsham, N. B. Forrest, J. M. Crews, A. P. Merrill, D. B. Malloy, R. M. Kirby, John Martin, C. W. Frazier, J. B. Robinson, D. G. Feger, H. Volentine, W. C. Anderson, W. S. Pickett.

July, 1861 to July, 1862:—Mayor, John Park. Aldermen, Samuel Tighe, G. M. Grant, M. E. Cochran, S. T. Morgan, L. Amis, Jr., C. Kortrecht, A. P. Merrill, L. J. Dupre, J. O. Greenlaw, R. M. Kirby, D. H. Townsend, C. M. Farmer, John B. Robinson, J. M. Patrick, H. Volentine, F. M. Gailor, T. S. Ayres.

July, 1862 to July, 1863:—Mayor, John Park. Aldermen, S. Tighe, J. C. Powers, Paul Schuster, G. D. Johnson, L. Wunderman, B. F. C. Brooks, H. B. Henghold, M. Mulholland, Wm.

Harvey, James Hall, S. Ogden, John Gager, B. Fenton, S. T. Morgan, M. McEncroe, A. P. Merrill, C. M. Farmer, J. O. Drew, H. T. Hulbert, S. A. Moore, C. Deloach.

July, 1863 to July, 1864:—Mayor, John Park. Aldermen, J. Donovan, J. Glaney, G. D. Johnson, S. T. Morgan, L. Amis, L. Wunderman, A. P. Merrill, C. A. Stillman, M. Mulholland, W. W. Jones, G. W. Harver, M. McEncroe, M. Kelley, W. P. Evans, H. T. Hulbert, H. Volentine.

July, 1864 to July, 1865:—Mayors, Lieut.-Colonel Thos. H. Harris and Captain C. Richards. Aldermen, J. P. Foster, A. Renkert, G. D. Johnson, S. T. Morgan, B. F. C. Brooks, A. J. Miller, I. M. Hill, J. G. Owen, W. S. Bruce, W. W. Jones, J. E. Merriman, C. C. Smith, G. P. Ware, Jos. Tagg, Patrick Sherry, H. T. Hulbert, J. B. Wetherill, H. G. Smith, W. R. Moore, W. M. Farrington.

July, 1865 to July, 1866:—Mayor, John Park. Aldermen, John Glancy, E. V. O'Mahoney, S. T. Morgan, J. H. Reany, Louis Wunderman, Thomas Leonard, I. M. Hill, A. P. Burdett, A. Hitzfield, M. Burke, R. K. Becktell, Wm. M. Harvey, John S. Toof, M. Kelly, J. F. Green, G. D. Johnson, D. R. Grace, Thomas O'Donnell, S. P. Walker, R. W. Creighton.

July, 1866 to July, 1868:—Mayor, Wm. O. Lofland. Aldermen, J. J. Powers, John Glancy, G. D. Johnson, M. E. Cochran, E. W. Wickersham, L. Amis, R. P. Bolling, H. J. Lynn, T. W. O'Donnell, J. C. Holst, A. T. Shaw, D. H. Townsend, H. Lemon, T. O. Smith, W. H. Passmore, H. T. Hulbert.

42nd Corporate Year, 1869:—Mayor, John W. Lelfwich. Aldermen, Thos. Foley, E. Marshall, James O. Durff, L. E. Dyer, Thos. W. O'Donnell, James Gallager, S. Ogden, L. M. Wolcott, L. D. Vincent, J. E. Williams.

43rd Corporate Year, 1870:—Mayor, John Johnson. Aldermen, Owen Dwyer, Phil. J. Mallon, J. O. Durff, I. T. Cartwright, J. C. Holst, Thos. B. Norment, A. J. Roach, Thomas Moffatt, J. P. Prescott, James Rounds. Councilmen, John Glancy, Patrick J. Kelly, William Chase, J. M. Graves, O. F. Prescott, James Birmington, R. P. Duncan, M. Pepper, Owen Smith, M. Cohen, R. A. Parker, H. M. James, J. B. Signaigo,

Patrick Twohig, John Hallum, William Hewitt, William Miller, M. Doyle, George Dixon, D. F. Boon.

44th Corporate Year, 1871:—Mayor, John Johnson. Aldermen, Owen Dwyer, Phil. J. Mallon, T. F. Mackall, I. T. Cartwright, J. C. Holst, P. A. Cicalla, H. G. Dent, Thos. Moffatt, A. C. Bettis, M. J. Pendergrast. Councilmen, John Zent, John Walsh, William Chase, R. W. Lightburne, Lewis Amis, Jr., Henry Eschman, R. P. Duncan, J. M. Pettigrew, N. Malatesta, James Bachman, J. B. Signaigo, Patrick Twohig, J. D. Ruffin, W. M. Harvey, J. Genette, J. R. Grehan, Gus. Reder, J. F. Schabell, J. H. Smith, M. Boland.

45th Corporate Year, 1872:—Mayor, John Johnson. Aldermen, John Walsh, Phil J. Mallon, T. F. Mackall, J. M. Pettigrew, N. Malatesta, P. A. Cicalla, H. G. Dent, M. Burke, B. F. White, Jr., M. J. Pendergrast. Councilmen, John Zent, Thos. Foley, S. B. Robbins, William Schade, Jacob Steinkuhl, A. D. Gibson, C. A. Beehn, J. L. Norton, James Bachman, W. P. Martin, J. Halstead, W. M. Harvey, A. J. White, A. H. Dickerson, J. Genette, H. Marks, J. F. Schabell, Gus Reder, J. H. Smith, P. Colligan.

46th Corporate Year, 1873:—Mayor, John Johnson. Aldermen, John Walsh, S. B. Robbins, Andrew Davis, J. M. Pettigrew, N. Malatesta, P. A. Cicalla, J. J. Busby, M. Burke, B. F. White, Jr., P. Colligan. Councilmen, John Zent, M. V. Holbrook, William Hewitt, Wm. J. Chase, C. A. Beehn, J. L. Norton, A. R. Droescher, John A. Roush, Edward Shaw, Joseph Clouston, Jr., Benj. Bingham, C. E. Clark, S. C. Toof, Turner Hunt, A. J. White, John P. Hughes, Geo. M. Grant, P. S. Simons, J. H. Smith, Turner Mason.

47th Corporate Year, 1874:—Mayor, John Logue. Aldermen, Owen Dwyer, S. B. Robbin, Andrew Davis, N. Malatesta, H. G. Dent, J. T. Hillsman, H. S. Lee, Mike J. Doyle, P. Culligan. Councilmen, P. J. Kelly, J. Walsh, W. J. Chase, William Hewitt, C. A. Beehn, A. G. Tuther, J. A. Rourke, C. E. Keck, J. Clouston, I. Thomas, W. M. Harvey, J. Happeck, J. S. Carpenter, T. Hunt, J. W. Hagley, B. E. Bounds, J. T. Walters, C. E. Page, G. A. Morti, J. H. Moon.

48th Corporate Year, 1875:—Mayor, John Loague. Aldermen, Owen Dwyer, S. B. Robbins, C. W. Metcalf, H. G. Dent, J. T. Hillsman, I. Happeck, H. S. Lee, Mike J. Doyle, P. Culligan, G. A. Morti. Councilmen, John Zent, P. J. Kelley, William Hewitt, H. Caso, S. J. Camp, A. G. Tuther, S. W. Green, Henry Luehrmann, R. Dougherty, J. Clouston, Jr., Charles G. Fisher, William Gay, S. Solari, J. S. Carpenter, J. W. Moore, J. W. Cochran, L. D. Grant, J. D. Danbury, T. A. Ryan, Jacob Moon.

49th Corporate Year, 1876:—Mayor, John R. Flippin. Aldermen, John Zent, W. A. McCloy, James Elder, S. W. Green, H. G. Dent, W. O. Harvey, W. N. Brown, J. W. Cochran, L. D. Grant, Thomas Fleming. Councilmen, P. J. Kelly, J. W. Kerns, J. M. Rourke, John Donovan, Thomas Doyle, James Speed, H. M. Neely, J. T. Blaise, R. Dougherty, E. Hardin, Jacob Weller, A. W. Otis, R. C. Wenson, W. H. Bates, H. Seessell, Sr., R. B. Denson, E. J. Karr, W. B. Glisson, W. M. Hill, George Hutchinson.

50th Corporate Year, 1877:—Mayor, John R. Flippin. Aldermen, John Zent, W. A. McCloy, James Elder, S. W. Green, H. G. Dent, W. O. Harvey, W. N. Brown, J. W. Cochran, L. D. Grant, John A. Strehl. Councilmen, John Bohan, P. J. Kelly, J. M. Rourke, E. Worsham, Thomas Doyle, J. B. Dillard, R. Britton, S. T. Carnes, R. Dougherty, G. E. Evans, T. J. Beasley, M. Jones, W. H. Bates, R. C. Williamson, H. Sessell, Sr., J. P. Hughes, A. W. Newsom, John Scheibler, E. W. Clapp, P. Culligan.

51st Corporate Year, 1878:—Mayor, John R. Flippin. Aldermen, W. J. Chase, J. M. Rourke, James Elder, J. B. Faires, H. G. Dent, W. N. Brown, J. W. Moores, William Benjes, John A. Strehl. Councilmen, W. P. Proudfit P. C. Rogers, James Bohan, A. Renkert, Herman Caro, D. F. Goodyear, C. Quentel, H. L. Brinkley, I. N. Snowden, W. J. Crosbie, C. G. Fischer, Charles Kortrecht, W. H. Bates, R. C. Williamson, M. Selig, J. P. Hughes, L. Lanborn, James Brogan, P. O. Wood, Willis Radford.

52nd Corporate Year, 1879:—Mayor, John R. Flippin. Aldermen, W. J. Chase, William Hewitt, Thomas Doyle, S. W. Green, H. G. Dent, M. Jones, W. N. Brown, W. F. Kennedy,

William Benjes, P. Culligan. Councilmen, James Bohan, J. C. Powers, J. M. Rourke, S. L. Barinds, N. Hooth, C. Geis, P. Twohig, N. N. Speers, G. E. Evans, J. H. White, D. Gensburger, W. H. Bates, S. Solari, M. Selig, W. H. Bunford, J. Pickering, L. Lanborn, J. Sweeney, P. Slogan. (The board of this year had only served a month when the city charter was repealed, a new form of government established and new officers installed.)

Taxing District, 1879:—President, D. T. Porter. Fire and Police Commissioners, John Overton, Jr., Michael Burke. Secretary, L. C. Pullen. Supervisors of Public Works, C. W. Goyer, chairman; John Gunn, W. N. Brown, J. M. Goodbar, Robert Galloway.

Taxing District, 1881 to 1883:—President, John Overton, Jr. Fire and Police Commissioners, Michael Burke, R. C. Graves. Secretary, C. L. Pullen. Supervisors of Public Works, W. N. Brown, chairman; John Green, J. M. Goodbar, Robert Galloway, Henry James.

Taxing District, 1883 to 1885:—President, D. P. Hadden. Michael Burke, R. C. Graves. Secretary, C. L. Pullen. Supervisors of Public Works, James Lee, Jr., chairman; Henry James, M. Gavin, Charles Kney, Lymus Wallace.

1885 to 1887:—President, D. P. Hadden. Fire and Police Commissions, James Lee, H. A. Montgomery. Secretary, C. L. Pullen. Supervisors of Public Works, Charles Kney, Lymus Wallace, R. F. Patterson, T. J. Graham, John E. Randle.

1887 to 1889:—President, D. P. Hadden. Fire and Police Commissioners, James Lee, H. A. Montgomery. Secretary, C. L. Pullen. Supervisors of Public Works, Charles Kney, Lymus Wallace, R. F. Patterson, T. J. Graham, John E. Randle.

1889 to 1891:—President, D. P. Hadden. Fire and Police Commissioners, James Lee, Jr., J. T. Pettit. Secretary, C. L. Pullen. Supervisors of Public Works, Charles Kney, Lymus Wallace, Samuel Hirsch, T. J. Graham, John E. Randle.

1891 to 1893:—President, W. D. Bethell. Fire and Police Commissioners, J. T. Pettit, Martin Kelly. Secretary, Henry J. Lynn. Supervisors of Public Works, T. J. Graham, Samuel Hirsch, E. J. Carrington, Geo. Haszinger, Geo. H. Herbers.

THE NEW YORK
PUBLIC LIBRARY

ASTOR, LENOX
TILDEN FOUNDATIONS

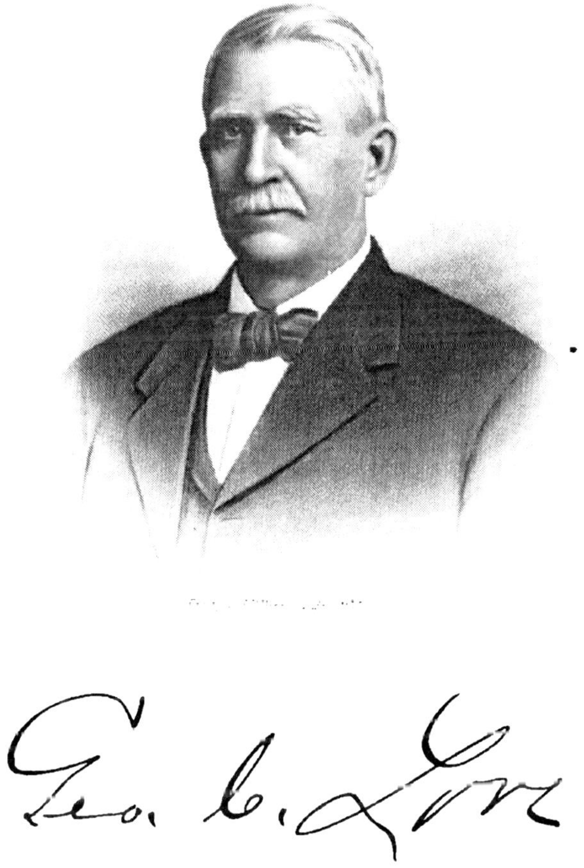

1893 to 1895:—President, W. L. Clapp. Fire and Police Commissioners, R. A. Speed, Martin Kelly. Secretary, J. J. Shea. Supervisors of Public Works:—J. T. Walsh, A. T. Hayden, E. J. Carrington, George Haszinger, G. H. Herbers.

1895 to 1897:—Mayor, W. L. Clapp. Fire and Police Commissioners, J. M. Fowlkes, vice-mayor, Hugh L. Brinkley, J. F. Walker. Supervisors of Public Works, J. T. Walsh, A. T. Hayden, E. J. Carrington, George Haszinger, G. H. Herbers.

1897 to 1898:—Same as preceding.

1898 to 1900:—Mayor, J. J. Williams. Fire and Police Commissioners, D. P. Hadden, vice-mayor, Hugh L. Brinkley, J. F. Walker, secretary in 1898 and W. B. Armour, secretary in 1899. Supervisors of Public Works, J. T. Walsh, E. J. Carrington, Thomas Clark, B. R. Henderson.

1900 to 1902:—Mayor, J. J. Williams. Fire and Police Commissioners, D. P. Hadden, vice-mayor, H. L. Brinkley, W. B. Armour, secretary. Supervisors of Public Works, E. C. Green, W. LaCroix, H. H. Litty, G. D. Raine, P. J. Moran.

1902 to 1904:—Mayor, J. J. Williams. Fire and Police Commissioners, B. R. Henderson, vice-mayor, John Armistead, W. B. Armour, secretary. Supervisors of Public Works, E. C. Green, Wm. LaCroix, H. H. Litty, E. B. LeMaster, G. R. James, W. D. Moon, E. F. Grace, David Gensburger.

1904 to 1906:—Mayor, J. J. Williams. Fire and Police Commissioners, B. R. Henderson, vice-mayor, John T. Walsh, W. B. Armour, secretary. Supervisors of Public Works, D. Gensburger, A. B. Caruthers, G. C. Love, Thomas Dies, E. F. Grace, G. M. Tidwell, W. D. Moon, E. B. LeMaster.

1906 to 1908:—Mayor, James H. Malone. Fire and Police Commissioners, John T. Walsh, vice-mayor, H. T. Bruce, B. G. Henning, D. S. Rice. Supervisors of Public Works, G. C. Love, Thos. Dies, G. M. Tidwell, Louis Sambucetti, E. H. Crump, J. S. Dunscomb, A. H. Frank, F. F. Hill, R. A. Utley, W. T. Winkleman.

1908 to 1910:—Mayor, James H. Malone. Fire and Police Commissioners, J. T. Walsh, vice-mayor, H. T. Bruce, B. G. Henning, E. H. Crump. Supervisors of Public Works, G. C. Love, Thomas Dies, C. W. Edmonds, Louis Sambucetti, P. J.

Moran, J. S. Dunscomb, A. H. Frank, F. F. Hill, R. A. Utley, H. F. Henderson.

Commission Government, 1910 to 1912: Mayor, E. H. Crump. Department Public Affairs, E. H. Crump. Department Accounts, Finances and Revenues, C. W. Edmonds. Department Fire and Police, J. M. Speed. Department Public Utilities, Grounds and Buildings, Thomas Dies. Department Streets, Bridges and Sewers, G. C. Love.

Commission Government, 1912:—Mayor, E. H. Crump. Department Public Affairs and Health, E. H. Crump. Department Accounts, Finances and Revenues, E. R. Parham. Department Fire and Police, R. A. Utley. Department Public Utilities, Grounds and Buildings, Thomas Dies. Department Streets, Bridges and Sewers, G. C. Love.

Memphis has given to the Nation a number of distinguished characters, civil and military. Among these are:

Luke E. Wright, Governor General of the Philippines; Ambassador to Japan; Secretary of War.

United States Senators:—Isham G. Harris, Thomas B. Turley and E. W. Carmack.

Governors:—James C. Jones, Isham G. Harris and M. R. Patterson.

Congressmen:—Frederick P. Stanton, W. T. Avery, W. J. Smith, Wm. R. Moore, Casey Young, Zach Taylor, Josiah Patterson, E. W. Carmack, M. R. Patterson, G. W. Gordon, K. D. McKellar.

Military Men:—Lieutenant General Nathan Bedford Forrest, Lieutenant General A. P. Stewart, Major General Marcus J. Wright, Brigadier General Preston Smith, Brigadier General John Adams, Brigadier General John L. T. Sneed and General William H. Carroll.

In addition to the above, were the following distinguished colonels, whose deeds shed luster on Memphis:

Colonels:—Michael Magevney, Charles M. Carroll, Ed. Pickett, Jr., J. Knox Walker, T. W. Preston, Kit Williams, Luke W. Finley, Wm. F. Taylor.

# CHAPTER XIV

## Architecture and Public Buildings.

THE architecture of the city of Memphis, like all other American cities, has passed through various stages, from the log hut and frame dwelling, crude at first and without any claim to distinction, step by step, to the palatial homes of our present day.

Public and business buildings have likewise developed from a mediocre beginning to the beautiful structures which are now erected to house our people in their business and public life. Among the first buildings claiming any distinction whatever were those erected for business houses, mostly in the fifties, a row of three or four stories, with little or no variation, and if any, only in a minor treatment of window and door openings, with a cornice of metal in imitation of a more permanent structure. A number of these buildings still exist on our principal streets and with the exception of perhaps the lower stories, which have been modernized to suit present needs and conditions, they still serve their original purpose.

A departure from this style of building brought about another class of structures overladen with crude, meaningless cornices and ornamental work, claiming no merit except the individuality of the architect or master builders who were responsible for their creation.

To this period of our city's history likewise belongs the early frame dwellings, a few of which are still in existence. The greater number, however, have disappeared as the business center of the city has expanded; but a few homes, although erected in frame, were well designed in Colonial or Neo Greek style of architectures which prevailed in this country at the times these houses were erected.

At the time Richardson, the architect, was erecting his buildings in a castellated or American adaptation of Romanesque style of architecture, the Cossitt Library was built and this building is an example of the style of architecture prevalent at this time. This style supplanted the so-called Queen Anne, of which there are very few examples in this city; for while it was well adapted to frame dwellings it was but little used here.

The iron front for business buildings, of which various cities in this country contain innumerable examples, was used here in a limited number of cases for such purposes. One of the largest erected in this country at the time, 1858, we claim to have in this city, on Second Street, between Adams and Jefferson Avenues. If they may be classed in any particular style of architecture it belongs to a renaissance period consisting of a superimposed order of architecture with a crowning cornice of classical profile.

Architecture, since the periods enumerated above, has steadily improved in quality, as the conditions justified more expensive and permanent buildings. The Porter Building marked a new epoch in construction, inasmuch as it was the first building erected of steel and skeleton construction in this city. Of later years we have many examples of this same class of construction represented by both public and business or office buildings, among them being the Tennessee Trust, Memphis Trust, Central Bank and Exchange buildings.

During recent years the architecture of the public schools has likewise kept pace with the improvements in other lines of buildings until at the present time our schools are excellent examples of scholastic architecture. The improvement, however, has been most noticeable in our domestic architecture until at present we number among our homes some of the most beautiful residences erected in this section of the country.

It would hardly be permissible to review the architecture of this city without making mention of the churches which have been erected within the past few years and of which we have some very beautiful examples. These, however, owing to changing conditions, are gradually being removed to the suburbs or residential sections of the city.

To the business and public buildings belong the credit for the most decided change and improvements and the one most likely to impress the visitor to our city, and an historical sketch of Memphis would not be complete without special mention of the beautiful Court House and Municipal Building recently erected, which is treated further on in this chapter.

The office buildings are purely commercial structures but have played a very important part in the architecture of the city. Our business section is rapidly assuming a metropolitan condition as a result of the buildings that have been erected for office and commercial purposes within the past few years.

With the exception of the small bust of Andrew Jackson in Court Square, we were entirely without monuments until the erection of the General Forrest statue in Forrest Park a few years ago. This statue, the work of the sculptor Charles Niehaus, is a beautiful example of his work. Within more recent years a memorial fountain and pergola have been erected in Overton Park; likewise a bust of Captain Harvey Mathes in Confederate Park; but with these exceptions Memphis is unfortunately lacking in works of art of this nature.

Taking an unbiased view of the architecture of the city of Memphis, we feel that we can compare favorably with other cities of our class, that the conditions and continued improvements are most encouraging and that our city will eventually be a city beautiful.*

The public buildings of Memphis will be treated of only as they exist at present. There are few in the remote past worthy of attention. Indeed, for a period of about thirty years of her existence it was playfully said by Memphians that there was but one building in the city in which they could take a pride and that was their jail.

Beginning with the most important building of the city, the new Shelby County Court House, it is in wonderful con-

*For the details of this sketch of Memphis architecture the editor is indebted to Mr. M. H. Furbringer, of Jones & Furbringer, prominent local architects.

trast with the little log structure of 1820, costing $175.00. The present enormous but classic structure occupies the whole square bounded by Adams and Washington Avenues and Second and Third Streets. This court house is surpassed in symmetry of design and convenience of arrangement by no county building in the United States, though several actually cost two or three times as much. The description embodied in the report of the Court House Commission which built it cannot be improved upon and will here be given in part:

"The exterior of the building is classical, a modified Ionic. The southern front presents a lengthy portico with fourteen Ionic columns, the shafts left unfluted, resting on pedestals of the same height as a heavily latticed balustrade. The principal entrances are three, one at each end of the southern front and one at the southern extremity of the western side. These entrances are joined by the front portico; they project slightly from the front and side and rise two stories to pediments, each of which is supported by two columns of the same order as those of the portico. Preserving the architectural unity, there has been introduced a similar entrance at the southern extremity of the eastern side as well as the northern extremities of both sides but on account of the height of the bases, these entrances have been converted into balconies which, but for the additions of balustrades similar to that of the main portico, correspond in every respect with the main entrances. * * * * All columns are so placed as to come between windows and thus in no way interfere with light or ventilation. * * * * The sides are severely plain except for the introduction of pilasters the full height of the two stories between the windows and recessed panels between the second and third rows of windows. All the side windows are simple plain openings in the walls but the lower tier in the front has plain mouldings around the tops and sides; the ornaments of the upper tier of windows in the front are formed by the interior frieze of the portico and by sills of plain mouldings. The extremely long lines of the cornice all around the building, with the exception of the parts pertaining to the pediments, have been interrupted by the introduction of lion's heads at frequent intervals. The plain surface of the frieze except that on the sides between the pediments, has been relieved by the addition of wreathes near the end. The cornice is topped by a comparatively high parapet capped with simple mouldings. All door openings are ornamented with carved mouldings on the lintels and jambs and covered with richly carved canopies. The apex of each pediment supports a collossal head of Minerva from each side of which drops a richly carved cresting entirely to and around the eaves. * * * *

"On the cornice of the six-column portico of the northern front are placed six figures representing Integrity, Courage, Mercy, Temperance, Prudence and Learning. They are cut from the same kind of stone as that in the building and are more than double life-size.

"Life-size groupes are carved in high relief on the webs of the pediments. They represent Religious Law, Roman Law, Statutory Law, Common Law, Civil Law and Criminal Law.

"The approaches on the east and west side of the main front and that at the south of the west side are imposing flights of granite steps flanked by heavy walls which finish at the tops at the sides of the entrances in massive pedestals on which rest seated figures of heroic size, cut from single stones of Tennessee white marble, representing Wisdom, Justice, Liberty, Authority, Peace and Prosperity. These sculptures are said to be the largest figures in the country cut from single blocks of marble.

"The floors of all corridors and public parts of courtrooms and offices are Tennessee gray marble. The sides of all corridors have base and high wainscoting of beautifully veined Tennessee marble. The courtrooms, entrance halls to offices and public parts of offices have similar bases and wainscoting but not quite so high as that of the corridors. The marble, a variegated grayish red, in addition to veins of undecided coloring carries heavy veins of pronounced dark red. In the pannelings the slabs have been so joined as to match the veinings into a variety of surprising beautiful effects.

"The interior woodwork, doors, partitions, rails and general finishings are mahogany, with bronze lock, hinges and trimmings. Chipped glass is used in all doors opening on the corridors and frosted glass in office partitions. Electric light and gas fixtures are bronze, in heavy ornamental designs. Floors are laid with rubber tile or cork carpet, the former in all the courtrooms and the latter in the private parts of all offices. The beautiful front corridor looks directly on the front portico and receives the southern sun through thirteen windows. The principal decorative effect has been successfully attempted in the design and execution of this really magnificent entrance hall. Seven different marbles from Vermont, Pennsylvania, Alabama and Tennessee have been used in its embellishment. The design satisfies the anticipation excited by the exterior and maintains the architectural unity. A Grecian ceiling is divided into 15 panels, two at the end and 13 corresponding to the front windows. The panels are marked by beautiful cornices with beds ornamented by guilded Grecian borders and rosettes enclosing heavily gilded plain frames. On the cornices one moulding only on the sides and one only on the lower faces are gilded. The ceiling is supported by marble pilasters in pairs corresponding to the cornices of the ceiling panels. These pilasters are a beautiful combination of the various marbles, red sub-base, black-base, green shaft and white capital. White marble with trimmings of the other, completely covers the walls between the pilasters. On the walls opposite the windows and corresponding with them as well at the ends, Alabama white marble, beautifully veined, has been arranged in matched and figured panels of remarkable beauty. The floor is Tennessee marble, gray and light red; squares of gray are arranged diagonally with light wide red borders. Heavy ornamental electric light brackets further adorn the walls.

"The material used in the entire exterior of the building is blue Bedford limestone. This is an even, close grained stone, slightly oily and practically impervious to frost and moisture. The color is a light grayish blue, which under the sun first bleaches to a shade much ligher than when first quarried and finally weathers into a pleasing dark gray. For building purposes it is not excelled by any stone in the country. The material of the court is a light buff brick with white terra cotta trimmings."

The commission further say of the building that it is an adaptation of a classical design to modern utilities and conveniences. The exterior is intentionally simple; extreme care was exercised to avoid over-ornamentation and painstaking consideration was used in preserving conveniences above designed. The general appearance should prove not only pleasing for the present, but satisfactory for a long time to come. The building is fire-proof, practically indestructable and should endure for ages. It follows a style which has never grown tiresome and one which has survived to satisfy and please through unending and unsuccessful attempts at improvement and innovation. In unity of composition, simplicity of arrangement and combination of design and use, the structure is not believed to be surpassed by any modern building.

This great building, with a frontage of 270 feet and nearly as deep accommodates at present within its luxurious interior the city and county government, the State courts and the various boards of health and other accompaniments of municipal administration.

Historically the scheme to erect this court house was conceived in 1904, when at its October term, the County Court passed a resolution memorializing the General Assembly of the State to grant authority to the county to issue one million dollars of bonds with the proceeds of which a site might be procured and the building erected. This authority was granted by an act passed on February 2, 1905, authorizing the issuance of $1,000,000 of fifty year bonds and containing other powers including the right of condemnation of lands for its site. Other amendatory acts were passed on April 13, 1905 and on March 15, 1907, changing the details of the original act in several respects and authorizing additional issues of bonds to the amount of half a million dollars. The court appointed on April 17, 1905, the Building Commission, composed of N. C. Perkins, W. G. Allen, John Colbert, John T. Walsh and Levi Joy, of which the first named three were then members of the County Court.

These were all well known Memphis citizens of large ability and earnestly set about the performance of their great work. N. C. Perkins was elected chairman and Levi Joy, secretary. This organization continued until May 13, 1907, when John Colbert was elected secretary.

The site for the construction of the building was obtained by purchase and condemnation for the sum of $323,882.78, which was reduced by rents received, etc., to $319,361.91. Hale and Rogers, architects of the highest skill and character of New York City, were employed to design the building and the contract for general construction was awarded to the John Pierce Company for $792,820.00. The laborious work of construction will not be narrated here. It is sufficient to say that the entire work was finally completed and equipped and the building occupied by the public offices and courts by December, 1909.

The entire expense of the building amounted to $1,588,871.71, of which the ground cost $319,361.91. The construction, including sculptures and decorating, amounted to $1,119,208.84 and the furniture and fixtures $118,406.41, while the salaries and incidental expenses were $30,863.50. After completing the building the commission had on hand a cash balance of $1,924.98. The excess of this cost over the million and a half dollars in bonds was made up of premiums and accrued interest on the bonds and interest on the deposits of the funds in bank during the construction, with some additional minor items.

It may be added to this statement that the entire furniture equipment of the building is made of solid mahogany.

The new building for the Memphis Central Police Headquarters designed by Mr. G. M. Shaw, a prominent local architect, located at the corner of Adams Avenue and Second Street, is now completed.

Built of white Carthage marble and reinforced concrete, with fire-proof floors and construction, it will endure as a monument to the civic pride of Memphis for the remainder of the century.

Not only is it a creation of masterly architectural design

from the standpoint of beauty, but it contains every modern equipment which could be devised to make it adequate to the needs of the department for all time.

The first impression one gathers on approaching the building is its appearance of strength, durability and simplicity; upon entering the main rotunda however, the observer discovers there is ample consideration given to the artistic side of the construction. The oval rotunda, with its green marble columns and mosaic relief work, is indeed a thing of beauty. The offices throughout are tastefully decorated and furnished complete with the latest design of imperishable furniture of metal; but it is upon entering the courtroom that the crowning impression is given; finished throughout in English oak, with panels of immense size and magnificent arched, ribbed and decorated ceiling, it gives one the impression of dignity, simplicity and taste.

In the construction of this building reinforced concrete played an important part; the floors, foundation walls and footings are all reinforced concrete; while the columns and girders are of steel. The cell rooms are equipped with tool proof steel cells, similar in material and workmanship to those in use in the most modern penitentiaries. So hard is the steel in these cells that the finest steel saws have no effect upon them.

The arrangement of the building sets a new standard of design for central stations, being settled upon after an extended trip by the commissioners and architects throughout the principal cities of the United States. In addition to offices for all the officials there are club and sleeping rooms for the policemen; charity rooms for the unfortunate; a room for the convenience of visiting officials from other cities; a gymnasium; a shooting gallery in the basement, and a lavish supply of shower baths for the inmates of the building.

Taking into consideration the cost of this building, which was less than $308,000, the city has a right to be proud of the magnificent structure, which will stand as a monument for many years to come.

Memphis has been the recipient of several noble benefactions donated by as many of her sterling citizens who loved and were loyal to their city. Among the most valuable of these was the founding of the Cossitt Library by the heirs of Mr. Frederick H. Cossitt, a philanthropic man from Granby, Connecticut, who adopted Memphis as his home in 1842 and remained here engaged in successful business pursuits for eighteen years. After his death, September 23, 1887, at New York where he was then residing, there was found among his private papers an informal memorandum expressing his intention to give the city of Memphis the munificent sum of $75,000 for the purpose of founding the nucleus of a public library. This memorandum was not in any sense a will but merely expressed an intention. But that intention was held sacred by his children and his three daughters, Mrs. Elizabeth R. Stokes, Mrs. Helen C. Juilliard and Mrs. Mary C. Dodge, who soon after his death took steps to carry it into effect. When a board of trustees had been appointed and incorporated as a library commission two of these noble women, Mrs. Juilliard and Mrs. Dodge, and Mr. Stokes, the husband of the third who had died, each gave to the trustees a check for the sum of $25,000 for the purpose of carrying into effect the contemplated bequest of their father.

The city contributed a part of the promenade, a lot 162 by 300 feet on the bluff south of the United States Custom House, with the approbation of the Legislature of the State, as a site for the building. The Cossitt Library was incorporated by charter, dated April 6, 1888, the Board of Trustees having been suggested by Mr. Cossitt prior to his death being as follows: Carrington Mason, David P. Hadden, Wm. M. Randolph, Samuel P. Read, Wm. M. Farrington, J. T. Fargason, J. C. Neely, Napoleon Hill and Elliston Mason. The officers of the board elected were Wm. M. Farrington, president; D. P. Hadden, vice-president; S. P. Read, treasurer, and Carrington Mason, secretary.

To the donation given by the Cossitt family there was added $1,000 to the building fund by the estate of W. H. Wood of Memphis, $75.00 by the Union & Planter's Bank of Memphis; $500 by E. W. Barnes of New York; $20.00 by Jacob

Schaaf of Memphis; and $550.00 by the Portage Red Sandstone Company of Cleveland, Ohio.

The declared purposes of the corporation in its charter are:

1—To establish and maintain a free public library within the city of Memphis, Shelby County, Tennessee.

2—To establish and maintain a free public art-gallery within said city.

3—To establish and maintain a free public music-hall within said city.

4—To establish and maintain a free public lecture-room within the said city.

5—To establish and maintain a free public museum within the said city.

Subsequently to the incorporation the sum of $5,000 was bequeathed by the late Mr. Philip R. Bohlen, to be used for the purchase of books for the library. The library building is a beautiful structure of red sandstone, the style being a castellated or American adaptation of Romanesque architecture and the building is skillfully arranged for the storage and convenient use of books with splendidly ventilated and lighted reading-rooms, while the nucleus of a fine museum has been installed on the second floor.

Among the buildings devoted to the public welfare, the Goodwyn Institute is notable not only for the munificense of the donor who conceived and provided for its construction and equipment, but for the great benefit it has proved to be to the citizens of Memphis of all classes.

This institute was formally dedicated to the public use on September 30, 1907, the address being delivered by Gen. Luke E. Wright, one of the illustrious citizens of Memphis. The institute was the gift of Mr. Wm. A. Goodwyn of Nashville, Tennessee, formerly a citizen of Memphis, who in his will, after making sundry provisions for his family, declared that after the death of his wife his property should vest in the State of Tennessee, as Trustee, for the uses pertinent to said institute. The will provided further that the Governor and State Senate should nominate and appoint three commissioners to be known as Commissioners of Goodwyn Institute, their tenure of office to be four years. The commissioners were to purchase a suitable lot in Memphis and erect suitable buildings thereon, expending part of the funds derived from his estate for this purpose and applying the balance for the purchase of a library and apparatus and making provision for an endowment fund. The whole scheme was to be subject to the supervision of the State Legislature at all times and the title to the property should be in the name of the State of Tennessee.

It was further provided that a portion of the building should be rented for the purpose of providing a maintenance revenue for the library and public lectures; another part should be devoted to lectures and still another part to library purposes, the use of the library to be free to all, as should also the lectures which, however should be for instruction and not for entertainment merely. It was further provided that no part of the building should be used for political gatherings, but the lecture hall, when not in use otherwise, might be rented for musical concerts, art exhibitions or other purposes likely to elevate public morals and taste. The first Board of Commissioners were suggested to the Governor by the testator and was composed of Samuel P. Read, Bedford M. Estes and Rufus Lawrence Coffin.

Mr. Goodwyn at the conclusion of his will, thus stated his reasons and wishes as to the splendid institute which was to bear his name:

"My whole wish and desire as respects this Goodwyn Institute is to afford to future youths, who may desire it, information upon such practical and useful subjects as will be beneficial in life. My reason for locating it in Memphis is, it was there I spent much of my life in the happy circle of my wife and children. The latter sleep near her borders as I and my wife expect to do when we die. Here I made the first friends of my early life; many of them are dead, but their descendants, many of them, remain, in Memphis and were playmates of my children, and to them or their descendants I hope this may be of great benefit. This legacy for the benefit of my old home has long been thought of by myself and wife, and took shape in a will written by me in November, 1887 and now repeated. It became necessary to write this will on account of necessary changes and to destroy that of 1887. And I mention this fact in order that my old friends at Memphis may know that I have long cherished this idea.''

The institute as finally constructed, is on the southwest corner of Madison Avenue and Third Street in Memphis. The lot was purchased on July 21, 1903 for $75,000. The building fronts on Madison Avenue and is seventy-five feet wide and one hundred and seventeen feet deep. It is a modern, fire-proof construction of steel, stone, brick and terra cotta, seven stories high with a basement of 5,768 square feet. The auditorium or lecture hall occupies the second and third floors, and will seat nearly one thousand people. The library occupies the seventh floor, while the basement, first, fourth, fifth and sixth floors are used for different business offices and other rental purposes. The cost of the building and equipment was more than $300,000. The exterior construction is of stone up to the second floor and above that of ''Harvard Gate Brick'' being of the same type as that first used at Harvard University. The brick work makes an artistic mosaic appearing old and weather-stained, which effect is secured by the varied colorings of the bricks. The trimmings are of white terra cotta. The building possesses a spacious lobby forty-five feet wide, fifty feet deep and fifty feet high, adorned with beautifully tiled floors, lofty pillars, wide marble steps and artistic marble newels. The institute has been self-sustaining from the beginning and has paid all expenses for lectures, besides providing for the purchase of necessary books for the splendid library which, by the order of the trustees, is limited to the purposes of a reference library only. The trustees at present are Messrs. S. P. Read, John R. Pepper and J. M. Goodbar and the superintendent is Mr. C. C. Ogilvie, all of Memphis. One of the principle and most benificent features of the institute are the lectures and lecture recitals which ''cover a wide range of subjects and relate to art, science, literature, music, travel, history, biography, philosophy, sociology, economics, education, commercial, municipal and governmental affairs. The highest grade of lecturers obtainable in the land are annually secured for these purposes, and, it has been remarked, afford interest, amusement and instruction for a more varied class of citizens than seem to attend upon other benefactions in the city.

The city has a new Union Station on Calhoun Street, completed and opened to traffic April 1, 1912. It is owned and operated by five railroads, namely, the Southern Railway Company, the Louisville and Nashville Railroad Company, the St. Louis, Iron Mountain and Southern Railway Company, the Nashville, Chattanooga and St. Louis Railway and the St. Louis, Southwestern Railway Company.

It was at first planned to have all the trunk lines centering at Memphis construct and occupy one building at the corner of Main and Calhoun Streets, but differences arose among the several companies, growing out of the nature of the transportation service and that plan fell through, the other railroad systems undertaking to build independently a station at Main and Calhoun Streets. The Memphis Union Station Company, composed of the above five mentioned railroads, was organized and incorporated on the 30th of September, 1909, and the work of construction on the present station was begun April 1, 1910. Its incorporators and the first board of directors were M. H. Smith, Fairfax Harrison, J. W. Thomas, Jr., C. W. Nelson and J. L. Lancaster.

The new depot of the Memphis Union Station Company, which cost something like $3,000,000, was built on Calhoun Avenue and Fourth Street, about three blocks east of Main Street. The building is of gray stone, the architecture presenting old colonial lines, and is three stories in height. Grand stairway approaches of stone spring from the avenue to the general entrance on the second floor, this entrance being embellished with six stone columns about fifty feet in height. The waiting room for whtie passengers is in the center of the building on the second floor and is one hundred feet by fifty-one feet eight inches in dimensions. The colored waiting-room, more than half as large, is to the east of the general waiting-room, while the ladies' waiting-room is on the west side of it and surrounded by the dining-room, lunch-room and other arrangements for personal comfort.

Over the general waiting-room the ceiling springs to a height of forty-six feet and is exquisitely ornamented with buff terra cotta, in which are myriads of artistic electric lights arranged in rosettes. The wainscoting is finished in terra cotta, with a solid marble base extending around the entire room and the floor is of vari-colored marble tiling in beautiful natural tints. The woodwork is mahogany on the second floor and quarter-sawed oak on the ground floor. The terra cotta finish is something new in depot construction, and the coloring is soft and restful to the eyes.

The whole arrangement of the station building from ground-floor to attic is very convenient, adding vastly to the comfort of the traveling public. In the rear of the main building on the second floor is a grand concourse, seventy-five by two hundred forty feet in dimensions, from which passengers enter trains, twenty tracks being provided for this service. The concourse may also be used for a promenade, a thing much needed in all large passenger stations, but rarely provided. The station has its own light, heat and water plant, the water being derived from artesian well three hundred feet deep. The architect of the station was J. A. Galvin and chief engineer, J. Weiness.

Most extensive provisions have been made for the care of baggage and express, numerous elevators being provided for lifting it from the ground to the second floor. Beside the rooms on the second floor and the baggage and express rooms on the ground floor, the latter floor is provided with numerous capacious apartments for special purposes necessary to a complete Union Station, such as a drug-store, barber shop, billiard-room mail-room and rest-room for employes, besides numerous smaller quarters for other purposes. The upper floor is taken up almost exclusively with offices and file-rooms. It is conceded that no more commodious, comfortable or handsome Union Station can be found in the entire South and it is hoped that it may be surpassed by the other Union Station nearby, now about to be put under construction.

In January, 1877, the State of Tennessee passed an Act ceding to the United States for the purpose of having erected thereon a United States Custom House, a large lot of land on the promenade or bluff overhanging the Mississippi River, having a frontage on the west line of Front Street of three hundred sixty-four and one-fourth feet, extending from the north line of the first alley south of Madison Street to the south line of the first alley north of Madison Street and extending thence westward between parallel lines three hundred feet.

On this lot was erected a stone building, the basement being of pink granite and the superstructure of white Tennessee marble and large enough to accommodate all the offices of the United States government, including a post-office, Custom's offices, the United States court-rooms, inspectors' offices, etc. The architecture is of modified Italian design and the finish is of cherry. The floors of the public parts of the building are tesselated. The windows are of heavy plate glass, the stairways of iron, with slabs of slate. The building is thoroughly fire-proof and has an independent sewer system. The grounds surrounding the building are adorned with lawns and trees and are supported with a heavy retaining wall constructed of great blocks of stone.

The original cost of the building was approximately $500,000, but it has been recently greatly enlarged on the west side, as the demands of the Government service in Memphis have quickly outgrown the structure first devised and it was found imperatively necessary to nearly double the size of the building.

# CHAPTER XV

## Parks and Promenades.

WHEN the proprietors of Memphis conceived the plan of the infant city on January 6, 1819, as mentioned in the agreement of that date, as recorded in the Register's office, and caused William Lawrence to prepare a plan and map of the town, they also had a vision. These shrewd men foresaw that the little town which they had planted would at some future day become a great metropolis in the nation and emphatically declared that it would rival its ancient namesake on the Nile in beauty and grandeur. They also foresaw that reservation must be made in advance for the civic adornment of the future queen city so that a landscape unsurpassed in the great southwest should be rescued from commercial obstacles on the river front and be reserved forever to the dwellers in this great metropolis of their dream. So they made generaus provision, not only for the future commercial convenience of its inhabitants, but for their comfort and enjoyment as well.

Hence on this plan and map, as will be seen on inspection, they provided not only four handsome squares called Auction, Market Exchange and Court Squares, but they provided also a grand promenade or river-front park from Jackson Avenue to Union Avenue, a distance of 4,197 feet, and extended it east and west so as to embrace all the land between the west line of Front Street, then Mississippi Row, and the then edge of the bluff overhanging the river, except a roadway along the edge, the dedicated promenade being 572 feet wide at the south end and 180 feet at the north end of the plat and containing something like thirty-six acres. They also dedicated the streets and alleys of the new town and a splendid landing extending along the Mississippi and Wolf River front, from Jackson Street north to Bayou Gayoso and from the then water's edge, as shown on the map, eastward to Chickasaw Street, the northern extension of Mississippi Row. And they were so particular in preserving these civic dedications for park and promenade purposes to the future people of Memphis that on September 18, 1828, they executed a carefully drawn deed of confirmation, which is here given in full.

"The undersigned proprietors of the land on which the town of Memphis has been laid off, having been informed that doubts have arisen in relation to their original intention concerning the same, for the purpose of removing such doubts, do hereby make known and declare the following as their original and unequivocal designs and intentions in relation therto:

"First. All the ground laid off in said town as streets or alleys, we do say that it was always our intention that the same should forever remain as public streets and alleys, subject to the same rules and regulations as all streets and alleys in towns or cities, forever obligating ourselves, our heirs, or assigns, and by these presents, we do bind ourselves, our heirs, etc., that the above streets and alleys shall continue eastwardly as far as lots are laid off, and the streets, though not the alleys, as far east as Bayou Gayoso, agreeably to the last survey and sale.

"Second. In relation to the ground laid off in said town as public squares, viz: Court, Exchange, Market and Auction Squares, it was the intention of the proprietors that they should forever remain as public grounds, not subject to private appropriation, but public uses only, according to the import of the above expressions, Court, Exchange, Market and Auction Squares.

"Third. In relation to the piece of ground laid off and called the 'Promenade,' said proprietors say that it was their original intention, is now, and forever will be, that the same should be public ground for such use only as the word imports, to which heretofore, by their acts, for that purpose it was conceived, all right was relinquished for themselves, their heirs, etc., and it is hereby expressly declared, in conformity with such intention, that we, for ourselves, heirs and assigns, forever relinquish all claims to the same piece of ground called the "Promenade," for the purpose above mentioned. But nothing herein contained as to the promenade shall bar the town from authorizing one or more ferries to be kept by the proprietors, their heirs or assigns, opposite said promenade and the mouth of any of the cross streets on Mississippi Row.

"Fourth. In relation to the ground lying between the western boundary of the lots from No. 1 to 24 inclusive, and the same line continued in a direct course to the south bank of the Bayou Gayoso and eastern margin of Wolf and Mississippi Rivers, and between Jackson Street extended to the river and the said south bank of the bayou, it was the original intention of the proprietors that there should, on said ground, forever be a landing or landings for public purposes of navigation or trade, and that the same should be forever enjoyed for these purposes, obligatory on ourselves, heirs and assigns; but all other rights not inconsistent with the above public rights incident to the soil, it never was the intention of the proprietors to part with, such as keeping a ferry or ferries on any of the public ground, an exclusive right which they always held sacred, and never intend to part with in whole or in part."

The two succeeding sections numbered 5 and 6, relate to a gift to the city of a block at northwest corner of Poplar and Third Streets, theretofore used for a burying ground, which was to be discontinued, and the dedication of another site for a burying ground on what was known then as Second Bayou, since known as Winchester Cemetery.

This conveyance was dated September 18, 1828, and was signed by John Overton, John C. McLemore, George Winchester and William Winchester, surviving owner, by M. B. Winchester, attorney in fact.

This deed of dedication and confirmation apparently vested in the people of Memphis the perpetual right to the use and enjoyment of the squares and promenade as far as legal skill and the agency of human language could accomplish the purpose of the founders. But as the town and later, the city, grew, human ingenuity was employed successfully to undo the plans of those wise promoters of civic beauty and enjoyment and to rob the luckless people of Memphis of their birthright. And these schemes always came in the guise of an alleged blessing.

In 1844, as we have seen above, the city government conveyed to the United States the splendid navy-yard property, embracing for two blocks the north end of the original promenade. This cession covered all the land between Market and Auction Streets and from Chickasaw Street to the river. But the navy yard was receded by the United States to Memphis in 1853.

In 1847 the city made a lease to W. A. Bickford, of Exchange Square, for 99 years, the consideration being $10,000 of city bonds and provision for a city hall and offices during that period in the building to be erected thereon. This lease has yet 34 years to run.

Before this date the city had extended the public landing from its original location above Jackson Street steadily down the river front, by cutting away the face of the bluff and thus reducing the public promenade one-half or more from Jackson Street ultimately to Union Street. This appropriation of the west part of the promenade, however, though reducing greatly the privileges of the people as to the extent of their splendid pleasure grounds, yet cannot be assailed as a mistaken exercise of clear business judgment, as the traffic privileges thus given to steamboats and river commerce undoubtedly made Memphis what it became before the railroads came to supplant the steamboats.

In 1876 the city and state ceded to the United States as a site for a Custom House that section of the bluff promenade fronting the western terminus of Madison Street and embracing a lot 364¼ by 300 feet, which was also originally part of the ground dedicated by the founders of Memphis.

Later, in 1888, the city donated a lot 162 by 300 feet adjoining the Custom House grounds on the south and extending to Monroe Street for the use of the Cossitt Library. This was a splendidly endowed institution founded by the generosity of Mr. Frederick H. Cossitt, a former citizen of Memphis. As the surrounding grounds of both the Custom House and Library have been handsomely parked and opened to the people, the loss is not great to the public.

At a later period still, the city appropriated a part of the promenade lying between Union and Monroe Streets for the erection of a central fire-station.

The city also, on October 1, 1881, leased for 25 years to the L. & N. Railroad Co., the north half of Auction Square, for $500 per annum, the railroad company undertaking to defend itself against all efforts to set aside the lease by the public without cost to the city.

Besides granting track privileges, over the whole length of the levee embraced in the promenade limits, to several railroads, the city on April 26, 1881, leased to the Memphis, Paducah & Northern Railroad Company for 55 years that part of the public promenade between Poplar and Market Streets and Front and Promenade Streets for an annual rental of $500, and on which grounds are now located the depot buildings used by the Illinois Central Railroad.

So also on August 3, 1899, the city leased to the Choctaw, Oklahoma & Gulf Railroad Co., for $1500 per annum, that part of the public promenade from Washington to Jefferson Streets and between Front Street and the line of the Illinois Central Railroad right-of-way, for a period of 50 years to be used for depots, yards, etc.

These contracts are set out here in brief abstract form for the purpose of illustrating the extent of the inroads made thus far upon the original splendid park and promenade system of the founders of Memphis by the succeeding city governments. The courts have in some instances sustained the rights of the city to thus lease these grounds and the present lessees feel no uneasiness about their right to retain the leases and licenses to occupy the ground and have erected splendid improvements thereon in some cases.

However, the Park Commissioners have rescued such bits as are still left of the once magnificent domain and have taken charge of one-half of Auction and all of Market and Court Squares and that part of the promenade still unused, which lies south of Jefferson Avenue and have created out of the latter beautiful Confederate Park, and the little plat called Chickasaw Park, adjoining the engine house between Monroe and Union Avenues. The people may yet by alert action, come into their own again at the termination of these leases.

But after this grewsome review of the disintegration of the beautiful park and promenade system of our founders and the repeated sacrifice of the civic pride and comfort of the people to the utilities of commerce, we are now about to tell of a brighter day for Memphis and her splendid park system. On March 31, 1899, the Legislature of Tennessee passed an act amending the Taxing District Act of 1879 so as to empower cities organized under said act to acquire, improve and maintain parks for the benefit of the public, and also authorizing such taxing districts or cities to establish by ordinance a park commission composed of three members to be elected by the Legislative Council. By the terms of the act the commissioners were to "have the entire control of the parks, park-lands and parkways acquired by such Taxing District or city under the provisions of this act. It shall be their duty to direct the laying out, improvement and maintenance of said parks." They were also empowered to open or close up any streets, alleys or roadways running across such park or parkland, and this power was to extend as well without as within the limits of such city.

Under this act Judge L. B. McFarland, John R. Godwin and Robert Galloway were appointed the first Board of Park Commissioners. These gentlemen organized the Board in September, 1900, by electing L. B. McFarland, chairman, and on November 14 of the following year they had succeeded in floating $250,000 of four per cent bonds with which to begin the acquisition of the beautiful grounds now composing the Memphis Park system.

When the board was organized there came under its control by direction of the city government certain remnants left from the original park system of the founders of Memphis, as well as the several donations mentioned below, the whole constituting the following properties:

L. B. McFarland,

ties south of Jefferson Avenue and have created out of the latter beautiful Confederate Park, and the little plat called Chickasaw Park, adjoining the engine house between Monroe and Union Avenues. The people may yet by alert action, come into their own again at the termination of these leases.

But after this grewsome review of the disintegration of the beautiful park and promenade system of our founders and the repeated sacrifice of the civic pride and comfort of the people to the utilities of commerce, we are now about to tell of a brighter day for Memphis and her splendid park system. On March 31, 1899, the Legislature of Tennessee passed an act amending the Taxing District Act of 1879 so as to empower cities organized under said act to acquire, improve and maintain parks for the benefit of the public, and also authorizing such taxing districts or cities to establish by ordinance a park commission composed of three members to be elected by the Legislative Council. By the terms of the act the commissioners were to "have the entire control of the parks, park-lands and parkways acquired by such Taxing District or city under the provisions of this act. It shall be their duty to direct the laying out, improvement and maintenance of said parks." They were also empowered to open or close up any streets, alleys or roadways running across such park or parkland, and this power was to extend as well without as within the limits of such city.

Under this act Judge L. B. McFarland, John R. Godwin and Robert Galloway were appointed the first Board of Park Commissioners. These gentlemen organized the Board in September, 1900, by electing L. B. McFarland, chairman, and on November 14 of the following year they had succeeded in floating $250,000 of four per cent bonds with which to begin the acquisition of the beautiful grounds now composing the Memphis Park system.

When the board was organized there came under its control by direction of the city government certain remnants left from the original park system of the founders of Memphis, as well as the several donations mentioned below, the whole constituting the following properties:

L. B. McFarland,

lies south of Jefferson Avenue and have created out of the latter beautiful Confederate Park, and the little plat called Chickasaw Park, adjoining the engine house between Monroe and Union Avenues. The people may yet by alert action, come into their own again at the termination of these leases.

But after this grewsome review of the disintegration of the beautiful park and promenade system of our founders and the repeated sacrifice of the civic pride and comfort of the people to the utilities of commerce, we are now about to tell of a brighter day for Memphis and her splendid park system. On March 31, 1899, the Legislature of Tennessee passed an act amending the Taxing District Act of 1879 so as to empower cities organized under said act to acquire, improve and maintain parks for the benefit of the public, and also authorizing such taxing districts or cities to establish by ordinance a park commission composed of three members to be elected by the Legislative Council. By the terms of the act the commissioners were to "have the entire control of the parks, park-lands and parkways acquired by such Taxing District or city under the provisions of this act. It shall be their duty to direct the laying out, improvement and maintenance of said parks." They were also empowered to open or close up any streets, alleys or roadways running across such park or parkland, and this power was to extend as well without as within the limits of such city.

Under this act Judge L. B. McFarland, John R. Godwin and Robert Galloway were appointed the first Board of Park Commissioners. These gentlemen organized the Board in September, 1900, by electing L. B. McFarland, chairman, and on November 14 of the following year they had succeeded in floating $250,000 of four per cent bonds with which to begin the acquisition of the beautiful grounds now composing the Memphis Park system.

When the board was organized there came under its control by direction of the city government certain remnants left from the original park system of the founders of Memphis, as well as the several donations mentioned below, the whole constituting the following properties:

L. B. McFarland,

|  | Acres |
|---|---|
| Market Square, now called Brinkley Square | 1 |
| Auction Square, Remnant | ½ |
| Court Square | 2½ |
| Confederate Park, part of Promenade | 5 |
| Chickasaw Park, part of Promenade | 1¾ |

The tracts donated or acquired by the city since the original dedication by the founders of Memphis, were:

|  | Acres |
|---|---|
| Old Hospital ground, now Forrest Park | 10 |
| Gaston Park, donated by John Gaston | 5 |
| Bickford Park, donated by W. A. Bickford | 2½ |
| Annesdale Park, donated by R. Brinkley Snowden | 1 |
| Belvidere Park | 1-6 |

Forrest Park was originally the ground of the old Memphis City Hospital and was kindly donated by the city for park purposes at the instance of the Confederate Historical Association of Memphis, which desired to and subsequently did erect a splendid bronze monument to General Nathan Bedford Forrest, costing $30,000, on the grounds when the park had been laid out. The suggestion to obtain from the city this ground for a park, to be called Forrest Park, first came from Captain R. J. Black of the Historical Association.

With this nucleus the Park Commissioners began with great enthusiasm to plan for the acquisition of far larger bodies of beautiful lands in the suburbs of Memphis in order to complete a system of parks and parkways which for beauty and artistic design is probably surpassed by only three other systems in the United States and very slightly, if at all, by these.

The first purchase of the Park Commissioners was a tract of 335 acres then known as Lea's Woods, which lies on the east limits of the city at the northwestern intersection of Poplar Boulevard and Trezevant Avenue, now the Parkway. This tract, an exquisite greenery, slightly broken and with several running streams, was purchased for $110,000, or about $330 per acre on November 14, 1901. There was a competition organized by a city newspaper, the *Evening Scimitar*, for the purpose of selecting a name for the new park, which finally resulted in giving it the name of Overton Park, in honor of Judge Overton, one of the founders of Memphis.

The Park Commissioners also acquired a tract of 367 acres of land adjoining the city limits on the south and fronting on the Mississippi River on a high bluff overhanging the water. Soon after the County of Shelby donated 60 acres more, the two tracts constituting a body of land with a river-front 50 or 60 feet high, and about 4800 feet in length, called Riverside Park. This tract is more broken than Overton Park and intersected with deep dells, affording sites for winding driveways of exquisite beauty. In some respects it surpasses Overton Park in natural beauty and scenic effect, besides containing nearly 100 acres more of land, the whole body covering 427 acres.

The next enterprise of the Park Commissioners was to obtain by purchase and condemnation a magnificent parkway varying from 100 to 250 feet in width and containing 11.11 miles of roadway and 182.23 acres of land. Including the double drives there are in this parkway 19.35 miles of roadway. The embellishment of the parkway, which encircles the entire city and connects Overton and Riverside Parks, is exquisite in character, the highest effects of landscape architecture having been brought to bear in its construction, and it is believed that no city in our nation can surpass it in comfort and scenic beauty as a pleasure drive of that length.

The commissioners now have completed negotiations with the owners for the purchase of a new park-site to be known as DeSoto Park, in honor of the daring Spanish soldier who first saw the Mississippi River at the present site of the city of Memphis and whose discovery has been treated fully in the initial pages of this history. This tract embraces some thirteen acres of land and includes Chisca's Mound or fortress, from which that doughty Indian chief hurled defiance at the Spanish invaders, and another or smaller mound, probably of more recent construction.

The opening of this historic spot as a public park will prove a notable achievement for Memphis, through her present park commissioners Robert Galloway, J. T. Willingham and

B. F. Turner and it is contemplated making the new park a place worthy of its historic importance and ultimately it is believed that a magnificent bronze monument will be erected to the wonderful Spaniard who first brought the great bluff on which Memphis stands under the searchlight of history.

It is believed that no rivals can be found among the parks of the United States to contest with Overton and Riverside in elements of natural beauty. Throughout a large part of Overton Park nature has been left undisturbed, except by minute footpaths, to develop its trees, plants, and shrubs and its infinite wild flowers, each after its own kind. More than thirty kinds of native timber are to be found here. Rare wild plants, vines, grasses and flowers spring up in bewildering luxuriance and infinite variety to attract the scientist and lover of nature and where children can roam next to Mother Earth and her own immediate handiwork, as in the days of our first parents. It has been observed that plants and wild flowers, which had long since disappeared from the environs of the city, have reappeared in lavish abundance and brought with them numberless new species. It is in spring and summer a paradise for the botanist. Trees that were here when DeSoto came rear their mighty heads at intervals, and one buried in the green wilderness can discern no evidence that despoiling civilization exists anywhere near.

This park of 335 acres is nearly an equilateral parallelogram, its western side being embellished with driveways, lakes, flower-beds, lawns and pavilions, with a splendid zoological garden in the forest at the northwest corner. This zoo contains 405 selected animals, birds and reptiles installed with their buildings, dens, etc., at a cost of $31,726.58.

Riverside Park differs materially from Overton in several respects. It fronts about 4,800 feet along the high bluff overhanging the Mississippi River, giving a water view of exquisite beauty, the mighty river with its hazy veil unfolding for miles to the enchanted eye. This tract of land containing 427 acres, is broken into deep, winding dells at frequent intervals, heavily wooded throughout, with wide expanses of almost level plateaus along the river bank, here more than 60 feet high, and between the dells to the eastward. These high levels have been exquisitely improved with plants, shrubs and flowers, and from them the white driveways dip at intervals into and thread the shady dells, affording natural scenery of wierd and strange beauty. This park is off of the highways of travel and overlooks the ever silent river, so majestic in its grandeur as to evoke from its awed Spanish discoverers the impressive name of Rio Espiritu Santo, or River of the Holy Spirit. No more restful place of retreat for the city-tired man or woman can be imagined than quiet, beautiful Riverside, where the flowers bloom and the mocking birds sing and nature seems "in silent contemplation to adore" one of the mightiest handiworks of the Creator, the great inland river of America.

### RIVERSIDE PARK.

By tawny tide,
At Riverside,
We walk and dream and softly bide,
While far below,
Deep, stately, slow,
The yellow waters swirl and flow.

Around us nods
The golden-rods
And purple in its feathery bloom,
The giant grass,
On stems of brass,
Like banners, flaunts its glossy plume.

The sumac burns
In leavy urns
Fired by the torch of Autumn's sun;
And by the woods
Its scarlet hoods
Tell of the summer's battle won.

In Riverside,
At eventide,

We wander through the deep, brown dells,
Where leaves unfold,
In tints of gold,
Sun-painted groups of fronded bells.

About the balks
Of tangled walks
The autumn creeper twines its spray,
And nestling there,
In tiny lair,
The sylvan locust trills its lay.

Far o'er the dell
The broad hills swell
And giant poplars crown their crests,
Where mocking-birds,
In wondrous words,
Talk love to mates in swinging nests.

High on the vine
The muscadine
Suspends its globes of honied wine,
And festooned grapes
In purpling shapes,
About the massive oaks entwine.

Oh dells, deep, wide,
At Riverside,
We would in thy sweet peace abide,
Far from the throngs,
The rush, the wrongs,
That stifle life on urban tide.

For 'mid thy peace,
The pulses cease
To beat the fevered life's quick blow,
And love and truth
Renew their youth
Beneath the autumn afterglow.

The smaller of the town parks are scarcely less beautiful than their larger sisters, especially Forrest Park, where the grand equestrian statue of the South's mightiest cavalry leader, Nathan Bedford Forrest, towers amidst the trees.

All these splendid pleasure grounds are the creations of the distinguished landscape architect and scenic artist, George E. Kessler, of Kansas City, Missouri, than whom no one has done more to beautify Memphis. In little Confederate Park on the riverfront north of the Custom House, a touch of wartime is added in the monster but now obsolete cannon and mortars, relics of the great strife between the States. These guns point over the waters as they did fifty years ago, but the birds are nesting and the spiders are weaving their webs in the black cavities whence issued at that time sounds transcending thunder and missiles of awful destruction.

Beside these parks there are other small plats of ground ranging from five acres down to one or less. Among these are Gaston Park, the donation of John Gaston, long a citizen of Memphis, and holding her in grateful remembrance; Bickford Park, of two and one-half acres, generous donation of W. A. Bickford; Chickasaw Park of one and three-fourth acres; Annesdale, Belvidere and Astor Parks, all of them oases in the deserts of buildings and homes, and jewels in the order of park construction.

It has been proposed by Mrs. S. H. Brooks, widow of the late S. H. Brooks, prominent merchant of Memphis, to build in Overton Park a Memorial Art Gallery to the memory of her husband, to cost $100,000. The proposal has been accepted by the Park Commission and the site designated. This will perhaps be the beginning of the great scheme for an Art Museum for Memphis planned by the late Carl Gutherz.

The several boards of park commissioners, since the first one was organized in September, 1900, have been by years, as follows:

1901:—L. B. McFarland, chairman, J. R. Godwin, Robert Galloway. 1902:—L. B. McFarland, chairman, John R. Godwin, Robert Galloway. 1903:—Robert Galloway, chairman, L. B. McFarland, John R. Godwin. 1904:—Robert Galloway,

*R. Galloway*

chairman, L. B. McFarland, John R. Godwin. 1905:—John R. Godwin, chairman, L. B. McFarland, Robert Galloway. 1906:—John R. Godwin, chairman, Robert Galloway, L. B. McFarland. 1907:—Robert Galloway, chairman, J. T. Willingham, John R. Godwin. 1908:—Robert Galloway, chairman, J. T. Willingham, John R. Godwin. 1909:—Robt. Galloway, chairman, J. T. Willingham, Dr. B. F. Turner. 1910:—Robert Galloway, chairman, J. T. Willingham, Dr. B. F. Turner. 1911:—Robert Galloway, chairman, J. T. Willingham, Dr. B. F. Turner. 1912:—Robert Galloway, chairman, J. T. Willingham, Dr. B. F. Turner.

# CHAPTER XVI

## Military History

THE military history of Memphis presents some quite graphic as well as tragic features, as it was a sort of storm center during the War Between the States. The early military career of the city began with the Mexican War, 1846. The various military operations which took place on the Chickasaw Bluffs before the beginning of the Nineteenth Century, under DeSoto, Bienville, Gayoso, Captain Guion and others are given fully in the preliminary chapters of this work.

When the Mexican War broke out in 1846 the fires of patriotism were fiercely lighted in the little city on the bluffs and six military companies were organized here for service in that conflict but only three were accepted and went to Mexico. These were the Gaines Guards under Captain M. B. Cook; the Memphis Rifle Guards under Captain E. F. Ruth and the Eagle Guards under Captain W. N. Porter. The two first named companies became part of the Second Tennessee Infantry, the Rifle Guards, as Company D, and the Gaines Guards as Company E. The Eagle Guards was organized as a cavalry company. The two infantry companies were engaged at Monterey and Vera Cruz and at Cerro Gordo, April 18, 1847, lost several men, the Rifle Guards losing their first lieutenant, F. B. Nelson and Private C. A. Sampson killed and Ben O'Haver, Isaiah Prescott and C. C. Ross, wounded. The Gaines Guards lost Lieut. C. G. Hill, Sergeant A. L. Bynum, J. J. Gunter, E. Y. Robinson and R. L. Bohannon, killed, and Burton Plunkett, Abram Gregory, John Gregory and John P. Isler, wounded.

Between 1852 and 1859 there were nine military companies organized, several of which subsequently became famous in the

Civil War. These companies were the Clay Guards, Captain Charles M. Carroll, 1852; the Washington Rifles, Captain Ringwald, 1853; Young American Invincibles, Captain S. H. Whitsitt, 1855; the Steuben Artillery, Captain William Miller, 1858; Memphis Light Guards, Captain Jones Gennette, 1859; Jackson Guards, Captain M. McGeveney, Jr., 1859; Harris Zouave Cadets, Captain Sherwin, 1859; Memphis Southern Guards, Captain James W. Hambleton, 1859; and a cavalry company, the Memphis Light Dragoons, Captain T. H. Logwood, chartered by the Legislature in 1860. Nearly all of these organizations which survived became noted companies in famous Memphis regiments during the War Between the States.

After the establishment of the Confederate States in February, 1861, the city became rapidly a great military camp. The tramp of armed men was heard on the streets and the people, intensely Southern and quickly imbued with the war spirit then burning fiercely throughout the whole South, sprang to arms almost as one man. No city of its size, then containing only 22,600 population, white and black, furnished so large a proportion of the adult male inhabitants to the armies of the South. More than fifty companies of infantry, cavalry and artillery were enlisted, the minimum number for each company being eighty-three and the maximum one hundred and three.

The ladies also caught the spirit of the hour and at a meeting by resolution declared to her warlike sons: "Though we cannot bear arms, yet our hearts are with you and our hands are at your service to make clothing, flags or anything that a patriotic woman can do for Southern men and Southern independence." The Board of Mayor and Aldermen at the same time voted $59,000 "for the defense and the protection of the city of Memphis."

It would be interesting if the historian could give all of the details of this period of excitement and preparation for war in the little city on the Mississippi River, but that would require a space not warranted in the chapter on the Military History of Memphis. As far as possible the military organizations, regiments, battalions, companies and batteries will be here compiled, the names of many of the companies being indicative of the spirit of young Memphis men of 1861, though oftentimes fantastic. Among the infantry companies of that day which sprang into being in response to the first ominous gun fired at Fort Sumter on May 12, 1861, were the Shelby Grays, the Bluff City Grays, the Crockett Rangers, the Jeff Davis Invincibles, the Garibaldi Guards, the Memphis Marine Guards and the Memphis Light Dragoons. Some of the old companies were the Memphis Southern Guards, the Harris Zouave Cadets, the Washington Rifles, the Jackson Guards and the Memphis Light Guards of infantry, and the Steuben artillery, which were at once sworn into service. Following these were the Greenwood Rangers, Tennessee Mounted Rifles, Shelby Mounted Rifles, Hickory Rifles, Tennessee Guards, Tennessee Star Grays, Emerald Guards, Carroll Guards, May's Dragoons, The Beauregards, and Capt. W. D. Pickett's Sappers and Miners.

Memphis furnished the Confederate service several regiments and representative companies to several other regiments in that service. Indeed, almost her entire voting population joined the ranks and boys of from fifteen to men of fifty-five were common in the lines. Those regiments made up in whole or in part of Memphis men were chiefly the Second, Fourth, Ninth, Fifteenth, Twenty-first and One Hundred Fifty-fourth Tennessee Infantry and two companies of the Seventh Tennessee Cavalry and one company of McDonald's battalion of Forrest's old regiment. A roster of the Memphis companies in these regiments, as complete as possible to make it at this date, follows:

*Second Tennessee*—Colonel Knox Walker. Company A, Capt. F. A. Strocky. Company B, Capt. W. B. Triplett. Company C, Capt. Chas. E. Cossitt. Company D, Capt. E. Marshall. Company E, Capt. John Wilkerson and E. C. Porter. Company F, Capt. Sam Vance. Company G, Capts. J. Welby Armstrong and R. A. Hart. Company H, Capt. R. E. Chew.

*Fourth Tennessee*—Lieutenant Colonel Luke W. Finlay. Company A, Shelby Grays, Capt. James Somerville. Company H, Tennessee Guards, Capt. B. F. White.

*Ninth Tennessee Regiment*—Company I, Capt. Hal Rogers.

*Fifteenth Tennessee*—Colonel Charles M. Carroll. Company A, Capt. A. C. Ketchum. Company B, Capt. Frank Rice. Company C, Capt. Charles E. Rose. Company D, Capt. Ed. S. Pickett. Company E, Young Guards, Capt. John F. Cameron, later in 3rd Confed. Company F, Capt. E. M. Cleary. Company G, Capt. O'Carroll. Company H, Capt. Jos. Keller. Company I, Washington Rifles, Capt. Nick Frick.

*Twenty-First Tennessee*—Colonel Ed. Pickett, Jr. Consolidated with Second Tennessee to constitute Fifth Confederate, as follows:—

*Fifth Confederate*—Major R. J. Person. Company A, Capt. Thomas Stokes. Company B, Capt. Chas. W. Frayser. Company C, Capt. W. H. Brown. Company D, Capt. L. D. Greenlaw. Company E, Capt. J. H. Beard. Company F, Capt. John Fitzgerald. Company G, Capt. W. H. Carvell. Company H, Capt. A. A. Cox.

*One Hundred Fifty-Fourth*—Colonel Preston Smith. Company A, Light Guards, Capt. Jones Gennette. Company B, Bluff City Grays, Capt. J. H. Edmondson. Company C, Hickory Rifles, Capt. J. D. Martin. Company D, Southern Guards, Capt. J. W. Hambleton. Company D, (2nd), Beauregard's, Capt. Moreland. Company E, Harris Zouave Cadets, Capt. Sterling Fowlkes. Company F, Crockett Rangers, Capt. M. Patrick. Company I, Maynard Rifles, Capt. E. A. Cole.

*Cavalry*:

*Seventh Tennessee Cavalry*—Company A, Memphis Light Dragoons, Capt. T. H. Logwood. Company C, Shelby Light Dragoons, Capt. S. P. Bassett. Company D, (Battalion) Tennessee Mounted Rifles, Capt. Josiah White.

*Forrest's Old Regiment*—Colonel N. B. Forrest. Company C, Forrest Rangers, Capt. Charles May.

*Artillery*—Bankhead's Battery, Capt. Smith P. Bankhead, Capt. W. Y. C. Humes, Capt. J. C. McDavitt. Steuben Artillery, Capt. Wm. Miller, Capt. W. H. Jackson, Capt. W. W. Carnes, Capt. Louis G. Marshall. Rice's Battery, Capt. T. W. Rice, Lieut. B. F. Haller, Lieut. D. C. Jones.

It is not the intention of the editor, nor would it be practicable to follow and narrate the careers of these companies and regiments through the Civil War. To do so would be practically to write the history of the Army of Tennessee and Forrest Cavalry. It is sufficient to say that these commands each and all acquitted themselves gloriously on almost every battle-field of the West, and they were cut down by hundreds until only the merest fragments remained to reach home at the close of the great conflict. Many of them still survive, 1912, battle-scarred and bent with age, but still men of heroic mould and unquenchable love of country. Only the military operations and engagements which have a strictly local coloring will be recorded in this narrative.

The first active demonstration of warlike activity was an incident which occurred in Memphis on March 28, 1861, when several companies of Mississippi volunteers passed through the city, bound for Pensacola, Florida, to become part of Col. James R. Chalmers' 9th Mississippi Regiment in the Confederate Army. These troops were handsomely uniformed and carried Mississippi State and Confederate flags. They were escorted from the old Mississippi & Tennessee depot to the Memphis & Charleston depot by two Memphis militia companies, the Memphis Southern Guards, Capt. J. W. Hambleton and the Harris Zouave Cadets, Capt. Sherwin, the latter companies wearing the uniform and bearing the flag of the United States.

On April 28, 1861 the Southern Mothers, a patriotic band of women were organized for the purpose of nursing the sick and wounded soldiers. Their work was notable and continuous until the city was captured by the Federal forces in 1862, when they turned their attention, as far as permitted, to aid the Confederate prisoners in the Federal prisons. Some of these noble women yet survive, true Mothers in Israel, revered of all men.

Louisiana sent April 28, in response to an appeal through W. G. Ford, a prominent citizen of Memphis, a battery of 32-pound guns, 3,000 Mississippi rifles and 500,000 cartridges to aid in the defense of Memphis.

The old Quimby & Robinson foundry on the river-front where the sand bar now extends at the foot of Adams Street and the Memphis & Charleston Railway shops on Adams Street now the Southern yards, were utilized for the casting of brass and iron cannon, shell and grape-shot, and laboratories were improvised at various places for the manufacture of cartridges and fixed ammunition, many women and girls being employed in this business, whose nimble fingers were especially useful.

General S. R. Anderson had been sent in April by Governor Harris to command the post here and he was succeeded on May 3, by General John L. T. Sneed. On July 13, Major-General Leonidas K. Polk, the soldier bishop of Mississippi, Louisiana and Arkansas, who had been commissioned by President Davis, arrived and took command of the military department in the name of the Confederate States.

On November 7, 1861, the first battle was fought in Memphis territory at Belmont, Missouri, opposite Columbus, Kentucky. Many Memphis soldiers were killed or wounded here, three of the Memphis regiments, the 2nd, 21st and 154th Tennessee losing an aggregate of 31 killed and 138 wounded. This loss of their own flesh and blood brought great grief to the people of the devoted city, which was not relieved by the sight of the large detachment of crest-fallen Federal prisoners marching up Main Street a few days after the battle. The hospitals, under the care of the Southern Mothers and sisters of St. Agnes Academy, largely took care of the Confederate wounded.

After the fall of Fort Donelson and Nashville the state government was removed to Memphis and was located in a building at the northeast corner of Second and Madison Streets, the State Legislature was convened here and preparations were at once made for the defense of the state and city. In April, 1862, fearing the capture of incomplete boats by the Union fleet, then endeavoring to force a passage down the Mississippi River, the Confederate government ordered the removal of the iron-clad gunboat and ram Arkansas, which had been constructed under the bluff at Fort Pickering at the debouchment of the Kansas City railroad incline, to New Orleans, but her commander, finding New Orleans occupied by the Federal fleet, carried the boat up the Yazoo River where she was completed and put in commission.

But the dreadful front of war was drawing nearer to Memphis. For several weeks in May, 1862, the deep bellowing of the big guns on the Federal mortar fleet, engaged in shelling Fort Pillow, forty miles north of Memphis on the river, could be counted by the citizen all through the night, as his head rested on his pillow, and then there was a pause at Fort Pillow and suddenly, on the morning of June 6, 1861 the Federal ironclad and ram fleet appeared at the very doors of the city and the war-cloud burst in uncontrolled fury over the homes of her devoted people.

This being the first naval engagement, or other deadly operation of war, which had ever occurred here, a careful narrative will be here given of the gunboat battle, in all its tragic details.

Before describing this most notable of gunboat battles on the inland waters of the continent it is proper to narrate something of the invention and necessity for what were then called steam rams, or gunboats with prows of wood or metal, so constructed as to be used for sinking an enemy's vessel by deliberate collision or raming its hull.

The Confederates were the first inventors of these novel craft and had by means of the first completed one, the Virginia, constructed of the old U. S. frigate Merrimac, attacked on the 8th of March, 1862, the Union fleet lying at anchor in Hampton Roads, Virginia, and destroyed the Congress and Cumberland, two famous war vessels of the olden type. This disaster called forth from Mr. Charles Ellet, Jr., a civil engineer, a pamphlet on the 6th of February, 1862, in which he called attention to the fact that the Confederates possessed five of these powerful engines of destruction, including the Merrimac at Norfolk, the other four being at Mobile and on the lower Mississippi River. He predicted that if these vessels got at large on the high seas they would prove a very dangerous factor in the Civil War, as well as very destructive to the Commerce of the United States. This pamphlet called attention to Colonel Ellet's scheme and he was called to Washington and soon after authorized to construct an unarmored ram fleet for use upon the Mississippi River and tributaries and at once, by authority of the Government, purchased a number of steamboats and by reinforcing the hulls and prows and building a bulkhead of heavy timber around the boilers, made of them very efficient naval monsters, able to destroy the most powerful gunboat, if it could be reached without first subjecting the ram to destruction by its gunfire.

Colonel Ellet, with the rank of Colonel of Marines, was in command of these improvised rams, viz: the Dick Fulton, Lancaster, Lioness, Mingo, Monarch, Queen of the West, Sampson, Switzerland and Horner. These were assembled by May 25, at Fort Pillow, forty or fifty miles north of Memphis and which was then being besieged by the Federal gunboat fleet.

In the meantime the Confederates had been busy along the same lines and on the 16th of January, 1862, Captain J. E. Montgomery selected at New Orleans twelve large tow boats and two ocean steamers then lying in the river and proceeded to fit them out as steam-rams and gunboats.

The eight boats designed for service on the upper Mississippi were the General Bragg, the General Price, the General Van Dorn, the General Lovell, the General Beauregard, the General M. Jeff Thompson, the Little Rebel and the Sumter. These boats were completed between March 25, and April 17, 1862, and were ordered to Fort Pillow as completed. When they left New Orleans they only carried two guns, a thirty-two and twenty-four pounder smoothbore, on the whole fleet, but at Fort Pillow each boat received a thirty-two pounder smoothbore and later four eight-inch guns were added.

On the morning of the battle, June 6, 1862, Fort Pillow having been evacuated June 4, the Federal gunboat fleet, consisting of six heavily iron-plated gunboats, namely, the Benton, Essex, Cairo, Carondolet, St. Louis and Louisville, and the above named Federal ram-fleet, were assembled in the bend a couple of miles north of the city and the Confederate ram and gunboat fleet above named, were lying in front of the city at daylight, each busily engaged in clearing ship for action.

Captain Montgomery, in command of the Confederate

fleet, not having coal enough to enable his boats to proceed as far as the next Confederate stronghold at Vicksburg, but having enough for the purpose of maneuvering through a gunboat battle, determined to try conclusions with the enemy and bring on a spectacular engagement, in front of the city of Memphis, with almost the entire population of the city on the bluffs as spectators. With this purpose a bit before sunrise, on the morning of June 6, 1862, the gunboat General M. Jeff Thompson, Captain J. H. Burke, and the gun-boat General Lovell, Captain J. C. Delaney, had taken positions at the foot of the bend above the city as an advance guard of his fleet. The Federal ironclad gunboat fleet was at once observed in battle formation across the bend, with four of the Federal rams, viz., the Queen of the West, Monarch, Lancaster and Switzerland in the act of making a landing at the bank above. Just at sunrise a few minutes before five o'clock, Captain Burke of the Jeff Thompson being within easy range, fired on the Federal fleet with his eight-inch gun, which replied ere the reverberation of the great gun ceased to repeat itself along the bends of the river. The action at once became furious. The Confederate fleet, as stated above, only had fourteen guns in the entire fleet, while the Federal ironclad fleet carried 84 guns of the heaviest calibre. The noise of the engagement exceeded anything in volume ever dreamed of theretofore in the little city by the riverside. The sound of the cannon was almost continuous and the belching of smoke soon formed a wall of haze across the river, obscuring the enbattled gunboats from each other. It was the purpose of Commodore Montgomery, as he was then called, to use his boats as rams and thus destroy the Federal gunboat fleet by attacking their six ironclads with his eight rams. But he made the fatal mistake, or perhaps his subordinate commanders did, of stopping to fire their guns. At the sound of the first Confederate gun Colonel Ellet instantly gave orders to his ram fleet, calling out, "It is a gun from the enemy! Round out and follow me! Now is our chance!" The Queen of the West swung around, followed by the Monarch, in obedience to this order, and glided rapidly towards the openings between the Federal ironclads for the purpose of getting to the front. "Some of the officers of the Lancaster, the next boat in the line, became excited and confused and the pilot erred in signals, and backed the boat ashore and disabled her rudder. The captain of the Switzerland construed the general signal order to keep half a mile in rear of Lancaster to mean that he was to keep half a mile behind her in the engagement and therefore failed to participate; hence the whole brunt of the fight fell upon the Queen and the Monarch."*

These two steamers gallantly passed through the blazing line of Federal ironclads and through the belt of smoke in which only the tall chimneys of the Queen could be seen and came out in front of the entire Confederate fleet. Selecting the General Lovell, Captain Delancey as the nearest Confederate craft on which to try the power of his ran, Colonel Ellet signalled his brother, Captain Alfred W. Ellet, of the Monarch, to ram the General Price, Capt. J. E. Henthorne, which was at the extreme right of the Confederate line, and steamed swiftly toward the General Lovell. The Lovell accepted the challenge bravely and moved forward head on for the prow of the Queen of the West. But here the first accident of the battle occurred. The engines of the General Lovell got out of order and the boat became unmanageable, drifting half way round and exposing her side, which the Queen of the West struck amidships, crushing in her hull. For a few minutes the Queen of the West and the Lovell were entangled, and as the Queen of the West withdrew her prow the General Lovell, with a lurch, sank quickly beneath the muddy waters. A striking incident was witnessed from the shore at this moment by the cheering crowds of citizens. As the Lovell went down the bow gunners were loading the big eight-inch gun and unwilling to be denied, attached the lanyard and fired the gun for the last time at the enemy, while standing waist-deep in the water on the deck of the sinking vessel. The crew of the Lovell all escaped by swimming to the landing at the old Navy Yard.

As the Queen of the West stood by to see the Lovell sink

*Report of Secretary, Capt. A. B. Hill.

she was attacked by the Sumter from the east side, which struck her a heavy blow and disabled her wheel, leaving her helpless in the battle. Just at the moment of collision Colonel Ellet was shot in the knee with a pistol by Signal Quartermaster J. Sullivan on the Confederate vessel, receiving a wound which at once disabled him and a short while later resulted in his death. Lying helpless on the hurricane deck Colonel Ellet gave the order to run his boat on one wheel to the Arkansas shore, where she was grounded and took no further part in the combat.

The Monarch had in pursuance of her first order from Colonel Ellet singled out the General Price for ramming and was met by the Price in the onset with the like purpose of ramming the Monarch. They struck each other glancing blows which resulted in injury to neither. The Monarch then proceeded to attack the Beauregard which had turned and was coming down the river and was herself assailed by the General Price, but the Monarch being much the swifter of the boats moved past the Beauregard and Price and the Beauregard struck the Price, cutting off her wheel. The Price then crossed over to her and was run aground near the disabled Queen of the West and her unarmed crew was captured by the armed marines from the Queen, who had gone ashore for that purpose.

The Beauregard then endeavored to escape downstream and rejoin the remaining boats, but was intercepted by the Monarch and struck a heavy blow which wrought serious damage to her hull. The Beauregard was immediately hit by a big Federal shell in her waist, which completely disabled and almost wrecked her and she signalled to the Monarch her purpose to surrender. But the Monarch, which actually did most of the ram fighting and inflicted the greatest amount of injury or damage upon the Confederate boats sighted the Little Rebel, the flagship of Captain Montgomery, and headed for her. The Little Rebel was then endeavoring to ram a gunboat and was struck by a shell below the water-line, which passed through her boilers, completely wrecking her. The crew sprang into the river to swim ashore on the Arkansas side and the boat being near the shore, the Monarch attempted to ram her, but having only slight headway pushed her hard aground in shallow water. The crew of the Little Rebel escaped by swimming to the shore. The Monarch then returned to the Beauregard and towed her ashore with the hope of saving her, but she sunk to her boiler deck and later proved a total loss.

The Sumter and Bragg, like the other vessels of the Confederate fleet, had relied rather upon their guns than their prows, except when the Sumter assailed the Queen of the West near the beginning of the battle, with disastrous results to the latter, and being much cut up by the shot and shell of the Federal fleet, and manoeuvering to escape, both got aground in the shallow water of the bar on the Arkansas shore, and were soon after captured.

The Jeff Thompson fighting gallantly and assailed now from every side by an overwhelming force, was run ashore around the bend by Capt. Burke and set on fire, his men escaping to the shore, and soon blew up with a tremendous explosion.

The Van Dorn, the last of the Confederate vessels, having a good supply of coal and being uninjured in the fight, showed a clean pair of heels and escaped down the river. The storeboat Paul Jones also escaped in company with the Van Dorn, both going up the Yazoo River. This left the hapless city on the bluff at the mercy of the enemy's fleet and the crowds extending from Poplar to Union Streets along the river front sorrowfully waited in silence and humiliation to see what next would happen.

They did not have to wait long. Towards the close of the engagement Colonel Ellet was informed that a white flag had been raised in Memphis and sent his young son, Medical Cadet Chas. R. Ellet, ashore to demand the surrender of the city. It is curiously enough stated by Capt. Alfred W. Ellet, brother of Colonel Ellet, and in command of the ram Monarch during the battle, that Cadet Charles R. Ellet, was sent ashore in a rowboat with a party of three and a flag of truce and demanded the surrender of the city. The editor, then a boy of fifteen years, was a spectator on the bluff at the close of the engagement and, tumbling down from the face of the bluff as a Federal ram approached the shore about the foot of Court Street, ran down the levee and reached the edge of the river just as the ram touched the shore and ran out a stage plank. The ram carried a small flag of truce, not larger than a pocket handerchief on her jack-staff peak, and a number of marines were on duty in front of the bulklead about the bow of the boat. Some other small boys threw pebbles at these marines, calling them blue-bellies, which only provoked a smile and a warning. The editor's recollection is that this boat bore the name Monarch on a board at the top of the front cabin deck. A moment later a young man, who appeared to be eighteen or twenty years of age, came out on the gang-plank, not with a flag of truce, but with a United States flag tightly rolled up and tucked under his left arm with the staff extending behind him and without any escort of any sort, commenced to ascend the levee, followed first by the writer and perhaps two dozen small boys and three or four men, and proceeded rapidly up the bluff across Front Street to the then Federal Building or Post Office, now the Woman's Building, at the northeast corner of Jefferson and Third Streets, on reaching which the young man ascended the stairways and attic ladder to the top of the building, where he unfurled the United States flag. In the meantime the crowd accompanying him grew to several hundred in numbers but were perfectly orderly until the flag was unfurled. The mayor met the young cadet at the postoffice building and accompanied him to the roof with one or two policemen. When the Stars and Stripes were unfurled on the building the crowd below became noisy and attempted to reach the roof with a view to throwing the bold intruder off the building. A Confederate flag was soon obtained with a strong new, ashen staff and was carried up by a young man to replace the Federal flag, but the trap-door at the roof of the building was fastened down with a big policeman standing upon it, and all the efforts of the muscular young man to break the door with the aid of his ash flag-pole, proved unavailing. The crowd or mob then returned to the street and Mr. George W. L. Crook, then a young man, but afterwards quite a prominent citizen of Memphis, ran over to the southwest corner of Jefferson and Third Streets and ascending the steps at the front wall to the elevated yard of the Cummings Johnson residence, fired two or three shots with a revolver at the bold young cadet on the building. These proved ineffective and did not seem even to startle the cadet, who stood imperturbably by his flag, and the crowd left hurriedly to return to Front Street and see what further might be going on there. These are the personal recollections of the editor after fifty years and are still very vivid in his memory.

The young cadet Ellet bore with him a written message from Col. Charles Ellet to the mayor and civil authorities of Memphis, which was as follows:

"Opposite Memphis, June 6, 1862.
"To the Civic or Military Authorities of Memphis:

"Gentlemen: I understand that the city of Memphis has surrendered. I therefore send my son with two United States flags, with instructions to raise one upon your Custom House and the other upon the Court House, as evidence of the return of your city to the care and protection of the Constitution.

Chas. Ellet, Jr., Colonel Commanding."

The Mayor's reply was as follows:

"Mayor's Office, Memphis, Tenn., June 6, 1862.
"Col. Charles Ellet, Jr., Commanding, &c.

"Sir:—Your note of this date is received and contents noted. The civil authorities of this city are not advised of its surrender to the forces of the United States government, and our reply to you is simply to state respectfully that we have no forces to oppose the raising of the flag you have directed to be raised over the Custom House and post-office.

Respectfully,

Jno. Park, Mayor."

Later in the morning Flag Officer C. H. Davis, commanding the Federal fleet, also sent the following communication to the Mayor of the city:

"U. S. Flag-steamer Benton,

Off Memphis, June 6, 1862.

"To His Honor, the Mayor of the City of Memphis:

"Sir: I have respectfully to request that you will surrender the city of Memphis to the authority of the United States, which I have the honor to represent.

"I am, Mr. Mayor, with high respect, your most obedient servant, C. H. Davis,
Flag-officer, Commanding, &c."

To this the Mayor replied:

"Mayor's Office, Memphis, June 6, 1862.
"C. H. Davis, Flag-officer, Commanding, &c.

"Sir: Your note of this day is received and contents noted. In reply I have only to say that as the civil authorities have no means of defense, by the force of circumstances the city is in your hands. Respectfully,
John Park, Mayor"

Later in the day another communication was sent ashore to the Mayor as follows:

"U. S. Flagsteamer Benton, Off Memphis,
June 6, 1862.

"To His Honor, the Mayor of the City of Memphis,

"Sir: The undersigned, commanding the military and naval forces in front of Memphis, have the honor to say to the Mayor of the city, that Colonel Fitch, commanding the Indiana brigade, will take military possession of the city immediately.

"Colonel Fitch will be happy to receive the coöperation of his honor the mayor and the city authorities in maintaining peace and order, and to this end he will be pleased to confer with his honor at the military headquarters at three o'clock this afternoon.

"The undersigned have the honor to be, with high respect, your most obedient servants,
C. H. Davis, Commanding Afloat,
G. N. Fitch, Colonel, commanding Indiana brigade."

To this the Mayor replied:

"Mayor's Office, June 6, 1862.
"To Flag-officer C. H. Davis and Col. G. N. Fitch,

"Sirs: Your communication is received and I shall be

happy to coöperate with the colonel commanding in providing measures for maintaining peace and order in the city.

Your most obedient servant,

Jno. Park, Mayor."

And thus the possession of the city of Memphis was transferred forever from the control of the Confederate Government to that of the United States.

After the naval battle at Memphis the city remained quietly, as a garrison town of the Federal army, frequently congested with large bodies of troops assembled here preliminary to some important movement on the chess-board of war and at all times occupied by Federal officers pertaining to the garrison and to transient armies and who in many instances, fortunately not in all, caused great annoyance to the people of the town by petty persecutions and sometimes by wanton outrage.

The citizens of Memphis as a whole were unquestionably loyal to the cause of the South and did all in their power to aid it. They would go to great extremes, especially the devoted women of the town, to smuggle through the lines salt, medicine, clothing and other indispensables for their families in the Southern Army and this fact called down upon their heads the frequent wrath of the Federal officers. This wrath was exhibited in various ways. Sometimes refined women of prominent families were arrested and confined in the Irving Block prison, a place so horrible in its appointments that it subsequently abated by order of President Lincoln; the Commandant, Capt. Geo. A. Williams, being cashiered, but subsequently restored to duty as not being mainly responsible for the condition of the prison. An excerpt is here made as part of the history of the city, from a report made by Judge Advocate General J. Holt to President Lincoln, by whom the matter of the condition of the prison had been referred to him for report. General Holt says:

"According to a report of inspection made to Colonel Hardie by Lieut. Colonel John F. Marsh, 24th regiment Veteran Reserve corps, under date of April 28, 1864, the prison which is used for the detention of citizens, prisoners of war on their way to the North and the United States soldiers awaiting trial and which is located in a large block of stores is represented as the filthiest place the inspector ever saw occupied by human beings. The report proceeds thus:

" 'The whole management and government of the prison could not be worse! Discipline and order are unknown. Food sufficient but badly served. In a dark wet cellar I found twenty-eight prisoners chained to a wet floor, where they had been constantly confined, many of them for several months, one since November 16, 1863, and are not for a moment released, even to relieve the calls of nature. With a single exception these men have had no trial.'

"The hospital is described as having a shiftless appearance and the guard dirty and inefficient. It is also stated that there was no book or memorandum showing the distribution of the prison fund."

If the curtain of forgetfulness could be drawn back and all the stories, romantic, pathetic, pitiful, which originated in that dire dungeon during the several years in which it was occupied as a military prison by the Federal authorities disclosed, humanity would be shocked by the tragic narration. A few years ago when the building was being repaired and the kalsomining scraped from the walls in the upper stories the walls were found to be covered with legends written there by the victims of military oppression, giving their names and dates and sometimes details of their experiences. All this makes a dark chapter in the story of the Federal occupation of the city. The officer of the guard, a man named Lewis, wantonly shot a prisoner, Lieutenant Colonel Wood, of an Arkansas regiment, while asleep in bed. Lewis was arrested and ordered to be shot but escaped and disappeared. This is the only known or recorded instance of an attempt to punish any of those petty military tyrants for their crimes committed in connection with the Irving Block prison.

Sometimes ladies were sent to the state penitentiary at Alton, Illinois, and sometimes they were transported through the Federal lines and set adrift without protection. When the Confederate troops undertook to prevent the operation of trains on the Memphis and Charleston Railroad by attacking and capturing the trains and guard, groups of prominent citizens were arrested by orders of General Sherman and confined in passenger coaches on the trains, that they might receive the fire of their Southern friends in case the train was attacked. Occasionally, when scouts were fired on in the vicinity of Memphis, General Sherman would send a detachment with orders to burn all the houses in the vicinity and to shoot the male inhabitants. When steamboats were fired on, while engaged in military duties in the vicinity of Memphis, the nearest town was burned in retaliation and in this way Hopefield, opposite Memphis, and Randolph some forty miles above Memphis, met with a fiery doom. These are not merely baseless charges, growing out of legends or rumors which have survived the war, but the facts in these several cases are fully set out in the reports of the Federal commanders, printed in the Records of the Rebellion now to be found in every public library.

In order to make the town impregnable a great fortress was built in the southern part of the city on the river-bank known as Fort Pickering, probably named for the old fort built in that quarter about 1803, by General Wilkinson. This fortress was built in a broken line beginning at or about the foot of Vance Street and running somewhat southeastward and turning in towards the river again below the site of the Marine hospital, as at present located. The greatest distance from the river reached by the eastward extention of the fort, was at an angle about or near the corner of Railroad and Pennsylvania Avenues, some fifteen hundred feet from the river-bank.

Brig. General Z. B. Tower, in a report made of this fortification, on May 25, 1865, says among other things:

"Fort Pickering, with its keep, has a crest of about two miles and a half in length. If we except Washington, upon which immense labor has been expended, no city has been so thoroughly defended with redoubts and infantry lines upon a development of six miles as indicated above. * * * * This fort is mostly a broken line. Its ditches are therefore swept. It is fairly constructed, has a good command, so that the parapet gives excellent cover to the defenders; some traverses along the crest and some within the work would have been judicious, furnishing excellent resting places for portions of a garrison not on duty. The ditches are from six to seven feet deep and excavated on so steep a slope (which the tenacious soil permits) that it would be difficult to get over the parapet without ladders, and especially so under canister and musketry fire. The work therefore may be pronounced strong as an obstacle, which obstacle has been increased in portions of the contour lines by inclined palisades placed in advance. It would be difficult to assault Fort Pickering. * * * * There are some magazines near the parapet and under its cover. At the south end of the fort two ancient mounds are used as barbette batteries, which have a fine command over the country."

These mounds, it will readily be seen, are the Chisca Mounds, remaining just as they were discovered by DeSoto, as stated in the early part of this narrative, and the magazines referred to by General Tower are constructed of brick and cement and are still to be seen deep in the bodies of the mound.

This great fort which, next to Fortress Rosecrans at Murfreesboro, was the most powerful fortress constructed by the Federal armies in the South during the Civil War, was armed with 97 pieces of artillery ranging from six pounder field-batteries to thirty-two-pounder rifle cannon and eight-inch columbiads and siege-mortars.

And so, as the war went on from year to year, the people were more and more antagonized by their conquerers and became more and more resentful, but with the exception of some skirmishes on the outposts, or an occasional alarm caused by a rumor of a descent of Forrest, there was no real fighting or bloody drama of war enacted within the limits of the city until the 21st of August, 1864.

At this time General Forrest, who had been engaged for several months in conducting formidable raids into West Tennessee, or in defending the great grain section in the prairie regions of Mississippi from repeated Federal endeavors to destroy it and being confronted with a large army of infantry and cavalry which was rapidly forcing his small command of about 3,500 men southward in the vicinity of Oxford, Missis-

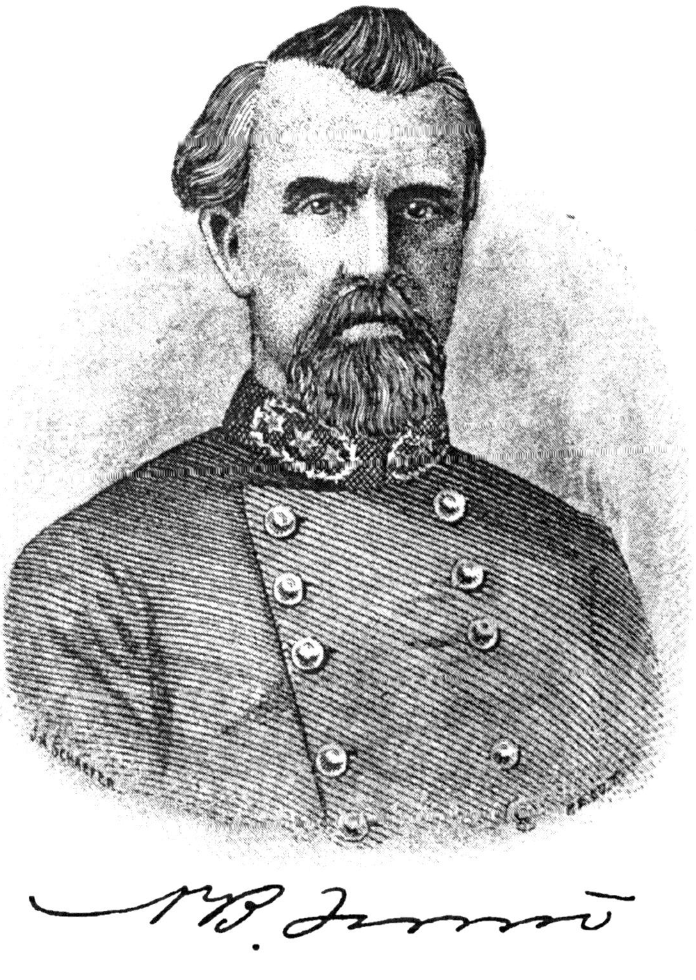

sippi, conceived the idea of riding past the Federal column commanded by General A. J. Smith, attaining his rear and making a rapid descent on Memphis, his great base of operations, and by capturing it with an irresistable charge at daybreak, force his overwhelming competitor to withdraw from Mississippi. This scheme once conceived by Forrest, was carried out with lightning-like rapidity and the troopers of the famous Confederate cavalry commander were actually dashing through the streets of the city of Memphis a hundred miles to Smith's rear, shouting, shooting and riding down their terrified enemies before General Smith had discovered his adversary's absence from his front.

Forrest, in order to carry out his brilliant conception, had taken about 1500 of the 3500 men under his command at Oxford, the detachment being of picked men and horses of Bell's, McCulloch's and Neely's brigades, and a section of Morton's battery, and left Oxford at five o'clock on the afternoon of August 18, 1864, in a pouring rain and started to Memphis, being compelled to make a circuitous route by Panola in order to make a crossing of the swollen Tallahatchie River. The march was made with tremendous speed in mud and rain, Panola being reached at seven o'clock on the morning of the 19th, and Senatobia on the same afternoon, where he stayed all night. Stopping next morning at Hickahala Creek and then at Cold Water, over which formidable streams he was compelled to improvise bridges constructed of logs, telegraph poles, grape-vines and the floors of gin-houses, by nightfall Forrest was at Hernando and after stopping to feed and water his tired horses took the direct road for Memphis in a drizzling rain with a great fog prevailing.

The command approached the city by way of the Hernando Road and was at Cane Creek about four miles from Court Square, by three o'clock in the morning. Meantime Forrest had, with his usual foresight, ascertained through trusted scouts and spies the exact condition of things in the menaced city, the number of troops there, the location of the encampment, the positions of the picket posts and, more important than all, the exact locations of the places of abode of the three Federal commanders, Generals C. C. Washburn, S. A. Hurlbut and R. P. Buckland. Calling his brigade and detachment commanders together Forrest gave detailed and explicit instructions as to the part each one was assigned to perform in the approaching drama and distributed among them the necessary guides. His brother, Captain Wm. H. Forrest, was directed to surprise the picket on the Hernando Road, if possible, and then to dash forward into the city without being diverted for any other purpose, and following the most direct route to the Gayoso House, to capture Major General Hurlbut and other Federal officers known to be quartered there. Colonel Neely was directed to charge impetuously the big encampment of one hundred days' men bivouched across the Hernando Road in the southern outskirts of the city and to use for this purpose his command composed of the Second Missouri, Lieut. Col. Bob McCulloch, 14th Tennessee, Lieut. Col. R. R. White and 18th Mississippi, Lieut. Col. Ham Chalmers. Col. Thomas H. Logwood was to follow rapidly after Captain Forrest with the 12th and 15th Tennessee regiments, leaving detachments for observation at Main and Beale and Shelby and Beale Streets, and to establish another at the steamboat landing at the foot of Union Street. Lieut. Col. Jesse Forrest was ordered to move rapidly down DeSoto Street to Union and thence westward along that street to the residence of Major-General C. C. Washburn, then in command of Memphis, on the north side of Union at the alley east of Third Street in the building now known as the Blood residence, 206-8 Union Avenue, the General's headquarters being then in the residence of Gen. Joseph R. Williams, later the Y. M. C. A. building and now the University of Tennessee building on the south side of Union Avenue opposite the intersection of Third Street. Colonel Forrest's orders were to surround the residence and capture General Washburn at all hazards.

General Forrest ordered to be held in reserve Newsom's and Russell's regiment and the Second Tennessee under Lieut. Colonel Morton, with Sale's section of artillery, which force was designed to cover the movement and keep the highway open for retreat, when the troopers who had entered the city had accomplished their purpose. Everything being ready the command was formed into column of fours and moved forward at a quarter past three a. m., Captain William H. Forrest, brother of the General, being in command of the vanguard, a picked body of forty men.

It was still dark, a heavy fog having settled over the environs of Memphis following the three days of rain and this fog was so dense that neither man nor horse could be distinguished at more than thirty paces, as the column headed by Captain Forrest filed noiselessly across the Cane Creek bridge. General Forrest, who left nothing to chance, after a half-mile march, halted his column and sent his accomplished aide-de-camp, Captain C. W. Anderson, to see that each officer "understood precisely and clearly the duty that had been specially entrusted to his execution." When Captain C. W. Anderson reported, showing that all was clearly understood by the commanders, General Forrest put the column in motion again at a slow walk. He had enjoined upon all commanders and soldiers the necessity of the most perfect silence until the heart of the town was reached and the surprise was complete.

Captain Forrest, with ten picked men rode some sixty paces ahead of his command until the first picket was reached, about two miles from Court Square on the Hernando Road. When the challenge of the picket came in the stillness of the morning calling out, "Halt! Who comes there!" Captain Forrest was ready with an answer and quietly replied, "A detachment of the 12th Missouri cavalry with rebel prisoners." Instantly came the usual response of the picket, "Advance one!" Captain Forrest rode forward, telling his men to follow silently but closely behind. When he reached the picket mounted in the middle of the road Captain Forrest rode up familiarly beside him as if to explain who he was but suddenly, with his heavy revolver, struck the unsuspecting picket such a crushing blow on the head that he reeled from his saddle to the ground. His men sprang forward and captured the picket-post a few steps rearward to the left of the highway with scarcely a sound above their voices. One of the pickets, however, a little apart from the others, fired his gun, which was heard with no little concern by General Forrest, who was riding at the head of his column one hundred yards to the rear of his brother. Captain Forrest instantly pressed forward with his detachment and a quarter of a mile rearward was received with a volley by the next picket-post which had been given the alarm by the firing of the single gun. Captain Forrest instantly charged this post, scattering the pickets in every direction and, without waiting to secure them as prisoners, and knowing that he was now past the picket lines, dashed forward with his little squadron towards the city. But the boyish troopers in their enthusiasm forgot the injunction of silence and when within, as they soon were, the suburbs of the city they began shouting in the wildest fashion and the contagion spreading, the whole column was soon madly riding forward on the Hernando Road at full cry like a pack of eager hounds.

The day was just breaking when a long line of tents stretching across the highway in front and occupied by sleeping Federal soldiers became visible through the fog. The alarm having been given by the shouting against the express orders of General Forrest, nothing could be gained by further silence, and calling to his favorite bugler, Gauze, always at his elbow in battle, Forrest directed the charge to be blown and instantly every regimental bugle took up and repeated again and again the inspiring notes. Captain Forrest's detachment discovered just short of the encampment the Federal battery in bivouac besides the road to the left and immediately left the highway and charged the sleeping artillerists, shooting some 15 or 20 of them as they sprang from their blankets, and without stopping to secure the guns, galloped on in their mad rush for the heart of the city, not drawing rein until they had reached the Gayoso Hotel, the place of abode of Major General S. A. Hurlbut. Meantime Col. Thos. H. Logwood, who had been ordered to take two regiments, the 12th and 15th Tennessee and dash for the heart of the city, deploying his men when he reached the position on Beale Street, from DeSoto to the river in order to present a barrier to any Federal force attempting to drive the two detachments away which were hunting for the Federal generals in their residences, had succeeded in reaching his goal, but passed en route, through a column of infantry, formed across the Hernando road in haste following the alarm of the attack, and finally galloped down Hernando Street to the market-house and up Beale across to the Gayoso Hotel. The men, wild with excitement, and many of them for the first time since the war in their native town again, shouted like demons as they rode and thousands of citizens, aroused from their slumbers by the unwonted din, and finding their streets occupied by gray-coated troopers, threw off all timidity and men and women in their night-clothes filled the galleries and windows of residences, waving handkerchiefs or pillow-slips and shouting in unrestrained glee, "It's Forrest! It's Forrest!" As narrated by an eye-witness soon after, "Memphis was the home of many of those gray-coated young riders who suddenly burst into the heart of the city that August morning; and the women, young and old, forgetting the costume of the hour, throwing open their window blinds and doors, welcomed their dear countrymen by voice and smiles and every possible manifestation of delight inspired by such an advent."

In the meantime Lieut. Colonel Jesse Forrest, another brother of the General's, had with a detachment by direction of the General, ridden rapidly and silently through the streets to the residence and headquarters of General C. C. Washburn, the residence being now known as the Blood House, No. 206 Union Avenue, but at that time the home of Mr. W. B. Greenlaw, a prominent citizen, which had been seized by General Washburn in the absence of Mr. Greenlaw for his own domicile and that of his family. The building is the large two-story brick structure on the north side of Union Avenue nearly a block east of Third Street and the headquarters was at the residence of General Joseph Williams, which was subsequently known as the Y. M. C. A. Building and later the University of Memphis Building, No. 177 on the south side of Union Avenue, nearly opposite the intersection of Third Street. Col. Jesse Forrest's detachment, including some Memphis boys familiar with the premises, reached and surrounded the building, but the bird had flown. General Washburn had been notified by a courier sent by Col. M. H. Starr of the 6th Illinois cavalry, of his danger, and being warned by the courier that the firing nearby was by Forrest's men, had slipped down the interior basement stairs in his night-clothes and going into the alley between Monroe and Union Streets, had fled bare-footed to the river bluffs at the foot of Union Street and thence along under the bluffs to the Federal fortress, the north end of which touched the river-bank about the foot of Vance Street. The General escaped from his residence while or just before the gray-clad troopers under Col. Jesse Forrest were climbing the front and rear steps of the building, leaving his uniform, boots, hat and sword in his bed-room where his wife was also found, and these articles of attire, together with his private papers, were secured by the Confederate troopers. The dramatic incident and narrow escape caused General Hurlbut to remark next morning, when he heard of it, as narrated by General Chalmers, "There it goes again! They superseded me with Washburn because I could not keep Forrest out of West Tennessee, and Washburn cannot keep him out of his bed-room!"

General Forrest, later in the day, courteously returned by flag of truce, the uniform and sword of General Washburn to that doughty commander with the message that he, a Federal Major-general, would probably have more need of them than Forrest had and incidentally another message, that he had 600 Federal prisoners barefooted and hatless down on the Hernando road and would like to have some clothing and provisions for them, which request was promptly granted by General Washburn, the supplies sent being so lavish that after feeding his prisoners General Forrest was enabled to give a full meal to each of his own men.

In the meantime, Captain Forrest, with his detachment of forty bold riders, had reached and surrounded the Gayoso Hotel with the hope of capturing General Hurlbut and staff, as before stated. Captain Forrest, with the instinctive individuality of the Forrest family, rode with several of his companions mounted into the rotunda of the hotel from Shelby

Street and calling for the hotel register and a cigar, both of which were promptly furnished by the frightened clerk, he registered his name as a guest. He then began a systematic search of all the rooms for Federal officers and found and put under guard a number but failed to find General Hurlbut, that officer lodging that night as reported by General Washburn, with Col. A. R. Eddy, assistant quarter-master. A Federal officer, hearing the disturbance in the rotunda and supposing it to be caused by some drunken Federal soldiers leaned over the balcony and called out to know what the trouble was. Captain Forrest startlingly made him aware of the nature of the trouble by a pistol-ball which caused the untimely death of the Federal officer.

While these dramatic occurrences were happening in the city, General Forrest, who had remained behind with the remainder of his force in the suburbs to look after the Federal forces in that quarter and to prevent his daring columns, then in the heart of the city, from being cut off in their effort to rejoin him, had found much to do along the line of the Hernando road and eastward on McLemore Avenue in subduing the now thoroughly aroused Federal troops in that quarter. Neely's men after Colonels Logwood and Forrest, had broken through the line of Federal encampment reaching across the Hernando Road, had charged eastward of that road into that part of the encampment and met with serious resistance after the Federal soldiers had recovered from their first alarm. The two regiments of one hundred day men and some other troops in that quarter, about a thousand strong, had succeeded in deploying and received Colonel Neely's men from the rear of their tents with a hot fire. Upon observing this General Forrest led the other column of reserves under Colonel Bell to Neely's aid, intending to attack the Federals on their left flank; but he here unexpectedly came across a cavalry camp from which he received a withering fire. This command was extended along in the grove just north of McLemore Avenue, General Forrest, without waiting for the reserves still to his rearward, instantly charged this encampment with his escort, dispersing the Federals and capturing all their horses with many prisoners. Neely at the same time charged dismounted upon the hundred-day men in his front, driving them pell mell northward. Many of these and most of the cavalry detachment took refuge in the State Female College buildings, several hundred yards eastward, the strong brick walls of which afforded them perfect shelter. Unable to dislodge them General Forrest directed Lieutenant Sale to bring up this section of artillery and shell the enemy out of the buildings which were then vacant. A number of shells were fired and several exploded in the main building. But finding the place very strong and not worth the loss it would cost to capture it General Forrest withdrew his reserves back to the Hernando road so as to prevent the reassembling there of Federal troops who might cut off the retreat of his men from the city.

In the meantime, having accomplished the objects for which they had been sent into the uptown districts, the Confederates in that quarter had been ordered to retire and rejoin General Forrest on the Hernando Road. The detachments uptown had become much scattered in their enthusiastic rushes about the city and it required some little time to collect them, but having at length rejoined their respective columns, Colonels Logwood and Forrest effected a junction on DeSoto Street and moved out together. When they had reached the vicinity of the Provine house on the Hernando Road they found a strong line of infantry formed across that highway as a support for the batteries there, the same whose gunners had been twice dispersed in the rush into the town, but had once more rallied and taken position commanding the road. When this force was reached it was instantly charged mounted by Capt. Peter Williams, Company I, 15th Tennessee, who received a check, but being reinforced by Company H, Lieutenant Witherspoon of the same regiment, another charge was made, and this time the brave gunners were again driven away and the guns captured, but for want of teams could not be brought away. All the Confederates were now out of the city except the small number which had been killed, wounded or captured and a few stragglers who were soon chased out by a body of several hundred Federal cavalry. This force found some other of Forrest's men still in the infantry camp, engaged in equipping or feeding themselves on the abandoned rations, and these endeavored to mount and get away. Finding them in peril General Forrest, taking a small detachment of the 2nd Missouri Cavalry nearby charged in turn and drove the Federal detachment back. An incident strikingly characteristic of Forrest occurred here. Col. M. H. Starr, of the 6th Illinois cavalry headed this detachment and bravely confronted Forrest in the charge. Colonel Starr rode out in front of his command as if to challenge General Forrest, whom he recognized, to personal combat between the lines. Forrest instantly accepted the challenge and leaving his detachment halted, turned the head of King Philip, his famous war horse, toward the brave Federal commander and rushed forward alone. At this juncture however, a detachment of the 15th Tennessee, under Col. Hugh D. Greer of Memphis, which was nearby, observed the apparent rashness of their General and fearing that he would be himself killed by the Federal line after disposing of Colonel Starr, which none doubted he would do, were ordered by Colonel Greer to end the strange combat by firing on Colonel Starr. This was promptly done by several dismounted riflemen and Colonel Starr was mortally wounded. Forrest, enraged at being thus deprived of his opportunity as a swordsman, galloped rapidly to the front of the 15th Tennessee detachment and denounced them vehemently in no choice language for shooting Colonel Starr, saying that the latter was a brave man and that he intended to meet him as a soldier and give him every chance to defend himself.

The Confederate troops were then withdrawn quietly and deliberately to Cane Creek, a mile from the scene of this last fighting, and halted there, where they were not further molested by Federal soldiers. There were many interesting incidents which occurred uptown during the wild ride of these boyish troopers through the heart of the city. Several endeavored to release the Confederate prisoners in the Irving Block, still standing near the northeast corner of Court Square, but found it strongly guarded and barricaded. Private James Stokes of the Bluff City Grays, a Memphis company in Forrest's old regiment, went as far as the Federal building or post-office, now the Woman's Building, at the northeast corner of Jefferson and Third Streets, and was killed by a shot from the Federal barracks just eastward on Jefferson Street. His gun, a breech-loading carbine, was picked up by a citizen and preserved, and is now a valued relic in the hall of the Confederate Historic Association, recalling as a souvenir of those bloody days the death of a brave son of Memphis fighting for her release from captivity on one of her prominent streets. Many Federal horses and equipments were gathered up by the bold riders as well as several hundred prisoners, the latter being largely taken in the charge upon the encampment south of the city. When the Federal battery was first charged in the onset into the city the guns were abandoned by the frightened gunners but a colored sergeant, Benjamin F. Thacker, who was detailed as a recruiting officer of Company I, Second U. S. Colored artillery, with Lieutenant B. Halley of Company K, 61st U. S. colored infantry, boldly ran among the guns, charging one with canister shot and fired it at thirty paces into the flank of Forrest's escort just then passing, Private Tom McCord, of the escort, with his horse receiving the entire charge of thirteen canister shots, by reason of which he lost his leg. Mr. McCord was living until recently in Bedford County, Tennessee, wearing a wooden leg as a souvenir of this terrible experience. His horse was literally torn to pieces. This brave negro sergeant, Thacker, was a half hour later seriously wounded in the fighting in front of the State Female College and at a barricade across College Avenue, between the college and Elmwood Cemetery.

It is proper now to give some statements of the Federal side of this unique conflict and to this end excerpts will be made from the reports of several of the Federal commanders. General C. C. Washburn, commanding the district of Tennessee and whose capture was one of the main purposes of this dash into the city, after stating that General Forrest had attacked the city on the morning of August 21, with 2,500 or 3,000 men, adds:

"A force consisting of about one-third of Forrest's command was detached by him and ordered to dash over the pickets and into the city, while the remainder engaged our forces outside. This detachment came in on the Hernando Road, driving in the pickets and riding past a regiment of 100-days troops that was there stationed, and rode with the utmost rapidity to my headquarters, which they at once thoroughly invested, giving me barely a moment's time to escape. Another party rode to the Gayoso House, where they expected to find Major-General Hurlbut, but in this they were disappointed, he lodging that night with Col. A. R. Eddy, assistant quartermaster. Another part went to attack General Buckland's headquarters, but making a mistake in the street gave him also time to escape.''

Col. W. H. Thurston, assistant-inspector general of the 16th army corps, thus reports:

"Memphis was entered about 5 a. m. by about 400 of Major General Forrest's command. They moved on Memphis by the Hernando Road, and drove in the pickets on that road, One Hundred and Thirty-seventh Illinois (100 days) volunteers, and easily broke their lines and entered the city, dividing into two squads of about 200 each, one under the command of Lieut. Colonel Logwood, the other under Jesse Forrest, or Bill Forrest (reports conflict); one squad surrounded the Gayoso House, the other occupied Union Street, on which Major General Washburn has his headquarters and resides. Major General Washburn, having been notified by Colonel Starr, 6th Illinois cavalry, of their approach, left his residence as early as possible, and made his way to Fort Pickering, without having given any command as to what should be done by our troops. He could much more easily have retired to headquarters of provost guard than to have gone to the fort, as the fort is full one-half mile from his house, and but three squares to the provost marshall's office. On the 23rd the whole town was stampeded at about ten a. m. by a report being circulated that Forrest had returned in force and was again in town. It was the most disgraceful affair I have ever seen, and proves that there is demoralization and want of confidence by the people in our army and our army in some of its officers. No blame can be attached to Brig. General Buckland that I can hear of. On the 23rd, so far as I can learn, no Confederate troops were nearer than Forrest's rear, which was probably not less than twenty-five to thirty miles distant, and the alarm was probably caused by some of the troops firing off their guns which had been loaded since Sunday."

The result of this daring venture was that General Forrest, after entering the city and demoralizing the large Federal army stationed here, almost to the point of panic and scaring their generals out of their rests at daylight, had prudently left the telegraph wires untouched until General A. J. Smith, with his army of 13,000 men, whom he had left at Oxford, Mississippi, could be thoroughly informed that he had captured Memphis, and then had them cut. General Smith, alarmed by this information, immediately began a rapid retreat to Memphis with his whole army, which was exactly what General Forrest had planned by this daring movement to compel him to do and which result he had completely accomplished. And so it was that General Forrest, unable to obstruct Smith's great army in any way on its movement into the heart of Mississippi, by stratagem had compelled his retreat to its starting point.

When we consider the immense odds against Forrest it will be realized that this was one of the most brilliant moves of his career. Only Forrest could have conceived and executed it. As to the forces engaged, the report of Major General O. O. Howard, inspector-general of that military department, shows that the Federal force in Memphis from the return of August 24, exceeded eighteen thousand men, including those with General A. J. Smith at Oxford. This report was made to General Halleck by General Howard on August 24, 1864. The field returns for September 1, 1864, shows that General Smith had with him present for duty 8,427 infantry, rank and file, and the report of General Washburn, dated September 22, shows that he had in addition to this 4,800 cavalry, making a total force of 13,227 in Smith's army at Oxford when Forrest left the front of it to attack Memphis. Deducting this from the eighteen thousand and odd hundred men reported by General Howard, as stated above, we find that on August 24, there was a force of 5,000 infantry encamped in Memphis, besides cavalry, reported by Lieutenant Colonel George Duffield, commanding the Second brigade, as 650 troopers. There were also 2,000 armed and equipped militia present for duty as shown by the report of Brig. General C. W. Dustan, their commander, the report also being signed by Captain Alfred G. Tuther, A. A. A. G., our late prominent citizen. This gave a total Federal force in the city of 7,650 infantry and cavalry, besides numerous batteries of artillery and the garrison of the great fort or fortress at Fort Pickering.

As above stated, the troops brought to Memphis by General Forrest were detachments of the Second Missouri and Eighteenth Mississippi regiments of McCulloch's brigade; the 12th, 14th and 15th Tennessee cavalry regiment of Neely's brigade and Russell's and Newsom's regiments of Bell's brigade. These detachments from said regiments were of picked men, having serviceable horses, deemed able to stand the fatigues of the long ride in the rain and numbered all told, about 1,475 effective men, of which not exceeding 500 entered the city, the remainder staying with General Forrest to cover the retreat. The operation against Memphis was brilliantly conceived by her great cavalry commander Forrest and brilliantly carried out, the exploit costing him a total of nine killed and twenty-six wounded. The losses of the Federal forces were reported by General Washburn as fifteen killed, sixty-five wounded and one hundred sixteen captured. But the detailed report of the several commanders show the total losses to have been two hundred and seventy-three killed, wounded and missing. Of these one battery alone, the 7th Wisconsin, which was run over at the outset in the charge, lost four killed, two wounded and nine prisoners, besides 64 artillery horses. General Forrest, after the fighting was over, retired leisurely to Hernando, Mississippi and thence to his command at Oxford. In return for courtesies extended him by General Forrest, through Adjutant General J. P. Strange, in sending back his uniform and sword, General Washburn had made a beautifully engraved sword of the highest finish and sent it as a present to Major Strange. This sword is now in the possession of the daughter of Major Strange, Mrs. W. R. Barksdale, of this city.

The subsequent military history of Memphis during the remainder of the War Between the States has been fully treated in the chapters on municipal history in previous pages of this book. After the close of the war the military history of Memphis is continued in the achievement of her celebrated militia companies, the Chickasaw Guards and Bluff City Grays and later organizations, which will now be briefly described.

The Chickasaw Guards became, possibly, the most famous militia organization in the United States, owing to its wonderful efficiency in drill and discipline, they having in their career overcome in competitive drill and inspection nearly all the most noted bodies of citizen soldiery in the land.

This company was organized on the 30th day of June, 1874. Its officers were R. P. Duncan, captain; W. P. Martin, first-lieutenant; James R. Wright, second-lieutenant; P. A. Ralston, third-lieutenant; John Poston, ensign; and L. Mix, sergeant. The company was unfortunate in its first competitive drill and was defeated by the Porter Rifles of Nashville in May, 1875, but being reorganized in October of the same year and with R. P. Duncan as captain; S. T. Carnes, first lieutenant; T. A. Lamb, second lieutenant; and J. S. Richardson, third lieutenant, they retrieved their reputation and easily defeated their late antagonists.

In May, 1878, S. T. Carnes became captain and the Chickasaws in the same month defeated the Bluff City Grays of Memphis, a noted company of that day. In September of the same year, when they drilled at St. Louis, against the best ten companies in the United States, they were overcome by but one point in a possible 300 by Company C of Chicago. After exhibition drills at Indianapolis, Cincinnati, Columbus, Chicago and Louisville to raise money to aid the yellow-fever sufferers in Memphis, they took first prize at a great drill at Chattanooga, Carnes still being captain and N. B. Camp, Harry Allen and W. L. Clapp, lieutenants. In October, 1879, the Chickasaws were pitted against a field of eight companies at St. Louis and won first prize over all. A few days later they were first in another prize competition at Columbus, Ohio, and on May 19, 1880 defeated the Rock City Guards and Porter

Rifles of Nashville and Company K of St. Louis, at the former city. At New Orleans in 1881, the Chickasaws defeated the Crescent Rifles, League Guards and Nichols Rifles of New Orleans, the Mobile Rifles and the Houston Light Guards. *Harper's Weekly* of July 2, 1881 published a cut of the Chickasaw Guards in line, with this legend: "The Chickasaw Guards of Memphis have now the reputation by decision of West Point officers of being the most perfectly drilled company of citizen soldiery in the United States. In 1879 General Sherman witnessed their drill at the contest in St. Louis and pronounced them superior to anything in or out of West Point."

The Drill Teams of 1878 and 1879 were taken from the following list:

Sam T. Carnes, captain; N. B. Camp, 1st lieutenant; Harry Allen, 2nd lieutenant; W. L. Clapp, 3rd lieutenant; Richard Wright, 1st sargeant; T. A. Lamb, 2nd sargeant; A. R. Taylor, 3rd sargeant; R. W. Harris, 4th sargeant; S. A. Pepper, 5th sargeant; W. W. Talbot, 1st corporal; Jno. C. Henderson, 2nd corporal; Sam J. Hayes, 3rd corporal; A. H. Proudfit, 4th corporal. Privates: Allen Asher, Richard H. Allen, Jno. Bradley, Henry J. Bailey, J. W. Clapp, Jr., Walter C. Chidester, A. L. Duval, L. R. Donelson, Howard Edmonds, J. B. Jones, Pete Jones, Chas. Joseph, Walter M. Johnson, Tom Johnson, C. H. Raine, John Sanoner, Ralph Semmes, John S. Speed, W. J. Steel, W. A. Sneed, T. H. Allen, Jr., B. I. Busby, Lamar Chappell, Haze Chiles, Geo. W. Crook, C. Q. Harris, Harry A. Hunter, Joe B. Houchens, Fred Hessig, James Kirkland, John Kirtland, I. F. Peters, James Proudfit, S. H. Phillips, H. J. Parrish, Chas. Patton, P. C. Smith, John W. Tyler, Will Warren, Chas. M. Waldran, John D. Waldran, L. B. Wright, T. A. Wright, Tom A. White, J. A. Wooldridge, R. T. Cooper, Jefferson Davis, Jr., Sam I. McDowell, Branch Martin, John Newsom.

On June 28, 1882, however, the Chickasaws were defeated by the Crescent Rifles of New Orleans, but in the same drill defeated the Porters of Nashville and the Quapaw Guards of Little Rock. At Indianapolis on July 5, 1882, the Chickasaws defeated the Crescent Rifles, Porter Rifles, Quapaw Guards,

Asbury Cadets of Indiana, Indianapolis Light Infantry, Company K, of St. Louis and McKean Cadets of Terra Haute, Indiana. In the drill at Louisville the Chickasaws won the championship of Tennessee by defeating the Porter Rifles and at Indianapolis the championship of the United States. Owing to weather conditions the Chickasaws met with bad luck in 1885 at Mobile and New Orleans.

Among the noted militia companies of Memphis of that day were the Bluff City Grays, organized October 1, 1876, with J. F. Cameron, captain; F. T. Edmondson, first-lieutenant; T. C. Rogers, second-lieutenant. In 1879 J. F. Cameron was still captain; Herbert Rhett, first-lieutenant; Hugh Pettit, second lieutenant; and R. B. Armour, second lieutenant. In 1880 T. A. Lamb was elected captain and was followed by Herbert Rhett in 1881.

The Memphis Light Guards, thirty-eight strong, were organized July, 1877. The officers were E. B. Moseley, captain; E. M. Apperson, Jr., first lieutenant; and H. S. Trezevant, second lieutenant. This company was consolidated with the Bluff City Grays in 1882 and became the Porter Guards with J. D. Waldran, captain; Kellar Anderson, first lieutenant; H. G. Getchell, second lieutenant; M. T. Cooper, third lieutenant.

Another company called the Porter Reserves, was organized in 1879 during the epidemic, with Frank Lamont, captain and W. J. Freeman, G. M. Guerrant and W. J. Jones, lieutenants. It disbanded in about two years.

In June, 1882, the Waldran Guards were organized with L. V. Dixon, captain, and E. C. Campbell, T. Hawkins and C. Kellar, Jr., lieutenants. This company was disbanded after a year or two's service. Another company called the Memphis Light Infantry was organized in May, 1885, with B. F. Hollenberg, captain, but was disbanded soon after.

In September, 1886, the Memphis Zouaves were organized with F. K. Deffry as captain; Charles J. Rauch, James D. Proudfit and B. C. Sawtelle, as lieutenants.

These companies were organized and fostered with little or no authority of law, Tennessee having no settled militia laws at that time, but in 1887 on act was passed providing for

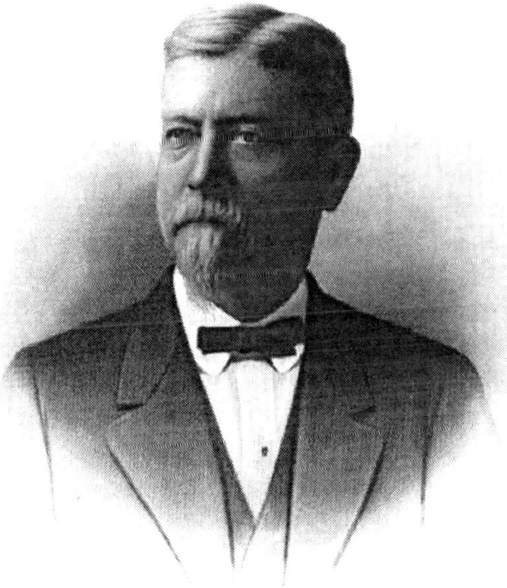

Eng by F. G. Williams & Bro. N.Y.

A. R. Taylor

a thorough organization of the militia and the Second Regiment of State militia was organized, in which there were four Memphis companies. Of this regiment S. T. Carnes was elected Colonel, and when he was elected Brigadier General of the State Militia in 1889, Hugh Pettit was elected Colonel and A. R. Taylor became Lieut. Colonel of the regiment and I. F. Peters, Major. In this regiment were four Memphis companies, namely, Company A, the Chickasaw Guards, Junior, Captain W. A. Kyle; Company B, Neeley Zouaves, F. K. Deffrey, captain; Company F, the Forrest Rifles, Wright Smith, captain; Company G, Kellar Anderson, captain, was nominally attached to this regiment but was on detached service during the Coal Creek troubles in 1891 and 1892. During the insurrection of the miners at Coal Creek, Captain Kellar Anderson was appointed to command the forces there after the return of the main body of the militia which had been present there under the command of General S. T. Carnes and Colonel A. R. Taylor and was in command of the fort or redoubt overlooking Coal Creek during the skirmishing with the miners in the vicinity of the fort. Two boys were killed in these disturbances, namely, Lee Waterman, Junior, killed by the premature discharge of a howitzer, and Private Smith, who was waylaid and shot by the insurgents while on post as a picket. In 1894 Colonel A. R. Taylor was elected Brigadier General, the term of Brig. General S. T. Carnes, having expired. All of the officers of the Second regiment resigned and the regiment and companies led an anomolous existence for several years without regular organization.

At the beginning of the Cuban War in 1898 the Second regiment was reorganized, with Kellar Anderson as Colonel, T. E. Patterson, Lieutenant Colonel and M. E. Walker and F. K. Deffrey, Majors.

The Memphis companies in the regiment at this time numbered three, commanded respectively by George A. Chighizola, W. R. Derrick and John Hampton as captains. The regiment, however, never reached the front, being kept on garrison or post duty during the remainder of the war, but Colonel Kellar Anderson, its commander, was transferred to the Forty-seventh

United States infantry as major, and served through the remainder of the Spanish War in the Philippines.

After the Cuban War the Fifth Tennessee regiment was disbanded and the Second regiment was reorganized, taking part of the Fifth regiment, and Captain J. W. Canada of the latter regiment was made colonel. In the Second regiment after reorganization there were three Memphis companies, namely, A, the Neely Zouaves, Captain Kit Deffrey; E. Frazier Rifles, Captain John Hampton; 1, Forrest Rifles, Captain Singleton; and M, Governor's Guards, formerly commanded by Captain Canada.

About 1906 Company G, the Patterson Guards, were organized by Captain Hearn Tidwell, of Memphis, giving Memphis five companies in the regiment.

In 1908 the Second regiment was again reorganized, being consolidated with the First regiment and taking the name of the latter. This regiment now contains all the Middle and West Tennessee companies, the companies retaining the same letter designation. The first colonel of the new regiment was W. C. Tatum of Nashville, the lieutenant colonel R. L. Beare and the majors, C. P. Simonton of Covington, J. B. Horton of Memphis and R. E. Martin.

During the Reel Foot Lake disturbances, growing out of the night riding of people living on the banks of Reel Foot Lake, two Memphis companies were detached for special service under Major Horton; Company E, Frazier Light Guards, under Captain B. L. Capell, and Lieutenants Ike Rosser and Jack Starr; and Company L, Captain James W. Hunt, with Lieutenants Allen H. Miller and George W. Peters. Captain Ed. W. Kinney was on special duty for these companies. Major Horton's staff was composed of Lieutenant W. L. Terry, Adjutant, and Second Lieutenant, Arch Well, Quartermaster. While at Reelfoot Lake the battalion was engaged in post and picket duty, scouting and arresting night-riders, in aid of the civil authorities. Colonel Tatum, commander of the regiment, died and was succeeded by Col. Tom C. Halbert, and Major Horton resigned in 1909. Capt. Roane Waring, regimental quartermaster, was promoted to Lieut. Colonel, taking the place of Colonel Beare. W. L. Terry of Memphis, Otto Robinson of Clarksville and John Samuels of Nashville were commissioned as majors, the latter taking the position of Major R. E. Martin, resigned. Captain Tidwell resigned and was succeeded by John D. Martin as commander of Company G, and Captain Martin resigning, was succeeded by Captain George Hoppe. In Company E, Capt. Ben Capell resigned and was succeeded by Capt. M. L. Rawitzer. The regiment and companies still retain this organization.

# CHAPTER XVII

## Transportation

SITUATED as Memphis is river transportation has naturally been an important mode of travel for the vicinity, both passenger and traffic. In the early days traveling on the river was chiefly accomplished on flat-boats and, although that was very slow, it was better than land travel. It has been shown in another part of this work how important the flat-boat trade was until far into the Nineteenth Century. These boats only floated downstream and, after their produce and lumber of which they were built, were disposed of, if the owners wished to go back it was necessary to go on foot or horseback.

There were trails of travel—many of these being old Indian trails—for pedestrians and horses and there were many long journeys made by foot. Very early in the century traveling through the woods was unsafe to traveler and property, because of wild beasts and robbers, though the trip was often made from here to Baltimore on horseback, as the travel was quicker than by river, even on the occasional steamboats. It was necessary to employ a guide to conduct the traveler through the wilderness from Memphis to Jackson, Tennessee, pilot and passenger going well armed for protection. But even precaution did not prevent frequent cases of robbery and murder. Robbers also infested the trails along the river, that they might plunder returning flatboatmen, having with them the gains of their sales.

These robberies became so frequent that the boatmen organized companies and made their return trips in large numbers, well armed for battle. Flatboats also often descended the river in fleets and the landing of one of these companies made quite a stir in young Memphis and her environs, farmers' wagons coming in from all directions to patronize the owners of the boats.

But when the prow of the steamboat began to plough the yellow waters of the Mississippi River as commercial and freighting craft the destiny of the little city on the lower Chickasaw bluffs was assured.

It is true that one steamboat, the New Orleans, the first on inland waters, was built and puffed down the great river past the bluffs before Overton, Jackson and Winchester had laid off the town of Memphis. This steamer was constructed at Pittsburg, Pennsylvania, the boat being launched March 17, 1811, and left that port October 20, 1811 for New Orleans, only four years after the trial trip of Robert Fulton's boat the Clermont, in 1807. When the New Orleans passed the Bluffs in December, 1811, the great New Madrid earthquake was prevailing along the river, the banks were caving, the timber falling into the stream and islands disappearing before their eyes. Nature seemed, with all her awful forces, to protest against the installation of steam power on the great inland river.

After the voyage of the New Orleans there was little steam navigation for some years but about the time Memphis was incorporated in 1827, numbers of steamers were plying the waters of the river. By 1835 the list had increased to over two hundred and many of the boats were of pretentious size and luxurious accommodations.

About this time also several steamboat disasters occurred at or near Memphis. The Helen McGregor, a Louisville and New Orleans packet, on February 24, 1830, exploded her boilers at the landing here, killing fifty people, many of them citizens of Memphis, and injuring as many more. On April 9, 1832, the Brandywine was burned just above the city, in which disaster one hundred seventy-five lives were lost and on May 15, 1835, the Majestic blew up at the Memphis landing, in which accident fifty-six passengers were killed or seriously injured.

Between 1840 and 1850, lines of steamers were established between Memphis and Cincinnati, Memphis and Louisville and Memphis and New Orleans, and a little later a line was placed between Memphis and St. Louis. Between 1850 and 1860 lines were also established between Memphis and Nashville, Little Rock, Vicksburg, Napoleon, Arkansas, and up the White, St. Francis and Arkansas Rivers. Captain Ad. Storm was the pioneer in the Little Rock trade in 1858.

The splendor of the Mississippi River packet service was maintained largely in the fifties by the great St. Louis and New Orleans and Louisville and New Orleans steamers which, when the stage of water would permit, sent out such palatial stearers as the Eclipse, A. L. Shotwell, Diana, Southerner, Moselle, Ingomar, H. R. W. Hill and Pennsylvania and in the bends by the splendid packets Daniel Boone, Capitol, Kate Frisbee, Glendale and the first Belle Memphis. The larger of these steamers were never surpassed for luxury and speed and the visits of the rich planters to this port on steamers bearing great cargoes of cotton and from the lower coast sugar and molasses, rapidly brought Memphis to the front as a trading port of vast importance.

In the semi-decade, 1865 to 1870, following the War Between the States, when the cotton and sugar plantations were reopened, even greater steamers began to ply the Mississippi and carry its commerce to the doors of Memphis. Among these the most splendid were the Great Republic and its successor, the Grand Republic, the largest and most beautiful craft ever seen on western waters, the Imperial, the Richmond, the Natchez, the Robert E. Lee, the Mary Belle, the James Howard, the J. M. White, the Mississippi, the Von Puhl and a score of others of almost equal note.

The Lee and Natchez were famous for speed and made the celebrated race from New Orleans to St. Louis in 1870, which resulted in a victory for the Lee and gave her the certificate as the fastest steamboat that ever turned a wheel on the Mississippi River.

In the last half of the sixties there were a large number of steamboat lines terminating at the Memphis wharf, among them, the Memphis and Ohio River Packet Company, the Arkansas River Packet Company, Southern Transportation Company, White River Line, Hatchie River Line, Mississippi River Line, St. Francis River Line, New Orleans Line, Osceola and Hailes Point Packet Company, Memphis & Friars Point Line and Memphis and Forked Deer River Line.

As a matter of interest to the host of river men in Memphis and many of the old inhabitants, the steamers running in these lines at those dates will be given: In the Arkansas River Line were the T. H. Allen, Ozark, Caldwell, Fort Smith, Fort Gibson, American, Guidon and Clarksville. In the White River trade were the Natoma, Desarc, Liberty Number 3, Mayflower, Commercial, Legal Tender and R. P. Walt. The St. Louis Line had the Belle of Memphis, Marble City, City of Cairo, Belle St. Louis and City of Alton. The Friars Point Line ran the G. W. Cheek, Dan Able, A. J. White and General Anderson. The steamer St. Francis ran to the St. Francis River. The Memphis and New Orleans Line had the Belle Lee and Magenta. The Arkansas River Packet Co., in addition to those named above ran later the Mary Boyd, Pat Cleburne, R. P. Walt, J. S. Denham, Dardanelle and Celeste. The St. Louis Line, in 1876, called the Anchor Line, besides the five above named, had added the Grand Tower, City of Vicksburg, City of Chester, Julia, Colorado, St. Joseph and Rubicon; Independent New Orleans Line, Richmond and Mollie Able; Forked Deer Line, Sallie V.; Cincinnati Line, Alice Dean, Robert Burns, Silver Moon, Sam J. Hale and Minneola; White River Line, Hard Cash, Chickasaw, Alberta, St. Francis, Belle, Ella and Milt Harry.

The first Memphis road on record was ordered by the County Court in 1820, when Thomas H. Person, Charles Holman, Joshua Fletcher, M. B. Winchester, J. C. McLemore and William Irvine were authorized to "mark out a road from Memphis to the county line, in the direction of the settlement on Forked Deer River."*

The next year another road was made from Memphis to

*Vedder.

a settlement on Big Creek and Loosahatchie and on to Forked Deer River. The men who established this important road were Jesse Benton, John Ralston, John Reeves, Robert Meckleberry, D. C. Treadwell, Nathaniel Kimbrough, Edward Bradley, E. Deason and F. Kimbrough.*

In 1827 there was only one long wagon road to Memphis, called The Great Alabama and State Line Road, but despite its high-sounding name it was a very poor road, and almost an impassible one in spring. Later in this year a road was cut out to Somerville, Tennessee, through Raleigh, but was not completed for two or more years.

In 1829 roads were more numerous and, although still only dirt roads and usually very muddy or very dusty, received more attention and were constantly being improved. This year a line of stage coaches was established via. Nashville, Charlotte, Reynoldsburg and Jackson, to Memphis. These stages ran three times a week, making travel easier and therefore more frequent, while each coach brought happiness to many and strengthened business by delivering the mail.

A year later, when the Somerville road was completed, James Brown & Company started a line of four-horse post coaches, the starting of which made a great epoch in Memphis history.†

As land travel improved river facilities became better also and some very handsome steamboats began to ply the river and improvements grew apace.

The *Gazette*, a small news sheet of the time, had these words in the issue of April 30, 1830: "The facilities of intercourse are increasing daily by the construction of bridges, turnpikes, the running of stages and steamboats and the astonishingly improved moral condition of the people."

Railroads at this time constituted a new mode of travel and were yet only heard-of accommodations to most Memphis people, though a few of her inhabitants had not only seen the trains but had ridden on them. The total railroad mileage in the United States at that time was twenty-three miles, but

*Vedder.  †Old Folks Record.

even as early as 1830 some of the progressive men of Memphis endeavored to get a railroad line here.

By 1834 stages had become very lucrative and were formidable rivals to the steamboats, especially as they were considered safer. Numerous steamboat explosions in the early thirties had taken hundreds of lives, which put the boats into disrepute with many people.

At this time a line of packets ran between Memphis and New Orleans, making two trips a month, and independent boats were numerous, so that river accommodations were to be had every week.

In 1835 some Memphis and LaGrange citizens appealed for a charter to build a railroad between Memphis and LaGrange and obtained it, but before really getting a railroad much more work had to be done than obtaining the charter. Some subscriptions were raised in Memphis but the enterprise met with much opposition, as all new ventures do, and work was not begun on the road until 1838. It progressed slowly and in 1842, six miles had been completed.

This road entered the city on Washington Street and Mr. Vedder says that "where the street crosses Main the cut was so deep as to require a bridge." The rails were of bar-iron laid on longitudinal beams or "stringers," and these were laid on transverse ties. This road, never finished, proved more a curiosity and pleasure scheme than a business advantage and after operating a few months, failed.

Later the road was lengthened and its projectors again tried to make it a success, but Memphis was not ready for railroads and this venture was followed by failure also.

These failures confirmed the timid in their belief that railroads were not feasible and discouraged some who had favored them before, so that it was impossible to arouse enough interest to secure another line for several years, though the public-spirited tried to make the people understand the importance of this new mode of transportation in building up a place.

That railroads had become popular throughout the country was evidenced by the fact that in 1840 the mileage in the United States had increased to 2,888 miles, and by 1849 to

7,365 miles. But by this latter date Memphis had herself become such a convert that she was said to lead Tennessee towns in her quota of railroad increase.

In 1846 the Mississippi and Tennessee Railroad Company was chartered.

During this same year a line of boats was established between Memphis and Louisville, with trips every three days, and a packet line between Memphis and New Orleans started, first with two well-fitted boats which were soon increased to four and later to six, each of these making the trip every two weeks.

The river was now used for long trips or as the starting place of long trips, and in 1845 the "Muskingum" arrived in Memphis, this boat having left Cincinnati for Liverpool, England. It took her forty-seven days to make the trip. The "Marietta" of Marietta, Ohio, and bound for Boston, Massachusetts, arrived at Memphis, March 21, 1846, and then continued successfully on her long journey.

In the latter forties there was much agitation of a railroad from Memphis to Charleston, South Carolina, one of the prime leaders in this movement being ex-Governor James C. Jones. This road succeeded in getting a charter in 1846, but not until 1850 did the enterprise bear fruit. In that year the Memphis & Charleston Railroad Company bought the charter of the Memphis and LaGrange road and commenced work. The state appropriated $2,202,000 for this road and Memphis subscribed $500,000 toward its building. But the work was slow and not completed until 1857. Its completion brought about one of the greatest demonstrations the Bluff City ever had, which has been described in the general history.

During the years in which the Memphis and Charleston road was being put through, other railroads for connecting Memphis with different points were agitated and on October 23, 1849, a convention was held in the Exchange Building for the purpose of considering a railroad from the Atlantic to the Pacific. Delegates attended this convention from Louisiana, Arkansas, Mississippi, Alabama, Kentucky, Missouri, Texas, Illinois, Pennsylvania, Massachusetts, New York, Virginia, South Carolina and Tennessee. Commodore M. F. Maury of the United States Navy was chairman of this convention and Colonel Jefferson Davis was an enthusiastic member from Mississippi. Colonel Keating says, "Mr. Davis was a zealous advocate of a transcontinental line of railway in the Senate and as Secretary of War. During his tenure of the latter office as a member of President Pierce's cabinet he ordered and organized a survey for such a line under Captain George B. McClellen (afterwards Major-General) within the limits of latitude indicated by the resolution adopted by the convention as expressive of its objects and purposes."

The fifties saw much progress in railroads and Colonel Keating called 1852 the railroad year in Memphis, as so many roads were projected and much work done on lines already begun. One of these was the Mississippi and Tennessee Railroad, chartered by Mississippi and Tennessee. For this project Tennessee made a loan of $97,500 and Memphis subscribed $250,000 of the stock.

At the same time the Memphis and Ohio Railroad was projected from Memphis to Louisville and the first section completed about 1855. The name of this road was subsequently changed on being absorbed by the Louisville and Nashville, which has become a great system.

In 1853 the Board of Mayor and Aldermen voted $350,000 for a railroad to Little Rock, Arkansas.

As railroads were being extended in all directions over the country Memphis was recognized by many as the most central point for an eastern terminus of the proposed Pacific railroad. Colonel J. T. Trezevant wrote of this:

"Memphis is nearer to the South Atlantic and Gulf States than any town on the Mississippi above the mouth of the Ohio, and nearer to the North Atlantic and Lake cities than any town on the river below the mouth of the Ohio. In other words, Memphis is that point in the Mississippi Valley where the lake, the Atlantic and the Gulf cities can, and soon will, meet by the shortest and most direct line of railroad."

Colonel Trezevant was enthusiastic over railroads and had succeeded in convincing people in his speeches and otherwise, but many were still sore over the LaGrange failure and this kept some from lending help that might otherwise have done so.

However, time proved the necessity of keeping up with the whole country and also proved Memphis to be the most central city of the South or Southwest for a connecting link between West and East, South and North.

Coal, iron and other minerals were discovered in the East Tennessee mountains and this discovery, by aid of the railroads, was an advantage to the whole State and section of the country. Southern railways increased in number and direction and brought more activity to the city in increased commerce, railway stations, yards, new employments, etc.

The railroads injured steamboat traffic a good deal but the boats kept railroad rates within bound by competition and the balance was well maintained. The railroads also spurred the steamboats and they increased in numbers and improved accommodations until some of them were denoted "river palaces," where passengers had such good attention that many trips were taken on them just for the comfort enjoyed.

By 1860 the railroads and improved river transportation had brought much prosperity to Memphis and population had increased so much, as well as area, that in June of that year Memphis citizens petitioned the council to permit the street railway to lay its tracks on Main Street, and several years later, after much dallying, street-car service became one of the the city conveniences.

The war of course affected transportation of all kinds. Of the river Mr. Vedder said that "the period from 1850 to 1861 was the most extensive and profitable in the history of navigation upon the Mississippi and its tributaries," but that "the four years of war following 1861 caused almost an entire suspension of legitimate river commerce."

After the war river commerce and passenger transportation were resumed but never regained the precedence of ante bellum days. One of the first river lines to resume regular traffic after the sectional upheaval was the Memphis and St. Louis Packet Company, with six first-class boats. In 1876 this line was extended to Vicksburg, Mississippi, and called the St. Louis & Vicksburg Anchor Line. In 1883 it was again extended, this time to New Orleans, and called the St. Louis & New Orleans Anchor Line.

Other lines were inaugurated and did good business. One of the most important of these was the first line of steamers from Memphis to Friar's Point, Mississippi, established by James Lee, Sr., in 1866. His son became a partner and this company ran a number of boats with such success that the line continued to grow until it became one of the most noted lines on inland water. The senior James Lee was identified with Mississippi Valley river traffic for over fifty years, until 1885, when he retired. But the Lee Line continued under the Lees and is today,—nearly fifty years after the establishment of the line,—one of the most successful and noted on the river, its growth having been a part of Memphis history.

In 1870 there were forty steamboats enrolled and owned at Memphis, with a tonnage of 10,306. During the year ten boats had been sunk and two dismantled.

The total import of cotton by river had been during the year ending June, 1870, 115,730 bales and the export, 162,343.*

During the War Between the States railroads had been so wrecked that it was some time before people had energy or means to push railroads or any other enterprises, but before many years tracks begun to go down in different directions and by 1870 several of these were under way. In 1871 the Memphis and Little Rock road was completed and was an accomplishment of great satisfaction to the two cities at its termini. The Selma, Marion and Memphis, later the Kansas City, Memphis and Birmingham railroad was organized by General Forrest under an efficient board of directors and Memphis subscribed $200,000 to the Mississippi River Railroad. Shelby County subscribed $50,000 to the Raleigh Railroad and its little train made Raleigh Springs a popular resort to Memphians. A Memphis union station was also contracted for,

*Vedder.

the many railroads coming to and leaving Memphis at that time requiring it.

In 1873 all energetic business action in Memphis had a check when the epidemic and financial panic prostrated the city, the latter catastrophe extending throughout the country.

Some of the projected railroads were never revived and some other not for years. The Mississippi River Railroad, which was under contract but had been stopped, was resumed and finished, but some others that had been begun were left in their unfinished condition.

After all the epidemics were over and the Taxing District launched in its government, railroads grew so rapidly here that it would be tedious to follow them all, but each road filled an important part of the city's growth, and smoke and noise of many engines means expansion and prosperity to city commerce, and manufacturing grew as quick transportation came to hand. Memphis handled more and more of the products of the states surrounding her and was the center of long shipments from and to all directions. She became a railroad center of importance to the whole country and by 1887, eight trunk lines, or main branches of trunk lines entered here and seventy-six trains arrived and departed daily to and from the city, carrying millions of dollars worth of products.

City transportation had also received its share of attention. Soon after the War Between the States citizens reverted to interest in street-cars and in 1865 the Citizens Street Railroad Company was chartered and incorporated with these gentlemen as incorporators: Messrs. Wm. M. Farrington, president; Wm. R. Moore, I. M. Hill, S. B. Beanmont, R. Hough, Frank Taft, G. P. Ware, S. R. Wood, Fielding Hurst, P. E. Bland, Joseph Bruce, Abner Taylor, Thomas R. Smith, H. B. Mills, Joseph W. Eystra, Wm. C. Bryan, W. P. Hepburn and Frank Brooks.

The line first traversed Main Street only, with less than four miles of single track. On this track ran short one-mule cars that never became famous for their speed. The first extension was the red line of cars to the south gate of Elmwood Cemetery, a single track with occasional switches, where cars waited for one another to pass, the waits often trying the patience of passengers. By the close of 1866 the lines had more widely extended and covered ten miles of track.

The first fare charged on Memphis street-cars was five cents, but in 1867 it was raised to ten cents. This caused a great deal of dissatisfaction and it was later reduced to six and one-fourth cents. In 1875 it was again made five cents and has continued so until the present time.

In 1869 Mr. R. C. Floyd, who published a short history of Memphis, wrote: "Street railways now stretch to all parts of the city, making travel from the Memphis and Louisville Railroad depot, in the northern part of the city, even as far as Elmwood Cemetery in the furthermost southern limit, cheap and speedy."

That travel would be far from "speedy" to us today, but it was an accommodation then so superior to walking that people without private vehicles considered the tinkling bell of the street-car mule indicative of time saved and comfort enjoyed, even as the whirr of the electric car indicates to us today.

Differences arose among men interested in the street-car lines which ended in litigation that brought much disturbance and enmity. The car service grew to be so wretched that the poor cars and slow mules became a theme of ridicule. This went on until 1885, when a new company was organized, called the Citizens' Street Railway Company, with Napoleon Hill, president; Sam Tate, Jr., vice-president and general manager; Raphael Semmes, superintendent; George Vance, secretary and treasurer.

This company pushed its work and the day the new service was opened for the public, passengers were carried free all over the city, the cars being filled with merry people who made a gala day of this opening one. The new lines interfered with the old ones, paralleling them on most streets, and competition became strong and even bitter. The new cars were freely patronized from the beginning and were immediately put on a paying basis, which forced the old company to improve its accommodations.

In 1887 competition and hard feeling were ended by the two companies consolidating their interests, under the name of the Citizens' Street Railway Company. The price paid for the old company's property was $1,000,000, one-half in stock in the new company and the other half in bonds. In the reorganized company Napoleon Hill was president; Thomas Barrett, vice-president; Raphael Semmes, superintendent; S. P. Read, Jr., secretary and treasurer.

Soon after this union the Main Street line was extended to Jackson Mound Park, which was then thrown open to the public and became a popular resort.

Two years later the street-car company again changed hands, when Mr. C. B. Holmes of a Chicago syndicate bought the Citizens' Street Railway Company for $2,000,000, borrowing money for the purpose from Mr. James Billings, a Chicago millionaire. Later the company was about to fail when Mr. Billings came to Memphis to investigate the street railway property. He concluded that prospects here were good for any sort of business and pronounced Memphis the "Chicago of the South." He bought the street-car company's stock and determined to change the system to rapid transit, gained by means of electricity, then a comparatively new mode of travel rapidly growing in favor all over the world.

Mr. Billings found his new undertaking filled with thorny problems and every project he proposed met with opposition. After months of trying to adjust matters he was about to abandon all idea of starting anything in Memphis when an agreement was settled upon and, by adding new capital to the amount of $1,500,000, a contract with the city, by which the street-car company was ceded the right to all streets occupied by tracks for twenty-six years, with the right to erect poles, wires, etc., for a new electric system. This transaction passed in April of 1891, and the new electric lines were rapidly instituted. By the close of 1892 Memphis had sixty-five miles of street railroads with more tracks going down in many directions. Forty miles of this distance was controlled by the Citizens' Street Railway Company, with its new electric lines on which had been established sixty motor cars and one hundred trailers.

But steam served the city passenger traffic also. In the spring of 1887 the Memphis, Greenwood and Prospect Park Railroad Company had been organized with a capital stock of $100,000, for the purpose of running a small steam-railroad line from the city to some of the suburbs. This road was known as the Dummy Line and proved a great convenience for people living several miles from the city, especially for people who worked in Memphis and lived beyond the city limits.

The incorporators of this company were T. J. Latham, president; J. A. VanHoose, vice-president and general manager; T. A. Lamb, secretary and treasurer; S. H. Lamb, E. F. Adams, Major John D. Adams of Arkansas, Wm. J. Smith, F. M. Nelson and F. H. White.

Another steam-dummy, instituted in 1887 at a cost of $150,000, was the East End Railway, leaving town at Monroe and Third, and going through a suburban residence district to East End Park, a pleasure resort, and thence to Montgomery Park or race track. This line was an independent one under the management of Mr. W. M. Sneed.

Suburban traffic became a great builder of the city in general and along its lines attractive residence communities sprang into being. Nothing helps the growth of a city more than her street-car service. Extension of the lines and their assurance of transportation enables inhabitants to have their homes away from the city smoke and noise, going and returning each day in short time to and from business. By 1892 some of the residence additions of importance were Madison Heights, Gladstone Heights, Lenox, Ingleside, Idlewild and Mt. Arlington. The property in all these places was greatly enhanced in value by reason of the improvements accomplished and the certainty with which they could be reached from the city.

Raleigh Springs, nine miles distant, was also brought seemingly close to the city by an electric line being extended to that attractive resort.

The great cantilever bridge built across the river at the southern part of the city and completed in 1892, has already been described in detail. Its value was inestimable to railroad traffic and it was used by several routes. During the time the bridge was being completed some railroad companies had spent thousands of dollars in the city on terminal improvements, among these being two new stations.

By this time people generally recognized railroads as a powerful agent in progress, and Memphis had become the greatest railroad center of the South, besides being the tenth railroad city of the country.

The ten railroads entering Memphis at that time were the Illinois Central, a branch of which ran from Memphis to Grenada, Mississippi, this road being successor to the old Mississippi & Tennessee Railroad; the Louisville & Nashville Railway, which afforded wide communication in many directions and connected Memphis with many important cities; the Mississippi Valley Route or Louisville, New Orleans & Texas Railway; the Iron Mountain Route of the Missouri Pacific Railway Company; the Cotton Belt Route; Kansas City, Springfield and Memphis, another trunk line. The Kansas City, Memphis and Birmingham; East Tennessee, Virginia & Georgia; the Tennessee Midland; the Little Rock & Memphis Railroad, connecting these two cities; and the projected Belt Line, belting the city from the bridge at the southern extremity to Wolf River in the north, and connecting all lines centering in Memphis. Tennessee had at that date 2,901 miles of railroad.

Trains of these various routes entered the city at different points but street-cars and transfer accommodations connected passengers, baggage and freight with the different stations. Transfer companies operating at that time were the E. G. Robinson Transfer Company, with Mr. E. G. Robinson president; and the Patterson Transfer Company, with carriage and omnibus departments, Mr. R. Galloway, president; Mr. P. M. Patterson, vice-president and Mr. B. A. Wills, secretary and treasurer. This company had been organized in 1856 by Mr. P. M. Patterson, Sr., with a line of stage coaches. When this mode of travel became an accommodation of the past the company changed its function to transfering city traffic.

Of the river packet lines in the early nineties, the St. Louis and New Orleans Anchor Line boats had an agency in Memphis and landed three times north and three times south each week. Captain A. Storm was in charge of this line, a man of long river experience. This was one of the finest lines of boats that ever traveled the river and it was said in 1892 that it "guages the highest point of progress made in inland navigation." Its passenger boats were designated "floating palaces," and equaled the ante bellum boats that had once been a glory of the river. It had seven boats, with Captain Isaac M. Mason president of the line and Captain John A. Scudder, vice-president.

The Lee Line, with Captain James Lee, manager, also ran seven boats with 2,500 tonnage. This was a very important line, especially in commercial traffic up and down the Mississippi and on its tributaries.

The Cherokee Packet Company plied two boats between Memphis and St. Louis at that time and had an excellent trade. The president of the line was Mr. Ferd Harold of St. Louis and the Memphis agent was Mr. H. C. Lowe.

The Memphis, Arkansas City and Bends Packet Company ran one boat, the Kate Adams, between Memphis and Arkansas City. This boat was managed by Captain John J. Darragh and was one of the swiftest on the river, with 800 tonnage. It was a passenger, freight and mail boat. The president of the line was Thomas Darragh of Little Rock and the secretary and treasurer, J. M. Peters of Memphis.

The Memphis & Cincinnati Packet Company had four regular boats and an occasional one plying the Mississippi and Ohio Rivers. This line had been established in 1866 and had been an important one since its beginning, both for passenger and freight carriage. F. A. Laidley of Cincinnati was president and Captain C. B. Russell, an old river captain, was the Memphis agent.

The Arkansas River Packet Company, with Mr. James

Rees, president, ran two boats from Memphis to Pine Bluff, Arkansas, each having a tonnage of 350.

The Memphis & White River Packet Company ran a steamer on the Mississippi and White Rivers from Memphis to Augusta, Arkansas. Mr. Sam Brown was president of this line.

All through the nineties railroad facilities continued to increase and before 1900 Memphis boasted eleven trunk lines. In the new century belt railways were added, with many miles of terminal and lineal tracks and in 1910 Memphis was pronounced one of the best and most important terminals in America, with eleven lines of railroad and two complete belt lines.

Over these operate the Union Railway; Illinois Central; Louisville & Nashville; Nashville, Chattanooga & St. Louis; Yazoo & Mississippi Valley; Frisco; Southern Railway; St. Louis, Iron Mountain & Southern; St. Louis Southwestern; Chicago, Rock Island & Pacific.

Memphis has the best terminal, switching and freight facilities in the country and there is little conflict between the different roads as the law here requires that each road switch for every other and any switching charge is included in the general freight rate.

The Bureau of Publicity and Development of Memphis state: "No American city is so well adapted for quick and economic distribution of articles manufactured in the North and East and consumed in Arkansas, Mississippi, West Tennessee, Western Kentucky, Northern Alabama, Louisiana, Texas and Mexico, as Memphis."

Delivery of freight must be made here in from one hour to one day, with a maximum of twenty-four hours, and this law is strictly enforced.

While these improved advantages are enjoyed by the business world, passenger accommodations have improved even more than any other branch of railroad service. Once people traveled on railroads for quick transportation and on boats for comfort, but now sleepers, drawing-room, observation and dining-cars make railroad travel a delight as well as convenience, as is proved by their vast patronage, while boats have degenerated in passenger service and the "floating palaces" are no more on the Mississippi River, though some prophets say they are coming back as inland water travel revives.

With all the growth and improvements of railroads Memphis has continued to have poor station facilities and as travel and business increased in volume the necessity for a union station became a cry with citizens, newspapers and business organizations. This cry continued for many years without avail and Memphis, with all of her other city improvements, stood a laughing-stock as to railway stations, those here having the appearance of belonging to small towns. Finally, in 1907, the Memphis Railroad Terminal Company applied to the city authorities for an ordinance allowing them to condemn property, close streets and alleys and build a Union Station. The ordinance was elaborately drawn and met with numerous objections. After months of discussion it was passed but met with denial from the Terminal Company. This was discouraging but agitation again arose the following year, another ordinance was drawn up and this time accepted by the Terminal Company.

The people rejoiced at the prospect of a great central station benefiting a city the size and importance of Memphis, but again disappointment came. The railroads disagreed as to the share of expense each should assume and once more the building of a new station was abandoned. This brought such great disappointment to the city that there were steps taken to sue the Terminal Company, but a new organization was formed, called the Memphis Union Station Company, and they applied for another ordinance to build a new union station.

This new ordinance, after much consideration and discussion was granted and approved by Mayor Malone November 29, 1909. This to-be $3,000,000 structure was at last assured, but was not strictly a union station after all, as some of the railroads refused to join in the scheme.

However, the great structure was begun and has since been completed. It is a splendid edifice and, when improvements and clearings are made around it, will be an ornament to Memphis and this part of the country. The building itself is described in the chapter on buildings.

This beautiful new station was opened March 30, 1912, and the five roads using it for the arrival and departure of their trains commenced this utility on the following day. These roads are: the Southern Railway Company; Louisville & Nashville Railroad Company; St. Louis, Iron Mountain & Southern Railway Company; Nashville, Chattanooga & St. Louis Railway and the St. Louis Southwestern Railway Company.

There are five directors of the Station Company and each company using the station has the privilege of selecting one of these directors, so that each road may have a voice in the management and control of the property. The first board of directors, who were also the incorporators were: Messrs. M. H. Smith, J. W. Thomas, Jr., Fairfax Harrison, C. W. Nelson, and J. L. Lancaster. The capital stock is owned equally by the five railroads.

The present directors are: J. W. Thomas, Jr., H. B. Spencer, F. N. Fisher, C. W. Nelson, J. L. Lancaster, and the officers are: J. L. Lancaster, president; F. N. Fisher, vice-president; C. R. Alexander, secretary; H. C. Ashley, treasurer; R. E. Kimball, auditor; J. W. Canada, general counsel; J. Werness, chief engineer; J. A. Galvin, architect; and W. F. Schultz, engineer of construction.

Despite the fact that railroads have displaced river trade to an extent, business people have never lost sight of the immense advantages afforded by the Mississippi River and at the present time this great waterway is receiving much attention. All know of the long-sought movement for making a deep waterway from the Great Lakes to the Gulf of Mexico in order that all these miles of water passage might be used for large boats. It is thought that this would be a great advantage to the whole country and Memphis would be one of the great centers of the vast trade so carried on, even as she is now such an important center of railroad traffic.

Development of waterways is popular all over the world now and Germany and France especially have improved their water facilities very greatly.

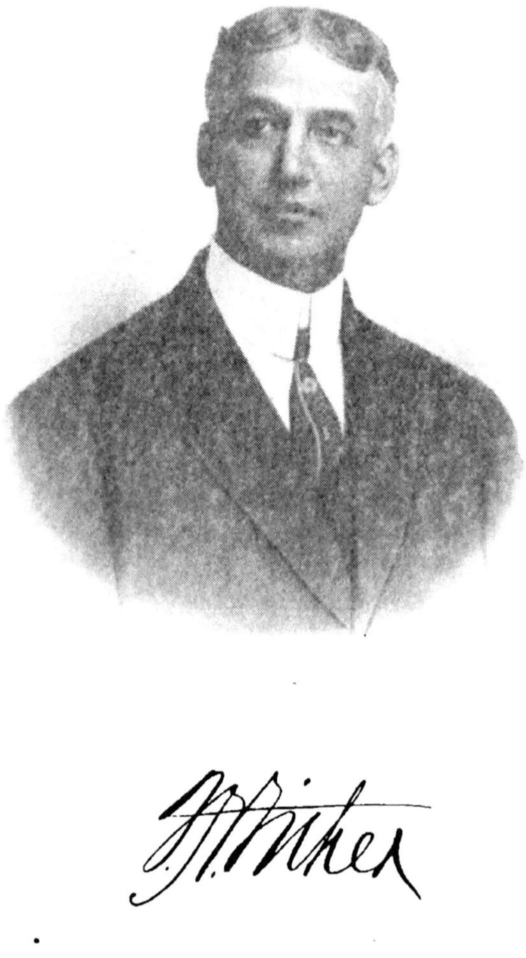

and this part of the country. The building itself is described in the chapter on buildings.

This beautiful new station was opened March 30, 1912, and the five roads using it for the arrival and departure of their trains commenced this utility on the following day. These roads are: the Southern Railway Company; Louisville & Nashville Railroad Company; St. Louis, Iron Mountain & Southern Railway Company; Nashville, Chattanooga & St. Louis Railway and the St. Louis Southwestern Railway Company.

There are five directors of the Station Company and each company using the station has the privilege of selecting one of these directors, so that each road may have a voice in the management and control of the property. The first board of directors, who were also the incorporators were: Messrs. M. H. Smith, J. W. Thomas, Jr., Fairfax Harrison, C. W. Nelson, and J. L. Lancaster. The capital stock is owned equally by the five railroads.

The present directors are: J. W. Thomas, Jr., H. B. Spencer, F. N. Fisher, C. W. Nelson, J. L. Lancaster, and the officers are: J. L. Lancaster, president; F. N. Fisher, vice-president; C. R. Alexander, secretary; H. C. Ashley, treasurer; R. E. Kimball, auditor; J. W. Canada, general counsel; J. Werness, chief engineer; J. A. Galvin, architect; and W. F. Schultz, engineer of construction.

Despite the fact that railroads have displaced river trade to an extent, business people have never lost sight of the immense advantages afforded by the Mississippi River and at the present time this great waterway is receiving much attention. All know of the long-sought movement for making a deep waterway from the Great Lakes to the Gulf of Mexico in order that all these miles of water passage might be used for large boats. It is thought that this would be a great advantage to the whole country and Memphis would be one of the great centers of the vast trade so carried on even as she is now such an important center of railroad traffic.

Development of waterways is popular all over the world now and Germany and France especially have improved their water facilities very greatly.

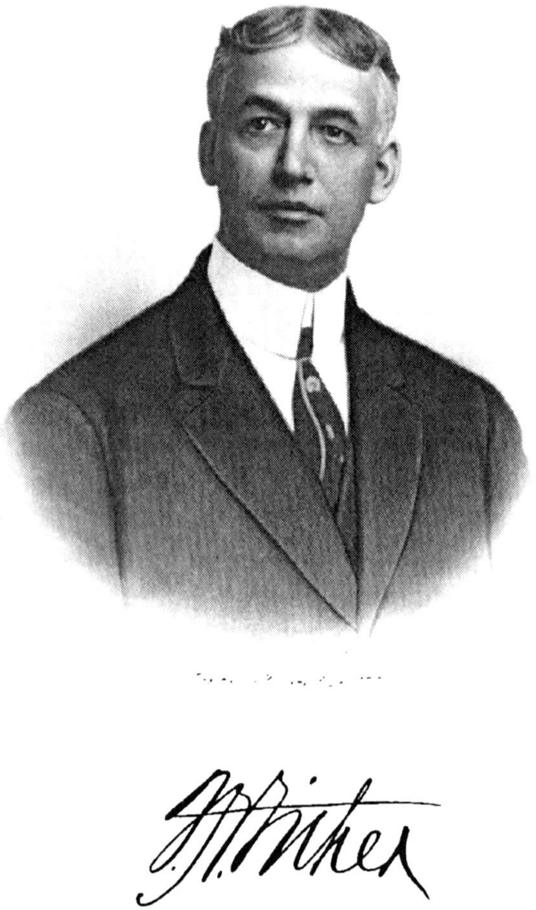

Some of the European engineers declare that this country has a wonderful advantage in the Mississippi and its tributaries, which might be developed into the greatest and most important water system on the globe. One writer says that "The Mississippi River and its tributaries constitute the most magnificent system of internal waterways on the face of the earth."*

Even now it is claimed that "the river alone is equal in carrying capacity to 1,000 railways, and that this large capacity gives shippers the advantage of low freight rates.

Another proposed form of river transportation is the use of large barges. This system had been agitated to some extent and in April, 1911, the first large steel barge was sent down the river by the Mississippi Valley Transportation Company. One of the advantages claimed for this line is cheap freight rates and another, low rates of insurance. This latter, the promoters say, is obtainable on account of the superior structure of the barges, as they are built of steel, which makes them fire-proof, and in such a manner as to make them "nonsinkable." Mr. W. K. Kavanaugh is president of this company and he is also president of the Lakes-to-the-Gulf Deep Waterway Association.

There are now 175 steamboats operating from the Memphis landings. Some of these are independent steamers but most of them are operated by companies.

The Lee Line has a large number of steamers that run north to Ashport, Tennessee; Cairo, Illinois; St. Louis, Missouri; Cincinnati, Ohio; and south to Friar's Point and Vicksburg, Mississippi. Captain R. E. Lee is the general manager of this line and the wharf boat is situated at the foot of Gayoso Avenue.

The Little Rock Packet Company also have their wharfboat at the foot of Gayoso. This line runs boats for Pine Bluff, Arkansas and Arkansas River landings.

The Memphis and Arkansas City Packet Company is a United States mail line and have their wharf boat and office at

*Bureau of Publicity and Development.

the foot of Union Avenue. The boat runs to Concordia and Arkansas City, Arkansas.

The Planters Packet Company also land their steamer, City of St. Joseph, at Union Avenue. This boat goes to Whitehall, Arkansas.

Railroads in the northern part of the city find it more expedient to transfer their trains across the river by ferry, so transfer boats are kept for this purpose. One of these, the General Price, is at the foot of Washington Avenue and transports trains of the Chicago, Rock Island and Pacific Railroad, and the other, the Little Rock & Memphis Railroad Ferry, is at the foot of Concord Avenue and transfers freight from Memphis to Hopefield, Arkansas.

At the foot of Wisconsin Avenue lies the United States Government Fleet.

The West Memphis Packet Company at the foot of Court Avenue, runs the steamer Charles H. Organ several times daily to Hopefield, Mound City, President's Island and Wyanoke. This boat is much patronized by excursionists and pleasure seekers.

Another excursion boat is the Pattona, run by the Bluff City Excursion Company.

The Street Railway service has made great strides since we left it in 1892. A city's growth along its street-car lines has already been mentioned and this fact has been demonstrated in Memphis as street-car facilities have grown. To quote from the *News-Scimitar* of May 3, 1912: "Hundreds of comfortable homes have been built and beautiful residence neighborhoods have grown up in places where nothing but farms or vacant land were to be found until extensions of the street railway made them desirable for building sites. Every one of these new homes adds to the property value of the city and wealth of the city's population.

"New districts have been opened to the uses of business by improvement of the street railway and betterment of the service, and every day transportation is becoming more and more a factor in the city's industrial and social life."

March 28, 1895, all the street railway companies in the

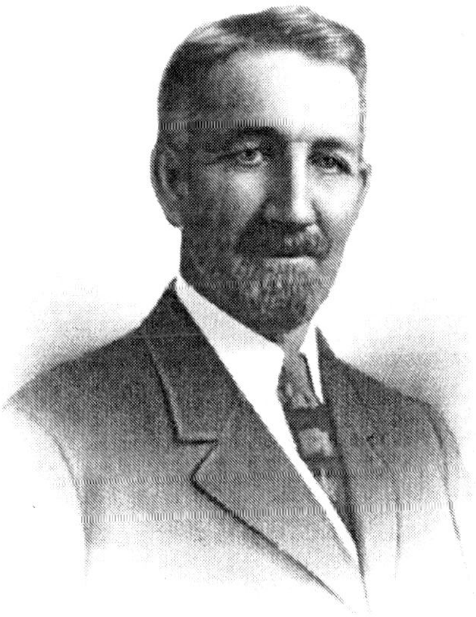

city consolidated and were incorporated as the Memphis Street Railway Company, under a fifty year franchise, with Mr. Frank Jones, president. This charter brought much new street-car property to Memphis and improved service.

After a decade of ownership under this organization the company again changed hands December 18, 1905, when the capital stock was increased to $2,500,000. This company does the entire street railway business of the city and has numerous lines running beyond the city limits.

Since this last purchase and reorganization under the old charter, $23,500 has been spent on fenders, gates, window-guards and other devices for safety, while many thousands of dollars have been spent on improved tracks and new cars, until 120 miles of trackage are owned by the company and 313 cars.[*]

The service is at present better handled than ever before and a general good feeling exists between the Street Railway Company and the citizens in general.

The greatest problem this company has now to meet is the congestion of passengers on Main Street, especially at Madison, but a system of loops is now under way, covering portions of Front and Third Streets from Union to Market Avenues, that will greatly help to obviate this trouble.

The validity of the franchise of the Memphis Street Railway Company being questioned, a law suit was instigated and decided in favor of the company, which decision was upheld by the Supreme Court of Tennessee in 1907. This franchise is valid until 1945.

The present officers of the Company are Mr. T. H. Tutwiler, president; General Luke E. Wright, vice-president;[†] Mr. W. H. Burroughs, secretary and treasurer, and Mr. E. W. Ford, superintendent.

The directors are: Messrs. George Bullock, New York; George H. Davis, New Orleans; A. H. Ford, Birmingham; Percy Warner, Nashville; T. H. Tutwiler, Luke E. Wright, R.

[*] These figures obtained from reports of the Street Railway Co.

[†] General Wright took the place of his son, Major E. E. Wright, after his decease.

A. Speed, W. B. Mallory, James E. Beasley, J. R. Pepper and Dr. W. B. Rogers, all of Memphis.

Public highways and city streets have undergone such vast changes in the last quarter of a century that a volume could be written on their development. Street improvements have been somewhat elaborated on in the general history and roads leading from the city have received no less attention. Great dangerous ruts and mud-holes, large enough to drown animals, are no more seen in our vicinity.

The Department of Public Highways keeps its work up to the standard which, in this generation, is high. Much thought and money have lately been spent in pushing the project of a highway from Memphis to Bristol, work on which has been begun and the West Tennessee end of the road is being rapidly pushed. Another project of this department is to have a first-class highway from Memphis, west through Eastern Arkansas, which it is hoped can be carried unbrokenly to Little Rock

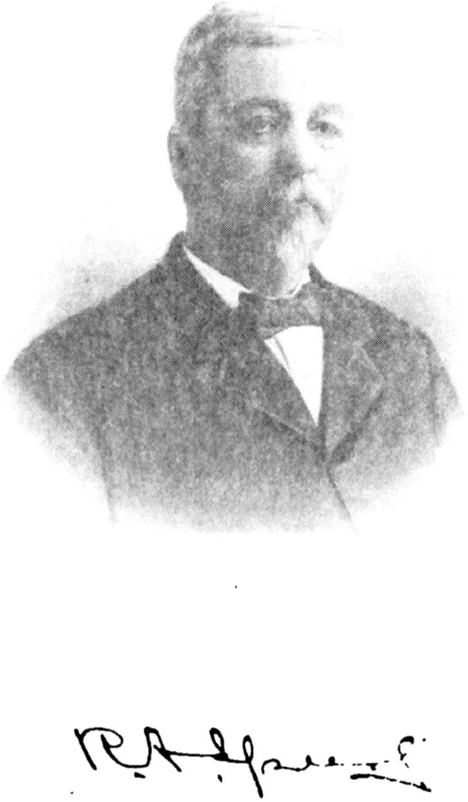

# CHAPTER XVIII

## Education

THE charter of 1826 that incorporated Memphis made provision for public schools and their maintenance, showing that even in her earliest days Memphis had citizens alive to the necessity of equipping future citizens by giving them educational advantages; but the real establishment of schools requires more than the convictions of the few and the majority of the inhabitants of a new town are usually of the rugged sort who think first of merely physical necessities. The moral and mental advantages are added by the few more profound thinkers and only by degrees become part of the regular system.

So, although the first charter allowed public schools, the only schools Memphis knew for a number of years were private ventures and they were at first of a rude character, until 1831, when the Garner School, conducted by a teacher of that name, was started at the corner of Auction and Chickasaw Streets. This school did not continue many years but performed its valuable part in the upbuilding of education.

Soon after the Garner School opened another followed, taught by Mr. Williams, in Court Square. He used the log building that had been erected for a church and had been used by several denominations in succession, each of which had outgrown the little log room and built buildings of their own. Mr. Williams had this rude structure weatherboarded and otherwise made more comfortable for his pupils.

The next Memphis teacher of note was an Irishman, Mr. Eugene Mageyney, a most excellent gentleman and scholar.

His school became popular and a real force, in which were educated numerous boys who later became substantial citizens of Memphis and several, encouraged by their teacher, pursued their studies in higher schools and colleges of the land.

There were several primary schools taught by women for small girls and boys, but the Magevney School was the one of greatest note in Memphis at that time and it was only for boys.

In 1846 the Reverend B. F. Farnsworth came to Memphis to take charge of a school of arts in Fort Pickering, which was to be a university and an educational pride to Memphis and to Tennessee. Dr. Farnsworth brought with him a valuable library, a chemical apparatus that was at that time the most complete in the Southwest, and a natural history collection that was one of the finest in the United States.

This pretentious school occupied a building in Fort Pickering that had formerly been erected for a hotel, and provided departments outside of the regular literary courses for law, medicine and the fine arts. The Board of Trustees of this school comprised, Rev. B. F. Farnsworth, president ex-officio; Seth Wheatley, Lewis Shanks, M. D., Geraldus Buntyn, Jeptha Fowlkes, M. D., Hon. Frederic P. Stanton, Henry G. Smith, Thomas J. Turley, Nathaniel G. Smith, Wm. A. Bickford, E. F. Watkins, M. D., Walter B. Morris, W. W. Hart, Dr. Wyatt Christian, J. J. Finley, and Thos. H. Allen, Secretary.

In 1847 the Misses Young had a school for girls and the St. Agnes Academy was incorporated by the Legislature in February of this year, though that Catholic institution did not really open as a school until four years later, when its building was completed.

In August, 1847, there was a teachers' convention in Memphis and the talks, lectures and general interest shown at this convention proved growth in the true spirit of teaching.

The public school spirit had grown in favor and early in 1848 Col. J. W. A. Pettit urged the Board of Mayor and Aldermen to use their right, given in the charter, and establish a system of free schools. His eloquence won, though the plan had much opposition, and each member of the Council established a free school in his ward.

Colonel Pettit, himself an alderman, opened the first of these schools at the northeast corner of Third and Overton Streets, in the home of Mrs. Moore, whom he made teacher, and in April following he was allowed, after much urging on his part, to employ an assistant teacher at half the salary of the principal, the school having grown so much that an assistant was badly needed.

The next public school opened was on the corner of Main and Overton Streets, taught by Mrs. Walker. These schools were in the first and fourth wards, and they were soon followed by schools in the second and third wards.

Some members of the Board of Aldermen had objected to these schools in the beginning and, like hindering spirits, continued to object until June, 1848, when much dissension arose at a board meeting, when a resolution was offered to discontinue the free schools. Fortunately the schools had increased in general favor and this resolution was voted down.

The four little schools passed the experimental period and on June 19th, just a few days after the above resolution to abandon them had been defeated, an ordinance was introduced and passed, making the public schools a fixture and strengthening them. "The main provisions of this ordinance were as follows: Section 1, divided the city into school districts; section 2, provided that the school tax should be one-eighth of the city revenue as provided by the charter, and that the schools were to be equally free to all white children between the ages of six and sixteen; section 3, that all that part of the city north of Poplar Street should be the first district, and all that part south of Poplar Street should be the second district; section 4, that the board of education, then called the board of managers, should consist of the mayor, two aldermen and two citizens, one from each school district; section 5, that there should be two school-houses in each district; and section 7, required the board of managers to report to the board of mayor and aldermen."*

On August 1, 1848, the office of Superintendent of public schools was created and Colonel Pettit, the first superintendent, entered upon his duties with much earnestness and without compensation.

He opened schools on Market, Poplar, Adams, Court, Madison, Gayoso, Main, Hernando and Third Streets and Brown Avenue.†

The unselfish and successful work of Colonel Pettit has caused him to be called the Father of the free schools of Memphis.

In 1850 a recommendation was made to pay the superintendent a salary and a vote on the question showed how the public-school spirit had broadened in two years, the vote giving the superintendent a salary of $600.

Colonel Pettit was retained as superintendent and labored unceasingly for what he considered the most important factor in building up a city, and spent the money allowed, always, to the best possible advantage. He importuned the city authorities to purchase school sites while property was cheap, but he had poor success, as the city in later years had reason to regret. He worked against many disadvantages and much ignorance, often failing to get the support of people who would be most benefitted by the success of the schools.

Colonel Pettit's report for the year ending June, 1851, showed a fairly good condition of twelve schools with 580 pupils and an expense account for the year of $4,891.50, which some of the tax-payers of that generation considered not only useless, but a great imposition on the citizens of Memphis.

About this time Dr. A. P. Merrill moved to Memphis from Natchez, Mississippi. Dr. Merrill was an ardent student of his profession of medicine, but he was also deeply interested in the subject of education for all the people. In Natchez he had

*Quoted by Vedder.
†Vedder.

been instrumental in starting a central public school which had caused much improvement in the little Mississippi city, commercially as well as educationally. After taking up his residence in Memphis Dr. Merrill became one of the public-spirited men of his adopted town, and did much to advance the cause of public education.

Dr. Merrill's pet scheme was a large central public school such as Natchez had at that time, but free education in any form being the great need, in his opinion, he was willing to abandon the one central school idea and work with Memphis educational workers for the general good, and this man's force in the community did much for the cause of free schools, and the equal education of all classes of people.

Colonel Pettit served as superintendent until 1852, when he moved to Germantown, Tennessee. He was succeeded in the office by Dr. Isaac Ebbert, who served the schools in this capacity one year. The following year Mr. J. F. Pearl took his place and in 1854 Mr. Pearl was succeeded by Superintendent Tarbox, who went to Nashville before his term expired. Mr. Tobey filled out the term and the next year, 1855, Dr. A. P. Merrill was persuaded to accept the position.

The school year beginning the first Monday in September, 1855, was auspicious and by the last of the month 1108 pupils had been entered in the nineteen schools, but yellow fever became alarming about that time and the school attendance continued to decrease until in a few weeks it was useless to try to conduct the schools with any sort of regularity. One school after another closed until fifteen had ceased operations, leaving only four running in an irregular manner. Nearly all the teachers had left the city and general fear prevailed among the parents who were left.

On May 4, 1856, the Memphis city schools were incorporated by an act of the legislature. This Act provided "That immediately after the annual election and organization of the Mayor and Aldermen of the City of Memphis, they shall appoint a suitable person for each ward of the city, and one for the city at large, as visitors of the city schools, who shall be appointed for one year; but no one shall be a member of the Board of Visitors unless he will declare his intention to discharge the duties of his position with fidelity."

Dr. Merrill was appointed Visitor for the city at large, and the other members of the Visiting Board, representing each ward, were Dr. L. Shanks, Dr. J. W. Maddox and Messrs. I. B. Kirtland, Leroy Pope, H. L. Guion and Robertson Topp.

The expenses of the schools for the year ending in June, 1856, were $1,500 for the Superintendent's salary, $10,563.34 for teachers' salaries, $2,745.99 for rents and repairs, $400.15 for furniture and $1,030.13 for incidentals. This total sum of $16,239.61 represented an expenditure of $10.29 for each pupil admitted to the schools during the year.

In 1857 Mr. Leroy Pope became superintendent and the Board of Visitors consisted of Messrs. Thomas D. Eldridge, the visitor at large, S. W. Jefferson, Fred Baxter, George R. Grant, B. F. Dill, W. J. Tuck and H. F. Farnsworth.

There were 1,313 pupils admitted to the schools during the term of 1856-57, and nineteen teachers were employed. Of these Mr. P. H. Davie was teacher of the "Senior male school," at a salary of $1,000, and Mrs. Annie C. Bradford was teacher of the "Senior female school," at a salary of $800. The male junior teachers received $600 and the women junior teachers, $500. The primary teachers, who were all women, received $500 each. All the salaries from Superintendent down had been increased that year.

The revenue collected for school purposes for the year ending July, 1857, was $24,000.

In 1860 the school-tax was increased to $15 for each white child between the ages of six and eighteen years of age. The same Act that made this provision authorized the Board of School Visitors to spend $75,000 for building school edifices, the Board of Mayor and Aldermen being given the authority to issue bonds for the amount to be so expended.

The Board of Visitors that year were John A. Nooe, president; J. F. Johnston, secretary; Thos. H. Allen, treasurer;

P. T. O'Mahony, Charles Scott, George R. Grant, F. S. Richards and N. B. Holt.

In 1861 the War came with all of its terrors and disadvantages and general interest in schools naturally slackened with the masses, immersed as they became in national affairs, but it is good to be able to relate that during the whole four years, with no money in the treasury and business and other interests in upheaval, the Memphis schools remained open and the attendance was fairly good all the four terms during the conflict. Buildings and school supplies were neglected, but some of the citizens furnished money, the Board of Visitors continued their duties and each year had a faithful superintendent. The teachers were paid and the terms lasted ten months.

The term ending in 1861, with Mr. Leroy Pope, Superintendent, showed an enrollment of 2,073 pupils and an average daily attendance of 1,019, while the expenses of the year amounted to $29,977.

The next year Dr. Merrill was again superintendent, and Mr. G. R. Grant was president of the Board of Visitors. This year there were 1,791 pupils enrolled with an average daily attendance of 755, and the cost of running the schools was $20,030. Dr. Merrill said that the pupils decreased considerably that year "from the disturbing influences of the war; and especially by the near approach and final capture of the city by the Federal troops." Another reason for decrease in attendance that year was the withdrawal of Catholics of their children, that they might attend the newly opened Catholic parochial schools, where they were to be taught the church catechism in addition to the regular school studies. The senior boys' school became so depleted that it was discontinued, but the senior girls' department, because the girls could not be soldiers, was well attended and very successful.

The year of 1862-63 had an enrollment of 1,495 and an average attendance of 607. Mr. Richard Hines was superintendent this year and Mr. James Elder president of the Board. The expenses amounted to $20,038.09.

The next year Mr. Elder became superintendent and was

succeeded as president by Mr. S. T. Morgan, and they remained in office two years. $23,707 were spent on the schools that term and 2,216 pupils were enrolled, while an average attendance of 902 was shown.

The year of 1864-65 had an enrollment of 2,418 and an average attendance of 1,036.

When the war closed a census was taken, which showed a school population of 3,865, and the enrollment in the public schools at that time was 2,523, with an average attendance of 1,209.

The amounts contributed towards the schools during the war, while very generous from some of the contributors, were inadequate and the treasury was empty, so in 1863, at a meeting of the Board, a committee was appointed to devise ways and means for carrying on the schools. The committee framed this resolution, which the City Council passed: "That the certificate of indebtedness issued monthly by the Board of School Visitors to their officers and teachers in settlement of their claims for services rendered as officers and teachers, be and the same are hereby declared receivable by the tax collector and city treasurer in satisfaction of any and all claims due the city."

Public education was thereby kept going, but a heavy debt was incurred which embarrassed the schools for years after the war and retarded their progress for a time. In 1864 provision was made for maintaining public schools for colored children, the only education they had had prior to that time having been private instruction. The colored schools were afterward incorporated with the system of white schools and in 1865 there were nearly 2,000 pupils in this department of the public schools.[*]

At the close of the war J. J. Peres became President of the School Board and W. Z. Mitchell became Superintendent.

An Act of the Legislature in 1866 increased the Board of School Visitors two members for each ward, and increased

[*]Vedder.

their time to two years instead of one. Public schools were placed under the exclusive control of the Board of Visitors, who were vested with power to purchase and hold property for city school purposes, and do whatever was needful for the good and advancement of the schools. They could purchase buildings and lots to the amount of $75,000. This Board was to submit a budget each year to the Board of Mayor and Aldermen. A school tax of $15 was to be levied by the Board for each child of school age in the city.

For the year ending in the summer of 1868 we find the public schools progressing under Mr. H. D. Connell as President of the Board and Mr. W. Z. Mitchell, Superintendent. The Board had been forced to limit expenditures to salaries, rents and necessary repairs, and money was not at all times available for these purposes. The President said: "Every other interest has been better protected" than the schools, "the paltry sum of $11,285.05 for school purposes" having been all collected for the year. He also said: "Memphis has continued to have her schools taught in temporary and uncomfortable buildings. Our teachers have faithfully worked on, while the Board is largely in debt to them for their salaries."

This year when the Board asked for an additional $10,000 to meet extra expense brought on by the extension of the city limits, Mayor Leftwich vetoed the request, giving as his excuse, enforced economy in every department of the city government.

Mr. Mitchell in his report this same year said that the schools had made marked improvement in organization and classification of the pupils, despite "difficulties heretofore unknown in your school history." Organization among the teachers was good, too, and the requirements for thoughtful teaching became more strict. A teachers' institute met the first Saturday of each month, when it was required that they should be "at least three hours in discussing methods of discipline, methods of instruction, and conferring together respecting the general interests of the schools." So imperative was it made that teachers attend these meetings that absence from any of them forfeited one twenty-fourth of a month's salary.

A teachers' library was begun and enducational periodicals were subscribed for.

The pupils enrolled in the public schools this year numbered 2,884, out of a scholastic population of 5,555, and the average daily attendance was 1,583. There were forty-two teachers, and Mr. Mitchell gave the "average salary of male teachers, $1,361.11," and the "average salary of female teachers, $971.43."

In 1869 a new charter was granted to the city schools, placing them under the "exclusive management and control of a board of education consisting of two members from each ward."

So the School Board began the new decade with what had been long desired, the dignity of controlling its own affairs, which has ever since proved an advantage to the schools and to public education in Memphis. But the Board depended still upon the General Council of the city for all funds, as the School Board had no taxing power. A small amount of the county tax levy came to the city schools.

The reports of the President and Superintendent following this action made July, 1870, show the beginning of real growth in the schools. Superintendent J. T. Leath said that the scholastic year of 1869-70 "may be considered in all respects as the most prosperous which our city schools have experienced since their organization in 1852. For the first time since I have been acquainted with the financial condition of the School Board, its treasury has been in a state sufficiently sound and healthy to pay off and discharge in full the pay-roll of its teachers and employees of the year."

President Thomas R. Smith also congratulated the Board "on the healthy state of its finances." During this year fifty-one schools had been maintained at an expense of $54,027, and the Board had reduced the debt of $58,702.64 to $30,569.25, and they had on hand cash to the amount of $311.89; State warrants to the amount of $9,761.32; taxes due by the city $56,635.23; city bonds belonging to the building fund of $20,000; city ledger balance $900. The Board also now owned buildings, lots and school furniture to the amount of $125,-825.50.

The buildings were still inadequate for school purposes and despite acts that had authorized funds for school buildings, the city still did not own a good educational building nor a site for one. Under the conditions of the new charter the School Board commanded more money, and in 1870 a lot was purchased at the corner of Market and Third Streets and the following year the first real school-house owned by the School Board was erected, costing, with the lot, $80,000. The next year another good brick building went up in the southern part of the city, named for the great philanthropist and school promoter, George Peabody. This building cost $30,000 and was a pride to the city, as the one of the previous year had been.

In 1872 Dr. R. B. Maury was President of the Board and Mr. H. C. Slaughter Superintendent of the Schools. The reports tendered by these two leaders showed good condition of the schools. Sixty were maintained that year at a cost of $72,195. Dr. Maury's predominating idea was to make the schools "everything they ought to be," to use his own words.

Mr. Slaughter expressed satisfaction for the schools in general, but urged better teachers for the colored schools and means of making pupils in those schools attend more regularly.

The yellow fever in 1873 was a great set-back to the schools as it was to all Memphis enterprises. Several members of the Board, several teachers and many of the pupils died during the epidemic. The schools were forced to close, but reopened in November and continued through the term, meeting all current expenses, but were otherwise embarrassed as school taxes were poorly collected. Even salaries and other necessary expenses could not have been met but for a contribution from the "Peabody School Fund," which was a great help in time of trouble.

Mr. Charles Kortrecht, who was now President of the School Board, insisted that Memphis ought to have new school buildings, as all used for that purpose, except the two recently built, were a disgrace to the city, another exception being one for colored children on Clay Street, a building similar to the Peabody School, built in 1874.

Most of the buildings were still rented from private owners and wholly unfitted in their construction for schools. In mentioning the male and female high schools, where young men and women were prepared for society and business, Mr. Kortrecht said: "It is a shame and a disgrace to our city, to this Board, and to the municipal authorities of Memphis, that these, the first and most important schools in our city, and in our system, should be kept in old, dilapidated, abandoned dwellings, and their outhouses, with leaky roofs and ceilings, with openings around the doors and windows, through which sunshine and storm alike penetrate, both in summer and winter."

Mr. Kortrecht urged that the Board assert their right to use the building fund of $500,000 provided by the Legislature for the Memphis city schools, "to be furnished in sums of not exceedings $50,000 per annum, for the term of ten years, from and after January 14, 1869."

Still pursuing this subject he said: "In part compliance with this requirement the city authorities furnished this Board, for the four years, 1869, 1870, 1871 and 1872, toward this building fund fifty thousand dollars each year—not in money as the charter requires, but in time bonds of the city, worth at their highest market price, sixty cents on the dollar. For the year 1873, the city government furnished the schools on account of building fund, not fifty thousand, but about the sum of fifteen thousand dollars."

The Superintendent, Mr. A. Pickett, corroborated all that Mr. Kortrecht said in regard to new school buildings, adding from his aesthetic point of view the beautiful to utility, in order to attract children and to make them happy as well as comfortable. "The place where children study," he said, "should be attractive, convenient and healthful. * * * Children especially live on hope; they always want something attractive before them, and they will labor and endure much to reach the desired object. A building is the first point of interest. If the other things that combine to render a school a success are all of the highest order, without the building, much, both of labor and other expense, will be unavailing. Can the city afford to build? is scarcely a question,—can the city afford to do without? is a question that needs most careful consideration."

Mr. Pickett considered culture a higher factor in keeping up or increasing the values of civilized communities than mere physical necessities.

During this year there were 4,258 white children enrolled in the schools and 1,565 colored, out of a scholastic population of 6,479 white and 3,902 colored children. The daily attendance of these averaged 2,092 and 658, respectively.

Drawbacks notwithstanding, the schools went on with growing success, several sites were purchased and modern school-buildings were planned, but in the latter part of this decade of the seventies all school enterprise was stopped by the two terrible scourges that visited the city.

During the epidemic of 1878 the Market Street, Court Street and Lauderdale Street schools were used by the Howard Association for hospitals.

1880 found the school wards of the Taxing District very short of funds and suffering with all of Memphis from the terrible devastation recently made. This year there were ten public school buildings, seven of which had been built for schools and the other three were old residences. Six of these buildings were brick and four frame. Nearly all were defective in ventilation and other essentials, having been built or remodeled simply for the purpose of housing the children during school hours. The converted residences were wholly unfit for schools, with poor sanitation, poorly arranged rooms, lighting, etc., and they were all crowded except Market Street. There were 4,105 pupils enrolled and sixty-seven teachers employed, white and colored.

There were thirteen private schools in Memphis in 1880. Miss Higbee, who had been a public-school teacher and principal, had started an efficient school for girls; Miss Murphy had a popular school and the Catholics conducted LaSalette and

St. Agnes academies, Christian Brothers' College and five parochial schools; Miss Conway, another public-school principal and intellectual woman, had a school for girls; the Germans had a Lutheran school; and Le Moyne was an institute that had been opened for colored students. These schools had an enrollment of 842 white and 200 colored pupils, giving a total enrollment of pupils in all the Taxing District schools of 5,147.

In 1883 the Legislature passed an Act repealing the Act of 1869, or amending it so much as to amount to a repeal, and created a new Board of Education, to consist of five commissioners, having the powers possessed by the old Board, but with modifications. The school officers were to receive salaries—the President $500 per annum, and each of the other members of the Board $200 per annum.

The first Board of these School Commissioners, who were G. V. Rambaut, R. D. Jordan, P. M. Winters, Henry J. Lynn and Alfred Froman, were appointed by the Governor and held office until their successors were elected in 1884 by the people, three of them for two year terms and two for four year terms.

1885 found all the available schools filled to overflowing and President R. D. Jordan pleading for new buildings, saying that "The overcrowded condition of the rooms is a positive hindrance to successful instruction and enforcement of the rules laid down for the governance of the schools, to say nothing of its deleterious influences on the health of the children and teachers."

The enrollment for that year was 5,143, of which 3,352 belonged to the primary department, 1,635 to the intermediate and 156 to the senior department. The total income for the year was $48,699.37, which was $4,038.58 less than for the previous year. Of the amount received $1,012.32 had come from "pay pupils."

In 1886-87 a school site was purchased in Chelsea and a substantial school building was erected thereon at a cost of $10,416. Besides this two other sites had been bought and the United States Government had given a lot on the corner of Jefferson and Third Streets.

Captain Collier considered this year as a whole a successful one with the students and he mentioned the success of some of the pupils in competitive examination, in which merit alone could win, he said: "Two of these young men, high-school graduates, received appointments to West Point and Annapolis. Another won first honor in her class at the Normal College in Nashville, and a colored girl of Clay Street school had led her class in the Roger Williams College."

In the school year of 1890-91 the five commissioners managing the school affairs had been elected by the citizens, and Captain Collier, elected by the Board in 1885, still filled the position of Superintendent. The President of the Board was Mr. R. D. Jordan.

The city now gave the annual $50,000 appropriation for the schools and other funds came from State and County appropriations, bringing the school fund to $175,000 a year.

In 1889 an Act of the Legislature invested the Board with authority to issue coupon bonds to the amount of $100,000 for providing ways and means for school buildings and grounds.*

In order to erect schools in all parts of the city at once instead of following the slow process of erecting one a year, the Board, after issuing the bonds allowed by the Act, placed them upon the market publicly for thirty days, after which time they were sold to the Manhattan and First National Banks at a premium of four per cent, netting $104,000.

This sale was "executed by the President and Secretary of the Board, with the seal attached, under a resolution of the Board, conveying all property owned by the Board of Education, valued at $350,000, by the Valuation Committee last appointed by the Board, to Thomas B. Turley, W. F. Taylor and J. W. Cochran, trustees."

In consequence of all these transactions handsome and well-adapted schools were springing up all over the city, much to the satisfaction and profit of all concerned. Equipments were constantly being improved and the Memphis schools were

*Acts of 1889, Chapter 185.

becoming a pride to the city and offering better and better advantages to those to be educated.

The amount spent on buildings that year was $118,616.69, and all the expenses of the schools amounted to $185,354.84.*

There were now two high schools with excellent teachers of higher and special branches, such as elocution, music, drawing, bookkeeping, and the Superintendent recommended introducing manual training as a practical part of education, asking that stenography and type-writing might be started right away.

1891 showed a register of 6,220 pupils, the average attendance being 4,263, of which 2,798 were white and 1,465 colored. There were 107 teachers employed with salaries ranging from $30 to $117 per month, and ten aid teachers at $15 per month.

In 1892 the Hope Night School was taken in as part of the Public School System. This school has an interesting history and has been a valuable factor in training Memphis boys. It was conceived in the fall of 1878 by Mr. J. C. Johnson, after the terrible scourge had left so many Memphis children fatherless. Many boys so left were forced to go to work and could not take advantage of the day schools. Mr. Johnson pondered on means for providing for a continuation of the education of such boys, which ended in his decision to open a night school. That took money, and knowing the impoverished condition of the city he would not solicit aid from others. He determined to make the venture alone and fitted up a room for the purpose in a store he owned on Main Street. After this outlay he obtained a teacher, whose salary he paid, bought books and other school-room necessities and invited the boys to come. They came and the school grew so rapidly that larger quarters were needed before many sessions had passed. The school was moved to the "Bethel," where four teachers were employed with Miss Smith as principal. The record of this school was excellent year after year and some of the most influential citizens of Memphis today were once students in the Hope Night School.

*Report of Secy., Capt. A. B. Hill.

When Mr. Johnson's daughter, Miss Lillian Wyckoff Johnson, returned to Memphis from school in 1887, she became a teacher in the Hope Night School. When her father moved away from the city she was not only principal of the school but, with her father's enthusiasm for the success of the institution that had become an expensive one to run, this brave young teacher collected from Memphis merchants $1,500 every year for its maintenance till it became one of the public schools in 1892.

Captain Collier, after having served as Superintendent twelve years, was succeeded in 1893 by General George W. Gordon.

The expense account of the schools for 1893 was $96,878.58, making a cost per pupil of $13.96. The scholastic population was 17,831, while the public school enrollment was 7,087, with an average attendance of 4,252.

Major G. V. Rambaut was President of the Board, the other member being Captain A. B. Hill, the Secretary.

The following year Mr. F. B. Hunter was elected President of the Board and in 1895 Mr. J. E. Beasley had that distinction, General Gordon still serving as Superintendent.

The total expenditure for 1895 was $95,156.79, teachers' salaries taking $63,062.65 of that amount. The enrollment was 7,095 with an average attendance of 4,483.

Mr. Beasley was succeeded in 1897 by Mr. A. W. Higgins but returned to the office the following year. This year the Legislative Council allotted to the School Board $90,000, to meet the demands made on the schools by the territory recently annexed to the city and in view of raising the salaries of a number of the teachers. With the mentioned annexation ten white and seven colored schools were added to the care of the City School Board.

In 1899 Mr. Israel H. Peres was elected President of the Board and served in that capacity until 1900, when Mr. Beasley was again elected.

The century closed promisingly for the schools, with indications nowhere visible of the terrible struggles that had been endured in previous years. Secretary Hill's report of 1900 showed an expense account of $143,551.01, the amount for teachers' salaries now amounting to $100,150.65. There were twenty-eight schools—the extension of the city limits in 1899 having given sixteen additional ones—and two hundred and eight teachers.

The scholastic population then was 27,325, of this number 11,071 being enrolled in the public schools. The enrollment of the white high-school was 441 and that of the colored—Kortrecht—was 86. There were 37 graduates in May from the former and 13 from the latter.

In 1901-2 Mr. J. M. Steen was President of the Board and his reports showed progress in both white and colored schools, as did those of General Gordon for the same time. In 1902 there were thirty-three graduates, eight of whom were boys.

The work of the schools was so great that the Board elected Prof. Wharton S. Jones Assistant Superintendent.

In 1903 Mr. C. J. O'Neil became President of the Board. Territory that was annexed in 1901, gave more children to be provided for, but the same Legislature that annexed the city territory authorized the issuance of additional bonds, and in 1902 the Board issued under this Act $70,000 of four per cent bonds which were sold at a premium.

Mr. O'Neil urged the introduction of manual training into the schools and reported the night school as doing satisfactory work and having a good attendance. He recommended a more central location for its accommodation, that more young people might be benefitted thereby. This year the school term was increased to nine months. Another year was also added to the school course and each year has added to the care with which text-books are selected and assigned to different classes, with the prescribed courses of study.

In the year 1903-4 Mr. C. W. Edmonds was President of the Board and he stated that Memphis schools had been brought to a standard that entitled them to be "the equal, if not superior, of any city of like size in our whole country."

It was planned this year to abolish a number of small schools and concentrate their forces into larger and better equipped schools.

In his report for the year 1903-4, Professor Jones showed much work accomplished. Besides conducting examinations, with the assistance of Professor N. M. Williams, he prepared questions for the examinations of many of the grades and inspected grade work in all the schools. That year he visited 596 grades and the following year he inspected the work of every grade in the schools. This familiarity with the work done in the school-rooms proved beneficial to pupils, teachers and school efficiency.

President O. I. Kruger's report for 1905 showed the income for the building fund for three and a half years to have been $292,721.20, and expenditures to have been $291,691.57. There were some splendid buildings and much valuable school property to show for this expenditure. During the three years ending with the 1904-5 term, ninety-nine school rooms had been added, making two hundred and seventy in all, but when some of the small schools were consolidated into larger ones, seventeen rooms were abandoned, leaving two hundred and fifty-three rooms in use; but these really gave better accommodations to the children than the two hundred and seventy rooms had done, poor and scattered as some of them had been. There were 207 white and 85 colored teachers that year, with a payroll of $147,773.05. The payroll of other school employes then amounted to $25,803.15, and other school expenses amounted to $56,999.84.

President Kruger considered the night school one of the most important departments in the free school system and recommended central and first-class quarters for its accommodation.

In 1905 the Legislature authorized the issuance of $125,000 Bonds for "providing ways and means of construction of school buildings and grounds and for improvements and repairs to school property."

School bonds were to be issued in such denominations as

the Board of Education should consider "best fitted to accomplish the object in view," and to bear a rate of interest not to exceed four and one-half per cent.

This Act further provided that "Said bonds shall be in such form as may be fixed and prescribed by said Board of Education, and shall be signed with the signatures of the President and Secretary of such Boards, the interest coupons attached to such bonds bearing the engraved or lithographed signatures of the President and Secretary of such Boards; provided, however, that said bonds shall not be sold for less than par, and no commission shall be paid for the sale of said bonds."

In this Act the Legislative Council are "given the irrepealable power and authority, and are directed in addition to the taxes levied by them for the building of said schools, or the payment of bonds heretofore issued by said School Boards and now outstanding, to annually levy a tax sufficient to pay the interest on such bonds authorized to be issued by this act as the same mature, and to create a sinking fund sufficient to pay the principal of said bonds at their maturity."

When the term ended in June, 1906, Dr. G. B. Malone was President of the School Board. Dr. Malone, like many of his predecessors, realized the importance of the public schools as educative and municipal institutions. He said on this point: "No other branch in our municipal government will compare in usefulness and permanent benefit to the general welfare of our people with that of our public school system. It should therefore be both the duty and pleasure of every citizen to inform himself as to the needs of the schools and co-operate with the Board in making them the best in the land"

Dr. Malone recommended manual training in the schools, saying: "It is the duty we owe to our children to prepare them for the higher positions in life. Why should the industrial institutions of our city have to send to other States for trained workmen when we have the material at home, and which only needs opportunity for proper training?"

The Secretary of the Board, Captain A. B. Hill, was

elected to that office September 12, 1881, and has noted the constant upward growth of the schools since those early Taxing District days, as no one else could.

In 1907, Dr. E. A. Neely was appointed President of the Board.

Manual Training had been made part of the public school curriculum and proved in its first year of experiment, a success, with an able supervisor in the work, Mr. E. E. Utterback.

The Legislature of 1907 passed an Act amending the Act of 1903, in regard to efficient management of the public schools, and the Commissioners governing them, thus:

"That said Commissioners shall be elected by the qualified voters of such taxing district, and that election shall take place at the same time that members of the General Assembly are elected, viz., on the Tuesday next after the first Monday in November, 1908, and every four years thereafter, and the term of office of said Commissioners shall be for a term of four years, and they shall hold their office for such term, and until their successors are elected and qualified four years thereafter; *provided*, that the present two Commissioners, whose term of office expires January 1, 1908, shall hold their office until the election and qualification of their successors, as above provided."

General Gordon, who had been Superintendent of the schools for nearly fifteen years, was succeeded as Superintendent in 1907 by Mr. I. C. McNeill, an educator of wide experience.

The schools had now grown to such proportions that the Board needed every dollar they could command to carry on expenses and erect new buildings demanded by the stress of necessity. For two years the school term had ended with a deficit of considerable figure that had been incurred in building, and other improvements had been needed, and needs continued to multiply as each year enrolled more children and modern education made heavier demands. The City Council refused to grant all that the law allowed to the schools and the Board won a suit for $40,000 due them.

Mr. Ogilvie, then President of the Board, plead for the

highest standard for the Memphis public schools in all branches of moral, intellectual and physical advancement, believing, as many of his predecessors had done, that improvement of the schools meant improvement of the city in every way.

A great need for normal training was felt at this time and the subject of a normal school was agitated. Mr. McNeill said, "Memphis needs a normal school. Untrained additions to the teaching corps are expensive at any salary. The loss of pupils' time and the waste of their energies when not guided by professionally trained teachers cost more than a normal school would." He also said, "The teacher is the vital element in the school. The best trained person, with all the natural and acquired graces of character, is none too good for the schools of this city. * * * Experience has shown that expert service is the most economical as well as the most profitable to employers."

Professor Jones conducted a normal class that year which met Tuesday and Thursday afternoons of each week. This class was formed for the aid teachers, but a number of regular teachers attended the lessons. One of the advantages these classes enjoyed was a course of lectures on music by Miss Marie Leary, the school supervisor of music, and a course of lectures on primary work by Miss Mabelle Solly.

Still another normal advantage given the teachers that year was a psychology class, from which the many teachers who attended derived much benefit.

The Conference for Education in the South met in Memphis in 1908 and Mr. McNeill called it "an instrument of mighty power for the educational uplift of this country."

The teachers gained benefit from their institutes, from the Teachers' League, the Story Tellers' League and a school magazine published in Memphis, "The Cornerstone."

The Superintendent considered the Teachers' League of great value.

Miss Cora Ashe, principal of St. Paul Street School, was president of the League and many teachers took active part in furthering and broadening its helpful scope. Among its benefits to the teachers were excellent educational lectures, some of which were "William Tell," by Rabbi Samfield; "Intellectual Reactions," by Superintendent McNeill; "Education at Public Expense," by M. W. Connolly; "The Source of a Teacher's Effectiveness and Power," by Rev. Hugh Spencer Williams; "The Appreciation of Parliamentary Law," by Mr. Israel Peres; and a number of physical lectures by eminent physicians.

The Story Teller's League was of inestimable value, as there is no surer way of reaching the sympathy of children or of appealing to the best in them than through stories.

Industrial and physical training had by this time become a very important part of the schools and had brought forth excellent results in developing the children and enlarging the attendance of the high schools, white and colored.

The industrial training linked the physical and mental by giving "doing with thinking," that paramount rule of the great Kindergartner, Froebel. The three-fold plan of Froebel was to train children equally morally, mentally and physically, thus making a wholly rounded character and this principle had grown to be part of the public school aim of Memphis.

The growth of the high school had been so rapid that the elegant stone building provided for that purpose had become much too small, so another building, the Fowlkes Grammar School, was taken for an annex, that the high school children might be accommodated, and the grammar children were assigned to other schools.

The high school course had been added to, so that graduates were enabled to enter many of the leading universities and colleges from this school, without further preparation or examination, which caused more students to plan to complete their school course in the Memphis High School. In a letter from Chancellor J. H. Kirkland of Vanderbilt University, received by Mr. McNeill, were these words:

"You certainly placed the Memphis High School on a sound basis, and the course of study * * * would be creditable to any city. It seems to me that it completely covers all requirements to college, and I trust some of your graduates may have their attention directed to this institution."

Mr. McNeill also had a letter from Professor Miller of Tulane University, in which he said:

"I have examined your course with great care, and am glad to tell you that everything seems to be up to the standard of the best schools, not only in the South but in the country. We are very glad to place your school on our accredited list. I trust that some member of our faculty may be able soon to visit your school and to come into personal touch with your work; and I hope, too, that we shall have the pleasure of welcoming here some of your graduates. The President instructs me to inform you that a scholarship in the Academic Colleges is open at any time to the boy who will make the best record at your school in his senior year, or, if your best boy can not come, the same offer is open to the second best."

An Act of the Legislature in 1907 authorized Memphis to issue coupon bonds to the amount of $500,000, "for the purpose of providing ways and means for the construction of school buildings and grounds and for improvements and repairs to school property."

These bonds were to be in such form as the Board of Education should prescribe, not to be sold for less than par and no commission to be paid for their sale.

It was further enacted in Section 3 of this Act, that the Board of Education should be authorized and empowered to secure the payment of each and all of said bonds and coupons authorized by this act to be issued, ratably and without preference, by mortgage or trust deed upon any and all real estate and buildings thereon. The property of said Boards of Education and said mortgages or trust deeds may contain such terms or provisions as such Boards of Education or any of them so issuing said bonds may deem most expedient and best, not inconsistent with this act."

Section b provided that the Legislative Council be "given the irrepealable power and authority and are directed in addition to the taxes levied by them for the building of said schools, or the payment of bonds heretofore issued by said School Boards, and now outstanding, to annually levy a tax sufficient to pay the interest on such bonds authorized to be issued by this act as the same mature, and to create a sinking fund sufficient to pay the principal of said bonds at their maturity."

This Act was passed April 23, 1909 and approved by Governor Patterson three days later.

Mr. McNeill was again Superintendent in 1909 and Mr. J. M. Steen president of the Board. They were succeeded in 1910 by Dr. J. P. Bailey, as superintendent and Dr. Malone as president. Dr. Bailey resigned his position August 31, 1910, and Assistant-Superintendent Jones was appointed to fill his place, "pending the election of a Superintendent." June 1, 1911, Mr. L. E. Wolfe was elected Superintendent, but Professor Jones made the report for the year, as he had done the work of that session.

Professor Jones' report for this year was one of the fullest ever given and showed much advancement in every direction.

Four elegant new buildings were completed that year, the Snowden School, corner of Speedway and McLean Avenue; the Peabody School, corner of Young and Tanglewood; Lenox School, in the part of the city known as Lenox; and the A. B. Hill School, corner Latham and Olive Streets, the largest of the four.

Extensive additions were made to numerous other schools and many of the school grounds were beautified. Dr. Malone said: "The cultural value of such beautiful buildings and attractive grounds is of inestimable value in the training and development of the young people of the city."

The new Central High School was also nearly completed. This splendid and most costly of the buildings yet erected by the Board was to fill an urgent need and was looked forward to with much pride by the Board, the teachers, pupils and interested citizens generally. It has thirteen acres of ground and is said to be the most complete high school building in the country.

A bond of unity of the Memphis High School graduates not before mentioned is the Memphis High School Alumni Association organized in 1897, with Miss Mary V. Little, President. This organization has brought students of many of the school terms in touch with one another.

The officers elected in 1910 were Mary V. Little, president; Alice O'Donnell, first vice-president; Oscar Haaga, second vice-president; Elizabeth Wills, secretary; Emanuel Klein, treasurer; Martha Michel Martin, press representative; and Effie Wright, historian.

In 1911 Mary V. Little, president; Alice O'Donnell, vice-president; Tom Mitchell, second vice-president; Clarence Moore, secretary; Cecil Elliot, treasurer; Clara McCorkle, historian; Ernest Johnson, press representative.

During the year of 1910-11, 16,636 pupils were enrolled in the public schools, an increase of 920 over the preceding year. The average daily attendance was 11,842.

The year closed with the schools in good financial condition, having on hand $4,680.76. Professor Jones attributed the good financial management to the Board of Education which, he said, "has been ever alert and vigilant in caring for the welfare of the schools. With this Board every member has lived up to the principle that the holding of a public office is a public trust."

Of course a great help was the Legislative Act of 1909, allowing the Board more money, and the winning of the lawsuit, which gave an extra tax to the schools.

Dr. R. B. Maury, Tennessee President of the Audubon Society for the protection of birds, aroused interest in the schools that year, so that auxiliary societies were formed among the pupils with an enrollment of 1,600, which was then the largest membership of any State in the Union.

Another work that interested many of the children was the introduction of school gardens, under the direction of Mr. O. M. Watson.

There are many difficulties to meet in such work in a city, but Mr. Watson was very much in earnest. He visited each school grade from the fourth grade up, explained his plan to the children and called for volunteer gardners. 126 children volunteered but later 23 dropped out, so the work commenced with 103 children and 85 gardens. Some of these gardens failed for lack of proper attention or other reason, and the number was reduced to 64, while the membership was 85. In June, 23 of the gardens made exhibits of their products and Mr. Watson considered this good work for a first year. He said: "In almost every home where the gardens have been made in the back yards the front yards have been beautified."

Industrial work was greatly strengthened in this year and Mr. Utterback expressed the opinion that it had been very successful.

Hand and machine sewing were added in the white high school and much good work was produced. In the colored school this work had been a feature for over two years and the girls had done creditable work there.

Mr. Utterback's idea in the industrial work was to keep it "abreast with the progressive industrial work outside the school."

The new high school was provided with every convenience for elaborate industrial work, as for all other branches of the work of the higher grades.

Women were admitted to the Hope Night School in the session of 1910-11, which caused its enrollment to increase very much. Bookkeeping, stenography, typewriting and manual training were added to the course and they attracted many students. The literary course was also enlarged and free textbooks were furnished. The night school has become a great force and many young men and women who must work during the day and who started to work early in life, derive valuable educational advantages here that they could not otherwise have.

Summer schools were held in 1911 when many children made up their terms, which they would have lost, as some had failed in examinations or had been otherwise retarded in their school work. There were 2,294 pupils enrolled in this summer school.

As so much extra work is required of teachers and many of them have no income except their salaries; and as they can do no extra work in vacation and still keep up with the required school work demanded by the Board during that time to fit themselves as better teachers and keep up with modern methods, the Board voted to allow them salaries every month in the year. So these men and women were given a chance to do good summer work without the strain that lack of money for necessary living, and perhaps supporting others, brings. Such strain hampers any worker and prevents his giving his best effort to his work.

The reports for the year 1911-12 are not yet prepared for the public but enough has been written of the past few years to show the marvellous growth and extent of the Memphis city schools. The school year just closed is not behind any other and with its splendid corps of officers and teachers and the modern buildings and equipments equal to that of any city its size and ahead of many larger cities, Memphis is not behind in the educational advantages she offers. Of all her city advantages and improvements none stands out more than her Educational Department.

The school property now amounts to a valuation of $1,800,000, and some of the buildings are among the handsomest and best equipped in the country. The standard of the teachers is high, some of these being graduates of the first colleges of the land, while others have taken special courses to fit them for special work and all are required to keep abreast of the times. The curriculum, as has been stated before, is high and Memphis High School graduates can enter some of the best colleges without further preparation.

There are twenty-three valuable brick, one stone and eight frame buildings. One other frame house was burnt April 25, 1912, and will be replaced by a more substantial school building.

In addition to these schools the Board has for two years furnished two teachers for the Church Home School and for three years two teachers to the Leath Orphan School.

The present Board of Education comprises, Dr. G. B. Malone, president; P. H. Phelan, Jr., vice-president; O. I. Kruger, W. C. Edmondson, Chas. J. Haase, A. B. Hill, secretary; Melvin Rice, assistant secretary and M. S. Buckingham, treasurer.

The superintendent is Professor L. E. Wolfe; assistant superintendent, Professor Wharton S. Jones, and Miss Ella Orr is the superintendent's secretary.

There have been and are numerous good private schools in Memphis, some of which have already been mentioned.

One of the oldest of these, as heretofore shown, is St. Agnes Academy, a Catholic school for girls. This institution is now in its sixty-first year, having been founded in 1851, by Father T. L. Grace, and chartered in 1852. It was first placed under the care of six Dominican Sisters from St. Catharine, Kentucky, with Mother Superior Veronica Roy as supervisor.

In May, 1878, most of the buildings of St. Agnes were destroyed by fire and a valuable library lost, but the following year a substantial building was erected.

St. Agnes is delightfully situated, having kept a large part of its primitive forest trees, and its large grounds and groves, besides making a beautiful park for the students, is a joy to the thickly settled neighborhood in that part of the city. In those trees birds nest with the freedom and safety of the country, and delight the surrounding neighbors with their home-making songs and calls.

By 1868 St. Agnes had grown so in popularity and its buildings had become so crowded that another Catholic school for girls was opened on Third Street between Poplar and Washington Streets. This institution was called LaSalette Academy and was also conducted by Dominican Sisters. This school grew rapidly and its curriculum included a collegiate course.

During 1878 and 1879 both this and the St. Agnes buildings were used as hospitals and several Sisters succumbed to the yellow fever after having given their services to the care of the stricken. After the epidemics were over LaSalette again opened its doors as an academy and the Sisters taught successfully for several years, but it has since been abandoned as a school and its large building is now used by the Nineteenth Century Club as studios for teachers of arts, while St. Agnes, with its large, well-equipped building accommodates more pupils than both schools formerly did.

The Mother Superior of St. Agnes Academy is Mother Mary Pius.

Later another Catholic school for girls was established in the old Clara Conway Building on Poplar Avenue, the Sacred Heart Institute. This school is also under Dominican Sisters, with Sister Alphonse, superioress. Girls are here prepared for Vassar, Trinity and other colleges.

In 1858 the Reverend Stephen G. Starke founded a girls' school, the State Female College, on McLemore Avenue. He interested seven citizens who bought seven acres of land for the college and buildings were erected costing $60,000. President Starke died a year after the establishment of the school and the Reverend Samuel Watson took his place. This president was succeeded by the Reverend Charles Collins who, after conducting the school successfully for a while, purchased it, becoming thus its owner as well as president. The school was very successful and girls from many States attended its sessions. It was in flourishing condition when the war broke out and continued its work uninterruptedly until the Federals occupied Memphis. They then took possession of the buildings and grounds and continued to use them to the end of the war.

After the war the school was reopened but had a struggle to continue its work and the yellow fever epidemics completed its ruin. After the siege of 1879 there was an attempt to continue its existence but the people of the city were so depressed and impoverished that the school failed for lack of patronage. When the charter expired the property was divided into lots and sold. In one of the buildings Miss Mollie Marshall started a private school which she conducted for several years.[*]

The main building has since been remodeled and converted into an apartment house.

On November 19, 1871, the Brothers of the Christian Schools, an order founded in France in 1680, by St. John Bap-

[*]Vedder.

tist de La Salle, opened a college in Memphis under the direction of a few of the Brothers, with Brother Maurelian as president.

The first installment paid on their school property was by popular subscription, and many furnished money for the advancement of the school. Bishop P. A. Feehan, then of Nashville, Tennessee, was largely instrumental in obtaining these subscriptions and in getting the college established in Memphis. One of the first financial aids these Brothers had was the proceeds from a lecture by the Reverend Thomas N. Burke, on "The Ruins of Ireland."

The property purchased by this institution was formerly occupied by the "Memphis Female College," which had been established and chartered in 1854 by Rev. C. G. McPherson. This school had ceased to exist and in 1872 its charter was amended to provide for a college for boys.

The Christian Brothers College was well patronized from the first and the accommodations were soon extended. In 1886 improvements were made to the amount of $20,000 and additional improvements have been made from time to time since then. A good gymnasium has been provided and the facilities for out-of-doors athletics are excellent.

On June 7, 1912, the boys had their sixteenth annual Field Day exercises in which much proficiency was shown in physical training.

The revised charter of 1872 empowered this college to confer A. B. and A. M. degrees.

Brother Maurelian continued the faithful president of the college until a few years ago when he felt the need of rest and retired. He left Memphis for a while but was made President Emeritus and continued to be revered as the father of the school. He is again with the institution, as faithful as ever in the work.

Brother Maurelian is justly proud of the Christian Brothers' schools and of the one in Memphis especially, which he has seen grow from infancy to its present manly proportions.

The year closing June 18, 1912, the College conferred degrees upon ten young men and commercial diplomas on four.

The present officers of the College are the Reverends Brother Maurelian, president emeritus; Brother J. Edward, president; Brother C. Victor, vice-president; Brother Athanasius, secretray; and Brother Leander, treasurer.

In 1873 three Episcopal Sisters of the Community of St. Mary's Episcopal Church, were sent from New York to Memphis, at the request of Bishop Quintard. These good women nursed through the epidemic of that year and after it was over they opened a school for girls in the residence of the Bishop on Poplar Street, next to St. Mary's Church, calling the school St. Mary's School.

Its patronage enabled the supervisors to extend their quarters the next year beside the cathedral. In 1878 a brick building was commenced but the epidemic interfered with its completion; however it has since been completed since which time it has been the school home of many girls and young women.

During 1878-9 the three Sisters of the institute gave their services to nursing the sick and two of these brave souls forfeited their own lives in the cause, one being the Sister Superior and the other Sister Thecla. Sister Hughetta survived and resumed the school work later, where she continued to labor in the cause of education many years, when Sister Mary Maud took her place and she was succeeded by Sister Anna Christine.

The standard of this school has been high from the beginning and many of the noblest women in Memphis received their moral and intellectual inspiration under the good women of St. Mary's.

The Sisters continued to teach in St. Mary's school until 1910, when a change in the Sisterhood caused the Sisters here to be withdrawn. They then turned the school over to Misses Helen E. Loomis and Mary H. Paoli as principals, with an excellent corps of teachers throughout. Miss Loomis, having had much experience in the school, could easily take its management in charge, and Miss Paoli is a first-class primary teacher, which means in this day of high primary advancement, that she fills a very important place as teacher-mother to the little ones under her care. Beside these two finished teachers there are eight others, all efficient and equal to maintaining the high standard of the school, and girls are accepted from here into the best colleges. Out of six graduates this closing year, four of the young ladies have determined to go to Cornell next year. The school had nearly one hundred students in 1912, from tiny tots to young ladies preparing for college.

In this institution special attention is given to English, music and dramatic work, the teachers of these departments having had splendid advantages and experience in their arts.

The school property at present belongs to Bishop Gailor, who purchased it a few months ago from the Sisters.

In 1875 the Presbyterian Grammar and High School for girls was founded by the Reverends W. E. Boggs, Eugene Daniel, J. O. Steadman and E. M. Richardson, and Messrs. J. L. Welford, G. W. Macrae, J. C. Neely, Wm. Joyner and J. M. Goodbar.

The principal selected for this new school was Miss Jennie Higbee, who had for ten years been principal of the Memphis High School. The school was opened in the Bethel Building, corner of Adams Street and Charleston Avenue, and the first year one hundred and fifty pupils were enrolled, of which number sixteen graduated at the end of the term.

After conducting this school successfully for three years Miss Higbee resigned and established a school of her own in the St. Mary's building on Poplar Street, but in 1880 the Sisters occupied all this building and Miss Higbee moved to a beautiful site on the corner of Lauderdale and Beale Streets, in the old Robertson Topp home.

In 1892 the officers of the Board of Trustees of this school were Messrs. John Overton, Jr., president; N. Fontaine, vice-president; John Johnson, secretary and J. A. Omberg, treasurer.

In its new home the Higbee school continued to expand and became one of the best girls' schools in the South. Miss Higbee, in addition to being an excellent teacher and school manager, was a good business woman, and while the school was fortunate enough to have some of the leading men of the city for its trustees and stock-holders, the chief management was carried on by the principal until her death in 1903. At this time the school had a large corps of teachers and had won for itself a high reputation. Miss Higbee will always be revered as one of the early educators of Memphis and a classic monument in Overton Park is one proof of how her memory is held in Memphis.

The city has become compactly built all around the Higbee School, but the buildings of the institution hold their solemn dignity on the hill that overlooked woodlands when it became a school. Now there are few old trees to be seen in the neighborhood besides the grand old veterans of this hill.

The home building of the original owners still stands, a picturesque old colonial house, and is used as the home of the school-boarders, where it is the aim of the teachers to throw around the girls a home atmosphere. The school building is a large brick structure fronting on Beale Avenue, well ventilated and heated.

On the demise of Miss Higbee, one of the valuable teachers, Miss Mary E. Pimm, was appointed business manager and another experienced and valuable member of the faculty, Miss Hattie L. White, was elected principal by the Board of Managers, who were: Messrs. G. W. Macrae, president; O. B. Polk, E. Carrington, E. L. Menager and H. H. Higbee.

In 1908 the board dissolved and Misses White and Pimm leased the school, which is at the present time under their management. The Higbee School occupies three buildings and has three acres of ground. The enrollment is limited to one hundred seventy-five and the number of boarders to thirty. The principal lives on the place and the boarders are under the care of an efficient matron and two governesses.

The curriculum begins with Kindergarten and is taken from this important foundation of education to preparation for college. Graduates are accepted by Wellsley, Smith, Agnes Scott and other colleges. One Kindergarten principle carried throughout the grades is that of learning the individual nature of and peculiar bent of each pupil and basing her management on this knowledge.

In 1877, Miss Clara Conway, a woman of high intellect and splendid education, and who had also been a teacher and principal in the public schools, established a girls' school on Poplar Street with one assistant and sixty-eight pupils. Her aim was to give advantages such as had not yet been introduced into Memphis. In this school a Kindergarten was conducted, and many people who had before known nothing of Kindergarten work, or looked upon its method of teaching as useless or even absurd, learned of the vital principle underlying Kindergarten training, which had taken Frederick Froebel many years to formulate. The little children learned unconsciously and surely, getting comprehension and knowledge that gave them a substantial foundation for future education and life, while seemingly they only played, used their little hands as well as minds, and were happily occupied.

Miss Conway also introduced into her school physical culture, free-hand drawing and other branches that required mind and hand, and tried to impress on her patrons the importance of educating children in their three-fold nature—moral, mental and physical.

This school grew rapidly and by 1885 had 270 pupils enrolled. In this year a stock-company was formed for the purpose of founding an incorporated school. The trustees were Messrs. H. T. Lemmon, J. C. Neely, G. W. Macrae, T. H. Milburn, J. K. Speed, W. F. Taylor, W. A. Collier, P. McIntyre, Elias Lowenstein, E. L. McGowan, John Johnson, George Arnold, Clara Conway, Henry Frank, Z. N. Estes, W. S. Bruce, W. M. Randolph, S. Hirsh, A. W. Newsom, T. J. Latham and Reverend H. A. Jones.

Under this incorporation the school was named the Clara Conway Institute and a large school building was erected on Poplar Street. The school soon outgrew this building and a large modern brick structure was erected, most beautifully fitted up, among its treasures being some rare pictures and sculpture.

In 1888 there were over 300 pupils in the school and a corps of 26 teachers besides Miss Conway, who was principal, many of the teachers being graduates of the institution. The officers of the Board at this time were Messrs. John K. Speed, president; T. J. Latham, vice-president; J. H. Shepherd, secretary and T. H. Milburn, treasurer.

The classical course of the school consisted of eleven years' work, and the last year included trigonometry, Horace, Herodotus, history of philosophy, history of art, English literature, course of historical reading, political economy and civil government.

This institution flourished for years, standing for refinement and intellectual progress, many leading educators of the country complimenting its work, but too much ambition on the part of the principal for all school and aesthetic advantages caused the business part of the enterprise to fail and finally an institution that had become a power, succumbed, at a time when financial conditions of the country were at low ebb.

Miss Conway still persisted in educational work and had private classes of high rank. This educator would no doubt have had another school but the same year that took Miss Higbee from human work took Miss Conway also and, like her contemporary, she has been honored with a beautiful memorial in Overton Park by grateful pupils and admiring friends.

Professor Wharton S. Jones came to Memphis in 1881 and opened a school for boys. This venture prospered and four years later Professor Jones bought the old Grace Church on Hernando (now South Third) Street and had the building converted into a school-house. This school was known as the Memphis Institute and had a good enrollment every year for many years, but Professor Jones broadened his sphere of action and benefitted Memphis education still more in 1903 by joining the public schools where, as assistant-superintendent, he has given faithful service, as already shown in the part of this chapter given to the public schools.

The year following the establishment of the Memphis Institute, the Rolfe Grammar School was started by Robert Mayo

Rolfe, B. A., principal; Lawrence Rolfe, B. A.; and Theophilus Root, B. A. This school prepared boys for college and had a commercial department. The original number of pupils was limited to twenty-four but there was so many applications for admission that the school was enlarged and flourished for a number of years but the teachers have since connected themselves with other interests.

"The University School was established in Memphis in 1893. The purpose is to provide a school where boys and young men may be prepared for the leading technical schools and colleges of the country, or given substantial training in the various branches of a liberal education which will fit them for the duties and responsibilities of life, and at the same time develop them into Christian gentlemen."

This is the opening paragraph of a chapter in the year-book of the Memphis University School. This institution of learning has kept up its high standard and only admits boys of good moral character to its advantages, and that boys may receive individual attention, the number is limited.

Graduates of this school are accepted by the highest colleges, and Vanderbilt, Harvard and Princeton have allowed students to take their examinations here for acceptance into their own doors. The Washington and Lee University "has conferred a scholarship upon this school, which entitles the winner thereof to a free tuition in the University." Hampden-Sidney, Tulane and Central Universities also give scholarships to this school.

In 1899 a brick building was erected on the splendid site at the corner of Madison and Manassas Streets for the use of this school and each year the campus has been beautified, making the school and its environs an additional attraction to the city.

Facilities for athletics, both indoors and outside have received much attention and every boy in the school is urged to take part in one branch of the school athletics while each is required to take instruction in gymnastic work. This school has carried off honors in a number of athletic contests.

The faculty of the M. U. S. comprises: Edwin Sydney Werts and James W. S. Rhea, principals; Howard G. Ford,

Charles C. Wright, John B. McAlister, Robert E. Denny, Arthur T. Brown, Lee McB. White and W. T. Watson.

The average enrollment for the year just closed was between one hundred forty and one hundred fifty pupils.

A more recent girls' school than the ones written of above, is a select school for young ladies on Adams Avenue, conducted by the Misses Thomas. Miss Lida G. Thomas is principal and she is a teacher of high attainments. This institution, though one of recent establishment, has already won success and gives promise of most excellent future work and results.

Another recent school—one for boys—is the Miller School on Madison Avenue. Professor Phipps Miller is principal and he has high ambition for the young boys entrusted to his care. This is a school that gives promise of expansion and at present it is accommodated in temporary quarters only.

A number of schools in the city are maintained for the purpose of giving business education only and these have had good patronage that has ever advanced with the growth of the city. The oldest of these was opened in 1864 by Prof. T. A. Leddin, an efficient teacher and promoter of business education, who conducted it until 1887, when he sold out to Professor W. T. Watson, an L. L. B. graduate of Cumberland University. Prof. Watson gave new impetus to the school, introducing advanced methods, and had a good enrollment. Under this management the school prospered many more years, when Mr. Watson in turn sold out to Mr. R. M. Hill, who is the present proprietor. Under Professor Hill's direction the school is rapidly expanding and is now one of the best business colleges in Tennessee.

Another well established and well-equipped business institution is Draughon's Practical Business College, with Mr. Wm. T. Davis as manager, a practical school, conducted for the purpose of training practical business people.

Nelson's Business College is also an institution that has fitted many men and women of Memphis and the surrounding country for the business world, and it has an efficient corps of teachers. Professor Threlkeld, the principal, has long been an inspiring genius of this institution.

Two excellent competitors of these business schools are the Macon and Andrews College, of which Professor G. A. Macon is president and Prof. A. A. Andrews, vice-president; and the Memphis Business College, with Prof. John T. Thomas, principal.

Still another business college is connected with the University of Memphis, one of the numerous branches of this enterprise established in Memphis under an Act of the Legislature of 1909. George B. Frasher, C. P. A., is dean of this business department.

The various medical schools are mentioned in the Medical chapter, and another professional school that shows the ever broadening sphere of education in Memphis is the College of Law established in 1909, as one of the departments of the University of Memphis. This school fills a long-felt need in the city and vicinity, and has a faculty of most excellent professional men. For the session ending 1911, these were:

"Hon. S. Walter Jones, Dean, a well-known author of law text-books; Hon. Julian C. Wilson, ex-Chancellor of Mississippi; Hon. Royal E. Maiden, ex-Judge of Tennessee, trial attorney for the Memphis Street Railway Company; Hon. Allen Hughes, ex-Judge of Arkansas; Gen. David A. Frayser, one of the best criminal lawyers in the State; Hon. John E. McCall, United States District Judge, and Hon. H. Dent Minor, Judge of the Chancery Court and authority on law."

The first noteworthy educational advantages for colored people were offered in the public schools before the war closed, as already shown, and the first private school of any magnitude was Le Moyne Institute, which was established in 1871 by the American Missionary Association. This Association had conducted a few private schools here before, but in 1870 Dr. F. Julius Le Moyne donated $20,000 for founding a school in Memphis, and the following year the Missionary Association, in whose charge the money had been placed, erected a building on Orleans Street, spending $9,000 of the fund and leaving $11,000 for an endowment fund. This school has continued operations ever since, receiving in addition to annual money from the fund, tuition from the pupils, though this is not a great amount.

A good literary course is provided from the primary to normal training. Manual training was introduced early into the school, the leaders recognizing the fact that this practical need was the greatest among the colored people. In the eighties there was a printing-shop in which the pupils were taught to set type, etc., and a carpenter-shop, where boys learned the use of tools and how to handle them. An experimental kitchen was fitted up for the girls, where they were taught cooking and other household duties, and a sewing-room, in which plain and fancy sewing were taught.

In the beginning all the teachers of this institution were white, furnished by the Missionary Association, but as colored students became fitted for imparting knowledge they were made teachers and now only the principal and two or three other teachers are white. Many good teachers have been trained in this school, some of whom are now teaching in the city and county schools with satisfaction, and it is commonly said that a servant trained in Le Moyne is usually a good one.

The pupils are taught industry, self-respect and respect for others, which makes of them good workmen and law-abiding citizens. Some of the brightest and most upright members of the colored race in our midst are the products of Le Moyne teaching. The principal is Ludwig T. Larson.

On St. Paul Street is to be found another colored school that is doing splendid work. This school was opened in 1891 by the American Baptist Home Missionary Society, for the purpose of educating colored children for intelligent, capable workers, and trying to counteract the indolence and consequent mischief so prevalent with this race.

Peter Howe of Illinois gave an endowment to the institution, not sufficient to support it, but a very substantial foundation for the work. The pupils are charged a nominal board and tuition, and positions are obtained in families for boys where, mornings and evenings, they can earn money to pay their way through school, and they can help themselves still more if room and board can be obtained from their employers. Girls are required to board in the school dormitory or at some place approved by the principal, though they are allowed to work by the hour in order to earn or help earn their way.

Special attention is given to industrial work, as an important part of the education of the race. The Gas and Electric Company has fitted up a room with electric and gas ranges free of charge, where girls are taught cooking and economical and prudent use of fuel and materials generally.

The principal of Howe is a minister, T. O. Fuller, a man who came to the institution recommended by Hon. R. B. Glenn, the Governor of North Carolina, who called him "an industrious citizen and a safe leader of his race." It is Principal Fuller's plan to add continually to the industrial features which he says are not adequate to the demand, and he is having an efficient teacher trained at Tuskegee to take charge of the trades. He wants the boys to study carpentry, kalsomining, paper-hanging, brick-laying, painting, grading, gardening, upholstery, printing and other useful trades, and the girls to become intelligent and skilful dress-makers, plain-seamstresses, domestic servants, nurses, etc.

Out of two hundred graduates in sixteen years, 13 have become stenographers and typewriters, 16 teachers, 5 physicians, 5 ministers, 1 music-teacher, 2 dentists, 2 seamstresses, 1 trained nurse, 1 printer, several first-class domestics and several others skilled workmen. The school boasts that "Hundreds have worked their way through Howe, and are living lives of honor and usefulness."

The new dormitory building in which are also the experimental kitchen, sewing-rooms, reception-room and assembly hall, was built with $5,000, given by the General Education Board and $4,200 by Mr. Charles Howe, son of the founder. Each room in the dormitory is maintained by some church.

Much good work has come from this school and in September, 1911, the Howe school took first prizes at the Knoxville Appalachian Exposition over colored schools of eight States in basketry and manual training, these being for the most unique invention, the best collection of wood furniture, the best single piece of wood furniture and the smallest basket, while the Howe Orchestral Club furnished music for the colored department at this exposition.

This year the school had forty-eight graduates in the academic, normal and industrial courses. All the teachers in Howe belong to the colored race and they are men and women of upright character, who are earnestly trying to bring out the best in their pupils and make of them desirable citizens for the communities in which they are to live.

There are still two other subjects to be treated in this chapter of great importance to both the City and County in educational equipment, namely, the State Normal School for West Tennessee, and the Industrial and Training School of Shelby County.

The Legislature on April 26, 1909, passed an Act, Chapter 580 of the Acts of that year, providing that counties and municipalities should be authorized to issue $100,000.00 of 5 per cent bonds, each, for the purpose of purchasing and erecting and equipping buildings for a State Normal School.

This act gave a great stimulus in West Tennessee to the cause of education, and, inasmuch, as Chapter 264 of the Acts passed at the same session had provided for the establishment of one school in each grand division of the State, there was great rivalry among the counties in West Tennessee in the effort to obtain the site for this school. As early as the 10th of May, 1909, at a meeting of the City Board of Education, Mr. C. C. Ogilvie of the Board offered a resolution that the Board declare itself in favor of a location of the State Normal School of West Tennessee at Memphis, and directing a committee to be appointed to confer with the County and Municipal authorities, and educational, patriotic and business organizations, and obtain their financial and moral support in the effort to secure its location here. The committee was appointed and conferred with representative bodies and individuals with the result that a meeting was called to assemble at the Board of Education rooms. At this meeting it was determined to make a winning fight for the great school for

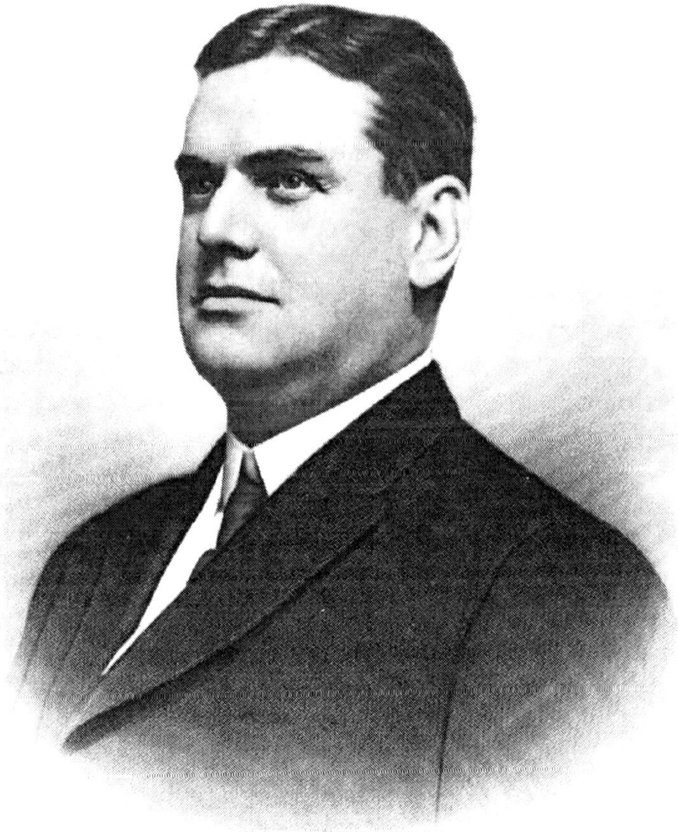

Eng. by E. G. Williams & Bro. N.Y.

C. Hanson

Memphis and Shelby County, as the State had never done anything for Memphis up to that time in the way of providing educational institutions. A strong executive committee was appointed to carry out the plans, composed of the following well-known citizens:

C. C. Ogilvie, City Board of Education, Chairman; Wharton S. Jones, City Schools; Ernest Miller, County Board of Education; Miss Mabel C. Williams, County Schools; Mrs. J. M. McCormack, Tennessee Federation of Women's Clubs; Dr. Lillian W. Johnson, Chairman of the Education Committee of the Tennessee Federation, and Nineteenth Century Club; Miss Cora Ashe, Miss Mamie E. Caine, Teachers Educational League; F. W. Faxon, President, and Francis Fentress, Jr., Business Men's Club; James F. Hunter, vice-president of Union and Planters Bank and Trust Company; O. I. Kruger, Workingmen's Civic League and Board of Education; Abe Cohn, president Y. M. H. A.; J. W. McClure, secretary Lumbermen's Club; Rev. John C. Molloy, Pastor's Association; Dr. R. B. Maury, C. C. Hanson and E. B. LeMaster, City Club; Tate Pease, Merchants' Exchange; J. S. Williams, Cotton Exchange; Dr. B. F. Turner, Civic League; A. G. Kimbrough, County Court; Mayor J. H. Malone, City Council; Thomas B. King, Y. M. C. A.; Robert Galloway, Park Commissioner; D. M. Crawford, Builders' Exchange; C. P. J. Mooney, Commercial Appeal; W. M. Clemmens, News Scimitar; R. B. Young, The Press; Dr. G. B. Thornton, Medical Association; Judge J. P. Young, Brother Maurelian and Rabbi M. Samfield.

This Executive Committee organized a Finance Committee of one hundred and fifteen prominent business and professional men and women with Mr. J. F. Hunter as chairman, and Miss Mabel Williams, County Supterintendent of Education, and later Mr. John W. Farley, as secretary, and work was begun in earnest. The County Court was applied to by a special committee and promptly agreed to issue the $100,000.00 of bonds authorized by the legislative act. The city likewise was gracious and directed a like issue of bonds.

It was at first planned to raise by a popular subscription

$100,000.00 cash to supplement the bond issue, but when about $25,000.00 had been subscribed the plan was abandoned, and it was agreed to appeal to the City and County to issue each $50,000.00 additional of bonds to complete the dormitories and other improvements and make the burden fall equally upon all of the people. This was done and the County Court granted a further bond issue of $50,000.00, and this was followed by the City with a like subscription when the legislative approval had been obtained in both cases. And still later the County Court increased its supplemental bond issue from fifty to one hundred thousand dollars, making a total of $350,000.00 raised for promoting the great school.

Various sites were tendered, eleven in number, including one offered by J. H. Creath, three miles east of the City on the Southern Railway, which carried with at a donation of $50,000.00 in value of real estate. Seige was then laid to the State Board of Education for the award of the site. Competition in other counties was strong and the Board hesitated. In October, 1909, they made a visit to Memphis and were given a banquet at the Gayoso Hotel at which urgent addresses were made in behalf of Memphis by Hon. Luke E. Wright, Bishop Thomas F. Gailor, Professor Wharton S. Jones, J. P. Young, Dr. Lillian Johnson, and other citizens.

On December 1st the State Board met at Nashville to select a site. A committee composed of C. C. Hanson, Prof. Wharton S. Jones, and Thos. C. Looney, went up from Memphis with instructions to stay until the fight was won. This was done, and after a continuous session of more than two days, in which the Governor, Hon. M. R. Patterson, a member of the State Board, strongly supported his home city, the Board unanimously awarded the site of the school to Memphis.

The State Board of Education appointed a building committee composed of Professor R. L. Bynum of Jackson, Tenn., and J. F. Hunter of Memphis, members of the State Board of Education, S. A. Mynders, president of the school, J. P. Young and C. C. Hanson of Memphis.

Work was begun in June, 1911, and pressed forward with

all diligence. The buildings have just been completed and will be ready for occupancy and the opening of the school on September 10, 1912. The total cost of the school buildings and equipment, including thirty-two acres additional of land purchased, will be over half a million dollars. The buildings at present include the Main or Administration Building, a magnificent structure with a frontage of 330 feet and embelished with massive stone columns in front, and being several stories in height, with ample room for administering a Normal School of two thousand or more pupils; a dormitory three hundred feet in length, containing one hundred thirty rooms for the accommodation of young women; a president's house of splendid design; besides power house and other equipment features. The building is located three miles eastward of the city limits on a site unsurpassed for picturesque surroundings, and it is the determination of the people of Memphis to make of it, both in construction and equipment and beauty of surroundings, a Normal School unequalled by any other in the entire South. The School is furnished with artesian water from a well four hundred feet deep, with electric lights, gas, sewerage, and all other modern features for proper comfort and sanitation.

The members of the Executive Committee and Finance Committee, as loyal builders of Memphis, individually and collectively, worked with all energy and devotion, and are entitled to equal credit for this grand achievement in behalf of Memphis. The city, itself, will gain, both in educational and financial blessings, from this school in the years to come more than can now be estimated.

In accordance with an Act passed April 10, 1895, the County Court of Shelby County considered in the summer of 1903 the question of establishing an Industrial and Training School for Shelby County. The Act provided that such school might be established by any county or municipal corporation. In this case it was inaugurated by the county. But as Memphis, owing to its great population and wealth is essentially Shelby County and as it has supplied with few exceptions all the inmates and trustees in charge of the school, it may be treated as a Memphis institution.

This scheme was promoted by and was brought about by the activity of certain ladies of the Needy Circle of The King's Daughters in this City, who persisted in their labors until the County Court finally took hold of it and provided the means for establishing the school.

When all the obstacles had been cleared away and certain litigation disposed of, the judges of the Courts of Law and Equity in the County, appointed, under the provision of the law, the trustees for administering the school. The first board of trustees consisted of Judge C. W. Heiskell, Mistress Percy B. Russell, Mistress W. A. McNeill, and James A. Omberg, Sr. W. H. Bingham, chairman of the County Court was ex-officio a member of the Board. At organization on September 10, 1903, Judge Heiskell was made president of the Board, Mistress W. A. McNeill, secretary, and Mr. Omberg, treasurer. On November 21, 1903, the Board deceded to buy the farm of 395 acres known as the Asa Hatch Place near Bartlett and about fourteen miles from the city as a site for the school, the sum paid being $9,000. December 1st, 1904, the trustees awarded the contract for the new brick building to be used as a dormitory and school, for $14,973.00.

The grounds selected for the buildings are very beautiful, being a rounded hill of gentle slope and covered with a forest of splendid oaks. The railway station on the L. & N. Railroad at the foot of the hill in front has been aptly named Altruria. The buildings are of brick with dormitories, school rooms, etc., and afford accommodations for seventy or eighty boys. Recently $15,000.00 has been appropriated by the County Court to build an annex for the accommodation of girls, also an auxiliary building for colored boys.

The school has excited much interest among the people of Memphis and since its foundation nearly three hundred wayward boys and homeless little orphans have been provided for in the institution and given a course of moral, mental and physical training to their vast benefit. The commitments of boys

*Walter H. Harrison*

were under the original law made by the Judges of the Law and Equity Courts, and the trustees have been appointed by the same judicial officers thus obtaining a very high grade of men and women for this important board. Under an act passed in 1911 the Juvenile Court of Memphis is also given the power of commitment.

The trustees, since the establishment of the school, have been Mistress W. A. McNeill, Mistress Percy B. Russell, Mistress Eugene L. Milburn, Judge C. W. Heiskell, Mr. J. A. Omberg Sr., Mr. J. F. Hunter, Judge A. S. Buchanan, Cyrus Garnsey Jr., T. B. King, F. T. Edmundson, B. R. Miller, C. C. Hanson, and Walter H. Harrison. The Chairmen of the County Court, who have been ex-officio members of the board of trustees have been W. H. Bingham, J. H. Barret, A. G. Kimbrough, J. F. Williams and W. A. Taylor. The present Board of Trustees are: Mistress W. A. McNeill, Mistress Eugene Milburn, Mr. C. C. Hanson, Mr. Walter H. Harrison and Mr. W. A. Taylor. When the new girls' annex and colored boys' building, recently provided for, have been constructed and equipped and the tillable lands brought into use, the institution will be one of the most important and valuable of its kind in the Southern States.

Walter H. Harrison

were under the original law made by the Judges of the Law and Equity Courts, and the trustees have been appointed by the same judicial officers thus obtaining a very high grade of men and women for this important board. Under an act passed in 1911 the Juvenile Court of Memphis is also given the power of commitment.

The trustees, since the establishment of the school, have been Mistress W. A. McNeill, Mistress Percy B. Russell, Mistress Eugene L. Milburn, Judge C. W. Heiskell, Mr. J. A. Omberg, Sr., Mr. J. F. Hunter, Judge A. S. Buchanan, Cyrus Garnsey, Jr., T. B. King, F. T. Edmundson, B. R. Miller, C. C. Hanson, and Walter H. Harrison. The Chairmen of the County Court, who have been ex-officio members of the board of trustees have been W. H. Bingham, J. H. Barret, A. G. Kimbrough, J. F. Williams and W. A. Taylor. The present Board of Trustees are: Mistress W. A. McNeill, Mistress Eugene Milburn, Mr. C. C. Hanson, Mr. Walter H. Harrison and Mr. W. A. Taylor. When the new girls' annex and colored boys' building, recently provided for, have been constructed and equipped and the tillable lands brought into use, the institution will be one of the most important and valuable of its kind in the Southern States.

# CHAPTER XIX

## `The Press

THE GROWTH of a modern city is more or less dependent upon the Press. Newspapers convey the news to the people, act as a medium between people of all classes and trades, give notices meant to reach the populace, talk for a community or part of a community, and if the editors are broad and intellectual and have the ability to impart their wisdom through the columns of their papers, these papers become a great educational force.

The first newspaper was established in Memphis when the Bluff City was a very small village and largely made up of people who did not read. But Memphis has always had some cultured people from her earliest days and these citizens have sought to build the city along elevated lines. Some of the early fathers deemed journalism an essential and in January, 1827 "The Memphis Advocate and Western District Intelligencer" was established, with Thomas Phoebus as editor. This paper was set up in the old meeting house, becoming the center of much curiosity and some attention. It appeared once a week, and notwithstanding its name, had a fairly good circulation, but it was generally considered a useless expense and was not taken by the citizens at large.

Mr. Phoebus had a partner and they maintained the paper until 1833, when they sold out to James and McLellan. When the *Advocate and Intelligencer* was about four years old the "Western Times and Memphis Commercial Advertiser," another weekly, was published by T. Woods & Company, but Memphis could not, or did not, support two papers, and after a short life the *Times* was consolidated with the *Advocate*, the joint publication becoming *The Times and Advocate*. Later still, after these papers had been published jointly, a little over a year, they separated and tried individual existence once more, each taking its original name, but separation must have been disadvantageous because in a few months one of them failed and soon after the other succumbed.

Perhaps a new paper that appeared in 1834 had something to do with their demise. This new sheet was *The Memphis Gazette*, with Mr. P. G. Gaines, an able editor, and Mr. McMurray a partner in the enterprise. This paper was Democratic and vigorous in its support of Andrew Jackson and his administration. In 1838 the *Gazette* also ended its existence.

The same year that saw the birth of the *Memphis Gazette*, witnessed another infant newspaper at Randolph,—the then rival of Memphis,—called *The Recorder*. The editor of this sheet was F. S. Latham, who tried to make Randolph popular and to set it above Memphis, but the Fates favored the latter town and Mr. Latham, seeing the possibilities of the more southern village, sold his little paper and came here. In 1836 he issued a new Memphis paper, *The Memphis Enquirer*, that became rival to another paper that had issued its first number a few weeks before. This rival paper was *The Memphis Intelligencer*, which soon acknowledged the superior power of the *Enquirer* by selling out its stock to the latter. *The Enquirer* was a Whig organ, opposing Andrew Jackson in his campaign of 1836 and advocating Hugh L. White of Tennessee for the presidency.

In 1838 Mr. Latham took a partner, Colonel Jesse H. McMahon. These two able editors continued the paper for three years, when Mr. Latham sold his interest to Messrs. J. B. Moseley and D. O. Dooley. The paper continued under the new firm, with Colonel McMahon as editor, and it became a semi-weekly, so adding to its strength. It continued a Whig organ and supported Harrison and Tyler for the head of the government in 1840. *The Enquirer* continued successful and four years after this exciting campaign between Harrison and Van Buren, followed a still more exciting one between Clay and Polk, and the little Memphis paper upheld the Whig candidate, Clay, who was probably the most popular man ever defeated. Polk, the Democratic candidate, was that year elected.

There was also a Democratic paper here at that time, the *Appeal*, which will be noticed further on, with Colonel Van Pelt as editor. He and Colonel McMahon were formidable rivals, each being a man of force of character and strong convictions. Each man was enterprising too and did all in his power to make his sheet a shining mark of the locality.

Another strong Whig paper which had been started in Memphis January, 1842, was the *Eagle*. After Mr. F. S. Latham had withdrawn from the *Enquirer* he set up this new paper in Fort Pickering, first calling it *The Weekly American Eagle*. Its existence in that locality was short-lived and Mr. Latham moved to Howard's Row (now Union Avenue), at that time just on the south line of the city limits. Mr. H. L. Guion bought an interest in the *Eagle*, and it was published by Latham & Guion, the former being editor. After its removal the *Enquirer* became a tri-weekly and a year later a daily, its name then being changed to the *Memphis Daily Eagle*, the first daily of Memphis. In 1845 Mr. Latham bought the entire paper and continued its sole proprietor and editor until 1848, when he accepted a partner in Mr. Edward J. Carroll. Two years later the paper was sold to John P. Pryor and Mr. Pryor became its editor, publishing the daily and weekly until the *Eagle* and *Enquirer* consolidated.\*

Colonel McMahon and his partner, Mr. Moseley, introduced the first steam-power press used in Memphis, having it set up in the office of the *Enquirer*. In 1847 the *Enquirer* became a daily, at which time Colonel McMahon was still editor. Mr. D. O. Dooley was publisher, he having bought out Mr. Moseley. In 1848 Mr. Charles Irving became assistant-editor but before the end of that year both he and Colonel McMahon retired from the paper. On this change Mr. R. J. Yancy became editor and one of the owners. In 1850 this little paper again changed hands, D. O. Dooley & Company becoming owners, with Colonel McMahon again editor.

In 1851 the two Whig papers consolidated and became *The*

---

\*Mr. Pryor many years later became joint editor with Gen. Thos. Jordan, of a Life of Forrest.

*Eagle and Enquirer.* In 1848 each of these papers had supported Zachary Taylor for President, as they had four years previously supported Henry Clay.

The *Appeal* was again stanch for the Democrats and the two leading Memphis papers made thrusts at each other and at the opposing parties quite equal in force to those of our own day.

Colonel Keating said of the papers of that day, "Very few papers in the West surpassed those of Memphis at that time." The *Appeal* had been a power since its beginning and had been one of the first papers to advance advertising. In 1837 it had printed bills, advertising for sale the property just south of Exchange Square and interest thus being brought to the locality many of the lots were sold and Memphis grew southward from that time.

As years passed the *Eagle and Enquirer* changed hands several times and political disagreements among members of the staff had become so bitter by 1855, when Pryor, Stockdale & Gray were the proprietors, that Colonel McMahon withdrew, after having served as editor for seventeen years. Two years after this time the paper with all of its equipment, was sold to the Franklin Typographical Union. Mr. L. D. Stickney was president of this company and Mr. J. J. Parham, secretary. In 1859 another change occurred when the firm became L. D. Stickney & Company, with Dr. Solon Borland and Honorable Jere Clemens editors. The following year Doctor Borland bought the paper outright and was its proprietor and editor until 1861, when he sold out to Gallaway & Clusky, editors of the *Avalanche,* a Democratic paper that had been established January 12, 1858, by Col. M. C. Gallaway, and Southern in every sense of the word. Thus the *Eagle and Enquirer* was merged into the *Avalanche,* after having existed for twenty-five years.

The telegraph had become an important factor of newspapers by this time, and news was obtained from all the important cities of the Union; while foreign news, after reaching New York or other seacoast cities was immediately telegraphed to inland towns. Memphis thus obtained foreign "news" in a little over half a month.

*The Memphis Weekly Appeal* became a member of the Memphis press on April 21, 1841, with Colonel Henry Van Pelt its editor. This paper was successor as above stated to *The Western World and Memphis Banner* of the constitution,* and continued to assert the Democracy of its parent, which as a Democratic paper had succeeded the *Gazette*. In 1851 the *Appeal* was still flourishing under Colonel Van Pelt, though it had changed hands several times during its existence and in April of that year it celebrated its anniversary by thanking Democracy and the people for their long support. A few days after this anniversary Col. Van Pelt died and his loss was greatly felt, as he had been a force not only in newspaper growth but in the city's development. Colonel Keating has called this ardent newspaper man the "Father of the Memphis Press" and Mr. Vedder said of him: "His editorial ability was of a high order, and both as a thinker and writer he commanded the respect of political opponents as well as of party friends."

After the decease of Colonel Van Pelt the *Appeal* was edited by Messrs. Edward Pickett & McClanahan, and in 1852 Leon Trousdale became associate editor. The paper continued and grew, though several times during its career the *Appeal* had been burnt out. After one of these disasters on Front Row, near Madison, in 1855, the *Eagle and Enquirer* had tendered the *Appeal* the use of their press, type and other materials, which courtesy enabled the paper to appear at its stated times uninterruptedly until setting up its own office again on Main Street, opposite the northwest corner of Court Square in an adjoining building with the *Eagle and Enquirer*. Both of these offices were later destroyed by fire and the *Bulletin* came to their assistance by lending its materials. So, even though the papers did denounce each other politically, in time of need they were brothers and friends. In 1860 Colonel Trousdale withdrew from the *Appeal*, which left Messrs. McClanahan & Dill, proprietors.

When hot differences arose between sections of the country the *Appeal* never wavered in its stand for the Southern Confederacy. Hence when the Federals were seen coming down the river in the first days of June, 1862, and their superior force was known, it was thought that the *Appeal* had better be moved

*Keating, page 213.

southward for safety as, if the Federals took Memphis, operations of the little paper that had grown to mean so much to the Army of Tennessee and the Southern States, would be stopped, or the office might be taken possession of and the paper turned into a Federal organ.

To Mr. S. C. Toof, who was at that time connected with the *Appeal*, is due the expedition with which the paper's property was packed up and put onto a south-bound train. Mr. Toof had come from Canada when a lad of fourteen and had first started in his business career in Memphis as a printer boy for the *Eagle and Enquirer* in October, 1852. Since then he had espoused the cause of Memphis on all occasions and cast his lot with her fortunes.

On the afternoon of June 5, the Federal boats were seen descending the river slowly and indications pointed to a river fight or a siege of the city. As night came on rockets illumined the sky and Memphis inhabitants were much wrought over the impending danger. Mr. Toof, after ascertaining that his wife and little children were safe, and that the fears of Mrs. Toof were allayed, went to the *Appeal* office where, with assistance, he worked until four o'clock the following morning getting the press and all the paper's outfit packed and on the train for Grenada, Mississippi.

Thus the little Confederate organ was saved and in Grenada was published for several months, still a voice of the Southern people. The Federals again drove it away from Grenada, when it moved to Montgomery, Alabama. There its work was continued only a short time, when another removal was necessary and this time Atlanta was its refuge. In that city the plucky little paper was still published on any sort of paper obtainable, wall-paper being used when more suitable materials were exhausted, just as carpets were ripped from floors and heavy curtains were taken from windows to serve as covering for Confederate soldiers who had no blankets.

Despite this exiled existence the paper was still published, under the name of the *Memphis Daily Appeal*, with correspondents in all the armies, when Sherman and his destructive soldiers besieged Atlanta. When that city fell still another move was hurriedly made and the paper taken to Columbus, Georgia, where it was at last captured and destroyed.

The editor who had thus faced many dangers that the Confederacy might retain a newspaper and the Southern Army be kept informed, was Mr. B. F. Dill. When the paper was finally captured he was arrested and placed under a $100,000 bond not to edit another issue of the *Appeal*. This occurred on April 16, 1865, when the war was practically over. After the surrender the *Appeal* returned to Memphis and on November 5, 1865, Mr. Dill set up his paper again, still the *Appeal* and still Democratic, though the cause of secession was lost. Colonel McMahon became assistant-editor, and these two faithful newspaper men kept the Southern people informed of Southern news and feeling so far as it was possible in that reconstruction time of upheaval.

The following year Mr. Dill died and his wife continued the paper until 1867, when Mr. J. S. C. Hogan, General Albert Pike and Mr. John Ainslie bought it. In 1868 the firm was again changed, this time being Ainslie, Keating & Company, with Colonel J. M. Keating as editor.

Colonel Keating had, in June, 1865, started a Democratic paper, the *Commercial*, the other papers here during that unsettled period being the *Post*, a radical paper published by John Eaton; the *Bulletin*, which represented the Unionists; the *Ledger*, edited by Whitmore Brothers; and the *Argus* which, during the entire period of the war had held neutral ground.

The Avalanche continued to be published as long as possible after the war broke out, but being managed by strictly Southern men, it could not continue operations after the Federals captured Memphis. In the latter part of 1861 it was consolidated with the *Bulletin* and in April, 1862, Colonel Gallaway sold his interest to Jeptha Fowlkes and Samuel Bard. He himself entered the Confederate Army, where he served to the close. Just as soon after the war as he could get ready for work, which was January 1, 1866, he reopened the *Avalanche* office and the paper continued its career along with its contemporary, the *Appeal*. Its new firm comprised Gallaway, Pollard & Company, with Colonel Gallaway, editor-in-chief.

In 1870, after several changes had been made in the ownership and staff, Colonel Gallaway sold his interest in the *Avalanche* to Colonel A. J. Kellar.

Soon after the war the Southwestern Press Association was organized at the Gayoso Hotel, with Colonel J. H. McMahon, chairman. At this meeting Colonel Keating was elected president; J. W. Kingsley, secretary; and J. M. Roberts, treasurer. The object of this association was to facilitate methods of getting news quickly, but the association had difficulty in carrying out its plans as, although the war was over, the Federals still controlled the telegraphs and railroads, and prevented Southern papers, to a great extent from getting reliable reports of facts and opinions expressed by Southern people.*

This Northern control caused many misrepresentations to be published of Southern occurrences and thought, and these were taken advantage of by unscrupulous workers of the press. If the Association could have had their rightful power much comfort would have been rendered the defeated Southern people and their burdens lightened. Colonel Keating says: "Abuses that grew apace as they were encouraged by Congress might have found a quicker remedy, and the Union have been really restored some years earlier," if the Press Association had had free play.

In 1868 Memphis papers were doing fairly well, but the carpet-bag rule was still in sway, so Southern editors were often punished for daring to express themselves. Gallaway, Rhea & McClusky were editors of the *Avalanche* at that time and they did not hesitate to criticise the manner in which justice, so called, was administered. The criminal judge in Memphis that year, Judge William Hunter, was a Northern man and bitter partisan, and he showed his contempt for the Southern people on several occasions. The *Avalanche* censured him in its columns, representing him as Southern people considered him, which was not flattering.

For this all three editors were arrested for contempt of court. Each man was fined ten dollars for the first contempt of court and ten dollars each again for the second contempt, with imprisonment until fine and costs were paid and for ten days thereafter. That was for two cases and for a third citation the

*Keating.

judge issued against them, he caused imprisonment until certain interrogatories should be answered. This revengeful justice also fined the city-editor of the *Avalanche*, Mr. John M. Campbell, ten dollars and imprisonment for "libel." Two days after the above decision this judge ordered that in four other cases standing against Gallaway, Rhea & McClusky, each defendant be fined fifty dollars in each case, with imprisonment until fines and costs in all cases be paid and until the defendants answered interrogatories of the court. These defendants demurred and they were taken to jail, but were released on a writ of *habeas corpus*, sued out before Judge Waldron. Judge Hunter was so furious at this proceeding that he ordered the arrest of Judge Waldron, having the order served late at night.* But human endurance, even of the defeated, has a limit, and this arbitrary act of Judge Hunter's proved the last straw for some of the citizens. The city-editor and sixteen companions disguised themselves as members of the Ku Klux Klan and visited the arrogant official. After this visit Judge Hunter closed his court until his personal safety was assured.

The cases of the accused editors "hung fire," as the lawyers say, for several months, the defendants being alternately remanded to jail and released on *habeas corpus* or *supersedeas*. All this dallying of the defendants' counsel was a "fighting for time," Colonel Keating says, Judge Hunter all the while losing favor in the community. The case was taken up by the Memphis bar and in a meeting of the bar association July 11, 1868, a report and resolutions on the "Avalanche contempt case," were passed. The committee reported:

"The law provides the remedy for private and public wrongs by defamatory publications, by an action for damages and by indictment, and the defendant may give the misconduct of the bench in evidence. But a judge must submit to the same test of truth as other men, all being equal in this respect before the law. He has no right to drag an offender before him for a libelous publication not coming within any of the specifications of the code, and to act at once as the accuser, witness, judge and jury. To

*Keating.

do so calls for the most earnest and emphatic rebuke of the profession."

The Supreme Court later held that "There are no punishable contempts of Court in Tennessee, except those specified in the statutes."

So the case ended, bringing disrepute to injustice or tyranny, and popularity to the *Avalanche*.

In 1870 Colonel Gallaway gave up his interest in the *Avalanche*, as before stated, and became editor of the *Appeal*.

The *Avalanche* continued unsavory to the carpet-bag element and a few months after Colonel Gallaway left the paper an attempt was made to mob its office, but the effort was unavailing.

The *Bulletin*, which had had a varied experience during the war, and a new start after the war, with Raphael Semmes, editor, sold out in 1868 to J. M. Currie & Company, who continued to edit it for about a year, when it ceased to be, but had a successor, the *Memphis Daily Sun*, published by W. A. McCloy. This paper only lived about two years.

In 1870 the *Appeal* became the property of the "Memphis Appeal Company," with Colonel Keating and Colonel Gallaway, eidtors. In 1875 both of these able editors became owners of the paper and it continued successful under their management for more than a decade.

In 1887 Colonel Gallaway sold his interest in the *Appeal* to Messrs. W. A. Collier, M. B. Trezevant, A. D. Allen, Laurence Lamb and T. B. Hatchett, Colonel Keating still retaining his interest and becoming editor-in-chief. The managing-editor was Mr. G. C. Matthews, and the city-editor, F. Y. Anderson. In closing his history of the *Appeal* Mr. Vedder said, in 1888:

"For nearly half a century this journal has been within itself the history, not only of a city, but of the South, in all of the potent, social, political and economical factors that before and since the war have formed the internal motives of the South's progress and its present prosperity. At the same time it has been the reflection and record of the thoughts and events of this period, it has itself been a power in moulding this thought, and controlling these events."

Through all the years of their existence and the turmoils of much of the period, the *Appeal* and the *Avalanche* remained Democratic, though other political differences arose between the two papers. It was one of these differences that caused Colonel Gallaway to dispose of his interest in the *Avalanche* in 1870 to Colonel A. J. Kellar, and become an editor of the *Appeal*.

In 1876 Mr. R. A. Thompson became a partner with Colonel Kellar, and remained with the paper until 1878, when he forfeited his life in the awful epidemic of that year. In the latter part of 1878 Mr. F. S. Nichols became editor of the *Avalanche* and remained so through the epidemic of 1878 and 1879.

In 1884, on the death of Mr. Nichols, the paper was purchased by Mr. James Phelan. Mr. H. M. Doak became the next editor and he was succeeded two years later by Mr. A. B. Pickett, who was then the youngest newspaper manager in Memphis. But Mr. Pickett's youth did not prevent his being an excellent manager and the paper grew and improved rapidly under his supervision. The paper was sold by Mr. Phelan in 1889 to Mr. W. A. Collier and others owning the *Appeal*, and consolidated with this paper.

In 1865 an evening paper, the *Public Ledger*, was organized by Edwin and William Whitmore, with Colonel F. Y. Rockett, editor. Colonel Rockett was a successful editor for three years, making the *Ledger* the first successful evening paper maintained in Memphis. After that time he was succeeded by J. J. DuBose, who edited it for three years, when he retired and Colonel Rockett returned to the editorial chair. Mr. Edwin Whitmore, after the death of his brother, became full owner of the *Ledger*, and remained so until 1886. Captain J. Harvey Mathes was city-editor much of this time, he and Mr. Whitmore working together harmoniously. Upon the death of Colonel Rockett, Captain Mathes became editor in 1872. The *Ledger* continued through many years of success while other evening papers came and went in periods of brief life. Captain Mathes, a man of learning and a soldier of high type made much of the success of this little paper. It was Democratic, but as Mr. Vedder says, "Very independent as well as liberal, fearless as well as bold, a leader in progressive development and the social and educational advancement of Tennessee."

In 1878 Mr. Whitmore sold his interest to Captain Mathes and Mr. W. L. Trask, after which the paper was continued under the firm name of Mathes & Company, with Mr. C. G. Locke as business manager. After a trip to Europe Captain Mathes returned to Memphis in the midst of the yellow fever epidemic of 1878. He and his wife both had the disease, after having given themselves unselfishly to the assistance of others, but both recovered to continue their useful lives.

Nearly a decade later,—1887,—Mr. Trask sold his interest in the *Ledger*, and Captain Mathes organized a stock company, of which he was made president; Henry F. Walsh, secretary and associate-editor; and R. J. Black, treasurer. Mr. A. B. Pickett became city-editor, which position he held until he transferred to the *Appeal*. Then Mr. H. C. Ricketts was city-editor until he went to the *Avalanche*.

The *Ledger* at that time had one of the best equipped newspaper establishments of the South. Its largest stockholder was Captain Mathes and he was assisted in the publication of the paper by a staff of talented men. On the death of Captain Mathes the paper was reorganized with Mr. John T. Harris as president and business-manager; Mr. M. W. Connoly, editor-in-chief, and Mr. D. A. Frayser, secretary and managing editor. The *Ledger* was discontinued in 1894, being at that time the oldest evening paper in the South.

The *Memphis Scimitar* was established in 1880 by Attorney-general G. P. M. Turner, as a weekly. In 1882 it became a Monday morning paper and the following year an evening sheet, with a Monday morning issue. Miss Hattie A. Paul became its active business manager, she having contributed to its editorial columns from its beginning. She remained business manager until 1887, when the paper was sold. Then it came under the control of a stock-company with Sam Tate, Jr., president; Napoleon Hill, vice-president; S. L. Barinds, secretary; and W. D. Bethell, treasurer. N. Pickard was editor-in-chief, Reau E. Polk, city-editor and S. L. Barinds, commercial editor.

In 1884 Walker Kennedy and O. P. Bard, established a

weekly society and literary paper called the *Sunday Times*, which was successful from the start. In 1885 Mr. Bard sold his interest to Mr. Charles L. Pullen, who became business manager. Mr. Kennedy, as chief editorial writer, used his learning, wit and polished style to good advantage, making the paper very popular, especially with cultured people. Every Sunday morning families and individuals looked for the *Sunday Times* as many people looked for the *Spectator* early in the Eighteenth Century. This paper continued until Mr. Kennedy became chief editor of the *Commercial Appeal*.

In 1890, when the *Avalanche* was sold to the *Appeal*, Mr. Pickett bought most of the stock in the *Scimitar*, and became owner and general manager of the "Daily Scimitar Publishing Company." Sam Tate was president of this Company and Ben H. Porter, secretary and cashier. Mr. Picket made great changes in the *Scimitar* and it became and has remained one of the best newspapers in the South. Two years after the new management the circulation had increased from 3,000 to 10,000, which has grown steadily ever since.

In 1889, when the city was stirred up over the Hadden-Bethell campaign, the *Scimitar* was against Hadden, as were the *Ledger*, the *Avalanche* and the *Appeal*. All these dailies fighting the late president of the Taxing District, a paper was started in his interest by friends, called the *Evening Democrat*, with Walker Kennedy as editor.

In November of that same year a new morning paper was established, the *Commercial*, with Col. J. M. Keating as editor. The same company printed both the *Democrat* and *Commercial*, and was styled the "Commercial Publishing Company." The *Democrat* was short-lived but the *Commercial* continued.

In 1890 Mr. Phelan became ill and sold his interest in the *Avalanche* to the *Appeal*. These two papers then became consolidated as the *Appeal-Avalanche*, with W. A. Collier president of the new consolidated daily.

In 1891 Colonel Keating resigned his editorship of the *Commercial* and his place was filled by E. W. Carmack, who retained the position until 1896, when he resigned to take up a political career. Mr. Carmack was sent to Congress from the

Tenth District and later, represented his state in the United States Senate.

In 1894 the *Appeal-Avalanche* was sold to the *Commercial,* and the newly consolidated paper was called the *Commercial-Appeal,* which name it still retains. Mr. C. P. J. Mooney became managing editor of this paper, with Messrs. Walker Kennedy and W. M. Connelly editorial writers. This was the arrangement until 1902, when Mr. Mooney went to New York and F. Y. Anderson took his place. Later Mr. Anderson gave up the management and George McCormick succeeded him. In 1908 Mr. Mooney returned and reassumed the management of his old paper. Mr. Kennedy was then chief editorial writer and remained so until 1910, when death claimed him in the midst of a successful career that promised to be a brilliant one. After his decease his editorial work was divided between Mrs. Walker Kennedy and Mr. Hugh Huhn, who now do about half of this writing, Mr. Mooney doing the other half. The *Commercial-Appeal* still continues, a progressive Democratic paper, one of the best in the country, and in a handsome new building at the corner of Court Avenue and Second Street, one of the best equipped newspaper buildings of the time. Mr. W. J. Crawford has been president of the Commercial Publishing Company since its organization.

May 5, 1902, a new morning paper was started, called the *Memphis Morning News,* with A. C. Floyd, editor. G. D. Raine bought the *News* and it had very good success.

The following year Mr. Pickett died, when his paper, the *Scimitar,* was taken charge by a board of trustees who controlled it until 1904, when Mr. Raine, owner of the *News,* bought the *Scimitar* also. The two papers were consolidated December 25, 1904, under the name of the *News-Scimitar,* and has so continued to the present time. This is an afternoon paper with no Sunday edition,—an independent, Democratic paper. Its present staff comprises: G. D. Raine, editor-in-chief; M. W. Connolly, managing editor; T. W. Worcester, business manager; E. C. White, circulating manager; and R. S. Eastman, city editor. The *News-Scimitar* has its home in a costly building at the corner of Madison Avenue and Third Street, not surpassed by any other newspaper building and press equipment in the state.

In 1907 the *Memphis Press,* was started, a sprightly evening paper published daily except Sunday. This paper claims to be "Independent politically, financially, commercially." Its editor-in-chief is Mr. R. B. Young; business manager, Mr. J. A. Keefe; and city-editor, Mr. H. Leech. This evening sheet is the workingmen's friend, and while it voices scathing sentiments sometimes, its aim is to be just and to befriend the down-trodden on all occasions.

There have been many papers published in Memphis,—so many that it would take a volume to treat them all from the beginning. Even within the last generation the number has been legion. Mr. Mooney says, "Within twenty years half a million dollars has been lost in Memphis newspaper ventures," but he adds, "within the last ten years most of the losses have been recovered."

A number of German papers have been published, among them, *The Memphis Journal,* issued by Charles Weidt in 1876, which was well supported by the Germans until the 1878 epidemic, when the publisher left the city. It continued to be published by C. Twanzig. Later it was united with the *Southern Post Journal,* and was edited by Otto and F. Zimmerman, becoming a popular paper.

A German paper was established in 1854 by August Kattman, entitled *Die Stimme die Volks* (The Voice of the People). On the death of Mr. Kattman in 1860, it suspended. Mr. Kattman was a German protestant minister who came to the United States about 1850. His paper opposed slavery and expressed rational views.

There have been numerous religious papers. One of these, the Baptist, originated in Nashville in 1834, and had a successful existence until the war, when it was suspended. After the war it was removed to Memphis and started a successful career under Graves, Jones & Company.

A Catholic journal under the name of *Adam* was established in 1885, under the management of Reverend William Walsh. It was afterward controlled by the "Adam Publishing Company," with John S. Sullivan, president.

In the early fifties the *Memphis Daily Whig* was published by S. P. Bankhead, J. M. Parker and A. H. Avery, with Colonel Bankhead as editor-in-chief and Mr. Avery commercial and local editor. It lived three years and during that time was very popular with its party, having quite an influence in the community.

In 1856 a purely literary paper made its appearance,—the *Memphis Diamond*. The chief aim of this little paper was to improve taste and stimulate desire for education in the community, and its publishers, Messrs. C. B. Riggs and H. S. Millet, used their influence to good advantage.

Under the firm name of Priddy, Hays & Brower, the *Memphis Daily Argus* was established in 1859, with W. P. McQuillan, editor. He was succeeded by Robert J. Yancey, formerly connected with the *Enquirer*, who, after a year's service gave place to Colonel John P. Pryor. A number of noted Memphis men were connected with this little paper at various times.

Quite a deluge of papers came to Memphis right after the war, but most of them were short-lived.

Colonel J. M. Keating founded the *Daily Commercial* in 1865 and the next year it was consolidated with the *Argus*, but the united paper did not live long.

A number of Republican papers were among these after-the-war publications but were not popular and so short-lived.

The *Masonic Jewel*, edited by A. J. Wheeler, a popular paper among the Masons and with other people too, died during the yellow fever epidemic and was not revived.

In 1874 the Old Folks Society issued a monthly, which they called *Old Folks Record*, devoted to preserving early Memphis history. It was only published one year but during that time preserved many interesting facts for future generations. It has been largely quoted from in the present work.

Several papers in the interest of farming have been started with varying success. Some of these, published for short intervals after the war were: *The Southern Farmer*, by Dr. M. W. Phillips; the *Practical Planter*, by Messrs. Gift and Anderson;

the *Southern Farm and Home*, by W. W. Browne; the *Shelby County Journal*, by Messrs. I. B. Wright and Marcus J. Wright; the *Patron of Husbandry*, by W. H. Worthington; and the *Mississippi Valley Farmer*, in 1887, by W. A. Battaile and Thomas Marshall.

Some religious papers published in those early days were the *Christian Advocate*, edited about 1856, a weekly, by Reverend Samuel Watson. In 1871 its name was changed to the *Western Methodist*, R. W. Blew & Company, publishers. This paper had several changes, cessations and revivals and finally ceased in 1885. In 1875 Dr. Watson started the *Spiritual Magazine*, which lived three years. Reverend F. A. Taylor edited the *Presbyterian Sentinel* in 1859-60. The *Memphis Presbyterian* was edited by Reverend A. Shotwell in 1872. In 1876 the *Southern Catholic*, published by Harrington & Powell, appeared. The *Jewish Spectator* was established in 1885 by Rev. Max Samfield, which has proved a successful paper to the present time. This paper was first managed by a stock company, but in 1886 it was purchased by Messrs. Samfield & Pickard.

The first Memphis paper published for colored people was the *Mississippi Baptist*, established in 1872 by C. C. Dickinson. It was a semi-monthly for four years, when it became a weekly. In 1883 it changed hands and became the *Memphis Watchman*. Another paper devoted to the interests of this race, the *Living Way*, was started in 1874, with W. A. Brinkley, editor, and R. N. Countee, business manager.

A number of society papers have been started in Memphis at intervals but they were usually of short duration.

In 1886 *The Council* was a publication that enjoyed temporary popularity, edited by women, but contributed to by the pens of men and women both, chiefly local talent, and many superior articles, stories and poems appeared in its pages. The editors were Mesdames Olivia H. Grosvenor, Margaret Minor, Jennie D. Lockwood and Misses Jennie M. Higbee and Louise Preston Looney; and those in charge of departments were Mrs. Lucy W. Bryan, literature; Mrs. Elise Massey Selden, education; Mrs. Samuel Watson, church work; Mrs. S. B. Anderson, philanthropy; Mrs. Lide Meriwether, temperance and reform; Miss Mildred Spotswood Mathes, history.

*The Torch*, also published in 1896, was another popular monthly. The business manager of this periodical was Mr. W. T. Watson, and the editors, Messrs. Anton Ankersmit and George Storm. The secretary and treasurer was Mr. S. S. Preston, Jr.; the manager of the Advertising and Circulating department, Mr. Clyde W. Winn. This paper delved into the political questions of the day and, while a Southern paper, was an American one too, and its tone was optimistic.

Papers published in Memphis at the present time, not already mentioned, are: *Elkdom*, a magazine published for the Elks, a very entertaining little periodical, often containing superior productions; *Good Tidings*, a religious paper published on Oakland Avenue; the *Memphis Magazine*, dealing chiefly with local matters; the *Medical Monthly*, published in the Rogers Building; the *Bluff City News*; the *Catholic Journal of the New South*; the *Commercial Advocate*; *Deutsch Zeitung und Suedliches Post Journal*; the *Memphis Herald*; the *Progressive Farmer*; the *Southern Lumberman*; the *Sunday Plaindealer*; the *Early Bird*; the *Memphis Daily Record*; *The South Today*, "published in the interests of the Memphis District, under contract with the Bureau of Publicity and Development of the Business Men's Club;" and the *Cornerstone*, an excellent educational paper published by the Teachers' Educational League." Besides these are a daily *Hotel Reporter and Register* and a *Daily Abstract Sheet*, published in the Courthouse.

There are two news associations, *The Associated Press*, with headquarters in the Scimitar Building, and the *Western Newspaper Union*, 261 Court Avenue. These associations are invaluable to the dailies for their assistance in obtaining news and obtaining it quickly. Cities do not wait half a month now, as they did a few decades ago, for foreign or any other sort of news, but through concerted action news comes to all the world from all the world every day.

# CHAPTER XX

## Literature

IT WILL be impossible to embrace in a short historical sketch all the fugitive poems and magazine articles, many of them beautiful and some brilliant, which have graced the columns of the daily Memphis Press for more than half a century and in more recent years, the pages of magazines, opened so generously to Memphis writers and the historian must for the greater part be content to note the writers of books only.

Beginning with didactic and professional works and historical writings Memphis took high rank in the first of a series of law books produced here since the Civil War. Mr. R. B. Hutchinson, a learned lawyer of her bar, wrote in 1877 "Hutchinson on the Law of Carriers." This splendid treatise, published after his death in 1879, was from the first approved and adopted as a text book and hand-book of law in all of the United States. There were several other law books printed about that time, among them, "The Law of Telegraphs," by W. L. Scott, and the "Law of Self-Defense," by L. B. Horrigan and Seymour D. Thompson, "Heiskell's Digest," by Joseph B. Heiskell and "King's Digest" by H. C. King, and in 1896, "Telegraph and Telephone Companies," by S. Walter Jones, an excellent and accurate treatise.

In polemics and controversial literature Memphis has been prolific of books. The first of these of note was "The Great Iron Wheel," by Reverend J. R. Graves, a learned divine, which was published in 1855. The same writer in 1861 published "Tri-Lemma;" "Bible Doctrine of Middle Life," 1873; the several subjects of his great debates with Ditzler at Carrolton, published in 1876; "The Work of Christ in the Covenant of Redemption," 1883, and "Parables and Prophecies of Christ," 1887.

The Reverend Samuel Watson printed in the seventies "The American Spiritual Magazine" and in 1872 he published a work on Spiritualism called "The Clock Struck One," and this was followed in 1873 and 1874 by two other volumes entitled, "The Clock Struck Two" and "The Clock Struck Three." In 1874 he also published "A Memphian's Trip to Europe," and in 1884, "The Religion of Spiritualism."

Among historical works of the period are "A Complete History of Memphis," 1873, by James D. Davis; "Old Times in West Tennessee," Joseph H. Williams; "A History of the City of Memphis," 1888, by J. M. Keating, a very comprehensive historical study of early Memphis, as well as contemporary history in its bearing on Memphis and her welfare. This book is a great mine of local historical data and reflects high credit on the illustrious editor who compiled it. O. F. Vedder's volume, published in connection with and as a part of Keating's history, is a very valuable compilation of great interest to Memphians.

In 1867 General Thomas Jordan, Chief-of-Staff to General Beauregard, and John P. Pryor, a noted Memphis editor, wrote a valuable military narrative entitled "The Campaigns of Lieutenant General Forrest and Forrest's Cavalry," with an introductory note by General Forrest, approving the narrative.

Judge J. P. Young, in 1890, published a military history entitled "The Seventh Tennessee Cavalry."

In biography Captain J. Harvey Mathes, 1897, published "The Old Guard in Gray," a series of sketches of Memphis Confederate Veterans, and later, 1902, contributed to the Great Commander Series, "The Life of General Forrest."

Captain J. M. Hubbard published a little book containing narratives and sketches of the Seventh Tennessee Cavalry, entitled "Notes of a Private," 1911.

In 1904 T. B. Edgington of the Memphis Bar, printed a treatise on the "Monroe Doctrine."

In books of travel the late Judge John R. Flippin contributed in 1889 a delightful series of "Sketches from the Mountains of Mexico," in which a vein of quiet humor embellishes the exquisite word painting of the observant traveler.

But in Memphis, curiously enough, for it is yet but a youthful civilization, the principal tendency of intellectual endeavor has been to poetry. Turning recently the leaves of some volumes of the old time blanket newspapers of Memphis, the pages were found to be lavishly embellished, as was the custom then, with numerous short poems, nearly all musical, and frequently of exquisite mould. Those inside pages of the fifties were the embryos of the modern magazine, a daily repository for aspiring bards and rhapsodists of their mental products, the difference mainly lying in the obvious superiority of much of the matter in the old newspaper columns over that customarily admitted to the modern magazines.

Later the aspiring young Memphian turned to the novel, as offering a wider field of endeavor. But some have clung affectionately and successfully to their first love, and the occasional lyric poems have broadened into heroics and epics and the fugitive pieces with other more ambitious efforts, into volumes of poesy.

Almost the first to grace the young city, ere it was a third of a century old, with the music of their lyric measures, were two sisters, Virginia born, who came to Memphis in 1843 to teach. Both were soon married to Tennesseeans and became known to the literary world as L. Virginia French and Lide Meriwether. The latter still survives in Memphis, a silver-haired matron, whose mind and fancy are as clear and bright as in youth. Mrs. French, who wrote her early poems under the widely known nom, L'Inconnue, was a voluminous writer and became widely known through her early poems: "The Legend of the Infernal Pass," "The Lost Soul," "The Misarere of the Pines," "Unwritten Music" and "Alone."

In 1856 she published a collection of poems under the title, "Wind Whispers." Later she published a five-act tragedy, "Iztalilxo," and contributed voluminously of prose and poetry to the literature of that day. She also wrote a novel, "Darlingtonia," a book of force.

Mrs. Lide Meriwether likewise was not idle and in early life contributed many beautiful poems to the press and magazines and in middle life published, in conjunction with her sister, L. Virginia French, a volume of poems entitled "One or Two." Subsequently a little volume called "Soundings," a repertoire of pathetic experiences gathered by her in her work among unfortunate women. Her subsequent writings have been devoted largely to her life work in promoting temperance, in ameliorating the condition of woman and in elevating her status in the economic and political world.

In 1859 a little volume was published in Memphis by William Atson, entitled "Heart Whispers," probably the earliest effort of the Memphis book press. There were also three other writers at a somewhat later day who entertained Memphians with grateful verse,—Mrs. Mary E. Pope, who published a book of "Poems," in 1872; Mrs. Annie Chambers Ketchum, who brought out "Benny," New York, 1870 and "Lotus Flowers," New York, 1877; and Mrs. Martha Frazer (Brown) whose poems were signed "Estelle."

Miss Clara Conway published in 1876 a novel entitled "Life's Promise to Pay," and Miss Lulla Vance at a later date, "Lois Carroll."

Mrs. Elizabeth Avery Meriwether published in 1880 a very striking sketch of reconstruction days entitled, "The Master of Red Leaf." Her other books were "Black and White," "The Ku Klux Klan" and "My First and Last Love." In 1904 A. R. Taylor & Co., Memphis, brought out for her "Facts and Falsehoods Concerning the War on the South." In 1883 Mrs. E. Collins printed a book, "Poems."

Among the writers during the tenth decade of the last Century, whose work attracted attention were Howard Hawthorne McGhee, writer of poems and short stories; M. W. Connolly, who printed for private distribution in 1890, "Poems, Wise and Otherwise;" Will Hubbard Kernan, the wierd composer of Poe-like measures who, in 1892, gave one book of poems of high merit, queerly entitled "The Flaming Meteor;" and Mrs. Minnie Walter Myers, who published in 1898 "Romance and Realism of the Southern Gulf Coast."

In 1894 a story appeared by Sister Hughetta, called "Dear Little Marchionness;" and this was followed in 1895 by a Norse Idyl by Adolyn Gale Horne. The year 1896 brought forth two books, "A Strange Friendship" by Frances K. Wolf, and "Ten-Nas-Se," by John Clay Johnson. The next year appeared "The Escape and Suicide of John Wilkes Booth," by F. L. Bates. In 1909 Gilbert D. Raine published "Life;" and in 1910, William S. Bond brought out "His Struggle Magnificent."

Louise Preston Looney published "Tennessee Sketches" in 1901. Dr. William M. Guthrie published "Modern Poetical Prophets" in 1897 and "Songs of American Destiny," in 1900. Augusta Kortrecht, a Memphis writer now living in New York, has written an interesting Southern novel, "A Dixie Rose," and recently she has followed it with "A Dixie Rose in Bloom."

Among the best known Memphis writers not yet mentioned and whose works require no introduction to the reading public, are Mrs. Virginia Frazer Boyle, Judge Walter Malone, Mrs. Sara Beaumont Kennedy and Mrs. Annah Robinson Watson. Virginia Frazer Boyle is both poet and novelist. She has written widely for newspapers and magazines, beginning quite early in life. Her first book appeared in 1893, entitled "The Other Side." This was a study of the Civil War and its causes. In 1897 followed "Brokenburne" and in 1900, a series of folk-lore stories called "Devil Tales." "Serena," a novel depicting Southern life, appeared in 1905 and her latest work, a volume of poems entitled "Love Songs and Bugle Calls," was published in 1906.

Mrs. Boyle has contributed much to magazine literature, writing at intervals for Harper's Magazine and Weekly, the Century and the Delineator. She also wrote the Centennial Ode for Tennessee in 1896, which was awarded the prize. In 1909 Mrs. Boyle was selected by the Philadelphia Brigade Association, a patriotic military organization, to write the centenary Ode to Abraham Lincoln, which was received with marked approval, and in 1910 she was elected Poet Laureate of the United Confederate Veterans. A loyal Southern woman, yet her range of writing makes her a daughter of the North too, so, as a Northern paper stated, she belongs to her whole country.

Walter Malone has confined his literary achievements almost exclusively to poetry. At the early age of sixteen he published a book of poems entitled "Claribel and Other Poems." This was published in 1882 and in 1885 another volume of his appeared, "The Outcast and Other Poems." "Narcissus and other Poems was issued in 1892, "Songs of Dusk and Dawn" in 1894 and "Songs of December and June" in 1896.

In 1897 Judge Malone published "The Coming of the King," (short stories); in 1900, "Songs of North and South," and in 1904 there appeared a volume entitled "Poems," which included, besides his latest work, much that had appeared in his four preceding volumes. This book attracted wide attention not only in America, but in England and Scotland as well. Judge Malone is now engaged in writing an epic entitled "De Soto," which will give the coloring of lofty poesy to the march of that great Spanish soldier and adventurer across the Amercan continent, 1539-1541, and his discovery of the Mississippi River at the site of Memphis.

Walker Kennedy, a noted and able local journalist, and his wife, Sara Beaumont Kennedy, gave to Memphis several novels which attracted much attention. The first of this series was by Mr. Kennedy in 1893, and entitled "In the Dwellings of Silence." In 1898 Mr. Kennedy published "Javan ben Seir" and in 1899 he wrote and published "The Secret of the Wet Woods." Mrs. Kennedy, who had written quite extensively for leading magazines, her stories appearing in Harper's, McClure's, Everybody's, Outing and Ladies Home Journal, and a number of poems, largely patriotic lyrics of the Revolution, published her first book in 1901, "Jocelyn Cheshire." In 1902 she also published "The Wooing of Judith." Several years later, 1908, another volume appeared, "Told in a Little Boy's Pocket," and her last work, "Cicely," appeared in 1911. Mrs. Kennedy continues to print in the Commercial Appeal, the journal of which her late husband was editor, little gems of poems.

Another well known writer of Memphis, Mrs. Annah Robinson Watson, has published several works. The first of the series was "Some Notable Families," 1898. Then came "Passion Flowers," in 1901; "A Royal Lineage," 1901; "On the Field of Honor," 1902, a series of sketches from real life of Juvenile Confederate soldiers, and their boyish adventures. A later and more pretentious work, "Of Sceptered Race," appeared in 1909. It was of unusual order and at once attracted much attention. Mrs. Watson's latest book, "Victory," is a poem.

# CHAPTER XXI

## Art, Music and the Drama

THE majority of people who make up a new town are of the rugged type whose chief considerations are how to obtain the practical necessities of life. First utility, then comfort and then embellishments is the general order of development in a settlement, though the love of beauty is never wholly dead in the roughest human breast. The eye is unconsciously attracted by color and form, the ear by sound and the feeling by reproduction of life in story or acting.

So in the homes of early Memphis,—except those of the cultured few,—could be seen rude prints or gaily colored pictures, and spare change was spent for china dogs, vases or other gay ornaments that could occasionally be bought from peddlers, or when some member of the family made a visit to a distant city.

Music had its expression in the banjo and violin, or "fiddle," as it was known. The style of music was in keeping with the gay prints and china ornaments, and rollicking, jerky tunes could be heard from the above two instruments. Some of the favorite pieces of 1826, given in "Old Folks Papers," were "Old Zip Coon," "Row, Boatman, Row," and "Arkansas Traveler." The last of these was popular for dances, these consisting of jigs and reels.

When military companies began to be formed the drum and fife were introduced. Patriotic airs then became popular, the favorite of these being "Yankee Doodle." "Jay Bird Dies with the Whooping Cough," was another popular air of that time. None of these songs can be called elevating, but they gave expression to the desire for harmony and this desire was sometimes better satisfied in love songs, the sentiment of these and music always gravitating toward one another.

The drama was the first of the arts to receive serious attention in Memphis, and as early as 1829 a theatrical society was organized, called the Thespian Society. This society brought some really good actors to Memphis, among them Sol Smith, who was induced to stay in the town as an amateur director and in 1830 he reorganized the Thespian Society into the Garrick Club. Later, as Mr. Smith's talent became more marked he left Memphis for broader fields, but he had laid the foundation of the drama here.

The first building used for theatrical performances was on the northwest corner of Jackson and Chickasaw Streets,[*] and here some very good performances were had from amateurs who had grown from the Garrick Club, and from occasional professionals who came to the "far West." Some of these notables were among the first actors of the time.

In 1838 a more commodious theatre was fitted up on the south side of Market Street, between Front Row and Front Alley. An old frame building was converted into this theatre and a stage erected with some tolerably good scenery and a drop curtain to use between scene changes, this part of the performance heretofore having been conducted before the audience.

In 1841 a large stable on Main Street, near Adams, was converted into a "very genteel looking theatre,"[†] by John S. Potter, where new and good scenery was introduced and some very good plays performed. This theatre grew in popularity and by 1845 we are told that Shakespearian plays were produced there by good talent and to appreciative, large audiences. Some of the actors brought to this stable-theatre in the forties were the elder Booth, Eliza Logan, Julia Dean, the famous Hackett, Charlotte Cushman, Charlotte Crampton, Chanfrau, Neafie and on this crude stage the afterward world-celebrated Adah Isaacs Menken began her career as a child.[‡]

[*]Chickasaw Street was North Front Row, now Front Street.
[†]Old Folks Magazine.
[‡]Floyd.

Here was presented "Pizarro," and "The Fall of the Alamo, or the Death of Crockett," a play which was immensely popular on account of the historic interest then still fresh in the minds of the people.

This building was later burned and in 1849 Thomas Lennox, familiarly known as "Old Tom," converted the church building on the corner of Washington Street and Center Alley into a very good theatre, where only first class productions were presented. After Mr. Lennox had conducted his theatre for a while Charles & Ash became managers and they brought some of the first stars of the time to Memphis boards. Among these were the elder Booth and his famous son, Edwin Booth, Eliza Logan, Hackett, known as the great Falstaff, Charlotte Cushman and others.

In 1859 this playhouse discontinued use as a regular theatre and subsequently lost its high caste and was changed into a varieties theatre.

During the existence of the Washington Street theatre a building was erected for the express purpose of a theatre by James Wickersham. This was called the New Memphis Theatre and was opened October 19, 1859, by W. H. Crisp, who continued the management for several years. Its plays were produced by a stock company.

By this time many cultured people had come to or had grown up in Memphis, and the need was felt for high-class entertainment. Occasional musicians were brought and grand opera was enjoyed at intervals.

March 14, 1851, the great "Sweedish Nightingale," Jenny Lind, gave a concert in Memphis and people from all the surrounding country flocked to hear her wonderful voice. Newspapers descanted on her vocal and ventriloqual powers, and those who heard her could think of little else for days after but her wonderful voice and singing.

In April, 1851, "Master" Thomas, a violinist of note, gave a concert here and was later persuaded to take up his residence in Memphis and teach music. He taught successfully for a while but patronage was not large enough to give him continued and broadening success, so he went to wider fields.

On April 22 of this year, Parodi gave a concert and was almost as enthusiastically received as Jenny Lind had been. Colonel Keating says that "The cultivated musical people were especially enthusiastic over her."

While music and the drama made headway and the attendance at good concerts and plays was usually good and often crowded, painting and sculpture made little advancement among the people before the War Between the States. The only monument erected in Memphis worthy of note was Frazee's bust of Andrew Jackson in Court Square, and that appealed to the majority of people largely because it represented Jackson, and not because of its artistic value. Drawing and painting were taught in some of the schools but the outcome of that was small and much of the artistic talent of young girls in those days was directed in the monotonous, almost senseless lifelessness of wax and hair flowers and other inartistic time consumers, which were preserved under glass cases. If the time spent on these had been given to really reproducing nature, no matter how crudely, in drawing, which always speaks so keenly to young minds, or in color, or reproducing form in hand-adaptable clay, the result would have been far more elevating to the growing youth of the city. No record is found of a Memphis boy or girl developing into a real artist in the early days.

During the War Between the States even music and drama received little attention in the distressed South, though musicians and actors continued to flourish in the North. In 1864 Maginley & Solomon built a theatre on the southwest corner of Jefferson and Fourth Streets, naming it the Olympic Theatre. It was opened by Kate Warwick Vance in "Mazeppa" and pronounced a sort of success, but its managers could not make expenses, so the theatre closed ingloriously. After the war this theatre was reopened by a circus company that had tolerably success for a while.

After the war was over places of amusement were reopened and by the end of 1865 all were well attended. Laura Keene appeared for a successful week and she was followed in December by Mr. and Mrs. Charles Kean. After the Keans came Edwin Adams in "Hamlet," and played to appreciative audiences.

The Greenlaw Opera House, finished toward the last of the decade, supported some good attractions, among them Ghioni-Susini Italian Opera Troupe, which gave their performances for a week to good audiences. Each season following gave good attractions, though Memphis still did not give large support to the theatres.

In 1867 Lawrence Barrett was here, and in opera, Patti-Strakosch Italian Opera Company. The next year Lawrence Barrett and Laura Keene were here together, each having become a favorite of Memphis audiences before this partnership.

Home music was growing and numerous amateur concerts were creditably given for charities and churches.

The end of this decade also gave Memphis people such actors as Edwin Booth, Frank Mayo, Mary McVicker, Edwin Forrest, Joe Jefferson, Isabell McCullough's Opera Troupe and the Frederica Opera Troupe, popular in that day. Leo Wheat, a famous pianist, also gave a concert.

During the seventies the drama and music increased in favor and other forms of amusement came. There were musical entertainments and educational as well as entertaining lectures given at the theatres and churches; spiritual mediums and other mystery-loving performers gave seances, and Mardi Gras became a popular annual festival.

Among the lecturers were George Francis Train at the Greenlaw Opera House; a blind preacher, Mr. Milburne, who also lectured there to large audiences; Father Burke, who gave a series of popular lectures at St. Peter's church and was feted by all classes of people; Lilian Edgarton, who lectured on "From Fig Leaves to Dolly Varden;" Olive Logan, at that time a noted actress and journalist; John G. Saxe, the poet; and Horace Greeley, whose lecture was well attended and he himself was hospitably received by Memphis people. The Confederate soldiers sent a committee to greet him at the Overton Hotel, corner of Poplar and Main Streets.

Of the actors some of the most celebrated came to the

Bluff City at that time, among them being Lydia Thompson, a famous burlesque actress of her day; Janauscheck, another actress who had gained fame; and the talented Sothern.

Blind Tom, a negro genius who could imitate with his voice every sound he heard and who could play the most difficult compositions on the piano after having heard them once, even imitating the time and expression, gave several concerts, which always brought crowded houses.

The Thomas Orchestra came to the Greenlaw Opera House; Patti and Mario gave very successful concerts there; Ole Bull charmed hundreds with his violin, and the great pianist Rubenstein, came.

After the epidemic of 1873 the theatre was reopened with the play "Watch and Wait, or Through Fire."

In 1874 Ben DeBar was Falstaff at the theatre; the extremely popular "Lotta" was here; T. C. King, a noted tragedian of the time, presented Hamlet; Lawrence Barrett charmed old and new audiences; George D. Chaplin gave Monte Christo; McWade gave Rip Van Winkle; Marion Mordaunt gave Oliver Twist; and there were many others of less note.

On March 13, 1874, a benefit was given for the monument to be erected to Mattie Stevenson, a beautiful young woman who had come to Memphis to nurse the yellow fever victims and after nursing many patients through the disease took it herself and died. This heroic deed appealed to Memphis people and at a later date the monument was erected. It is today a conspicuous tribute near the North gate of Elmwood Cemetery.

Professor Perring trained amateurs for the "Messiah," which was rendered with great credit to himself and the singers. Another amateur performance was "Jarley's Wax Works," given for charity.

Mr. Tom Davey that year assumed charge of the theatre and it thrived under his management.

Mardi Gras, celebrated according to the old French custom on Shrove Tuesday, grew to be quite as much a part of Memphis as of New Orleans, where it has been celebrated for many years. Besides the masking and ball-room festivities that were not always conducive to the best behavior, there were day and night pageants that were usually educative and the floats of these spectacular processions were works that required art and skill in the construction. In 1875 the floats were the most pretentious Memphis had yet attempted. The subject of the night parade was "Ferdinand and Isabel," and as may be surmised, told the story of these two monarchs and Columbus in costly, artistic scenes on wheels. General Colton Green, a man of learning and artistic skill was the designer of this beautiful display.

After the yellow fever epidemics people were too sad over their recent bereavements and the general city depression to have the gay Mardi Gras, but in the late fall of 1879 the theatre was opened and Mary Anderson, then under the rising star of her fame, played to a Memphis audience.

In 1880 the Memphis Theatre was purchased by the Lubrie Brothers, who fitted the play-house up and named it Lubrie's Theatre. They conducted it five years and sold out. Upon this change the theatre had its original name restored and again flourished as the New Memphis Theatre. Many were the stars and lesser actors that played on its boards; many operas were there rendered and numerous lectures entertained and edified Memphis people as the theatre was conducted by different managers. Mr. Vedder gives its successive managers from the Lubries to 1888 as Messrs. W. C. Thompson, C. D. Steinkuhl, Spalding, Bidwell & McDonough, C. A. Leffingwell, T. W. Davey, Davey & Brooks, Joseph Brooks and Frank Gray.

The Greenlaw Opera House was burned in 1884. This theatre had been very popular in its day and was missed by the theatre-going people.

During the eighties the Higbee school gave its girls a high standard of music and art by employing teachers from advanced schools. Other schools were also giving attention to this part of education and art was receiving more general recognition in the city.

The first teacher of note of whom we find record was

Mrs. Morgan, who first taught in the Memphis Female Institute on the site where now stands the Christian Brothers College. Mrs. Morgan did some good work herself and imported knowledge successfully. In the sixties this artist did a book in water-colors of flowers collected around Memphis, which was considered valuable, both from an artistic and a useful point of view. This interesting book was lost in a fire in the seventies.

The pupils of Mrs. Morgan progressed notably and one of them showed genius which was brought out and afterward ripened into world-wide reputation. This pupil was Miss Mary Solari. The talented girl studied with Mrs. Morgan until 1882, when she went to Florence, Italy and studied ten years. After working a year in Casioli's studio he thought her work ought to be exhibited in the Academia di Belle Arte, but owing to the fact that she was a woman her work could not be entered. However, as pictures were entered anonomously Casioli exhibited some of her work. One of these pictures in black and white was a decorative piece that showed such strength that it took a first prize and another—heads of different types of peasants, took a prize also. When it was learned that the artist was a woman some of the Board of Awards did not want the decision to stand but others said it would be a disgrace for it not to stand and would cast a reflection on the Academy. The press took up the subject and it ended by the young girl receiving her fairly-earned prizes and honor and opened the door of the Academy to women. Colonel Keating says of this achievement of Miss Solari's, that she "surpassed Savonorola in this, that she conquered the prejudices of Florence and commanded that the gates of the Academy of Art be opened and remain open to women forever."

Cavallucci, president of the Academy, expressed fear that this entrance of women would distract the attention of men artists and bring about a deterioration of art but the opposite effect was experienced and it was found that men and women stimulated one another to their best. So the Academy remained co-educational, made so by a young Memphis woman through the real merit of her work.

Miss Solari returned to Memphis in 1892 and in 1893 she was appointed one of the Board of Judges of the Fine Arts Department of the Chicago World's Fair. She was the only woman on this jury and the only representative from the Southern States. She displayed such good judgment in the work performed by this board that she was designated the "business woman," an unusual title for an artist. Mrs. Potter Palmer invited Miss Solari to exhibit some of her pictures at the Woman's Building at this Fair, which she did.

In 1896 Miss Solari had several pictures and an antique collection at the Cotton States and International Exposition at Atlanta, Georgia. Here her collection of antique tapestries and curios took a gold medal. She also received a silver medal for water-color, a diploma of honor, diploma of honorable mention and a bronze medal for other work.

At the Tennessee Centennial in 1897 she took the first prize for oil painting, second for water-color, first for crayon, first for landscape and first for antique collection. At this exposition Miss Solari had charge of the art exhibit in the Memphis building and some of her pictures hung there as well as in the "Parthenon," the general art building. One picture in the latter building, "The Cloister of St. Marc" was commented on by the Nashville American, which article asserted that this picture "cannot be surpassed." Another of her pictures exhibited there was "Hopefield Under Water, 1897."

In 1894 this gifted and energetic artist opened a school of Fine Arts in the Randolph Building in Memphis. A partner in this school was M. Paradise, the French juror on the world's fair board. He taught sculpture; Miss Freeman, wood-carving and Mrs. Fry, china-painting. Miss Solari taught oil, water-color, pastel and tapestry painting.

In 1898, at a concourse of the whole Academy in Florence, one of Miss Solari's decorative compositions took the one hundred pound prize.

Miss Solari considers her best picture a life sized Magdalene, painted from life in Florence. This is an oil and has attracted much notice. Rabbi Samfield of Memphis, lectured on this wonderful production and Mr. G. C. Matthews, of the *Memphis Appeal* wrote an editorial on it. Another of her pictures that has received much favorable comment is an oil of an old man and woman begging, also from life, named "Two Mendicants."

Before Miss Solari opened her art school Mr. and Mrs. Longman, two gifted artists, had a studio here, where some excellent pictures were produced and where pupils received careful and intelligent instruction. Mrs. Longman was a Memphis resident for many years. She was the daughter of Adjutant General Lambert May, a Frenchman and a Confederate soldier.

On December second and third, 1892, the Longman studio was open to visitors and there were many creditable pictures displayed. Some of these were works of the students, some the work of Mr. and Mrs. Longman and a number had been loaned by artists or owners for the exhibit.

In this same year Miss Ashe had an art school and both her own work and that of her pupils received high commendation.

In 1895 the Nineteenth Century Club gave a water color exhibit, where some excellent pictures were shown. Among them were two of James Henry Mosler's scenes; a gorgeous sunset by J. C. Nicholl, "well handled," the *Commercial Appeal* asserted; "A Judean Mill Stream," by W. H. Gibson; Theodore Robinson's "Salvation Girl," which was called "one of the gems of the collection;" and some good studies in life. A visiting artist to this exhibit made the remark, "There is not a weak picture in the collection."

An Art League was inaugurated and chartered about 1900. The object of this League was to promote painting, sculpture, etching, designing, etc., and to hold exhibitions at intervals.

Of course art was taught in many of the schools and the standard was continually raised.

An artist of note who spent much of his life in Memphis and never lost interest and love for his home city, was Carl Gutherz, who was born in Switzerland. In 1851 his father, a cultured man, left Switzerland and located in Ohio, where he founded Tell City. There he lost all he had in establishing works for terra cotta, after which he moved to Memphis. He was an artistic man and an excellent draughtsman. Carl gave indications of talent at an early age and at sixteen was placed in a school of mechanical drawing. When the warship "Alabama" was built Carl Gutherz designed all the machinery. But he was an artist of higher light and while the mechanical training benefitted him it did not prevent his soaring nor keep him from giving expression to his dream world. In later years he said that his first inspiration to become a real artist came while viewing the magnificent sunsets from the Memphis bluffs.

When a young man it became possible for him to go to Paris to study, where he entered the Ecole de Beaux Arts. He studied with Pils, Jules Lefebre and Boulanger. He dreamed and did good work in Paris in the atmosphere of art. He was working on a copy of the "Lost Illusions" of Glyre, in the Luxembourg, when the war between France and Prussia broke out. He left France and went to Munich. In that city a vision came to him which proved to be that of his first great picture,—the "Awakening of Spring," but he did not paint it until he went to Rome,—walking most of the way there because he did not have the money to ride. In Rome he studied in the Villa de Medici. His "Awakening of Spring" was painted and was well received. This picture was afterward bought by an American and now hangs in a private gallery in Boston.

In 1880 Mr. Gutherz married an Alabama lady and returned to Paris. They remained there until 1896, during which time the artist produced numerous pictures and became one of a circle of the gay city's best artists. All the salons were open to his pictures and he received several medals. He also received the magic parchment certificate, entitling him to be forever *hors concours* in the Salon. Some of his greatest pictures are "Lux Incarnationis;" "The Evening of the Sixth Day," one of the great mystical paintings of the time; "Ad Astra," which he didicated to the French astronomer Flammarion; "The Temptation of St. Anthony;" "Ad Angel-is," representing an earthly figure being carried by two angels to heaven; "Midsummer Night's Dream;" "Ecce Homo;" "Sappho;" and the "Golden Legend."

To go back: after the War Between the States Mr. Gutherz made his home in Memphis and having been in sympathy with the Confederacy and fought for it, after its sad fate he loved it still and his first great painting after the conflict, "The Flight of the Warrior's Soul," embodied his feeling. This picture was reproduced on cards and thousands of these copies were sold in the Southern States. "Sunset After Appomattox," is another picture in which his sentiment for the "Lost Cause" is given expression. In this picture, which hangs in the Tennessee Club of this city, General Lee sits on a fallen oak,— a fallen oak himself but, like an oak of sound wood, still destined for usefulness. It is all over—he has performed what seemed to him to have been his duty, and although surrender was inevitable, his head is not bowed. His army was a respectable one; there had been no pillage, no barbarous cruelty, no unnecessary taking or destruction of provisions. Civilized warfare was ever his method. In this picture the great warrior sits deep in thought, his old war-horse Traveler standing behind, perhaps expecting the usual call to action and wondering at the deep, unusual silence in the evening glow. General Lee looks ahead, into the future, not knowing how it will be with his loved land and his people, but he has the optimism of a true Christian and philosopher and knows that right will finally triumph and so he looks ahead and not down.

In 1896 Mr. Gutherz and his family moved to Washington, where they continued to reside until the artist's death. In the Congressional Library are mural paintings of his that have attracted world-wide attention. In the reading-room of the House of Representatives, greatest of its beautiful decorations are seven panels in the ceiling by Carl Gutherz representing "The Spectrum of Light." Each of these panels has a figure in a rainbow color, representing a special achievement, all combining the seven colors of the spectrum. His decorations are also to be seen in other public buildings, all characteristic in their coloring and the mystical charm of Mr. Gutherz's rare touch and feeling.

But all of his pictures are not mystical; some are very real and very life-like. Portraits from his brush hang in art galleries and elegant homes, "speaking likenesses" indeed. He said of his own taste that portraiture and ideal creation both had "a subtle fascination" for him.

Several years ago when Mr. Gutherz was in Memphis, Mrs. E. A. Neely telephoned him that she wished to lay before him a project she had for establishing an art gallery in Memphis. He was to leave the city that night and told Mrs. Neely that he could give her one hour. She thanked him for that and he went immediately to her home. Mrs. Neely, after welcoming him, launched straightway into her subject. She told him how, one day while sketching in Overton Park, a strong impulse had come to her that Memphis *must* have an art gallery; how she had since dwelt upon it, talked about it and tried to scheme to devise ways and means for it. Either the plan itself or her intelligent manner of explaining it appealed to the artist who had come to her for a limited time, for he lost his hurried manner, became interested and his one hour grew to two and a half hours. He returned to the hotel full of the scheme and remained in Memphis that night. Indeed most of the night was spent drafting a plan for the proposed Art Museum and before morning he had drawn a ground plan which he later submitted to Mrs. Neely. Subsequently he drew another and improved plan in which he provided for a series of buildings to be joined by pergolas which, as the Museum should grow, could be walled up into more housing space for the pictures, statues or curios. These two persons, with their desire to have a lasting good for the people, grew enthusiastic and aroused some interest but where were funds for even the first of such a pretentious scheme to come from? Mr. Gutherz had to leave and the project lagged but never was given up by Mrs. Neely. Often while engaged in domestic duties for her large family or otherwise employed, this enterprising woman was wondering how to go about getting money for the museum. Very trifling things sometimes serve as promoters of big thoughts and one day when Mrs. Neely was in her front yard she stooped to pick up a scrap of paper that had been thrown down by a school boy and marred the neatness of the surroundings. At once she thought of the carelessness of children in scattering trash about instead of being taught to have civic pride and to practice orderliness. This particular scrap was a page foom a drawing book on which a crude school-boy drawing appeared. The drawing brought to the lady's mind her pet scheme. "In some cities," she reflected, "waste paper is collected and brings money; why can we not gather it and make money for a nucleus for the museum?" That same day Mrs. Neely talked with Miss Ashe and Miss Cain of the school near her home and a plan of collecting waste paper was really formulated. The Park Museum Association was then and there formed with Mrs. Neely president and Miss Cain secretary. These ladies have not been idle and now they actually see an open way for collecting, baling and selling thousands of dollars worth of waste materials of the city, from schools, homes, factories, stores, laundries, etc. Already many Memphis men and women are interested in this scheme of furthering art culture in Memphis.

Mrs. Bessie Vance Brooks' $100,000 proposed memorial building to her husband, S. H. Brooks, mentioned in a previous chapter, now seems to be an assured fact and this will be a great beginning for the plan of the great artist who has physically passed to the Great Beyond. This splendid bequest and the scheme for a continuing art fund, are expected to secure for Memphis the great Museum of which Mr. Gutherz dreamed, to adorn and elevate our already lovely Overton Park. His plan was to have a park-museum where all arts shall be gathered together. "The sciences and muses all should and will come to favorable environment," he said, and "a cluster of associate arts and sciences will be attracted towards one another and it will be but reasonable that finally the Park Museum will represent a great nucleus and center of aesthetic interests."

Yet another great artist received early training in the Bluff City and went to distant countries and to fame. This was Katharine Augusta Carl, born in the South and a longtime resident and teacher of Memphis. When a young girl Miss Carl went to Paris to study, her first teacher there being Bouguerean and later she studied and worked abroad eighteen period of her life she studied and worked abroad eighteen years.

In 1903 Miss Carl and her mother went to China to visit her brother and while there she was invited to paint the portrait of Si Ann, the Empress Dowager of China. She accepted the commission and took up residence in the imperial palace, a distinction not before enjoyed by any foreigner since the Twelfth Century, when Marco Polo was a resident guest there. She remained the guest of Court for eleven months during which time she painted four portraits of her majesty. Special apartments were set aside for the artist in both the summer and winter palaces. Of the four portraits painted the largest was sent to the St. Louis Exposition, where it was unveiled during the visit of Prince Pu Lun to the Fair. This portrait was set in a handsomely carved frame that cost $40,000. The picture received much comment during the Exposition and was later presented to the United States. It now hangs in the Corcoran Gallery in Washington. The idea of painting this portrait originated with Mrs. Conger, wife of the American Minister to China, who desired a correct picture of her majesty presented to America, where she had been so grossly misrepresented.

Since 1895 Miss Carl has lived in Paris. Her work is well known there and has won her the honor of membership in the French Academy of Fine Arts.

Miss Carl formerly had a studio in Memphis and this city still holds many close friends, admirers and students of the gifted woman. Several of her pictures hang in Memphis homes also; one of these, owned by Mrs. D. P. Hadden, "Bubbles," is a life-sized picture of charming children blowing bubbles. This picture hung in the Cossitt Library for a long while and so is well known to many Memphians.

The standard of music in Memphis rose also and the jigs and reels of early days gave place by degrees to cultivated music, as the people became more appreciative of harmony and its high sense.

A Mendelsohn Society was formed in the early seventies and the study done in this society not only improved the members but caused them to give several public concerts and bring artists to Memphis, so reaching the people. Later the Mozart Society was organized with twelve prominent business men of Memphis of the board of directors, and this society did a great deal of work. In 1883 they gave a music festival with the Theodore Thomas Orchestra and a well-drilled chorus of two hundred fifty voices in "Elijah." The following year the "Redemption" was given, having the same orchestra and two hundred fifty voices; and excerpts were given from Midsummer Night's Dream, Lohengrin, the Meistersingers and the Valkyrie. The great singers brought for this festival were the "Wagnerian trio," Materna, Wilkleman and Scaria, besides Christine Nilsson and Emma Juch.

A few seasons later the Appollo Club gave the "Messiah," the "Creation" and several less pretentious productions, under Alfred Ernst, with the St. Louis Symphony Orchestra and these were very successful.

In 1888 a musical organization was formed that has done a great deal for the musical development of Memphis. This is the Beethoven Club, which is treated as a club in another chapter. These women have brought many musical artists to Memphis among them, Eurico Campobello, Johanna Gadski, William H. Sherwood, Schumann-Heink, Lillian Nordica, Josef Lhevinne, Emil Liebling and the Spiering Quintette, New York Symphony Orchestra, under Damrosch and the Dresden Philharmonic Orchestra.

A Musical Festival was given at the Auditorium in May, 1895, which gratified the music lovers, especially as every performance was greeted by a large audience. In this concourse of singers were many renowned artists and an immense chorus of home talent, making it the greatest concert troop ever gathered in Memphis before. The Messiah was given one night and received applause and demonstrations that must have gratified even those artists who were accustomed to applause.

While the clubs were improving taste in music the theatres interspersed their dramatic with musical productions and in the nineties their managers brought many first-class and some famous musical artists here. January 20, 1890, William H. Sherwood gave a concert at the Lyceum and the Thompson Opera Company gave "Said Pasha." In April of that year this theatre also had a series of operas by the Boston Ideals, who gave Rigoletta, Il Trovatore, Faust and Lucia.

March 7, 1892, the Second Presbyterian Church gave a concert, conducted by Signor Campobello, made up of home talent and the result showed that Memphis at that time had some excellent musical ability.

Miss Marie Greenwood, now Mrs. Worden, a talented young Memphis woman who had made a name in the musical world, gave "Amorita" at the Lyceum in August, 1893. Her voice was wonderful and when the audience could forget the singing and forget the woman they were glad indeed to know she was a Memphian.

In January, 1894, the great Adelina Patti, with her wonderfully preserved voice, was at the Grand, drawing an audience from many miles around Memphis.

Bands had become popular and in 1895 Gilmore's Band gave concerts at the Lyceum, Sousa's Band, with their many instruments, gave a rousing concert at the Auditorium and the same year the Damrosch Opera Company was at the Grand.

Ellen Beach Yaw greeted a large and appreciative audience in March, 1895, charming her hearers with her marvelous range of voice.

In the summer of that year East End Park gave a series of operas and dramas that were well attended and much enjoyed by the people who stayed in Memphis during the warm months. One of the drawing numbers of that year's park entertainments was the McKee Rankin-Drew Company in "Arabian Nights." That same season the East Park Company gave the great spectacular "Last Days of Pompeii."

Madame Tavary in November, 1895 gave "Lohengrin" at the Lyceum, when fashion attended in large force and the house was filled to its utmost capacity. She was assisted by an excellent company. During that same month there was a week of Grand Opera by the Tavary Company, which was so well attended that there was no longer doubt about the uplift of musical taste among the people.

The May Festival was repeated in 1896 and was a great success. On the opening night "Creation" was given, greeted by nearly three thousand people. The "Messiah" was the last night's performance and brought forth much enthusiasm from the audience.

In November of that year Lillian Nordica, with the Linde Concert Company, came to the Auditorium. In this company, besides the great Nordica, were William H. Rieger, John C. Demsey and Signor C. DeMacchi.

When the Bostonians came to the Grand in 1898 Memphis greeted them with a crowded and enthusiastic house. There were two Memphis girls with the company, Eunice Drake, who took the leading soprano role and Nellie Chapman, who showed her ability as a pianist. The friends of these young women gave them an ovation and they deserved all the attention they received as they were both artists of no mean pretension.

Many Memphis girls were on the stage at that time, all doing creditable work and some holding positions as stars. Among these, besides the two above, were Maud Jeffries, Dorothy Sherrod, Bessie Woodson, May Montedonico, Charlotte Severson, Emma Miller, Laverne Meacham and Florence Kahn, whom the great Irving had complimented so highly, and who played in his company.

May Montedonico appeared in Memphis in 1898 in "Miss Francis of Yale" and was enthusiastically received.

In the summer of 1898 two parks gave opera and vaudeville to the "stay-at-homes"—East End and Jackson Mound Parks, and were well patronized.

The drama kept pace with music during the nineties and the managers of the different play-houses endeavored to bring attractions to their stages to please all the people. Of course that meant a wide range, from cheap vaudeville to high-class drama, but the general tendency was ever toward elevating the stage.

In January of 1890 the popular little actress, Annie Pixley, came to the Lyceum and she was followed by the inimitable Sol Smith Russell in "A Poor Relation."

February brought "Little Lord Fauntleroy," for the children, the Primrose and West minstrels, Cora Tanner, Fanny Davenport in "La Tosca" and Clara Morris. Marie Wainwright followed in March in "Twelfth Night."

Later in the season some Memphis amateurs gave "Uncle Dick," for the benefit of the Jefferson Davis monument and it was cleverly done.

As new theatrical stars rose and others waned Memphis was not behind in learning the strength and weakness of most of them. In 1892 Margaret Mather, with a strong company, was here; Otis Skinner, in "Joan of Ark," "Romeo and Juliet" and "Leah the Forsaken;" E. H. Sothern in "The Highest Bidder;" DeWolf Hopper in "Wang;" Robert Downing in "Ingomar."

Downing opened the year 1893 at the Grand Opera House with "Virginius," and the Lyceum opened with "The County Fair." These were followed by Robert Graham in "Larry the Lord;" Harry Lacy in "The Planter's Wife;" Annie Pixley in "Miss Blythe of Duluth;" James O'Neill in "Fontenelle;" Richard Mansfield in "Beau Brummel;" Fanny Davenport in "Cleopatra;" Marie Wainwright in "School for Scandal" at the Grand; and at the Lyceum, by Frank Daniels in "Dr. Cupid;" Patti Rosa in "Dolly Varden" and "Miss Dixie;" Daniel Frohman in "The Wife;" Lillian Lewis in "Lady Lil."

The Grand gave summer opera that year where light opera and drama were enjoyed under electric fans.

The following fall Ward and James gave a heavy repertoire, which was much appreciated; the commedians Sol Smith Russel and W. H. Crane followed one another; Katie Emmett gave Irish plays that were charming; and then came Lewis Morrison; Roland Reed; Thomas Keene in Shakespeare; Herman the Great with his wonderful feats of legerdemain; Clara Morris; Wilson Barrett and Maud Jeffries in Shakespeare;

Alexander Salvini; and Joseph Jefferson in the play that made him famous and which he made famous, "Rip Van Winkle." Mr. Jefferson was invited to lecture in the Peabody Hotel dining-room which he did and there he was given an ovation. This ovation continued in the evening at the theatre when he appeared on the stage.

In 1896 the large Auditorium, corner of Main and Linden, was converted into a theatre and it was opened in September with "The Streets of New York." This building had formerly housed street-cars and mules and was afterwards fitted up for a lecture hall to accommodate large audiences.

The coming of Mrs. Fiske to the Lyceum in 1897 brought a treat to theatre-goers and she was well supported. In her company were James M. Colville, Clara Morris, Barton Hill and Mary Maddern.

Later Clara Morris came to the Grand, appearing in "Camille," and those great actors, Henry Irving and Ellen Terry came and drew large and appreciative audiences to their Shakespeareian performances.

The closing years of the century saw an increase in theatrical attendance and brilliant stars shone here and there in the plays given. It would be tiresome to name them all but nearly all of those mentioned returned and many others were engaged and came.

Mardi Gras was revived and lasted a couple of seasons but did not bring its old-time favor and died.

Some of the lecturers who gave their elevating sort of amusement during these years were Thomas Nelson Page, at the Grand; Henry Watterson on "Money and Morals;" Robert Burdette with his wit; Will Allen Dromgoole, with her charming Southern stories; Hamlin Garland; Susan B. Anthony; Carrie Chapman-Catt; "Bob" Taylor with his "Fiddle and Bow," and on another occasion this popular lecturer and his brother "Alf" together, giving their well-known lecture on "Dixie and Yankee Doodle."

Several amateur entertainments of credit were given during this decade, notably those of Miss Lewellyn and Mrs. Wiltshire, afterward Mrs. Hammond.

Miss Grace Lewellyn is one of the educators of Memphis to whom the city owes a debt of gratitude. Miss Lewellyn came to Memphis in the early seventies, a young girl graduate from Nazareth, Kentucky, after the death of her father, who left her entirely orphaned a short while after the death of her mother. Through the influence of friends of her father, Dr. Lewellyn, she obtained a position as teacher. She taught for several years in Miss Conway's school in regular literary work but her talent in elocution and her success with children in this line of work brought her much praise so, encouraged by teachers and friends, she took vacation courses and made a specialty of dramatic work. After becoming absorbed in her new labors she took several leading roles in plays in which she was so successful that she became stage-struck and accepted a theatrical position in New York. This life did not prove the paradise of ease and fame in reality that it had in her girlish imagination, so she gave it up and returned to Memphis. She obtained the position of elocution and physical culture teacher in the Memphis City High School, where she taught for a number of years, in addition to having private classes in her home.

Miss Lewellyn's entertainments, given by herself and pupils, under her supervision, grew to be very popular and her own popularity grew apace. In 1895 she opened the Memphis Conservatory in the new Lyceum Building, with a corps of teachers for the different arts, chosen from the best talent of Memphis. She conducted the elocution and physical culture departments herself and made a great deal of money, but with a heart full of sympathy for the world and an ever-ready attention for those in need, her money went out as fast as it was earned. Many men and women owe their start in life to the sympathy and material help of this generous woman.

Many of Miss Lewellyn's pupils went on the stage and became successful actors, some even stars of note. These students never accepted stage life because of their teacher's encouragement but because they desired the profession themselves. She considered the life too trying, especially for young girls, and always advised her pupils to use their talents in other directions, which many did, but when they persisted, then she did all she could to make them proficient and her teaching has borne as good results as that of any other teacher of Memphis.

In the summer of 1904 Miss Lewellyn became ill and went to New York in search of cure, but died while there. She made one of a trio of good teachers lost to Memphis within that year, the others being Misses Higbee and Conway. Would that a monument stood to her memory in one of the parks, as to the other two, but even if no such tribute is ever erected to her memory, many hearts will revere her so long as life lasts, and the good that she did will go on bearing fruit even after her name might be forgotten.

The Memphis Conservatory, organized by Grace Lewellyn in 1895, was the first Memphis school devoted to the arts and here were concerted a corps of teachers who did much to advance culture. To the arts was added languages and later a practical department in which stenography and typewriting were taught.

The first faculty of the Memphis Conservatory consisted of: Miss Grace Lewellyn, director, elocution and physical culture; Mrs. Cary Anderson, vocal culture; Professor George Gerbig, instrumental piano music and harmony; Professor Wm. Saxby, Jr., violin; Professor Edgar Sellec Porter, mandolin, guitar and banjo; Miss Ida King, guitar and mandolin; Professor Henry Vorsheim, German Language and Fencing; Professor P. M. Rodet, French language; Miss Anna Rhea, painting in oil, water-color and China; Professor Wm. Saxby, Sr., and Misses Saxby, dancing and deportment;; Miss Katherine Southerland, stenography and typewriting.[*]

All art work begun and accomplished in the Nineteenth Century has borne good fruit and in our little more than a decade of the Twentieth Century Memphis ranks as one of the most appreciative cities of higher arts in the country. The advancement in music has been more marked than in the others but they too, give promise. There is at least a large appreciation

---

[*]During later years Mrs. Marie Greenwood Worden taught vocal in the Memphis Conservatory and other artists were added or took the places of retiring teachers.

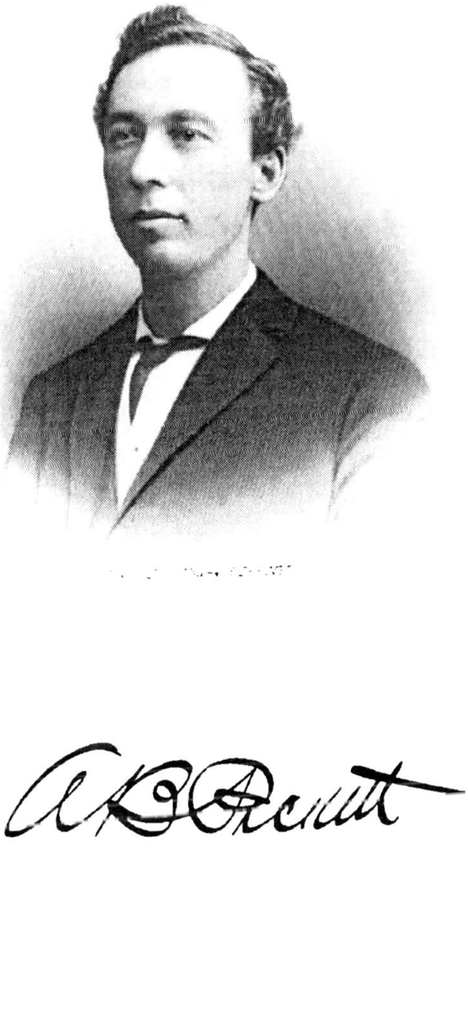

of form, color and conformity in art, many beautiful pictures and statues—some of them master-pieces—adorn Memphis homes, a few good public monuments have been erected in the city and children are receiving an art foundation by having art instruction in the public and private schools.

In 1904 Miss Solari received a second appointment on a jury of judges at a great world's fair, that of the Louisiana Purchase Exposition, when she was made one of fifty-six jurors of awards in the Fine Arts Building. At this Exposition her work was again awarded prizes and perhaps it will not be amiss here to state that when the Daughters of the American Revolution were having their Liberty Bell moulded Miss Solari sent her finest medals to become part of the bell.

In May, 1901 the Mozart Society gave their third Music Festival at the Auditorium, which was truly enjoyed. This Festival had the Chicago Symphony Orchestra and the Mozart Society chorus.

1901 and 1902 brought Paderewski, the wonderful Russian pianist; grand opera at the Auditorium by the Metropolitan Opera Company, with the great Sembrich as one of its singers; French opera at the Lyceum; Creatore and his famous band; and the renowned Josef Hofman at the Lyceum.

Four Memphis girls appeared in Drama in their home town during the season of 1902-3, namely: Bessie Miller as Bonita in "Arizona;" Edna Robb in "Sweet Clover;" Myrtle McGrain as Minna in "Rip Van Winkle" with Joseph Jefferson; and Adele Luehrmann, all talented young women.

The dramas of course had many of the best and continued to bring great tragedians, comedians and all sorts of actors from over the world. In recent years we have had Louis James and Kathryn Kidder together; Mary Mannering; Julia Marlowe; Sarah Bernhardt; Richard Mansfield; Maude Adams; Victor Herbert and his orchestra, brought by the Beethoven Club; and many other shining lights of the advanced stage.

In 1904 the Auditorium was again overhauled, refitted, the stage enlarged and reopened to the public as the Bijou Theatre, adapted for large productions. It continued to be used for various kinds of attractions until it was burned in 1911.

The Goodwyn Institute has been another great factor for culture in Memphis, its advantages being such as few cities of the world are possessed of. This building and its purposes have been treated in another chapter so here will merely be mentioned some of the many attractions that have been enjoyed within its walls by citizens of all classes of society, entirely free of charge, according to the will of its donor.

This institute was opened to the public on the night of September 30, 1907, and every season since has added its important quota to Memphis advancement and Memphis culture. The lectures given at the Goodwyn are selected for their educational value and cover a wide range, carefully selected by the Goodwyn Institute superintendent, Mr. C. C. Ogilvie. Some of these that have helped artists of the various sorts and benefitted all the hearers in the season of 1908-9 were: "An Evening of American Fiction," by Mrs. Isabell Cargill Beecher; "Seeing Things," by Pitt Parker, cartoonist and crayon artist who worked before his audience; "In a Sculptor's Studio," by Lorando Taft, showing the interior of a studio and its work in clay; numerous literary lectures and some with stereoptican views of high merit.

During 1909-10 the Goodwyn gave us such artists as Henry Turner Bailey in "The Town Beautiful," "Not Fancy Work but Handicraft;" Frederick Warde in four lectures on Shakespeare; Mrs. William Calvin Chilton on "Southern Stories from Southern Writers;" Dr. Eugene May on the "Passion Play of Oberammergau;" Ross Crane, showing drawing and clay modeling; and Lester Barlett Jones, A. B., on "The Growth of Song," "The Analysis of Song," "Folk Songs," "Masters of German Song," "Songs from Scattered Lands," and "Songs of England and America," all these lectures accompanied on the piano by Professor Gerbig of our city.

The season of 1910-11 was so rich in attractions that it is difficult to leave out any, so only three will be mentioned. These:—William Storling Battis gave three fascinating lectures on "Life Portrayals," from Charles Dickens' characters, in costume, "Oliver Twist" and "Nicholas Nickleby;" A. T. Van Laer, an artist of note, gave five lectures, "Painting in Italy," "Painting in the Netherlands," "In Spain," "In England" and "In America;" and Garrett P. Serviss gave four astronomy illustrated lectures that were a perfect delight and were the cause of an astronomy club being formed in Memphis. These were "The Beginning of Things," "The Sun as a Star," "Evolution in the Solar System," "The Planets," and "The End of Things,—Comets, Meteors and New Stars."

The season lately closed held more delights which we will again illustrate by three only. Edward Howard Griggs of New York gave six delightful lectures on "Socrates," "St. Francis of Assisi," "Victor Hugo," "Carlysle," "Emerson," and "Tolstoi." Margaret Steele Anderson gave four art lectures on "The Great Presentations of Faith," "Modern German Romanticism," "The Spirit of Later French Painting," and "Impressions of Modern French Sculpture." Carl Fique gave four of the most charming lectures on music ever given here or elsewhere. Mr. Fique illustrated his lectures on the piano and gave his listeners the delightful sensation of listening to Fairy-stories, with his simple narratives and simple and exquisite illustrations. These four lectures were "Rheingold," "The Walkure," "Siegfried," and "Gotterdammerung," (The Dusk of the Gods.)

The Beethoven Club has kept up its work and among other things organized the Symphony Orchestra of thirty musicians, which has done much toward the upbuilding of Memphis music. In 1909 this orchestra withdrew from the club and became an independent organization. Its name was changed to the "Memphis Symphony Orchestra," and its good work is still continued.

In 1907 the Beethoven Club entertained the National Federation of Musical Clubs.

While Mrs. Gilfillan was president of the Beethoven Club in 1910 she agitated giving monthly concerts to the public free of charge in the Goodwyn Institute Building. This generous movement won the approval of the club and last winter these concerts were enjoyed by many who could not belong to the Club. Teachers especially commended these musicals, as they were given at an hour when they and the pupils could attend. Of course only first-class music is given and that counteracts much of the "rag-time" heard in this generation.

At the instigation of this Club a piano was placed in the Front Street Mission for men, Mr. O. K. Houck furnishing the piano for this purpose. A man is employed to play this instrument and the benefit already accomplished by giving the members good music, is marked.

Still another benefit from this organization is tuition furnished to talented children who would perhaps not otherwise cultivate their gift.

In 1910 a grand Musical Festival of five concerts was given at the Auditorium, conducted by Mr. Frederick Stock. The chorus of adults comprised 250 voices and that of children for the Wednesday afternoon concert, 300 voices. These children as well as the grown singers were most excellently trained and rang out in the big Auditorium a clear, happy whole that was a joy to the listeners. The choral director was Alfred Hallum and his work was never better than in Memphis at this grand musical treat—a festival indeed. The number of Memphis people interested in this great musical enterprise and who worked for it, both in and out of the club, women and men, and the large audiences that attended all the concerts, certainly showed a high order of musical taste in the inhabitants of this vicinity.

We have mentioned East End Park, that gave pleasure in the nineties. This pleasure park closed for several seasons but Colonel D. Hopkins, who controlled large theatrical interests, reopened it in the spring of 1904. At first the park was only experimental but the original outlay of money reached into the thousands as the park grounds were barren fields save the old dance pavilion which had housed summer opera, vaudeville and other entertainments with varying success. The opening of the park was a dazzling occasion with its thousands of incandescent lights, which was an innovation to local amusement seekers.

The park was operated by the Hopkins Company until 1909. Then Mr. A. B. Morrison, with the aid of several business men, organized a local corporation and took all the effects of the old company. The park has grown steadily and is a substantial part of summer recreation and amusement for Memphis people—a Mecca for children and grown-ups. Mr. Morrison says "The street railway extensions and the growing population of the city have caused the enterprise to become one of vast proportions and there is every indication that East End Park is a fixture for years to come."

The officers of the park are W. H. Carroll, Jr., president; John H. Moriarty, vice-president; J. S. White, treasurer; John V. Bruegge, secretary; A. B. Morrison, general manager.

In 1908 a three-story, fire-proof building was erected at 291-3-5 Madison Avenue, by the Madison Avenue Theatre Building Company, for a theatre and leased to the Jefferson Theatre Company November, 1908. This theatre is an ornament to the city with its cream-colored brick and terra-cotta trimmings and an artistic marquee of iron and glass stretching across the sidewalk. The lobby is of variegated Tennessee marble and the interior finishings and seating are in mahogany and leather.

This new theatre was opened with a dramatic stock company and presented standard and popular plays at popular prices, under the management of Mr. A. B. Morrison.

Mr. Stainback follows the history of this new play-house, thus:

"In September, 1909, the Jefferson opened as a link in the chain of vaudeville theatres under the direction of William Morris. For six weeks high-class vaudeville at popular prices remained the policy of the house, but a few weeks later the theatre again became the home of a stock organization under the management of Mr. Morrison and as such finished the season 1909-1910. During the memorable summer of 1910, when plans for the theatrical war between Klaw and Erlanger (known as the Syndicate) and the Shubert's was formulated, Klaw and Erlanger secured a long term lease on the Jefferson in which to play their attractions; so the opening in September found the pretty Jefferson presenting the Syndicate shows at high (or standard) prices. At the close of the season 1910-1911 quasi peace was declared between the warring factions of the theatrical world.

May 1, 1911, Mr. Stainback, then operating the Bijou Theatre, secured the lease of the Jefferson. The Bijou Company then made some improvements to the theatre and renamed it the Lyric. Under this management it opened in September, 1911, with Mr. Jake Wells, president, and Mr. B. M. Stainback, an experienced theatre man, manager.

Again quoting Mr. Stainback:

"On June 29, 1912, the Lyric closed its first season, the longest and most successful in the history of the theatre. Standard dramas and musical comedies at popular prices, booked through the Stair and Havlin agency, was the policy of the Lyric for the season 1911-1912."

A form of entertainment that has become very popular in the last few years is Moving Picture Shows. These cheap shows reach so many tens of thousands of people that their power for good or evil is very great. Some people who produce these plays, like some novel writers, pander to the vulgar or brutish taste and harmful scenes portrayed as vividly as the moving pictures portray, are calculated to do more evil even than low novels. On the other hand, these pictures can be used for real education and the taste of onlookers raised rather than lowered. So, those who have the good of communities at heart and especially of growing boys and girls, can do no better moral work than to raise and enforce a pure standard for these shows, that are presented to the eyes and imaginations of so many thousands of young, middle-aged and old people.

It is well to know that in Memphis we have a Board of Censors, whose duty it is to see that no immoral or brutish or lowering plays of any sort, either in moving picture theatres or theatres where real people do the acting. This board consists of J. M. Brinkley, chairman; John M. Dean, secretary and I. B. Myers. It is the duty of this board to exclude from public exhibition all moving pictures or other plays which they consider unfit to be presented before the public. Still further, this board has authority to prosecute the performers of objectionable plays. Surely no work is more important than that which keeps the minds and thoughts of the people clean and elevates them.

Memphis has good art teachers today,—many who are building on beauty and truth and it would be a pleasure to name them all and tell of their individual work if space permitted.

The Society of Arts and Crafts is a school and sale-shop that teaches art work that is both practical and beautiful. This society was organized in 1907 by young women, Miss Grace Heiskell being the leader in the movement. She was made president and remained so until the last year, when she was made honorary president for life and Miss Mary Love elected acting president. Mrs. S. A. Wilkinson is vice-president; Miss Estelle Lake secretary and Miss Octavia Love, treasurer. The shop was first conducted by Misses Louise Fleece and Rostand Betts and many pieces of beautiful work produced and sold there. Miss Betts later withdrew to pursue other work and now the shop is kept by Misses Fleece and Bessie Blanton. Miss Clara Schneider teaches art and Miss Fleece metal and jewelry work. Work from this school has taken first prizes at Knoxville, Chattanooga and Memphis fairs.

Still another practical art that has been introduced into Memphis is stained-glass work, which is conducted by Mrs. Stanbro, a true artist in the line. Mrs. Stanbro has done some really beautiful work and is fast making a name for herself. Miss Bessie Searcy, as assistant in this shop does excellent work too and at present she is designing work in a manner which pleases even the finished teacher, Mrs. Stanbro.

Mrs. Marie Greenwood Worden, once so successful as an opera star, has left the stage and is teaching vocal in her home city with great success. Other artists teach our people and those who come from other places to be taught. There are a number of music and dramatic studios as well as of painting and sculpture, and the few artists in this line hope to see their important work grow as music has grown.

The Southern Conservatory of Music in the Masonic Building is doing good work under its four co-directors, Professors Jacob Bloom, who teaches violin; J. G. Gerbig, piano; Ernest F.

Hawke, piano-organ and theory; and Herman Keller, vocal. Besides these leaders there are numerous other first-class teachers in the Conservatory of different branches of music, besides complimentary branches in languages, expression and physical culture.

Band concerts have done much to build the musical taste of Memphis. These were inaugurated in 1904 with seventeen men, Professor William Saxby as director. These open-air concerts were so successful the first summer that they have continued ever since, Professor Saxby being the leader every season but two. There are now twenty-five men in the band and the Park Commissioners are spending $7,000 a year for music for the Memphis public. The chief object of the Commissioners is to improve the musical taste of the city and the improvement has come. Professor Saxby says: "It is a frequent occurrence to hear people humming or whistling snatches from the classics who, before the band concerts knew only rag-time."

# CHAPTER XXII

## Churches of Memphis

THE early history of the churches of Memphis is involved in much obscurity and is based largely on memory and tradition. Many articles relating to the first ministers, or preachers as they were popularly known, in the frontier town, have been written, some amusing, some scurrilous, and some with a modicum of truth. But they were manifestly unreliable and those stories will not be noted here.

The first minister of the gospel who is known to have begun active work in Memphis was Rev. Thomas P. Davidson, of the Methodist Episcopal Church, familiarly known in later life as "Uncle Tommy Davidson." While Mr. Davidson did the first religious work in the then small village about 1826, he did not establish the first church. Religious meetings were held by him in a rough structure near the mouth of Wolf River, the landing place for Memphis at that date. Services were held in Memphis at intervals until 1832 by Methodist "Circuit riders," of whom in 1830, on the circuit including Memphis, were Reverends Thos. P. Davidson, M. S. Morris and J. E. Jones. In 1832 the Methodist Episcopal Church put forth a strong effort and determined to erect a house of worship in Memphis. Rev. Francis A. Owen was commissioned as minister and a lot having been purchased from M. B. Winchester on the east side of Second Street, near Adams, and a church building erected thereon called Wesley Chapel, the work of the Methodist Church was fairly begun. This Chapel is claimed to have been the first actual church structure built in Memphis. As the Methodists began first, their churches will be noticed first.

When *Wesley Chapel,* referred to above, was nearly completed services were held in it in June, 1832. The membership at first was only eleven persons. But it soon increased and in 1845 the First Methodist Church was erected on the site of the chapel. It was a handsome building for that era, but was replaced in 1886 by the splendid granite edifice which stands on the adjoining lot at the corner of Second and Poplar Avenue, one of the handsomest of Memphis churches.

The Pastors of the church since 1832 have been: Revs. Robt. Alexander, 1832; W. Phillips, 1833; T. P. Davidson, 1834; S. S. Moody, 1835; W. D. F. Sawrie, 1836; Isaac Heard, 1837; T. C. Cooper, 1838; followed the same year by Joab Watson; Samuel Watson, 1839; P. T. Scruggs, 1841; S. S. Moody, 1842; Doctor Thweat, 1843; S. G. Starkes, 1844; Wesley Warren, 1845; M. F. Blackwell, 1847; S. J. Henderson, 1848; Jas. L. Chapman, 1850; W. C. Robb, 1852; J. W. Knott, 1853; Thos. C. Ware, 1855; Jas. E. Temple, 1855-56; J. T. C. Collins, 1857; A. H. Thomas, 1858; W. T. Harris, followed by Samuel Watson 1860; J. W. Knott, 1862; D. J. Allen, 1863; A. H. Thomas, 1865; A. P. Mann, 1866; E. C. Slater, 1869; S. B. Suratt, 1873; E. C. Slater, 1877; R. H. Mahon, 1878; S. A. Steel, 1882; and R. H. Mahan, 1886; S. A. Steele, 1887; R. H. Mahan, 1888; Warner Moore, 1889-90; W. G. Miller, 1891-92-93; C. B. Reddick, 1894; R. D. Smart, 1895-98; J. C. Morris, 1899-1902; W. E. Thompson, 1903-1906; Lewis Powell, 1907-1910; T. W. Lewis, 1911-1912.

*Asbury Church* was founded in 1843. The early organization was weak and worshipped in a private house and in John Brown's carpenter shop on the corner of Hernando and Vance. Then a lot was purchased on the corner of Hernando and Linden at the instance of Rev. Moses Brock and a rude structure erected, little better than a shack, which was called Asbury Chapel in honor of Bishop Asbury of the M. E. Church. In 1847, a somewhat better frame building replaced the first one, in which worship was held until 1882, when the present brick building was erected, which is quite a handsome Gothic edifice.

The pastors of this church have been Revs. Benj. A. Hayes, 1843; D. W. Garrard, 1845; L. D. Mullins, 1846; W. C. Robb,

1847; A. H. Thomas, 1849; J. Henderson, 1850; Jos. H. Brooks, 1852; Jas. W. McFarland, 1853 (died and was succeeded by B. M. Johnson); J. T. C. Collins, 1854; Phillip Tuggle, 1857; J. T. Meriwether, 1858; E. B. Hamilton, 1859; Robt. Martin, 1860; Guilford Jones, 1861, who left on the Federal occupation in 1862 and his pastorate was filled by D. J. Allen; Guilford Jones, 1865; F. T. Petway, 1867; L. D. Mullins, 1869; J. H. Evans, 1871; E. E. Hamilton, 1873; J. C. Hooks, 1875; Guilford Jones, 1877; Warner Moore, 1879; David Leith, 1882; J. M. Spence, 1886. H. B. Johnston, 1890-93; G. T. Sullivan, 1894-96; E. B. Ramsey, 1897-98; R. W. Hood, 1899; W. A. Freeman, 1900-02; G. W. Banks, 1903-06; G. B. Baskerville, 1907-10; Robt. A. Clark, 1910-11.

When the brick church was erected in 1883, the name was changed to Hernando Street Church and upon the change of the street names the church name was changed to Second Church.

*Central Methodist Church* was organized in 1860 and a church building, a small wooden affair, was dedicated by Bishop Geo. F. Pierce, in the same year. The church was organized by Rev. J. T. C. Collins. In 1868 a splendid brick structure was erected on Union Street, which cost $40,000, with a seating capacity of 750. The church had only temporary supplies during some years, but since 1868 the pastors have been as follows: Revs. W. M. Patterson, 1869; A. L. Prichard, 1871; P. T. Scruggs, 1873; S. B. Suratt, 1873; E. C. Slater, 1874; J. A. Heard, 1875; W. D. Harris, 1877; S. W. Moore, 1879; S. B. Suratt, 1880; J. H. Evans, 1881; R. H. Mahon, 1882; R. W. Erwin, 1886; R. H. Mahon, 1887; R. W. Erwin, 1888-1890; Alonzo Monk, 1891-93; C. F. Evans, 1894-95; W. F. Hamner, 1896-98; E. B. Ramsey, 1899; R. H. Mahon, 1900-1901; W. K. Piner, 1902-1904; W. T. Bolling, 1905-7; Wm. E. Thompson, 1908. In 1909 the Central Methodist Church moved to their new church on Peabody Avenue and renamed it St. John's Church: Wm. E. Thompson was pastor in that year and 1910; T. E. Sharp, 1911-1912.

*The Harris Memorial Church* began its useful work in Memphis in 1899, with Rev. G. W. Banks as minister, followed in 1900 by Rev. W. J. McCoy who served three years. These were followed by G. H. Martin, 1903; W. W. Adams, 1904; R. W. Hood, 1905-6; J. C. Wilson, 1907-8; W. C. Waters, 1909-10; W. W. Armstrong, 1911 and H. W. Brooks, 1912.

The *Madison Heights Church*, came into the Memphis corporation in 1899, with O. H. Duggins as pastor. J. C. Wilson followed him in 1900 and stayed with the church until 1903; E. B. Ramsey succeeded in 1904 and served until 1908 when C. A. Warfield succeeded him. John T. Myers came to this church in 1909 and is still serving as her pastor.

*Saffarans Street Methodist Church*, in 1867, a colony from the First Methodist Church, under the leadership of Rev. A. H. Thomas, organized a church on Saffarans Street, near Seventh Street, in Chelsea, and a small church building was erected there. The first pastor was Rev. M. Thomas, who, was followed in succession by Revs. J. C. Hooks, S. M. Roseborough, L. D. Mullins, W. R. Wilson, L. H. Holmes, J. P. Walker, R. S. Maxwell and J. S. Wiggins. Rev. W. H. Evans was pastor in 1886; W. W. Adams, 1892-94; C. D. Hilliard, 1895-96; G. W. Banks, 1897-98.

The *Springdale Methodist Church* became one of the churches of the city in 1899. Her pastors since that time have been Reverends, Warner Moore, 1899-1902; J. J. Thomas, 1903-4; George Kline, 1905; R. M. King, 1906-9; W. W. Armstrong, 1910-11; David Leith, 1912.

*Olive Street* or *Olive Dale Church*, formerly outside of the corporation, became a Memphis Methodist Church, with G. W. Evans, pastor; he was followed in 1903 by B. S. McLemore, who was succeeded in 1906 by S. M. Griffin; in 1909 by J. M. Maxwell; 1910 by C. Lee Smith and he still serves this church.

*Annesdale Methodist Church*, corner of Rozell and Euclid Avenues, began its Memphis service in 1904. Its ministers since that time have been Reverends J. M. Maxwell, 1904-6; B. S. McLemore, 1907-8; R. B. Swift, 1909; S. M. Griffin, 1910; J. G. Williams, 1911-1912.

*New South Memphis Methodist Church* is an active and far-reaching little church, beginning its career in the city in 1906. The ministers have been the Reverends T. S. Stratton,

1906; J. T. Myers, 1907-8; E. R. Oberly, 1909; R. M. King, 1910; F. H. Cummings, 1911.

The Methodists in South Memphis had a place of worship before the Civil War known as Davidson Chapel. This was destroyed during the war and in 1872 another building was erected and a congregation organized by Rev. W. M. Patterson on Georgia Street near Tennessee Street. The pastors of this church have been Revs. W. M. Patterson, 1872; T. P. Davidson, 1872; Edward Slater, 1873; D. R. S. Robeborough, 1874; L. D. Mullins, 1875; J. D. Stewart, 1878; J. E. Treadwell, 1879; J. W. Knott, 1880; J. A. Moody, 1881; W. S. Malone, 1883; D. D. Moore, 1884 and W. H. Evans, 1886; D. D. Moore, 1887; W. H. Evans, 1888-1890; R. M. King, 1891-93; S. H. Williams, 1894-96; F. M. Leake, 1897-1901; J. M. Maxwell, 1902-3; A. F. Stein, 1904-5; I. D. Cannaday, 1906-7; B. S. McLemore, 1908-11; J. L. Hunter, 1912. In 1899 the name of this church was changed to *Pennsylvania Avenue Methodist Church,* when the church was moved to that street.

The *Mississippi Avenue Methodist Church* was organized in 1893, since which time the following pastors have served its people: H. C. Johnson, from 1893 through 1896; W. W. Adams, 1897-99; G. W. Evans, 1900-1903; G. H. Martin, 1904-7; E. B. Ramsey, 1908-11; C. Brooks, 1912.

The *Lenox Church* became a Memphis church in 1898, with Rev. O. H. Duggins, pastor. He was followed by P. H. Roberts in 1899; H. C. Johnston, 1900-1903; W. C. Sellers, 1904-1907; G. H. Martin, 1908-11; H. O. Hofstead, 1912.

*Washington Heights Methodist Church* on South Wellington Street, though not old, is wide-awake and its members exert influence for good among old and young in and out of its congregation. Rev. A. C. Bell became first pastor in 1909 and has remained with the church ever since.

The *Galloway Memorial Church* was inaugurated in 1910 with Reverend J. M. Maxwell as pastor. His successor in 1911 was Reverend M. F. Leak and this helpful leader is still with the congregation.

The *Kentucky Street Methodist Church* is only two years old, having begun its work in 1910. Reverend B. S. McLemore began its work as pastor and he still serves in making the new organization a strong one.

Two Methodist Churches were born only this year, 1912, one, the *Parkway Church*, and the other, the *Pepper Memorial Church*. Of the former Reverend C. Lee Smith is pastor, and the latter, Reverend F. H. Cummins.

The *First Presbyterian Church* was probably the second church in the city of Memphis to effect an organization. This was done June 17, 1828, under the direction of Rev. W. C. Blair, aided by Mr. L. Henderson, one of two gentlemen in the membership, who was chosen as ruling elder. As in the case of the First Methodist Church noted above, this congregation had great trouble in finding a place to rest. The first record obtainable states that the members held their worship in the old log house which had been erected in Court Square just southwest of the fountain and was variously used by churches, schools and as a place of public meeting.

In 1834 the church secured a lot, by donation, adjoining the old cemetery, which was on the corner of Third and Poplar, and a small church was erected. In 1850, a handsome brick structure was built at the northwest corner of Third and Poplar on lot 378, the Old Cemetery lot. This cemetery had been removed in 1828, as stated in the general history, to Winchester Cemetery on Second Bayou, and this lot on which it had been located was donated by the deed of John Overton and others, successors of the proprietors of Memphis, to the city, on condition that it should no longer be used as a cemetery. The property of the First Presbyterian Church now stands on this ground. The original brick church was destroyed by fire in 1883 and the present edifice was erected on its site and dedicated in 1884. The pastors of this church have been Rev. Wm. Patrick, stated supply, from December, 1829 to February, 1830; S. M. Williamson from November, 1830 to November, 1833; Rev. Samuel Hodge, February 1834 to March 1837; Rev. J. Harrison, March, 1837 to July, 1843; Rev. Geo. W. Coons, 1844 to 1852; Rev. S. Kay, 1853; Rev. J. O. Steadman, May, 1854 to May, 1856; when he became pastor and continued until March, 1868; Rev. J. H. Bowman, 1868, to October, 1873; Rev. Eugene Daniel, April,

1875 to 1893; E. A. Ramsey, 1894 to 1898; W. H. Neel, 1899 to 1908; C. H. Williamson, 1910 to 1912.

The *Second Presbyterian Church* was organized December, 1844, with Alexander S. Caldwell and wife, Dr. Joseph N. Bybee and wife, Dr. R. H. Patillo and wife, Misses M. A., M. C., P. C., and M. L. Patillo, Mrs. Eliza Houston, Jas. D. Goff and wife, Miss L. C. Boyd, Scipio, Miss Boyd's slave, T. Pritchett, M. F. Pritchett and J. S. Levett. J. N. Bybee and R. H. Patillo were chosen elders; A. S. Caldwell and J. S. Levett were the first deacons and J. N. Bybee the first clerk.

Rev. John H. Gray was the first pastor. Rev. R. C. Grundy held the pastorate from 1857 to 1861, and Rev. Jno. N. Waddel and J. H. Gray then supplied the pulpit for a time. Rev. T. D. Witherspoon was pastor from 1865 for several years and was succeeded by Rev. W. E. Boggs, who was pastor till 1879. In 1881 Rev. J. M. Rose became pastor and was succeeded in 1882 by Rev. J. F. Latimer. In 1885 Dr. Boggs was again elected pastor. He served the church until 1890, when Rev. N. M. Woods was elected to the pastorate. Dr. Woods stayed with the church until 1903, when he was succeeded by Rev. A. B. Curry, who is still with the congregation.

*Alabama Street Presbyterian Church* was a colony led by Rev. J. O. Steadman, pastor of the First Church, which organized in 1868. The lot was donated by J. C. Johnson, at Alabama and Jones Avenue, and a small house erected. In 1872, the present brick structure was built in place of the cottage church. Rev. Dr. Steadman was pastor until 1880, when he was succeeded by Rev. E. E. Bigger, and he in turn by Rev. Wm. C. Johnson, who died the same year. The next pastor was Rev. Wm. Darnall, who held the pastorate about a year and was succeeded in July, 1885, by Rev. J. L. Martin. Doctor Martin was succeeded in 1891 by Rev. W. McF. Alexander, who was succeeded in 1900 by Rev. T. A. Wharton. In 1903 Rev. W. M. Scott was pastor and he served until 1909, when Dr. L. E. McNair succeeded him. In 1911 Rev. T. M. Lowry was elected pastor and he is still with the church.

*Third Presbyterian Church* was organized October 7, 1856, with four members. Rev. Edward E. Porter was stated supply for four years and became pastor on the 20th of October, 1860. In 1862 he resigned to enter the Confederate Army and the church was without a pastor until 1866, when Rev. Wm. Sample was elected, who served for two years and Rev. E. M. Richardson was then chosen pastor and installed June 13, 1869.

In 1859, a church building was commenced and completed and dedicated October 21, 1860. It is a brick building with a seating capacity of 500 and stands on Sixth Street at the corner of Chelsea.

In 1892 Rev. J. H. Lumpkin was chosen minister and he succeeded Rev. E. M. Richardson, who had been in the service of the church for a great many years. Rev. W. L. Caldwell became pastor in 1896, Dr. J. H. Lumpkin succeeded him in 1897 and he in turn again succeeded Doctor Lumpkin in 1898, since that time Doctor Caldwell has remained in the church.

*Lauderdale Presbyterian Church* or *Westminster Presbyterian Church* began as a mission in 1868, on Union Street, at which time a small chapel was erected. Rev. Mr. Wycoff was the first Minister and was followed by Rev. J. F. Latimer. In 1874, the mission was organized as a church under the name of Union Street Presbyterian Church, and Rev. A. Shotwell was its pastor for about a year, followed by Rev. Jno. N. Waddel. Later a lot was purchased at Beale and Lauderdale Streets and a brick edifice was erected in 1876, after which the name was changed to Lauderdale Street Presbyterian Church. Doctor Waddel was succeeded by Rev. N. M. Long and he in 1881 by Rev. R. A. Lapsley. In 1882, Rev. Sam'l Caldwell was elected. About two years ago the church was removed to Lamar Boulevard and Bellevue Avenue and a handsome building erected and the new church was dedicated and named the Westminster Presbyterian Church.

From 1887 to 1889 Rev. S. C. Caldwell was elected minister and when he returned to his old church, the Third Presbyterian, Rev. J. H. Boyd became pastor and served until 1894, when Rev. C. R. Hyde was elected. In 1898 this pulpit was filled by Rev. W. W. Akers and he was succeeded in 1909 by Rev. J. C. Molloy. In 1911 Rev. C. O. Groves became pastor and he is the present incumbent.

We find the *Porter Street Presbyterian Church* in 1896, with

Rev. J. D. Fleming as pastor and he was succeeded in 1901 by Rev. J. L. Bowling. In 1906 to 1908 Rev. J. H. Morrison was pastor of this church.

In 1906 the *McLemore Avenue Presbyterian Church* was organized and Rev. J. H. Morrison was the first pastor. He remained in the service until 1912, when Rev. W. W. Harrison was elected to serve the church.

*Idlewild Presbyterian Church* was originally organized June 2, 1867, as the Park Avenue Presbyterian Church, on Park Avenue, in the eastern suburbs of Memphis. The organization was effected by a commission appointed by the Presbytery of Memphis and composed of Rev. J. O. Steadman, Rev. A. W. Young and Rev. Jno. S. Park and ruling elders J. L. Dennison of the First Church and R. H. Patillo of the Second Church.

On June 10, 1867, Rev. John S. Park was chosen as stated supply and elected and installed on July 7, 1868 as pastor. In 1879 Rev. Horace M. Whaling became pastor and was succeeded about a year later by Rev. Nicholas M. Long, who in a few months was succeeded in turn by Rev. Chas. Heiskell. Within a year Mr. Heiskell left Memphis and Rev. R. R. Evans of Germantown became stated supply. In 1886 Rev. Lee H. Richardson was elected pastor and was succeeded December, 1888 by Rev. H. M. Pointer, who served until March 1, 1889.

In the fall of 1890 a movement was started to organize a church in the eastern suburbs to be called the Idlewild Presbyterian Church, and after several conferences the old organization of the Park Avenue Church changed the name of the church to the Idlewild Presbyterian Church and in January, 1891, purchased a lot on Peabody Avenue and constructed a small church there at the corner of Barksdale, which was dedicated October 11, 1891. The first pastor was Rev. Hamilton A. Hymes, installed July 14, 1892. He was succeeded January 20, 1895 by Rev. Sterling J. Foster, who was installed May 12, 1895. In the same year the church was removed to the corner of Union and McLean Avenues and the building was remodeled and reopened for worship August 25, 1895. The next pastor was Rev. W. C. Alexander, installed November 8, 1903, who continued to serve the church as pastor until July

10, 1910. In 1909 the congregation erected the present handsome brick structure on McLean Avenue at the corner of Union, at a cost of $26,000, which was dedicated December 12, 1909. The next pastor was Rev. Wm. Crowe of Abingdon, Va., who was installed April 30, 1911, and is pastor at the present time.

*Calvary Church* has been called the Mother Church of the Episcopal faith in Memphis, the Parish having been organized in 1832, and the church existed for a number of years as the only one of this denomination in the city. The first church building stood on Second Street between Adams and Washington. In 1841 the present edifice on the corner of Adams and Second Street was erected and was much enlarged and improved in 1880, and now contains a seating capacity of 750. The early history of the church is rather obscure, but Rev. Thos. Wright seems to have been the first rector of the parish, followed by Rev. George Wells. He was succeeded shortly after by Rev. Phillip Alston and Doctor Alston was in turn succeeded by Rev. D. C. Page. Bishop Jas. H. Otey and Bishop C. T. Quintard in turn served this church, but the dates of services are not clear. They were succeeded by Rev. Dr. Geo. White, who was rector for years. Doctor White was succeeded in 1883 by Rev. David Sessums, who resigned late in 1886 and was succeeded by Rev. Dr. E. Spruille Burford. Doctor Burford was succeeded by Rev. F. P. Davenport, who was in turn succeeded by Rev. James Winchester, who is now Rt. Rev. Bishop Winchester, of Arkansas. The present rector is Dr. W. D. Buckner.

*St. Mary's Parish* was founded in 1857 by colony from Calvary Church under Rev. C. T. Quintard. The church lot was donated by Mr. Robt. C. Brinkley and is located at the junction of Poplar and Orleans, running back to Alabama Street. For fourteen years Rev. Richard Hines was rector and at the close of his rectorship the parish was made a cathedral or church of the bishops of the diocese. Rev. Geo. C. Harris was called from 1871 to 1881, when he resigned. He was succeeded by the dean, Rev. Wm. Klein, who was succeeded in 1894 by Rev. H. M. Dumbell. In 1887 Rev. C. H. B. Turner became dean and in

1900, Rev. S. H. Green, who served until 1902. In that year Dean Morris was chosen and he is still with the church.

*Grace Church* was organized in 1853, but the Parish did not become a member of the Diocesean Convention until 1858. The first church building was on Hernando Street and in this the congregation worshiped until 1865. The property was then sold and a building on the corner of Vance and Lauderdale Street was purchased in which worship was from thence on held.

In 1876 Grace Church, and the Parish of St. Lazarus were united and the new organization now called Grace Chruch was admitted into union with the Diocesean Convention in 1879. The rectors have been: Rev. Geo. P. Schelky, 1857; Edward McClure, 1859; Jno. A. Wheelock, 1864; B. F. Brooks, 1867; Jas. Carmicheal, 1869; Chas. Carroll Parsons, 1878, died of yellow fever same year; W. T. D. Dalzell, 1879; Edgar Orgain, 1881; Wm. Page Case, 1884; Geo. Patterson, 1885; and this forceful man stayed with Grace Church until his decease in 1900. Rev. Granville Allison was pastor from 1903 to 1907. Rev. R. M. Black was elected to succeed him and served until 1911. The present incumbent is Rev. John B. Cannon.

*Church of the Good Shepherd* was organized as the outgrowth of a mission in Chelsea in 1865, by Rev. Jas. A. Vaux. The worshippers first met in private houses, but during the same year a lot was purchased on Mill and Fourth Streets and the present structure was erected and dedicated in 1866. Mr. Vaux continued as rector until 1870, when he was succeeded by Rev. Chas. C. Parsons, who remained until after the church was admitted as a parish in the diocese in 1872. Subsequent rectors have been Revs. Ruth, Tupper, Gee, Yeater, Grantham, Jury, Young, and H. Dunlap, who was rector in 1886; R. C. Young, 1887; Jos. C. Berne, 1892; H. M. Dunkell, 1893; S. B. McGlohon, 1894-7; J. P. McCullough, 1898-9; J. M. Northrup, 1900; J. D. Windiate, 1901-6; R. W. Rhames, 1907-11; George L. Neide, 1912.

*St. Luke's Mission* Episcopal Church was established in 1891, and in 1898 the church had grown so that it was able to have a regular pastor. Rev. C. A. Chism was pastor in 1898 and he was followed by Reverends E. S. Bazzette-Jones, 1899-1900; H.

L. Marvin, 1900; H. W. Armstrong, 1902; F. D. Devall, 1903-6; H. W. Wells, 1907-11; E. Bennett, 1912.

The *Church of the Holy Trinity* on Cummings Street is a thrifty little church, not very old. Its pastor in 1904-6 was Rev. Peter Wager and he was succeeded by Rev. Prentiss A. Pugh in 1907, who is still in the service.

Another recently instituted Episcopal Church is *St. Alban's Chapel*, on Florida Avenue. Rev. Craik Morris became its pastor in 1905 and he is the present incumbent.

*The First Baptist Church* was organized the 4th day of April, 1839. The preliminary meeting was held at the house of Spencer Hall and the persons signing the articles were Geraldus Buntyn, T. Carpenter, S. M. Isbell, Spencer Hall, Martha F. Carpenter, Rebecca Walton, Martha O. Mosby, Pamelia A. Fowlks, Mary Land, Dorcas Hall and Sherwood Walton. The organization meeting took place in the old Magevney school house in Court Square. Rev. Jno. C. Holt and P. S. Gayle officiating. It is not shown in the record where the first meetings were held, but in 1845 a Committee was appointed to secure a site and erect a building. A lot was purchased on Second Street between Washington and Adams and a temporary house of worship was fitted up. About 1847 the brick building so well known was erected and remained in service until 1888, when a new church edifice was built on the same site. This building and site was appropriated by Shelby County as part of a site for a new court house in 1908 and the church purchased the lot and erected a handsome modern building at the corner of Linden and Lauderdale Streets.

The records show that Rev. L. H. Milliken was pastor in 1840, B. F. Farnsworth in 1842, E. C. Eager in 1842, and Rev. S. S. Parr in 1843. Rev. P. S. Gayle was called to the pastorate in 1846. Rev. John Finley in 1849, Rev. C. R. Hendrickson in 1852, Rev. F. J. Drane in 1857 and Rev. S. H. Ford in 1862.

The church was used as an army hospital by the Federal Army during the occupation of Memphis and no services were held in the building. But in 1863, Rev. A. B. Miller was elected pastor, followed by Rev. D. E. Burns in 1868, and he was followed in turn by Revs. J. T. Tichenor in 1871, Geo. A. Lofton in 1872, R. B. Womack in 1877, W. A. Montgomery in 1879 and

R. A. Venable in 1880. From 1887 to 1892 Rev. R. A. Venable was pastor; in 1893 he was succeeded by Rev. R. J. Willingham. Rev. E. A. Taylor came to the church in 1894 and served until 1899. In 1900 Rev. A. U. Boone was elected to the pastorate and he is still with the church.

Before the Civil War the Baptists had a church on Beale Street and a mission down in Fort Pickering, but at the close of the war there was but one Baptist Church in Memphis, and that in the northern part of the city. It was determined at that time to organize the *Central Baptist Church,* to which the Beale Street Church conveyed their property and the First Church gave a liberal donation. The new church was organized December 1, 1865, in the First Church and Rev. S. H. Ford was chosen pastor. The Central Church then obtained a lot on Court Street and erected thereon the Tabernacle, a wooden building which was used until 1868. The site for the present church was purchased in 1867, on Second Street North of Beale for $22,500, but only a basement structure was erected, which was completed in 1868, and was used as the church for 17 years. The building was completed, after long delays, and dedicated December 6, 1885, the total cost being $130,000. The pastors have been as follows: Rev. S. H. Ford, from 1865 to 1871; Rev. Sylvanus Landrum, October 1878 to July 1, 1879; Rev. Thos. L. Rowan, January 1, 1880 to July 29, 1882; and he was followed November 1, 1882, by Rev. A. W. Lamar. In 1888 Rev. J. A. Dickerson became pastor; in 1891, Rev. F. R. Boston; in 1894, Rev. B. A. Nunnaly; in 1896, Rev. T. S. Potts; in 1911, Rev. J. L. White, who is still with the church.

*Chelsea Baptist Church* was also organized as a mission church in 1860, by Dr. W. G. Lawrence, with ten members and R. M. C. Parker and A. G. Thompson as deacons. The first place of worship was a dwelling house located on the old factory lot, as known at that day, and in 1861 a small frame building was erected on Front Street between Mill and Sycamore. The Mission became an independent congregation in 1865. The following pastors served at different periods in this congregation: Revs. Lancaster, Harbin, Caperton, Butler, Mitchell, Tragett, Powell, Crews, Stewart and Lipsey.

The *Rowan Memorial Baptist Church* was instituted in 1891, with Rev. J. H. Snow, pastor. He was succeeded by the Reverends W. L. Slack, 1893-4; W. L. Norris, 1897; R. N. Lucado, 1898; I. W. Page, 1899; Charles Lovejoy, 1900; R. W. Richardson, 1901-3; W. J. Bearden, 1904-7; W. L. Savage, 1909; D. D. Chapman, 1910; W. J. Bearden, 1911; O. A. Utley, 1912.

The *Johnson Avenue Baptist Church* had five years existence, with the following pastors: Reverends W. T. Hudson, 1898; A. P. Moore, 1899-1900. T. T. Thompson, 1901-2.

*Trinity Baptist Church* came into being in 1891, with Rev. M. D. Early as pastor, who served until 1894. His successors were Reverends W. F. Dorris, 1895; G. B. Thrasher, 1896-7; ——Hamlett, 1898; E. L. Smith, 1900; J. W. Lipsey, 1901-4.

*Seventh Street Baptist Church* was started in 1903. Rev. T. T. Thompson was pastor and served the church until 1906, when Rev. I. N. Strother succeeded him. Doctor Strother is still with the church.

The *Lenox Baptist Church* became a member of the Baptist Church organization in Memphis in 1904, with Dr. K. W. Reese as pastor who remained so until 1908. He was then succeeded by Rev. Davis W. Bosdell in 1909 and in 1911 by Rev. E. L. Watson, who is still with this church.

*La Belle Place Baptist Church*, started in Memphis with Rev. George W. Sherman, pastor. In 1908 J. N. Lawler became pastor. He was followed in 1909 by Rev. J. E. Dilworth, who served until 1911, when Rev. D. A. Ellis became pastor and he is now in this service.

The *McLemore Avenue Baptist Church* came into being in the city in 1906, the Rev. T. T. Thompson being pastor. In 1908 Rev. W. J. Bearden was pastor and he was followed in 1911 by E. C. Ross who was succeeded in 1912 by the first pastor, Rev. T. T. Thompson.

The *Bellevue Boulevard Baptist Church* has been within the corporation of Memphis since 1909, since which time Rev. H. P. Hurt has been pastor.

*First Cumberland Presbyterian Church* was organized in August 1840 with 18 members at a time of the revival held by Rev. Sam'l Bennett and Reuben Burrow. Of the early members of the church are Jno. D. White, Sam'l D. Key, W. D. S. Garrison, W. B. Waldran, Mrs. S. A. Waldran, Jas. White, A. Hutchinson, Albert White and Jno. D. White, Jr., Mathilda James, Maria Stewart, Chas. Stewart, Sabra White, Eliza Key, Ann Waldran, P. Hutchinson, Mary C. Stewart and Sophia E. Garrison. A lot was purchased the same year in September, 1844 the cornerstone of the church was laid with Masonic ceremony, but the house was not finished until 1845. The first pastor of this church was Rev. Sam'l Dennis, elected the first week after its organization; Rev. Robt. Donnell for a part of the year 1845, then Samuel Dennis again until 1851, followed by Herschell S. Porter and in 1856 by A. M. Bryan, who resigned in 1859. Mr. Bryan was followed by Rev. C. A. Davis, who was pastor till 1867; Rev. L. C. Ransom in 1868 to 1874, Rev. G. T. Stainback, 1875 to 1879; when Rev. H. A. Jones became pastor. Just before the Civil War the present church building on Court Street was erected, a brick structure with a seating capacity of 1200. In 1887 Rev. H. A. Jones was elected pastor; in 1897, Rev. Hugh Spencer Williams and 1910, Rev. W. J. King.

*Chelsea Cumberland Church* was organized in 1872 by Rev. L. C. Ransom. Mr. E. T. Keel donated a lot on Fourth Street and the church was built thereon. Up to 1879 the pastors were Rev. L. C. Taylor and M. O. Smith. Rev. G. B. Thomas was pastor for a short while and was followed in 1886 by the Rev. D. T. Waynick.

*The Third Cumberland Presbyterian Church* was established in 1894 with Rev. H. A. Jones, pastor. He was succeeded in 1897 by Rev. A. K. Burrow.

The *Georgia Street* or *Institute Cumberland Church* was instituted in 1897, with Rev. J. O. Davidson, pastor, who is still guiding this flock.

The *Central Cumberland Church* was inaugurated in 1898, when Rev. G. W. Martin was chosen pastor. He was succeeded in 1901 by Rev. R. Thompson; in 1908 by Rev. C. H. Walton who is the present incumbent.

The *Memphis Tabernacle* (Cumberland) is a little church that existed during 1909 and 1910, with Rev. R. M. Neel, pastor.

The *Walker Heights Cumberland Church* also existed during 1909 and 1910, with Rev. Richard Inge, pastor.

About 1841 Father McAleer became the first resident Catholic priest and steps were taken to build a Catholic Church. Previous to that time irregular worship was held by the Catholics, as by the other church organizations, in the Magevney School House in Court Square and later a small wooden house was used, standing on the site of the Convent of the Dominican Fathers. In 1843 a small brick edifice costing $5,000.00, was built on Third Street near Adams.

In 1845 this church, called St. Peter's, was under the care of the Dominicans and Father Jas. S. Alemany, afterwards Arch-Bishop of San Francisco, was appointed the second Catholic pastor in the city, assisted by Rev. Thos. L. Grace. Father Alemany was succeeded by Father J. H. Clarkson, who died in 1849. Father Thos. L. Grace was then placed in charge and assisted by Father J. A. Bockel and J. V. Daly.

In 1852 Father Thomas began the erection of the present St. Peter's Church, a splendid edifice, and it was dedicated in February, 1858 by Bishop Miles.

In 1886, Rev. J. P. Moran was priest in charge, assisted by Revs. J. V. Edelen, F. A. Ryan and E. Ashfield.

In 1887 Father M. D. Lilly became pastor of this church and he was succeeded by Reverend Fathers J. P. Moran, 1888-93; M. A. Sheehan, 1894-5; M. A. Horrigan, 1896-8; M. A. Sheehan, 1899-1902; F. A. Gaffney, 1903-6; J. P. Heffernan, 1907-1910; E. J. Farmer, 1910-12.

The German Catholics of Memphis organized in 1852, the Society of St. Boniface. In that year Father J. Bockel purchased a lot on Union Street, but sold it in 1856 and another was purchased at Third and Market Streets as a site for the *St. Mary's German Catholic Church*. A small frame house was built and fitted up in which Rev. W. J. Repis was installed as resident pastor in 1860, and he was followed in 1862 by Rev. Cornelius Thoma. In 1864 a brick building was commenced, which was completed in 1867, when Rev. L. Schneider succeeded Father Thoma. In 1870 Rev. Father Eugene Priers, of the Order of St. Francis, was sent as a minister and he was succeeded the same year by Rev. Killian Schlaser, and he in turn, in 1871, by Rev. Ambrosia Jansen, by whom a monastery was built in the rear of the church. In 1873 Rev. Lucian Bucholz became pastor until 1879, when he was followed by Rev. Aloysius Weiner. Father Weiner remained until 1885, and was succeeded by Rev. Nemesius Rhode, from Chicago, and he was followed in 1887 by Rev. Frances Moening. Father Nemesius returned in 1887 and his successors have been Fathers Francis Moening, 1888-1894; H. Fessler, 1895-8; P. Kohnen, 1899-1900; H. Japes, 1901; H. Fessler, 1902-8; Isidore Fosselman, 1909; H. Fessler, 1910-1912.

Rev. Martin Riordon was sent in 1865 to take charge of a mission among the Catholics in southeastern Memphis. He founded a school on Wellington Street and in 1866 built St. Patrick's Parsonage, in which services were held on Sundays until the church could be completed. Subsequently a frame church building was erected on the corner of DeSoto and Linden Streets. Calvary Cemetery was founded by Father Riordon in 1867. In 1878 Father Riordon died and was succeeded by Father Edward Doyle, who also died in 1879 of yellow fever and Father Quinn became pastor until 1881, when he was followed by Rev. Father Veale. Father John Veale watched over this church and its parish until his death in 1899, when the church lost a valuable pastor and many of its members and other people a true friend. Father Veale's successor was Father F. T. Maron, who stayed with the church until 1904, when Father F. T. Sullivan became its pastor. He was succeeded by Father D. J. Murphy, who is the present incumbent.

*St. Bridgid's Church,* erected at the corner of Third and Overton Streets, was opened for worship on Christmas day, 1870, by Rev. Martin Walsh, the first pastor. He was succeeded by Rev. Wm. Walsh, after the death of the former from yellow fever in 1878, assisted by Rev. Michael Ryan and Rev. Jno. J. Walsh. Father Walsh remained with this church until 1889, when Father Francis took his place. In 1896 Father J. K. Larkin came to the church and stayed with it until 1897. Father J. F. O'Neill succeeded him in that year and he is still with this parish.

*St. Joseph's Church* was constructed in 1878, the cornerstone being laid March 17th, and the building standing on the corner of Georgia and Seventh Street. Rev. Antonia Luiselli was installed as pastor and continued so for many years. In 1902 his successor became Father E. Gazzo and Father Gazzo is still with the church.

*Sacred Heart Catholic Church* was opened for worship with Rev. Father P. L. Mahony as pastor and he has remained with the parish ever since.

The latest Catholic Church inaugurated in Memphis is *St. Thomas Church*, 1912, with Rev. Father S. A. Stritch, pastor.

*Linden Street Christian Church* was founded in 1846 and incorporated in 1850. The original members were Mr. and Mrs. Egbert Wooldridge, Mr. and Mrs. E. W. Caldwell, Mary McIntosh and Ann McGuire. The lot was bought and the church was organized on the southeast corner of Linden and Mulberry and a small frame building standing on it was remodeled and made into a house of worship. In 1860 a brick edifice was erected, but not completed until after the war, and the parsonage was erected in 1877.

The pastors have been Elders B. F. Hall, 1846 to 1853; R. E. Chew, to 1855; W. J. Barber until 1861. During the Civil War services were held without a pastor and after the war the pastors were Rev. R. A. Cook, 1864-6; T. W. Caskey, 1866; Curtis J. Smith, 1869; David Walk, 1870; J. M. Trible, 1879; G. W. Sweeney, 1882; J. B. Briney, 1886-9; J. W. Ingram, 1889-1893; J. A. Brooks, 1893-95; W. E. Ellis, 1895-97; W. H. Sheffer, 1907-1912.

The *Mississippi Avenue Christian Church* was organized in 1891, with Reverend S. P. Benbrook, pastor. His successor in 1893 was Rev. S. B. Moore. Mr. Moore was succeeded by Revs. Joseph Severns, 1895-97; L. D. Riddell in 1907, who has been with the church ever since. In 1909 this congregation erected a new church building on McLemore Avenue, when one of its earliest and most liberal supporters, Mr. S. C. Toof, furnished the greater part of the funds for this new structure. Mr. Toof was such a strong arm of this church that his decease in 1910 was a great loss and the church held special memorial services in his honor. At this time the expressions of love and veneration for him were the outpourings of many individuals who expressed gratitude for his generous support and unselfish work and several for personal help received from him.

The *Third Christian Church* was inaugurated in 1899, with Rev. J. E. Willis, pastor. His successors have been Revs. E. L. Crystal, 1900-1902; J. E. Gorsuch, 1904-11; S. F. Fowler, 1912.

*Decatur Street Christian Church,* established 1910, has had two efficient ministers, Rev. H. F. Cook, 1910, and R. H. Love, 1911-12.

The latest church of this denomination is *Harbert Avenue Church,* established in 1912 with Rev. W. S. Long, pastor.

In 1855 an effort was made to establish a Lutheran Church in this city and Rev. W. Fick, of New Orleans, came to Memphis and ministered at intervals to the worshipers of that faith. Following him a student of the Concordia Theological Seminary of St. Louis, Paul Byer, was placed in charge. The *German Evangelical Lutheran Trinity Church* was organized in July, 1855, and N. Frech, F. Steinkuhl, H. Glindamp and W. Ringwald were chosen elders. Mr. Byer was installed as pastor and continued until 1858, when Rev. G. M. Gotsch became pastor. He died in 1876 and Rev. H. Lieck was selected, who resigned in 1879. The congregation was supplied for awhile by Rev. E. S. Obermeyer of Little Rock, when Rev. Theodore Benson was elected pastor, but died in 1881. A Theological student named Caspar Dorsch, from St. Louis, then ministered to the congregation, assisted by Mr. Obermeyer, and in September, 1881, Rev. I. G. Pflantz became pastor. He was succeeded in 1886 by Wm. Dau. The congregation purchased a house and lot on Main Street in 1856, at number 210, but in 1874 they obtained a lot and built the first story of the present church on Washington Avenue near Orleans. Doctor Dau stayed with the church a number of years. In 1899 his successor was Rev. L. Buchheimer and he in turn was succeeded by Rev. J. Broders in 1903, serving until 1908, when Rev. M. J. Brueggemann was elected pastor and is still with the congregation.

The Lutheran *Church of The Redeemer,* was first noted in 1910, with Reverend Theodore Stiegemeyer as pastor. Doctor Stiegemeyer is still serving this congregation.

*The First Congregational Church* or *Stranger's Church* was organized in 1863. Up to 1864 the congregation worshipped at Odd Fellow's Hall and in the Greenlaw Block and other places, but in the latter year purchased the site on Union Street on which a building was erected dedicated June 20, 1865 by Rev. T. E. Bliss, the first pastor. In 1868 Mr. Bliss was succeeded by Rev. A. E. Baldwin and in turn in 1875 by W. D. Millard, who was pastor for two years. Church services were suspended during the yellow fever epidemics and in 1881 Rev. N. M. Long held evening services and soon after reorganized the church, its name being changed to Stranger's Church. The church was much enlarged in 1882 and Mr. Long was called as its pastor, since which time he has remained in the service.

*Congregational Church of the Children of Israel*, the first Jewish congregation was established in 1854 under a charter. The incorporators were J. I. Andrews, Moses Lemmons, Jno. Walker, D. Levy, Julius Sandac, T. Folz, M. Hamberger, N. Bloom, Joseph Strauss and Simon Bernach. Being aided by a donation from Judah Touro, of New Orleans, a lot on Second Street was purchased, but not used and in February, 1858 an edifice at the corner of Main and Exchange Streets, the old Farmer's & Merchants Bank Building was rented and dedicated by Rev. Dr. Wise. Later the lot was bought and the house used as a Synagogue until 1884, when the present Jewish Temple, was built on Poplar Street at a cost of $50,000. The building was dedicated by Revs. J. M. Wise, H. Senneshein, and Max Samfield. On July 6, 1860, Rev. S. Tuska was elected Rabbi of the congregation, but died on December 30, 1870, and was succeeded by Rev. M. Samfield, who still presides as Rabbi of the congregation.

*Baron Hirsch Temple* is another Jewish Church on the corner of Washington Avenue and Fourth Street. The pastors of this church have been Rabbis M. Springer, 1898-1906; Maycrovitz, 1907; M. Springer, 1909; Aaron Schwartz, 1910; Benjamin Filbish, 1911-12.

*First Church of Christ, Scientist*, was organized in Memphis September 11, 1892, in the Randolph Building. The old Central Methodist Church on Union Avenue was purchased in 1907 and services were held there from April until December of that year, when the church building burned. Services were then held in the Woman's Building until December, 1908, when the congregation moved to the crypt of their new building corner Dunlap Street and Monroe Avenue, where services have been held ever since. The church building is now being completed.

The first readers of this church were Mrs. Rosa T. Shepherd, First Reader and Mrs. Hattie Caldwell, Second Reader. They were succeeded in 1903 by Miss Mamie Gafford, First Reader, and Mr. J. W. Stotts, Second. Miss Gafford resigned in March, 1905, when Mr. Stotts became First Reader and Mrs. Julia H. Edwards, Second. In 1906 Mr. Edward S. Stapleton became First Reader and Mrs. Ida G. Tate, Second. They were succeeded in 1909 by Mr. John M. Dean, First Reader, and Miss Mary V. Little, Second. They led for the allotted three years, when, January 1, 1912, Mr. Charles N. Churchill, became First Reader and Mrs. Emma Galloway Craft, Second.

The *Associate Reform Presbyterian Church* is situated on South Pauline Street, corner Eastmoreland Avenue. Its pastor is Rev. W. B. Lindsey.

The *Hebrew-Christian Church* is on Poplar Avenue. Rev. Joseph Rosenthal is its pastor, or missionary, as he is called.

The *Pentacostal Holiness Church* is on the corner of Latham and Simpson Avenues. Rev. B. S. Todd is its pastor.

*Faith Mission Church* is on Seventh Street and its services are conducted by W. P. Day, pastor.

*Church of God*, is on Pennsylvania Avenue. R. B. Burl is its pastor.

The *Seventh Day Adventists* hold services at the corner of Dunlap Street and Greenlaw Avenue. The pastor is W. R. Burrow.

# CHAPTER XXIII

## The Bench and Bar

NO CHAPTER in the history of Memphis surpasses in interest or in the splendor of achievement of the actors the story of the Bench and Bar of Shelby County. The founding of the great city was conceived by Judge John Overton, a noted jurist of the Supreme Court of Tennessee, and its charter and all the details of all its early career were carefully and studiously prepared by this able lawyer, one of the most brilliant lights that our state has produced. Many great lawyers have sought the "City by the Great River," since the days of Judge Overton and shed the luster of their fame not only upon the place of their chosen residence but, in numerous instances, upon the whole United States; and some of these jurists and lawyers have stamped their name and fame indelibly upon the history of our country.

In this little chapter it will be endeavored to select the salient points in the lives of these able jurists and lawyers without entering into tedious detail. Beginning with the courts we find that the Legislature of Tennessee on November 24, 1819, six months after the laying off of young Memphis, passed an act establishing a new county to be called Shelby, in honor of Governor Isaac Shelby of Kentucky, one of the heroes of the Battle of King's Mountain in the Revolutionary War and who had, in the preceding year negotiated with the Chickasaw Indians in company with General Jackson, the purchase of all their lands in West Tennessee and Western Kentucky, lying between the Tennessee and Mississippi Rivers and north of the line of the Mississippi Territory. This same Act established a tribunal called the Court of Pleas and Quarter Sessions. The court was composed of a chairman and four commissioned justices of the peace. William Irvine was its first chairman and the other members were Anderson B. Carr, Marcus B. Winchester, Thomas D. Carter and Benjamin Willis.

It had four terms a year and a general jurisdiction over county affairs in both criminal and civil cases, the intermediate appellate court being the Circuit Court of Humphreys County. As this court was established as a tribunal to be held upon the lower Chickasaw Bluff there was some question as to the proper situs for its organization, and this question was settled practically and literally by organizing the court in the open air on the top of the bluffs where Memphis now stands, the great forest trees being the only covering from the elements. This court was removed after the January term of 1827 to the new county seat at Raleigh, where it continued as the Court of Pleas and Quarter Sessions until the April term of 1836, when its title became simply the County Court of Shelby County. This court still exists, but there has been a wonderful change in its surroundings since its organization under the trees on the edge of the bluff, and its final evolution and present ensconcement in probably the most beautiful courtroom in the Southern States, under the roof of the new Shelby County Courthouse.

On July 22, 1836, the Legislature passed an Act creating a county judge for this county, to be elected by the people. This office continued with numerous legislative changes until the establishment of the present probate court of Shelby County by the Legislative Acts of 1870 and the Amendatory Act of 1881.

The first circuit court in Shelby County was held in 1827, this county being then in the Eighth Judicial Circuit, presided over by Judge Joshua Haskell. Shelby County also received its first special court in 1846, called the Commercial and Criminal Court, the presiding judge being Honorable E. W. M. King, who was succeeded in 1850 by Judge J. C. Humphreys. Many changes have been wrought in the Circuit and other Shelby County courts by Legislative enactment since 1827.

By the Act of 1853 it was provided that the voters of Shelby County should elect a judge of the Common Law and Chancery Court of the City of Memphis, and that the voters of Shelby, Fayette, Tipton and Hardeman Counties should elect a judge for the Eleventh Judicial Circuit, constituted of those counties, and that the voters of the Fifth, Thirteenth, and Fourteenth districts of Shelby County, in which Memphis and Fort Pickering were situated, should elect a judge of the Criminal Court of Memphis, and also an Attorney-general of said Court.

For some time there were no Chancery courts in Tennessee, the first Legislature which convened on the 8th of March 1796, establishing only a Supreme Court of Law and Equity. By enactment of 1822, Chapter 13, it was directed that one of the judges of the Supreme Court of Errors and Appeals should, at stated times, hold a court of equity at several places named in the Act. This Act was repealed in 1827 by Chapter 79, the State being divided into two Chancery divisions, called the Eastern and Western, presided over by two Chancellors elected by the joint ballot of the General Assembly. In 1835 the chancellors were increased to three and Fayette and Shelby Counties were constituted the Seventh Chancery District of the Western Division, the court being held at Somerville, Fayette County. On December 15, 1845, Shelby and Tipton Counties were constituted a new chancery district with the court at Memphis and Honorable Alexander McCampbell, Chancellor of the Western District, was its first presiding officer. The first case entered on the docket of this court May 26, 1846, was styled James O. Hutchins vs. R. K. Eskridge, and its purpose was to enjoin the collection of a note for the hire of a slave. The counsel for complainants were Delafield, Massey and P. G. Gaines while Sylvester Bailey appeared for the defendant. There were one hundred and five cases docketed in this court in 1846.

Shelby County was at first, as above stated, in the Eighth Judicial Circuit, presided over by Judge Joshua Haskell as far back as 1827, when Memphis was incorporated, but after that date the courts were held at the county site at Raleigh. Judge Haskell was succeeded by Honorable Valentine D. Barry, a native of Ireland and who was the first circuit judge to reside in Shelby County. After Barry came the Honorable Perry W. Humphries, Judge William B. Turley, L. M. Bramlett, W. C. Dunlap and William R. Harris, who were fine types of old-school, thoroughly trained lawyers and upright judges.

Of all of these circuit judges the most striking character perhaps, was Hon. Valentine D. Barry. He was not only striking in his personal appearance and upon the bench but also in his private life. He was an earnest, accurate and laborious Judicial officer, highly cultivated in all branches of literature and a man far ahead of his age and time in his southwestern home. As is the case with most men whose minds approach genius he had great capacity for detail and his office and library were model arrangements for carrying on the duties of his position, being noticeable for the neatness, order and arrangement of the judicial resources in the nature of books, briefs and digests collected by him for his own personal convenience. Judge Barry was also an eloquent speaker and a most attractive conversationalist. He was the fast friend of the new beginners at the bar, patiently instructing and training them and always ready to aid the youngsters in their perplexing legal troubles.

Another of these early and bright judges on the circuit bench was Hon. Wm. B. Turley, who was a Virginian, but first licensed to practice law at Clarksville, Tenn. He was a judge of this judicial circuit for several years and then became justice of the Supreme Court of Tennessee in 1836 and continued in that position until 1850. He declined re-election and voluntarily sought and obtained the judgeship of the Common Law and Chancery Court of Memphis and held that office until his tragic death from an accident some years later. He was a colleague on the Supreme Court bench of those great judges Green and Reese.

Another early judge on the Circuit bench was Hon. W. C. Dunlap, who was a native of Knoxville and born in 1798. In early manhood he was prominent in political affairs, having served fourteen years in the State Legislature and several terms in Congress, where he showed high ability. He was later circuit judge for about ten years. He might have worn the title of the "Equable Judge," sitting as he always did, with perfect composure and unruffled temper throughout the most trying wrangles at the bar before him but, never losing his grip on the case and steering it, as a skilled pilot would his craft, through all breakers into the still harbor of certainty and law. This amiable justice was of course loved by every attorney and practitioner and especially by the younger members of the bar to whom he was in their practice a delight Judge Dunlap died November 17, 1872 in this county.

Hon. Wm. R. Harris was a North Carolinian, born in Montgomery County in 1802. When a boy he earned his means for attending school by working on the farm during the summer and studied law at Lawrenceburg, Tenn., beginning his practice at Paris in Henry County. Coming to Memphis in 1851 he succeeded by appointment Hon. Wm. B. Turley and became judge of the Commercial and Criminal Court of Memphis until 1854. He was then made, after an interval, judge of the Supreme Court by appointment and subsequently by election. His splendid career was tragically cut short on the 13th of June, 1858 as the result of an accident, the explosion of the Steamer Pennsylvania a short distance below Memphis and he died a week later, on the 20th of June. His record was one indicating great ability and strength of character.

Another judicial officer of striking personality and unusual ability was Hon. E. W. M. King who was appointed the first judge of the newly established Commercial and Criminal Court in 1846, and held the position until 1850. Judge King was of a fiery temperament, resentful and sometimes rash, but exceedingly tender and gentle with those who were fortunate enough to be loved by him. His enforcement of the criminal laws, while entirely just, was rigorous in the extreme and this trait characterized his prosecution of criminals while attorney-general before he became judge.

The successor of Judge King on the Commercial and Criminal bench was an Alabamian named B. F. McKiernan who had come to Memphis in early life. Judge McKiernan was of gentler mould than Judge King but died no great while after being made judge of this court.

Honorable John C. Humphries was his successor. He had been splendidly trained for the bar and was well equipped for the duties of the bench. Judge Humphries was noted for his splendid personal appearance and attracted much attention because of that fact. His career was one of honor and purity and his death occurred at Somerville in 1868.

There were no courts while Memphis was a garrison town during the War Between the States. Honorable W. G. Reeves was Circuit Judge from the opening of the courts in 1865 until the court was abolished December, 1869.

The Common Law and Chancery Court of Memphis were separated by the Act of 1865 and 1866, Chapter 32, and made separate jurisdictions.

Among the judges of the Law Court of Memphis following the separation, was Judge Thomas G. Smith, who occupied the bench in 1866 and 1867. Judge Smith was far beyond the average in ability and was very popular both with the people of Memphis and with the bar. James O. Pierce, of Wisconsin, became judge of the Law Court in 1868, but occupied the bench only a short time and was succeeded by Captain H. S. Lee in 1869. Both the last named gentlemen had been officers in the United States Army during the Civil War and remained after the conclusion of peace between the sections. On the 4th day of December, 1869, by an act of the Legislature, the Circuit Court of Shelby County, as then existing, the Law Court of Memphis, the Municipal Court of Memphis, the Chancery Court of Memphis and the Criminal Court of Memphis, were abolished. By Section 3 of said Act there were created two circuit courts and one criminal court in said county and two chancery courts, the said courts to be known as the First and Second Circuit Courts of Shelby County, the Criminal Court of Shelby County and the First and Second Chancery Courts of Shelby County.

By Section 4 of the Act, the Circuit Court absorbed the civil business of the old circuit court, the law court and the municipal court. The dockets and business of the Circuit Court going to the new First Circuit Court; the records of the law court going to the Second Circuit Court and the records of the Municipal

Court going to the First and Second Circuit Courts, while the criminal business of the circuit and municipal courts were passed to the new Criminal Court.

With the reorganization of the State Courts under the new Constitution in 1870 the carpet-bag government disappeared and the people of the state came into their own again. New judges were elected in all the courts. Honorable Carrick W. Heiskell was elected Judge of the First Circuit Court and Honorable Irving Halsey, of the Second Circuit Court.

Judge Heiskell had been a distinguished Confederate soldier, commanding the Nineteenth Tennessee Regiment in Strahl's Brigade, Army of Tennessee, and after the close of the War Between the States, was compelled to leave East Tennessee and come as a refugee to Memphis in 1866. He had been admitted to the bar at Knoxville, Tennessee, in 1857.

These two judges, men of great vigor and learned in the law, continued to occupy the benches of their respective courts, Judge Heiskell until the end of his term in 1878 and Judge Halsey until his court was abolished in 1875. Judge Heiskell was succeeded by Judge J. O. Pierce former judge of the Law Court in 1878, who served his full term until 1886, when he was in turn succeeded by Hon. L. H. Estes, judge-elect who occupied the bench for two terms until 1902. In that year the present incumbent J. P. Young, succeeded to the Circuit Court bench and still occupies the same.

In 1905 three divisions, known as 2, 3 and 4, were added to the Circuit Court to meet the requirements of the enormous increase in business, which had come with the growth of the city, and as judges of these courts Hon. Walter Malone was appointed to Division 2, Hon. A. B. Pittman to Division 3 and Hon. W. H. Laughlin to Division 4. All of the four judges of the several divisions were reelected in 1910.

After the Civil War, Hon. Wm. M. Smith, who had been a Unionist during the great strife but was greatly loved by the people of Memphis, was made chancellor in 1866 and continued so until the reorganization of the courts in 1870, when Hon. R. J. Morgan was elected chancellor of the First Chancery Court and Hon. Wm. L. Scott of the Second Chancery Court.

Judge Morgan served out his term on the bench and was succeeded by Hon. Charles Kortrecht in 1878, who died of yellow fever soon after his election and was succeeded on the bench of the First Chancery Court in the fall of 1878 by Hon. W. W. McDowell, by appointment, and this Chancellor was soon after elected by the people and served the remainder of the term in this division. In 1886 Hon. H. T. Ellett, a former Supreme Judge of Mississippi and one of the ablest of modern jurists, was made chancellor at a great personal sacrifice to himself and took charge of the First Chancery Court. Judge Ellett presided with the most distinguished success until 1889, when he died suddenly in Court Square while on the rostrum receiving President Cleveland on behalf of the citizens of Memphis.

Judge Ellett was succeeded in that court by his law partner Hon. B. M. Estes, one of the ablest lawyers at the Memphis bar, who held the position until September 15, 1891, when he resigned and Honorable W. D. Beard was appointed Chancellor in his place. Judge Beard continued Chancellor until 1893, when he resigned and was soon after elected to the Supreme Bench of Tennessee, where he became Chief Justice. Upon Judge Beard's resignation Honorable John L. T. Sneed, a former justice of the Supreme Court of Tennessee, and a learned and distinguished man, was appointed Chancellor and was elected to that position by the people in August, 1894. In 1900 Judge Sneed resigned and Honorable F. H. Heiskell, the present incumbent, was appointed to succeed him and he was reelected in 1902 and also in 1910.

In the Second Division of the Chancery Court, Honorable W. L. Scott resigned in 1871 and was succeeded by Honorable Edwin M. Yerger. During the last illness of Judge Yerger, Honorable Sam P. Walker was appointed Chancellor in August, 1872 and reelected in August, 1874. Chancellor Walker resigned July 10, 1875 to accept the appointment of City Attorney and Honorable F. D. Stockton was appointed July 15, 1875 and continued on the bench until the Second Chancery Court was abolished in October of that year.

In 1895 the Chancery Court was, by Act of the Legislature, divided into two parts, known as Part One and Part Two. Honorable Sterling Pierson was appointed Chancellor of Part Two of this Court and continued to preside until October 15, 1898, when he resigned. Honorable Lee Thornton was appointed October 17, 1898 and held the position until Part Two was abolished by the Legislature, and retired May 8, 1899.

By an Act passed April 3, 1909, Part Two of this Court was reestablished and Honorable H. D. Minor was appointed Chancellor on May 6, 1909. He resigned August 8, 1910 and on August 4, Honorable Francis Fentress was elected Chancellor by the people and was inducted into office on September 1, 1910, and still holds the position.

Honorable William Hunter was first judge of the Criminal Court of Shelby County after the Civil War, from 1867 until December, 1869, when the existing Criminal Court was abolished and the new Criminal Court established as an auxiliary of the Circuit Court and for a brief period Honorable A. T. Henderson presided over that tribunal. After the Constitution of 1870 Honorable John R. Flippin was elected Criminal Judge in August of that year. Judge Flippin was a man of great strength of mind and character and his accession to the criminal bench marked an epoch in the judicial history of the county and city. There were no slipshod methods of practice and few loopholes left by which criminals could escape from the meshes of the law. To him the criminal law meant justice, firm, even-handed justice, acquitting honorably when the juries found there was no crime and punishing unsparingly when they found the culprit guilty. Immediately the Criminal Court became one of great importance under the guidance of Judge Flippin and his vigorous young attorney-general, Luke E. Wright, and the ablest members of the bar, were constantly found engaged in the numerous causes and state prosecutions, sometimes of distinguished citizens, which were being carried on there. Men like Duncan K. McRae, Emerson Ethridge, George Gantt, T. W. Brown, L. B. Horrigan, E. M. Yerger and John Sale, great lawyers as they were, engaged in battles royal with the vigorous young attorney-general at this bar during Judge Flippin's term and the state and county were vastly the gainers by the workings of this court at that period.

Judge Flippin held office until December, 1875 when, having resigned to become mayor of Memphis, on December 28, of the same year Honorable John D. Adams was appointed judge and held the position until Honorable Thomas H. Logwood, elected August 3, 1876, assumed the bench on September 1, 1877. Judge Logwood held office until 1878 when in August, Honorable P. T. Scruggs was elected in the summer but died before assuming the bench and Honorable J. E. R. Ray was appointed in his place. Upon the reopening of the court, after the yellow fever of that fall, Judge Ray himself died in the summer of 1879 of yellow fever and in the fall the Honorable L. B. Horrigan was appointed to succeed him.

Judge Horrigan was a master of the science of criminal law and a stern, unyielding man who made life a burden to evil doers of all grades. He invariably inflicted the maximum penalty for pistol-carrying, his judgment in such cases being eleven months and twenty-nine days confinement in the County Workhouse. Judge Horrigan's career was of great benefit to the people of Memphis and a constant source of terror to malefactors of all sorts.

Judge Horrigan died in 1883, and Hon. J. M. Greer was appointed to succeed him. Judge Greer served until September, 1884, when Honorable Addison H. Douglass was elected and assumed the bench. Judge Douglass served out the constitutional term to September 1, 1886 and was succeeded by Judge Julius J. DuBose, who was impeached before the Senate of the State Legislature in 1893, for malfeasance in office and was deposed and Honorable T. M. Scruggs appointed to his place. Judge Scruggs declined to stand for reelection in 1894, and Honorable Lunsford P. Cooper was elected and served for the remainder of the constitutional term until 1902, when Honorable John T. Moss was elected and served his full term of eight years.

On April 11, 1907, Division Two was added to the Criminal Court of Shelby County with a limited jurisdiction and Honorable J. W. Palmer was appointed judge of said Division Two, but on May 1, 1909 the jurisdiction was made coordinate.

At the election held August, 1910, Honorable Jesse Edgington was elected judge of Division One and Hon. James W. Palmer of Division Two, of said court and these gentlemen are still in these offices.

The Probate Court of Shelby County was established July 7, 1870 and Honorable J. E. R. Ray was made judge, serving until 1878, when Honorable T. D. Eldridge was elected judge. He served until 1886, when Honorable J. S. Galloway was elected judge and he still holds this position. In 1896 the Second Circuit Court of Shelby County was established, having limited jurisdiction and Honorable J. S. Galloway was made judge *ex officio* of said court and remained so until 1905, when the Second Circuit Court was abolished.

After the Civil War a court had been established in Memphis, called the Municipal Court, which was presided over by George W. Waldron, who continued in office until 1869, when Green P. Foute became judge. This court was abolished December 4, 1869 and its business transferred to the Circuit Court, as above stated.

Passing now to the bar of Shelby County, which has ever been one of the most notable in the Southwest, we find that the first attorneys to be admitted to practice on the third day after its organization, May 1, 1820, by the Court of Pleas and Quartersessions of Shelby County, were John Montgomery and John P. Perkins and these were the first lawyers to be recognized by the court in West Tennessee. Little is known of these gentlemen or their careers except that Perkins was at once elected County Solicitor. About the same time a prominent attorney of Mobile, Alabama, named Robert McAlpine, removed to Memphis. Remaining here for some years he finally returned to Mobile. While here he took a very prominent, perhaps a leading part in the litigation of that day. Other attorneys who were admitted to the bar about the same time were David W. Massey, John Brown, Wm. Stoddard and Robert Hughes. Nothing further is known of the professional careers of these gentlemen. P. T. Gaines early came to Memphis. He was a lawyer and Democrat bitterly opposed to "whigery" as then called, was a man of striking presence and more devoted to politics than to the practice of law. Being rarely ready for trial at the terms of court, he was dubbed by the young attorneys whose cases were blocked, "old Continuendo." Although described as a genial gentleman, he had at least one serious short-coming, he lived and died a bachelor.

Among the most distinguished lawyers of that day however, was Wm. T. Brown who came from Middle Tennessee to Memphis and formed a law partnership with Frederick P. Stanton. Judge Brown was a tall, dark-complected, black-eyed man with nervous temperament and rapid, vigorous habit of speech.

Contemporary with him was Granville D. Swarcy, who came from Somerville, Tennessee. Possessing great power as a lawyer, with much ready wit, he made a dangerous rival to Judge Wm. T. Brown in the practice of that day.

James Wickersham was a product of the North and was not only a good lawyer but a very thrifty man as well. It is narrated of him by Judge L. B. McFarland that he got indebted to his landlord for board but soon after securing what he called an "admiralty case," an attachment on a flatboat, he made a good sized fee and bought some of his landlord's depreciated notes with which he paid his debt. He came to Memphis in 1844. Spencer Jarnagin swooped down from East Tennessee on Memphis in 1847. He was an able lawyer of lazy habit, fonder of fishing than of practicing law and caused much trouble by his dilatory tactics. Of a different type was Col. James B. Thornton of Virginia who came to Memphis in the same year. Colonel Thornton was a man of many attainments in literature and of splendid education and much reading. Several books were written by him, one of which, Thornton on Conveyancing, was made a text-book at the Cambridge Law School of Massachusetts and passed through several editions. Colonel Thornton joined the Confederate service at the beginning of the Civil War, and served throughout. Colonel Thornton was the father of Dr. G. B. Thornton of Memphis and by a later marriage of Judge Lee Thornton of this city, both of his sons still residing here.

About this same period there were a number of successful lawyers in active practice in the courts of Memphis, some of whom became very distinguished at the bar in later years. From 1845 to 1850 these learned men saw in the growing young city a great opportunity and flocked here in considerable numbers, winning both fame and money in their energetic practice. Among those who came to Memphis during the period named, were Leven H. Coe, Walter Coleman, Thos. J. Turley, Wm. K. Poston, David M. Currin, Edwin M. Yerger, John L. T. Sneed, John Sale and Henry G. Smith. What a galaxy of ability and power was represented by that group! L. H. Coe, the aggressive lawyer and active partisan; Walter Coleman, of splendid presence, and an eloquent orator; Thos. J. Turley, the partner of Archibald Wright and father of the late distinguished Senator Thos. B. Turley; Wm. K. Poston, wise, prudent and strong at the bar, who gave three sons to the law to become distinguished at the bar after their father's death, in W. K. Poston, Jr., David H. Poston and Frank P. Poston; David M. Currin, from Murfreesboro, Tennessee, able lawyer and politician and Confederate Congressman, who died during the Civil War; Henry G. Smith, one of the most profound of our attorneys and councellors, who came from Connecticut to North Carolina and thence to Memphis, and who ultimately served a term by appointment in 1868 on the Supreme Bench, and lived a long, useful and laborous life of 33 years in the city of his choice. Judge Henry G. Smith was more than a great lawyer; he was possessed of the keenest wit and while sometimes wrapped in the most painful abstraction when struggling with a great thought, he would arouse to humor and abandon in the battle at the bar and while striking his heaviest blows and inflicting the most dangerous wound upon his opponent's case, would so entertain by his versatility and scintillating humor as to retain the good will even at the time of the man whom he was overwhelming with his clear logic and flood of eloquence. Away from the bar he was the most genial of companions, his polished manner and graceful courtesy winning one unconsciously to him. Judge Smith died suddenly, after intense argument to a meeting of citizens upon a matter of great civic importance, and Memphis in his death lost one of her greatest lawyers and ablest citizens.

Edwin M. Yerger, one of the brilliant men of the early forties, at this time shed his rays by the light of his genius upon all the courtrooms of this city. Mr. Yerger was what was called a natural lawyer, which only means that, with a wonderfully retentive mind, he had so mastered the principles of law and of equity jurisprudence in his early years that his keen powers of reasoning enabled him to break away from precedents and citations of cases and to declare *ex cathedra* the correct rule of law or equity in any case which he was arguing. This was done in language eloquent and forceful, and which seemed to crystalize the thoughts of other astute thinkers into scintillating diamonds of pure reason for use in that particular case. Mr. Yerger was appointed Chancellor to succeed Honorable W. L. Scott, who had resigned in 1871, but he himself died in August, 1872, after a brief but able career on the bench.

John Sale was the law partner and inseperable companion of Judge Yerger, and during their copartnership they were rarely seen apart on the street. Mr. Sale came to Memphis in 1846 and became attorney-general for four years in the Criminal Court. He was a great criminal lawyer. In eloquence and forensic ability he was the equal of Judge Yerger, but did not possess the latter's wonderful reasoning powers. As an advocate before the jury he was overwhelming, and when the logic of the case was not with him his withering sarcasm and ability for lingual castigation often won for him where other men would have failed. Colonel Sale would not hesitate where he had the least opening, to attack the character of the opposing litigant and so trenchant was he in the use of this weapon that Attorney-general Luke E. Wright on one occasion turned to the jury and arraigned Colonel Sale at the close of his argument by declaring him to be "the great and original dirt-dauber of creation." Of this unique character Colonel M. C. Galloway, the brilliant newspaper editor, wrote at his death in November, 1872: "John F. Sale was great in his frivolities, great in his burlesque, great in his humor, great in his common sense, the great lawyer, the great orator, the great black-guard, the great companion, the great friend, the great worshipper of ladies, the great spendthrift. In nothing was he little."

Of the old Memphis bar in the later fifties there were W. D. Beard, afterwards Chief Justice of the Supreme Court; B. M. Estes, in later life the great Chancellor; R. J. Morgan, also a Chancellor after the Civil War; J. M. Gregory, L. D. McKisick, B. A. Massey, Charles Kortrecht, Henry Craft, Luke W. Finlay, Howell Jackson and Archibald Wright. Immediately after the close of the Civil War there came to Memphis other able and ofttimes brilliant lawyers who, combining with the survivors of the fifties, became a bar in the latter sixties, which has probably never been surpassed or even equalled by that of any single city in the whole land. Among these last named gentlemen who came in 1865 or 1866 from other sections of Tennessee were Colonel George Gantt, Thomas G. Smith, M. R. Hill, W. H. Stephens and Thomas R. Smith from West and Middle Tennessee, Landon C. Haynes and Joseph B. and C. W. Heiskell and S. R. Gammon from East Tennessee, Duncan K. McRae and R. M. Heath from North Carolina, James Phelan, Judge Henry T. Ellett, J. W. Clapp and Colonel Wm. Harris from Mississippi; Judge Tom W. Brown from Kentucky; Charles W. Adams, W. M. Randolph and General Albert Pike, from Arkansas and a little earlier, W. Y. C. Humes, of Virginia, but who had lived briefly in East Tennessee.

What a school of law this great galaxy afforded for the young law student and practitioner of that day! Sketches cannot be afforded of each of these great lawyers, nearly all of them cast in the same mold, and giants as they were in forensic debate.

One of the greatest lawyers which Memphis ever knew was Colonel George Gantt. With an intellect sparkling and scintillating like a diamond, hard study had wrought out of him a master of the science of law, and his versatility and love of the law caused him to master every branch of it. He was equally at home in a great struggle for a human life before the able criminal courts of that day; amid the quietly flowing waters of equity practice; in the din and heat of the battles royal for preeminence and success in the contests in the courts of law, or in the humble office of some justice of the peace, illuminating with his genius the intricate question of obscure common law practice, which would often cause the untrained magistrate to forget himself and become the active partisan of the keen lawyer, who had perhaps for the first time brought him to understand the nature of the litigations daily waged before him.

Extremely unlike Colonel Gantt, but a foeman worthy of his steel, was Judge Tom W. Brown of Kentucky, the erudite and classical scholar, the polished rhetorician and the extremely well-grounded lawyer, who richly embellished with his learning, wit and polished language the cases tried by him in the courts and whose eloquence and beauty of diction made him famous not only at the bar but on all other occasions where a great mind and a highly trained orator were needed in public affairs.

Another giant of that day was Judge Archibald Wright, the massive man and massive mind, which had at one time dominated the deliverances of the Supreme Court of Tennessee, at a period when it was strikingly great both in its makeup and its opinions. Judge Wright, while plodding and laborious in his research, at the bar resembled Vulcan, wielding his sledge-hammer with crushing effect upon his less-careful prepared antagonist. Judge Wright knew his own ability and while never vainglorious, exacted unsparingly of his clients due compensation for his labor. He was great as a judge, great as a man, great as a lawyer and advocate and transmitted to his posterity many of the elements of his own massive and imperious mind.

Thomas R. Smith, originally from the State of Maine, though he died young and had but a brief period of development at the bar of Memphis between 1865 and 1872, forged rapidly to the front and became before his death one of the master minds of the great bar of Memphis of that day. He was a man of wonderful resource, clearness of judgment, quickness of perception and indomitable in attack. He was in almost every great case before the Memphis courts between the close of the Civil War and his death in 1872; and his continual successes won for him the greatest distinction.

Landon C. Haynes was a man of winning eloquence and unsurpassed in the beautiful figures of speech and flowers of rhetoric which he lavished upon every audience. Almost every address was a poem, and his love of his native district in East Tennessee with its purple mountains, its dimpled valleys and above all, of the "beautiful blue Wautauga," which he would manage to weave, in some way, into every speech which he made, caused Mr. Albert M. Stephens, one of the young lawyers of that day, to speak of every beautiful and flowery address which he heard as "Blue Wautaugaism."

Two other striking characters of that bar were Duncan K. McRae, of North Carolina and General Albert Pike of Arkansas. Colonel McRae was learned, logical, incisive and intense in every law-suit, conceding no such word as failure, yet striking his tremendous blows with the chivalry of a Bayard, and pleasantly saluting the antagonist he was about to overwhelm. General Albert Pike was a soldier, pioneer, poet, journalist, statesman and last but not least, a lawyer. In all of these he was great and a more striking figure or personality never arose before the bench of a court in Memphis than this tall, broad-shouldered man with bold, high forehead, keen but calm eyes and hair flowing over his shoulders, in appearance, a reincarnation of some of the great jurists of the Elizabethan period in England. General Pike was a child of nature, a child of the forest and a seasoned soldier, but as refined at the bar as any polished courtier, or any grave and dignified gentleman of the early American school of statesmen. He was universally loved and universally respected.

Judge Henry T. Ellett was still another type of the elegant and polished lawyer of that day and, with Judge Henry Craft, like himself from Mississippi, by their suave manners and beautifully expressed thoughts and above all by their unbending dignity and sweetness of manner were examples to all the younger generation of struggling, ambitious attorneys. If either ever lost his balance on the bench, or at the bar it escaped the writer's notice.

Judge J. W. Clapp and Judge Howell E. Jackson were two other notable figures of that day. They both took high position at the Memphis bar and in the affairs of the Memphis public, and Mr. Jackson became a Justice of the Supreme Court of the United States by sheer force of merit, for he was a Southerner of intense loyalty to his section and such men were rarely in favor at that time in administration circles at Washington.

All of these great lawyers have passed on to another world, leaving a memory that will ever be mellow in the minds of those who knew them, and a record that will be historical in the annals of Tennessee and Memphis.

Of this same coterie were Judge John L. T. Sneed of the Supreme Bench, J. M. Gregory, T. B. Turley, R. B. Hutchinson, J. A. Taylor, R. D. Jordan and George B. Peters. Robert Hutchinson was a quiet, gentleman but one of the most thorough equity lawyers of his day. He was a student and writer of high merit and his work on carriers is a standard handbook and textbook in every State of the Union.

Judge Sneed was a gentleman of the olden time, very tall, powerfully built, with a large head and Websterian features. His career was almost coextensive with Memphis, being one of the earliest lawyers to shed lustre upon her name and serving her as lawyer, soldier and jurist in a long career of scholarly endeavor and patient devotion to duty.

General George B. Peters was one of the most brilliant of the corps of brilliant attorneys-general, who have represented the interests of Shelby County and of the State of Tennessee in her courts.

There were yet others noted in that decade of able lawyers, among whom were L. D. McKisick, E. S. Hammond, for a quarter of a century judge of the Federal Court; General W. Y. C. Humes, the genial and able Charles W. Frazer, Ed Beecher, Charles W. Adams, W. T. Avery, Judge E. R. Ray, George Phelan, William M. Smith, R. F. Looney, Judge John P. Caruthers and Emerson Ethridge, who by their earnest and ambitious endeavors added to the fame of the Memphis bar.

And then of the more recent dead we have Luke W. Finlay, brave soldier, able lawyer and good man; Judge W. D.

Beard, learned and wise and who graced the Supreme Bench as Chief Justice of the Supreme Court; John R. Flippin, lawyer, jurist, earnest and faithful mayor of Memphis, who first came to her relief when her interests had been wrecked; D. E. Myers; Eldridge Wright, one of the most brilliant of the generation of lawyers who had reached middle life, when crushed to death in a railroad accident, and last, W. A. Percy, not only a lawyer of great ability, but a man of preponderating influence in public affairs and on whose recent grave the green grass has scarcely yet appeared. In these shining marks chosen by the angel of death, Memphis suffered irreparable loss when the sudden blow fell.

Memphis still has an able, nay, a brilliant bar, embracing a few of the men of the later sixties and a far larger number of young but intellectual giants who are worthy successors in life and character and intellectual ability of the great men recorded above, and who will preserve the name and fame of her bar to other generations. But it is merely possible that prototypes will be found among them of those colossal lawyers, whose striking personality and individuality, and it may be added originality, born of the surrounding conditions and stormy scenes amid which they developed, shed such luster upon the life and story of the bar of that day.

E. E. Wright

# CHAPTER XXIV

## Medical History of Memphis

MEDICINE and surgery have undergone vast changes in Memphis, as they have the world over, and no set of natural scientists have been more persistent in investigations and changing theories than those of the medical profession.

When Memphis was a very small village in the early twenties Indian Medicine men still used their queer practices for relieving the sick and there is record of several white people who, unable to find a white physician, resorted to the help of their red brethren. The methods of the Medicine men were carried on by incantations and invocations to the Great Spirit, but they also used herbs and often gave their patients very strenuous physical treatment.

A writer in the Old Folks Record tells of a process the medicine men had of bleeding by drawing needle points, fixed securely in a quill up and down the patient's arms and legs. The desired end of "bleeding," was attained and the patient would lie abed for days after, unable to walk or move. For some ailments these physicians of the forests believed in blistering and this process was performed by holding hot embers over the patient's abdomen until the blistering was accomplished, it usually taking several helpers to hold the victim in place during the performance.

We learn of no white physician here until late in the twenties, when there is record of Dr. Frank Graham, an intelligent worker for health, with considerable knowledge of medicine.

In 1827 Memphis had an epidemic of dengue, or break-bone

fever, and in 1828 yellow fever visited the town, for the first time since July, 1739, when Bienville's army was attacked while on the way to this point from New Orleans and decimated, by what many now suppose was yellow fever.

When Doctor Graham came he found many new conditions to meet and used his skill in the young town with varying success.

In 1834 two other physicians came to the growing village, Drs. M. P. Sappington and Wyatt Christian, and in 1835 Dr. John R. Frayser was added to the list. Doctor Frayser was a good physician and commenced that year a residence and practice in Memphis which lasted through a long life, in which time he witnessed the vicissitudes of Memphis from those early days until he died an old man, near the close of the century. He also witnessed the marvelous growth in his profession and in 1888 Mr. Vedder said of him, "he still lives, and around him clusters much of the medical history of our city."

Other physicians followed and one, Dr. H. R. Robards, was a surgeon of no mean ability and became the surgeon not only of Memphis, but of the surrounding country.

In the early days Memphis was not a clean city, as has been shown in the general history, and in the thirties Doctor Frayser and his brother physicians thought a board of health should be organized, that sanitation and other provisions for the health of the town might be instituted, and August 6, 1838, the first board of health was formed, composed of Doctors Wyatt Christian, M. P. Sappington, John R. Frayser, DeWitt, Maybry, Lewis Shanks, and     Hickman.* This board did not gain the influence they desired in order to enforce cleanliness and make other hygienic demands of the community, but they accomplished some good and worked together for the common benefit.

Asiatic cholera reached Memphis from New Orleans in January, 1849 and caused much alarm, but the disease was confined chiefly to the flatboat neighborhood and to people of dissipated habits and enervated condition.† In other places

*Vdder. †Keating.

visited by this plague that year results were more serious than in Memphis.

In the Railroad Record of 1854, these lines appeared concerning Memphis health: "Its high position has secured its health so far that neither cholera nor yellow fever have visited it in the severe forms in which they have prevailed in almost all the Southern cities. This immunity is likely to continue, for it lies on both high and dry ground, and has purer and better air than any other place in that region.

But the sanitary condition of the town was poor and Dr. A. P. Merrill, a physician and citizen of high rank, who has also appeared in these pages as an educator, in response to a discussion between the Board of Aldermen and the Board of Health carried on in the newspaper in the fifties, advocated a sewer system. In this discussion Doctors Watkin and Booth reported:

"Memphis has for the past two years been alarmingly sickly, and the sickness has been alarmingly fatal. No sort of explanation can weaken the force of these facts. They have become notorious, and if allowed to become her permanent characteristics will brood over the city like an eternal incubus, destroying its pleasantness, arresting its growth and paralyzing its commercial prosperity."

The coming of Doctor Merrill brought another physician of high standing and impetus to the profession generally. Dr. William V. Taylor, took up his abode here in 1850. He was followed at intervals by his four sons, all physicians and all standing for the best in their profession. Still other physicians came and soon Memphis had doctors of all the schools existing at that time.

As early as 1846 it was thought that Memphis could support a medical college of her own, and the Memphis Medical College was instituted and proved very successful. Doctor Shanks was elected dean, and all the teachers were men well versed in the profession, some being physicians of wide repute. In 1853 Dr. John Millington was made professor of chemistry, and he was ranked one of the best chemists of the world, having had broad experience both in America and England.

Another able teacher in this institution was Dr. H. V. Wooten, recognized far and near as an authority on the principles and practice of medicine, which was his branch of work in the college. Doctor Merrill was appointed professor of *materia medica* and Mr. Vedder says of him that he "has had few superiors, before or since his time." Dr. C. T. Quintard taught physiology and anatomy and gave promise of being one of the first in this branch of doctor's work, but he abandoned medicine and went into the ministry. Dr. Arthur K. Taylor then taught anatomy with excellent results until he moved to Hot Springs, Arkansas. Dr. Daniel F. Wright, one of the best workers for the State Board of Health, was also a teacher in this college.

Colonel Keating mentions a closing term of the Memphis Medical College in February, 1852 "under circumstances of exceptional *eclat,* Dr. Charles T. Quintard delivering the valedictory address."

During the following summer this college was consolidated with the Memphis Institute and opened in the fall under splendid auspices, Doctor Merrill giving the introductory lecture and Congressman F. P. Stanton delivering an able address.

The Botanical School of Medicine was very popular in the early half of the last century and several physicians of that practice came to Memphis. The system grew in favor and about the time the Memphis Medical College was established the Botanico-Medical College was opened here and became popular.

Dr. M. Gabbert of this school gave his life in 1855, during the yellow fever epidemic that came to Memphis that year. He had been very successful as a practitioner and had grown to be much beloved by many Memphis families who relied on his skill and sympathy during their trials of sickness. Doctors T. C. Gayle and G. W. Morrow were also successful followers of this school and had extensive practice.

Homeopathy came to Memphis in 1856 with Doctor Edmonds who won the confidence of many people and gained a large practice. Homeopathy became popular and numerous good physicians of this school followed Doctor Edmonds at intervals to Memphis. They, with physicians of other schools, battled with the yellow fever of 1855 as well as later epidemics.

The best physicians in Memphis, being broad-minded men, did not allow the different theories of practice to interfere with the general professional harmony, and when the Memphis Medical Society was formed, physicians of all schools were admitted, and we find the principles of this society laid down by Doctor Merrill in an address given in 1857. He stated that all reputable physicians could belong to the Memphis Medical Society, but no one who practiced charlatanry would be recognized. One of the articles of the constitution of this organization read:

"All graduates of respectable schools of medicine, of good moral character, and willing to adopt the Code of Ethics of the American Medical Association, and scrupulously to adhere to its teachings, may become members of this society."

Also, "No individual shall be considered eligible to membership in this society, who divides responsibility with a known empiric, or associates with any such in consultation, or practices with nostrums or secret patent medicines, or who exposes, vends or advertises such medicines either in his own name or that of another."

Doctor Merrill thought that in the true physician it was narrow and unscientific to inhere inviolably to one class of materials for cures, and the members of this society were urged to keep no good discovery secret, but to share with the brotherhood every new good that could in any way aid the profession.

He thought that the Board of Health should be a substantial organization of the city; to attend to sanitation and make the city a healthful place of residence, and an attractive place which would encourage and invite immigrants of a solid and beneficial sort.

Of the physicians here at that time Doctor Merrill said:

"Memphis contains, as compared with other cities, its full proportion of medical talent and learning. Fatal diseases are not more fatal in the hands of physicians here, than are the same diseases in all our principal cities. Those terrible epidemic scourges of modern times, cholera and yellow fever, have been treated even more successfully in Memphis than in most other places. * * * * Our surgery compares favorably with New York and Philadelphia."

Physicians not mentioned above, practicing in Memphis in 1860, are given by Mr. O. F. Vedder, as follows: Drs. R. R. Ball, C. C. Berry, Field & Berry, B. F. C. Brooks, R. W. Creighton, E. W. Davis, P. E. Dickinson, Abner Dayton, James Hall, Zeno Harris, C. Spiegel, J. M. Sledge, G. H. Smith, A. Thumel, William J. Tuck, J. S. Williams, F. M. E. Faulkner, J. Fowlkes, E. P. Frains, M. B. Frierson, Frederick Hartz, Hopson & Martin, R. P. Jones, T. Keefe, J. M. Lane, F. H. Leroy, J. W. Maddox, E. R. Marlett, Thomas Peyton, J. S. Pearson, Milton Sanders, James Young, W. T. Bailey, D. M. DeBose, C. S. Fenner, S. & S. T. Gilbert, W. H. Hawkins, D. Herndon, J. R. Hill, H. J. Holmes, J. J. Hooks, J. T. Marable, W. D. Tucker, A. B. Washington, R. T. Webb, J. S. White, W. W. Wright, Charles McCormick, J. D. Martin, W. H. Pickett, R. H. Redmond, A. A. Rice, Shanks & Cobb, L. D. Shelton, Snider & McGinnis and John Wilson.

During the sixties the medical profession kept pace with other Memphis progress and the two schools of Homeopathy and Allopathy, directly opposite in their theories, grew powerful, but rivalry sprang up and as time advanced the schools became antagonistic.

Some of the most noted of both these schools during the years succeeding the War Between the States were: Drs. John R. Frayser, R. W. Mitchell, S. P. Green, Emmett Woodward, A. L. Kimbro, Wm. Hewett, C. F. Snyder, John R. Pitman, H. P. Hobson, E. A. White, W. E. Rogers, Josiah S. White, Frank Rice, George R. Grant, Arthur K. Taylor, R. C. Malone, W. T. Irwin, R. F. Brown, S. H. Brown, E. Miles Willett, Alexander Erskine, G. B. Thornton, D. D. Saunders, R. W. Mitchell, Paul Otey, W. C. Cavanaugh, J. M. Keller, J. H. Nuttall, Richard H. Taylor, R. B. Maury, W. B. Avant, H. W. Purnell, J. Joseph Williams, J. Murray Rogers, Robert P. Bateman, Joseph Lynch, B. M. Lebby.

All medical organizations had been abandoned during the Civil War and most of the physicians joined the army. After the war people of all professions and callings in the South were heart-sick and disorganized, but by degrees order came again and the Memphis doctors started afresh to pursue their professions and to be interested in the growth and prosperity of Memphis. Besides many of the old resident physicians a number of new ones took up their abode here and while secular feeling and distrust lasted for several years after the close of the war, few physicians allowed personalities or feelings of hatred to interfere with the work of helping humanity in which they were engaged.

Organization again did its part in bringing the M. D.'s together, helped them in their work and by degrees the ravages of war and their effects were forgotten, or at least put in the background, and new life was infused into Memphis.

But in 1873 another check came in the yellow fever epidemic and many brave physicians who stayed to fight the fever and to learn to handle it gave their lives as toll, while many others had severe attacks of the disease.

Doctor Thornton gave the list of deaths that year in Memphis as 1,244 out of 4,204 cases, as the nearest estimate, but he stated that many other cases were not recorded or were called something else. 1873 was a trying year but one soon followed that eclipsed both it and the War Between the States in the devastation it wrought.

The epidemics of 1878-9 have already been so fully treated in the general history of this volume that they will not again be dwelt on here. Suffice it to say that the doctors of both schools were tried in the fire and proved pure metal. Some gave their lives, most of them were attacked by the plague and many lived to continue serving Memphis and their fellow men. Dr. G. W. Overall is said to have been the only physician who escaped the fever altogether. Dr. G. B. Thornton, in charge of the City Hospital, who had had the disease in 1873 nearly lost his life from it in 1878. Dr. John H. Erskine, health officer of Memphis, was cut down in the midst of official duty, and Colonel Keating says of him, that "He was an inspiration to his friends, an example of constancy, steadiness and unflagging zeal. To the sick room he brought all these qualities, supplemented by an unusual experience, an inexhaustible stock of knowledge, and a sympathy as deep as the sad occasion."

Would that an eulogy might be here given every brave physician, and nurse, who gave his or her life during that awful time.

Among other physicians who came here and volunteered services during the 1878 epidemic was Dr. R. H. Tate, the first negro professional who had ever come to Memphis. His services were accepted by the Howard Association and he worked faithfully among his own people until himself overtaken by the fever. He died September 21, with the crown of martyrdom, so many white physicians and nurses bore that fatal year.

We have already dwelt upon how the city was impoverished in 1880, but physicians as a rule are not people to be daunted and our Memphis fraternity was one of the best. Most of the surviving doctors took up the reins with new vim and new men of the profession came. Among these were three negro doctors from the Mcharry Medical College of Nashville, all reputable men and a benefit to their people morally as well as physically. These were Doctors T. C. Cottrell, A. S. J. Burchett and Y. S. Moore.

Many of the physicians devoted themselves to specialties as this mode of practice grew in favor, and infirmaries were established for the treatment of special diseases. An important one of these was established by Dr. W. E. Rogers for surgical cases, assisted by his son, Dr. W. B. Rogers. After the death of the senior member of this firm the son, together with Doctors B. G. Henning and H. L. Williford, founded a better equipped surgical infirmary on Madison Avenue.

Soon after this Doctors Mitchell and Maury opened an infirmary for women at Third and Court Streets, which was soon outgrown and these enterprising men in 1886 erected a four-story building costing $40,000, with baths, operating rooms, laboratory and every convenience for such an institution. Dr. R. B. Maury and Dr. R. W. Mitchell and his son, Dr. E. D. Mitchell conducted this infirmary, and later Doctor Maury's son, Doctor Maury came into the partnership. In 1903 the firm name was changed to Maury & Ellett, when improvements and additions were made to the institution and recently still further improvements have been instituted.

Dr. T. P. Crofford opened another infirmary of this sort on Main Street which in its turn had to be enlarged. In 1891 this infirmary was largely extended, a building costing $75,000 being erected on Third Street. This institution was operated by Doctors Crofford, Rogers & Henning, three physicians standing very high in the profession.

Dr. G. W. Overall, believing strongly in electricity as an agent in curing disease, opened a sanitarium in 1888, where electrical appliances were used. Later E. D. Peete entered into partnership with Doctor Overall.

Other infirmaries, sanitariums, sanitoriums and hospitals have operated at intervals, all performing their share of benefit to suffering humanity.

Of public institutions the City Hospital on Madison Avenue stands first, but it has been so fully treated in the general history, as part of the growth of the city, that mention is sufficient here. Its present superintendent is Mr. Edward Nowland, Jr., and its corps of physicians and nurses is one of the finest in the country. The hospital now has three wings besides the central building and contains 250 beds. There is a training school for nurses and thirty nurses are at present in the hospital. Seven finished nurses graduated in the class of 1912. These devoted women have become an important factor in nursing serious cases of disease and physicians rely upon them to a very great extent for success in treating their patients. As with the doctors, nurses of this time must earn their diplomas by high efficiency. The head nurse of the City Hospital is Miss Frances O. Spencer, who also has charge of the training school.

The City Hospital has eight internes, seven of whom serve in the hospital and one in the police station. Something of the amount of work done in this institution can be imagined when it is known that 2,300 patients have been received and cared for since January 1, 1912. The present trustees are Messrs. R. O. Johnson, chairman; M. M. Bosworth, St. Elmo Newton,

C. R. Mason, superintendent; S. T. Wharton, assistant-superintendent; and J. F. Ward, bookkeeper.

The Baptist Memorial Hospital opened July 20, 1912, under excellent auspices. Reverend Thomas S. Potts is general superintendent of the hospital and there is a good corps of workers under his direction, as he himself says, one of the best to be found. Mr. A. Q. Gillespie is assistant superintendent and Miss Florence Bishop, superintendent of nurses and principal of the training school for nurses. Miss Dorothy Hughes is surgical nurse and both she and Miss Bishop are nurses of experience and recognized efficiency.

The City Dispensary, 222 North Front Street, is a very useful branch of medical work in Memphis.

St. Joseph's Hospital, situated on Johnson Avenue, is in charge of the Sisters of St. Francis, Sister Alexia being the Superior. Although a Catholic institution patients from all or no denominations are cared for alike, religious considerations not controlling them in sickness. This hospital, like the City Hospital, has pay and free patients, according as the patient is able or not to pay for his treatment. This institution can accommodate 150 patients.

The Lucy Brinkley Hospital, 855 Union Avenue, in charge of Miss Lavania Dunnavant, is quite an old institution, but has only occupied its splendid new quarters since June, 1907. The Board of Directors is made up of Mrs. C. F. Farnsworth, president; Mrs. Grant, secretary; Mrs. M. L. Selden, treasurer; and the Staff comprises Doctors W. W. Taylor, president; Moore Moore, secretary and treasurer; Ed. Mitchell, J. A. Crisler, W. S. Anderson, M. B. Herman and E. M. Holder.

The Presbyterian Home Hospital has for one of its chief aims the desire to throw around the patients as much of home atmosphere as possible in an institution of this sort. This hospital is situated on Alabama Street and is in charge of Doctors G. G. Buford and James A. Moss. The institution was founded in 1903 by Doctors Buford, Thomas and Morrow, Doctor Buford later buying the whole interest. Later still he took Doctor Moss as a partner and now these two physicians have charge of the work. Miss Buford is head nurse.

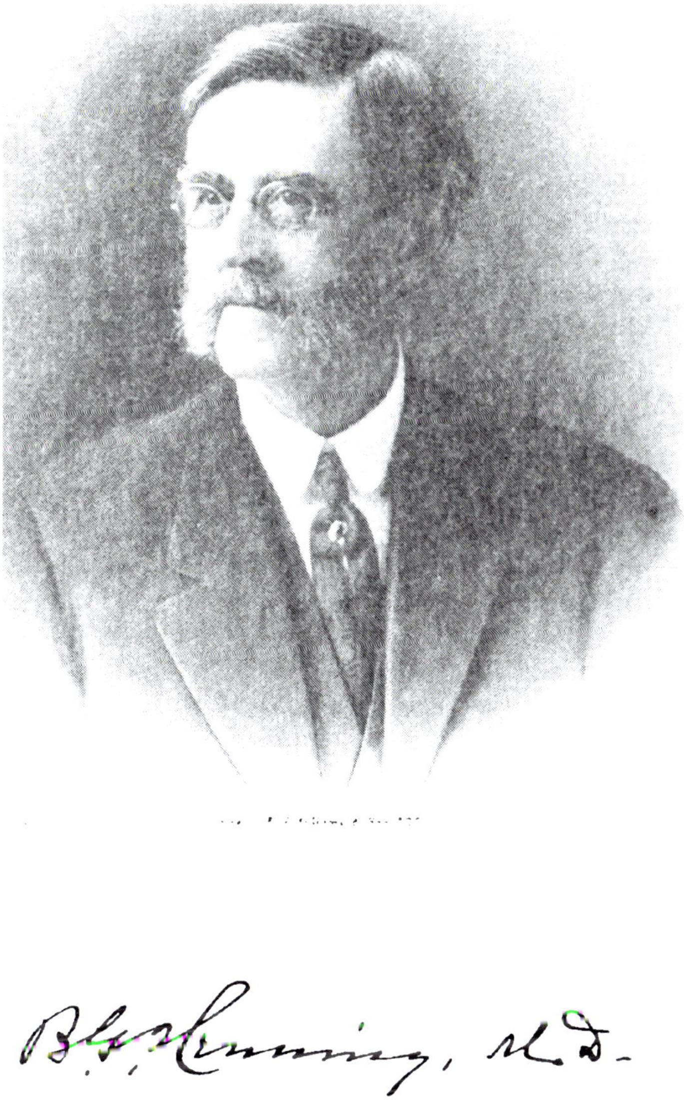

The Home for Incurables, 1467 E. McLemore, is a beautiful place where the aim is to make the last days of their patients as pleasant as possible. Mr. Re H. Vance is president of this institution and Mrs. Olive Marshall, matron.

There is a Tuberculosis Hospital on Riverside Boulevard, at the corner of Rhode Island Avenue, whose name designates its purpose. The city and county are now jointly preparing to build a public tuberculosis hospital on a large scale.

On West California Avenue, overlooking the river, is the United States Marine Hospital, where river patients are made comfortable and carefully tended. Dr. P. C. Kalloch is the surgeon in command.

At 698 Williams Avenue is the Negro Baptist Hospital, in charge of Dr. C. A. Terrell, where patients of this race receive good attention from well-trained physicians and nurses.

Another good Negro institution is the Hairston Hospital at 628 South Orleans Street.

Not least of Memphis institutions for the sick is the Pest House, where contagious diseases are treated and tended. This hospital is in charge of Mr. W. F. Kimbrough.

Memphis has some excellent medical schools, which have many graduates every year. The Memphis Hospital Medical College is the oldest of those now in existence. In 1876 Doctor William E. Rogers thought Memphis should have a medical school and consulted with some of his fellow physicians on the subject. Dr. G. B. Henning and Dr. W. B. Rogers agreed that such a school had become a Memphis need and by 1878 considerable interest had been aroused. A lot was purchased on Union Street opposite the old City Hospital, now Forrest Park. This school was ready for work by the fall of 1878, but the yellow fever epidemic prevented its being opened. The same fate served it the following autumn but in September, 1880, the college was thrown open to students and has ever since been successfully operated. It has several times been added to and at present a large, efficient establishment is maintained at 718 Union Avenue. This last building was erected in 1902 at a cost of $100,000.

In 1886 the college lengthened its course of two years to

three years, and again in 1900 to four years. This school grew steadily and by the school year of 1900-1901, had 750 students, being at that time the second largest medical school in the United States. Last year the school had 380 matriculates and from its beginning, 2,625 graduates have left its training. Many of these men now occupy high positions in the profession all over the Union, some being employed in the United States army and navy.

The advantages for study and practice of the students here are excellent and before a student can enter the college he must be of good moral character, at least eighteen years of age and a graduate of a high school.

Professors Emeritus of the college are Dr. Alexander Erskine and Dr. A. G. Sinclair and many other members of the faculty have had long experience in the institution. The present faculty comprises Drs. W. B. Rogers, B. G. Henning, B. F. Turner, Elmer E. Francis, J. L. Minor, F. D. Smythe, Frank A. Jones, J. L. Andrews, J. B. McElroy, J. J. Huddleston, J. A. Crisler and J. L. McGehee.

The Board of Directors are: Col. Wm. H. Carroll, president; W. B. Rogers, secretary and treasurer; A. C. Treadwell, Capt. J. W. Dillard, W. B. Galbreath, P. P. VanVleet, W. H. Bates, R. T. Cooper, Bolton Smith and Doctors W. S. Smith, B. F. Ward, Zach Biggs and B. G. Henning.

Another successful medical school is the one connected with the University of Tennessee, which college is in a splendid new building at 879 Madison Avenue. This College of Physicians and Surgeons, includes a School of Pharmacy and a College of Dentistry.

The location of this college is admirable for its purposes, having the City Hospital opposite, the splendid new Baptist Memorial Hospital within a stone's throw of its doors and the new Methodist Hospital to be soon erected 150 feet south, and still another institution to be erected in this neighborhood this summer is a 50-bed emergency hospital. With these four hospitals surrounding the school the students will have clinical and other medical advantages surpassing the neighborhood of any other college in America, it is claimed.

The students here are eligible for eight positions as internes at the City Hospital, house-surgeon and assistant-house-surgeon at St. Joseph's Hospital, assistant physician to the County Hospital and six internes at the Baptist Memorial Hospital. The faculty is a most excellent one, with Dr. Brown Ayres, president; Dr. E. C. Ellett, dean; and Mr. E. F. Turner, registrar. Dr. Heber Jones is Dean Emeritus and also professor of clinical medicine. The other members of the faculty are Doctors E. M. Holder, M. Goltman, G. R. Livermore, A. R. Jacobs, John M. Maury, Richmond McKinney, G. G. Buford, Marcus Haase, R. S. Toombs, Louis Leroy, Wm. Krauss, W. H. Pistole, P. W. Toombs, H. T. Brooks, W. C. Campbell, E. C. Mitchell, E. D. Watkins, Robert Fagin, O. S. Warr and Robert Mann.

In order that they might work together for the common good the dentists of Memphis have an organization called the Memphis Dental Society. It is the object of this society to bring about courtesy and coöperation among the dentists of Memphis and, to quote from their constitution, "to agitate and discuss all new questions, both theoretical and practical, in the science and art of dentistry, that we may always be in touch with those who are leaders of our profession, thereby enabling us more readily to recognize that which is for the best interest of our patient, and more able to meet the obligations which honor and integrity demand of us."

In 1909 the College of Dental Surgery was organized in Memphis by Doctors Justin D. Towner and M. Goltman, as a department of the University of Memphis. The aim of this college is high and its standard chosen from the regulations prescribed by the National Association of Dental Faculties. The course requires three years of study and practice. The first faculty was made up of Doctors Justin D. Towner, dean; David M. Cattell, registrar; M. Goltman, Wm. E. Lundy, C. J. Washington, J. A. Gardner, J. L. Mewborn, C. H. Taylor, E. Edgar West, J. A. Crisler, Louis Leroy, Percy W. Toombs, E. D. Watkins, W. H. Pistole and E. C. Mitchell.

In 1911 this college consolidated with the University of Tennessee Dental Department of Nashville, operated as the

University of Tennessee Department of Dentistry at Memphis. The present dean is Joseph A. Gardner, and the registrar is David M. Cattell. The present faculty comprises, Doctors H. A. Holder, J. A. Gardner, Justin D. Towner, D. M. Cattell, M. Goltman, Wm. E. Lundy, C. J. Washington, Elbert W. Taylor, Eugene A. Johnson, Louis Leroy, Edwin D. Watkins, E. C. Mitchell, Robert Mann, Robert Fagin, Raymond Manogue, J. L. Mewborn, L. J. McRae, L. M. Matthews, H. C. Rushing and R. E. Baldwin. This college, as well as all other departments of the University of Tennessee, is co-educational.

This department occupies the historic building at 177 Union Avenue, occupied by the Y. M. C. A. before moving into their elegant new home, and the building has been remodeled for its new purpose.

The James Sanitorium is a well known institution devoted to the curing of alcoholic and drug addictions. This institution was beautifully situated at Raleigh Springs in what was formerly the Raleigh Springs Hotel, until it was burned and completely demolished a few months ago. Now the sanitorium is located at 692 Alabama Avenue in pleasant and attractive grounds and buildings. The president of this institution is Charles B. James.

Doctors Petty and Wallace also conduct a sanitarium for the treatment of unfortunate people habituated to drugs or alcoholic drinks, at 958 South Fourth Street. Dr. Petty is the medical director of this institution.

# CHAPTER XXV

## Societies and Clubs

MANY social gatherings were enjoyed by the pioneers and sometimes these were conducted periodically, but the first society organizations in Memphis of which we have record, were fraternal. The first of these was a lodge organization by Masons in 1836-1837, known as Memphis Lodge Number 91. This lodge grew and became a strong organization in the community. Their first recorded lodge rooms were on the west side of Second Street, corner of the alley, between Adams and Washington Streets. Washington Chapter Number 18 was formed later and met in the same rooms. . Both these lodges surrendered their charters about 1851 but before they discontinued many other Masonic lodges had been born and they continued in their work, ever increasing in numbers.

The Masons have a handsome building on the corner of Second Street and Madison Avenue, covering 80 by 148 feet. This building was erected in the seventies, being much hindered in its progress by epidemics and financial depressions that followed. In August, 1870, the stockholders of the Masonic Temple Association elected officers to purchase a site for the temple. These officers were H. H. Higbee, president; A. J. Wheeler, secretary; T. R. Farnsworth, treasurer; and the directors were John Pettigrew, John Lent, C. B. Church and George Mellersh.

These men purchased the lot corner of Second and Madison, and on June 24, 1873, the cornerstone was laid with much ceremony, and on April 6, 1880, the Masonic Temple was finally dedicated, since which time it has held an important place in Memphis for lodge-rooms, offices, studios, etc. The first six years of its use the first floor was used as the post office and, upon its removal, served as store accommodation.

There are numerous Masonic lodges in Memphis at present and the order has ever held a dignified place among secret organizations.

Another fraternal order whose benefits have been felt since the early history of Memphis is the Independent Order of Odd Fellows, which was organized here on January 30, 1843, with O. E. Wilcox, Harlan L. Leaf, James M. Howard, Abel B. Shaw and John Y. Bayliss as charter members. This first lodge was called Memphis Lodge Number 6 and two years after its establishment another lodge, "Chickasaw Lodge Number 8," was organized with six charter members,—William K. Poston, Thomas S. Brown, William Badgley, William F. Davis, James M. Howard and D. S. Wilder.

This order, like that of Masonry, grew rapidly and spread its influence around. Many of the members of this order, as stated in the general history, were among the tried and sacrificed of the epidemics and after those scourges many people who had been left destitute were again given a start in life by the Odd Fellows. In 1873 the call of this order for funds brought from sister lodges all over the Union $30,000 in excess of the expenses incurred during the epidemic. This surplus money was used for building an addition to the Leath Orphan Asylum, besides supplying the needs of many widows and children of Odd Fellows left destitute.

1878-1879 also found many of these men at their self-appointed posts of duty and after each epidemic their help was extended to the destitute.

The Odd Fellows have a beautiful building on North Court Avenue, in which the different lodges of the order meet.

The Maccabees is a beneficiary order of women, organized in 1893 in Memphis, a society for "truth, love, fraternity, progression and benevolence." This society's emblem, a beehive, is significant of thoughts of industry and elevation.

The German Benevolent Society was organized in 1855 and continued its operations through all the mutations of war, pestilence and scarcity of money. This organization has paid many thousands of dollars in benefits to members and has done much work outside its membership.

The "Memphis Gruetli Verein" is a Swiss beneficiary order established in 1855. The war and fever weakened its ranks but after these disasters were over it took new life and grew prosperous again.

A Scotch organization, St. Andrew's Society, was chartered in 1866. Its membership is composed of Scotchmen, their sons and grandsons. All their meetings are solely for business except one a year,—the birthday of St. Andrew, when social, literary and musical entertainments are held.

The "Societé Francaise de Secours Mutuels," was organized in 1855, but not incorporated until ten years later. Its incorporators were John Pelegrin, Felix Leclerc, Francois Lavigne, F. Faquin and Pierre Deputy. After one of the epidemics its membership was reduced to six, but it afterward resuscitated.

The "Sociata di Unione e Fratellanza Italiana" was incorporated in 1870 by Italian citizens for social and helpful purposes. The secretary of this order is F. T. Cuner.

Other nationalities have their representations also in benevolent societies, as nearly all nationalities of the earth are represented in Memphis.

The Knights of Honor was established in 1873 and it was the first organization giving death benefits to families of the members at their decease. Its membership grew even more rapidly than the other relief societies, made up largely from both Masons and Odd Fellows. The first lodge in Memphis was Memphis Lodge Number 196, which was established in 1875, with the following gentlemen as charter members: William R. Hodges, Lucien B. Hatch, Thomas J. Barchus, John C. Scronce, J. Harvey Mathes, E. H. Martin, S. O. Nelson, Jr., John A. Holt, John W. Ward, P. R. Cousins, E. J. Carson, J. P. Young, Jerome Baxter, James S. Wilkins, and Joseph E. Russell. Its first officers: L. B. Hatch, P. D.; J. Harvey Mathis, D.; John Preston Young, V. D.; Dr. W. R. Hodges, A. D.; Thomas J. Barchus, Rep.; Joseph E. Russell, I. Rep.; John Loague, treasurer.

The first severe test of this lodge came in 1878, after which epidemic so many of its members had died that $385,000 was required to fulfil its obligations but they were all met.

Many lodges of this order have been established since and all have been faithful sponsors of their trusts.

On March 23, 1878, an order called the "Knights and Ladies of Honor," was formed, in which both men and women carried policies for their beneficiaries. There were sixty-one charter members to this lodge and the first officers were: Phil Maurer, P. P.; Jacob Braun, P.; Henrietta Saupe, V. P.; Max Herman, secretary; J. R. Kleiner, F., secretary; L. Ottenheimer, treasurer.

In 1878 the lodge lost five members and many members of families. At their next appointment of officers Clara Unverzagt was elected P. P.; G. W. Lippald, P.; Rose Lippold, V. P.; William Souhr, secretary; Fred Siedel, treasurer. By that time there were 223 members. Since then the lodges and membership have increased and the order is a strong one.

Equity Lodge Number 20, of the Ancient Order of United Workmen, was organized June 8, 1877, with fifty-four charter members. The first officers were D. F. Goodyear, P. M. W.; S. S. Garrett, M. W.; S. C. DePass, F.; Joseph E. Russell, O.; D. G. Reahard, recorder; N. L. Avery, financier; Ad. Storm, receiver.

Tennessee Lodge Number 5, of this order was organized in 1872, with twenty members. The first officers were J. E. Russell, C. C.; W. K. French, V. C.; H. C. Bigelow, R. S.; E. R. Jack, F. S. The object of this society was to "disseminate the great principles of friendship, charity and benevolence," and was open to all sects and political parties, men's private opinions having nothing to do, the order claimed, with the general brotherhood of the world. It also has an endowment fund. The lodges of this order increased rapidly.

As Catholics were not allowed to belong to secret organizations and many of them wanted the privilege of providing an endowment for their families, an order was formed in the church called the "Catholic Knights of America." Five per centum of the benefit fund is used to form a sinking fund.

The first officers were Reverend Father Francis Jansend, Bishop of Natchez, S. S. D.; Honorable James David Coleman, S. S. P.; S. O'Rourke, S. V. P.; John Barr, Lebanon, Kentucky, S. S.; J. O'Brien, Chattanooga, Tennessee, S. T.; E. Miles Willett, M. D., Memphis, Tennessee, S. M. E. The Supreme Trustees were: J. J. Duffy, John H. Zwarts, M. D., and B. C. Eveslage, chairman of the sinking fund commissioners.

There are numerous branches of this Religious-Fraternity order in Memphis and they do a great work.

The Ancient Order of Hibernians, which was organized in 1885, is a beneficiary society for Irish people, instrumental in doing much good for its members.

The Knights of Innisfail was organized in 1873 and chartered in 1878. It is an Irish organization of brotherhood with the double object of encouraging feelings of "fraternity, temperance and respectability" amongst its members and relieving misfortune wherever they can. The early officers were Anthony Walsh, president; M. T. Garvin, vice-president; Jeremiah Sullivan, secretary; and P. J. Kelly, treasurer.

The Benevolent and Protective Order of Elks was instituted in 1884. This order originated among actors but the membership soon extended to men of all professions and vocations. While it is a benevolent society, its social advantages appeal to many of the members and the order has grown to be a great power. In 1904 the Memphis lodge erected a modern building on Jefferson Avenue, a beautifully fitted-up clubhouse with parlors, library, dining-room, etc. The officers are: George Haszinger, Jr., Exalted Ruler; J. D. Cella, secretary and E. B. Sullivan, treasurer; and the trustees are: William H. Dean, chairman; P. Harry Kelly, Matt Monaghan, D. F. Balton and John C. Reilly.

There are many charitable institutions in Memphis, each and all doing good work and ever tending toward making our city one of charity, justice and equalization.

First of these comes the Associated Charities, with headquarters in the new Police Building. This organization, under the name of United Charities, was organized November 15, 1893. The first year of their work 1600 persons living in

Memphis were relieved and the work has grown to enormous proportions since then. This association has a wide field, which is very well known, and its organized work is well managed. The president of the Associated Charities Board is R. O. Johnson; the secretary, Reverend P. A. Pugh; treasurer, John M. Tuther; chairman of the financial committee, June H. Rudisill; and the general manager, James P. Kranz. The directors are Mrs. Ben Goodman, Mrs. J. M. McCormack, Dr. Lilian M. Johnson, Rabbi W. H. Fineshriber, Reverend T. W. Lewis, B. G. Alexander, F. S. Elgin, J. V. Rush and P. H. Kelly.

In 1860 Jewish women organized the "Hebrew Ladies' Benevolent Association," and much charitable work has been done by the members of this association ever since. Their meetings are held in the Poplar Avenue Temple.

In 1868 the United Hebrew Relief Association was organized. The membership of this society is large and each member makes his voluntary contribution yearly. This association relieves indigent Jews to the amount of thousands of dollars every year in their quiet, unobtrusive way. The present officers are Reverend Max Samfield, president; Samuel Slager, vice-president; H. Bluthenthal, secretary.

In 1875 the Womans Christian Association was organized in Memphis and did noteworthy work from the beginning, although the association was not chartered until 1883. The object of these women was to help unfortunate women and to prevent neglected children from being led into evil. Their work is widespread and the thousands of dollars contributed every year to the association have saved many women from lives of degradation, bettered the lives of little children and helped respectable young women to obtain positions and to live protected from snares that so often beset the paths of inexperienced young people seeking a place in the work-a-day world. The present officers of this association are Mrs. M. C. Reder, president and Mrs. Maria McElroy, general secretary.

April 26, 1883, the Young Men's Christian Association was chartered in Memphis and grew rapidly in popularity and strength. Its object was to reach all the young men possible and to hold out incentives to them to be upright and to grow mentally, morally and physically. Rooms were secured in which a parlor, library, gymnasium and auditorium were fitted up. In five years the organization had outgrown its quarters, having gained a membership of three hundred. The officers at that time were R. G. Craig, president; L. H. Estes, vice-president; J. H. Thompson, secretary; George S. Fox, treasurer; and William D. Laumaster, general secretary. The association continued to expand, outgrowing more and more commodious apartments, until its final move into its own elegant club building on Madison Avenue, one of the handsomest and most convenient Y. M. C. A. buildings in the world. The present officers are E. B. LeMaster, president; B. G. Alexander, general secretary and G. C. McCollough, secretary. The membership in Memphis at present is over three thousand.

The Young Men's Hebrew Association is an organization for young Hebrew men similar to that of the Y. M. C. A. It was organized in 1881 with only a few members, for the purpose of creating sociability among young Hebrew men and encouraging them in moral and literary improvement. After a while of struggling to keep together and several misfortunes, one of which was the burning of their well-equipped rooms and property, not protected by insurance, the club became a power and has remained so, at present having nearly 500 members. The first president was Dave Gensburger.

In November, 1910, the Association took up its headquarters and club home in the Y. M. H. A.—Rex Building, corner of Madison Avenue and Dunlap Street, a building fitted up commodiously and elegantly for both these associations,—the one an intellectual and general improvement club and the other a social organization.

The present officers are, Otto Metzer, president; Jacob H. Foltz, vice-president; Emil C. Rawitser, secretary; Edw. E. Becker (reelected for the twenty-ninth term), treasurer; Israel H. Peres, librarian; Emil Kahn, auditor. The Board of Control is composed of Charles J. Haase, Henry D. Bauer, Elias Gates, Dr. Harry S. Wolff, Dave Sternberg, Clarence N. Frohlich.

The Young Men's Institute was organized July 19, 1891

by twenty-six young Catholic men whose object was to form a club for social intercourse and intellectual advancement. George D. Hook was made president and much of the club's early popularity was due to Mr. Hook's unselfish efforts in its behalf. The society gave entertainments to its friends which were instructive as well as enjoyable and the work among themselves was always helpful. It has grown until there are now 100 members, who have rooms at 198 Washington Avenue. The present officers are John E. Colbert, president; P. M. Canale, 1st vice-president; R. J. Regan, 2nd vice-president; H. W. Neff, recording secretary; B. C. Cunningham, corresponding secretary; E. M. James, marshal; E. F. Longinotti, general secretary. The Board of Directors are G. W. Dichtel, chairman; T. J. Noonan and E. P. Colbert.

The Poor and Insane Asylum is six miles northeast of the city on the Old Raleigh road and serves the city and county as such institutions are wont to do. Its labors are great but much lessened by the numerous private and church institutions supported for charity. Dr. J. C. Anderson is superintendent and physician in charge of this Asylum.

The Girls' Friendly Society is an organization established by the Episcopal Church for girls, "to encourage purity of life, dutifulness to parents, faithfulness in work and thrift," according to one of the by-laws of the society. The secretary of the Girls' Friendly is Miss Ada Turner; the corresponding and recording secretary, Miss Nettie Barnwell; and the treasurer, Mrs. A. Y. Scott. The Executive Board consists of Mesdames Brinkley Snowden, William Somerville, J. A. Evans and A. Y. Scott and Misses Rostand Betts, N. Barnwell, Turner and Montgomery Cooper. The matron is Mrs. Donald MacGillivray. The Society maintains a lodging house on North Main Street for its members who have no homes, and on South Main Street lunch and rest rooms for working women and girls. Good influence is thrown about the members and much done for their social pleasure and uplift. Evening classes are also conducted in which girls employed during the day are able to improve their minds or pursue school studies which were cut off by the urgency for bread-winning.

In 1840 the Shelby County Bible Society was organized for the purpose of distributing bibles and six years later was changed to the Memphis and Shelby County Bible Society. The organization is auxiliary to the American Bible Society and its work extends to all of Tennessee, Mississippi and Arkansas.

The Nineteenth Century Club was founded in 1890 by Mrs. Elise Massey Selden and two years later it was incorporated. Naming the departments of its work will give an idea of the scope of the club's undertakings. These are art, civics and health, children's story hour, current topics, domestic science, education, French, history, music, literature, philanthropy and work for the blind.

It was through the efforts of the Nineteenth Century Club that a matron was placed in the Police Station, that women prisoners might have proper attention; that the Juvenile Court was first agitated and established; that a shop and entertainment were provided for the blind and numerous other benefits, the value of which are felt throughout the city. The present Board of Directors consist of Mesdames Wharton Jones, J. H. Watson, J. S. Ellis, Earl Harris, William Omberg, Battle Malone, A. B. Pittman, Dudley Saunders, W. B. Mitchel, Jr., G. M. Garvey, Percy Finlay and Miss Frances Cole. The officers are Mrs. J. M. McCormack, president; Mrs. R. O. Johnston and Wesley Halliburton, vice-presidents; Mrs. Bolton Smith, recording secretary; Miss Frances Church, corresponding secretary and Miss Lettie Riley, treasurer.

The Teachers League, whose work has already been dwelt upon somewhat in the chapter on Education, was organized by Miss Cora Ashe, who was the first president and has since been made honorary president. The League now has over 250 members and the present officers are: Mrs. M. M. Ward, president; S. L. Ragsdale, vice-president; Emma Rogers, corresponding secretary; Nellie Lunn, recording secretary; Birdie McGrath, treasurer; Charl Field, librarian; Marie Leary, musical director; Roane Waring, Jr., legal adviser; Olyve Jackson, historian.

The Memphis Deaf Mutes Association was founded in October, 1910 and this organization gives benefit and entertainment to people who live in the silent world. The meetings are held in the Y. M. C. A. Building. N. E. Harris is president; Mrs. N. C. Harris, vice-president; John A. Todd, secretary; E. P. Jones, treasurer.

There are several medical associations for the purpose of advancing that profession. Of these the Memphis and Shelby County Medical Society affords profit and social intercourse to its members. They meet in the Odd Fellows Building. W. T. Black is president; J. C. Ayres, vice-president; B. N. Dunavant, secretary.

Many Memphis clubs and some of the most popular have been organized for purely social recreation and are maintained to that end. These are far too numerous to name in sketch of limited length but some of the most popular and best known will be mentioned.

The Chickasaw Guards Club was originally organized in 1874 by the men of that day who made the Chickasaw Guards Military Company so famous. In 1886, after Memphis was on her new road to progress, the Club reorganized under the old charter. The chief promoters of the newly organized club were Captain S. T. Carnes, Lieutenant Kellar Anderson and Sergeant Richard Wright. The club became very popular and many high-class business and social men joined its ranks. The first president of the 1886 club was Colonel H. A. Montgomery and Professor R. O. Prewitt was secretary. The Club has ever retained its high standing. The present officers are: H. H. Crosby, president; J. R. Flippin, vice-president; B. H. Finley, secretary and treasurer and Albert B. Baumberger, assistant secretary. The Directors are B. H. Finley, J. B. Goodbar, S. P. Walker, E. C. Turner, W. G. Thomas, W. A. Bickford, J. D. Martin, H. H. Crosby, J. R. Flippin, L. L. Heiskell.

The Tennessee Club is another social organization for men which is somewhat exclusive and offers comfort and other advantages to its members. This club was organized May 7, 1875, by Colton Green, C. W. Metcalf, I. M. Hill, H. C. Warriner, D. W. Miller, and D. P. Hadden. Colton Green was made president; R. B. Snowden, vice-president; W. M. S. Titus, secretary; H. C. Warinner, treasurer. By the close of the first year of its existence the Tennessee Club had nearly two hundred members. It now has a beautiful home on the corner of North Court Avenue and Second Street, where members meet socially, dine, discuss questions of the times and occasionally entertain their friends with balls or other receptions. The present officers are N. C. Perkins, president; William Ball, vice-president and treasurer; Julian E. Heard, secretary.

The Rex Club is a social club for Jewish men, with high-class club advantages and they have recently moved into an elegant new building on the corner of Dunlap Street and Madison Avenue, where the members enjoy the club privileges and frequently entertain their friends. Abraham Cohn is president of the Rex Club and Leopold Hirsch, secretary.

The Germans have several societies and improvement clubs. One of these, the German Casino Club, organized in 1856, making it the oldest in Memphis. In the Casino the members all speak the German language and one of the objects of the club is to preserve their language and German institutions. Entertainments are frequent and the members of this club have had more share in cultivating taste for good music than is generally known. Among its membership are many of the best business men of Memphis and some of the most progressive in all civic undertakings. The club rooms are situated at 190 Jefferson Avenue. Louis Schumacher is president and L. G. Fritz, secretary.

The German Turn Verein holds its meetings in Germania Hall on Jefferson Avenue. The club has an efficient physical trainer and for many years this organization held precedence in interesting Memphis men and women in physical culture. Gustave A. Lott is president of the society, Otto Rahm, vice-president and G. H. Pfaff, instructor.

The Maennerchor is another German organization that was started in 1871. Its purposes are to perpetuate the German language, German songs and to create sociability among the members. Its founders were Otto Zimmerman, S. Damstadt, P. Kahler, A. Goldsmith, M. Gotlieb, D. Schmivels, and A. Schmivels. The club meets in Germania Hall and its president is Harmon Starkey.

The Country Club has a beautiful country home at Buntyn,

a suburb of Memphis. There the men and women who are fortunate enough to be members enjoy the comfortable clubhouse and grounds. In the house, books, magazines, games, conversation and other social diversions are enjoyed, while the spacious grounds afford out-of-door games. The golf-links especially are good. The president of the Country Club is S. T. Carnes; first vice-president, F. G. Jones; second vice-president, Joseph W. Martin; secretary, Homer K. Jones; treasurer, N. C. Perkins.

In 1857 the Old Folks Society of Shelby County was founded by old Memphis residents who wished to preserve for future generations authentic history of early Memphis. The society gathered numerous valuable records and continued to work until the war between the sections broke out. In 1870 the society reorganized and continued its work for a number of years. In 1874-1875 the members issued a monthly magazine in which are preserved many valuable articles on the early days which will be read with increasing interest as the decades come and go. The society was never so active as during the year of the publication of its paper. In 1880 the Old Folks acquired the possession of Winchester Cemetery and rescued the remnants of that old resting place of the city's early dead and created a fund for its care. In fact, their efforts did much to arouse indignation at ruthless destruction of cemeteries and so brought about legislation in regard to the preservation of cemeteries.

In 1874 the officers of the Old Folks Society were W. B. Waldran, president; J. Halsted, vice-president; J. G. Lonsdale, treasurer; B. Richmond, financial secretary; J. P. Prescott, recording secretary; James D. Davis, historian. These officers and the 150 members have made the people of Memphis their debtors for the invaluable stories, reminiscences and records they have left. Much of the information of the present volume was obtained from the Old Folks Record.

Memphis was one of the first cities of the South to form an association for the perpetuation of Southern history, joining this object to the charitable cause of aiding disabled Confederate soldiers and the widows and orphans of Southern men who gave their lives in the cause. The first society was the "Confederate Relief and Historical Association of the City of Memphis," was organized and incorporated in 1867 and exists to the present day. The Association is comprised of ex-Confederates whose records as soldiers were clean, and their male descendants. The relief duties of the society were soon unnecessary and it became historic only. These men have accumulated many records and manuscripts pertaining to the war, all of which are carefully preserved and much that would have otherwise been lost has been kept for future generations. In its early years the Association had only a few interested members but that small number persisted in having meetings at homes of the members, in discussing events, gathering records, placing true statements of Southern chivalry before the world and in interesting their fellow soldiers of former days.

Officers of the early organization were C. W. Frazer, president; R. B. Spillman, vice-president; R. J. Black, secretary and John T. Willins, treasurer. Colonel Frazer who died in 1897, was succeeded by General George W. Gordon. General Gordon also passed to his reward in 1911.

As the sons became men they took up the work of their fathers and the association is one of interest and enthusiasm with its members of this day. It now has a room in the Shelby County Courthouse and its officers are, Edward Bourne, president; G. B. Malone, first vice-president; J. P. Young, second vice-president; I. N. Rainey, secretary and treasurer.

Immediately after the war a law was made forbidding monuments to heroes or soldiers who died on the Southern side, but Memphis women loved the dead men who had fought for home and every year when spring flowers were in bloom they mingled the youthful blossoms with hundreds of wreaths of evergreen and set apart a day to lay them on the soldiers' graves, at Elmwood. Later the unjust law was repealed and the Confederate Historical Association erected a granite shaft to the dead Confederate soldiers. But the more enduring shaft did not cause the women to cease their work of love and Memorial Day became and has remained a day of patriotic love and reverence of Southern women for Southern soldiers. This work has passed practically to another generation but it is continued no less lovingly and the monument and graves receive the yearly tribute of flowers and evergreen. The day has long since been recognized as a State holiday and Memorial Day is to Southern heart what Decoration Day is to the North. Indeed, Decoration Day was born after Memorial Day.

The association which inaugurated and continues this work is the Ladies Memorial Association. This association is successor to the Southern Mothers, which was organized in 1861 for the purpose of caring for wounded Confederate soldiers. Mrs. Sarah Law was president of that association. When the Federals took Memphis and the work of the Mothers stopped as an organization they nevertheless remained organized and the Mothers continued to work for wounded Confederate soldiers, Mrs. Law and some of the others following the armies to care for the wounded soldiers.

After the war their work was gone so these women turned their attention to perpetuating the memory of the brave dead, though without formal organization. The work of love was performed each year, so the ladies determined to make it perpetual. Accordingly, on May 16, 1889, Mrs. C. W. Frazer made a call at her home and the former Southern Mothers organized under the name of the Ladies Confederate Historical Association, as an auxiliary to the Confederate Historical Association and under the charter of that organization.

Southern Mothers who became active members of the Memorial Association were Mesdames Sarah Law, Flora Turley, W. B. Greenlaw, Phoebe A. Edmonds, Mary E. Cummings, Emily Ball, Mary B. Beecher, M. C. Galloway, Henrietta Bowen and J. H. Humphreys and Miss Betty Yancy. The officers of the new organization were, Mrs. C. W. Frazer, president; Mrs. Luke W. Finlay, secretary; Mrs. Eugene Whitfield, treasurer. When Mrs. Frazer gave place to another active president she was made honorary president for life and this brave woman still works with the Association. Presidents following have been Mesdames Luke E. Wright, Keller Anderson, Hugh L.

Bedford, J. C. McDavitt, Mary E. Wormely and C. B. Bryan. The secretaries have been Mesdames F. T. Edmondson, S. A. Pepper, Thomas Day, L. E. Wright, Ina Murray and Misses Mary Solari and Phoebe Frazer. The treasurers have been Mrs. Kellar Anderson, O. E. Bayliss, J. H. Moyston and Kate Southerland.

The chief work of the Ladies Memorial Association is perpetuating the memory of the Confederate soldiers and to this end money is contributed to monuments all over the South. These ladies built a pavilion in Elmwood to accommodate the speakers, band, etc., on Memorial Day and in conjunction with the Historical Association erected headstones at the graves of the soldiers.

The United Sons of Confederate Veterans is an association active in its work of perpetuation. The present Adjutant General and Chief of Staff of the "Sons" is N. Bedford Forrest, grandson of the illustrious cavalry leader.

There are several Chapters of the Daughters of the Confederacy here, among them the N. Bedford Forrest Chapter, with Mrs. N. Bedford Forrest, president; the Sarah Law Chapter, with Mrs. J. W. Clapp, president and Mrs. E. B. Moseley, secretary; Harvey Mathes Chapter, with Mrs. W. A. Collier, president and Mrs. Earnest Walworth, secretary; and the Mary Latham Chapter, with Mrs. J. L. Manire, president and Mrs. Henry Lipford, Jr., secretary.

On June 10, 1904, Mrs. Virginia Frazer Boyle, that true daughter of a Confederate soldier but still so American that the whole country loves her, organized the Junior Confederate Memorial Association with sixteen children.

The boys over fourteen were organized into a Drum and Fife Corps, under an efficient director, Mr. E. T. Atkins. At the Jamestown Exposition in 1907 this Drum and Fife Corps acted as escort to Company A, Confederate Veterans and during that visit, which was successful from the time they left Memphis until they returned, the corps scored one triumph after another, besides having a glorious trip.

The membership of the J. C. M. A. now numbers over

two hundred. Mrs. Boyle is honorary president; Mrs. P. H. Patton, president; Mrs. J. O. Flautt, vice-president.

In 1885 the Tennessee Equal Suffrage Association was organized in Memphis with Mrs. Elizabeth Lyle Saxon, president. Mrs. Saxon had been an earnest worker in the cause of Equal Suffrage for many years. She was succeeded in 1886 by Mrs. Lide Meriwether, another veteran worker for this cause. These two pioneers, both still living can remember when it was a brand of disgrace to stand up for the equal political and social life of women with men. Mrs. Meriwether remained president until 1899, when Mrs. Elise Massey Selden was elected to the office and Mrs. Meriwether elected honorary president for life. Mrs. Martha Allen became president in 1906 and she too has worked long for the cause. The present officers are Mrs. M. M. Betts, president; Mrs. E. W. Bowser, vice-president; Mrs. A. Apperson, treasurer; Mrs. J. H. Reilly, recording secretary and Mrs. J. D. Allen, corresponding secretary.

The musical clubs and their work have already been partly discussed in the chapter on Arts. They have been of great benefit both to their members and to Memphis at large. Of these the Beethoven is the most important and to this club is much of the musical culture of Memphis due. The charter members of the Beethoven Club were Mrs. Elizabeth Cowan Latta, Miss Isabella Gertz (now Mrs. A. J. Thus), Mrs. E. T. Tobey and Miss Mary Duke (now Mrs. A. H. Wisner). The present officers are Mrs. Eugene Douglass, president; Mrs. E. T. Tobey, Mrs. A. D. DuBose and Mrs. L. Y. Mason, vice-presidents; Mrs. William H. Barnes, corresponding secretary; Mrs. E. W. Taylor, recording secretary and Miss Annie Dickson, treasurer.

Mrs. Ben Parker has charge of the monthly concerts for the year 1912 and these promise to be as much or more pleasure and benefit to the public as were those of 1911.

There is also a Junior Beethoven Club, this organization coming into being principally through the efforts of Mrs. Napoleon Hill. This music-loving woman, who was for eight years president of the Senior Club, is known as the "Mother" of the younger club and she has done a great deal to encourage young people to cultivate their musical talents. She gives an annual gold medal as a reward to successful musicians of this club. After the club was on a substantial basis Mrs. Hill withdrew from active work and Mrs. Jason Walker became the active leader. Mrs. Chapman followed her and both these ladies were untiring in furthering the interests of the club and club members. This club is the largest musical organization for children in this country and perhaps in the world. It has over a hundred members, divided into chapters which meet each week in convenient neighborhoods to be trained by their leaders. The Mary Hill Chapter, named for the founder, is the governing chapter of the club and meets once a month for business. At this same meeting all the chapters meet and have a monthly concert. The junior officers of the club are: President, Juliet Graham; first vice-president, Avaligne Edgington; second vice-president, Jennie Evans; third vice-president, Marcelle Talley; treasurer, Ruth Gothard; recording secretary, Nell Lewis; corresponding secretary, Rebecca Spicer. The chapters, with their respective leaders, are as follows: Mary Hill Chapter, Mrs. W. P. Chapman and Juliet Graham, leaders; Mozart Chapter, Mrs. Rogers McCallum, leader; Haydn Chapter, Mrs. Stella Graham, leader; Chopin Chapter, Miss Alma Ramsey, leader; Ernest Hutcheson Chapter, Misses Louise Faxon and Elizabeth Wills, leaders; Arne Oldberg Chapter, Miss May Maer and Mrs. W. P. Chapman, leaders; Schumann Chapter, Miss Annie Dickson, leader; Symphony Chapters, Mrs. Ben Hunter and Miss Zoa DeShazo, leaders.

In 1909 the Memphis Symphony Orchestra Association was organized, composed of fifty professional musicians. Their object is to encourage musical talent and musical taste in Memphis and to give to the city each year a symphony orchestra. This association, in addition to the orchestra, presents vocal and instrumental artists. Some of the great musicians already brought by the Symphony Orchestra are Madame Louise Homer; Madame Johanna Gadski; Mrs. Francis Macmillan, violinist; Signor Alassandro Bonci; also the New York Symphony Orchestra of fifty players and four soloists, conducted by Walter Damrosche. The symphonies of this organization are all star entertainments and certainly do credit to the conductors, as their large attendance does to the taste of Memphis.

Civic clubs perform an important function in creating city pride and activity for city betterment. On November 7, 1908, The Civic Progress League of Memphis was organized. The object of this League, as set forth in the first section of the Rules and Regulations, is to provide "the improvement and betterment of Memphis in respect to rendering more beautiful her streets, homes and environment, to improve sanitary conditions, to render home life and conditions more comfortable and in providing outdoor recreation and sports for the better development of young children."

The Civic League has four departments,—Civic Improvement, Sanitary Science, Domestic Science and Children.

The following officers were appointed: J. P. Young, president; Mrs. H. C. Myers, first vice-president; Joseph R. Williams, second vice-president; Mrs. J. M. McCormack, third vice-president; Mrs. Wallace James, recording secretary; Mary V. Little, corresponding secretary and Mrs. J. W. Pumphrey, treasurer. The Governing Board comprised Joseph R. Williams, chairman; Mrs. M. M. Betts and Mrs. F. M. Guthrie.

The four departments were thus assigned: Civic Improvement—Judge L. B. McFarland, chairman. This includes Landscape Architecture, Shade-trees and Flowers. Sanitary Science—Dr. B. F. Turner, chairman. This includes Hygienic Laundries, Tuberculosis, Sanitary Groceries, Public and Personal Hygiene and professional Nursing. Domestic Science—Mrs. H. C. Myers, chairman. This includes Housekeeper's Club, House Furnishing and Interior Decorations, Delicatessen (prepared foods), Cookery and Dietetics.

Children—Mrs. M. M. Betts, chairman. This includes Fresh Air Parks, Playgrounds and Physical Culture. There have been many changes in this roster since organization.

A city as active as Memphis in a business way naturally has numerous business clubs. Of these the Bureau of Publicity and Development is a great factor in furthering the business of the city and in bringing new business to and within her borders. The following officers and working members are enough to prove the efficiency of this organization:

J. N. Cornatzar, chairman; F. W. Faxon, first vice-chairman; J. L. Lancaster, second vice-chairman; S. B. Anderson, D. M. Armstrong, O. C. Armstrong, H. W. Brennan, S. L. Calhoun, Sol Coleman, Carrol P. Cooper, E. B. LeMaster, L. W. Dutro, John W. Farley, F. N. Fisher, A. C. Floyd, Jacob Goldsmith, G. B. Harper, R. L. Jordan, C. P. J. Mooney, B. L. Mallory, H. C. Pfeiffer, Chas. A. Price, W. H. Russe, I. Samelson, T. H. Tutwiler, W. A. Turner, F. C. Johnson, W. F. Meath, J. K. James, S. H. Stout, R. E. Buchanan, J. S. Warren, John Parham, M. S. Binswanger, J. H. Hines, E. S. Sutton, Joe Isele, M. H. Rosenthal, John W. McClure, John M. Tuther, L. M. Stratton, J. F. Ramier.

The Business Men's Club has a beautiful building on Monroe Avenue, where its members enjoy social as well as business advantages. The work of this club for Memphis welfare is inestimable. The officers are: S. M. Neely, president; W. P. Phillips, first vice-president; A. L. Parker, second vice-president; James F. Hunter, treasurer; John M. Tuther, secretary. The Directors are: S. M. Neely, D. H. Crump, Calvin Graves, J. F. Hunter, A. L. Parker, M. G. Evans, C. J. Haase, W. P. Phillips, H. C. Pfeiffer and William White.

The Builders' Exchange, organized in 1899, is also a power in the Memphis business world. Its officers are Charles R. Miller, president; F. L. McKnight, first vice-president; J. E. Walden, second vice-president; J. W. Willingham, treasurer; Stuart H. Ralph, secretary; Miss Frances A. Taylor, assistant secretary. The directors are, L. S. Akers, I. N. Chambers, R. F. Creson, D. M. Crawford, F. S. Denton, H. J. Bartl, William M. Fry, P. A. Gates, W. T. Hudson and L. T. Lindsey. The headquarters of this Exchange is in the Goodwyn Building.

There is also an Insurance Exchange of Memphis, of which W. A. Bickford is president and Wm. F. Dunbar, secretary. Insurance has also become a business science and Memphis is not behind in handling this science.

March 26, 1860, the Chamber of Commerce was established

in Memphis, Thomas W. Hunt was made president and John S. Toof, secretary. Their first regular meeting was held August 24, 1860 in the Southern Express Building. This organization promised to be a power in the business of Memphis but the war between the sections interfered with its purposes. After the war they reorganized and did a great deal to further the business interests of the city, helping as no other force in having unjust carpet-bag laws repealed and stimulating a healthful business enterprise. The Chamber had several backsets from the calamities that visited the city and in 1878 it was disorganized.

In 1883 the Merchants Exchange was established with nearly 100 charter members. Since the disruption of the Chamber of Commerce a business organization was needed by merchants, manufacturers and other business men, that they might further the business interests of the city and have a means of reaching the Legislature and the public. As much of the progress of a city is built on the work of its business organizations the Merchants Exchange became a very important function from its beginning and its influence has never ceased, although it has many descendants, other business associations, all looking after the business and general improvement of the city.

The present officers of the Merchants Exchange are W. W. Simmons, president; M. M. Bosworth, vice-president; Nat S. Graves, secretary; S. M. Williamson, treasurer. The Directors are E. C. Buchanan, G. F. McGregor, W. C. Johnson, John Myers, S. M. Williamson, A. G. Perkins, J. B. Edgar, Julien L. Brode.

The Memphis Cotton Exchange was established in 1873, and, as its name implies, is the Exchange for the cotton men. This Exchange is of course a vastly important one and controls the biggest staple of our cotton country. Its force is felt through the entire business of Memphis and far beyond the city, throughout the country. In its early years the Cotton Exchange erected a building on the corner of Madison and Second Streets which was for a long time a pride of the city, but as styles change in clothing, so buildings become antiquated and the once proud exchange building became "old-timey" and inefficient, so it was torn down to give place to an elegant modern "sky-scraper," which not only houses the Cotton Exchange in commodious and elegant rooms, but many offices, a large club and numerous stores.

The officers of the Cotton Exchange are F. G. Barton, president; C. W. Butler, Gwynne Yerger and John Phillips, vice-presidents; T. O. Vinton, treasurer; Henry Hotter, secretary and superintendent. The Directors are John Phillips, Jr., J. F. Smithwick, M. J. Hexter, W. F. Meath, Carroll P. Cooper, E. G. Gibbons, C. A. Lacey.

The Lumberman's Club is an organization very useful to the many lumbermen here and abroad and of course furthers the interests of the lumber trade to a very great extent. Its officers are F. B. Robertson, president; C. B. Dudley, first vice-president; Phil A. Ryan, second vice-president; Robert T. Cooper, secretary and treasurer. The Directors are R. J. Wiggs, A. N. Thompson, C. W. Holmes, S. W. Nickey and J. D. Allen.

As Memphis has grown to be a manufacturing center it was necessary for her and her manufacturers to have a business organization, and the Manufacturers' Association of Memphis was organized in 1912. This Association promises to build Memphis as no other organization has done, by devoting its energies entirely to the manufacturing interests. The officers are S. B. Anderson, president; George R. James, first vice-president and treasurer; J. T. Willingham, second vice-president; John M. Tuther, secretary. The Governing Board is composed of Frank R. Reed, Silas Riggs, H. P. Boynton, Milton H. Hunt, J. E. Stark, Owen Lily, C. P. J. Mooney, J. H. DuBose, T. J. Clark, H. O. True, L. D. Falls, W. W. Simmons, C. B. Clark, L. P. James, Thos. R. Winfield.

Most important among the civic bodies which have from time to time sprung up in Memphis has been the City Club. In all municipal corporations there is need for a body, independent in action and free from political motive, which can operate as a sort of balance wheel in the machinery of government and aid without antagonizing the officials charged with municipal administration. Such a body is the City Club of Memphis. Since its organization its influence has been only for good.

Its organization was brought about in the following way:

On Saturday, the 11th of May, 1907, the following gentlemen, at the request of Dr. R. B. Maury, lunched together at Luehrmann's: H. M. Neely, J. M. Goodbar, Jno. R. Pepper, W. H. Bates, Bolton Smith, H. L. Armstrong, Jas. S. Robinson, Dr. R. B. Maury.

A temporary organization was effected; H. M. Neely, chairman; Bolton Smith, secretary. Organization of bodies of citizens interested in municipal affairs of other cities was considered. The records of the City Club of Cincinnati, Ohio, seem to have interested the meeting most. Result: It was decided to organize a similar organization to be called the City Club of Memphis.

Saturday, May 25, 1907, the gentlemen lunched together in the private dining room of the Royal Cafe; the attendance had increased to about twenty in number. The City Club was organized and the following officers elected: Dr. R. B. Maury, president; Jno. R. Pepper, vice-president; Jas. S. Robinson, second vice-president; Geo. R. James, treasurer; Bolton Smith, secretary; W. H. Bates, member board of governors; J. M. Goodbar, member board of governors.

The officers of the club and the last two gentlemen named constituted the Governors. The objects of the club, as stated at organization was to bring together frequently men who believe in the complete separation of party politics from the administration of all local public affairs, in order that, by friendly acquaintance, exchange of views and united activities, intelligent and effective coöperation in the work for good government in Memphis and Shelby County may be secured.

Having affected an organization the Club lost no time in getting to work. It has met regularly every Saturday at luncheon since the election of its officers, and the membership has now increased to about three hundred. The custom of the club is to invite from time to time to meet with it, those persons most interested in the matters under consideration, and also to call into conference at these meetings citizens, promi-

Richard P. [illegible]

THE NEW YORK
PUBLIC LIBRARY

ASTOR, LENOX
TILDEN FOUNDATIONS

nent in business or professional life, and to carefully consider and discuss all subjects before final action.

One of the chief, early subjects considered was the Commission Form of Government for the City of Memphis, and the effect upon the municipality of the Legislative Acts of 1905 and 1907, fully treated elsewhere in this history. The momentus question was frequently debated before the club both by the members and by the friends of the measure, and was finally happily brought about as a great municipal reform.

The club was also in sympathy with the Front Foot Assessment Plan of paving the streets and took an active interest in its development.

It was also responsible for the formation of the Bureau of Municipal Research, the story of which will be given following this narrative.

The City Club realized in the autumn of 1910 that the invasion of the Memphis trading territory by the boll weevil constituted a great menace to the prosperity of the city as well as the surrounding country, and made it imperative that the farmers prepare themselves for crop diversification. For the purpose of aiding this movement the Club, in co-operation with the U. S. Government acting through Dr. Seaman A. Knapp of the Department of Agriculture, raised $5,000.00 for the purpose of establishing the Boys' Corn Club work in the Memphis territory.

The City Club has considered and acted upon practically all of the important municipal questions coming before the city government or the people of Memphis for solution from the time it was organized until now. Among others we will mention:

Street and alley cleaning and drainage, street railroads, city streets, normal school, poll taxes, errors in public inscriptions, weights and measures, amendment to constitution of Tennessee, changes in the revenue law, public service commission bill, Turner anti-fee bill, Memphis street railway franchises, Madison Avenue paving, turnpike expenditures of Shelby County, purchase of the Tri-state fair grounds, disposal of Turnpike funds turned over to the city for street purposes, tuberculosis, Tri-state Audubon Society, smoke nuisance, new state constitution for Tennessee, new Memphis bridge across the Mississippi, law enforcement, house screening, plans of Circuit Court judge for reduction of jury expenses, and numerous other minor matters.

The present officers of the City Club are: Dr. R. B. Maury, honorary president; C. C. Hanson, president; R. O. Johnson, first vice-president; J. Z. George, second vice-president; E. O. Gillican, secretary; Abe Goodman, treasurer. Directors: C. C. Hanson, R. O. Johnston, J. Z. George, Abe Goodman, J. M. Goodbar, C. F. Farnsworth, E. O. Gillican.

The Bureau of Municipal Research is an off-shoot of the City Club. The conception originated with Dr. R. B. Maury, president of the City Club, who, in the fall of 1908, became interested in the work of the New York Bureau of Municipal Research. Upon his invitation Dr. W. H. Allen, director of the New York Bureau, visited Memphis, and at a dinner given at the Business Men's Club on December 5, 1908, explained the purposes and methods of that organization. As a result of this meeting a group of interested citizens invited the New York Bureau to make a brief study of the business procedure and methods of the City of Memphis. In accordance with this request, a preliminary survey was undertaken by a well-known New York investigator, and a report thereon submitted on February 9, 1909, which indicated the advisability of a more extensive study and outlined a definite program of work to cover a period of six months.

It was the unanimous decision of the men interested that the work should be continued as outlined in the report, and a committee of fifty was formed, the members of which pledged themselves to provide the necessary funds. The following officers were appointed:

President, Dr. R. B. Maury; vice-president, Albert S. Caldwell; secretary, W. A. Buckner. Executive Committee: Cyrus Garnsey, Jr., chairman; Geo. R. James, Caruthers Ewing, R. Brinkley Snowden, Jas. S. Robinson.

The purposes of the bureau are thus stated in the announcement made at its organization:

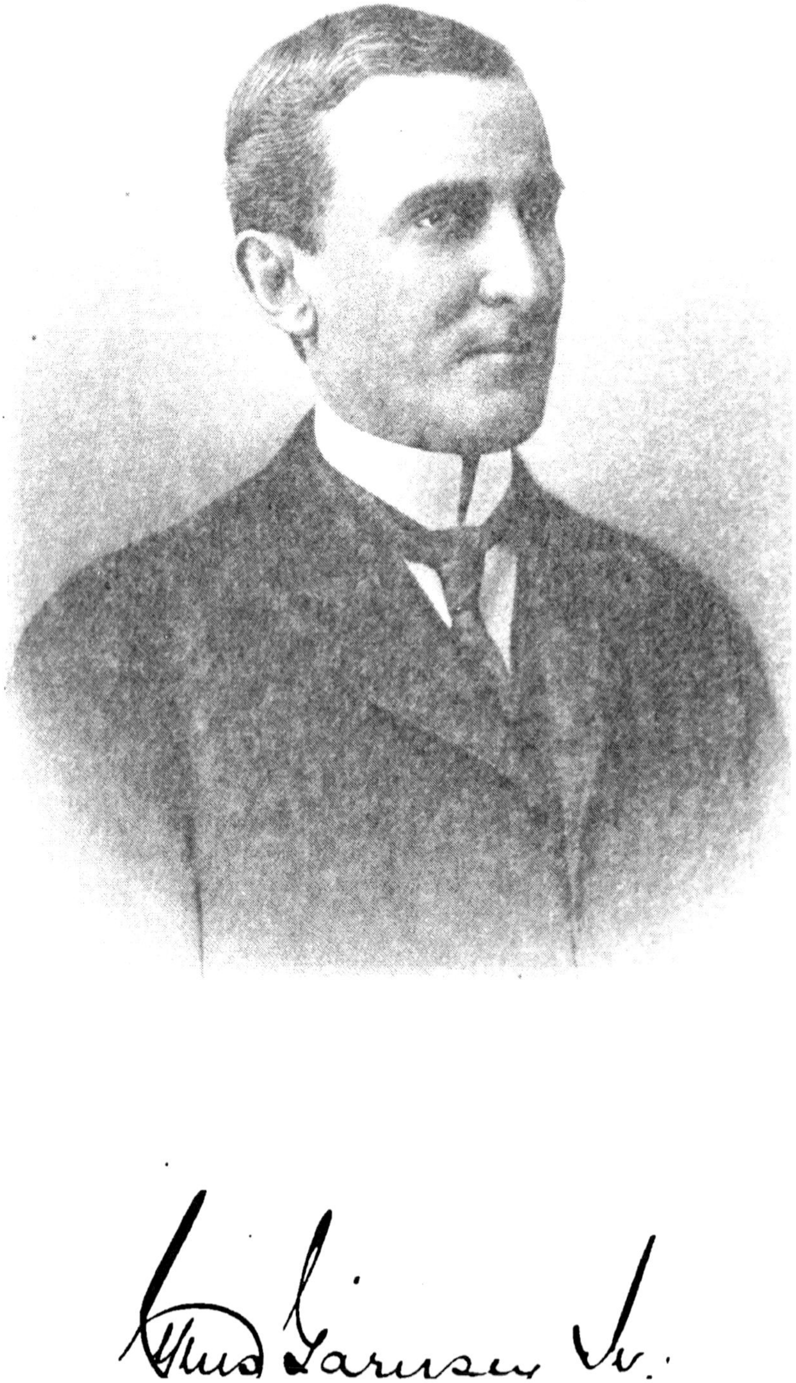

THE NEW YORK
PUBLIC LIBRARY

ASTOR, LENOX
TILDEN FOUNDATIONS

"To serve Memphis as a non-partisan and scientific agency of citizen inquiry, which shall collect, classify and interpret the facts regarding the powers, duties, limitations, and administrative problems of each department of the city and county government and public school systems; to make such information available to public officials and to citizens, in order that inefficient methods of administration may be eliminated, and efficient methods encouraged; and to promote the development of a constructive program for the city, county and schools that shall be based upon adequate knowledge and consideration of community needs."

Work was promptly begun and a systematic investigation prosecuted, and in October, 1910, the executive committee published an elaborate report entitled: "Memphis, a Critical Study of Some Phases of its Municipal Government, with Constructive Suggestions for Betterment in Organization and Administrative Methods," an impersonal and critical analysis of public affairs as then existing and a clearly marked way to improvement.

In March, 1910, the Committee was reorganized by the City Club and was constituted as follows: C. C. Hanson, chairman; J. P. Young, vice-chairman; Marcus Haase, treasurer; C. F. Farnsworth, Bolton Smith, Thomas F. Gailor.

The Bureau was incorporated in December, 1910, at the instance of the City Club, thus making it independent of the Club and its present officers and directors are: C. C. Hanson, president; H. M. Neely, vice-president; R. O. Johnston, treasurer; E. O. Gillican, secretary. Directors: R. B. Maury, Thomas F. Gailor, J. P. Young, H. M. Neely, C. F. Farnsworth, R. O. Johnston, D. Canale, Jos. Isele, I. N. Chambers, C. C. Hanson.

Some work done by the Bureau has been, after investigation, to install an adequate system of accounting for the Memphis Board of Education.

Also to install a like system of accounting for the Shelby County Board of Education.

The Bureau, at the request of Mayor E. H. Crump and Commissioner Riechman, coöperated with the city officials in the preparation of the budget of expenditures for the year

1910 and conferred with them concerning the necessary steps to be taken to correct the defects in the then existing accounting methods of the city government. This was a work of great labor and care.

Of the report on city finances made by the City Commission in August, 1911, Mayor Crump wrote to the Chairman of the Municipal Research, August 24:

"Have you read the last city report, showing in detail the work of each department, and which was formulated along the lines suggested by the Bureau of Municipal Research?

"Of course, we realize that this report is susceptible of improvement, but in spite of that it is a great improvement over anything heretofore issued, and undoubtedly the Bureau of Municipal Research has been the means of bringing about a more definite statement for the information of the taxpayers and public generally."

The Memphis Bureau of Municipal Research is still a live organization and ready to take part in municipal and county improvements in administration whenever the occasion may require.

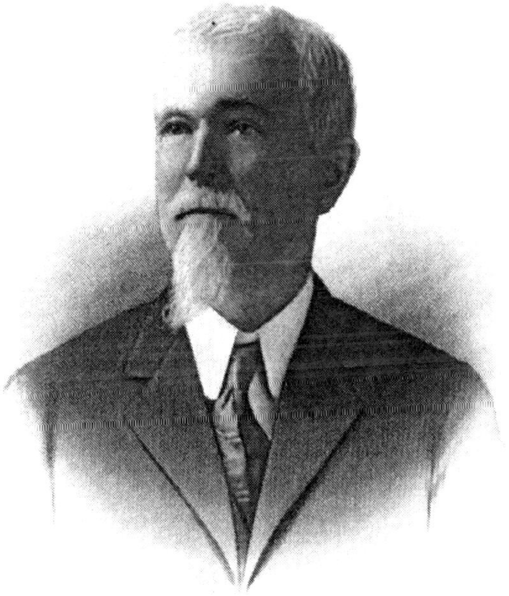

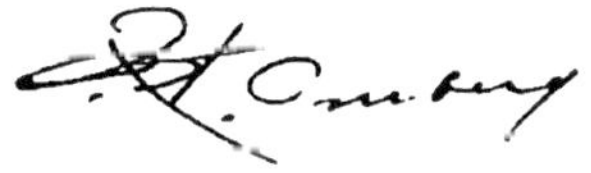

## ER XXVI

### and Insurance

T

...phis was curr...
...rolina and G...
... not equal to ...
... East or bough...
... only at a disco...
... dollar bill was ...
... cent pieces a...
... halves, making

impo...
lishe...
th...
was...
d...
it a...

and w...
much ...
Rawling...
in this ...
Mr. Raw...
young city ... sed to bear t...
man was s... streets was on the d...
election in ... Two negro men carri... 
chair on th... to vote and he cast his vote for
candidate ... ected and he lived long enough

*Vedder

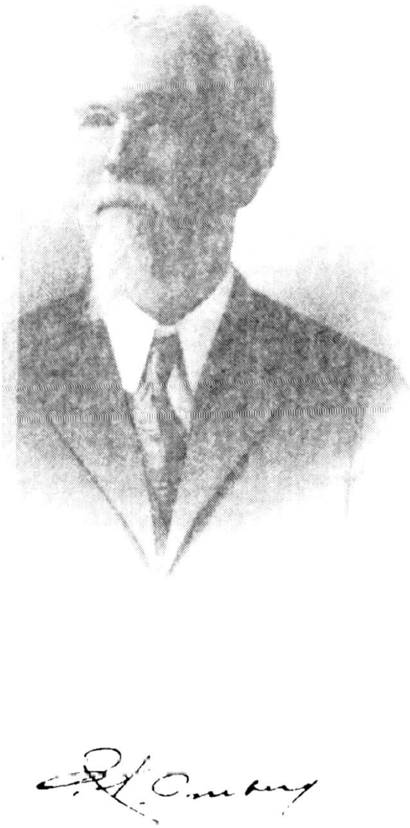

# CHAPTER XXVI

## Banks and Insurance

THE first money used in Memphis was currency of Tennessee, North Carolina, South Carolina and Georgia.* This was depreciated currency and not equal to United States coin and when Southern people went East or bought goods from the East their money could be used only at a discount of 25 to 30 per cent. To make small change a dollar bill was cut into four equal parts for quarters or twenty-five cent pieces and sometimes even these were again divided into halves, making "bits" or twelve and a half cents.

As the population grew in numbers and Memphis in business importance a bank was felt to be a necessity and one was established in 1834, under the charter of the State. This was called the Farmers and Merchants Bank, and its first acting manager was Ike Rawlings, that intrepid old citizen who, after once agreeing to the advancement of Memphis did all he could to bring it about.

This bank was a big stride for Memphis in those early days and was a source of pride with business men and the theme of much conversation in its beginning. After the death of Mr. Rawlings, Robert Lawrence was elected as president and served in this capacity to the satisfaction of the people. The death of Mr. Rawlings was a great loss to Memphis but his work for the young city has never ceased to bear fruit. The last time the old man was seen on the streets was on the day after the Presidential election in 1840. Two negro men carried him to the polls in a chair on that day to vote and he cast his vote for Harrison. His candidate was elected and he lived long enough to rejoice over

*Vedder.

the fact. He never saw another election and passed from life just when Memphis was fairly beginning her political history.

The president of this bank had the confidence of all the people, from the most intelligent business man to the most ignorant slave. Slaves in those days had much more liberty than in later days, when they had become a theme of bitterness between the sections of the country. Many of them had bank accounts and they were generally encouraged by their owners to save their earnings. It is recorded that Marcus B. Winchester opened a regular account with all of his slaves, charging them with their purchase money, food, clothing, etc., and crediting them with all of their labor, with the view to their buying their freedom.

Before the establishment of a bank almost everybody in Memphis was in debt and the rule was credit with long time, because money was loaned at such exorbitant rates, sometimes as high as six per cent a month.

The financial panic of 1837 brought distress to Tennessee and other Western States because of the unstable currency and "wild-cat" banks, with their unsteady and insufficient capital. Colonel Keating says of this time: "The whole financial system of the country was one of mere paper, promises to pay, the solvency of which depended upon the demand for payment being put off as long as possible. Speculation was rife, and the speculators who were to be found among all classes, were wild in their calculations as to the near future and all values were inflated beyond the ability of a generation to realize. This structure of paper yielded to the first breath of the storm and wholly disappeared, leaving people who had trusted to it and who had been the victims of its greed, rapacity and thieving operations, ruined and in despair."

In 1838 the Legislature provided for a State bank that was to have a main bank in Nashville with branches in different parts of the State. This bank was "Established in the name of and for the benefit of the State," and "the faith and credit of the State were pledged for the support of the bank and to supply any deficiency in the funds therein specifically pledged and to give indemnity for all losses arising from such deficiency."*

This bank had a capital of $5,000,000, with the State the sole stockholder. It was established in order to prevent a recurrence of the panic of the year before and Colonel Keating called this bank the "anchor of the State." It was named, the Bank of Tennessee.

After the establishment of this institution confidence was again restored in Tennessee and other banks were established in Memphis. By 1841 bank accommodations here were quite equal to wants of the trade and besides the State bank privileges Memphis had the Union, the Planters and the Farmers and Merchants banks, all having assets seven times greater than their liabilities.

In 1848 the Farmers and Merchants Bank closed its doors and almost caused a riot in the city, but this was kept down by the officers and peaceable citizens and affairs were afterward adjusted by the bank so that depositors were not entire losers. After this Memphis got on such a firm banking basis that when the financial panic of the whole country came in 1857 Memphis felt it but slightly and her prosperous condition continued until the breaking out of the war in 1861. During the four-year period that followed there was such a general disruption of Memphis banks that after the conflict it was necessary to reestablish a banking basis. Several banks were established and in some of them people deposited all the savings they could scrape together or save from necessary expenses in order to obtain a new start after their severe war losses.

In the latter part of 1865 the banking capital amounted to $400,000, and by 1870 it had increased to $1,700,781, still $300,000 short of what it had been in 1860. But in 1867, the Gayoso Savings Institution, and in 1872, the Memphis Savings Bank failed, bringing disaster and discouragement to many who had been saving all they could possibly spare in order to get a new start or to provide for contingencies.

After the yellow fever epidemic of 1873 the Freedman's

*Quoted by Keating.

Savings Bank collapsed, the First National Bank closed for a short while, the Union and Planters, the German National and the DeSoto Banks all had heavy runs and narrow escapes but they all succeeded in escaping failure. After the disastrous epidemics of 1878 and 1879 we know how Memphis fell off in business as well as in every way and for twenty years she was no longer a city but the Taxing District of Shelby County. This period of enforced economy and good management of the authorities brought the city to her own again and long before the close of the century good faith was established and numerous banks were running on a firm basis.

In 1893 the Memphis banks were on such a firm footing that when the financial panic of that year spread over the country Memphis was one of the few cities that had no bank failures nor suspensions. None of the Memphis banks even limited its payments during that trying period and the report of 1894 showed that there had been no change in any of the nine commercial banks with capital and surplus of over $6,500,000 and eight savings banks, with capital and surplus of over half a million dollars. Each of these had declared regular dividends. As one of the chief indications of a city's success is shown in the prosperity of her banks this spoke well for Memphis and gave confidence at home and abroad. The years following emphasized this stability and the combined capital of the banks in 1897 was $3,392,500.[*]

Memphis banking in the new century is without any striking history which is proof of its steady prosperity. There have been one or two bank waverings and suspensions for a short while but these have been rectified and the depositors' interests secured.

Memphis furnishes millions of dollars for handling the cotton crops and other business branches are all well supplied.

As sufficient yearly bank clearings have been scattered all through the general history of this work to show their importance and increase, such figures will not be reiterated here. The Memphis Clearing House was established in 1879, during a time of

[*]Report of Merchant's Exchange.

general business depression, and its reports have frequently been given in other chapters to show the increase in business. The Memphis Clearing House Association is now situated at 32 South Main Street. E. L. Price is president; J. D. McDowell, vice-president, and James Nathan, manager.

The present banks of Memphis are:

*Chickasaw Bank and Trust Company*, incorporated in 1902. George E. Neuhardt, president; T. J. Turley, vice-president; S. L. Sparks, cashier.

*National City Bank;* J. T. Willingham, president; W. Haliburton, J. Marlin Speed, vice-presidents; W. H. Kyle, cashier.

*Commercial Trust and Savings Bank;* Abe Goodman, president; Lem Banks, vice-president; Simon Jacobs, second vice-president; Dwight M. Armstrong, cashier.

*Continental Savings Bank;* Rhea P. Cary, receiver.

*First National Bank*, organized 1864. J. A. Omberg, president; S. H. Brooks, vice-president; P. S. Smithwick, active vice-president; C. Q. Harris, cashier.

*Germania Savings Bank and Trust Company;* Harry Cohn, president; Walter B. McLean, vice-president; J. A. Goodman, cashier.

*Manhattan Savings Bank and Trust Company*, organized 1885. Hirsch Morris, president; James S. Robinson, vice-president; James Nathan, cashier.

*Mercantile Bank of Memphis*, incorporated 1883. C. Hunter Raine, president; J. M. Fowlkes, Luke E. Wright, vice-presidents; Claude D. Anderson, cashier.

*North Memphis Savings Bank*, incorporated 1904. Anthony Walsh, president; Joseph Rose, vice-president; Mortimer G. Bailey, cashier.

*People's Savings Bank and Trust Company;* S. B. Anderson, chairman of board; J. H. Smith, president; S. M. Neely, vice-president; J. T. Wellford, second vice-president; Horace N. Smith, secretary and treasurer; A. C. Landstreet, assistant secretary and treasurer.

*State National Bank of Memphis;* Geo. R. James, president;

Cyrus Garnsey, Jr., and Frederick Orgill, active vice-presidents; M. G. Buckingham, cashier.

*State Savings Bank*, incorporated 1887. J. W. Proudfit, president; Philip Fransioli, vice-president; J. V. Montedonico, cashier.

*Union Savings Bank and Trust Company*, organized 1895, J. A. Ormberg, president; H. Bensdorf, vice-president; Noland Fontaine, Jr., cashier.

*Bank of Commerce and Trust Company;* T. O. Vinton, president; R. Brinkley Snowden, vice-president; E. L. Rice, vice-president; James H. Fisher, secretary; S. J. Shepherd, trust officer; L. S. Gwyn, cashier; G. A. Bone, auditor.

*Central Bank and Trust Company;* N. C. Perkins, president; J. F. Mathias, vice-president; J. C. Ottinger, cashier.

*Fidelity Trust Company;* Charles W. Thompson, president; D. D. Saunders, vice-president; P. Galbreath, cashier.

*Memphis State Bank and Trust Company;* W. J. Smith, president; J. S. McTighe, vice-president; E. E. Becker, cashier.

*Phoenix Trust Company*, organized 1911. John K. Mills, president; Marcus L. Saunders, vice-president; M. Orin Carter, secretary and treasurer.

*Security Bank and Trust Company*, incorporated 1885. O B. Polk, president; Theodore Reed, R. S. Taylor, C. T. McCraw, vice-presidents; W. R. Cross, cashier.

*Solvent Savings Bank and Trust Company* (colored), incorporated 1906. J. C. Martin, president; Thos. H. Hayes, H. H. Pace, J. W. Sanford, vice-presidents; Harry H. Pace, cashier.

*Fraternal Savings Bank* (colored), incorporated 1909. J. Jay Scott, president; R. J. Petty, H. C. Purnell, vice-presidents; A. F. Ward, cashier.

*Union and Planters Bank and Trust Company;* S. P. Read, president; J. R. Pepper, J. F. Hunter, Frank F. Hill, vice-presidents; J. D. McDowell, cashier.

*United States Trust and Savings Bank;* G. R. James, president; W. H. Wood, Miles G. Buckingham, vice-presidents; W. W. Stevenson, cashier

Steamboat accidents made life-insurance companies popular

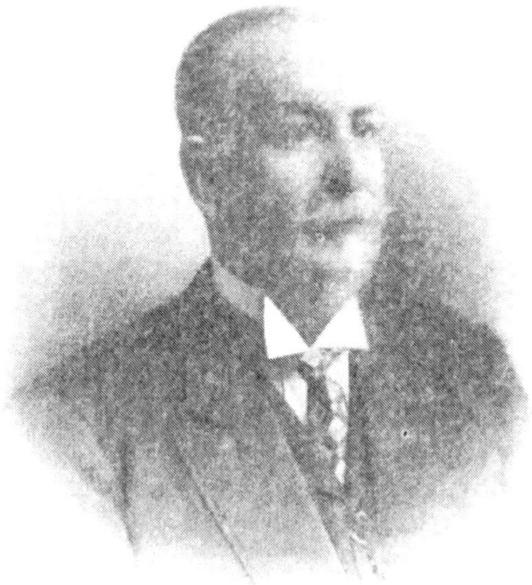

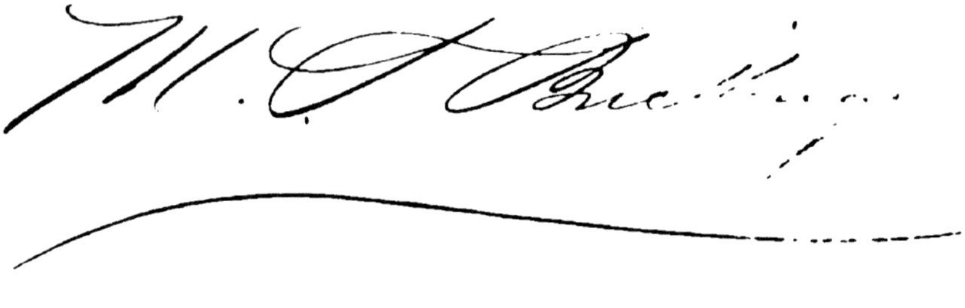

Cyrus Garnsey, Jr., and Frederick Orgill, active vice-presidents; M. G. Buckingham, cashier.

*State Savings Bank*, incorporated 1887. J. W. Proudfit, president; Philip Fransioli, vice-president; J. V. Montedonico, cashier.

*Union Savings Bank and Trust Company*, organized 1895. J. A. Ormberg, president; H. Bensdorf, vice-president; Noland Fontaine, Jr., cashier.

*Bank of Commerce and Trust Company;* T. O. Vinton, president; R. Brinkley Snowden, vice-president; E. L. Rice, vice-president; James H. Fisher, secretary; S. J. Shepherd, trust officer; L. S. Gwyn, cashier; G. A. Bone, auditor.

*Central Bank and Trust Company;* N. C. Perkins, president; J. F. Mathias, vice-president; J. C. Ottinger, cashier.

*Fidelity Trust Company;* Charles W. Thompson, president; D. D. Saunders, vice-president; P. Galbreath, cashier.

*Memphis State Bank and Trust Company;* W. J. Smith, president; J. S. McTighe, vice-president; E. E. Becker, cashier.

*Phoenix Trust Company*, organized 1911. John K. Mills, president; Marcus L. Saunders, vice-president; M. Orin Carter, secretary and treasurer.

*Security Bank and Trust Company*, incorporated 1885. O. B. Polk, president; Theodore Reed, R. S. Taylor, C. T. McCraw, vice-presidents; W. R. Cross, cashier.

*Solvent Savings Bank and Trust Company* (colored), incorporated 1906. J. C. Martin, president; Thos. H. Hayes, H. H. Pace, J. W. Sanford, vice-presidents; Harry H. Pace, cashier.

*Fraternal Savings Bank* (colored), incorporated 1909. J. Jay Scott, president; R. J. Petty, H. C. Purnell, vice-presidents; A. F. Ward, cashier.

*Union and Planters Bank and Trust Company;* S. P. Read, president; J. R. Pepper, J. F. Hunter, Frank F. Hill, vice-presidents; J. D. McDowell, cashier.

*United States Trust and Savings Bank;* G. R. James, president; W. H. Wood, Miles G. Buckingham, vice-presidents; W. W. Stevenson, cashier.

Steamboat accidents made life-insurance companies popular

*M. T. Buckingham.*

in Memphis as early as the thirties, but no Memphis insurance firm was formed until 1856, when the Home Insurance Company was incorporated. After this they continued to be added at intervals, but not rapidly until after the war. After that insurance of all kinds multiplied in the country and Memphis had her share of local companies. By 1887 there were thirteen substantial firms, with capital stocks as follows: Arlington Insurance Company, $100,000; Bluff City Insurance Company, $150,000; Factors' Fire Insurance Company, $250,000; Factors' Mutual Insurance Company, $130,000; Hernando Insurance Company, $150,000; Memphis City Fire and General Insurance Company, $250,000; Home Insurance Company, $100,000; People's Insurance Company, $200,000; Phoenix Fire and Marine Insurance Company, $150,000; Planters' Insurance Company, $150,000; Vanderbilt Mutual Insurance Company, $100,000; Germania Insurance Company, $150,000; Citizens' Insurance Company, $100,000.

The popularity and growth of this sort of protection since then has been phenomenal and at present there are over six hundred insurance companies represented in Memphis. These are general, accident, burglary, casualty, liability, fire, marine, guaranty, fraternal (Woodmen of the World), lightning, plate glass, sick, life, tornado, vessel, automobile, rental, and all kinds known to the science of Insurance. Insurance inspection is forced and this is under the charge of the Tennessee Inspection Bureau, William C. Sweetman, manager, located in the Tennessee Trust Building.

# CHAPTER XXVII

## Commerce and Manufactures

THE commerce of Memphis has been so generally treated in the municipal chapters of this book, as commerce has been such a vital part of the growth of the city, that it will be only briefly gone over here. Manufactures follow commerce and their interests are ever commingled.

As we already know early commerce here was carried on with the Indians in barter trade but as this portion of the country became more thickly settled with white people trade improved. We have seen how flat-boats brought their cargoes to our bluffs, sold their goods, then the lumber of their boats and returned home on foot or horseback. Those were crude days of small convenience. Seed-corn was packed on horses and sent to the country to be planted, it was then rudely tended until the corn came and then the grains were pounded into meal in a mortar with a pestle.

The first Memphis store was owned by Ike Rawlings. He was not pleased when rivals came but he soon grew reconciled as he saw increased business building up a town and it has been told how the latter part of his life was spent in furthering the interests of Memphis in every way he could and was one of the best friends of progress the young city had.

By 1830 there were numerous stores, mechanics' shops and other places of business and people had come to realize the importance of cotton to the locality, as it was learned that Memphis lay in the heart of the cotton zone, this zone extending one hundred miles north of the Memphis parallel. In the autumn of 1826 about three hundred bales of cotton were handled in

Memphis, coming chiefly from Hardeman and Fayette Counties.

Before 1830 Joseph L. Davis established a cotton-press and as the staple increased and improved with the years inhabitants came and Memphis grew rapidly. Enterprising business men realized that manufactures ought to go hand in hand with produce and early attempts were made in this way. A flour-mill was started, a saw-mill and a few unsuccessful attempts were made at manufacturing cotton. It has taken the people of this cotton country a long while to realize that right here where the fibre grows is the best place to carry on its manufacture.

Other industries, becoming necessities of the people, followed: groceries opened, a drug-store and bakery were successful and were followed by others, tailors came, shoemakers, dressmakers, milliners and other workers that made progress for a community and easier times for its inhabitants.

Goods were usually bought on time and bills settled once a year. If a man was unable to meet his indebtedness neighbors were willing and ready to go his security until he could pay and few ever lost by standing security for his neighbors in those days. A man's word then was considered as good as his bond and to doubt a man's word was to give him mortal offense.

In 1830, 50,000 bales of cotton were shipped from the district about Memphis and six years later Memphis alone shipped that many bales. This exportation of cotton caused enterprising merchants to consider the advantages offered by the then new telegraph in obtaining each day the condition of the markets all over the country, but a telegraph was not really completed from here to an important city until 1843, when a local company built a line through to New Orleans. Thomas H. Allen was president of this company.

The last years of the thirties seemed disastrous to Memphis, nearly all of her public ventures failing. Several leading merchants failed in business, the Farmers and Merchants Bank suspended, the building of important roads fell through and corporation credit was low, but it was a time of general depression over the country. About 1840 Memphis revived and even before the East had regained its equillibrium business here had greatly improved and by 1842 was quite lively, 100 flat-boats commonly lying at the wharf at that time.

In 1841-42, 60,000 bales of cotton were shipped from this point, and in 1845 over 100,000 bales were handled in Memphis. During this year a cotton convention was held in the Bluff City and did much to stimulate business. In 1846, 130,000 bales of cotton were shipped and the yearly increase continued.

Dr. A. B. Merrill urged manufacturing in 1851, saying that Memphis "ought not only to export the agricultural products of a large area of fertile country and import all the merchandise for the same region, but she ought also to contain the workshops from which should be sent out the cotton-gins, the cotton-presses, the sugar mills and corn mills, the wagons, carts and ploughs, the castings, the household furniture and many other things which planters have to buy. Memphis ought not only to supply these products of her mechanical industry to the district of country which has become, by geographical position, dependent upon her, but to all the vast delta which lies below us and all around us."

Manufacturing ought to be the natural outcome of agriculture but this cotton country has been very slow to give attention to any other industry but the growing of cotton. Occasional efforts would be made in the early days to inspire the desire for manufacturing but cotton men here knew only cotton in the bale and seemed not to care for it further than to ship it to American and European cities, where it was manufactured into all grades of cotton cloth, twine, bagging, etc., and the seeds often came back in the form of "olive oil."

In 1853 the great Commercial Convention met here and helped Memphis in many ways, as we have already shown in an earlier chapter. In 1856, 200,000 bales of cotton were shipped and about this average continued for several years.

The business of Memphis grew very rapidly between 1850 and 1860 and the population is said to have increased more during that decade than in any other city in the Union. Cotton of course was still king, but wholesale grocery business had grown and other business interests were being inaugurated with success. In 1860 business was the supreme subject but a few months changed the community from a business-building one to an aroused military center. The money-market was in almost a panic state, caused by the political upheaval of the country and enterprises that had given so much promise waned or died.

War came and it was the chief subject, although business continued in a modified way and even held the interest of good business men for a while. In 1860 the Chamber of Commerce had been established and September 1, 1861, its secretary, Mr. John S. Toof, published the first annual report. This report showed a sale of 369,633 bales of cotton valued at $18,481,650, $3,000,000 worth of manufactured articles and $9,700,000 worth of retail trade. This report was encouraging but the war continued, grew in proportions and absorbed business as well as all other subjects. The years following were paralyzed as to trade and even records of the little business left were not kept. The Chamber of Commerce that had been organized to benefit the city ended and the late city pride and progress were gone.

We know too well the fate of Memphis during the years of the war. When it ended the South was in such a distressed condition that it seemed all hope was gone. When Memphis soldiers who had survived returned they came to impoverished homes and had to submit to a new order of rule by people who had come from other places. The flourishing Memphis of four years ago seemed dead and chaos was dominant. There were no crops, the city had no credit, the form of labor had changed without a new form being established, hundreds of unemployed negroes loafed around expecting wonderful riches from the government. No city suffered more from the ffects of the war than Memphis.

The first year after "peace" had been declared might almost be said to have been a listless one and 1867 did not solve the problem. James F. Rhodes expressed the condition of this year. He said: "The South was in a state of agricultural and industrial distress and what little recovery there had been since the close of the war was neutralized by the unsatisfactory political conditions."

Exorbitant taxes were placed on cotton and other restrictions enforced which continued to hold the people down and retard development. But in time the Southern people lost their discouragement and, enraged at unjust measures passed upon them, began to assert their human and State rights. The Chamber of Commerce revived and it did a great deal toward having business restrictions abolished. The awakening once commenced of course business went straight ahead and in 1869 R. C. Floyd, in a little history of Memphis written at that time said: "Eight saw-mills are in operation, employing over two hundred hands; six foundries, with four hundred workmen; five marble yards, with fifty hands; three brick yards, with sixty hands; four sash, door and blind factories, with one hundred and fifty hands; flouring mills, with fifty hands; besides cotton gin factories and numerous businesses that give employment to the mechanic and laboring man. Street railways now stretch to all parts of the city, making travel from the Memphis and Louisville Railroad depot, in the northern part of the city, even as far as Elmwood Cemetery, in the furthermost southern limit, cheap and speedy."

1870 opened a new era for the city and disaster was forgotten in the bettered conditions and rapid growth of business. This year showed cotton receipts for 290,738 bales of cotton and led all the cities of the Union in the manufacture of cotton-seed oil. This product from all the mills amounted to 7,400 barrels of oil and 4,080 tons of cake.

This oil had become an important product and was used for many purposes, the one of use in cooking not at first being popular, but it always takes a while for people to become accustomed to change or to take to it favorably. However, the cleanliness and purity of this vegetable oil gradually won for it favor and now most housekeepers and cooks prefer it to lard. This once-wasted product has also served Memphis well in helping her to become a manufacturing city.

The new prosperity continued and Memphis had two years of rapid commercial growth but in 1873 came another check. This was overcome, business life came again and improvements increased. The Chamber of Commerce showed in 1875 that cotton, manufacturing and all the industries were in excess of any previous year. This was encouraging and the city again lauched forth on its sea of growth and prosperity, but the Fates seemed to frown upon our city in those days. 1878 brought the most direful calamity she had yet experienced, when the fearful yellow fever epidemic of that year laid her waste and the following year still another visit from the plague seemed to doom her as a city. We have dwelt upon this terrible period in former chapters, have shown the gloom and pall of the closing of this decade and the political and municipal adjustment which put Memphis above ruin once again. The city was cleaned up as she had never been before, an excellent sewer-system inaugurated and business not only revived but in a little while flourshed more than it ever had. Each year showed increased cotton receipts and, what seemed even better to many, all kinds of other business increased. A few manufacturers came and a growing industry, lumber, was becoming very important.

The year closing August 31, 1887, showed the general merchandise trade of Memphis to be—including exports and imports—, $160,000,000. Wealth was now rapidly accumulating and by 1890 it was said that for the past twenty years Memphis had,—despite the discouragements of the seventies,—surpassed any city of equal population in the United States in business and increase in wealth.

The lumber trade had grown very much and saw-mills buzzed in great numbers in woods surrounding the city, while in 1880 not a dozen saw-mills had been within one hundred miles of her environs, and none at all that had cut lumber for shipping. Great quantities of lumber were now shipped and Memphis was acknowledged the largest hardwood lumber market in the world and the largest cotton-wood market, as well as the largest stave manufacturing city and one of the largest barrel manufacturing cities. In addition she was the largest inland cotton market in the world; the largest producer of cotton-seed oil products, having seven mills in 1890; the sixth retail grocery market; the fifth wholesale grocery market in the United States and the sixth boot and shoe market in the United States.

Of course Memphis stood first in the cotton trade above her other industries, but it was an excellent indication to see how she was branching out in all trades. Promoters of these other industries were not trying to lessen cotton importance, but to bring all branches of trade to this center and to make the cotton interests even greater by having the staple manufactured as well as grown here. That Memphis was a natural cotton center was early seen by reason of her locality in a cotton territory on the most important river of the country, giving her excellent facilities as a cotton-market, for transportation or storage, and this situation also makes her the trading point of planters for many miles in all directions. At this period it was reported that this city furnished to these neighbors $16,150,000 worth of provisions annually.

The year 1891-2 showed 770,000 bales of cotton valued at $30,000,000 or more, as against 470,000 bales at $23,000,000 in 1880.

In 1893 one of the most severe money panics in the history of the country caused many failures of far-reaching disaster, but Memphis suffered less than most other cities, not having a single bank failure and no large failures among her merchants, though business fell off a great deal. The next year showed little improvement and "hard times" was a phrase with business men who had not used it before. Failures were so common over the country that they were not considered at all detrimental, as they had formerly been held, and all firms that kept intact were to be congratulated.

A report of the Merchants Exchange in 1894, stated that while the depression in cotton had caused the trade of Memphis to diminish, the leading wholesale dry goods houses had sold as much goods as usual, the grocery men had done a fairly good business, two large wholesale boot and shoe manufacturing houses had moved here, real estate had been fair and immigration from the north had added to the farming business of adjoining territory.

Memphis had never been a "boom" city and her sure growth

had caused her to stand firmly through this great business depression. This seeming calamity really brought a benefit to the cotton country by making some provisions so high that plantations and small farms raised necessary home provisions instead of putting all their land and labor in cotton.

The grocery business continued to grow in importance, this business being a natural outgrowth of the cotton factor business which supplied planters with provisions for the plantations in addition to the cotton department and in many instances the profits from the grocery equaled those of the cotton. Memphis also became a market for sugar and molasses, having by 1895 several sugar and molasses commission houses, and canning factories began to make their appearance.

All these new industries greatly benefitted Memphis as the increase of cotton growing was already tending to overstock the world with its supply. The cotton crop for the year 1894-95 aggregated 9,901,251 bales, which exceeded the requirements of the world's manufacturers. The next year the cotton sales in this market alone amounted to nearly $20,000,000, which represented 450,000 bales. Two thirds of this amount was for export and the remainder went to eastern and domestic spinners. Only 1800 bales of all this amount was used by local mills.

The Merchants Exchange report for 1896 stated that of thirty-two crops of cotton grown between 1864 and 1897, 14,620,000 bales had been sold in the Memphis market, realizing $825,000,000, an annual average of 456,210 bales, valued at $25,750,000. The most valuable of these crops had been that of 1870-71, when 511,432 bales had sold for $39,552,366, and the cheapest had been that of 1894-95, when 583,973 bales had sold for $16,125,225.

The cotton-seed industry grew greatly as the receipts for 112,932 tons for 1896 as against 76,694 the previous year will show.

The lumber trade grew so rapidly that in 1896 a lumber report of the Merchants Exchange stated that the lumber industry gave employment to more laborers and required three times as many cars for transporting their goods as cotton did.

The cotton crop for 1897 was stated to be the largest in

history, after an unfortunate spring start that had seemed to forbode failure.

1900 showed Memphis to have 826 industries and the past decade, despite the great business depression of much of the time, had brought an increase of sixty per cent in population. The city had become the greatest dry goods market in the South; the second grocery market; the greatest wholesale shoe distributing point; a live stock market of importance; and the largest producer of cotton-seed manufactures in the world. It had eleven trunk lines of railroad and led Southern cities in its street railway system, electric light service, water plants and telephones.

We have now lived over a decade in the new century and during that time commerce and manufactures have grown and improved as much in Memphis as in any city in the Union and more than in most cities. We have city-loving men and women such as few cities possess and these people have formed clubs for business, civic improvements and all the other requirements of a well-regulated city, the work of which is felt throughout the city. Some of our business men are about as near being human live-wires as can be found and they are untiring and unstinting in their efforts to make Memphis a first-class city in every respect. The different associations are treated briefly in the chapter on clubs and societies and our business clubs alone give an idea of the amount of work done for city betterment.

Cotton and lumber are our chief staples of business and these are bringing the different manufactures of their raw and finished materials rapidly to Memphis.

It has ever been the plea that the situation of Memphis makes her a good transportation city, a good central market for wholesale and retail business and a good home place, and now it is urged that her situation is no less advantageous to manufacturing. This fact is becoming more generally understood and factories are coming here steadily. In 1911 alone twenty new industries were brought to Memphis. It is conceded that this is an excellent location for all kinds of cotton manufactures and now, being quite as much of a lumber market, it is a most excellent location for furniture and all kinds of wood-work manufactures. That this fact is more and more recognized is evidenced by the mills and factories we already have and others that are coming.

A few statements taken from a manufacturing report will verify this: The Standard Oil Company is now operating the largest cooperage company in the world in Memphis; the third largest bridge company in the world chose Memphis, declining a $50,000 bonus to go elsewhere; the largest sash and door company in America is located here; the National Biscuit Company has one of its largest plants here; the American Steel and Wire Company has one of its most important plants here; there are in Memphis five box factories; two column factories; one coffin factory; two car factories; two wagon and carriage factories; four dimension stock factories; three furniture factories; nine handle, spoke and hard-wood specialty factories; one hard-wood flooring factory; one screen-door and wash-board factory; thirteen planing mills; three slack cooperage; four tight cooperage; five veneer plants; twenty yards handling retail yellow pine; thirty-one hard-wood lumber firms, without yards or mills; twenty-five wholesale lumber firms operating yards; twenty-seven hard-wood saw-mill operators. In all 155 business houses engaged in the one industry of lumber and its products.

Experts of the Illionois Central railroad state authoritatively that there is 600,000 feet of hard-wood lumber produced in Memphis every work day of the year. The annual production of Memphis hard-wood lumber was 125,000,000 feet. In 1909 receipts of logs at Memphis were 137,391,274 feet. Of this 91,850,318 feet was received by rail and 45,540,956 feet by water.

Quoting from the above report: "There is nothing into which enters either iron or wood that cannot be economically and successfully, peacefully and profitably produced in Memphis. Memphis has all the advantages of raw material, markets, transportation, traffic and distribution facilities, low cost of production, cheap and efficient labor, good health and good living conditions, good homes and low in cost, splendid street car facilities, good schools and colleges, churches and Sunday Schools of all denominations, and a contented and happy people."

According to the Thirteenth United States Census of Manufactures of Memphis, prepared under the direction of William M. Steuart, chief statistician for manufactures, the Bureau of

Census, Washington, D. C., "Memphis has increased in the per cent of manufactures for 1909, over 1904, 103 per cent in the capital stock invested; 76 per cent in the number of salaried officials and clerks; 71 per cent in the miscellaneous expenses; 57 per cent in the cost of materials used; 51 per cent in the value of products; 42 per cent in the value added by manufacture; 33 per cent in the salaries and wages; 14 per cent in the number of establishments; and 7 per cent in the average number of wage earners employed during the year. There were 329 establishments in 1909, an increase of 40, or 14 per cent. The value of products in 1909 was "$30,242,000, and $20,043,000 in 1904, an increase of $10,199,000 or 51 per cent. The average per establishment was approximately $92,000 in 1900 and about $69,000 in 1904."

The annual cotton statement of the Memphis Cotton Exchange gives the gross cotton receipts for the year 1910-11, 920,887 bales, and the net receipts 547,496, with a total value of the year's net receipts of $44,122,702.64.

Memphis is also becoming an important stock-raising point and some of our best business men predict that the future Memphis will be one of the greatest stock-raising centers in the country.

Front Street is almost entirely devoted to grocery, cotton and commission merchants, while Madison Avenue is called the Wall Street of Memphis, and Main Street is the greatest retail business street, on which is transacted many thousands of dollars worth of business every day.

The corner of Main Street and Madison Avenue is the great center of the business district and its usually congested condition and the despair it brings the street car company to handle its crowds, shows Memphis to be a true metropolis.

# INDEX

Abolition in Memphis .............................................. 76
Aborigines ........................................................ 10
Adams, Gen. John ................................................. 306
Akansea, towns ............................................... 34, 37
Alibamo, battle of ............................................ 20, 38
Allegheny, warship ............................................... 82
Anderson, Butler P. ............................................. 175
Anderson, Kellar ................................................ 371
Annesdale Park ............................................. 329, 334
Architecture and Public Buildings, 307; early architecture, 307; iron front buildings, 308; steel structures, 308; churches, 308; stature of Forrest, 309; bust of Jackson, 309; bust of Harvey Mathes, 309; new Shelby County Court House, 310; Cossitt Library, 316; Goodwyn Institute, 317; Union Station, 320; Central Police Station, 314; United States Custom House, 322.
Artesian Water Company, 209, 210, 211, 239, 251, 258, 267. Contract with City, 210; Commissioners, 267.
Artesian Water Department .................................. 272, 293
Art, Music and Drama, 469; early theatricals, 470-471; Jenny Lind, 471; first efforts in Art, 472; Laura Kean, Edwin Booth and Joseph Jefferson, 473; Old Washington Street Theatre, 471; Greenlaw Opera House, 473; Mardi Gras Festivities, 474; New Memphis Theatre, 471; Miss Mary Solari, 476-478; Carl Gutherz, 478-481; Katharine Augusta Carl, 483; Mendelssohn Society, 484; Appollo Club, 484; Beethoven Club, 484, 493; Musical Festival, 484; Grace Lewellyn, 489; Memphis Conservatory, 490; Nineteenth Century Club, 490; young Memphis actresses, 486-491; Bijou Theatre, 491; Goodwyn Institute, 492; East End Park, 494; Jefferson Theatre, 495; Lyric Theatre, 496; Society of Arts and Crafts, 491; Marie Greenwood Worden, 497; Southern Conservatory of Music, 497.
Astor Park ...................................................... 334
Atlantic and Pacific Railway Convention ......................... 380

Bailey, Sylvester, Mayor ......................................... 84
Bank Clearings, 1897 ....................................... 246, 257
Banks and Insurance, 579; Early Banking Systems, 579-582; Banking organizations, 583-584; Insurance companies, 584, 585.
Baugh, R. D., Mayor ............................................. 300
Beasley, J. E. .............................................. 193-413
Bellechasse, Captain ............................................. 46
Belvidere Park ............................................. 329, 334
Bench and Bar, the, 520; First Court in Memphis, 520; Circuit Courts and Judges, 521-525; Chancery Courts and Judges, 522, 525, 526, 527, 528; Commercial and Criminal Court, 524; Criminal Courts, 528, 529; Probate Court, 530; Municipal Courts, 530; Noted members of the Bar in the past, 530-538.
Bethell, W. D. ......................................... 216, 218, 304

Bickford Park ............................................... 329, 334
Bickford, W. A. ............................................. 326, 329
Biedma, 13; narrative of ........................................ 27
Bienville, LeMoyne ..................................... 36, 37, 41
Blair, Gen. F. P. ............................................... 150
Bluff City Grays ........................................... 338, 368
Board of Health ................................. 210, 216, 217, 287
Bond Issues ................................................ 243, 288
Boyle, Virginia Frazer .......................................... 466
Bridge, Mississippi River, 207, 225; Opening of ............. 226-228
Brinkley, R. C. .............................................. 93, 145
Brooks Memorial Art Gallery .................................... 334
Brooks, Mrs. S. H. .............................................. 334
Brown, James, 61; reminiscences of Memphis ................. 62-65
Brown, John, raid .......................................... 106-108
Bryan, C. M. ................................................... 287
Buckland, Gen. R. P. ........................................... 356
Bureau of Municipal Research ................................... 576

Canada, Col. J. W. .............................................. 372
Carmack, E. W. ..................................... 234, 306, 456
Carnes, Gen. S. T. .......................................... 368-371
Carnes, W. W. .................................................. 226
Carondelet, Baron ............................................... 43
Carpet-baggers ................................................. 148
Carr Grant ...................................................... 57
Carroll, Chas. M. ............................................... 306
Carroll, Gen. W. H. ............................................. 306
Celoron, Mons de ................................................ 40
Chicasa, town of, 19; battle of .................................. 20
Chickasaw Bluffs, 9, 12, 20, 21, 24, 31, 33, 36, 40, 46; under Spain, 42; under Great Britain, 42; part of Carolina, 42; Part of United States, 43.
Chickasaw Guards ............................................... 368
Chickasaw Park ............................................. 328, 334
Chickasaw Purchase .............................................. 57
Chickasaws, treaty with .......................................... 62
Chisca, 21, 22, 24; Mound (Jackson) ..................... 29, 38, 354
Churches and Ministers, 499; Baptist: First Church, 510; Central Church, 511; Chelsea Church, 511; Rowan Memorial Church, 512; Johnson Ave. Church, 512; Trinity Church, 512; Seventh Street Church, 512; Lennox Church, 512; LaBelle Place Church, 512; McLemore Ave. Church, 512; Bellevue Boulevard Church, 512; Christian: Linden Street Church, 516; Mississippi Ave. Church, 516; Third Church, 517; Decatur Street Church, 517; Harbert Ave. Church, 517. Catholic: St. Peters Church, 514; St. Mary's German Church, 514; St. Patrick's Church, 515; St. Bridgid's Church, 515; Sacred Heart Church, 516; St. Thomas' Church, 516. Congregational: Stranger's Church, 518. Cumberland Presbyterian: First Church, 512; Chelsea Church, 513; Third Church, 513; Institute Church, 513; Central Church, 513; Tabernacle Church, 513; Walker Height's Church, 514. Jewish: Jewish Temple, 518; Baron Hirsch Temple, 518. Lutheran: German Evangelical Trinity, 517; Church of the Redeemer, 517. Methodist-Episcopal: Wesley Chapel, 500, Asbury Church, 500; Central Methodist Church, 501; Harris Memorial Church, 501; Madison Heights Church, 502; Saffarans Street Church, 502;

Springdale Church, 502; Olive Street Church, 502; Annesdale Church, 502; New South Memphis Church, 502; Davidson Chapel, 503; Pennsylvania Avenue Church, 503; Mississippi Avenue Church, 503; Lenox Church, 503; Washington Heights Church, 503; Galloway Memorial Church, 503; Kentucky Street Church, 504; Parkway Church, 504; Pepper Memorial Church, 504. Protestant Episcopal: Calvary Church, 508; St. Mary's Cathedral, 508; Grace Church, 509; Church of Good Shepherd, 509; St. Luke's Church, 509; Church of Holy Trinity, 510; St. Alban's Chapel, 510. Presbyterian: First Church, 504; Second Church, 505; Alabama St. Church, 505; Third Church, 505; Lauderdale or Westminster Church, 506; Idlewild Church, 507; McLemore Ave. Church, 507. Scientist: First Church, 518. Miscellaneous: Associate Reform Presbyterian, 519; Hebrew-Christian, 519; Pentecostal Holiness Church, 519; Faith Mission Church, 519; Church of God, 519; Seventh Day Adventist, 519.

Citizens Street Railway .................................................. 384
City Club .................................................................. 573
City debt .............................................................. 161, 288
City Hospital ........................................................ 240, 268
Civil War, beginning of, 118; subscriptions for, 122, 125; Memphis in, 337.
Clapp, J W. .............................................................. 167
Clapp, W. L., 217, 230, 231, 232, 305; elected mayor ............. 239
Colbert, Chief ......................................................... 47, 48
Commerce and Manufactures, 586; barter with Indians, 586; primitive commerce, 586; Commercial Convention, 588; Chamber of Commerce, 589; the cotton trade, 589, 590; lumber business, 591; financial panics, 587, 590, 592; growth of cotton trade, 592; manufacturing industry, 594, 595, 596.
Commission Government, 277, 280, 281; Commission Government Act ................................................................. 277
Concord, gun boat ...................................................... 228
Conduit System ........................................................ 281
Confederate Park .................................................. 328, 334
Confederate Reunion .................................................. 255
Confederate troops, Memphis, 337, 338; regiments and officers .. 338
Conflagrations, great ............................................ 223-225
Connoly, M. W. ......................................................... 455
Conway, Miss Clara ................................................... 431
Cossitt Frederick H. .................................................. 316
Cossitt Library .................................................. 270, 316
County seat moved to Raleigh ........................................ 78
Court House, first, 68; Overton Hotel, 162; present ............. 309
Courts, Circuit and Chancery, established ......................... 94
Court Square ........................................................... 327
Crawford, W. J. ........................................................ 457
Crump, E. H., Mayor ........................................ 279, 289, 290, 306
Crump-Williams contest ............................................... 279

D'Artaguette ........................................................ 36, 38
Davila, Pedrarias ...................................................... 13
Davis, Capt. C. H. ................................................ 349, 350
Davis, Jefferson .............................................. 113, 160, 381
Davis, W. C. ..................................................... 270, 271, 289
DeSoto, 9; birth of, 13; in West Indies, 13; in Peru, 14; marriage of, 14; Governor and Captain-General of Cuba and Florida, 14;

Adelantado or Priest of Florida, 14; at Tampa Bay, 14; marched through Florida, 15; marched through Georgia, 16; turns westward, 16; battle of Mauvila, 17; enters Mississippi, 17; winters at Chicasa, 18, battle of Chicasa, 20; battle of Alibamo, 20; crosses the Tallahatchie, 21; the march to the Chickasaw Bluffs, 22; narrative of Garcilaso de la Vega, 21; narrative of the Portuguese gentleman, 25; the narrative of Biedma, 27; narrative of Ranjel, 28; at the Chickasaw Bluffs, 25; crosses the Mississippi River, 27.

DeSoto Park .................................................. 330
Dies, Thomas ............................................ 305, 306
Dil, B. F. ..................................................... 448
Doak, H. M. .................................................. 454

Education, 397; Primitive Schools, 397; Private Schools, 398, 425-438; Public Schools, 398-424; State Normal School, 438; Industrial and Training School, 441.

Electric Lighting ............................................ 239
Ellet, Col. Chas. Jr. ......................................... 342
Ellett, H. T. ................................................. 167
Engineering Department ......... 202, 213, 214, 219, 239, 251, 268, 287
Exchange Building .................................... 89, 326
Express Companies ........................................... 101

Fentress, Francis ............................................ 528
Ferguson, Kenneth ............................................ 49
Finlay, Luke W. ..................................... 306, 338, 534
Fire Department ...................... 109, 303, 223, 253, 286
Fisher, F N. ................................................. 392
Fitch, Col. G. N. ............................................ 350
Fitzhugh, G. T. .............................................. 234
Flatboatmen War .............................................. 81
Flippin Compromise Bonds ............................... 166, 265
Flippin, Jno. R. ................................... 155, 165, 303
Floyd, A. C. ................................................. 457
Forrest, Gen. N. B., 160, 306, 354, 355, 356, 357, 358, 360, 361, 362, 363-367; rescue of Able, 98; attack on Memphis, 355; forces and losses, 367; statue of, 309.
Forrest Park .......................................... 329, 334
Fort Adams ............................................. 44, 48
Fort Assumption ........................................ 37, 38
Fort Esperanza ......................................... 46, 50
Fort Ferdinand ......................................... 44, 46
Fort Pickering ........................................ 50, 353
Fort Pike ..................................................... 50
Fort Prudhomme .............................................. 40
Freedman's Bureau ..................................... 139, 148
Front Foot Assessment ................................. 269, 287

Gailor, Thos. F. ............................................. 256
Gallaway, M. C. .............................................. 447
Galloway, J. S., Judge ...................................... 530
Galloway, Robt. ..................................... 192, 229, 328, 334
Galvez, Admiral .............................................. 43
Gambling in Memphis .................................... 75, 231
Gantt, Geo ........................................... 186, 195, 534
Gaston Park .................................................. 329

Gayoso Don Manuel .................................................. 44, 46
Gayoso House, founded ................................................. 85
Genet, French Minister ................................................. 44
Godwin, J. R. ............................................. 205, 328, 334
Goltman, Max .......................................................... 287
Goodbar, J. M. ........................................................ 234
Goodman, Leo .......................................................... 287
Goodwin, Robt. B. ...................................................... 21
Goodwyn Institute ..................................................... 317
Goodwyn, Wm. A. ....................................................... 317
Gordon, Gen. G. W. ........................................ 226, 306, 413
Grant, U. S. .......................................................... 128
Greenlaw, W. B. ....................................................... 145
Greer, Col. H. D. ..................................................... 363
Guion, Capt. Isaac, 44, 50; seizes Chickasaw Bluffs .................. 47
Guion, H. L. .......................................................... 446
Gunboats for Memphis, 121; Confederate, 343; Federal, 343; battle before Memphis, 342.

Hadden, D. P. ................... 193, 204, 205, 206, 211, 213, 218, 304
Harris, Isham G. ........................................... 118, 160, 306
Health Department ..................................................... 287
Health Measures Committee ............................................. 195
Heiskell, C. W. ...................... 186, 188, 203, 205, 206, 234, 526
Heiskell, F. H. ....................................................... 527
Hermany, Chas. ................................................. 199, 207
Hickman grant ......................................................... 57
Higbee, Miss Jennie M. ................................................ 429
High School Alumni Association ........................................ 421
Highways, Shelby County ........................................... 377-379
Hill, A. B. ........................................................... 413
Hopefield .......................................................... 48, 79
Howard, Col. ....................................................... 48, 49
Howard Association, 157, 173; roll of dead ............................ 183
Humphries, J. H. ...................................................... 197
Hunter, F. B. ......................................................... 413
Hurlbut, Gen. S. A. .......................... 134, 356, 360, 361-365
Hutchison, R. B. ...................................................... 462

Indians, Chickasaw, 18, 33, 39, 41; Choctaw, 17; removal to West.. 77
Indian Tribes .......................................................... 11
International Improvement Convention .................................. 83
Interstate Drill ...................................................... 242
Irving Block Prison ................................................... 133

Jackson, Andrew, 51, 58, 60; bust of .................... 104, 109, 309
Jackson, State of ..................................................... 79
Jackson, Thos. H. ......................................... 267, 271, 272
Johnson, Andrew ....................................................... 149
Johnson, John, Mayor ...................................... 153, 301, 302
Jones, Sam ............................................................ 235
Jordan, R. D. ......................................................... 411
Juvenile Court ........................................................ 282

Keating, J. M., 78, 148, 153, 155, 158, 161, 165, 166, 169, 177, 178, 182, 183, 184, 193, 450, 456, 459.
Kellar, A. J. ......................................................... 451
Kennedy Sara Beaumont ................................................. 467

## 602    History of Memphis, Tennessee.

Kennedy, Walker .................................................. 455, 467
Kernan, Will H. ...................................................... 465
Kessler, Geo. E. ..................................................... 334
Ku-Klux Klan, the, 150; constitution and creed of ............... 151

Langstaff, A. D. ........................................... 173, 183, 193
La Salle, voyage of, 32; takes possession of Mississippi Valley .... 34
Latham, F. S. ........................................................ 445
Laughlin, H. W. ...................................................... 262
Lawrence, Robert, Mayor .............................................. 75
Lee, James, Jr. .................................................. 204, 205
Lee Line Steamers ......................................... 383, 389, 393
Leftwich, Jno. W., Mayor ............................................ 152
LeMaster, E. D. .................................................. 258, 305
Levee, North Memphis ................................................ 270
Linkhauer, J. A. ..................................................... 175
Literature, Memphis books and authors ....................... 462-468
Loague, John, Mayor ........................................ 161, 165, 302
Lofland, W. O., Comptroller, 135; mayor, ........................... 149
Long grant ............................................................ 57
Love, G. C. ...................................................... 305, 306

Mageveney, Michael .................................................. 306
Malone, G. B. .................................................... 416, 424
Malone, J. H., Mayor ......................... 263, 270, 274, 279, 305
Malone, Judge Walter ........................................... 262, 467
Map of Memphis ....................................................... 60
Margot River (Wolf) .............................................. 38, 47
Market Square ........................................................ 327
Marquette and Joliet ................................................. 32
Martial Law in Memphis .............................................. 135
Mathes, J. Harvey, 454; bust of .................................... 309
Matthews, G. C. ...................................................... 453
Maurelian, Brother .................................................. 427
Maury, R. B. ..................................................... 407, 574
Mauvila, battle of ................................................... 17
Mayors, Aldermen and Commissioners; table of, 1827-1912 ...... 296-306
Mayors Office restored .............................................. 238
Membre, Piere Zenobe ................................................ 32
Memphis, founded, 60; first map of, 60; name of, 65; first census, 63;
    incorporated, 70; first charter, 71; first officers, 72; first elec-
    tions, 72; first ordinance, 73; new city limits, 73; population,
    74; amendment of charter, 74; Isaac Rawlings, Mayor, 74; Wards
    established, 74; population, 1835, 78; slighted by State, 79;
    claimed by Mississippi, 80; census of 1840, 80; taxation in 1840,
    80; Spickernagle, Wm., Mayor, 81; war with flatboatmen, 81;
    boundaries enlarged, 83; Sylvester Bailey, Mayor, 84; population
    1846, 85; first bond issue, 89; leases Exchange Building, 89; new
    charter, 90; annexed South Memphis, 90; census of 1850, 92;
    plank roads, 92; amendment of charter, 94; census of 1860, 108;
    secession of from Tennessee, 119; John Park, Mayor, 125; cap-
    tured by Federal fleet, 126; exciting scenes, 127; under military
    rule, 128; hardships of people, 132; under martial law, 135; civil
    law restored, 137; distress of people, 138; great negro riot, 140;
    Northern estimate of, 146; boundaries enlarged, 149; boundaries
    reduced, 152; property values, 153; census 1870, 153; debt and
    bond issues, 155, 156, 205, 219; taxation troubles, 156, 159;

scheme to retire debt, 161; census 1875, 162; revised charter, 164; enormous debt, 164; bankrupt, 185; wasteful bond system, 190; census of 1880, 213; census of 1890, 213; mortality rate 1893, 217; rapid growth of, 222; wants name restored, 229; Back Tax Collector, 240; bonds refunded, 243; limits extended, 245, 249; power of taxation, 249; census of 1900, 254, rate of taxation, 1907, 264; real estate, 268; front foot assessment, 269; parks, 270; limits extended 273; Commission Government, 277, 280, 281; early militia companies, 237; late militia companies, 368-373; Memphis in Civil War, 337; Confederate troops from, 338; gunboat battle, 342; capture of, 350; under Federal rule, 351; Union Station Co., 320, 391, 392; street railways, 395; yellow fever epidemics 1867, 152; 1873, 157; 1878, 170-184; mortality of, 172; relief committees, 183; bands of workers, 175; incidents of, 180-182; 1879, 192-194; 1897, 243.

Memphis and Charleston Jubilee .................................. 95
Memphis Medical History, 539; early practitioners, 539, 544; yellow fever epidemics, 545, 546; medical institutions and hospitals, 546, 552; Memphis Medical Society, 543; noted physicians of the past, 544; first college of medicine, 542.
Memphis water supply, 207, 208, 209, 210, 267; contamination of... 293
Meriwether, Minor ............................................. 169
Meriwether, Mrs. Lyde .................................... 237, 464
Meriwether, Niles ............... 197, 201, 203, 211, 213, 214, 216
Merrill, A. P. ............................................. 400, 403
Mexico, war with, 85, 87; volunteers in ......................... 336
Military History .............................................. 336
Militia, early companies, 337; late companies ............... 368, 373
Minor, Judge H. D. ............................................ 528
Mission Home ................................................. 221
Mississippi River, discovery of, 24, 34; DeSoto crosses, 28; great overflow ............................................... 243, 289
Mitchell, R. W. ........................................ 170, 175, 182, 193
Mitchigameas, town ............................................ 33
Mizell, Wm. ................................................... 49
Montgomery, Commodore J. E. .................................. 343
Mooney, C. P. J. ............................................. 457
Moore, Wm. R. ................................................ 306
Morison, Sanford ............................................. 272
Municipal ownership ....................................... 258, 280
Myers, Minnie Walter .......................................... 465
McClanahan, Mr. .............................................. 448
McFarland, L. B. ......................................... 328, 334
McKellar, K. D. .............................................. 306
McKinley, President Wm. ...................................... 254
McLemore, Jno. C. ............................................ 325
McMahon, J. H. ............................................... 445
McNeill, I. C. ............................................... 417

Navy Yard ............................................ 82, 166, 326
Neely, E. A. ................................................. 417
Negro riot ................................................... 140
Nichols, F. S. ............................................... 454

Ogilvie, C. C. ............................................... 477
O'Haver, Geo. T. ......................................... 265, 270
Overton, John, Jr. ....................................... 192, 304

Overton, Judge John .................................. 59, 69, 325
Overton Park .......................................... 329, 331

Panics, money, 1837, 78; 1857, 96; 1873, 590; 1893 ............... 592
Park, John, Mayor,....................... 125, 144, 148, 349, 350
Parks and promenades, 232; dedication of, 324; Park driveway, 330; Commissioners, 334; Overton, 331; Riverside, 331; Forrest.. 329
Patterson, Josiah ......................................... 306
Patterson, M. R. .......................................... 306
Peoples Protective Union ............................. 164, 169
Peres, Israel H. .......................................... 413
Petit, Col. Hugh .......................................... 371
Petit, J. W. A. ....................................... 398-401
Phelan, James ............................................ 226
Phoebus, Thomas .......................................... 444
Piamingo, Chief ....................................... 47, 48
Pickett, A. B. ........................... 454, 455, 456, 491
Pickett, Ed. Jr. .......................................... 306
Pike, Capt. Z. M. .......................................... 50
Pike, Gen. Albert ......................................... 450
Pinch ..................................................... 84
Pittman, Judge A. B. ...................................... 262
Plank roads ............................................... 92
Police Department ............ 141, 143, 154, 203, 220, 251, 265, 286
Population ............... 68, 74, 78, 80, 85, 92, 108, 153, 162, 213, 254
Porter, D. T. ................ 183, 189, 191, 192, 195, 200, 204, 304
Portraits of Mayors ....................................... 276
Portuguese gentleman, 13; narrative of ..................... 25
Press, The, 444; Memphis Advocate, 444; Western Times, 444; Memphis Gazette, 445; Memphis Enquirer, 445; Memphis Appeal, 446-450, 451-454; Memphis Eagle, 446; Eagle Enquirer, 447; Memphis Avalanche, 447, 450-454; Western World, 448; Commercial, 450, 456; Post, 450; Bulletin, 450; Evening Ledger, 450; Evening Argus, 450; Public Ledger, 454; Memphis Scimitar, 455; Sunday Times, 456; Evening Democrat, 456; Appeal-Avalanche, 456; Commercial-Appeal, 457; Morning News, 457; News Scimitar, 457; Southern Post Journal, 458; Memphis Press, 458; Miscellaneous newspapers, 458-461.
Preston, T. W. ............................................ 306
Prohibition law ........................................... 282
Prudhomme Piere ........................................... 33
Pryor, John P. ............................................ 446

Railroad Jubilee .......................................... 95
Railroad lines ....................................... 378-384
Railroads, rapid extension ................................ 95
Raine, J. D. ............................................. 457
Rambaut, G. V. ........................................... 410
Ramsey grant .............................................. 55
Ramsey, John .............................................. 55
Randolph, town of ......................................... 78
Randolph, W. M. .......................................... 162
Raniel, narrative of .................................. 13, 28
Rawlings, Isaac ....................................... 71, 74
Rice grant ........................................... 52, 58
Rice, John ........................................... 52, 58
Ricketts, H. P. ........................................... 455

Rioting in Memphis ............................................. 97
Riverside Park ........................................ 330, 313, 332
Rocky Ford ............................................... 21, 22

Secession upheaval, 111; meetings, 108-115; directory, 116; of Memphis, 117; State vote, 120; Memphis vote, 120.
Sewer System ............................................... 196, 287
Shelby County, founding of, 66; early history of, 66, 69; first court house, 68; second court house, 162; present court house, 309; Court House Commission, 313; Highways, 377, 379.
Shelby, Gov. Isaac ......................................... 51, 58
Sherman, W. T. ............................................ 128-131
Slavery ..................................................... 93
Smith, Gen. Preston ........................................ 306
Smith, W. J. ............................................... 306
Sneed, Gen. J. L. T. ....................................... 306
Societies and Clubs, 553; Secret and benevolent orders, 553-559; Social organizations, 560-464; patriotic and memorial societies, 564-568; musical organizations, 568-569; civic clubs and exchanges, 571-573; city club, 573; Bureau of Municipal Research, 576.
Speed, R. A. ............................................... 396
Spickernagle, Wm., Mayor ................................... 81
Stanton, F. P. ............................................. 306
Starr, Col. M. H. .......................................... 363
State lines ................................................ 378
Steamboat Lines ................... 375-377, 383, 389-390, 393, 394
Steen, J. M. ............................................... 414
Stewart, Gen. A. P. ........................................ 306
Street Railways ..................................... 384-389, 394-396
Subways .................................................... 275

Tallahatchie River ......................................... 20
Taxation, unequal .......................................... 230
Taxing District, preliminary plans, 167; Taxing District Act, 186; creditors protest, 189; first commissioners, 191; engineering work, 202, 219; refunding Act, 205; progress of sewer work, 205.
Tax Rate, 1909 ............................................. 74
Taylor, Col. W. F. .................................... 234, 306
Taylor, Gen. A. R. ................................ 226, 369, 371
Taylor, Zack ............................................... 306
Telegraph, first line, 85; line to Nashville ............... 89
Tennessee admitted ......................................... 43
Thornton, G. D. ..................... 182, 203, 206, 211, 217
Thornton, Judge Lee ........................................ 528
Tombigbee, battle of ....................................... 17
Tonti, Henri de ........................................ 32, 36
Toof, S. C. ................................................ 449
Transportation, 374; steamboat lines, 375-394; railroad lines, 378-384; street railways, 384-389; 394-396; stage lines, 373.
Trask, W. L. ............................................... 455
Turley, T. B. ....................................... 205, 247, 306
Turner, Dr. B. F. .......................................... 335
Tutwiler, T. H. ............................................ 395

Union Station ........................................ 320, 391, 392
U. S. Custom House ....................................... 322, 326
Utley, R. A. ........................................ 289, 290, 306

Van Pelt, Henry .............................................. 446, 448
Vaudreuil, De .................................................... 41
Vega, Garcilaso de la, 13; narrative of ......................... 22

Walker, J. Knox ............................................... 306
Walker, Judge S. P. ................................. 165, 186, 205
Walsh, J. T. .................................................. 305
Waring, Col. Roane ............................................ 372
Waring, Geo. E. Jr., 196, 197, 198, 200, 201; sewer system,..... 196-201
Washburn, Gen. C. C., ................. 134, 356, 359, 360, 361, 364-367
Watson, Annah Robinson ........................................ 467
Weatherford, J. H. ............................................ 268
Wheatley, Seth, Mayor .......................................... 75
Wilkinson, General ............................................. 44
Williams, Col. Kit ............................................ 306
Williams, J. J., Mayor ............... 247, 250, 254, 257, 263, 279, 305
Williams, N. M. .............................................. 415
Willingham, J. T. ............................................ 335
Winchester, Gen. James .................................... 60, 63
Winchester, M. B., Mayor ................................. 71, 325
Wolfe, L. E. ................................................. 425
Wolf River Canal .............................................. 86
Wolf's Friend, Chief ...................................... 47, 48
Women, publish newspaper ..................................... 237
Workhouse ................................................... 154
Wright, E. E. ................................................ 538
Wright, Gen. M. J. ........................................... 306
Wright, Luke E., .................... 181, 182, 183, 193, 196, 306, 395

Yellow Fever, 1867, 152; 1873, 157; 1878, 170-184; mortality, 1878, 172;
    relief committee, 183; bands of workers, 175; incidents of, 180-
    182; 1879, 192-194; 1897, 243.
Young, Casey ................................................ 306
Young, J. P. ............................................ 280, 525
Young, R. B. ................................................ 458

Zimmermann, F. .............................................. 458

# CITY'S HISTORY TOLD BY JUDGE J. P. YOUNG

*Appeal 11/17-12*

## Work Is Valuable Contribution to South's Literature.

## MUCH NEW DATA INCLUDED

**Memphis Jurist Has Contributed to History of State's Greatest City a History Which Is Complete in Every One of Its Details.**

A historical work, a standard "History of Memphis," has just been issued from the press.

The author is Judge J. P. Young of this city, and in the book he has contributed a detailed history of particular value at this time, for much of it has been compiled from the recollections of some of the older residents of the city, which, in a few years, would no longer have been available. The work as a whole bears indications of the most painstaking research into the old records and public documents of past years, while later data has been secured from the files of the city's newspapers.

The volume is dedicated by Judge Young:

"To the pioneers who founded, and the brave sons who builded and loyally stood by Memphis in her hours of adversity and pestilence as in her days of victory and triumph."

In his introduction Judge Young voices the spirit with which he undertook the immense amount of labor and research which has gone into the making of his book. He speaks of the story of the nation's origin and growth and holds that "the same patriotic devotion, born of the same sentiment, does, or should, prevail in every city as in every nation."

### Early History Fully Treated.

It is this spirit which breathes throughout every page of Judge Young's work. One feels in reading the accounts of the past that every loyal son of Tennessee and every citizen of Memphis has a right to feel a pride in the achievements of the past and in the promise of the future.

The early history of the city itself is preceded by several chapters dealing with the years which passed before the real founding of the city. These chapters deal with the visit of the great Spanish captain, Hernando DeSoto, which it is noted occurred seventy-nine years before the landing of the Mayflower at Plymouth Rock and twenty-four years before the building of the first log hut and stockade at St. Augustine, Fla.

Following what may be considered almost ancient history, the author devotes much space to the details of the voyages down the great river of Joliet, Marquette and LaSalle, the arrival of Bienville and his building of a fortress on the Chickasaw Bluffs, where years before DeSoto had landed, and the later stories of the efforts made by the Spanish governor, Don Manuel Gayoso, to establish an empire in this section for Spain.

The romance of the days of old is embodied in these chapters.

Then the records become more those of modern days, the organization of the first government of the newly laid out city of Memphis and the history of its people, their early struggles, the dark days of civil strife, the days of terrible pestilence, and the coming of the better days of prosperity.

The history is brought down to the present time, with an account of the establishment of the commission form of government and what has been accomplished of good under the city's new charter. There follow a few additional chapters devoted to a special consideration of the city's public buildings, parks, its military history, transportation facilities, literature, art and music, churches, a brief history of the bench and bar, the medical profession, societies and clubs, banks, commerce and manufactures.

Those chapters contain valuable statistics brought down to recent date, which add to the value of the work as a whole.

A map showing the first site of the city and a number of illustrations serve to embellish the work.